MW00618451

The World of Tantra

It is a faithful presentation of personal experiences of a devoted man who has been throughout his life of 76 years searching for receiving an answer, an understandable logic behind those mystic events before which logic stands spell bound. These personal records—secret, mind boggling, enigmatic—-none the less reserve for the reader an unfailing touch of reliance. Man stands here face to face with the mystery which takes the mind above matter, and wonderment gasps although the Hamlet like assurance comes in time to point out confidently to 'more things between heaven and earth.' Chapter by chapter, the author unfolds layer after layer the secrets of the tantra world, as he has found himself in, at times to satisfy his quest, at times as just a beam of blessing.

The personal note of these pages, together with the lessons in tantric practices, some sweet and startling, some horrid and blood-curdling, make this book an addition to the authentic report of this much maligned but equally intimate world. Those who want to profit and learn of and about what is and what could be held in store by tantra will find *The World of Tantra* a secret mind of relevant information at first hand.

B. Bhattacharya, born in 1910 in Varanasi, received his first education in traditional 'toles' in Sanskrit and further did M.A. (English) from Allahabad University. He spent the best period of his life as an educationist in Guyana and Trinidad (West Indies).

His other works, *Saivism and the Phallic World,* 2 vols. (1993) and *Varanasi Rediscovered* (1999), both published by us are well-known. The persent work shows the range of his reach in the mystic sphere of tantra.

The World of Tantra

B. Bhattacharya

MUNSHIRAM MANOHARLAL

Munshiram Manoharlal
Publishers Pvt. Ltd.

ISBN 978-81-215-0968-8
Reprinted 2007, **2014**
First published 1988

PRINTED IN INDIA
Published by Vikram Jain *for*
Munshiram Manoharlal Publishers Pvt. Ltd.
PO Box 5715, 54 Rani Jhansi Road, New Delhi 110 055, INDIA

www.mrmlbooks.com

To
Dr. Stella Abid
Dr. J.H. Maurice
Two adored friends of the Spirit

Lokenath—Sugrim—Madhu—Jeevan—Mohan
Devoted and Beloved 'Seekers'
from the warm Island of Trinidad

Contents

Foreword

B. Bhattacharya is a distinguished and internationally renowned scholar of Saivism as well as allied subjects. He is a world-trodder and an adventurer in the areas of knowledge beyond mundane knowledge, the mystic experiences which are on the borderline of light and darkness. No wonder *The World of Tantra* explores the twilight-language (*sandhya-bhāṣa*) which has been so much misinterpreted and misrepresented in India and abroad by half-baked dealers in the exotic wares.

On Tantra, there were several questions asked by the students of philosophy as well as the laymen, which had remained like the proverbial Sphinx's enigmatic smile or the hieroglyphs of Indus valley seals. They are not only raised and touched, but very sympathetically answered in this eminently readable personalized account of the quest for the Secret Path, very authentically explained. When time stands still and life extends itself to 'before' and 'after' the writer philosopher, the mindless meditator, the beloved of the gods, carve for themselves a niche for lighting a candle to the joy of the soul.

Mysticism is proverbially Janus-faced. The one looks into the dark regions of the unknown and the occultish, the other looks into the gleaming face of Truth. As the author rightly says: "Truth scares—Even Arjuna got scared." Friendship, intimacy, love sacrifice, skin-to-skin discovery of the natural and the ever-invigorating joy which never stales, nor is consumed like momentary physical passion—are some of the key-words which reduce thinking 'down from hour to moments.' Another gem of a quote from this work is "Friendship is a gem, like a gem it is vulgar to display it." The Tantra uses the terms like MANI or PADMA, not without its hard and soft connotations, its solid and expanding meaningfulness, beyond Time and Space. The physical and the metaphysical do not remain two dichotomies. The sacred and the sensuous melt into one fusion. It is beyond reason and so there is no confusion. It is direct communion and atonement. Shelley's 'Love's philosophy' dances hand-in-hand with Jalaluddin Rumi's wave and the ocean mingling. Tagore sang about form and fragrance:

Roop a-panare milaite chaye gandhe
Gandha se chahe roopere rahite jure

Earth is called *gandhavati*, the perfumed, and the breath and space are colourless. The celebration of five senses and elements conquers Death. Sensations are thus transcended. The pilgrims who are on the march through this difficult terrain, but who, tempted by the grand silver glow of the sunbathed peaks of the horizon, keep on marching through challenges, limitations and the risk of being misunderstood.

In Tantras there is a special position given to the BHAIRAVI. In *Dhanvantaritantra-shiksha* she has been described as:

Udyadbhānu-sahasra-kāntimaruṇaṁ kshaumam-shiromālikām

"She is red like a thousand morning suns, she is having a red garment, she has a garland of skulls in her neck (the KĀLĪ in Bengal has 52 skulls as 52 letters of the Sanskrit alphabet—all literal knowledge is symbolically dead-head), whose breasts are blood-smeared, and who has a rosary and book in her hand. The author was fortunate to get his initiation in his young age in Varanasi, from the Lady in Saffron. All other characters in this autobiographical-cum-philosophical book of musings, like Narada, the Dutch girl or the many other female forms is a virtual galaxy of the possibilities of human infatuation and fascination for the wonder that is expressed by Goethe in the last lines of *Faust* (part II):

Das Ewig Weibliche Zieht uns hinan
(*the Eternal Female draws us upward*)

The philosophy of Tantra practised and propounded properly can serve us thereby, better than western self-hypnosis, psycho-analytical big-feedback and Sheldrake's 'memory-pool.' Human body has such morphogenetic fields of unrapped energy, which can be released and aroused by the appropriate contact. Old Testament said in *Proverbs* 'The way of a man with a maid' is too wonderful and which one knows not, as one cannot predict the way of the eagle in the air, the way of a serpent upon a rock and the way of a ship in the sea. Thomas Moore wrote—"My only books were woman's looks" and all they taught him was folly. Actually that impossible she is in Shakespeare's word lent such grace by Heaven that for Scott, she was 'a ministering angel' to the man wreathing in pain and anguish. These *yoginis* and *matrukas* had very venerable place in Indian divine worship. *Shri-pujā* in Tantra was a culmination of the same. According to Buddhist beliefs Kamarupa (Assam), Purnagiri (Nepal), Uddiyan (Orissa) and Jalandhar (Punjab) had important *yogini-piṭhas*. B-

Bhattacharya has referred to his first-hand experiences in these religious sites, and many more.

Historical and archaeological research has brought in the Austric, Scythian and Mongolian strands and elements in the Tantric practices. But the author of this work does not load the book with unnecessary exhibition of erudition and footnotes. What the author attempts is to break through the prejudices and makes the hesitant stand for a while at the closed doors of the divine mystery. Life source (*yoni*) and culmination of life in Death are viewed with equal detatchment and distance. Here fiction and fact, myth and materialism, mingle. Duality is dropped like a veil, and the real and etherial embrace each other. The Indian science of eroticism (*Kamasutra*) had described eight kinds of physical embracing postures. But this work has proved that the erotic can be eerie, and the dreadful can be delightful, the elusive could be eternally enthralling and enchanting. *Kato Vichitra tumichitra-rupini*!

The world of tantra has to be traversed step by step, incident by incident, region by region. Here the ordinary men and women assume extraordinary proportions, the innermost is externalised. Saints and angels brush skin with passion, horror and the uncanny. Flesh eating, wine drinking, gnome-like characters come along with mellifluous musicians, miraculous mendicants and magnetic maidens who are *chadinī* (joy forever, the rook of Rādhā). That woman-power is Shakti, as well as Nature's prettiest flower dust. Goldsmith rightly said 'Women and music could never be dated. The central figure of this work, the Lady in Saffron has such personal charm, grace, wisdom and spirituality that she is the guiding angel for the author. She has lent the author a sensibility which enables him to etch each incident with accuracy and aestheticism yet the intellectual atomsphere-aroma evokes admiration.

This work will be appreciated and read by the specialist and the common reader with equal enthusiasm and interest, as it is written in an intimate vibrant language. Another special feature of this work is that the author handles many incidents and situations in such a delicate manner that though they seem to shock one's sensibilities and tear off one's taboos, yet they arise in the reader empathy of a different kind, a mixed feeling of reverence, wonder, fascination, curiosity and sublime sadness all rolled in one flash of intuition. The author has humility, and nowhere does he pose as omniscient or superior, pontified or prejudiced. For the Western reader, particularly obsessed with the original sin complex and the dictionary of body and mind, this work should come as a balance-setter. The so-called rationalist and radical West led the world into Auschwitz, Atom-Bomb and Aides. Let us now hear to the soft, serene but soothing story of the East which is slowly stretching and spreading (literal etymology of Tantra is 'to spread' 'to weave') through a new awareness of Tantra and Yoga, Zen and Samadhi.

Much research is needed to see the parallels between the search endocrinological center of gland-secretions and the *Shaṭchakras* of the *Yoga-Sūtra* of Patanjali, between the auto-suggestion and practice of *Pratyāhāra*, between the cycle of sexual energy and the liberation of the libido on the hand and the *kuṇḍalini*'s slow rise and reaching the upper lobe of the cerebellum and cerebrum through the *medulla oblongata.* Our *Dharanā* is the psychologist's concentration. Mythology, the study of the form and structure of plants and animals in the first wholestic concept of science, as propounded in *Bhūta Shuddhi* in Tantras. Morphic resonance is an analogue to energic resonance inherited by all kinds of life. All living organisations contribute to a collective unconscious or 'memory pool' in this cosmos, which survives the death of an individual or decay of a species. Oriental wisdom concentrated on this timelessness in eternal love, the intense innermost moment of forgetfulness of the outer material enlivens "*KAMASTADAGRE*"... the Upanishad said about creation. Freud's *Beyond the Pleasure Principle* quotes *Bṛhadāraṇayaka*, and Carl Jung speaks of Patanjali—not without reason.

I for one, hail this noble work and the noble courage of the author who is a poet and novelist in Bengali and English, besides being a deep student of Indian and Western philosophies, religions and literatures. At such a ripe age of seventy-six he should command such energy to pen such a sustained spiritual study in spontaneous succinct style, speaks volumes about his equipment and erudition, enormous experience and easy expression. He is really blessed by some Tantric (magic-making) Guru. Guru in Indian tradition can be male or female. Like Chaucer's description "And gladly would he learn and gladly teach." Plato had said—"Those having torches, will pass on to others." But the difficulty with the Tantra is that it is more practice than philosophising. It is more silent, than eloquent. More action than word. So let me stop.

11 November 1987 Prabhakar Machwe

Preface

Tantra is an intimate subject; tantra is an open and universal subject. Tantra cannot be narrated; neither described. Tantra is to be communicated, conveyed and shared. Tantra is not story, gossip, hearsay; tantra is history, tradition, primitive. Tantra is personal, practical, empirical; tantra is social, communal, tribal. Tantra is objective-subjective. Tantra is materialistic idealism; realistic mysticism. Tantra is the Mother, Madonna, Gaea; Tantra is Cāmuṇḍā, Kālī, Circe, Erzulie.

Because it is extremely difficult to communicate tantric experiences, because an effective language for truthful communication of the mystic nuances of tantra has not yet been forged by man, I was more than reluctant in expressing myself in this complex field, specially in the first person. Accuracy, precision and clarity are always victims of autobiographical representation. In this case too, actual facts are destined to undergo some misrepresentations.

But friends had been insisting on my telling the tale, which, in their estimation, would be of immense benefit to serious students of tantra. I am completely unaware if such is the case; if anyone would indeed be benefited; but it was no longer possible to resist the pressure. Further keeping off seemed useless. Finally I decided to give way.

Remoteness of the events narrated, together with the gray age of the narrator, and the absence from life of some of the characters involved offer me some protective cover, so that I accept the challenge of the undertaking, and settle for the venture. The difficult task of presenting in the first person intimate autobiographical details of incidents and events, which involve others as well, makes the venture delicately embarrassing. But in this I depend entirely on the charity of the reader.

I only hope that the decision of revealing these treasured secrets stands justified by the gains of the seekers, who, I know, always look for assistance from every possible source for achieving success in the world of tantra.

Since the explosion of the atom bomb, particularly since the Vietnam fiasco, an era of nuclear competition has gripped the so-called affluent, aggressive and militant nations. An almost inexplicable pall of mistrust has been driving these self-styled dispensers of world peace to the dangerous borders of cynical desperation.

Queerly enough the inherent disregard reflected by this callousness of the affluent powerful has cast a gloom of utter pessimism over the bright and young minds of their society. Despite the claims of their affluence, power, progress and scientific advance, gradually the growing youth has been getting disenchanted by these tall claims, which they know are nothing more than the empty growls of old hounds bent upon tearing themselves apart.

This is not the place to dissect and analyse the causes of this deplorable malady, which has been engaging the thoughts of social thinkers and philosophers.

But our subject is concerned with this phase of the changing times. Simultaneously with the growth of this despondence and cynicism, a taste for the mystic and the occult has characterised the mental fascination, the spiritual quest and the physical degeneration of our growing stock. A mad craving for some kind of inner freedom (picturesquely expressed by the escapist howling word *trip*) has overwhelmed the beleagured youth.

He longs for coming into grips with an easy road to escape into the realms of the romantic mysterious, where to be, he hopes, is to forget the problems that stare him in the face.

Amongst other means of escape, he has turned his mind to that proverbial mysticism of the East, which, in times bygone had lured the Greek and Roman youth, until a Dark Age had wiped out the glory that was the Classical Age. Traditionally, with historic precision, whenever the West has looked for spiritual and cultural sustenance, it has looked to the East.

In tune with that historic tradition, the present post-atomic age too, having run into a crisis of spiritual vacuum, looks towards the East for an answer. Not the growth of science and commerce, nor the fantasies of the atomic age and its residual threat to human existence, nor the revolutionary ideas of neo-socialism has been able to contain this zealous search for an instant remedy to the crisis that is about to overwhelm man's mind and body.

Tricksters have tried to pass off as saints and magic men, who through their dubious devices promise quick, hand-to-hand remedies for all such mental and spiritual maladies. A readymade package tour to an escape to total freedom is generally held out by many 'experts' from the East; and history would have to record once again that of all the pretending rogues, the spiritual Tartuffes of society find their victims easy lambs for a senseless slaughter.

Almost all the Western capitals could boast of flourishing spiritual shops where the credulous youth burn in their search for an ever-elusive world of personal freedom.

This situation has encouraged a spiritual market to flourish unchecked, and flood the guileless minds of the seekers with books, charts, diagrams, *tankas*, besides the scores of instant gurus who go about trading peace and tranquillity. The more remote, the keener; the more occultish, the hotter; the more eerie, the merrier.

Minds genuinely in search of solace and strength rush towards the promised peaceful goal, where there is love for the world and fulfilment for life; where the elders do not set a double standard, and dupe their juniors, or trick them into going for global wars in the name of peace.

This crisis of the spirit of man has been fully exploited by cheap pedlars of spiritual calm. The spirit of man hits the lowest bottom when consummate tricksters make the agony of the soul a bargaining commodity for personal profit and power.

Tantra, unfortunately, has been one of those chosen commodities on the shelves of the spiritual traders. Books on this very serious and time-honoured mystic way deluge the market; and yet another addition to the heap could hardly be justified. On the face of it the attempt is suspect.

As these thoughts pass through my mind, I feel I have so far rigidly tried *not* to succumb to the persistent requests from friends to record these experiences. These, they feel, are treasures of a specific nature of data for aspirants who search for first-hand facts.

As I submit to this insistence, (and perhaps also to an author's neurotic itch for public correspondence) I must sound immediately a note of warning.

Those who are looking for any theoretical guidance in or metaphysical explanations of tantra or tantric events, would find this book entirely disappointing. It does not propose to offer any messianic panacea to the souls in distress, or to the spirit in turmoil.

The World of Tantra does not pretend to *teach* anything; or *preach* any message. It does not offer any short-cut map to tranquillity. It entertains no presumptuous claims on the sophistry of the art of the masters, or the wisdom of the philosophers, or the secrets of the wizards and the mystics.

It records in the first person some complex personal experiences of a common seeker along the tantric way, the way of the deadly coil of the female serpent. This book claims for its merit no special kudos. In fact it has nothing to relate except to expose a genuine heart-to-heart appreciation of a fellow traveller's mood of sharing and comparing extraordinary happenings, in the sacred spirit of exchanging experiences with a sympathetic brotherhood met at a spiritual caravanserai.

As such, the reader is requested to lay his trust on the veracity of the narratives. Time and distance must have inevitably driven the details into an area of mist and fog.

Some of those objects, seen through the fog of a fading memory, must look, of course, larger, dimmer, out of proportion or perspective. Never would they appear in their own nascent purity. Some of the incidents have been passed over, some have worn thinner, some have cast longer shadows and deeper colours: but by and large the author has tried his best to keep close to the facts as watched then, and recollected now.

The incidents described are admittedly difficult to be 'believed'. Indeed, taken at their face value they are likely to pose a challenge to human credulity. If the reader takes them to be nothing better than a yarn, I shall be the least surprised, or hurt. As the narrator, indeed, I feel the least bothered. Because I had watched these, *incredible* incidents with my own eyes, and because I have heard some of these things with my own ears, I felt obliged to narrate them. It is not for me to offer justifications, or formulate rationalisations for their credibility; neither do I possess the mental or intellectual capacity to do so. That kind of exercise falls within the court of the theosophists and the metaphysicians.

Since I do not attempt to hold a torch to credibility of the narratives, I owe it to my readers that I give them the option of discrediting the entire monograph, and declare the exercise as a piece of howling figment. I shall not, therefore, feel offended; neither shall I deem my efforts as casting seeds in a windless desert waste. In narrating them, in bringing these reports to the notice of the deserving, I shall be fulfilling a mission in my life, which is running through its last lap. I am pretty sure that there are many who have need for such reports of first-hand experiences in a field of enquiry which remains until this day, amidst all this fadistic hullabaloo about 'a scientific outlook', an absorbing area of discovery, rediscovery and self-discovery. Tantra and the tantric truth still lies closetted within a mystery room, the keys of which are difficult to come by.

The mystery of the unknown has yet some charms left. The most profound of the scientific enquiries, ancient and modern, (from Atiśa Srījñāna and Nāgārjuna to Thales and Empedocles; from Śankara and Abhinavagupta to Faust, Schopenhaur, Blake, Blavatsky, Oliver Lodge and Tagore) have been addressed to the courage of breaking into the closed doors of the world of tantra. To such kindred minds the book might not be entirely useless. Tantra, after all, has been handed down to us through this stream of traditional recordings of events experienced.

Whatever is said and done, in spite of the best attempts, time is bound to take its toll, and certain understatements, together with many overstatements, as also instances of wrong emphasis, rhetorical excess must have embarrassed the narration. A writer is a human being; in spite of his determination to stick to sheer objectivity, his subjective presence is bound to cast shades on the mirror of life's moving events, specially when the subject itself offers so much details verging on the romantic and the eerie.

Apart from those blemishes in narration, and minus the literary flourishes, what has been stated, incident by incident, chapter by chapter, is nothing but fact, yet alas, not the whole fact. The whole fact shall always remain hidden inside the mystic darkness of the legendary 'cave' (*nihitam guhāyām*); and the charm of tantra would always continue to lure the aspirant towards it, and drive him mad for securing the proverbial 'golden key' to the 'cave of mystery'.

Granted that one favour, viz., acceptance of the factual correctness of the narration, the reader is assured of the relative truthfulness of the 'things that happened' before the eyes of a person who had been trained from his childhood to keep his eyes and ears alert for receiving the flitting messages from the wide extending shores of the mystic continents.

As I said, I attempt to 'scientific' or psychological explanations, and I offer none whatsoever, for the events, as they happened, phase by phase, one after the other. The explanations, if any, shall have to remain beyond the reach of those who find themselves in the need of explanations. Scepticism has a dearer price to pay in terms of tranquillity and peace of mind than credulity, specially in an area where faith and submission of ego provides the pass to entry.

Those who would not be convinced by the statements made, are, and I repeat, absolutely free to describe the entire exercise as a legend from the land of nowhere. Let the very serious subject of tantra and the tantric world remain for them and to them a world of fantasy. No star or dog would shed a mournful tear thereby.

The record is for the faithful, the diligent, the tenacious, the determined hunter on the track. It is a mission fulfilled, and does not have to open a chapter on advocacy. If even a single member of this brotherhood finds in these pages some food for further growth, some faint light that could, amidst the surrounding darkness, locate the final destination, the authors shall be generously rewarded.

The reader shall have observed through the pages that the locale of these incidents have been primarily restricted to the city of Varanasi, and the river Ganges. This is so because most of the incidents recorded happened to have been staged in that city where the author was born, and where he grew into his manhood. Naturally that locale, and the particular period have received a closer attention.

Not that other regions have not been brought into the picture; but by and large the stage has been set around the time, stretched from the second to the end of the fourth decade of this century in the city of Varanasi.

Similar and much more varied incidents have cropped up in the life of the author in course of his travels through countries far-flung around the world: Japan and Mexico, Thailand and Haiti, Cambodia and Jamaica, Greece and Surinam, Trinidad and Peru. It is not yet sure if those strange tales shall ever be told, age being a handicap amongst many other types of hazards.

For the best part of the narrative I have tried to use the direct form of speech. Of course time and space must have often emerged as deterrents to a faithfully photographic reporting. One of the factors that has stood in the way of accurate narration is the language spoken by the correspondents. Most of them used only their native tongue. English has not been spoken even. As such the text has been severely handicapped. But as I try to re-live the time and the events, despite the handicap, I have tried to maintain the warmth of the speech of the actual dramatis personae, which I feel I recall even at this distance of time most vividly, and which sends sparks of intense power and spiritual vibration.

Depending on the actuality of those messages as I vivify them, I have tried my best to maintain the spirit of their talks, and preserve the substantial purity of their contents.

Thus the direct form of speech, wherever used, retain, I believe, their original tang and flavour as well as their verve, urgency, import and life, even if, I dare say, they had to lose in accuracy of vocabulary used, and in the inimitable native simplicity of the manner in which these were originally spoken. Native presentation of the 'uneducated' and the unsophisticated is a delight which no literary artifice or craftsmanship could ever dream to capture.

Wherever I have entertained serious doubts about accuracy of direct narration, whether in syntactical arrangements, or in the use of images and idioms, or about those untranslatable native phrases, I have, by keeping close to the contents, as well as to the spirit of presentation, used a reporter's form, and used my own language and indirect reporting. To this extent some pardonable deviations, possible inaccuracies, and personal touches have inescapably cropped up.

In spite of those liberties taken, I believe, the taste of the brew remains loyal to the palate. Even as this might be so, it must be borne in mind that the book none the less has been a sad loser because the simple dignity, the direct penetration and the touching familiarity of the language of the Lady in Saffron, the biting and incisive humour of the language of Nārada, the placid and quiet grandeur of the language of Saint Jiten have most certainly, in the course of narration, lost their genuineness, as does the description of God and God's greatness by the descriptive language that man uses to contain the uncontainable. The author's personal lack of a yogic restraint, and his limited knowledge of a foreign tongue must also have deprived the original of its due lustre.

Apart from the failings, some wrong emphasis, some dramatisation, some rhetorical colouring must have flowed into the wide and fast current. These personal shortcomings apart, the reports here presented remain to me facts of life. If the reader is still bent on rejecting the entire exercise as a dreamer's soliloquy he is welcome to his adjudgement, and perfectly entitled to safeguard his credulity.

In preparing this book I was inspired by a dear friend who is not with me now, but whose name (Ramprasad Jadoonanan) will remain a by-word with every good soul in Trinidad. I am indebted to my friend Sri B.N. Chatterji, introducing me to Sri Devendra Jain. But for the combination of these two I would still be in search of a reliable and responsible publisher. I must acknowledge the labours which my daughter Shrimati Atreyee Cordiers has put graciously in preparing an index, a glossary and checking through the proofs.

B. BHATTACHARYA

New Delhi
2 November 1987

1

The Mystic Lady

A Brahmin Family

My involvement with tantra has not been either theoretical or academic. It could be described as radical. It had to be practical, and down-to-earth natural; to me it was as swimming is to a fish.

For a Brahmin boy born in 1910 in the ancient city of Varanasi, in a Brahminically Sanskritized family, tantrism was the very air he had to breathe. Sanskrit was almost my mother tongue; chants and hymns hummed like scores of pulsating lullabies; rituals and seances were almost periodic occurrences, which I accepted with as much grace and tenderness as is accorded in a Christian family to the mystic customs of Christmas. No questions were asked, no doubts harboured, no replies expected and no explanations appeared to be needed at all. Hunger for interpretation and explanation is more or less a fad of the rational world, which, historically, appears to be a growth of the eighteenth century.

Scepticism is an intellectual exercise indulged in by a world that seeks escape from any kind of authoritarian control. The Hindu world of mystical practice is grounded in the concept of the guru, who by his experience, his personal sincerity, his charm of manner, elicits absolute submission and unquestioning devotion from the initiates, and establishes over them a supremacy almost as absolute and inviolable as that of the Godhead.

The entire world of the boy was permeated with this spirit of complete submission. This was an inevitable growth from that inner hunger which seeks knowledge of the unseen depths indicated by life but not made clear. Life itself is taken to be only a stage in the race for reaching the ultimate truth. That small boy could not have divined the intricate process underlying the mysterious urgency of this kind of search; but the awareness of this mystery, of its reality, of the absolute possibility of some power of exotic nature became, as he grew, a part of his very personality. So it was not strange that he staked all to get to the heart of the thing, and to get to it through some unchartered process, if necessary. Besides, his insistent hunger for knowledge was pervaded also with the spirit of a holy and sanctified aura which was at once compelling and attracting, agreeably mysterious yet vibrant with an inner expectancy which had a language of its own.

It was sublimely exclusive, and exclusively sublime. It was both personal and communal. Bathed in mystery, it was yet clear as crystal. It was bold as sunrise, awe-inspiring like the peaks of the Himalayas seen through the dream-swathed mantle of moonlight on the snows.

I can still visualize, still sense, still thrill at the recollection. Like John Stuart Mill, I had no childhood.

Feasts and Devotions

Probably it has something to do with our way of life. The family was dedicated to the deity, Kāli, the Dark Mystic Lady, who is invoked every time there is a special family occasion. And Tārā, the prototype of the Oriental Astarte, the Tibetan Sarasvatī, the fierce Mother of benign grace, used to be worshipped as a community deity at our doorstep. This was an annual event, which demanded nocturnal dances intensified with rituals, lasting from midnight to sunrise.

The members of the family have their pretty little niches and respective shrines, with their individual *āsanas*. Everyone, male or female, had to offer prayers to the Mother and to Śiva, her *alter ego*. "No prayers, no breakfast," was a rigid rule, from which none was exempt save when severely incapacitated by sickness, or handicapped by menstrual cycles. In such cases, however, their shrines had to be 'kept alive' by substitute worshippers. The rules were strict, and were strictly followed without any question. Chants, *japa*, *prāṇāyāma*, *āsana*, *mudrā*, were just orders of the day.

The Lady in Saffron

But I was different. I do not know why, but it was so; and everyone recognised and accepted this difference. Obstinate, said some, precocious remarked others; according to the more liberal, I was determined. I was a naturally misunderstood, wayward, on-his-own child, but I sensed that I demanded notice, attention and regard from more people than were ready to give me such compliments. Always governed by a mighty urge to discover more, seek more, know more, absorb more, I could dare experimentations, misadventures, and even a touch of vagabond disregard of form and of tiresome routine. I enjoyed being rejected as a hopelessly wayward child. Ah! for the joys of protestant solitude and earned loneliness.

Soon this was rewarded.

It was rewarded by the motherly sympathy of a strangely silent lady in saffron who used to ply her humble trade in the same lane we lived in. In fact, she was one of our closest neighbours. These lanes of Varanasi run parallel to the river Ganges, on which the ancient city is situated like a crescent moon. Varanasi is as old as history, more ancient than Athens or Troy, Peking or Cairo, Damascus or Nineveh. And these lanes still spread out as ancient arteries of an ancient city. History has been flowing down these arteries uninterruptedly for aeons. The thick walls, the narrow passages, the cut-stone monolithic flags that stretch across the lanes (and roof the most ancient underground sewage system in India), the roaming bulls and cows, the naked fakirs and singing minstrels, let loose a stream of life altogether fascinating and intriguing. Nowhere in the world could one set his eyes so casually upon the open pages of such a living encyclopaedia as lies open across these narrow lanes of Varanasi.

And here was situated her humble shop: a one-door tenement with a narrow receding inner passage which stored, besides the sticky, oozy, sooty darkness, a large heap of husky coconuts imported from Bengal.

Apparently, she was a coconut vendor. One could buy pieces of coconut for as little as a quarter-of-a-pennyworth. But she also sold the fibres and husks of the fruit, and strings twisted from the fibre. She herself did the arduous task of ginning and twisting the rough stuff; and I with my boyhood eyes of wonderment kept watching the nimble fingers deftly engaged at what looked to me the most complicated mode of producing something out of almost nothing.

The great wheel of the machine which she drove with her left hand went round and round with droning melody of its own, until gradually, very often, I rested my head in the hook of her ample thigh, and fell asleep. The picture of that very accommodating, plump and pliant body, tall and confident, afforded to my imagination a sense of fortified security.

This Lady in Saffron had been a fascinating mystery to all of us children of the locality. This mystery was in no way solved by the persistent whisperings, at times awesome, at times deferential, at times suspensefully sacrosanct or sanctimonious, whatever one would like to call it. She was head and shoulders above the common grist of humanity.

This distinctiveness was recognisable at every step by the way people discussed her; not always a gossipy way, but always with some amount of regard and wonderment. This indirect homage was accepted by her with supreme equanimity and unconcern. She appeared always to be sunk within her own interior; and her exterior was never within the reckoning of those who came near her, or of those who kept miles away.

She was a living legend of the locality: of Varanasi, I dare say.

How else could I comprehend the stream of mothers (at times of fathers too) bringing on certain evenings their sick babies, children, and even their own suffering selves, in solemn disregard of the surroundings, for a few drops of water that she could sprinkle on them? Whenever she entered into such singular rites, she seemed to be transported to some unfathomable depths; and all those who were concerned also appeared to be influenced by the solemnity of her deep abstraction.

But I felt drawn towards her by her sheer charm.

Naked Innocence

In those halcyon days of childhood I used to tramp about with no more clothes on me than my birthday suit, which I so loved that I actually struggled with my mother to have 'garments' cast away. She, poor darling was naturally embarrassed at such heady freedom in a child of my age; and my playmates were often thrown into perplexity by such antics from a boy who otherwise seemed likeable to most of them.

I had a natural contempt for any cover. I delighted to receive the sun in its hottest glory over my bare skin. I thought that the skin was meant for the kisses of the sun. I liked the air to sweep over me, and I liked the bare earth to roll upon. The grass with its green must be nearest my skin, as, I thought, the roots of the body and those of the grass were kindred.

And water called me, particularly the mighty majestic water of the flowing Ganges. To swim in its sensuous liquidity, smooth and cool, to roll and roll again in its bosom, like the beams of morning on its waves, was sheer delight of 'skin-music' reaching the very roots of the nerves. Nothing was more soothing than the naked roll in the waters that were always there to receive me. How very kind was the river. The clothed cannot receive nature in the full. I loved myself as a close neighbour of the sun, the air, the earth and the water.

This kind of closeness to nature, an utter contempt for the standards of the clothed human norm, implanted and fostered in me a type of barefaced boldness that shaped my language, my character and my images. I was rather doubtful of the daredevil reputation my playmates often bestowed upon me; today, in retrospect, I can discover myself as a congenital introvert.

In any case the kind of supposed association with the devil made me, perhaps, interesting to Lady in Saffron. She began to draw me closer and closer. I found myself often closeted with her in that inner part of her humble abode which others could only imagine, but none had ever penetrated.

Through the acceptance of this 'distinguished' lady, I became the elect of the locality; much of that awe and wonder with which she was associated, shadowed me. It appeared as if from nowhere a holy mantle had suddenly fallen on me. In the eyes of the people in general I become the uncommon, the chosen. My companionship was sought by many, even by my elders. I was regarded as the *alter ego* of the impenetrable mystery that was personified by the Lady in Saffron, she who was known more by her seclusion than by her sociability. Her silence was more familiar to people than was her eloquence. Her eyes spoke more than her tongue. Her frowns were rare, but her smiles were rarer still. Her rejections were endured; but her acceptance surprised all. That inscrutable Lady in Saffron, who studiously avoided all fraternizing and kept herself aloof from all, accepted an unclad urchin of the lanes, who suddenly looked (to the surprised onlookers) much taller, and who felt overwhelmingly blessed.

My Tantrik Uncle

It was at this stage that the thing happened.

My uncle was respected as a tantrik. In the practical field of tantra he was regarded a master by all and sundry. He was well known for his extremely straight and decent conduct in personal life; and the meticulously Brahmanical forms that he preserved drew attention from those who knew tantra. One of the greatest scholars and tantra *sādhakas* of modern India was Mahāmahopādhyāya Dr. Gopināth Kavirāj, an internationally recognised savant and tantrik. I have been a witness to his unabashed devotion to this uncle of mine. With his white bouncy curls descending well below the shoulders, and white silky beard to match, my uncle, satin-skinned and light-coloured, looked like an Oriental patriarch materialized from the spirit of the Vedas, or of the *Zend Avesta*.

My closeness to the Lady in Saffron did not escape his notice. Once he made a significant comment on this growing relationship, a relationship impermissible in those days in a really devout Brahmin family.

Why?

It was her shady past. She was supposed to have belonged to the sisterhood of the *Scarlet Letter*. But was it certain, or only an assumption built on hearsay? Who was she, really, socially, and speaking with the inescapable subject of caste in mind? What were her antecedents? The Lady in Saffron was not born as a lady in saffron. None is. All females of the Hindu fold are supposed to embrace the marriage sacraments, which are the only sacraments they are exposed to. And if there had been any reason for not falling in line, what could it have been?

Or was there something worse? Had she in fact been married, only to be abandoned and rejected, an outcast?

This, and reflections such as this, forced her to exist as an island in the sea of humanity. She was an extraordinary person with an extraordinary past, which was even more dark and murky than the apartment she lived in. In later life, I discovered, that she had indeed been a "fallen" girl (to me a fallen angel) who had run away from her widowed girlhood with a man of 'very low caste', and was later abandoned by him; to toss around for a while in the multitudinous waves of the streets, until she found her footing, and rediscovered herself in the light of her inner glory and grandeur. She had exiled herself in the remoteness and impersonality of the mighty Himalayas, significantly in the eastern frontier of that vastness, finding her last resort in the placid silence of Varanasi.

All this was discovered and reknitted by me from her confidences which she shared a few months before she got ready for her final departure. Surely some of the strands of this history must have been known to my uncle. Hence the pointedness of his comment.

This in itself stands as evidence of the absolute freedom of the tantric life, where there are no restrictions of any kind, but where success and realization is judged by the sheer standard of true achievement. The tantrik has no bars; he admits of none; and he defies all that human society has forged to clamp on man's essential recognition of his purest identity.

She is not of Us

"It is lucky", my uncle said, "that you are the favoured one, young man; but do not waste either your time, or her love for you. Utilise it. Be grateful to her. Absorb her."

While I was wondering what could I do to 'utilise' my time, he continued, "Her voice is angelic. She sings great hymns. Learn them, and you will learn a divine way of reaching the sublime. Further, you should bear in mind that besides the spiritual poise which everyone notices in her, her expertise in tantric rites and mystic sacraments could lead you far. Above all, remember that she is a great scholar in Sanskrit, a fact which very few suspect."

He paused. After a while he resumed, "And if the gods favour, what is started in music could end in treasures that all yogis seek, but few gain."

"What treasure?", I at once asked, alert like a wild dog suddenly sansing his quarry.

For a while my uncle did not find words. His eyes searched for something in the sky. Then in a deep and sonorous voice he said, "She is not of us. She belongs to the evermore. She is one with Space and Time. Does that make any sense to you? With her as a pilot across the ocean of strange silences, out in the sphere of heavenly sounds, you two could be riding together, as only few hear or read in books. You have an opportunity. Do not allow it to go waste."

"One with Space and Time!"

The words started buzzing within my brain. Strange rumblings of things to come disturbed the calm innocence of my years.

Soon it was dark. It was time for the evening prayers. But my mind was away, far away. I was quietly seated across the railings overlooking the majestic river which flowed out of nowhere, and coursed down to nowhere, across time and space.

I was lost within. I felt a touch.

It was my darling sister who always worried on account of my other-worldliness. My absence from the prayers had shocked her. I went with her to the shrine as one bemused, and joined the others. Soon the agony of the ritualistic prayers was over; and dinner was eaten.

Fervently I sought to be alone. I wanted to have all time to myself. I found myself again perched on my favourite spot on the railings, watching the dark moving flood, and watching for the inner meaning and significance of that strange phrase that had suddenly thrown me far away from my familiar world: "One with Space and Time!"

Who could tell me what that meant?

One with Space and Time

Soon my sister called me to bed.

But rest was not for me. In the seclusion of the dark bedroom where I shared a floor-spread with my sisters and brothers gradually I was getting warmer. The words "One with Space and Time" assumed strange dimensions, kept my eyes wide open, and my mind wide awake. "*One with Space and Time!*" Words of great import. "I must seek their meaning now," so I thought, "and not a moment later. I must make a move. My move." I waited.

Soon I became aware that the world around me, my folks and my room-mates all were asleep. I made sure that I was not watched. The bed bothered me, and I found myself slipping out of it like a cat in the dark.

Stealthily, cautiously, I opened the door, and stepped on the terrace, by then flooded with the liquid grace of the sliver moon.

The quiet Ganges looked a flood of mercury. A strange sensation whispered through my nerves. In the distant, atop the roof of the seven storeyed yellow house, Gopal, a half-crazed tobacconist, was celebrating the wondrous moon-bathed night by playing soft melodies on his reed flute. Deep within me I became aware of a stirring. I was almost on the verge of a discovery.

Who was this Lady in Saffron? She was so little spoken of. Yet the way my uncle had referred to her not only betrayed his deep reverence for her, but by recommending her to me had even rested his confidence in her. I recalled with some amount of concern that he had warned me against taking her for granted, and accepting her too lightly. She appeared to me like a secret mine. She kept covered somehow, within the folds of her soft skin, and those of the saffron cloth, ages and ages of secret knowledge, much as the caves had kept covered the secret treasures that Alladin had sought.

Open Sesame! The magic words. *One with Space and Time!* Magic words again. And she was my dear auntie, the cocount lady. The cast-away, the shunned, the living monument of hushed references.

Suddenly I became aware of a familiar touch.

My father.

He looked at me, and watched into my eyes. Tears could no longer be kept back. That touch had a special appeal. He would not ask questions. He just waited.

I held his comforting palm in my hands, and all I could do was to give a gentle pressure.

"What disturbs my son?" The gentle voice became one with the soft light around. The flute in the distance played on.

"I don't know; I feel very disturbed."

"So you are. So am I, though not very."

There is something in a moon-washed flowing river, watched from an altitude of a hundred feet or more; some mysterious pull, some mesmeric spell. One watches the flowing glory of light, and gets bemused. This could be called poetry in Nature, the allure of profundity, a peaceful serenity of light reflected on the mind. Was it a summons from the Immense to the Immense?

"You do not care to retire to bed?," asked the caressing voice. It sounded smooth, soothing, secure as milk.

"Bed?", I cried. "Oh no. But perhaps you could tell me something."

"To ease you?"

"To ease me, Dad."

He watched me. The moon was shining on his silvery locks and the Messianic beard. The skinny frame, so familiar to me, to the touch of my eyes, shone in strange contours. He appeared to have emerged from other times, a patriarch of the lost tribes.

"What is it?"

"The Lady in Saffron; my aunite......"

And I stopped. I do not know why.

"What of her?", he asked, a little intrigued this time. And I could feel the sudden tension.

Even though he was my Dad, he looked and sounded different.

I was sure. He too knew her secret.

After what seemed to be ages I collected myself and said, "She belongs to Space and Time; in fact she is one with Space and Time. Isn't she?"

That was a mouthful for me to say. And I could feel the old man tense, strung as a sitar-wire about to be played.

There was silence all around, until the gentle voice asked, "Who told you that?"

He knew that I could not have composed these words by myself.

Then there was a gentle hug, followed by a more eloquent and significant touch. Did his eyes too get moist? I was not sure. His looks were dewy with a strange liquid light. He became another father from another world.

Then flowed his familiar-unfamiliar voice, deep, sonorous and confiding.

The Inner Sense

"Your uncle loves you. He is a divine person. What he says is the word of God. There is no like of him in this house; in this world....He is right. He is true. He has a special concern for you; hence he has confided in you. He would not reveal the identity of the Lady to any one else...

"But you are bursting with suspense. You want to know. Now listen. You see that river. Do you? Watch it well. Where from does it come?"

"From the Himalayas," I said.

"Have you seen this, or have you only heard of this? Do the Himalayas exist for you, as does this river; or have you just accepted in your imagination a land mass, hilly, huge, forested and snow-capped? Or is it for you only a line on a map?"

"You mean if I could see the Himalayas as the Himalayas all at one time? Well, no. I was indeed once there with you, and saw the huge hills. But who could see the whole Himalayas all at one time?"

"Where and how then does it exist in your understanding?"

"Understand? Exist?" I murmured. But I did not give up, and continued, "Understanding is existence. Existence is a kind of understanding...I am getting confused, Dad. I imagine, and it exists. I understand, and it exists."

"Right. You are not confused. Remain truthful, and you will see everything. Truth is the eye infallible; the third eye. Remain steadily face to face with Truth, and you will capture understanding. You shall comprehend...

"Our eyes are not fit, not even competent, to see *All. Allness* is an existence in comprehension. If it were not there, it would not be anywhere. Our senses are not equipped to detect *All*; to comprehend *All*. Senses are not really meant for undertaking such a task. Senses can only work superficially..."

"Superficially? I feel confused. Senses are all to me."

"Now. Not for ever. With growth and maturity you will realise that what the senses comprehend is not real. Even the beauty of Nature and the world is but superficial. There is a Beauty over and above all this which lies beyond the senses. That is the Real. Understanding is existence. Real existence. That which comprehends is the basic and the most trustworthy sense; not what you regard as senses. When we want to see more we close our eyes... Senses are not enough. To try to comprehend with senses is to try ploughing the running waters of the Ganges with a needle...

"But do not become despondent. God is merciful. God has equipped man with all that life needs, and more; with all that even the supra-life needs and that we do not care for. There is a life within this life. When all life is satisfied, there remains something still unsatisfied. This is the problem with life. You are suffering from a want of satisfaction tonight; and yet you have all that life needs; food, shelter, sleep, company.

"Man is possessed of another and more enduring sense, the sense that awakens with an inner light. And with that Man could see *All*. You do not know from where the Ganges comes; you do not know where does the Ganges go. All is 'information', ideas that get '*formed... in*.' Nothing is 'experience.' You do not experience the total Ganges because of the limitations of your senses. Senses are a set of apparatus fitted for receiving little facts of our life. We call them information, not experiences. Experiences do not depend on these senses. Experience is something that you alone could receive, and receive beyond the senses. Absorb. It becomes a part of you. You are what you are in experience. If someone hates you, for instance, you feel pain. And in this communication no sense-organ has taken a part. You see? There is another sense *antah-karaṇa*. You have heard about it. It means 'that which acts within'. Our language is so truthful and sensitive. It does not have to lie...

"This is the inner sense. The *antah-karaṇa*. The sense that you could only sense, and not find anywhere to see or touch, as you could your eyes, tongue or ears. With sense you said that the Ganges comes from the Himalayas, and that the Ganges goes to the sea. You never see this; yet you are so sure of this. Aren't you? This is your other sense. Men call it *reason*. This is another apparatus of knowledge; but again like the senses this too is limited. We shall see..."

"Yes, reason; I know reason. But this too is limited . . .," I parroted.

"Not only reason, even our comprehension suffers from limitations. You know why? We ourselves are limited and incomplete. Man is naturally born incomplete. It is man's destiny to make himself a total man. To become a man in full is his birthright. To be a full man is to fulfil an urgent charge; to grow to a fullness."

I was never more confused. I understood every syllable uttered by that familiar presence, my father, and none else. Yet he appeared and sounded to me so very unfamiliar; and he had been using such strange diction. I did not realise where I lost the thread. But I went on, picked it up again; and got lost again. I was confused. He was another father; a stranger to me.

"I do not understand," I managed to articulate.

"Yet your reason is there. Because you are open, innocent and outright, because you love and trust me, and because there is an urgent demand deeply disturbing you, you come out flat with the simple confession that you do not understand. There are many who are afraid to say that. Be that as it may, you know now that reason too fails, as eyes and ears do. Reason in children fails like eyes and ears in the old. Nevertheless, failure of these, at one or another time, only proves that these are unreliable, and limited in capacity."

"Yes, so they are. So what?"

He smiled, and through a gentle pressure on my shoulder reminded me of my sudden impatience. I could not hold the tension any more. I was hungry for more knowledge.

He continued.

"Never get impatient. Lack of patience is an enemy to realisation. Patience and practice are the two faces of the coin we have to pay for realising unlimited knowledge, or the knowledge of the unlimited...

"You see the Ganges?... You do. So you said a moment back. And then you also said that what you see is not the Ganges, but only a part of it seen at a time, which is also a part of all time. Both time and the Ganges are flitting, and are partially experienced, only one at a time, although both are moving simultaneously. You see how limited is the mechanics of comprehension? The real Ganges, as the real Time, is unlimited. What you call its limit is in your mind, or that which fits your reason. Good. But you also know that your mind, as well as your reason suffer from a limit. Both are incomplete and inadequate. Because you are incomplete; but not inadequate. You are quite adequate to develop into a complete being. You are a man. You have this right."

I appeared to stir again. But he was too fast for me.

"Wait. Do not be impatient. I do not want to confuse you. Hold on, and listen carefully. *Sam gacchadhvam...Sam vadadhvam... Sam no manāmsi jāyatām*...(Together we proceed, together we more sombre and sterile. The quarrelsome cacophony of birds fighting for a nightly perch added to the surrounding grimness a vertical depth. The quiet Varuṇā placidly submitted to the dominant Ganges; and the evening orange sky looked on. I, a mere boy at the time, would watch my Lady at *āsana*; feebly imitate her posture, thus offering a poor spiritual parody of a serious event. This was indeed a boyish homage paid to the influence of the surroundings on a naturally brooding soul.

In these outings very often a strange and peaceful feeling of contentment dawned on me. Often did I feel what is popularly described as exultation, a sensuous form of supreme delight. Often my younger cousins, and elder sisters tittered mockingly, disbelieving that I could muster enough courage to sit by myself near a crematorium, with only a strange meditating old lady as my companion.

One thing must be made clear.

I never 'meditated,' not knowing what exactly it was all about.

Or, to be more precise, no idea of meditation ever came clear to me. Whatever I did at such times in those places could be best described in Cowper's language: 'to think down hours to moments.' I just imitated what (it seemed to me) she did. I hardly knew anything about the implications of meditation as I do now.

Yoga Shops

Nowadays, wherever I have been, in the West, in the East, I have found people extremely insistent on finding out how to *meditate*. Prospering in this craze for instant meditation, instant liberation, and instant joy, a caravan of seducers have opened 'shops' to put on sale their opportune commodities wrapped up in attractive silver foils of hope and success. Such *shops* are today as numerous as cinema houses and insurance agencies. These are specially located at those haunts in India where the touring westerners credulously throng, and look for the roadside taste of India on sale. These have also mushroomed in those Western cities which, like prehistoric monsters, suck out of life a people's faith in joys of life, in dreams of freedom, and in the music of human values. Pressurised by modern conditions of living, they inevitably get frustrated, and fail to know anything about how to fight the situation. They are trapped in the vast prison-house of the mammoth cities of our times.

These unfortunate victims seek in spiritual pursuits some form of escape from their suffocating existence in these commercial overcrowded dungeons. In our sick civilisation meditation has almost assumed a medical connotation. Meditation has become a fashion, a mania. A tonic? Perhaps.

Peace Descending

But I did not care. I did not even know if I did meditate. All I remember clearly is that I used to do what the Lady did, and I liked it to be done in the way she has taught me.

Often I got absorbed. The calm grandeur of a descending evening on the fevered brows of a great populous city gradually sucked me in; the feeling lulled me. If perchance any evening there happened to be a cremation on, the flames added further depth and colour to the evening sky. At times the dying embers, the left-overs from some unknown pyre, breathed with the wafting breeze. My wonderment at the grandeur of the spectacle of life got me involved in the embracing call of the place. Often I broke into melodies.

That peace descending from the Varanasi-sky by the confluence of the Varuṇā and the Ganges offered a blanket-feeling of contentment. Gradually, the world became totally obliterated; and a supreme sense of fullness kept consciousness at a zenith. Peace descended as it does, in the language of Masefield, 'in the Isle of Innisfree'; often I broke into the Ṛgvedic verse—"The winds are sweet; the waters are sweet; the green earth is sweet; sweet are the night and the dawn; sweet are the dusts; our father in heaven is sweet; sweet are the trees, the sun and the cattle."

Zero Point in Mind

Was this meditation? Judging by the results, it could not have been anything else. In the most ancient and authoritative treatise on Yoga (Yoga Sūtra of Patanjali) as well as in the thoughts contained in the Vedānta and in the Upaniṣads, the one point lauded over others, endlessly, emphasises on the realisation of contentment. A kind of satisfying joy alone has been the hallmark of a successfull meditative exercise.

But I wonder today what exactly did I meditate on. What did I think upon? What did I concentrate on? The Lady never taught me anything; I never bothered to ask. Yet no mind could ever be set on a zero point. Mind can never be entirely naturalised. It has something to adhere to; it has to keep itself engaged. The trick lies in compelling it to think of a single, specific, clearly defined item of thought: in other words it has to concentrate its operation on a central point, an idea. Without that, there could be no meditation.

What to Meditate on?

Then, what did I really meditate on? What was it? Often the bantering cackles of my cousins and sisters dug through my patience. Or, was it impatience? They mocked at my weakness for meditating. "What is it you think you do? You are a fraud," they bantered. So I ventured to ask. I could only ask the one who, I supposed, would indulge me, and who appeared to me as the best equipped person to provide me with a satisfying answer. The Lady in Saffron would neither mock, nor deceive.

The Light from Other Spheres

My first attempt at this enquiry on meditation evoked from her the familiar smile. Apparently, she did not have the least idea about what I meditated on, nor what kept me engrossingly occupied. "But one thing I am certain about," she said, "that in meditation the mind should be kept occupied, and that with a single clear thought. If it were more than one, then you could not have felt the completeness of joy, which not only you say that you get, but which you actually show by your exuberance.

"Everybody speaks of the remarkable beams of your eyes, your pleasant relaxed looks, your friendly smiles. Perfect joy is not something one could keep hidden. The darkest night would show the tiniest lamp. Fragrance announces itself to the world around without caring if it is noticed. I notice it; and I could assure you that others notice it too. They notice that you are a very happy child; you are absorbed within yourself. To attain even to this stage is by itself something remarkable in a boy at your age. It is difficult. It is a fact that 'feeling inwards' has become a natural life-style for you."

A yogi's demeanour is unique. 'He glows with inner light,' says the Gitā; 'walks with inward glory crowned,' says Wordsworth.

I was not convinced. I was not even elated. I was hungering. The hungry is difficult to be kept at bay. The hungry is difficult to be pleased on chaff. Was she avoiding a direct reply?

She sensed my doubts. "You do not believe me. Do you?," She asked. I was glum and quiet.

"All right, you don't. If so, then tell me what do you think on? Could you pin-point it?"

This time I was busy searching for a correct reply.

You must be thinking of something; something total...something absorbing and liked...something once clung to, is difficult to get separated from. Recall what is it? It cannot be something casual. It cannot be something that changes from day to day. It has to be one, single, constant, loved and adored subject. Now, what is it in your case? What could it be? Recall; recall and you shall hit upon it."

Love Plants New Meaning to Life

She was right. I had come to know what it was. It flashed through me. It could not be any other thing but the one it was.

"What is it?" came the insistent question. "I see that you have located it. Now, what is it? Tell me. Out. No hesitation."

I had no immediate answer; but I knew what I needed to say.

I took all courage and declared, "You! I love you...I love to watch you absorbed in delight."

"I love you too, dear one," she said. And with a soft, deep, intimately confiding embrace she appeared to draw a curtain over the topic.

She did; I did not. "How could I get absorbed," I enquired, "even in loving you without knowing meditation? My cousins tell me without a guru it is impossible to meditate."

I hardly realised that I was inadvertently posing my 'book learning,' i.e., my pickings from the gossips and the hearsay of Varanasi; but the Lady was quick to sense it.

"Is that so?" She wondered with her mock voice, her mockingly wide eyes becoming wider. (How I, even at this age, recollect and visualise the incidents that happened sixty-five years ago, or, was it yesterday?)

"Then how was it," she continued, as was her wont, in the familiar manner of a myth narrator, "that the boy Dhruva, who had never seen a book, never learnt an alphabet, never met a guru, could still achieve perfect peace, and see God? And what about the boy Śukadeva?"

"And Kapila and Mārkaṇḍeya...," I added with a faith that inspired me to add.

"You love me," she continued, "You watch me with love; and love gives a new eye to see, and you see in me what others see not. Love plants new meaning to life. Love makes you adhere to me as if you could not do otherwise. Love makes your attention sharp-pointed speak, together may we develop our minds.... The familiar chant from the Upaniṣad we recited every day at the Sanskrit lessons, assumed a new dimension at this moment, as he sang them under the silent sky.) You too are, as I am, incomplete, but with a difference. You are a Man. As Man you are destined to discover eventually this lost self, and become complete. There is a share of the same Self lying asleep within you. Asleep; not lost. Not absent. Not dead. You could retrieve this, by your efforts. So could I. This is, as I had mentioned before, your birthright. Do you follow? You could realise this Self. You could realise the Total, the ALL. You see the Ganges yonder; but there is a Ganges more real than this known stream of water. That is the source of all water; the Source from where all streams flow, and into which all flows disappear. Remember, and I will not misguide my own son, that you could see, swim, feel, drink and live in that water, that Source. This is a possibility; and you have to accept this. That is why you are a *man*."

It had been a long harangue; and throughout I had held my breath, hardly able to move. I was stunned.

But did we not drift?

"I asked with a dogged insistence, "What about auntie?"

"Yes your auntie! Now I could speak about her. She is the one who could, whenever she chooses to do so, live in, swim in, and enjoy that Source. She is in touch with the Immense, that Unlimited in the limited. The hurrying current you call the Ganges is the timeless motion; it is one with Time; and she knows it. She lives in it. She is Time. For her there is no break in time."

The Treasure

Entranced I could just repeat, "She is time!"

"And also Space. She is one with Time and Space! She is continuity. For her there is no death, no birth. She takes her body just as a body, and nothing more. She cares for it as we take care of our living room, our clothes. We enter a room and go out of it. So we enter the world, and go out of it. This has nothing to do with birth and death as we know birth and death. To put on a suit of clothes, or to step out of it has nothing to do with birth and death. She knows that Life is a force, and is never ending. She belongs to the never ending Time, the never ending Life; not to the waves. She belongs to the ocean that never changes. That is in Space and Time. She is it.

"Watch there, the moon. Look at the light she sheds. You could see and spot the moon; but could you spot the light? Yet these are the same. One is the source; and the other is a property, an active purpose, a fulfilment. You cannot pin-point the light. All this is lighted by the moon, reflected. But the light itself cannot be seen unless and until reflected from an object which is not light. Probably all objects are naturally dark, belonging to a world of darkness, to a world of limited ideas. The Unlimited alone is Light. Could you see the light which is not reflected from an object? Look at the space between here and the clouds? Do you see light? But just as you reach the obstruction of the floating clouds, you see the wonderful visions of moonlit clouds floating around."

"I see; I comprehend; but somehow I get scared to think that all this is not what I see..."

"Scared?", he smilingly asked. "Do not worry. Such is the scare of learning. Truth scares. Even Arjuna got scared. To understand Truth and face it, scares not a few."

"I hate to think that I live in a world of darkness."

"You do? But you also live in a world of light. In fact you *belong* to the world of light. We all are the children of Light. Indeed there is no darkness except when we choose to keep ourselves merged in this myth of darkness. That moonlight *belongs* to the Space. Wherever the Light spreads beyond the objects of the world, wherever the light exists...."

"But Daddy," involuntarily I had interrupted.

"Yes."

I shuddered to have disturbed the old man at that intense moment. Perhaps my voice betrayed the timidity at facing the awesome greatness of the revelation. None the less I persisted. "But that would be an immense space."

"You said it!" This time I could hear his contented chuckle.

He looked at me, and I looked at him. There dropped a moment of peace concealed like a drop of pearl from a world of pain. I held to his hand, this time in a firm and confident grip of utter friendship.

But he continued. "She is one with Time and Space. Your uncle was so correct. And you are so lucky that the Lady in Saffron has chosen you for a monopoly, and keeps you so near her."

"Why, Dad?"

"She knows best. Only do not lose that blessed affection she bestows. Deserve it, and preserve it."

"Perchance I need her," I sheepishly offered.

"Perchance she needs you. Watch and keep your peace. Personal secrecy is a bond of absolute honour in such friendly relations."

"It is too much to keep." I confessed with a voice that sounded like a warning.

"It is not. Friendship is a gem; and like a gem it is vulgar to display it. All precious objects, as all precious feelings, demand secrecy; real worth of such acquisitions is revealed in the joy that our behaviour and our conduct in public relations express. You will need this loyalty. And you shall keep this a secret."

I kept up this loyalty, and the secret was mine, until she had herself one day released me from the bond. I loved her as a treasure, as a boy's find.

Then came the day when she asked me to accompany her on a strange journey.

I hardly realised that by following her that day I was entering at the threshold of a world which even fancy finds hard to compose; or reason to decompose. We arrived at a strange temple where I had never been before, although it was so close to our neighbourhood.

And she asked me to be seated on her naked body.

But I am rushing the whole experience.

This should not be done. She was holy, and the experience was sublime.

So, at leisure, another time.

2

Initiation

Where Fires Consume Flesh

It was not the first time that I had gone out with the Lady in Saffron; I frequently had the pleasure of going out with her. In a holy place like Varanasi excuses for such excursions were numerous.

If we were not visiting a newly arrived saint, we could be attending a special musical function, or gone far away to attend a fair. Occasionally it could have been a boat journey to a remote shrine by the river.

One such was situated at the confluence of the Varuṇā and the Ganges. There stood Ādikeśava, an ancient place and a Jain temple with some secluded ruins of scattered temples here and there.

Long ago, even before the Greek invasion of India, Kāśi, the reputed principality of the epics, had here its capital. The remains of a fort and the citadel walls are still traceable. No wonder that the gods have refused to die with the ruins. Many images still yield to the ploughshares, or to the archaeologist's spikes.

The sombre and still wilderness is dominated by the ancient crematory grounds on the banks of the wide river. Though not in use now (in preference to the newly extolled Maṇikarṇikā) the grounds still become animated by a stray pyre burning by the sleepy stream. The flames reflect and dance on the quiet water as they did in the remote past.

Here lurked a dilapidated tiny shrine of the illustrious Bhairava-saint Dattātreya, the miracles of whose life have been sung over the subcontinent from the times of the epics. In *Vāma Tantra* traditions the names of Vaśiṣṭha, Paraśurāma, Dirghatamas etc., have left immortalised history. Speaking of both esoteric and occult doctrines, as well as of their *siddhi*, Dattātreya ranks with the very highest.

Often I have observed the Lady in Saffron sitting at an *āsana* near the tiny Dattātreya temple. All on a sudden she would grow entirely remote. I would know very little of her. She, I discovered, was not always approachable.

In the evening haze the lonely shrine appeared lonelier, remoter, so long. No more of that, in this context. I have seen in the forests of Mexico aboriginal tribals stealing their footsteps to the secret water holes (Cenoté) where naked they perform their rites even now. True they have given up human sacrifice and cannibalism; but in the churches of Mexico, Guatemala (in the entire Amerindian world, known as Latin America) I have seen strings and strings of human limbs decorating the well lighted and well dressed waxen cadavers of a Christ lying in state, presumably before the burial. All these human limbs have been 'offered' to god! The devout have sacrificed, and the church has accepted. This has been going on till today. Yet there is a difference, and that saves grace! The difference is that these limbs are made by goldsmiths, and the offerings mean tons of gold and silver to the coffers of an intelligent church. So the old wine continues to be served in new gold cups, and the church flourishes.

It is useless to criticise the fraud and hypocrisy underlying this world of religion, and the minds of the prelates, who conduct religions. That is not what we have set out here for; we want to investigate that passion in man, which all over the world, from time immemorial, stakes and risks his utmost in order to create images, and bring the devout heart all out for paying to their creation their sincerest homage.

Granted this is mistaken; granted that this should be corrected. But could wrong have such a long lease of life? Could it outlive centuries of repression, torture, fire and brimstone? How and why we find this homage paid in every known human society? Is there some pocket of human misery which is assuaged by the creation of such gods who cannot stand the glare of logic? How could they have outlived the glare? It is a fact that they have. I have found priests singing the praises of saints after saints, taking the faithfuls down the dark corridors along the various lighted (and suitably decorated) niches that adorn the churches. Each of the saints is supposed to hold 'very special powers' for bringing a 'special' brand of relief to human ills.

Why this persistence against so much odds?

Images have been derided by the intelligent, the fashionable, the logical, the progressive. Sophistication blushes to admit them; and intellectuals sneer at them, and shout 'primitive!' Rarely the critics make a sympathetic study of the human element involved in this persistence. They themselves appear to be as much forced, regimented and/or brainwashed as those whom they brazenly criticise. This is the greatest injustice; the highest illogicality. Claims of intellectualism and progressiveness based on opinionated cliches alone inflict an insult on intellect's admitted virtues of honesty and fairplay. These critics are themselves sordidly regimented in their mind, and thoroughly brainwashed; but they do not realise it, much less admit so. Understanding connotes sympathy.

Faith: A Victim of Religion

Everyone knows that there cannot be any good in regimentation of ideas and thoughts. Man is different from other animals; but even animals pause to think, distinguish, select and remember. They are atavistically more sensitive, reflexively more alert than the human beings. Thinking in itself does not distinguish man as a superior product of nature in the animal world. It is intellection, rationality, and a strange combination of reason and emotion that makes man different from other animals.

To be regimented in mind is to lose the quality of the mind to think independently. In other words, this is the same as to be demented, at least partially; or 'brainwashed', if one prefers the current politically motivated phrase. The mind of such a man has been pressurised into a particular mould of thinking which was not of his choice. Such a mind has been given a specified shape, like a lump of steel passing through the torture from some hydraulic pressure. This inflicted shape denies man of his supreme right of thinking for himself. The fundamental difference between the processes of democracy and totalitarianism lies in this curse of regimentation. This phenomenon is not new to modern politics, or to the growing commercial economics. It is the religious institutions which really invented and applied it with success. Faith is a victim of religion; and mind is a victim of totalitarian politics

Call of Religion

Religion and religious systems have been exploited to enforce and dictate a type of divine regimentation which credulous devotees hardly ever suspect. All they are concerned with is to find refuge in some form of mental peace by submitting to a professed religious form.

Religion has wielded from time immemorial an influence in the formation of human society hardly excelled by any other single social inducement. Hunger is perhaps the most compelling form of inducement which acts as the most powerful drive in any animal society, not excluding the human. And next to that brute and primal compulsion is the tremendous drive coming from the calls of sex.

Apart from these two animal impulses, there is no other factor that has influenced the human society (exclusively), and generated as much sensitive emotionalism, creative dedication and pious fervour as the religious attitude of man. Religion has thus been called 'the hunger of the soul.' Men aware of this hunger seek to satisfy their souls by creating music, poetry and the divine arts. For the artists and for art, the divine and the secular are not held as different. Art is the religion of the artist; and a glow of aesthetic satisfaction appears to him as divine grace. Indeed the creative arts have often been described as 'Gifts of the Divine.' Art has been identified with the skill of creation itself; artists have been regarded as divinely inspired by a message of their own. God has often been imaged (as in the Veda as the supreme perfect artist.

Art would not have been thus extolled unless, like religion, it were a soul-filling involvement.

No animal except man creates art as art, with a voluptuary's conscious satisfaction of perfect consummation. The subjective delight in producing a thing of art does not differ from the satisfaction of offering a filling touching prayer.

Organised Transgression of Conscience

As I am looking at the emotional and creative contents in religion, I am not unaware of the fact that the area of human spirit and conscience has also been vitiated by the poisonous greed of vested interest. Much fraudulent hypocrisy and intimidating superstition has tarnished the faith, tainted the conscience, and stained believers' loyalty. Fire, blood and perverse cruelty all at a time have tested the faithful's loyalty. An entire directory of humbug has been enforced on the simple minded with the aid of political systems abetted by military might. Laws enacted by vested interest have been applied to judge the conscience of the free thinker. Honest protestations against indecency, cries of inhumanity and tyranny inherent in the inhuman process have been suppressed with sadistic indifference, irreverence and finesse.

But all these demands on social patterns and individual liberty were caused, not by religion or spirituality, neither by any inherent defect, lack of logic, or any unethical content in religion; but because of vested self interest, regimented impositions, institutionalised authority, and unrestricted exploitation of the credulity of the masses.

In short, after realising the fact that religion's comforting wing is an essentially needed factor in human growth, institutionalised dictatorships heartlessly monopolised this ultimate refuge that man, by his own suffering, had finally discovered for his protection against an insufferable emotional agony, and spiritual vacuum. The vicious grip of institutionalised authority held human conscience by its throat with the sole objective of exploitation and domination. Religiosity does not fail man.

Such forms of regimented and institutionalised religions, instead of inspiring man towards progress and liberation kept man clamped in abject spiritual fetters of penury in this life, and fear for the next.

Some great souls like the Buddha, Jesus, Confucius attempted to push the wheel on to the right track; but so powerful was the conspiracy of the system in power, that eventually their teachings got circumvented, and the institutions 'undid' the good the reforms did, and re-established with greater vigour their vicious trade.

Love for the Beyond

The sad and perverse chapter in the history of man's conquest of the Rights of Conscience does in no way belittle the role of true religion in bringing the much wanted peace, and personal solace in the social order. Neither does it in any way deprive religion of the glorious role it has played through its excellent spiritual and emotional content. Besides the poetry of words, music and colour no other craving of man has evoked so much dedicated effusion of the charm of human feeling, of the intensity of human emotion as this love for the beyond, known as religion.

It must be admitted to the credit of human heart, and its spiritual determination that in spite of the threats and failures of institutionalised religions man has preserved the sanctity of individual freedom in responding to his inner spirit's call, and registered his success in this struggle by exposing his emotional and imaginative feelings through religion of art, and art of religion.

True Religion Discovers Its God

True religion has proved to be a source of supreme subjective delight. It comforts and sustains man at times of distress and grief, loss and humiliation.

To barter away this tremendous right and powerful means of sublimating the clumsy business of living, by allowing our efforts to be and keen; nothing else can or could interfere. You must realise the meaning of 'a point' in this context.

"A point is where there is no place for two. It is just one. As soon as it is two, not to speak of more, it is not a point. The thought of any 'other' in the field of love, as in the field of yogic concentration is a grievous trespass."

As she continued, the voice was gaining in depth and strength. There was a change. A transformation was taking place. That voice always cast a spell over me; from those intensely articulated series of cadenced sentences, pouring like a cascade of love, flowing and covering me, she soon broke into one of those captivating songs:

How much I have been searching for you,
Here and there;
All the while you had been just here,
Within me...

These songs always intrigued me. As she sang, like an angel she appeared to float on the wings of her melody, away into regions unknown to me.

I shall forget all sorrow;
And bow in defeat;
Without complaint, without tears;
I shall gladly keep to the corner
Allotted to me in this life;
Only be kind,
And keep ajar just one door,
So that at the end of the journey
I could hopefully expect
A communion...

And soon I used to join her.
And soon I used to forget myself.
I ran to her for the coveted embrace at the end of the song. She held me close to her breasts.

Words, Words

Time and again she would remind me of this power of devotion culminating in submission, which is the supreme expression of Love.

There is nothing that love would not dare; nothing that love could not achieve; nothing that love would not abandon. In true love there is no feeling of sacrifice, sin, crime, or even of atonement. It is, she used to emphasise, a fulfilment of a divine sort. Such love causes no hunger; and seeks no result. It leaves no regret or sense of frustration behind. The more such love is given, the more a soul becomes liberated.

Gradually this kind of love overflows the person, and covers ultimately the whole known universe, nay even the unknown cosmos, even if we do not become aware of the change. Love makes a saint of a man. Love transforms flesh into a divine offering.

But all these, again, are words, words.

Samagram Pravilīyaté

To feel was different: I felt the vibrations,—her vibrations. She embraced me; and from one such embrace I could realise what she was trying to communicate. It was no mere communication, but a total transmission, a kind of pouring out to fill an empty vessel. That divine outpouring kept on ringing within me, and a voice kept urging, "Take! Take! Take all that I have. Multiply; justify; deify! Become liberated; liberate me. Let nothing hinder; let nothing bar. What is in me, is all yours!"

It is quite impossible to describe that insistent mute appeal; the eloquence of that all abandoning deep embrace. It was language without utterance; it was fire without movement. Not a hair stirred; not a glance flashed. With eyes closed, we felt submerged in a sea of tranquillity. A thrill of joy electrified the being. It was like writing a poem across a dream-laden sky with words not known to human tongue. "*Samagram pravilīyaté* (there is a total oblivion in love)", says the Gitā.

I have tasted that kind of love. And having tasted that kind of love, nothing more is worthy of having. "Nothing could ever add more to that. And as the mind gets steadied at that state, no feeling of grief or sorrow, nay, not even of the severest kind, could ever penetrate into that supreme composure."—(Upaniṣad) The language of 'yoga' and *samādhi*, of the apex of transcendental meditation (TM) describes this in a hundred similes, in a hundred poems, in a hundred ways. For language gets baffled to hand out a full and true description; the very mind is at standstill.

True it is that to the uninitiated these outbursts of description appear as mere words, words, words! What else?

One could not expect more from cynics, those pillars of wisdom who have been deprived of the simple joys of life. Those who live in the deserts of closed harems, have no alternative but to drive delight from geometrically drawn flowers and foliage. Those who seek the real delight must find it in the openness of Life. "If the deeps so fascinate you, tarry not, nor stumble; dive!" The seeming excess of words in itself turns the mind of the sceptic against its truth. It is a case of serving sweets to the spiritually diabetic. The initiated alone can appreciate the exulting spells of mystic delight.

Voyage to Innisfree

As I am on this topic, indulge me, dear reader, to recall here the entire philosophy of Love as expounded by her. I spent my entire growing youth in her company, and in a very close association. What I try to set forth here is what she had taught me carefully, diligently over those years.

Today I could unhesitatingly say that there is not and cannot be any tantra without this flame-swept message of love. The Lover and the Beloved, the Two in One and the One in Two, the Object-Subject turned into a purely subjective realization, *forms the very basis of tantra.*

Only idiots and charlatans view such idolatrous love as a blind submission of the foolish to some brass, clay, stone or wooden image. They even dare view this as hysteria, and reject such relationship as the expression of an imbalanced sex life. The compact relationship that the devotee gradually builds up through his single-minded devotion when warmed with the insistence and irresistibility of a loving impulse, turns his love into a spiritual power. It transmutes his emotional being to a purified state of ecstasy without body, music without words. This alone leads to the famed and coveted road to liberation, of which the wise speak, and which the suffering crave for. It is that utter freedom which *liberates the body and the agony of flesh from the slavery and servitude of the senses.* That terrible agony of flesh, which burns without satiety, and corrodes without repair gets cooled, and reaches a point of satiation at the touch of true love.

If there is a bliss to be conquered through effort, the way lies through this basic truth in tantra. That way alone the long long voyage navigates through the open sea of mystic realization, and reaches ultimately the destined Isle of Innisfree. The paradise lost to man could also be 'regained' through this understanding of, what is glibly termed as, tantra, as well as of the practice which is often sneered at as tantrism!

Idols and Images

But to continue with this love for idols, and images...

Images have often been derided by a section of 'religion vendors'. Images have been destroyed over the centuries, and over the length and breadth of cultures all over the world: Egypt, Mexico, Arabia, Syria, Greece, Rome, India, Indo-China, Siam, Java, name it, and images have been eradicated (!) from the pagan world, from the hall of the infidels; but images have been broken in Christian worlds too, and by Christians. The atrocities perpetrated in Holland, Belgium, France, Germany, in Rome itself, in the name of a truer and purer religion have turned pages of history into records of human agony, misery, humiliation and degradation. And to what end? Images and idols get broken; and like the legendary Sphinx and salamander survive their ashes, and rise up again, and in multitudes, with added vitality.

It is not the place to go into details of the political economy and commercial motivations of these organised carnages against the emotional creations of the peoples of different lands and times. But it is a moot question to be considered: why have men been found to create their own gods, and bring at their feet the best of their lives? Not wealth and freedom alone, but objects held far more dear than any worldly possession or interest. Why? Because even prior to Moses sacrifices, even of one's own children, were regarded as a normal way of expressing adoration and thanks.

Why? why the obviously illogical, the blatantly superstitious, the openly material forms of the various gods and goddesses do not end their tenure? Why and how do they get revived? Why? There must surely be some psychological justification for such 'senseless' devotion. These gods made of stone and wood, clay and brass must be fulfilling some inner need of man, without filling which man appears to remain unfulfilled.

Let us not go into the oft-beaten logic of explaining what is a true god, and what constitutes a servile submission to a world of superstition mesmerised by the magic wands of the clever priests and their skilful conspiracy.

Arguments like that have been droning into the ears of history ever dictated, is to act contrarily to the divine design. Like every other prized freedom, man also must cherish his freedom to accept a god of his choice, a god responding to the peculiar needs of his personal agony.

As such man is an exclusive individual in his pains, miseries, complaints, distresses, diseases and losses. Each man has to discover his own way of meeting the challenge he faces, and the situation that overwhelms him. In happiness the soul of man may become one with the seas and the sky; but in utter pain he is an island unto himself.

That which most answers his needs, that which responds by radiating intimate and confiding solace, is a man's own distinctive religion. Thus he creates and finds his own god.

As the artist's soul gradually discovers the medium through which he can best express himself, it would appear to be the height of foolish affrontary to command creative artists to accept an imposed canon or pattern of expression. Similarly, it would be unthinkable to impose a standard god on the famished broken soul of an individual, who is in search of his 'answering' god.

The body itself is a divine church; the soul, a shrine; realisation is the lamp, and what is retained there, in the sanctum sanctorum is his dearest God, his own Ideal. This is what tantra supports, believes, and preaches. This explains why in the tantra system there are so many deities, so many *dhyānas* and *mudrās*. Each aspirant under a threat of spiritual and emotional pressure creates his own deity, and prostrates before the ideal so crystallised. This is why the true tantric mind sings:

> I watch Thee, and Thou watcheth me;
> Let no other interfere between us.

This is the underlying concept of Hindu and tantric images. Intolerant iconoclasts could spare their outbursts by calmly understanding this point of view. As many individuals, as many individual ideas; as many ideas, as many ideals; as many ideals, as many *dhyānas*; as many *dhyānas*, as many *murtis* (images). Images are not idols. Deprived of their eternal values that are attributes of the divine presence, idols are mere lumps that man creates to raise up on a false pedestal.

We have heard of such idols: Alexander and Mardoch; Helen, Laila and Cleopatra; Caligula's horse, the Swastika of Hitler and the signs of the Zodiac. Each for a time has fascinated. The world of fascination still holds within its compass many such idols. Images that give to religions of the soul 'a local habitation and a name' must rise above the spell of mere fascination, and become one with the Soul.

Tantric images differ from mood to mood; from urge to urge; need to need; even from occasion to occasion. From the fierce forms of Chāmuṇḍā, Kāli and Nīla Sarasvatī to the milder forms of Lakṣmī, Sāradā and Prajnā-Pāramitā; from Viṣṇu, the sun-god, to Varuṇa, the water-god, and Śiva, the quiet static material image of absolute neutrality, every image is imbued with a subjective ideal, which if imaged successfully, holds the devotee's straying attention, and brings about the coveted concentration. This is just a method of setting the mind free of all inhibited pre-thoughts, and neutralising the world of the senses. The liberated alone are able to drive their consciousness inward. To them alone revelation becomes an achievement.

Images Bring Their Own Solace

This is the underlying secret of the many images of the tantriks, of the many ideals that aspirants nurse and adore. Each image represents an aspirant's soul-hunger congealed into a tangible form, so that he can establish a personal and rational bond between the outer form and the inner hunger.

This relationship knowing no better description, he emotively terms a Father, a Mother, even a Wife or, better still, an *alter ego*.

Even the lover who wants to reach the divine liberation, identification of the absolute type, must determine the kind of love that appeals to him the most; responds to his inner personality the most. There need never be any hesitation in accepting that which fits, suits and answers an inner hunger.

In selecting his own deity an aspirant could be confused; but he could always seek his guidance from a master-mind, or wait, strive, and discover gradually by himself what he needs.

Obviously, the accessibility of the expertise of a master-mind is a blessing to the enquirer and the aspirant. Arranged marriages as a system is a social extension of this method of expertise-guidance in spiritual field, which accepts at every turn of life the importance of having a guru. Those who do not appreciate the presence of a guru, cannot appreciate the spirit of guidance in marriage ties.

Let us not get lost to the sight of the fact that what is being discussed here is an entirely subjective quest, involving a subjective response. The response could not be objective. Poetry cannot be judged by weightage, binding or illustrations of a book of poems. If there is poetry in it, it would be self-reflective without the outward trammels that the publisher, or the binder might have bestowed on its production as skilful stage-managers.

Intellectual Disregard of Tantra

Often the so-called intellectuals view these images without the sympathising genius of that inspiration which a soul, struck with the inner hunger alone, could appreciate. Because these superfluous critics of tantra images and the tantric rites are more often than not regarded as 'educated and skilful,' what they opine on such forbidden matter (matter falling out of the orbit of their personal know-how) are easy to be misunderstood as valuable expert observations. These educated cynics, out of sheer frustration (traceable to bad health, shady upbringing, economic cramps, sex complexes etc.) parade their sophisticated writings under the cover of erudition, and make fun of the system, without ever attempting to go deeper into the subject. It often turns out to be a case of a dyspeptic person turned into a dietician.

Tantra, unfortunately, is not a subject that could be studied from books alone. It would be as dull an exercise in futility as the study of chemistry and physics without a laboratory, or a study of astronomy without ever looking at a star. To be knowledgeable in tantra is to get into it, and practise it with not only heart and soul, but with body too; for much of tantra is just rigour, much more than mere denial; but most of it is self-analysis, and a deep understanding of the self. Tantra educates a person how to fight and win in the battle of nerve, body and mind.

Tantra: A Negative Opinion

But the intellectual cynics, mostly unaccustomed to the real issues *the place of subjective power of Love in achieving a total transcendence*, find it a pleasant escapade to make fun of this demanding subject. Tantra is for the *vīra*, the strong-hearted person. The critics base their opinion on outward and superfluous observation, and what confirm their ill-based opinion are the numerous instances of the fake and fraudulent tantriks, who, like poetasters, by their total failure, only prove the importance and infallibility of real tantra. No empty claims could survive five thousand years of history. Generalisations based on disillusionments are bound to be negative in spirit, and inaccurate in fact.

Tantra is associated by these prophets of doom with charlatanism, debauchery, witchery, sorcerism and various forms of social crimes. (We shall describe some of these 'crimes' at a later stage.) From drug addicts to alchoholics, from perverts to maniacs all open their clubs under the undefined umbrella of yoga and tantra. Tantra has become an easy escape for the degenerate. But real tantra engages itself, heart and soul, with the submission of all sensuous emotions to the sub jective cause of discovering the true identity of the Self.

Neutralisation of all selfish emotive excesses through the complete dedication of the ego-bound self to the unattached liberated Self has been the aim of tantra. All rites evolved by tantra are but graded exercises for achieving this end. Cultivation of the impersonal sublime Love is yet another and sweeter process applied to the same end. The self offers the self at the feet of sublime Love.

Because of this, tantric treatises use copiously the imagery of Love, sex, and even of erotic pleasure; that is, it uses the language most easily understandable by man in functioning a 'union'; union of the mundane self with the unique sublime Self.*

By using sex-images in tantra expositions and hymnals two psychological purposes are served by tantra writers: (1) it dulls the erotic in unification, and wears out the effect of word-images through constant familiarity; (2) by imaging the erotically motivated pictures, tantra attempts to project a sublimated approach of the aspirant to the sex milieu. It is good to repeat here that tantra is meant only for the strong-minded positivist.

Adoration of the Human Body

Both body and senses are offered as items of sacrifice at the altar of aroused consciousness. The sublime voluptuaries alone could consummate the thrill of this pleasure. Under the spell of the power of this aroused consciousness (*chaitanya* or the *chit* power of *kuṇḍalinī*) they delight in the magic of creation. They are able to display with power their respective creative expressions, and leave to posterity such things of art as have been left by person like Shakespeare and Tagore, Leonardo and Pythagoras, Michaelangelo and Rembrandt, Sappho and

*For further treatment of the use of Eros in producing spiritual transcendence please refer to my *Saivism and the Phallic World*.

Meera, Beethoven and Ravi Shankar, all of them master voluptuaries, and master-artists in their own fields.

The cynical and discouraging remarks and reviews of sophists, who never bothered to take a sip of the drink before attesting the brew, cannot rob the value of the sublime gifts of these, who had acquired all they did through a type of tantra yoga about which they themselves could have been least aware. *Sādhanā*, or the skill of application, could be cultivated in a variety of ways. Yoga is to acquire that skill.

Many of them have actually been engaged in mystic rites and practices. Many of them had been arch voluptuaries. They turned the adoration and consummation of the wonderful and lively medium of the body and its senses into a vibrant material. They reached sublime truths through using body as a medium, and their creations were transformed into immortal works of art and science. Goethe or Rodin, Ramakrishna or Bhartṛhari, Lao Tsze or Tsangyang Gyatso have given first-hand information about his experiences of the use of the human body as a means of transcendental liberation.

Says Tagore:

My love becomes my god
My god becomes my love;
Where else could I realise this?
I see my love in god, my god in my love.

Tsangyang Gyatso, the Tibetan mystic is more specific:

The cuckoo bird from the land of Mön
Brings rain,
It descends from the sky,
It brings blessing to the earth;
Life grows and blossoms.
When the cuckoo bird comes from Mön
My lover and I join as One,
In body, heart and mind.

Tantra Calls for Stout Hearts

Yet all this cannot be just book knowledge. Neither has this been mere book knowledge for me. The practices to which I got initiated by the Lady in Saffron in my growing boyhood days remained enshrined within me like everlasting springs of ecstatic delight. I had the blessed fortune of coming into close contact with other *alter egos* in the course of my life, through whose assistance, grace and self-abandonment I had reached the apex of this realisation.

This is neither the epicurean delight in physical consummation, nor the voluptuary's glee at rolling in abundance. This is restrained, disciplined, extremely choosy and selective. It rejects opportunities, and accepts only the relevant.

Today I know, and I could say that this *could* be achieved through the 'hated-adored' *vāma-tantra* practices much more easily, and exquisitely, than through any other form of yoga. Those who feel too weak to face this, are at liberty to keep away from it. But to name this as blasphemous charlatantism is plain partisanism adopted in the negative interest of covering their own hesitation to face what is admittedly a difficult, demanding and testing situation. Tantra calls for stout hearts.

But of that later on.

Yoga-Vāśiṣṭha in a Broken Temple

Now to continue with the fascinating episode in that obscure lane of Varanasi where the Lady in Saffron had carried me. I said 'carried' me, because it was nothing less. I was swept away; swept off my feet; I was carried off in another realm.

To recall that event and that day (more than sixty-five years back) sets even now a series of vibrations within me.

The noon was simmering in a north Indian June sky. The merciless rays of the sun had got trapped by those tall buildings in stone on either side of a lane hardly eight to ten feet apart at its widest. Except during the noon the rays could not penetrate to the floors. The world seemed to be drowned in its post-lunch siesta. Only the stray dogs were at their unending rounds near the sweet vendors' shops; and sundry stray unfortunate beggars were seen still in search of a mouthful from a kind householder; here and there a pilgrim or two, disturbed the reigning coma of the miserable locality by their pious murmurings of hymnal piety.

The Lady in Saffron, a soft-spoken lady of few words, was walking at her easy placid pace of one engaged in some deep reflection (I was quite accustomed to this pace); and my boyish steps followed her close almost like a dachshund pup alert on a scent.

As usual, I had no clothes on; and as usual, her lustrous body was covered with only a single long, almost transparent, sheet in saffron, her various necklaces of beads and bones jingling softly now and then. In her hand she had a brass vessel filled with the water from the Ganges; and a basket containing odd things for lighting a ritual fire. In her other hand she had a volume of what turned out to be a copy of the venerated yogic treatise Yoga Vāśiṣṭha, written in Sanskrit.

These lanes still are, as they were then, some of the most crowded lanes in the world. In fact they were so crowded, and hazarded with the stray roaming bulls of Varanasi, that none ever noticed what might one be passing by. But as the same lane takes a turn towards the east where the Ganges flowed, all was peace. The turn to the east passed through an ancient stone gate about twelve feet high; and next to the gate was a mystically silent long room overlooking a three feet high veranda running parallel to the narrow lane. Inside this room behind some iron bars stood an image of Kāli.

For some reason or another even devotees did not tarry there long for offering prayers. All hurried through a ritual of bowing to the image, and if handy, throwing a few drops of water, seasoned at times by a few stray blossoms. There have been strange legends associated with this image, and stranger people have been seen moving inside when none was about.

Facing this rather mystifying image, which all were in a hurry to pass by, was a decorated royal gate. The occupants had at some distant past been related to Prince Pratapāditya of Jessore. We the urchins of the locality scrupulously avoided the inmates who, any way, could hardly be seen.

Passing these two rather grim landmarks we plodded on towards the Ganges. The right side of this secluded lane was bordered with a row of ancient dilapidated buildings occupied by a host of old and sick people. These assemble at Varanasi from all parts of Hindu India, each having rented his or her lodging in a single or double room tenement. Their one ambition was to breathe their last in holy Varanasi, so that they could be cremated in the famed Maṇikarṇikā. We viewed this row of houses rather grimly, as if we stood before the tenements of the dead.

Maṇikarṇikā, a Museum

The reputation of Maṇikarṇikā in the practice of tantra *sādhanā*, to the tantra *sādhakas*, is of supreme importance. To this day, any time during day or night, but specially through the nights, one could meet various types of tantric yogis engaged in their respective mystic pursuits with no holds barred. Maṇikarṇikā is a museum of a mixture of living saints and deadly frauds and charlatans.

It is here that I had observed one night a dark yogi with matted locks like so many reptiles flowing down his shoulders, and as naked as nature and sky, spooning with his cupped palms his own urine, which flowed down at ease, as he continued walking undisturbed, and drinking the fluid without stopping his progress even for a second.

It was here that I had a strange interview with a past master who was picking from the dirty water around, along with black pariah curs, charred pieces of bones. All these, man and dogs, were busy locating these bones amongst floating cinders, and chewing presumably whatever was left on them. A night long interview with that saint has been one of the most prized breaks in my spiritual life.

It was here again that I became fascinated with the devotional trance of an old yogini whom I used to watch in the dead of night, just sitting near and away from her. Night after night I kept a vigil, quite uncalled for, until one morning she happened to send for me through my father. That was a great experience again.

It was here that I met a later-day-famed yogi engaged in his penitential practice of crying aloud incessantly the repeated word, 'Mother!'. 'Mother!' until I used to get entranced. Often I found myself crying with him in sheer sympathetic vibration. In later life I had the good luck of receiving from him a fragment of his skill and grace. But I shall not crowd this chapter with those encounters at all. Space permitting I would like to narrate those vibrant experiences later, one by one.

Miracles

But I must make an observation for those who care: we know only a part of this life. Much of it is mystery to us; and what we view as miracles are but realities; only the dimensions of our own area of knowledge get exploded after we discover that our day-to-day life has its extended fields of consciousness and things do happen and could happen which to our three-dimensional experience look inexplicable and unreal. The most unreal thing in our life, to my belief, is our faith and belief on what we accept as reality.

(It is indeed a question of differing sense of dimensions. What are miracles to some, are facts and actualities to others. Once we accept that what we call life, and field of consciousness, do not start and end with the body, although we could realise these while in body alone. But once we accept the fact that the beginning and end of the life-force, as well as of consciousness, overlap our immediate awareness, we could regard these 'miracles' as happenings in the extended area of the accepted scope of our conscious field. Let us not forget that all our findings and conclusions are based on the limited scope of our senses reacting in a world of three dimensions. At no time we could see all the sides of a solid, although we infer the unseen balance from what we see. Human senses functioning under such limitations are naturally conditioned by the three-dimensional world which we hold on to as the only dependable and acceptable reality. This is the reality. This is the reason why our rational apparatus has so much to rely on inference, hypothesis, and analogies.

But a correct and scientific development of the latent faculties of the human brain could, of course, expand the scope of our consciousness. In this area functions the fourth dimension, generally signified by such words as Infinity or Time (*kāla*), the idea being represented by that single eye which the Tibetans use in their rituals, or the third eye which the Hindus put on their icons and images. To develop the faculty of the Third Eye is to acquire a passport to the realm of supra-consciousness. It is just an extension of the usually accepted field of consciousness. Viewing at the so-called 'miracles' from this field of extended consciousness, using the fourth dimension, one could realise that there is more substance in facts about these 'miracles' than in the facts we call substantial.)

This was the famed and mystic Maṇikarṇikā, the centre of tantric practices, and the Mecca for all the tantriks. To die in Varanasi and be cremated at Maṇikarṇikā is the one great ambition of each and every pious Hindu. Hence the phantom crowd in those ancient stone houses. They actually huddled there like so many bees in a hive; or were they like so many mummies on the move?

A little away from those houses, on the same side, is a strange shrine, one of the strangest, even in the shrine-infested Varanasi. This was the shrine of the Chatuhsaṣṭhi Yoginī (sixty-four yoginis). Let me explain.

Chatuhsaṣṭhī Yoginī

Eight is an esoteric number for the tantric yogi. Kṛṣṇa in the Gītā mentions the eight prakṛtis. The Yoga-lotus is eight petalled. The development of the inner power depends on the gradual control, development and grace of these eight prakṛtis in their eight facets.

Each of these sixty-four facets, also known as the *kalās*, refer to the conscious and subconscious tendencies which go to shape the personality of the whole man. Each of these also have their respective sources, or habitats, in the world of matter. To get a super control over the self, and over the world that covers the self (as if the world containing the self were a live-entity covered by the embryonic fluid of supra-consciousness), it is absolutely unavoidable to come to grips with these facts, and then like an extraordinary horse-man, control the sixty-four running horses tied to one harness. Hence these are called the sixty-four power-centres, the sixty-four yoginīs, the sixty-four facts of chaitanya. Naturally this shrine is considered to be extremely significant in the practice of tantra yoga.

The image itself is never to be seen. What is seen is but a golden mask of the great Mother, and the body is carefully covered with clothes and ornaments and garlands. The real image is one of Durgā, the buffalo-killing, lion riding goddess whose powers were respected all over the Mediterranean and Oriental cultures, inclusive of the Egyptian. (I have recognised this goddess in distant Thailand and Cambodia which I could understand to be a cultural expansion of Hindu tantra; but I have also noticed the same figure and its characteristics in the forgotten temples of Mexico and Peru, a fact which so far appears to be beyond an ordinary explanation.)

Just in front of the sacred shrine, on the opposite side of the small yard, and facing the Mother, is another unapproachable shrine. One could see the image of Mother Kāli in it; but few could reach near. For some mysterious reason devotees, at least the ordinary ones, avoid getting into the shrine. This is the shrine of Bhadrakāli, a form of the tantric spirit calling for the offerings of the extreme type which includes both the dead and the living, both blood and blood-red flowers. A Bhadrakāli altar is reputedly constructed over five cadavers of different animals, inclusive of a human cadaver. A saint has to perform the mystic rite of *śava sādhanā* (penance performed with a dead body as a seat) before a Bhadrakāli shrine could be consecrated.

Music at the Bhadrakāli Shrine

It had been a pleasure and a privilege for me to follow my father in the dark, through the lanes, and reach this double shrine in the sombre silence of the evening, when no other ordinary person usually visited it. Father would chant mildly a melodius hymn in Sanskrit, every word of which I knew by heart, and every word of which I repeated with him, which made him very happy, as I could sense it even through the immense dark.

I would have liked to translate that great hymn. But the space forbids. Tantric hymns in classical Sanskrit, because of their images, import, and their rhythmic sonancy, influence both mind and imagination, and generate a sustaining power of sheer tenderness and contentment. The emotional exuberance latent in the words and the melody overwhelms the mind with a tenderness that makes living a joy. This is perhaps known as exhilaration.

The role that sonic rhythm plays in soothing the nerves is well known. Latin, Sanskrit, and in a way, the ancient Celtic chants are particularly rich in this sonic effect.

The darkness around the shrine gradually became solid; and the awareness of a vibrant presence elevated both mind and body to a sphere far away from the known world.

Nearly about this precise time my father used to get lost to me. Invariably he would withdraw himself to an unknown corner, leaving me also on a stone seat which lay just at the threshold of the main shrine. Despite his absence I felt assured that he would be with me in a moment; but in the meanwhile, I was left to my own thinking.

I always thought of the Mother. And I repeated chant after chant in a suppressed voice. An oil lamp burned inside the temple. No sound except the chirpings of crickets and cicadas kept company of the lonely lamp.

I had got so accustomed to this feeling that in later years I found it very difficult not to halt at the appointed spot on my own, and get lost in that inner world which was all my own. Nowhere else I realise the supreme reward of meditation so fully and so quickly as at this temple.

In those days I hardly knew anything at all about meditation; neither had I ever heard of it. But today I could clearly recall those evening sessions by myself, and feel that my father taught me most practically, although indirectly, the secrets of meditation which thus had come to me as easily and naturally as swimming comes to ducklings. Even now at this hour, or in the depths of a moonlit night, the influence of that hymn overwhelms me, and I get merged into that spirit, losing myself totally in the embraces of the Mother.

Experience at the Pieta

(Once in the Vatican at Rome, kneeling before the image of the superb Pieta, forgetting myself, I got lost in that hymn, which had inadvertently bubbled out of me, and the Vatican establishment was thrown into a series of chained reactions.) For the people of the neighbourhood, as for most of the rubble, these nocturnal exercises were as good or as bad as adventures into tantric mysteries of a forbidden sort. But first because of the involvement of my father, and secondly, because of the common knowledge about the eccentric behaviour of a notoriously precocious urchin, people held their tongue, and did not as much as let fly a whisper. I do suspect that the umbrella of that presence of the Lady in Saffron, under which I thrived, also cast its influence.

On the contrary, I used to draw a kind of reverence from the people. I remember an old milkmaid, who used to sell in tiny earthen cups home-made sweet condensed milk. As we returned home, we had to pass by her wares. And she invariably offered me a filled cup, for which she never accepted anything. I knew that my father gracefully indulged in this acceptance. For the really spiritual being, an act of acceptance assumes at times the importance of conferring a touch of grace. It is possible to oblige even by accepting, which could be more humble than declining a gift of love.

The Temple in Ruins

Through this mysterious lane we had been proceeding. But I was quite taken aback when the Lady in Saffron guided me to another imposing building, then in ruins. We always observed the equally imposing gate. It fell to our right. But because of its extremely dilapidated condition we always thought it wise to keep away from this notorious den of poisonous snakes. Even at that young age I was aware of two fatal cases of snakebites from that area.

To this ruined heap she drew her steps. I followed mesmerised, as always, assured of her all-absorbing protective and motherly guidance. The inner yard held a wide space flooded with the bright scorching sun of a north Indian June. At a distance, and I could, assume, quite near the banks of the Ganges, rose the tall spire of a Śiva temple. She pushed open its broken doors. The ancient hook hinges gratingly groaned with a rusted protest. And there stood inside, the *lingam*, a black-stone chiselled shape, shining, glowing, towering above us a good height of at least five feet and more. The *Gaurī pattam* pedestal of the imposing *lingam* spread out in a wide circumference. Someone had put at the feet of the pedestal flowers which had dried up. The inevitable betel leaves humbly marked the silent offering from some devotee.

The Strange Initiation

Here she drew out from a crevice in the wall a piece of square straw-mat; and spreading it on the stone flags that covered the floor became seated. I made myself comfortable on the bare stone. Presently she lit a fire, and threw some incense into the leaping flames. The familiar aroma at once made the atmosphere come alive with a revered introspecting fragrance.

Then she closed her eyes, and was immediately lost in meditation. A light from another world shone on her face. Time passed. I had closed my eyes too.

After what could be ages, I felt her touch. On opening my eyes I was astounded to see what I did. The blinding glare was too much. I could hardly comprehend. In utter disbelief I looked again. My Lady in Saffron! What could have happened to her?

She was totally naked, and stretched flat on her back on the floor. Her legs were locked in a double lotus posture; her head was on the floor; between the belly's mound and the sloping valley, down to the bases of the feet and the heels there yawned a mysterious cavity where a moment back some flowers had been thrown. For the first time I knew that this area of the body too grew a patch of hair. Without minding my confusion she invited me to assume seat between her thighs, on the flowers, whilst she lay flat on her back with her eyes set up.

Her lap had always been my familiar sanctuary. But what amazed me was the strange fact that she had removed from her body her only garment. It lay folded into a bed-like arrangement over which her body lay. She appeared to me quite transfigured. Nothing was human about her. A gentle perspiration broke on my parched skin. The incense smoke was gradually covering the room. Her forehead as well as the grim hairy triangle were besmirched with ashes, and dabs of red and black.

The incense smoke was gradually invading the space. The

atmosphere in the room grew eerie. The chirps from the insects increased. Somewhere a lizard called. Again and again, I shivered, despite the heat outside. My hair stood on ends unexpectedly, and my goose flesh surprised me. The bare skinned form of the familiar Lady made her appear as a new being from another world. (I am trying to recall every second of that Grand Initiation.)

Her forehead smeared with the holy ash, with black and red marks between her brows, the heavy breasts hanging in fatty excess, the locks all spread about the saffron cloth, and that quite awesome space below the deep navel, sloping up to the hairy triangle, the mysterious darkness between the folded legs on which I was to assume my seat (!)—all rolled before my confused vision. I did not know how to respond to the situation.

(How many times I have undergone this exercise later at the subterranean Kāli shrine at the Tailanga Samādhi at Panchagangā, where stands the mosque that Aurangzeb had erected in his imperial defiance over a sacked temple of Viṣṇu Śakti.)

Another call came. This time heavy, unearthly, magnetic. "Tarry not, delay not dear one. This is your moment. Take what I alone give. Sit; and cover the *yoni*.

From the deep, sonorous, far-away nature of her voice I knew she was in trance. Her eyes were half closed. The little I could see of her eyes was all white.

I climbed over the sacred body, and sat over the dark space left by the folding of her legs. At the very first contact I was aware that her skin was burning. The heat was forbidding. But I knew it was not for me to question. I assumed the accustomed lotus posture. Her own legs were folded, as I said, into a double-lotus posture. Minutes passed; perhaps hours. Who cared? A stream of delight rippled through the 84,000 *nāḍīs* (nerves?) of which she had always spoken. At the base of my spine I experienced a half-tickling, half-singing urge which ran up and down my spine. I closed my eyes.

One Who Came from the Other Times

"Never mind," I heard her voice speaking to me, She did not, at that stage, appear as any tangible being. Just a solemn mystic voice. "I am here; I who am all yours to draw from as you need. What this piece of square (meaning the grass mat) is to me, is this body to you. You are a Brahmin child. A chosen child. One who came from other times. You are uncommon. You are all me; all me. In you persists the tradition of the Vedas. All you need is to open up what is closed You actually live what others only imagine to live. Be seated. Be at ease.

"I am the Lotus; you are the Brahman. I am the dead body, you are the living flame. I am in time; you are Time eternal. I am the sky, you are the sun. I am the sound, you are the sense. Now take up the book. Open it. Open. Carefully, slowly, deliberately read from it word for word. Start chanting aloud. Spread the book on my bare chest. Hesitate not. Tarry not. Proceed and progress. Be in me. I shall read through your tongue, your voice, oh my darling. Read. I am the dead matter; you are the spirit. I am stone; you are the message. I am dirt, you are the stream. Now! Now!! Open the book. Start. Start. No stopping, until you find a hymn, the first hymn."

And suddenly she was quiet. Her dark collirium-painted eyes opened. They were red-shot. The pupils had grown larger, and emitted fire. I was about to say something. But she indicated that I should keep seated. I should not interrupt. I hesitated. She kept looking at me. I read her approval. Yet I said, "If I cannot find the hymn; if I fail to. . . ."

"Fail you shall in nothing. You will not have to find the hymn. The hymn shall find you. Light the lamps at the base of the altar. Light them from the fire. Gather from the pit."

I did what she said as if bemused.

"Place them on each of my outstretched palms"; I did. "These are no lamps. The Sun and the Moon are keeping a watch over you. You shall see all; you shall know all that you read. Now. Start. Time is flying."

And entranced I started. Reciting Sanskrit verses was nothing new to me. The lines at the beginning were not so difficult; and I swept into the stream of verses as I loved to swim in the stream of the Ganges. . . . I continued with a power and vigour never known to me before. Time passed . . . I became aware of a new feeling of gold-garnered maturity. I felt as tall as the skies as it were. Time passed. Gradually and gradually I lost all sense of her presence. I lost sense of my presence. Against the light from the lamps, the pages, the verses swam in a luminous clarity of import. Then, at last, came the hymn, and came a strange delightful, absorbing, self-contained darkness. Time passed. . . . As the hymn was about to finish, I felt several strokes of gushing heat-waves lashing my eyes, my head, and what seemed to me very unbearable, deep within my bowels, my heart. The eighty-four thousand nerves were on fire. My heart seemed to jump out of me and float in the air, and mix with the smouldering smokes . . . . I lost consciousness. I became a zero.

Something was happening to the mound around my penis. A vibrating, thrilling, hot deep throb hammered beat after beat. The more it came in waves the more I was pushing out my spinal base. I sat straight as straight could be. [No! What people talk of erection, sex-urge, and reflexes, all, (even in a boy) as I had found, belong to a world which I had left long ago. I had shed my body; I was only a 'being'.]

* * *

But what a sense of relief when I came to myself. The Lady in Saffron was holding to my lips a cup of water mixed with honey. I have no idea from where she had materialised this superb drink. I was not only revived; but a strange feeling of completeness, fulfilment and ecstasy settled on my nerves. It was a soothingly caressing moment of life. I was staring at her with a new look, and gradually I broke into, what must have been, a pale and tired smile. She smiled in response, and kissed my cheeks as tenderly as only she could. I felt rewarded.

"Shall we now proceed to the Ganges? It is evening. A full moon is about to rise. There on the bank we shall sing together. It is a happy day, and we must celebrate. Follow me. Let us move out of here."

She was closing the broken doors. A couple of serpents wriggled past us.

But strange words fell out my lips. "When shall we come here again?"

She smiled again. Held me by the hand. "Yes again. And again, and again. A carpet also hungers for someone to sit on it. Another day. . . . To the bank now, and to music."

3

Areas of Sin

Conquest of Fear

The lessons on Yoga Vasiṣṭha continued. The *āsana* described before became a regularity. I became even an addict to the experience.

Gradually a change came over me. It was perceptible even to the less trained eyes. The changes were both physical and mental. The physical changes were noticed first, but the mental changes too were appreciated by those intimate to me.

I became aware of an internal change. Something was happening to me. I was gaining in courage. Besides going off and on to the Chatuhṣaṣṭhī shrine, even at night, all by myself, and without any qualms, I used to visit the forbidden shrine of the terrible Bhadrakālī too.

As others would view it, it must have been an act of serious daredevilry. Nothing at all posed any problem, specially of fear to me. I had no fear. I had no fear of the supernatural. I felt protected, secure. It was a novel feeling. A new life.

I had no fear of the Ganges at night. I used to swim across the river to the sand banks; and sat in an *āsana*, and meditated long hours, with only the stars watching me. Under a mantle of silver moonlight the familiar surroundings would assume unfamiliar dimensions. The lamps from the fishing boats would dot the distances over the flowing stream.

There I sat for hours and meditating how the Lady in Saffron had taught me to meditate. I took to these meditations with a seriousness as if my very life depended on them.

At about this time a singular episode added colour to my otherwise drab course of life.

* * *

The Call

One of these days at the peak of the noon sun, when I was engaged in Sanskrit grammar, I became aware of a sudden pull at my consciousness. I was much moved, and almost felt drawn forcibly towards a given point. The urge made me leave the security of home, and I found myself proceeding towards the shrine. The temple was empty, but for one or two stray devotees. 'This is not it,' said my restless mind, still under the influence of the pull. I stepped out, and proceeded towards the bank of the river which was close by.

On the way to the river stood an ancient boa tree. The sprawling branches kept the appoarch to the river spookily shady, yet not too dark. What thickened the mystery of the place were those strangely patterning movements of light and shade that the gnarled branches weaved and weaved, keeping the cool and quiet place in a state of perpetual animation. A coloured piece of stone, already engulfed in its twirling barks was supposed to hold powers of bestowing and protecting children.

The second factor that made this place distinctly eerie was caused by the innumerable crows, ravens, kites and even vultures, who generation after generation peopled the resort, and kept it always filled with a noise which had become a part of the rituals. People even left food for these birds. They were part of the shrine. Now and then the screechings reacted on the nerves, and the mind cringed in apprehension of some kind of mishap. Although nothing ever happened, yet in the nature of all mysteries, people in general used to attach unreal and unearthly values to the tree and the deity.

I climbed over the crumbling platform which surrounded the trunk as its base for about sixty feet. The roots had already dug their greedy jaws into the stone structure which had cracked at several places, and was in the process of crumbling. I stepped to the back of this huge trunk. There I confronted the source of the pull.

A Yogin

I stood face to face with a tall imposing man of great spiritual appeal. In aspect he looked more a man demented than a peaceful yogin. His locks, not matted, but flowing in black clusters, for some reason, had swelled into a moving mass. His eyes were red-shot and rolling, yet they held within the gaze a definitive purpose. He was wearing a long sheet of cloth, the end of which was wrapped around his neck, and allowed to fall over the shoulders.

As soon as my eyes rested on him, I was held by the fiery gaze; and the excitement of that inner pull was gone. I felt merged in a tranquil calm. I felt I belonged there; and I stood still, and carefully observed the charming apparition. Around us all was quiet. Not a leaf moved, no sound escaped, not even the breeze stirred, nor a squirrel flitted. Not a soul was in sight. Had some one strayed that way, we would still not be seen. I suddenly noticed the familiar hum of bees. Only then I noticed the huge hive hanging atop.

Not knowing what to do at this moment, and knowing that I must do something, nervously I broke into chanting a verse:

> Although one sees you in many forms
> The forms are but less than nothing;
> You are the One in all.
> The same in all.
> My father, mother, friend,
> Pride, wealth, and knowledge.
> You are all in all.

The man in white was not quiet either. Agitated by some inner fire he kept swaying; he reminded me of a candle in a stormy night, or of a cobra standing with its hood spread. His fingers drew strange figures, and the open palm moved up and down the sides. All he was uttering in an emotion filled voice was, "*Mā, Mā, Mā* . . ." incessantly, infinitely. Swaying like a cobra I said? But a cobra would strike. That swing is sinister. But the saint's swing was filled with submission, dedication, compassion. The fire and the flames would suggest burning heat. His voice was fervent, cool and consoling. As if a river of joy and cheer—rhythmic, regular, poised, and somehow remotely linked with some inner agitation—coursed from a distant mountain to a distant ocean of delight.

And while he was thus swaying from head to feet, his long hands which could reach to his knees, kept busy with fingers moving like petals of a lotus under a heavy breeze, bending on its long stalk. *Mā . . . Mā . . . Mā*. . . . The sound like a spell was reverberating in the moist atmosphere. Tears flowed openly down his bearded cheeks, and formed drops at the tips of the sandy brands. His body glistened in a light sweat. The pain and poignancy in his cry *Mā-Mā* reminded me of a deer struck with a hunter's arrow. I could not help standing petrified by that phenomenon. With no more volition than that of a torn rock, with no will of my own, I just watched and watched. There was something magnetic in the presence. Was it simply an expression of overwhelming joy? Was it the expression of a soul deeply merged in consciousness? An erasement of ego, time, space or will? Nothing like that had ever crossed my experience before. The mystic triangle of the Lady had been unique; but this erect male standing like a fascinating palm was quite another kind of experience.

For the first time I became aware of the sonic nature of a profound sound. I became aware of the syllabic formation which as *mantras* evoke respect, crystallise concepts, and radiate consonance. In some unknown way my nerves responded to the strange mesmeric effect of that sound.

Sound-effect of Mantras

In the interplay of body, speech and mind some specially conceived sound bubbles become effectively vibrant. This truth I arrived at much later. Much later in my life I was able to analyse the actual effect of *mantra*-sound on consciousness, and at the same time within the space we live in. I learnt later that like the *mudrās* (the positioning of the hands and the fingers to denote symbolically mental approach), like the various facets of rituals, (such as the *maṇḍalas*, the bells, the conchs, the stoles, even the uses of fire, water and special flowers), *mantras* too symbolise, direct, and crystallise the conceptual attitudes of the conscious being. 'Amen' as a *mantra* amongst some other Asian religions, the recital value of the Lord's prayer, the first sentence of the gospel of St. John have their *mantrik* effects. A *mantra*, by its effect, assists a mind to be totally dissolved; and then from the void's effulgence conjures up the dynamic power with which the reciter intends to come into contact; and he does. We shall have to come back to this subject of effect of sounds of chants (*japa*) on consciousness.

But on that day I was not aware of the dynamics of the philosophy of a *mantra*. That afternoon I was simply amazed, and carried away. The man stood over me several feet taller. Awed and overwhelmed I had to pay him a boy's sincere homage. He must have been a unique personality. A genuine Man.

Under a Spell

Hours passed. Suddenly he stared at me full in the face, which by then was also bathed in tears. Tears must surely be the unbarred expression of deeply felt stirrings of the soul. With his large and bare hands he dried my face. Then he took out from his heap of tousled hair a brown bead. It was the familiar *rudrākṣa* (*Elaeocaripus ganitrus*). And before I could say or feel anything he pressed the bead in between my brows as hard as he could. I could have cried for pain. But I lost my consciousness.

Somehow I was not much amazed at why this had to happen to me. I accepted the experience as one of the many adventures to which I had been exposed.

But the man haunted me. For years and years, at certain intervals, we used to meet. At times he even gave me valuable instructions. He spoke softly, and very little, if at all; but what he spoke was filled with intimate knowledge. With all this, however, I failed to establish a permanent rapport with him. Somewhere and somehow I could not fully communicate. But of that later on. But the saint for a long while continued to haunt my thought, and influence my life. Is he still with me? All memory is. Such is the nature of memory. But he is much more than a memory.

We might recall how my folks were rather surprised at the external changes in me. A change had been taking place indeed. But that was all a gift from the Lady in Saffron. Now, to what she had been giving, the man of the boa tree was adding. Soon we got closer, and he became a 'needed' factor in my life. I could not hide this from the Lady in Saffron. "Jiten is a saint," she assured very gently. He has to go far. Very far indeed. If he accepts you, I shall feel relieved." Nothing more; not a word again; but I came to understand that nothing in my life could happen, which the Lady in Saffron would not know.

My sisters giggled at the rapid growth of my size; my mother was satisfied that the blessings of the Lady in Saffron had been acting on me. My appetite pleased her immensely. She always remarked that my development was a standing example of what a regular course of *prāṇāyāma* could do to life. Yes, the great breathing exercise in itself is a friend to man, no doubt; but I wondered if every mother realised how happy I was with all that I learnt from the Lady in Saffron. I looked upon her, and loved her as my second mother, a spiritual mother.

Growing in Void

Any way, the change was there, and everyone noticed it. What I myself noticed was something different. Gone were those boyhood pranks; gone were the young tricksters, who, as my companions, used to draw me into silly games; gone was my interest in the subject of the tabooed areas of human physiognomy and the interplays involved in such rude engagements. I played little; but chose such sports which did not call for much company: swimming, boating, wrestling, lifting weight. Quite unlike a boy of my age I became more and more sedentary, although outwardly I continued to enjoy my natural popularity.

Yet it was true that like a person in the prime of maturity I avoided useless company, personal questions; I loved to be left alone. Loneliness was the tonic of my spirit. The Ganges held for me the highest relief; my first resort, and my last resource. All games connected with the river animated my desire to be near it all the time. The Ganges flowed as it were through my veins. I swam through a stream of delight. I boated on the stream of consciousness.

My language sounded precociously daring. My dreams were too personal and sacred to be exposed to others. I held on to myself. I realised that man in his seclusion and at peace with himself could enjoy within himself more colourful experiences. I loved and adored my lone moments.

Besides this love for seclusion, another change was noticeable. I loved this exercise of holding the breath up, and remaining still while at it. It gradually created a mindless void to live in. I can see in retrospect how much I owed to the Lady in Saffron for these strange passions which, however, I eagerly and readily nursed.

Such a state has a singular advantage in realising the supreme benefits of joy unbounded. Bathing in joy as it is said. A mind in void alone could create its own world of peace. For, did not creation itself emerge out of void?

Mind is never a supposition. It is a state of flux, undetermined and unidentified. It is identified and determined only where it suffers from cycles of actions and reactions. In that state we call it mind, and it is recognisable as mind. In the blank state the flux remains at still; man is free to enjoy his peace undisturbed. A peaceful mind would clearly reflect an image; but a disturbed surface would not do so. When a plane flies much above the clouds in void, because of the peace around, even the speed of the carrier is not realised. Obstruction animates mind. Void becalms it.

I have mentioned how lessons on Yoga Vāśiṣṭha continued undisturbed. The same *āsana* which had once invoked so much surprise and enquiry, gradually became a matter of routined acceptance. I no longer felt 'naked,' as I used to do before. Nudity meant nothing more to me. The feeling was not there. It appeared to me as something in the nature of a special spiritual uniform, with the difference that while other uniforms are to be put 'on,' this one is donned by putting away all garments.

Why Āsanas

But somehow I broke into the question one day. Why are *āsanas* necessary? Why are 'such' *āsanas* necessary?

The way she answered these questions has remained with me as striking examples of inductive teaching. She always referred me to the things I knew, and gradually brought me to the answers I wanted to know. In this our knowledge of the Hindu epics of the Mahābhārata and the Rāmāyaṇa helped us much. Anyone who tries to understand the Hindu way of life without going through these two epics is trying to read Hamlet without knowing about the Prince of Denmark. I am still strongly of this belief for the best understanding of the Western culture and Western mind a reading of Homer and the Bible is essential.

Besides depicting a feud between two sets of cousins for the control of a throne, the Mahābhārata itself is what it is, because of the classic grandeur and the Aryan nobility of the life pattern it describes. In fact, it stands today as an encyclopaedia of the social, ethical, aesthetic and the religious life of what we today term as the Hindu life. There are a thousand great episodes and narratives, with many thousands of characters. Every Hindu, some time or the other, refers to this book. Every writer of note in India must inevitably use this book as a source. The Mahābhārata, reputed to be the longest verse written in human language, is one of the lungs of the Hindu India; the other one, of course, is the Rāmāyaṇa.

The famed Bhagavadgītā is but an episode in the great epic Mahābhārata, and is not a separate book.

The stately verses moved on. I enjoyed the reciting. Questions kept bobbing up. I stopped; looked at her, and asked. And many questions she tackled. The method was supreme. Quiet, smooth, methodically graduated, enriched with motherly patience. I was encouraged to ask more and more by the very method of the approach.

One of these days the question arose around the yogic exercises of ascetics like Bhagīratha, lustful rogues like Jayadratha, or spiteful and cowardly avengers like Aśvatthāman. Were they not yogis, one and all? How could yogis then be so good and self-denying, and also so sinister and spiteful? Why the yogic power was used to harm other people?

How collected was her ease and mood as she expanded on the human views of good and bad, benefit and harm. As long as views rely on personal gain and loss, goodness in reality must always remain incomplete. Only the impersonal could be motiveless, selfless.

I came gradually to realise the fundamental difference between yogic blessings and grace, and the quest for occult, magic and the worlds of Origen and Delphos. I had come to acknowledge that a trance state could be a blessing as well as a sinister threat to peace. But we shall come back to this.

I particularly showed my interest in the profound mysteries in the human sacrifice of Aśvatthāman who wanted to immolate himself. All these cases involved an ethical judgement of good and bad, of end and means. And in all these the Śiva power was involved.

Magic, Voodoo or Obeah is something in which the actor, or actors are engaged in rituals that call for their concentration and expertise leading to induced trance. More or less these become partners in an elemental transposition of cause and effect. Metamorphic changes occur due to a combination of elemental forces induced by the studied practices of the leader. But in these cases the individuals had undergone severe rigours. At personal cost and extreme tribulation these individuals, otherwise great and high graded humans, had undertaken the path of tantra with a murderous resolution staking their individual lives. While Bhagiratha's penance and tantra practices involved the good of mankind, and life in general, the acts of the other two had no motive other than a spiteful destruction of adversaries who had achieved victory over the military skill of their enemeis.

Grace and Occult

I have no space here to explain further the knotty problems attached to these mystic narratives. Suffice it to say that from her lucid explana tions I was convinced that most of these acts were connected to tantra yoga. The effect may look like magic. But it is not magic at all.

There is no scope in these tantra practices for any spell as is commonly believed. Any individual by his practices and dourness could establish a communion with elemental or supra-natural powers. Once the rapport is established, and a steady stream of communication is laid out, the individual will be able to enact what the universal elements could. This is possible. Were this not possible the fraud in tantra would have been exposed long before this. It could not have outlived the oppressions and repressions of ages. After all, tantra and tantric methods are as old as the hills, skies and the elements. There is no religion worth the name which does not make use of 'miracles,' and which does not pay homage to the tantriks. Did not Jesus get into trances and bless the sick to health?

If these individuals had taken recourse to tantric powers, in order to achieve their ends, how is it that tantra does not distinguish between assisting the evil forces, and put them against the good ones. This might appear to be confusing.

I did not delay to place this question before her. The answer came in the usual quiet and easy rhythm. Even Kṛṣṇa was steeped with tantra powers. His powers were responsible for protecting the Pāṇḍavas at every crisis.

Evil and good are not different forces. All force is linked with a central power. But all concepts, or all objects grown out of the concepts have contrary sides. The sun, the moon, the universal movements of plants, climates, seasons, all have contrary sides, contrary pulls, this side and that side. It is in the nature of things that these have two sides. But once the sides are seen as proceeding from the same source, good and bad become but the reflections of passion and greed. Balance must be kept. This was what Kṛṣna was attempting to bring about.

The power of tantra, like any other power, could proceed forward, or reverse. The forces of progress must then stop the reverses. Tantra against tantra. This was matched in the battle of Kurukṣetra. There is no reverse; no bad. That which obstructs a balanced vision, a balanced life, a balanced ethics has to be brought to books. Balanced is that which makes room for better living, better understanding, better relationship in love. 'Better' than we know, that is. That is peace.

* * *

Āsana is Holding the Breath

Her answers were revealing. She was accustomed to spinning thread out of cotton fluffs on a hand driven wheel. On that afternoon she had been engaged in her routine exercise of spinning. She at once drew my attention to herself. "Watch me," she said, "I spin for hours at a time. It is a very delicate job demanding balance of touch and pull. The mind must be concentrated. The material must be well chosen for the very best results. Investments must be kept at a perfect condition. Efficiency depends on mind, material and instrument. Then come discipline and practice. All these combined, helps spin a thread of smooth consistency and extra-perfect refinement. A good thread has to be smooth, delicate and strong. It takes time to spin a quantity. No relaxation while the mind is on the job.

"Hence, it is absolutely necessary to select the very best posture for undertaking an arduous task. Selection of *āsana* is very important to a yogi. Some keep standing for years, as Gomateśvara Bahubalī did, Some sit for years, as Śākyamuni did. Some keep their hands stretched out above for years and years, while standing, as Bhagiratha did. For certain types of *mantras* certain types of *āsanas* are enjoined. I assume the spinning position after taking many things into consideration.

"Contrarily, when I sell at my shop, I do not have to assume the same poise and posture. My mind changes; attitude changes; so changes my posture too. When I cook, I make certain of my seat and my posture to suit the needs of cooking.

"When I sing I watch carefully what would assist my lungs and my breathing system. Even walking has its posture, and this changes too with the motive of the walk. Why are you walking, where are you going, what is the point of achievement, all these shall determine what posture shall one assume at walking. Do you agree?

"I hear that in the world of the white most people have forgotten to walk. I don't know. They must be paying for it in the end. They run and race, but do not walk. Funny. Isn't it? Perhaps they feel this to be the way of the wealthy. They feel that speed alone brings success. Thus they race and race. How to beat the front man at the back, and jump the rails first. They must pay the toll of having to live under such a pressure of having to jump the fellow man.

"They hardly walk. They pay for it later on, by jogging in the park, 'taking' a walk in and around the yard. Even motion has a posture, a rhythm. The rhythm for the static is *āsana*, the correct *āsana*; the *āsana* for motion is known as rhythm, *chhanda* for the *gati*, as we say in our language. But *sthiti* must assume a *sthāna*, or *āsana*. *Āsana* blesses the nerves with that essential pause which the nerves need for a ong long journey.

The Sex Āsana

"But you are concerned with the particular *āsana* in which we sit. You are more at a loss why this kind of total freedom from conventions. This question intrigues you because you have been taught to regard certain areas of the body as taboo, areas that are held as *dirty, bad* and *sinful.*

"You have heard the legend about two of God's children, who were thrown out of God's garden-house. Why were they thrown? Was it because they just ate a fruit of one of the trees against God's wishes? Which of us has not done this at some stage of our life? Is God so cruel? I do not think so. It is not what they had eaten that made God declare them unsuitable for a heavenly abode; they wanted to hide, lie and deceive. If they had come to God and told that they had eaten the fruit, and they had enjoyed it, perhaps God would have smiled on them indulgently. Hiding is sin. Falşehood is sin. Living a double life is hell. Considering a thing as worthy of hiding is the first sin which corrupts the mind. Sin is what gives complex to the mind; what creates tension. The result is untold suffering; loss of happiness! Destruction of all joy. This is living in hell. This is to be driven out of the innocent joy-world.

"Our mind has three very determined enemies. These come in the shape of joy; but what they leave behind is suffering. These three are anger, passion for sex union, and greed. None of these comes with any age; and therefore, none of these goes with age. Age has nothing to do with these contrary forces. And the cure for all these three is a clear understanding of things and values. Keep understanding at the driver's seat, and the car of life would never jump the path and go astray. When you keep these three, or any ony of these on the driver's seat, you are helplessly bound to be moved along paths 'they' would choose for you. You remain enslaved, imprisoned, deprived of your freedom for the rest of your life. To be in the full control of your own destiny you must get rid of these.

"But these are very powerful enemies. More powerful than you might think. They are not seen. They are not realised, until they are actually at action. They are carried as seeds from other times along with the seed of life. They determine the categories of the quality of personality that a life would develop into. More of their influence restricts your will.

"Freedom is *freeing the will force entirely from their influence.* The unfreed belong to the lowest categories. These categories are known as the *guṇas.* That which is free is *sattva*; that whicn keeps you totally bonded is *tamas. Rajas* is the state where these two are at conflict, and when *tamas* is at a lower ebb, and *sattva* is forcefully drawing the spirit up. Man's ideals are reached in *sattva*. An ideal is *sat*, the real.

"I was telling you that these are prenatal qualities, prenatal passions. Sex too is a prenatal passion. You conquer an enemy by knowing it well; by coming close to it; and then by weakening it gradually by tiring it out, or taking out of it its prenatal advantage of hidden power. Greed gets saturated, and is won by sacrifice, or learning to give things away, by sharing. Anger is the result of conflict and tension. Of the many reasons for anger sex is a very important reason.

Sex as Power

"Sex is a power that inspires man to become many through new creations. Create joy, create happiness, create art, literature, friendship. Create life. Enjoy sex. Joy is the power that guides and drives creatively. Sex is the *lhādinī* power; that which radiates joy and enjoys itself.

"But this power is restricted to certain areas of the body. So are the powers of seeing, hearing, tasting, smelling etc. All these refer to certain parts of the body. We do not hide them. We should. When I say we should, I mean a free unrestricted display of these powers, indulgence that is to say, shows the ugliness in man. A man without any control over his senses is an undependable creature. It shows his true ugliness. More than that an unrestricted indulgence of the senses leads to sorrow for others, and unhappiness to the self and to the body (in the long run). So, if we feel that we are civilised we should hide displaying the limbs that indulge in unrestricted excess.

These senses are body-located. The joy these senses give to the mind is restricted to an organ. But there are joys and sorrows which are mind-located; sex, anger and greed are the mind-located feelings. They drive the life of man to indulge, until man loses his grip over his control. It acts like a cycle without brakes descending a slope. Sure accident; even disaster; death.

"Of these three indulgences (greed, passion and sex) the last one, sex, is wrongly supposed to be located only to certain areas of the body, and equally wrongly we hide them. By feeling to hide them we give them reverse importance, and make of them a social taboo. This is utterly wrong. Let me explain.

"Why do we hide them? We want to keep them secure, because we regard them as extremely important to life. Two very important functions of life depend on these limbs. (This is besides their uses as drains of the body-abode.)

"One of these functions fulfills one of life's most important roles. This is to make life spread out of life, like lamps being lit from one lamp. One becomes, and helps to become, many.

"But this function is general to all lives, not specially to the human. The human is a special form of life. No other life is like it. Why? It is because the human alone, besides multiplying human life, also adds to the joy of life. Through creations of art, music, poetry, literature, painting, architecture, and through many other forms, the human joy of creativeness expresses itself. When would the Rāmāyaṇa and the Mahābhārata be without the human urge and effort to create joy.

"Like creation of a life from a life, creation of joy also owes its urge, power, inspiration to the power of sex. When you stop to consider this, you will see that to the human world, human need, for culture, society and posterity, this power is much more significant and important than making a man from a man, like any other animal does.

"You could now see that the physical role of sex in man becomes less significant than his brain or intellectual, perceptual, imaginative role.

"In the physical role the act starts at a point of the life: it also finishes at another point of life. But the intellectual expression of sex keeps the entire life involved. Giving birth to life is confined to an area of the body; but creating a work of art involves the entire man: his sensation, perception, memory, imagination. He, like a prophet, creates not only for the present, but more so for the future. *He creates the coming age.*

"You see, how important sex is to the human world. Without sex, without the *āvāhana* (invocation), *abhyāsa* (discipline), *prayoga* (application) and *bhoga* (consummation) of *lhādinī* (that is the sex, or the *kuṇḍalini* power) man's life has no purpose. Enjoy life in the given way; invoke the grace of *kuṇḍalini*. Spread joy to wipe away sadness of man.

"Since greed draws man to food, and distracts his attention from the value of food; since anger or passion draws man to revenge, or upsets man's balance of mind, and distracts his attention from the value of standing up against evil—these, greed and passion, are the greatest enemies for the development of man.

Why Hide?

"Similarly, sex could become one of the three greatest enemies of man unless man realises its real role in life. Instead of acknowledging the power of sex, *lhādinī*, as the fountainhead of all creative urge, *preraṇā* (inspiration), *ullāsa* (exhilaration), *ānandam* (ecstasy), they foolishly localise it to certain organs of the body, and get stuck to them, and in doing so feel excessively guilty. They want to hide this ill conceived and misused joy.

"Joy is not for hiding. Joy is for expression. Joy is for sharing. Joy increases by sharing, and continues to radiate joy from generation to generation. But like food-value giving way to greed and sickness, self-preservation giving way to anger, fight and pain—this wonder of sex has also been drawn deep into the lust for limbs and physically localised indulgences. It is totally disconnected with love, which of course is not a feeling to hide. It is totally disconnected with creative urge which claims a total dedication of all the senses.

"This is the reason why man wants to disown his responsibility for this misuse by drawing a curtain on it, and keeping everything in hiding, under cover. The acquired hypocrisy of hiding this so-called sex is a standing evidence of the evil in man. Man by his own misdoing has got himself driven out of the paradise which the tree of life, *kuṇḍalinī*, had made him heir to.

"Creation of life is a very painful process, specially for the mother. It is so painful that man would not willingly venture to procreate at all unless some intensely tempting reward and incentive were added to it. Hence sex is a power that gives to man the highest pleasure that man in body could experience. For experiencing this joy man goes to sex, although ultimately it adds to pain. Life is a poem of rhythmic pain and joy.

"Because there is joy in creation, man dares pain in life. In spite of the threat of pain we still seek this joy; so intense is this joy. It is the source of anger; it is the source of greed; it is the source of all our sufferings. Hence, it is absolutely essential to be in control of this power. No power is bad. Power is *śuddham apāpa-viddam* (immaculately pure). It is the source of all will. Will is power. But infected by selfishness, greed, we misuse and overuse, like a child misusing sugar-candy. It causes illness.

"Unrestricted use of this sex power makes the being feel sick. Whatever he does in the sick state becomes sickening. Will becomes loaded, and becomes wish; dynamism becomes domination; love becomes lust; ultimately joy becomes pain. It is most tragic that corrupted by misuse the very creative essence and the joy that creation is supposed to give, become overwhelmed by anger, sorrow, pain, enmity, conflict and tension.

"So I said that we must educate and train this power. We must be familiar with these areas. As we are instructed to keep away from higher voltage, we are also instructed to keep away from these areas. Only with the utmost preparation, and with the best of training we could expect to get from it the reward that it is supposed to bring to life.

"This is why we must, under strict supervision, be made to get familiar with these areas. These are the pure and sublime zones known as the erotic zones. *We regard these zones as the seat of the Mother Power. These become to us the zones of special pilgrimage to the shrines of joy and sublimity.* We do not at all feel dirty, sinful or guilty at approaching these areas, and using them for our full education, and for sublimation of joy.

"Many consider these areas as areas of sin. Sin is greed; sin is passion, anger, tension. Sin is lust, lousiness, cruelty, and above all disregard for the feelings of others. All these are the results of misunderstood, mishandled sex power.

"This is the reason my son, why I make you grow familiar with these areas; why I sit and make you sit skin to skin; why these zones on my body, and on your body come into the closest touch.

"We just make nothing of it, and yet concentrate. It is like acquiring resistance to heat by making the hand come into close contact with heat, as all cooks would tell you. A man from the northern polar regions, or from the heights of the Himalayas could stay bare skin even in December in Varanasi; we cannot. We could take the heat wave of June going up to 118 degrees, but that Himalayan man would die of heat stroke. Like the body, mind too could be acclimatised to the zones in the body which are the most vulnerable in breaking down your spiritual defences.

"Observe the very terms by which we in yoga describe these parts of the body. The triangular part with the slit we call *yoni-pīṭha* (the shrine of life-spring); the most sensitive flesh button within, we call *maṇi* (the jewel), and we recite the most significant *mantra* in the *Mahāyāna* and *Vajrayāna* calendar with this word *maṇi* as a seed word. *Maṇi Padme Hum*. Our final cremation takes place in *Maṇikernika* (the clitoric-jewel). The special flowers we reserve for tantra rites are distinguished by this clitorical (*maṇi*) reference to physical affinity so that we never forget to develop our solemn attitude to this part of the life machine: *vāsak* (Adhatoda vasica), *punnāga* (Alphousia speciosa), *nāgadamani* (Artemesia vulgaris), *Aparājitā* (Clitoria ternatia), *nāgakesara* (Messna feria) and *javā* (Hibiscus). The male part is known as *liṅgam* (the sign, the index); the output is known as *bījam* (seed), a word which the guru pours into the devout's ear most solemnly. Virgin, we worship. The menstrual female is known as *puṣpavatī* or *ṛtulā* (the female in blossoms or the one in season).

"You would observe from these terms the Hindu and the tantra attitude towards sex. In our books the act itself has been fully described as a sacrifice to the fire of the life-force, and the female body has been described as the altar and the pit. I find no kind of evil or lustful suggestion in this rite. And tantra feels not only clean about it, but divine. This body is the divine's own instrument for the fulfilment of the divine purpose.

The Nerve World

"Then there is another and more serious aspect of this kind of interlocked *āsanas*. I was explaining what related to the mind, and education of mental attitudes. I am about to tell you now something deeper. We call it esoteric. It relates to the spiritual personality alone.

"In course of time, and with experience and practice you will learn gradually, more and more, deeper and deeper, about this secret. This is the mysterious in *sādhanā*. This bears not too much explanation. This must be *experienced*. You will learn of it later. Directly! This knowledge is *pratyakṣāvagamam* (*per-tya-k-ṣa-ava-gamam* = realisable through personal experience). Yet I shall touch upon it, lest you might think—and such easy acceptance in thinking is dangerous and misleading—that this kind of preparation is all mental. It is not so.

"Yoga relates to the realisation of the purity of self by eliminating the mental world. Concentration alone makes consciousness free from the mind. The faculty of concentration depends upon the drawing in of all resources of the nervous being. The nerves, and the nerve centres play a very great role in concentrating our ego at one spot, and then burning it out of existence. Ego is the supreme sacrifice that could be offered in achieving the pure spiritual state.

"The nerve-body has special centres of operation. These are called *granthīs* (glands). Some glands are known, and recognised; some have not yet been known. In China there is confounding system of curing the body ailments, the mind ailments by needling certain precise spots on the skin. Even consciousness and awareness could be put to sleep and inaction by driving needles into some spots of the skin. Major surgical operations have been conducted with the help of such skin punctures.

"This shows that our yogić system was aware of these centres of the nerves. Nerves are the least detected systems of the body. The nerve-personality has yet to be understood by the Western methods of medical science. There have been ancient peoples living on this earth who had been practising brain surgery in ancient times without anaesthesia. Read the surgical treatises of *Suśruta* (Indian surgical treatise). In South America and Central America this incredible secret was known to the ancient cultures.

"There are the 'burning' spots, spots of awareness, zones of the sleeping power which have to be aroused, and put to action. It is in a way switching 'on' the power stream. Through these *āsanas* these power points are aroused. This much is sufficient to be known now.

"In course of time you will know of this more and more. There is nothing to be ashamed of, nothing to be excited about. You have the advantage learning this before your age of innocence has left you back. Others, who start to know this secret after their maturity, particularly after they have already mistreated and mishandled the sex zones, find the going forward an uphill task. Pictures are best drawn on a clean canvas. Minds already blotched over by bizarre images, psychic hallucinations, self-projected wishful conclusions find it very hard to keep to its proper course.

The Guru

"So you see that the problem of assuming the most convenient posture for the success of an undertaking is very important. In fact success in an undertaking that largely depends on assuming the most suitable posture. A wrong posture could deny success. This is true. It even could cause serious deformities, and ailments.

"But it is difficult to choose and select the right posture. It is not impossible; but it is difficult. Indeed very difficult. Life is too short for discovering everything that has to be known, by personal efforts alone. We have to depend on the experiences of others; and on certain guidelines they have left us.

"There are people who give you guidelines from reading books, but without having any personal experience. These are very dangerous second-hand sources, and make one waste valuable time for nothing. But there are some who speak direct from experience. These alone could be the gurus. Many of them might not have come across with a single printed line; yet they remain the maestros. Why? Because they have the experience.

". . . People mistakenly think that a guru is a spiritual preceptor who keeps the monopoly of 'guiding' others to heaven or to hell. This is a wrong view of the guru. A guru is more intimate than the most intimate; more belonging to the inner being than any being you love or adore; more precious than all the wealth you have, could imagine to have. His power, so far as the disciple is concerned is the most telling, most concerning and the most dynamic.

"Consider what and what he has to contribute to you. Things, treasures, experiences that are yours, and could become yours, through his guidance. And these experiences are realised through a sight without the eye, a sound without the ears, taste without the tongue, understanding and owning without mind. No words could talk about it; no limits could contain it. Death does not demolish it; time does not wear it; nothing to measure it; nothing to evaluate it.

"I am speaking this of all gurus. Only you have to accept the importance of the lessons accepted. The disciple could achieve far more than what the guru had achieved. Many students achieve far more in life than their teachers. But the guru remains a guru. You 'think' of the gods: the creative god, sustaining god, the assimilating god; but you 'have' the guru with you. He is all these. A guru might suffer a fall of the spirit; but what he has given to you does not fall down, unless you let it go down. A millionaire who has lent you a sum at a time of crisis may go bankrupt, and fall; but what he had done for you at your crisis has to be gratefully remembered; and the value of the sum lent does not fall because he has fallen. In fact you might well have raised it. You might have become a 'millionaire' due to timely help of the guru.

"Muni Dattātreya had many gurus. So had the Buddha Śākyamuni. Do you know that your mother has been my guru in cooking, in house management and public relations? She has the expertise, and is ready to part with her knowledge. Similarly your father, the great man with his nobility of soul, has been my inner guru in so many respects. Did you yourself ever realise the actual nature of the spirituality of your father? He is too near you. Yaśodā, the mother, was never convinced of the divinity of Kṛṣṇa, and even physically chastised him, as a mother would, for training her child. It is natural for people to lose perspective of greatness when they are too close to it.

"You know, when the people of a country named Judea became restless about the promised coming of a leader from heaven, a youngman, born and grown amongst them in very common circumstances used to tell them of many good things. But because he had been too near them they did not take him on, and ignored him and ridiculed him. He did not have much formal education of books. The book-people were held in great respect. His teachings, were thus resented by the elders, who took him for an upstart. In their eyes he remained 'uneducated,' since he was not one of those 'doctors of religion.' They took him for granted. They opposed him. A time came when infuriated at his methods of exposure of the frauds of the learned, their follies and superstitions, they decided to punish him. Do you know what these learned men did to this innocent young man who did what he did in all fearlessness out of his love for them? They got him involved in a false allegation; got a judgement from the government; and pinned him alive on a pair of crossed wooden beams, until they were satisfied that they had killed and buried him.

"But his lessons could not be buried. His voice rose out of the dusts and spread all over time and space. The message reached the millions, and millions sang of his tremendous sacrifice. Greatness found too near is often neglected as nothing.

"This was so because he kept no external fads. He was so simple that none expected him to be a spiritual man, much less a man blessed by God. Your father too is equally simple; equally filled with no personal motive in life; and ready to come to the assistance of the distressed. He is too approachable; he loves the crowd, and moves amongst them. Hence he is taken for granted. A man with no fads.

"When you read the Gitā you come to learn from Śri Kṛṣṇa that a divine man is often like this. But as and when such a man rubs his shoulders too close, too near, we still ignore and neglect him. You and I, and all the others around, make nothing of the divine charms of your father. Who would suspect this unassuming frail man for a yogi? Do you? Such a man is adorable to God. He is indeed a great yogin. He has all the attributes of a yogin. He has the most fascinating and the most difficult of the spiritual powers at his fingertips. He loves men without any distinction of class, age, sex or occupation.

The greatest spectacular power in life is demonstrated by the simple act of loving without discrimination. Love without effort, or self-interest. Ego-less love. Such a love is the greatest miracle that could happen to man. But we are not able to love without some motive. Motive to love is what fire is to a waxen doll. It destroys the very essence.

"Thus by observing your father from a distance I have learnt many virtues. This has left me much better equipped to suffer this miserable world, and yet discover and enjoy its fullness. It is the greatest amongst the yogis alone who could be singing with this misery around. A yogi feels free amidst thousand coils. He rolls on the high seas of passion of ecstatic enjoyment without ever being possessed by the spells of life's mesmeric glooms; without ever feeling 'trapped'.

"You must have heard how in the forests of Ceylon and Mysore they trap the wild elephants. They master the huge brutes not by snares, nets or drugs; but just by sending amidst them a trained cow elephant who trades love, and has them slaving for the rest of their life. Ask a horse trainer. He would tell you that for the sake of the gallantry of following a mare even hot blooded stallions would fall back in any race. The most effective trap in life is the charm of passions; the most trapping passion is the charm of sex. Of all agonies in flesh, sex is the most telling one.

"Man is bought and sold by money, power, wealth and this infinite draw for sex. Not the yogin. He, like Kṛṣṇa, enjoys the fullness of life, lives in the fullnes of life, yet remains sufficiently withdrawn to be constantly keeping in touch with his inner consciousness. Passionless love; heatless flame. The sense of duty of a yogi is too keen and real to admit of the least deviation. But living his life in its fullness he charges, as it were, an inner dynamo, a battery, so that he could effectively transform that power for the good of all. It demands a course of great discipline, astute and strict self-control; but that is expected of a yogin. No yogin seeks joy or heaven for himself. All his power is for the service of the suffering multitude. His self is not his. He discovers his self as a phenomenon found in each and every life, even in every object. This makes him actively non-violent, and non-violently active. In him violence and non-violence have become one.

"It is a great lesson my son; and before you could absorb it, I am sure, I shall have to repeat it to you many more times. This explains why we sing hymns, go for pilgrimages, visit shrines, recite the epics of the Rāmāyaṇa and the Mahābhārata. Recite and recite. To be self-abnegating is not enough. It is indeed less than enough. A yogin's life and conduct should be a fully involved one. Negation in involvement, and involvement in negation. 'Stand-offishness' is not his; a holy(?) negation is not his.

"In this tantra your father has been my silent guru, a burning yet a living example. He would never preach; he would read very little; but watch his enthusiasm for spreading learning.

The Bhairavas

"I have yet other gurus. I watch them from respectable distances. But I accept them, and learn from them. Govinda Pandit your uncle, for example. Everyone is afraid of him. He is the man of magic, the Aghori Bhairava, the fierce tantrik. No doubt he looks fierce, and talks fierce; but he is the greatest, and the kindliest doctor, specially when doctors are not available. Plague, cholera, smallpox, those ravaging epidemics devastate the town, and death-cries rend the air. You find this old man moving from home to home, bed to bed, fearlessly, tirelessly, uninvited, and reaching the stricken with his medicines, little globules of his own preparation, derived out of herbs, animal poisons and chemical ingredients. When he refuses to administer his medicine, people come to realise that nothing more could be done to the poor life. Of course, he is a man of miracle; but his demeanour is so forbidding that none dare approach him, and waste his time. He detests wastefulnes; he shuns sweet talks. The perfect yogin shuns crowd.

"I could list out a hundred gurus. There is no guru as a special guru, as the 'only' guru. Once you have chosen one for you, he remains yours for life. When you feel to bring problems, bring them to him. He himself would guide you to the specialists, if and when the specialists shall be needed. He would know it. Depend on him. You cannot love many loves."

She would have gone on; but she stopped as she noticed something in my eyes. And she broke into a tender smile. "But one could, as I said, love someone. You love me. I love you too. Such absolute love plants a trust in the soul. It is a mutual trust. Love purifies, chastens, teaches one to suffer, tolerates, adjusts, dares and shares. One could love only a guru like that. Such love is unbodied. It is love of, and for, another world. This love is not for this world.

"But all this does not mean that the great lessons of life cannot be learnt from several sources. That type of rigidity is contrary to a yogin. A real yogin is a relaxed being; he is a spirit of charity, compassion and humble acceptance of good from any source. A genuine yogin blooms like a lotus to receive the drink of light and life; and he withdraws his sense receptions like the limbs of a tortoise when he chooses. Keep the senses always open and alert. Receive as much of the gifts of God as possible. Who knows when, and in what form the divine essence would descend? Yoga sharpens the faculties of the senses. It is more rewarding to know how to care for them, deserve them; accept them and utilise them. Yoga is not dulling the senses. Do not waste power and skill chasing false pursuits.

"Remember to keep the senses awake. You hear the 'mad man of the morning' howling through the dawn '*Chet! Chet! Chet!*' (Awake, awake, awake). Keep the senses awake, but get not involved. This way you see, and meet many gurus. You remember Guru Dattātreya, the Mahābhairava. Don't you?" (*Bhairava* is an astute yogin feared for his unconventional ways or ritual ensemble.)

"Yes," I said the one at the crematory grounds on the Varunā. I know the shrine. You had taken me there."

"Then you must have noticed the various animal forms drawn on the walls of his shrine. He learnt from all animals, plants and even from the elements in nature. This is the way of the perfect Bhairava, of the *vāma-margīs* (left-path-followers). This is the way of *Mahāyāna*. Tantra adores this way. These are also known as the Aghoras, who keep contact with the abstract spirits in nature and supernature. Govinda Pandit is one such."

"And you . . . ," I added with caution.

The benign smile beamed again. The chubby palm rested on my head, and brushed along my spine. "Who? Me? An Aghora? No, not yet. Better by far is your aunite of the Maṇikarṇikā. A powerful lady. It takes a long long practice to rise up to that state. A time would come in your life, when you too shall have to realise this. Never despise an Aghora, only because his ways are not your ways. Judge them not by your habits, your forms, your tastes, norms and standards. You are nothing yet in the region of the spirit. You are just like one standing at the gates of a show house without having a ticket. What opinion would you have of the show that goes inside? Obtain the ticket first.

"The Aghoras (an extreme sect of Bhairavas) are neither despicable, nor perverse unless you put up a front, already made up by you. To be a yogin is to break up all fronts, and break through all fronts to perfect freedom. When through your uncontrolled anger you call a man a dog, a woman a whore, a beggar a vermin and a leech, you are much more perverse than you would accept. You are perverse when you have enough, yet fight for yet more; and you already have more than you need. You are worse than perverse when you sit over heaps and heaps of things which you do not need, but which keeps others deprived of the essential instruments for survival. You gloat and dote on women and men only for rolling on certain parts of the body, and act like living fungus, eczema. You are perverse in your thinking when you do not hesitate to plan mass killings of the innocents in the name of nation and patriotism. Political science is perverse; economy and commerce are perverse. What could be more perverse than to watch people die of hunger, children die without nourishment and medical care, souls die without education; and all this, my son, has been done under the silver cover of duty, religion, brotherhood, friendship and nationalism. No aid is aid if motivated as investments for future collection. No love is love when motivated by selfish designs.

"No my son, no! The Bhairavas are not perverse. They preserve within them some of the most impersonal blessings for the benefit of those who deserve them. A day would come when you would understand the Aghora way; you yourself would become Aghora. The unknown Aghora is more telling than the known Aghora.

"Such Aghories have their gurus everywhere. Only the correct disciple and the initiate could recognise their merits. Many of Magdala, the prostitute, knew who Jesus, the Christ was; Sujātā, the tribal maiden knew who Gautama, the Buddha was; Rādhā knew what Kṛṣṇa was; the little Sāradā knew what Ramakrishna was. It is very misleading and unjust to form opinion of a person from watching outward behaviour, specially if one were to judge his or her spiritual life.

(I remembered that in our locality most people abstained from coming close to the Lady in Saffron for her whispered past life.)

"The gurus teach; they instruct. They attribute and confide a heritage of immortal knowledge, but always to the right person at the right time. This is the practical knowledge of reality gained through experience. Having this, there is not else to be had.

"This is the Ultimate. *Śivam*; *Ānandam*; the ecstasy of feeling free. It is a tonic; a power that lifts, raises, transcends. Once this power is experienced, and stored within, man can love man without reckoning the fallen ones' sins, misdeeds and failings. Evil ceases to be an evil at the touch of a Bhairava, an *arhat*, a *muṣkil-āsān*. Were it not so, all this effort for attaining transcendental power and liberation would have been reduced to a selfish pursuit after personal ecstasy. That would become the hunt of a voluptuary for objects of personal enjoyment. No; Bhairavas are almost elemental in their generosity and sacrifice—but they are also elemental in their fury. Power that brings about cosmos from chaos could also send cosmos to chaos, when the time comes.

"Ecstasy is divine because joy goes out of the one to the many. It radiates. Consummation of the self, for the self, in the self is worse than being demonic. It is evil itself. It degenerates the will of man.

"But to reach up to this kind of impersonal power one has to exercise and practise; go through fire; hold the cobra by the hand, and swallow poison without the least hesitation. Laws that control objects and matter do not apply to spirit and soul.

"This is not often realised. One 'IS', because one's senses respond in a special individualised way to the world outside. This relation is established through the sense organs. But this is not all. The sense organs do not completely form our individuality. There 'is' also the other one; the other me, within me. The individuality and being of this other one does not depend on the responses of his outer senses. The presence and realisation of this other one depends on the feeler's supersenses, the senses beyond and deeper than the outer sense organs. There must be, therefore, some other set of apparatus which feels to respond to this inner being, the being that feels and responds in our dream, for example. Yes there is another being within us, more intimate, more vital, more concerned with our well being. That 'being' being imbalanced, we are severely imbalanced. That 'being' being becalmed we are completely at peace with ourselves.

"The obvious relates to the obvious; the initimate relates to the intimate set of senses. Man is a complete being; is a composite unit formed of these two sets of senses. But we fail to realise that, due to our blind fascination for the world. Hence it should not be difficult to understand why we fail so miserably to reach man in his acutest distress and agony; why we suffer, why we worry and why we break down under the pressure of tensions. We are not in touch with the inner being in us; with the 'I' within. We are not in control of the supra-senses within us.

"Those who have no senses cannot feel through their organs and instruments; those who do not have supersense cannot feel or measure the Reality. With instruments fit for measuring first, second and third dimensions one cannot measure the fourth, fifth, sixth and the seventh dimensions. One must cultivate humility for obtaining true knowledge. Ego of knowledge is the greatest enemy to knowledge.

Āsanas Again

"And for such exercise and rigours these *āsanas* were put up. These Aghorī *āsanas* have not come from one person, or one system. These did not come from even one people, or at one time. You see that the most treatises on this ancient knowledge have been recorded later, and in the most cryptic and mysterious language. These are known as tantras, the 'strands,' and are recorded in *sūtras*, the 'strands', again. Formed strands (*sūtras*) emerge out of a mass of silk or cotton, as truths come out of a mass of tradition, and to be carried over to other times. Long and unbroken is this strand; mysterious and pragmatic are these *sūtras*. 'Thread' of thinking, 'thread' of the spider's web. So is the web of tantra woven out of these strands of *sūtras*. Strand by strand a whole texture has been woven for expounding the efficacy of postures. One must assume a good and effective posture before one could sit for a long session on meditation. But the variety of *āsanas* that people find described with illustrations in commercial books are exclusively meant for a health therapy, or for those pompous minds which are engaged in the vain search for an easy way to concentration and meditation. There is no easy way.

"Besides, such book-knowledge which encourages the sprouting of the spiritual clubs, meditation centres etc. could become a further source of tension, unless conducted by the real experts, and attended by the serious and actual seekers. There is no such thing as a packet deal in spiritual involvement, or a portable spiritual experience. This could prove to be extremely arduous for an inner peace, because such superfluous participation might inflate the already inflated ego.

"In fact one or two *āsanas* should suffice to give a start to the novice. This *āsana* has to be selected by the guru with the complete diagnosis of the subject involved, and to his most comfortable acceptance. Hazardous ardour and forced compulsion are detrimental to the attainment of peace.

"Watch a typist. Because she has to sit for long hours at the machine, she adjusts her seat with great care. If she does not do so, besides affecting her performance adversely she would injure her sight, cause pain to her spine, ultimately becoming a victim to nervous discord and arthritis. You should by now realise how important it is to select . . . ."

I stopped her at this point, and broke out—"Did you select the *āsana* and the posture for me with that amount of deliberation? Was our nakedness and the complex seating posture something that you had intended for me?" I needed courage to ask; but I was determined.

Her eyes suddenly got stilled. Having kept quiet for a while she ultimately spoke. Her voice underwent a change. she spoke with a heavy depth, the voice rolling from afar.

"Why do you ask?"

"I must," I was forcefully dynamic.

"Why?" The same impersonal voice spoke again.

"Who else shall ask, if not I? Who else shall answer, if not you? I want to know for certain that this Aghora way, this *vāma* way is the only way for me. If I could be something else; if any other way would have done."

"What have you so much against the Aghories? Did I not explain? Aghories are the Buddhas, I told you. They have found out the secrets of *āsanas*. Gorakhnāth, Matsyendra, Aṣṭāvakra, Gheraṇḍa, Nakuliśa. Time will make you know.

"But the male-female circle of contact achieves a completeness of spiritual freedom which no man in body would achieve single-handed. This is the *vajra* way. This is the *sahaja* (easy) way, the way of feeling easy. The keen ascetic way remains incomplete; as it is a negative way.

"Why? Have I not been explaining to you the mystiques of the *vama*? It appears that the complex has not yet been removed. Let us then try to understand it in a different way. You know that the complete life cycle for a Hindu has been divided into four sections."

(i) *Brahmachāri* = Learner novice, practising the way to emancipation; (ii) *gṛhastha* = householder (who now accepts life as a testing ground of what he has been learning); (iii) *vāṇaprasthī* = the man retired and secluded in search for the Real (when he gives a further account of his basic preparation for enjoyment without attachment); and lastly, (iv) *sanyāsī* = the recluse (who now wants to discover himself, and thereby charge the human world with dynamism). The first stage is meant for application in the second; without this vital second stage there is neither the third, nor the fourth stage.

Why a Woman

"Then, must one marry? Must one have a woman?", I asked quite besides myself.

I was remembering the very many saints I had known. One of these was quite dear to me. He had been keeping the vow of silence for twelve years. Often did I see him in the Chatuhṣaṣṭhi shrine, almost waiting for me, and always smiling through his looks at me. But for a piece of loin-cloth he literally wore the shining robes of his wonderful health, the shine and glow of his skin and a divine glamour surrounding his tall form. I continued, "Without this man-woman tie could nothing be achieved? Are you telling me this?"

"Yes, I am telling you this," she repeated solemnly the words I had inadvertently let slip out. I was excited. "I am telling you this," she went on saying, "because I love you, and would not mislead you; nor set you on a path which would prove so much more difficult for a common person. Because I want to give you my all, I must never hide anything from you. Why are you so much surprised at this? The natural way is the ordained way. Nature is correct. The natural way; the *sajaha* way. The way of life. From life to Super-life. Rāma, Kṛṣṇa, Buddha—why, Ramakrishna, Śri Aurobindo, Śri Chaitanya,—well I could name so many. Which of the Vedic sages remained single? Those who did were the Bhairavas: Paraśurāma, Durvāsā, Dīrghatamas, Mārkaṇdeya, Dattātreya. This is the trend. The Great Mother desires this. . . . What happened to Jaratkāru, Aṣṭāvakra, Chyavana? You forgot?" (Hindu epic characters).

"Nò auntie. They had to get married at an old age to correct themselves, and then. . . ."

". . . and then achieve the goal. The female power actually assists the male power. The female is a special reservoir of power. This power they need to nurse and bear life. The seek life and motherhood. They feel incomplete without this motherhood. Because of this they have more power, inner power, emotional power. It is a forceful power, *tamas*. The Female power of *tamas*. The Mother is *tāmasī*. Females are moved by a greater urge; they suffer from greater cravings, greater upsets. *Tamas* is such. Power is power. To take power from power, and assist to get more light is a wise way. Through the help of this power the summit of spiritual realisation is attained within a shorter space. This is the *mahāyāna*, the *sahaja*, the natural way. This is the path of innocence. Those who achieve innocence in the male and female find in the *āsanas* (*mahāsana*) the peace of the ultimate.

"But in this age of greed and indiscipline many take to this path only to delude themselves. Their mind is corrupt. They are fraudulent and perverse of mind. They are cankers to the Great Spirit of Life. They sow the seeds of suffering.

"Hence we need caution. Hence the need for well tried directions. Directions from well tried gurus. Hence the need of dead secrecy between the guru and the disciple. Hence the need for a total dedicated control of the sensuous in life.

"Personality is a construction of the senses imaged by ego. Impersonality and total innocence is achieved when the ego is eroded through the discovery of joy freed from the sense organs. Who cares for the swim aids after the swimmer has achieved? Aids become encumbrances to the man perfected. Who cares for health tip, once the body functions tip top? What a man alone could give totally is but a half of 'Life'. What he must achieve must take a double time if he aims at completing it by himself. What man owes to woman must be recognised, respected and adored. What woman could bestow on man could cut his efforts by a half, or by more than half. Mahādeva needed Umā; Viṣṇu needed Lakṣmī. You and I need our opposites to complete the circle.

"This was the reason the great and sublime Bhairavas, age by age, discovered the *āsanas*. In the monasteries of Tibet, Nepal, Bhutan, Sikkim, in the books of secret tantra, one could still find elaborate descriptions of the *āsanas*. The Tibetan *tankas* are records of these *āsanas*, sometimes drawn geometrically through *maṇḍalas*. But books are poor substitutes for gurus. Gurus give you directly what you need. The Aghories are direct teachers who make nothing of the body, nothing of the body functions, nothing of fear, shame, scorn etc. They look like the rejects of life and senses; but they reject nothing."

I was merged. I was merged in on ocean of consciousness. Like the rains from the monsoon sky after the scorching months of summer the words poured, poured and poured. I was not only drinking, but also storing energy for future prospects, prospects for the future harvests. "Why then so many *āsanas*?," I asked.

"Why so many medicines? As many cases, as many diagnoses. As many ailments, as many drugs, as many methods. *Āsanas* are many. Aghories are many. Necessities are many. Methods are many. Each and every one of these has been well described by the adepts after full-measured experimentations."

You Are I

As if let loose from some height suddenly she climbed down to the level of life, and broke into a continued laughter without sounds. The atmosphere around became charged with a delightful vivification. She threw her hands around me, and gave me a gentle hug. "Dear one," she said, "come to me. Be fearless. You are mine. Very much mine. More than you could own or imagine. Why are you still at the cross-roads? Ask me further questions if you have any."

"I understand what you say. But still I feel that I cannot reveal or own such *āsanas* to others. I cannot speak of this to any."

"Why must you?," she looked surprised. "Every question need not be encouraged; every question need not be answered. It would not be worthwhile. You are you; more than you. You are me. You are I. All of you need not be for the showcase, or for the micro-scope. You have things essentially belonging to your inner self, and none needs know them; none could know them. Could they?"

"I follow you. I agree. But when I am hungry, sleepy, when I experience something exciting, or hear something interesting, I share my thoughts with others. Do I not? And in doing so do I not many times increase my joy in the things I receive and experience?"

"Yes there are things you do mention. But are there not some other things which you do not? This one is one such that you do not. You shall not. Secrecy is the key demand."

"Why?," again I insisted.

"Could you tell me how much do you love me?"

After considering the question for a while I said, "No!"

"How would you like to report to others about your love for me. And if you did, how far would you succeed in doing it accurately?"

This made me pause. I thought about it, and saw the futility of it all. I realised slowly that the most intimate experiences are bound to be lonely. These could not be reported, shared. Joy shared through reporting is like the reflected light from the moon. All descriptions must necessarily be tinged with colour. These are lies, and yet not lies. The effort being real and truthful, the effects are 'taken' to be honest. All art, all literature, all expressions must necessarily be a limited expression of the unlimited truth. Truth cannot be expressed. Reality is silent. Experience is entirely personal.

Experience is Lonely

She had been watching me carefully.

Then she gradually said, "My son, there are never two in the world of experience. Experience is always indivisible. Two might participate in an experience, but because the two are participating, it is not sure that the impacts of those experiences shall be identical for the two. Experience is individual. Sharing joy is always a vain attempt. Real joy is self-revealing in the self. Real friends do not have to be told. Friendship makes one transparent. A friend sees through the joy of a friend, like sunlight shining from behind the clouds. Men are at their best relations with the world of joy as long as they are not asked to speak of it; and what is more, as long as it is understood that a personal realisation cannot be spoken of. Consider the infants, the speechless infants. They speak with their radiance; and the mother understands. We are just like the little babies in the eyes of the Great Mother. And she alone understands whether we are famished or satisfied. There is no need to talk. Only communicate. Silent communication is the supreme bliss of love. The unspoken is always much sweeter than the spoken; and certainly more accurate. Hence in *japa* of *mantra* silence must be observed. Not even the tongue should move. In fact the tongue should be stuck to the area lying between the tonsils. Love is both blind, and dumb of tongue. Feel, and experience."

"Love also likes to express. To demonstrate. Is it not so?"

"Demonstrative love? That must be too thin. Spectacular and conventional. Better to avoid such love."

Why Rituals!

"Then why all these rituals? All these flowers, garlands, bells and singing of chants? Is the Great Mother deaf? Is she as weak as to need flattering praises?"

"Men often use demonstration for their own benefit rather than for the benefit of the worshipped. Such demonstrative practices assist the efforts, as the stick does assist the old and the cripple. Accept these as the necessary encumbrances; aides to achievement. Do not make a fetish of the aides, forgetting the aim and the objective. When one wants to speak the most in the least, one takes to poetical expressions. Hymns and *mantras* speak the most in the least. Only the writers and the poets know that having said all, much remains yet unsaid. There has never been a complete poet. Literature is a still born child."

I too used to try on versifications and short stories. I watched her remarks wide-eyed. The desire to talk and refute was rushing through my mind like a flood of sunlight overwhelming a closed room where a window has been suddenly opened.

But she continued. "We sing Her praises aloud. This is true. We bring Her homage in leaves and flowers, fire and water. This is also true. These are the methods through which we try to attach values and meanings to things we ourselves hold as valuable and meaningful. We would not have paid homage if we ourselves did not look forward to it. Ask the political leaders. They too receive the garlands. Ask the worshippers of birthdays, and those who observe anniversaries of Christmas and Valentines. Men glory and romance over these presentations, and feel that they could please their gods the same way. These are not entirely superficial. As I said, these are necessary as aids. These gifts offered through music, words, flowers, flames, candles, water, cards, food, even money have their psychological uses. Not superficial uses; real; almost medical and clinical. These expressions, made through the gifts, often iron out the crumpled complexes of the mind, and bring upon a disturbed mind the blessings of peace. They provide support of the cripple, as glasses do to the myopic. No, rituals are very much in place. Those who invented them were the wise of the earth. Never undervalue rituals; but also bear it in mind not to overvalue them."

Sex is a Sacrifice

"Is clothing too a convention, and unclothing a ritual?"

"No. More than that. Not clothing or unclothing, but the very sex. This is to be understood that the powers of sex, hunger and greed too, coming from the Mother, provide incentives to a purpose. But only when this is fully understood it is so; when misunderstood the incentive tempts indulgence, and becomes a source of serious danger. We have discussed that aspect already.

"The gift of anger is a great gift; the gift of greed is a supreme gift; the gift of sex is the most important of gifts. Unclothing is absolutely necessary when one practises rightfully the gift of sex. Let me explain.

"You make gifts of water and flower; of sweets and other food. And then you partake of the same flower, garland, food, drink. You claim that these are blessed. In Christianity they make gifts of bread and wine. And then partake of the gift. In this way we develop a rapport of veneration to the things we physically need, and mentally covete. This imposes on our sensuousness a kind of restriction through veneration and regard. When we offer our sex ritually to the divine, consider the sex as a divine gift, and then participate in it, automatically our attitude towards sex changes. Control over sex is the most difficult of controls. The more one preserves this control, the more one gains in accumulation of will power.

"This skin to skin *āsanas* close all the sex areas together; a state of intimate participation develops. Then this great offering leads to a consummate bliss of ecstatic realisation. After this, the attitude towards sex as well as to woman in general becomes so sublimated that in using this power we become divinely disposed. Power then is conserved. Do not flitter away the power. Do not waste the seed. This is tantra.

"Those who have prescribed these rituals knew very well what they were doing. Gunpowder was discovered for fun. Dynamite was discovered for the use of power for human service. Sources of more concentrated power shall be yet discovered. If these are used or misused for destruction and waste would you not call that an act of rascality? Vandalism? Barbarism? Sex too is a source of power. Only a very little of this power is needed for reproduction. But it is mostly wasted. If well preserved, this power could easily reach man to his ultimate goal of finding peace (to let others live in peace); it reaches the sublime heights without much difficulty. His actions would be inspired; his speech would be eloquent; his will would become dynamic; his love would become effective.

"But the wonder of wonder is that at the *āsana* or out of it, with woman or without her, amidst sex, gluttony, avarice, wealth and other sources of egotistic swell, man finally seeks loneliness. He wants to be secluded, alone. To be by his own Self. This is why we sleep. Nature has provided life with sleep to remain alone for a while. Without this resort in loneliness man would break down to pieces. Those who are not lonely even in sleep are subject to nerve-shattering dreams. They live in hell. They are the condemned of the earth.

Secrecy in Tantra

"Worry not about what others say about your intimate exercise. Where do those talkers and probers of your behaviour disappear when you are alone with me? Do they bother you then my child? During the sessions?

"When the world goes to sleep, the stars wake. When the stars go to sleep, the world wakes. That is why we find that the silence of the night appears to be more profound than the bustle of the lighted day. People regard saints and yogis, even me, as unrelated to the world. Yet these are most concerned with the life and beyond. A yogi is the one who though concerned, does not show it. He like the sunless silent night keeps a vigil of protection over a world that sleeps. He is silent. Silence could be very eloquent my son, as a crowd could be very lonely."

I recalled that the neighbourhood wondered at the vigilant silence of the Lady in Saffron.

Suddenly, I felt extremely ashamed that I had made her talk so much, and at length. I had asked her, what now appeared to me, a silly question about silence, secrets and hiding. Why must we always be fighting within for explaining ourselves?

But something else had still been bothering me.

She became aware of my disturbance.

"Do not stop now my son," she said. "I am about to lead you out to deeper seas. Ask now. What next? When we in tantra demand criminal secrecy, we do not mean secrecy in the sense of the criminal gangs. Secrecy like that cringes the soul; it makes the mind burrow deeper and deeper where light is denied. There is another kind of secrecy. It is the secrecy of the womb, where underneath deep covers, unseen and untended, the fruit of love grows. The time for revelation comes, and the fruit comes out to light and life. Some secrets are nursed for later revelation in their fullness; some secrets are preserved for the darkness alone.

"Look around, and watch. The world of nature secretly, under the earth, under the soil, conspires with wind and light and water for years and years, and going back far and farther back, eons and eons of time backward, until we fail even to measure the time and the cause, in total hush, prepares to spring out a bloom on a plant, and the fruit comes. We know that from the bloom the fruit comes. Do we know now the seed came? How the bloom came? What transmutations had to be gone through, before a grain of rice, or a cedar tree came to be what it is now? This is another kind of secret. The birth of a star is merged in another kind, and yet another deeper secret.

"The gaudy flower shows itself off; the juicy fruit tempts us. We stretch our hands to seize the one for its beauty and perfume; and the other for its juice and life giving properties. Watch the seed. The silent, insignificant, almost negligible seed. None imagines that, like the genii emerging from the insignificant little bottle that Aladin had picked up from the vast sea shore, from that little seed a whole generation of mangoes, and many more generations beyond, trees and mangoes would continue to emerge. The seed of the giant banyan tree is hard to be seen. Life is held in silence within the casket of an unseen seed. The life of *mantra* lies within a 'seed' sound. Hatch it; power would spring out of it. Who knows the source of life?

"Silence is a great virtue. Tantra believes in the 'vitality' (*prāṇa śakti*) of the seed. All its *mantras* are known as seed sounds. Great spiritual prospects are held within these insignificant syllabic sounds. Tantra has again enjoined on the great virtue of holding the tongue. The fraudulent beats his drums, makes a lot of noise, and attracts a crowd. Often sensation promoters get around a yogi, a miracle man, and keep up a big noise. For them noise is money. For others silence is a blessing; source of real wealth. The lion preys in utter silence, but the jackal that lives on the left-overs keeps on a lot of noise; and the crows and vultures attract the entire woodland of the kill that was made in silence. Promoters are like keen vultures. In no time at all the crowds flock around. The peace of silence gets eroded; its profundity gets deluged; and ultimately what had been an abode of peace ends up with the crescendo of a stage-managed variety performance.

"Tantra warns against such pitfalls. 'Secrecy has to be maintained," says tantra, "as the secret areas of one's own personal body."

That brought me to my real enquiry. My anxious reaction was visible. It appeared that the Lady in Saffron suddenly had grown larger in dimension. She had anticipated me, and beamed into a smile.

"You find the contradiction. Personal areas of sex, contrary to common acceptance, are not kept covered because there is any secrecy in them. There is no secrecy in milk; but we keep it secure from the cat. There is no secrecy in what we eat. But we keep them covered from flies and germs. Why then must you confuse between secrecy that has to be maintained in spiritual undertakings, and the physical nudity of the body? Those who make the body an object for exhibition and claim admiration, track, tempt and trap the onlookers. The motive behind makes an action vicious. By itself an action is not vicious.

"Take a good look at the world around you. Which other form of life, besides the human beings, makes a fetish of their nudity, or of the coverings? What brought about in the life of man the complex of shame? Lust for the surface of bodily joys motivates undeserved grabs;

and such thievings, when caught up, brings about the shame complex. The fear of public denouncement as a thief, or a grabber intensifies this shame which indeed is a guilt complex.

The Light Within

"Complexes, my son, result from problems. Problems are the products from misunderstandings and malhandlings of situations. Often we try to sweep out these situations, by keeping the facade smooth and clean, only by pushing the dirt under the bright carpet. The dirt however, corrupts and fowls the air. Purity of breathing is interfered with; and a complex is allowed to grow. Complex disturbs the mental health. Complex obstructs the light from heaven. This 'light from heaven' is not a legend. Heaven may be; but not the light from heaven. This light is a fact. It is within you. Call it intelligence, call it intellect. Without this unaccountable light, life would be dumb.

"This light is within you. This light is without you. Through this light you participate beyond your own limit. The light within enlightens you; the light without delights you. In the heavens and beyond it, on this earth, and what exists between the two this divine glory and light envelopes all life. Life is this light. This light enlightens your thinking as intelligence; in your eyes, it is sight; in your ears, sound (light is sound and *vice versa*); on your skin, touch and grace. This light becomes blessings coming through wishes; this light descends as joy in your smiles and popularity. Understanding is aglow with this light; darkness of mind and of soul is removed by this light. No secrecy could endure this light. The want of it brings out the beast in man; and one must secure life from the ravages of these beasts. God is *jyoti, go, bharga*—light.

"For further evidence of this 'light from heaven' one has to consider the secret springs of the faculty of clear thinking. Clear, direct, revealing reactions of the mind is described as 'coming to light.' One name of light (*jyoti*) is expression (*prakāśa*). *Jīvatām jyotih* (Let light prevail)."

Pain

"The mind that functions without pain or fear, specially fear, does not cause the self any pain and suffering. Pain and suffering are reactions of the mind. Even physical pain is a feeling. And feeling is the mind's only identity. Physical pain is the result of muscular sensitiveness and nervous intolerance. It is mind's failure to bear the unbearable.

Emotional pain could be neutralised by inner discipline. A disciplined mind regards all changes as casual and temporary. The balanced does not fluctuate, and does not suffer pain.

"Your Surendada admits members to his underground guerrilla club by putting them to physical tests against acute and severe tortures. He asks young boys and girls to hold out their fingers on candle flames until the skin begins to roast and peel. He drives sharp blades of knives through the flesh, and needles through the roots of nails as tests for dumb endurance. That is the passport for entering the club. How could they suffer the pain, and why? If one could suffer it; of course another could, or should. It is the pull of the objective that influences the nerves to gain in fortitude. With proper training understanding and subtle analysis, the cause of pain, as well as of suffering itself could be negatived. Do nor suffer.

Yogic Control Over Mind

"Knowledge, understanding, analysis and training are steps prescribed in yoga. Discipline, regulations, postures, control, decontrol, clear conception, absorption of the conceived ideal gradually step up the mind to gain the heights of impersonal concentration.

"Mental concentration first releases the mind free. The mind's place is then taken over by pure consciousness. Then the 'Fountain of Power' is released. Power is the greatest possession in human life. Else man would be only a glorified animal; a biological fact; a psychological chaos. The fountain of power must be discovered. It is within you. Love is within you: the love that does not get entangled, but is involved.

"Once the mind is free from the bonds of conditioned expectations, prejudiced conclusions, that is, from rooted superstitions, it is able to act as a subjective function. Thinking is a function that needs not be encumbered with mind. You know that mind does not do the thinking. It is illusory to suppose that the mind even remembers, retains or forgets. Those functions belong to memory. Mind only carries false impressions, and by doing so keeps clear thinking in a state of perpetual confusion. All mental conditions must be complex; because mind is a conditioned state of the personality. Consciousness alone is pure.

Clear Thinking

". . . But you are wondering. . . . Well, I am not surprised. Are you following?"

Indeed this was going partly over my head. The speed was too much for my tracing. I was on the verge of a breakdown. I hated to find myself in a position when she would be explaining, and I would be gasping for breath for survival. Following logical discourses was habitual with me. My birth in a classical Sanskrit school, environment had given me a training in following up the abstruse discourses. Our academy was a common meeting place in Varanasi of known logicians and grammarians.

But at her sudden halt, and query I felt a sort of relief, and I cried, "No? I don't".

"Yes, you do!," she asserted; and at the same time held my hand in hers, and gave me a gentle pull. Her right palm was on my eyes, which I closed. She rested her palm for a while on the eyes, and repeated, "Yes you do, you do. . . ."

In a flick, the tight feeling was gone. She continued as before "You do your arithmetic. Do you? Then you do think for arriving at the result step by step. Likewise you do your geometry. Don't you? Then again you are led to think, step by step until you are at the end of the solved problem. When you are asked to form a word from its roots, or construct a sentence, you have to go along the steps of grammar. This type of thinking is known as clear thinking, or mindless thinking. This is objective thinking.

"When the same brain is engaged in thinking about how to find food and shelter, how to escape punishment, or form lies, it is not engaged in clear thinking. This second kind of thinking is linked with self-interest, and is therefore prejudiced. It is, as it were, loaded with preconcieved conclusions, and wishes. Wish slaps a bond on free will. The thinker projects his wish through his thinking. He is walking under his own shadow. The thinker's conclusions are being foreshadowed by his thinking. The thinker himself, and not the problem, becomes the central commanding figure. The thinker gets himself emotionally involved. This severely stands against the course of free thinking.

"The aim of yogic concentration is achieving the freedom of mind; or if you prefer, achieving liberation from the world of mind. When the mechanism of thinking is thus liberated then, and not till then, one could realise what one really is. Once one realises the SELF in its fullness of glory, one is worthy of being called the liberated, the Buddha, the Paramahamsa. Else he remains a bonded slave to his emotional being and personality.

Power Ultimate

"This is the ultimate in manhood. Getting at the flush of this Fountain of Power. This is the aim of life. The ultimate in manhood is to drink directly from this final source; to bathe in this light from heaven. I have been talking to you of this. It is not difficult to understand this for those practised to keep their mind on the track of correct thinking. I hope you understand it now. It is inescapable."

". . . And when I get this power, what shall I do with it?"

"Why are you so anxious to "*do*" something at all? Why? Does the river ever think; 'Why must I flow?' Or, the sky, 'Why must I home the clouds?' Or, the cloud; 'Why must I float and melt?' Or, the trees, 'Why must we stand and grow and supply?' You will or you could say, that they have no mind, that they are parts of nature, and act under natural laws. Who says they have no minds? Is there any firm proof? How do we know? Are we not under the same natural laws? If the natural laws make us think of '*doing*', the other lives and other aspects and other forms in nature might be thinking too. You know about the existence of mind by the disturbances it creates in you. The undisturbed feels no mind. It is like a glass-door. Because it is transparent, because its purity is not disturbed by contrary substances, you do not realise that a door is there. And in your unconcerned attempt to pass through, you are obstructed; you bounce against it; you get vexed, as Duryodhana did. The unthinking cannot put up with obstructions, because he assumes too much. That which is itself, and no other but itself, must be free from all kinds of obstructions; so naturally, it has to be transparent in understanding. What is that thing which we might call as totally transparent? It is consciousness. You are not definite about the fact that there is no consciousness in nature. Are you?

"No action in nature waits for 'why.' Whys belong to us, men, who are doomed to reason out. Nature 'is'; there is very little of *why* in nature. It creates with perfect freedom, and open choice. Everything in nature fulfills a purpose and plays a definite role in the scheme of things. The universe is knit together into a unit in spite of its manyness; and each part of this well-knit unit fulfills a purpose in a well-laid out pattern. Nature sets its own pattern.

"If so, a man's life too must have a purpose; and if there is one, man must fulfil it. If man did not, imbalance would result. Imbalance in nature would bring disaster. The human world has brought down on its head disaster after disaster. The process is continuing, and would continue, as long as it accepts its own mind as the ultimate power, and considers it to be the last judge. It brings down disasters sometimes collectively, sometimes individually. But at its root lies some kind of an individual mind. Such a mind has to be a selfish mind chasing its preconceived conclusions. . . .

"I see you have not got it. We know that Rāvaṇa was an individual who brought about an imbalance, and disaster followed. True. But Daśaratha too had acted under the influence of an imbalance. Disaster had started from that act. He made vows in order to win the favours of a girl much younger to his age. Even Sītā was the victim of an imbalance mind when she had foolishly insisted on having the golden deer, Rāma knew well that the golden deer was a fake, a mental trap. He even tried to bring sense to Sītā. But she, with a woman's infatuation, was insistent. So carried away was she by her imbalance that she did not much worry to drive the loyal and godly Lakṣmaṇa away from his duty by stinging him with lashes of unmentionable accusations. These individual imbalances ultimately led armies of human beings to march in bloodshed, which could have been avoided. That process has not stopped yet. We have never known a year in the world without armies marching against armies due to the wrong thinking of individual; and armies would continue to march against armies. Mouthful names of justice and fairplay are always trumpeted. As long as man's thinking does not get clear, that is to say, does not get impersonally inspired, this disaster will continue to distress man. Man must learn to think about good through getting involved without personal interest, or personal gain. No gain is gain if it is only immediate. That which does not bear the stamp of the everlasting is a bad commodity.

"What are those functious for which man as a part of the universe exists? If purpose is not known, of course it could not be fulfilled. There is a fundmental difference between living and existing. A life that drags on and on, without a clear purpose ahead, only drags its steps to death. Living must be a joy in the fullness of life.

"Heaven's light obstructed, darkness and confusion must follow. This is an inescapable inference deduced from clear thinking. And through objective thinking alone the source of Power could be reached. There is no other way. This is tantra, the traditional way, that has been coming down from wise men to wise men like a continuous thread from a flux of experimental thinking. Call it Hindu, Aryan, Śaiva, Vaiṣṇava, Christian, Buddhist, Islamic, Judaic, Samman, Vāma,

Aghora, Vajra, Zen, Tao, or whatever you choose; it is tantra. All ways are tantra ways. These historical names or local names do not interfere with the basic contents of the search for the fountainhead of the Power of *kuṇḍalinī*, the peace of the thousand petalled lotus. Tantra, the name, signifies methodology and means 'method', traditional way', 'strain of continuity' and 'thread'.

Love does not Reason

"Now perhaps you would appreciate why it is vital for man to develop this power; how the acquisition of this power depends on guidance, special methods and special mechanics. We have lost that method, faith, and regard for guidance for, and control of patience. All we are engaged in this age is questioning, arguing, Why? Why and Why? As if man's ultimate peace is attainable through reasoning. As if reasoning would establish love between man and man. Love, funny to think of it, functions free of reason.

"The quest after the answers to reasoning led the heavenly pair of the legend to be driven permanently out of their beautiful and secured habitat, and miss God's own protection. They had to leave that protection because the anti-god taught them how to get at peace through enquiry and argument. Only after the two individuals lost the paradise, they realised that they were misled.

"The fact was that they naturally loved as two matured persons. They had not committed sin by loving. The sin was that they forgot to express innocently; they forgot to reveal; they did not take their most loving friend into confidence.

"Love felt hurt. Hurt at the trickery. Else how love could be wrong? All lives at their respective maturity have a mission to fulfill. Love ennobles this mission. Lives born in love find it easier to love. Lives born under duress, compulsion, haste, hatred or horror find it hard to generate love. There is so much lack of love in the world. Hence all this turmoil. The world has become a place of suffering. Love begets love. A mature life's mission is to multiply life; but it must be done with plan, preparation and love. There are seasons for flowers, fruits, animals, birds. Only the human beings do not have care or regard for the seasons.

"Love blossoms when the seasons are respected. Love is the finest blossom, and the cleanest to spread the perfume of understanding.

"This natural love of life for life, this urge for expression in joy, has acquired the special name of sex. I have spoken of the Power of *lhādinī.* This sex-joy, too, like all other forms of joy—food-joy, rest-joy, sleep-joy, creative-joy, is lifesome, healthy and natural. Through this joy the spirit of joy descends to the body level; there, out of the body it derives a limited joy which has unlimited potential. It springs out lives and more lives, and keeps the world drama supplied with actors. Joy is the sublimest and the most effective ingredient to make many come into one. Two become one in joy.

Life is Born

"Love-joy inspires, and sets the bodies into a hot heat of excitement. It churns the depths of the very beings. The egg of life then springs of the female, who receives the seed. The male costs the seed into the ovum-egg supplied by the female. A live seed is fondly put to sleep into the mother-soil almost as if an infant were put to sleep for nine months into a specially constructed cradle. This is so because in the male alone the seed forms. And all seeds need soil to germinate and grow. Seeds require soil, and soil calls for seed, and planting. The soil is provided by the female. Such is the arrangement in nature that the process could not be reversed. For the continuity of life the male and the female are interdependent. The male casts the seed, and the female, as soil, receives it. There it germinates, grows, and in time shows itself. A life is then born. This life, after the period of incubation, is cast into this world through a passage which we have chosen to call private. It is a wrong name given to a right fact. The parts of the body engaged in this process of generation of life are not so private as personal.

"It takes a period of nine months for the life-seed to germinate, and get strong enough to grow without the warming shelter of the mother's personal body heat. The constant watchfulness of men for the springing of a seed into a human life in nine months made the number nine assume a particularly meaningful esoteric importance in rites. In mystic calculations number nine thus became a mysterious number.

"By functioning as they did, the pair of human beings had acted in a natural function. So far this appeared to be all in form. Nothing had gone wrong. But the envious force which disturbed this innocent and noble fact did a mischief. Anti-god asked the pair to keep their joy and their subsequent love-making a secret from God, who actually would have been too pleased to find them in joy. Instead they presented to him a picture of criminal depression. They were led to believe that God did not want them reach the highest pinnacle of love, and create.

"This was not true, but only an assumption. They thought that they had gone against God. No one goes against God by loving. As they tried to keep their joy a secret from God, they had allowed themselves to be tormented by a guilty complex, and this made them lose the most important boon of life, the boon of innocence and universal joy of openness. Although they themselves had enjoyed, they did not want to include God's participation to their joy. Love can never be exclusive.

"It was a sad beginning for man. Man was born with a guilty complex, and was forced to find delight in the dark chambers of secrecy. Love and light were kept separated through a pervert scheme.

"But by definition God is a power that knows all, sees all and hears all. There was no question of 'keeping' a secret from him. Besides being foolish in feeling that they could keep a secret from him, they had acted also cruelly, because they had schemed to keep God out of their feast of joy. Real joy must be shared. In sharing it radiates and discharges streams of power.

"Thus the divine covenant was broken, and man forever lost the natural capacity to realise the absolute love of God. The spell of Eden had been broken. Man asked for his own misery. Since then men have been living in a world of mutual secrets, doubts and hidings. Animals do not have these secrets, neither do the babies. And they are the beloveds of God. They are without sin."

I was much moved by the contents of the legend which I had heard before. But the manner in which it was related, has brought the inner implications so vivdly that I could hardly resist my tears. It was indeed a tragic legend.

The Kancukas

The pigeons in the courtyard of the silent temple were busy in their own ways. In the Chatuhṣaṣṭhī shrine bells were ringing. The shadows had started lengthening. The Lady in Saffron appeared to have halted for breath. She had been talking now for about an hour and a half. I looked at her, and she knew that I wanted to hug her. She stretched her arms, and I was immediately lost in her motherly embrace.

"No, do not despair. God is kind. All was lost, but love was not lost. Love and hope. Love was still their. This love has to be liberated from its prison of many walls. We call them *kancukas*, or sheaths. These sheaths refer to vital stages which obstruct our growth; and obstruct us from getting completely independent of the world outside. We have a material personality which depends on food and drink; then we have an inner personality which depends on the environmental breathing; then we have our emotional being which depends on the actions and reactions of the people around us; then we have our personality of knowledge acquired from our own perception, and from informations left by others. And lastly we arrive at our own being, our real personality which depends entirely on our realisation. Unless we ourselves have realised, how the realisations of others could satisfy us?

"The walls of this prison-house keep growing around us because of our guilty complex, that makes us keep so much in hiding, and prevents us from living in the openness of life. Although man belongs to the family of the sun and the air, the water and the fire, he has forgotten the art of belonging to them. The links have broken. He dares not declare that like he, his other cousins in nature have the right to live in the openness of contact.

"The fun of life for the human animal so much depends on living a covered life that he almost worships this habit of taking cover, and living under a cover. God lives in the open. For God there is not, and there cannot be any cover. Our joys too, have been covered; our laughters are not free; neither our cries. To express one's emotions openly has been tabooed as contrary to form and culture. A free expression of the joys and sorrows of life is under a special licence. And this very damaging attitude has caused more problems in life than we would readily own; more complexes than we had bargained for have been brought about by blindly maintaining our wrongful attitudes to life.

"The only way to get over this is to try to get nearer God, get nearer nature. We are animals; and we must not feel small to own this. God is *paśupati*, the Lord over the animals. He loves the animals. All our gods and goddesses are represented as controllers of some kind of animal passion, and 'lords' of utilising the special powers of these animals for our own benefit. Look at the dog, the horse. How friendly these wild creatures have become to men. This is all due to our ability to control these animals. We could control all animalism of all the animals, inclusive of the animalism which we cover and nurse within us. To bring these to the open, and master them for our benefit, as we have mastered the bull for the plough, the elephant for carrying big loads across mountains and forests, the camels as ships of the desert, is the special gift of the human beings.

"Why must we not, then, take courage, and master the serpent, and many other animals, besides, which lie dormant and hidden within us? Let us recognise them, bring them to books, before they destroy all our joy in life. That would do so much good for our living, and dying, which is another way to living eternally at peace.

The Curse of Secrecy

"Men would still function in secret. Every one is aware of the functions of life and the relation of sex to life. Yet they would prefer driving these functions under the hypocritical pretence of secrets.

"Privacy? yes, of course. Every individual, every person is a sacred entity to himself. This sanctity enjoins the right to privacy. Most animals too, like to unite in privacy, although their love-life is for all to see. Most emotional demonstrations call for a special private expression. To exhibit emotions is a mark of crude taste. But secrecy? Why? No. Never refuse light, either within, or without. Light is life. Life is God. Men do not see this. Very unfortunate; but this is the Truth.

"Moreover, they would consider this attitude to be a better attitude, a more decent and natural attitude. Living openness, in loving fidelity, loyalty and friendliness washes out all complexes, or most of them.

"The highest wrong men do to their peace of mind is to help create an area of imbalance, crime, guilt, darkness by accommodating and compromising with these complexes.

"Men delight and take pride in nursing these complexes. It is difficult to believe it; but this is so. They must live under a mask of secretiveness. It is as it were a curse. They must create their own hell by refusing the penetration of light. Sex has remained with them an area of forbidden fruits. It ought to have been welcomed by them as an area of the highest joy that love and body could achieve through friendship, confidence, loyalty and togetherness. These are the sources of the highest spiritual joy in life.

"Forbidden fruits are taken to be, wrongfully though, sweeter than the openly distributed ones. It adds to excitement and to the perverse joy of living in danger. Thus the joy of sex too is often driven under the darkness of secret cover, and hurried secretiveness adds to the pep of this joy.

"As a result this joy is squeezed for joy alone. Man acts as a robber of his own rights. What a curse! It is never controlled; never accepted as normally healthy; its legitimacy in the world of spirit is corrupted by the complexes of guilt and fear; and the original motive of joy, namely, the joy of multiplying life, the joy of procreation is driven into a dark corner. Love gets depraved, degenerated. The greedy run after more food than could be digested. Similarly men run after more sex than the wonders and charms of life could even countenance. Continuity of life is a sacred duty enjoined on life. We have reduced that sacrament into a filthy sensation of a forbidden act.

"The Hindu mode of avowing a male and a female as man and wife is an extremely sublime and sacred sacrament. Their sex becomes veritably, an actual offering, a sacrifice, to the holiness of the life-purpose. The will of God is expressed through the continuity of life; and sex is a sacrifice to fulfil that will of God. One could go to sex only with that ideal in view, and no other. The hymn of the nuptials solemnly prays: 'Let us never seek a union aimlessly, frigidly, mechanically. Let our union remain a solemn offering from Love to Love. This all is for Love.' Ask your father. He would recite for you the whole hymn from the *Ṛgveda*.

"Men do not live by these laws and these ideals. They do not even follow the laws of nature. Instead they indulge in excesses, indiscretions and lust. Because they feel guilty, they want to cover up. Because they want to cover up, therefore they call for the covers. They cover and notify certain areas of the sacred human body as out of bounds, private parts, secret parts. What is in nature private, and what public? Secret to god? Secret to mind? How frustrating.

"Every yard of cloth on our body is an arrogant rejection of what God and nature had designed us to become. One day when you yourself shall be processed enough, educated enough, steeled enough, and when we shall call you fully matured, you shall personally realise the full and bountiful gifts of tantra. You shall be then convinced that all power implanted within our body and soul is for a cause. It is a greater cause than we, because of our lack of foresight and inner vision, could hardly visualise. One day you shall feel cleansed. You shall feel anointed. You shall come to me. You shall come to many like me. From much to more, from more to the most. One day this distinction of sex shall become non-existent to you. Your confusions regarding shame, secrecy, privacy, embarrassment all, all shall melt away at the powerful white-hot touch of tantric openness, and allness. This is true. Remember, tantra teaches the way to conduct life in a cleaner manner by respecting and following the laws of God and nature. Tantra is a regeneration, a resurrection, a revival. It admits of a mode of living with a positive purpose. It rules out the negative way. There is no negative in nature. It admits of no mysteries. Nothing is obscure in tantra, Obscurantism is the very antithesis of tantra. '*I am the Light. You all do not accept the Light. They remain fooled by their false involvements imprisoned within their prison of darkness. I run through it all unseen as does the thread run unseen to keep all the beads in the necklace held together.*' Remember the lines."

Of course, I did. The Gītā.

How Tantra Functions?

She continued: "This education comes gradually, because this knowledge is precious and vital, it has to be guarded with utmost care. Care, not secret. The indiscreet would misuse, because he would lack inevitably in proper care. When you have poison in the lab, or gasoline in stock, you take special care. That is nothing to be secreted. Just the training for the necessary care. Many researches are guarded by secrecy at the stage when it could not be made public without spelling danger to the public. The more precious a knowledge is, the more imperative becomes the need for keeping it under a strict supervision. The guru is the supervisory power.

"Tantra is not obscure. Were it so, the commonest of the tribals would not have been its custodians. You shall gradually realise that the more natural, uninhibited and simple a society is, the more reliant it becomes on tantric rites. The man of the soil and the man of nature are the closest adherents to tantra. Tantra and tantric rites reject too much learning and sophistry. It relies on the practical instructions from the guru. If one wants to accept this path after feeding his personal reasonings satisfactorily, one would find it much more profitable to reject this path completely. Reliance on the guru, and guru alone is the first, second and the third steps to this mystery-door of ultimate ecstasy.

"The training you are undergoing could be described as the tempering of steel, or the purification of gold. Unless you develop the right and proper attitude towards the body of man, you need not bother with tantra. What is the use of entering a church without having faith for the church? The sightseer's attitude is not for tantra, neither is the academician's. Unless man stands face to face with the body's function, and the designs of the life process, he cannot be liberated from the body, and specially from the mind. Obscurity of the mysteries does not stand in the way of the liberated.

"Man must reach the source of Power. You must reach this source of Power. You see now why you must develop the correct attitude to man and woman, manhood and womanhood, to the joy and bliss of life. You must have a very clear-cut concept about what is clean and what is unclean; what is private and what is public; what is essentially yours, and what belongs to all.

"The science of coming close to the bodies has to be learnt by you with as much zeal and care as the science of coming close to a blast furnace, a boiler, a raging fire-house ablaze. Else you would be burnt before the fire is extinguished. Expose, and the exposures shall not burn you. Sit long, and time would not bother you. Love the ideal with allness of heart, and concentrate on it, and temptation would not bother you. Learn it; master it. Only then you shall be fearlessly strong; expertly skilful; courageously valiant, and frank without complex, or any other keep-back. A perversion always has a correct version. Find that out. Follow that.

The Earth is a Maiden

"This is why the *āsanas* have been started. The body has to be trained along with the mind. Make *āsanas* of the body, and automatically the mind shall be subdued and controlled. The body would cease to bother you too much. This earth is the primal and the ultimate *āsana*. We are very close to it. We know it so much that we do not realise that we are the closest to it.

"The earth is a maiden that delivers life without getting corrupted. She absorbs corruption for the growth of life. This earth draws heat and moisture at the same time. How? Is it not amazing? How does she do the trick? As power draws power, body draws body. The ultimate in *āsana* depends on the body, in which the disturbance known as the mind sleeps or roars. In all cases mind is a deterrent to spiritual joy. Mind has to be kept under strict control. For controlling the mind the art of closeness of a body to a body has to be cultivated. The cultivation of aloofness, loneliness negates life. That is both impossible and unnecessary. Their is a surfeit of unnoticed power-current passing through the phenomena of the body, air, water, earth, heat and the atmosphere. Besides these, there are the three abstract phenomena of mind, intelligence and ego. The *āsanas* assist us to capture and store the powers from these phenomena, and re-circuit that power for the benefit of mankind.

"You are now being introduced only to one of the *āsanas*, and that coming close to one body. Soon you shall find other bodies, that is living bodies, as well as those bodies from which the *prāṇa* (life breath) has flown away. The living wood which we call a tree is as much wood as the dead wood. Both retain the power that wood has to retain. In time other *āsanas* shall come before you. Remember all *āsanas* are not for spiritual use. Some appeal to health; some to the removal of ailments; some to self-control; some are purely psychiatrically inspired. The mystic *āsana* in *latā sādhana* is a spiritual *āsana* of the ultimate type. A yogi needs them all.

I shall like to beware you at this stage, however, of the dangers of keeping these *āsanas* for the benefit of your physical needs alone."

Where Good is No Good

The warning surprised me. What dangers could there be in keeping the body in shape, or free from ailments?

She had observed my consternation, and she smiled again. Sundown was close at hand. The hot sun was no longer hot. Her quietly inspiring smile reminded me of the approaching evening. Was I not tired? Was I not eager to reach the river bank? I was not really restless, but it would be best to keep the discussion, no, the lesson, for another day.

She broke in. "Good health could be a threat to concentration, as good dress, good food and good feeling of well being also could be. I say good in the sense of indulgence and excess. Too much good is tempting. I say good in the sense of the accepted social behaviour. The Bhairava and the tantrik maintain other standards of good and bad. You must realise that by now. I shall educate you on that. Also I have to instruct you that in tantra we worship the body, adore the so-called unadorable; emphasise the obscure and extol the abhorring. Things terrible are our neighbours; souls without body are our consultants; the very phenomenal nature is our power house. We keep nothing behind the curtains. Pull at the cupboard hard my son. Let the dirty and smutty fly out. Let fly all that smell of moulds and fungi. Only then the freshness in air should vitalise your *prāṇa*. Only then we could sort out, and have our picks for the keeps. . . .

". . . but you are now thinking of the session on the river bank, and of the songs? Well, let us proceed. The sunset today shall look very beautiful indeed."

She held me by the hand; and we began to walk towards the river bank.

4

A Strange Nocturne

The Boy Sceptic

The training continued. New *āsanas* came to light. I could now feel that these *āsanas* were no common acrobatics, as are generally viewed on the hot banks of Varanasi, or in such cold prints.

And the songs and the hymns! After a considerable period of more than half a century, in retrospect, I feel so much indebted to those sheaves of songs and hymnals.

Songs and hymns are supposed to address themselves to the powers of the Infinite. To be in participation with these is to get involved in an act of religious solemnity. The bases of such reactions are so obvious that is does not take us much effort to realise how *mantras* could affect our subconscious and supraconscious beings, and bring about a change in us. These are automatically accepted by the spiritual aspirant. As an effective medium to get attuned to the cosmic, the value of *mantra* is immense, specially to the learner.

Even though a mere boyish youth, I used to feel quite a bit sceptic about the thin distinction between the religious and the spiritual. Because of the family traditions, and the almost continuous performance of a variety of rites and ceremonies at home, my idea of the religion was closely associated with the elaborate toss and tumble of the complicated and lengthy (often boring) Hindu rituals. The ensemble of various objects, sacrificial offerings, the layings of the *maṇḍalas*, the perfections of the *mudrās*, the difficult and laborious efforts of calculating the exactness of the time of the performance raised in my mind many awkward questions. Not that I always disliked them, but some of them imposed rigours on us, and made us work very hard indeed. We, the youngsters were kept on our run most of the time because of the demanding conditions of those rituals.

Today as I recall them I feel otherwise. I have come to experience, and learn from that experience, that these rituals by making demands on the devotees often chasten them, and condition them into a state of seriousness, self-control and reverence. Today, as I recall, I feel that besides the disciplinary overtone and the chastening influence, the attention associated with these rituals tones up the body as well as the mind. A solemn profundity elevates the soul, and a kind of satisfaction soothes the disturbed nerves. It adds interest to forms; and these forms, as well as the interest so formed, lead to sharpness of attention, concentration and even meditation.

In those days, however, the only points we the boys enjoyed through such exercises were two; one, the actual performance with solemn devotion. Gongs, bells and chantings with the ever-present aura of drama and show, captivated the boyish imagination. And two, the generally sumptuous dinner that followed. It was great excitement packed within a single day.

In retrospect, I think that what I call today as solemnity and awe, was more or less conditioned also by the personal involvement of my parents, both of whom, we noticed, were much worked up by such events.

We believed and held on to the fact that nothing that they would hold on to as precious could be anything other than precious. This singular confidence cast a halo around these events. Automatically the rites assumed a solemn grandeur irrespective of any personal mental differences. Rituals always follow a spoken (or even unspoken) vow undertaken for the performance of an act. And a vow is the mother of determination.

But this feeling of solemnity, and the aesthetic pleasure evoked by the paeans of gorgeous music of the great classical hymns stirred something deep within. Call it soul (for which we did not care much then), or call it heart, or anything else, (the choice is yours), the pull at our inner being at these ceremonies was undeniable, and now, unforgettable. The entire pursuit rested on a theory, and well it could be. But the effect it had in the formation of our attitude towards our life and living had the unmistakable imprint of a faithful conviction.

Spiritual Tooth Brush

This was then our *Religion* at the time. This religion held little or no scope at all for the *other-worldliness* on which, probably, most secular religions survive. Heaven or hell, God or Devil, life before or after etc., sounded no more than mere vulgar formalities, at times even deliberate designs for dumping and deluding. Do we not use similar terms in other contexts without the least involvement? Malaria, inflation, pollution, or ecumenical gatherings for instance? Religion too appeared to be one of those juicy and insistent terms in life. Just a routine conformity to things in vogue; submission to conventions. A kind of spiritual tooth-brushing without which the inside does not get ready, as it were, for chewing conscience raw.

Such conformities grow out of acceptance of sanctions, and force of habit. Fundamentally there is very little difference between a pull for the Saturday horse race, and one for the church. Under the forces of these social pulls, we act more as mere ball-bearings in a groove, than as independent protestants. Mysticism has no appeal to the worldly; the ability of taking delight in the unseen, or using it as a source of fulfilment of expectation is a special gift possessed by the hungry of soul. There is a hunger in the soul that craves for the elevating pleasures of music, sung or unsung.

Hymnal Effects

The hymns had a permanent effect on my soul. They moulded my character. I have tried and practised hymns in other set-ups: school gatherings, assemblies, even demonstrative responses to special requests. But the sublime feeling that the same hymns invoked against religious settings had invariably been much more satisfying, poised and fulfilling.

Hymnal sonance, I believe, divides the line between religious and spiritual feelings. Why has a kind of worldly gains and worldly success found clear mention in unabashed words within pious hymns? Religious rituals are designed for, and appeal to whatever gods there may be; ritualists expect worldly dividends in return. But I felt elevated with some reward more abiding, permanent and deep. Hymnal music changed the texture of my inner personality. I became not only more sensitive and vibrant, but I was also able in a very remote way to establish a relationship between the being within and the world around me. In agitation or peace, in dreams or realisation, in conflicts or tranquillity, in appreciation of beauty and creativeness I felt a fuller being. I felt to be one with the sun and the stars, the trees and the rivers, the valleys and the mountains. Men became my soul's neighbours. The world was my home. The sun was in my blood. The open sky and the sea my mental park. This was something more than religion. This was the gift of the spirit that runs between, and makes of individuals coefficients of Time and Energy.

This could be the possible border line between religion and spiritualism. This explains my natural attraction for hymns. I was getting more and more used to them.

The Lady in Saffron added to the stock from her own compositions and collections. Every time I sang them, particularly in natural solitude along the lonely hide-outs of the river bank, a soothing nervous stimulation drove me onward, and that spot, where the saint had pressed the bead, simmered. Before my closed eyes sparks in a multicolour glory shot through a quiet space, while unaccountable tears bathed my cheeks. I felt animated and flushed with a hot heat.

Now I must make a point clear. This sweet agitation, which became gradually a familiar experience, did not bear any deeper content. It was emotionally consummating, but spiritually shortlived. Since later in life a deeper content became a treasured experience, I could speak of this difference. Yet it was not entirely superficial.

Is there no pleasure in swimming on the surface? Is there no glory shared with the waves which the swimmer cuts through, with the myriad sparkles of the sun hitting, crumbling, swaying, floating around the liquid mass where the swimmer is also afloat? The freedom, the lightness, the ebullience, the levitating feeling of a riddance from the world-mass is a kindred feeling to some spiritual fulfilment. Yet the fact is that swimming is an exercise relates to the surface.

There are other types of fulfilment in the depths. The diver's excitement in coolness and coolness in excitement is of a nobler and sublimer texture than the surface joy of the swimmer. Deep down the deeps the known world gets blurred, and it recedes and recedes until it ceases to be. Memory alone remains in animated suspension—a faint link between the life and world that had been, and the world before and beyond. A life that was, has been transplanted by a life new, vital—and—*at peace* with itself . . . . The peace of the silences of the sun-clad snow-covered white Himalayan peaks could be described by silences alone. Silence is the only language of communication with the sublime and the ineffable. Dark mysterious figures jump out of sudden submarine rocks and bushes, caves and crevices. New lives flit about; new vegetations hold wonder in every quivering alga. Attention gets captivated, and keeps the mind focused to a perpetual quest for some strange and undefined revelation.

Yet in order to be an expert diver one has to be first an expert swimmer. So is the case with yogic liberation, sublime realisation and experience. Any experience to be deep must locate itself in the deep. Such is, then, the relation between the utility of rites, and the achievement of peace. Rites form the means, not the end of purpose.

The emotional content of these lonesome seances was in effect the combined result of well understood implication of the words, the sonic depth of the music itself and the peace in the atmosphere that always reigns supreme on the banks of the Ganges at Varanasi. Whatever that might have been, I must confess and record here that these songs assisted me much in leading me on to the spiritual experiences which again and again made me feel a tenant in the realm of the Infinite. It made me continue along the path of growth. The only difference, and this is a regrettable difference, between the feelings of a past master in yoga, a saint and my poor being was that I failed miserably in retaining those feelings over a long period.

Yet to this day, I owe an abiding indebtedness to those moments of thrill received through hymnal music and its emotive compositions. Often I myself burst into words couched in music, and sing them. If I compose songs and sing them, I do not do so with the remotest desire of gaining anything mundane, or ego-tickling, like fame, name or gain. I know such songs come to me as the myriad messages the breeze brings to the hungering expectant leaves of the forest wild. Such are the messages from the light, the heat, the drought, the flood, the sylvan cries, the vernal blossoms, the laughter of lovers, the smiles of babes, the wailing of the bereaved and lamentations of the storm stricken deeps of the Himalayan forests. I am life. I belong to life. I am only the one end of a correspondence; and I correspond. Is that not something? Something to be satisfied with? What a joy to be able to sing out a feeling newly born in life-bubbling word-structures!

But when my *āsanas* and songs were being scrupulously guided by the Lady in Saffron, a memorable episode brought my life face to face with certain realities. I have referred to this episode in one of my novels, using it as a stance to the plot; but here I want to describe it in greater detail. It had a tremendous effect on my spiritual education. Moreover, this made me understand another aspect of the Lady in Saffron, which till that day had been completely ignored by all who knew her.

Kālī versus Nila-Sarasvatī

Someone important in the locality had hit upon the idea of organising a common ritualistic prayer. The tantric deity to be invoked was the largely popular Spirit of Time, the Lady of the Dark, Kāli, the Mother. Such common prayers were held on the crossings of public streets, on a night of the new moon, when the moon rises with the break of the day.

Such a common prayer is known as *bārwārī pūjā* (community prayers) which is almost always a Kālī *pūjā*. It is a done with a great eclat, and with the concurrence of the community.

Now, Kālī (although she is fierce-looking and dark) is a familiar deity and the householder's favourite. Kālī, the Mother, stands for the fullness of life, for dissolution as well as for creation. She symbolises the Spirit of Time that integrates and disintegrates; the spirit that life-mystery is. Her image denotes the naked truth that reveals.

In the tantra calendar there could not be a more demanding prayer. Kālī *pūjā* as we know calls for solemnity, and absolute guarantee against any mistake in the correctness of the retualistic forms. Forms are of the utmost importance in tantra rites. With gradual progress, the adept sets aside those trammels of form, and their place is taken over by experiences of far significant importance. Stars fade into the background when the sun overwhelms the space.

If correct form succeeds in leading the adept forward, inaccurate or slighted forms could also lead to serious backfire.

Images and Models

Elaborate ritualistic prayers of this nature (tantra-*vājrayāna*) expect images of equally complicated and perfect forms answering to the descriptions already laid down in the scriptures. Exactitude is the very essence. There are astute master-artists who carve out these images from stones, wood or clay. These last ones are destined to be caste away in river or sea or even lakes after the rites performed. Tantra enjoins on the adept that no aspirant might forever cling to images. The place of images is supposed to be occupied by the thought image, and gradually by the thought itself, and later by just the feeling, which then becomes the very essence of the being of the adept. As long as there is a sense of duality, the adept's aim remains unfulfilled.

The modellers are adepts, and rarely make mistakes even in the minutest details demanded by the form of the deity. The precise details of the respective deities come down to the seekers from well preserved scriptural texts left by those ancient tantriks who had vivified the images through meditation. These are known as *dhyānas*; and each *dhyāna* has got to be mastered by the presiding priest who gets himself engaged in performing the rites. These *dhyānas* record the esoteric experiences of power in esoteric descriptions, each detail whereof symbolises aspects of the power inherent in the deitv

A Mistake or a Miracle?

The *Bārwāri* above referred to had been a particularly prestigious one, because of the involvement of some of the leading tantra experts of Varanasi. As the modelling progressed almost every day the image was being checked. The entire town became agitated over this rite, which had invited a top tantrik to perform the ceremony.

That afternoon father was casually visited by the Lady in Saffron, who amongst other humdrum enquiries and pleasantries let drop the question who would perform the proposed Tārā *pūjā* (rites to Tārā).

Tārā *pūja*! She could not have allowed so gruesome a slip of the tongue on such a subject. It could not be a mere slip. It must have been deliberate. But then why? Why she had spoken of Tārā? Father looked hard at her. "No Tārā *pūjā* has been planned," corrected he. "You of all persons should know what a Tārā *pūjā* involves, and what it means to a residential locality like ours. It is always meant for the crematory grounds; and is never offered in the open. Do you want the whole neighbourhood to turn into a graveyard? Do you? I hope not. Where should we find an adept in *vajrayāna*? Who would officiate in a *pūjā* like that? As it is we are still in search of an efficient adept for the proposed Kālī *pūjā*. No, you should not have let drop the suggestion of worshipping a Nīla-Sarasvatī Tārā! No!"

"Hum," grumbled she, and left nodding her head in half disbelief.

Imagine my surprise when after only a couple of days I found the whole locality, inclusive of the scholars of our popular academy, thrown into a state of excited disarray. The image had turned out to be that of a Tārā, and not of Kālī, as originally contemplated. Naturally, the unaccountable turn of events was a surprise to all. The mystery of the accidental change remained both gloomy and totally miraculous. There had been a vigilant check. The image was being modelled under the strictest supervision, and was in the hands of an astute and experienced modeller, who must have modelled a thousand Kālī images. That he had to develop a mistake in this case, and end up with a terrible forbidden image of Tārā, Nīla-Sarasvatī of *vajrāyana* had all the pundits astounded. The most significant, difference, and the most telling one was the placement of the feet. Tārā's left foot always rests on the earth (the right one resting on Śiva's lifeless body) as if in a state of startled commotion. The image was indeed not the familiar Kālī. This could not be rectified without seriously damaging the image itself, which would be a sacrilege to do; and the modeller would never agree to do so.

And all this happened when the modeller had been working under the direct and almost daily supervision of learned experts. The old modeller was dumbfounded. "She wanted to appear in this form," was all that he could say.

One day I was engaged taking a grammar lesson; and father was instructing some senior students, when the Lady in Saffron came again, and set close to him. His eyes wore a funny look, and all he could be heard to remark was, "So Tārā came. Tārā the mischief maker! You, and your mouth!"

Ignoring the rebuke she asked, "Who is going to officiate?" Her original question nagged. I still remember, almost see her, how easily and indulgently she received with a pleasant but apparently indifferent nod of the head all that father had to tell her.

The sparkle in her eyes kept an inner smile locked. But she was always a charming doll at times of such a crisis. To see her was to be rid of tension. She was personified welcome, peace and ample roominess.

"You should know," remonstrated father. "We are already hard in securing a qualified priest. And now for Tārā it would be a king-size problem. You perhaps could assist."

Without any further remark she took her leave. I left my grammar, and followed her to the temple. Yoga Vāśiṣṭha was almost finishing. Meanwhile I had grown into a pronounced boyhood entering the threshold of my glorious youth. No longer could I be ignored, or taken for granted. I was accepted by all with a very special consideration.

The Tārā Pūjā

I know that this Tārā *pūjā* once started had to be carried through three consecutive years; and these years would remain as years of great suspense. A blood sacrifice was indispensable; and no substitute would be accepted by a true tantrik. The mystery gripped the householders almost by their throat. They were scared, but did not know how to avoid the catastrophe.

An able priest had to be found.

That was the initial year; the all important year.

I had no idea about the arrangements; all I did was to be waiting for the event. It was the new moon night of the last week of April. From morning chants were being offered at every house. One hundred and eight priests were engaged on one hundred and eight separate *āsanas* spread at one hundred and eight different places. The whole day was spent in fasting by most of the elders. The actual rites were to start by ten o'clock in the night, and was to be carried through until sunrise.

The head priest who actually made his appearance by eight o'clock in the evening was quite new to me.

I would have liked to describe him here. But I must check the temptation. He was easily the tallest and the broadest man I have seen. His age I cannot recall now; but the respect my uncle paid to him (and my uncle was the oldest man in the community) easily put him much above him in age, and of course, also in esoteric importance. But neither his voice, nor his gait, nor his frame, nor the light in his eyes, or the sheen of his skin showed any decay due to age. But for the usual heap of garland and beads of a variety, and a piece of scarlet loin-cloth he was otherwise naked. Clothed or unclothed his body exuded a special personalised odour.

The only persons with whom he spoke familiarly were my uncle, my father, and the Lady in Saffron, with whom he appeared to have quite a fluid rapport.

A number of assistants were making arrangements for the elaborate rites.

Here I shall pause a little to let my readers have a cursory glimpse of the traditions of the Tārā rites.

Tārā Rites

Tārā is not peculiar to Indian or even to the Hindus. She is a deity worshipped in the traditions of the mystic Lady of the East. The Cannanites, the Egyptians, the Philistines, the Israelites, the Moabites, the ancient Babylonians, the Assyrians, the Phoenicians, the Tibetans, the Japanese, the entire South-East Asians all at some time or another had been under the spell of this demanding deity although under different names. Today the names are traced to the same source (*Astarte*, *Esther*, *Sitara*) all phonetically linked. In the Eastern Mediterranean and Egyptian mystic rites her spell still plays a dominant role (although under other names, other pretexts and other interpretations).

The genesis of the goddess Tārā is attributed by Western scholars to nature worship with the attributes of fertility and reproduction. The slant of sex, and openness of sex adoration, considered immoral by those who do not practise the cult in depth (but who take advantage of the form, and exploit the opportunity afforded) has imposed a hush-hush treatment of the subject which the rigid ardours of Christianity considers unmentionable. But the cults of Artemis, Aphrodite, Diana, Astarte, Juno and Venus, as of the traditional Cilestis and Urania are undying, because of their great hold on those who delight in mystic magic and spiritual liberation through associated rites.

Apart from the ancient cultures of Urania, the cult spreads through the mountainous veins of the Himalayas, and across the seas up to Fujiyama. The valleys of the Saluri, the Mekong, the Eastern Isles, observes to this day rites dedicated to the Spirit of the Mother, the universal or cosmic *Śakti*, symbolized by *vajrā* (the flaming thunder) and the sound of *hunkāra* (*HUM*).

As the female principle of creation as well as of destruction, blood is a common symbol. This is not really blood thirstyness, although the weak-minded think it to be so. Creation and destruction seen in togetherness cannot be held to be blood thirsty. Life is not blood 'thirsty'. But it would be more than weakness, foolishness to consider this intimate association of life-force with blood, symbolized by blood sacrifice.

The rites have been under a shade in certain parts of the world; while in other parts a deliberately sentimental attitude has called them perversion and orgy. Most of these are viewed as opinions of the weak-minded, who prefer to nurse pervert hunger of the mind and body under a thick cover of foggy informations and unfounded observations. A moral facade offers the most convenient shelter to hide sham and pedantry.

An Electric Situation

The facts of the case are that outside of sheer magic and charlatantism, outside the grievous misuses of a wealth handed down by mystic traditions, there is some area, which inspires man to search, strive, persevere, suffer and achieve. Achieve what? That is a flat question, loaded with impatient sneer. For that matter, what does the poet achieve? What does the artist achieve? What does the appreciation and creation of music achieve? What does beauty achieve over utility, emotion over reason, architecture or mathematics? An answer must be provided; and the answer must be total and comprehensive. Those who strive to acquire the supreme through these media are not deluded fools, or licentious voluptuaries. They want to achieve *liberation.*

There is something in man that feels stifled, unfinished, crippled. Those who feel the torture of having to live within the folds of this limited existence, and those who are suddenly awakened and carried away by an unaccountable whiff from the Infinite, break through their prison walls, crave for this liberation, and even stake their life and safety for it. This is how the rites for the acquisition of this ethereal power have remained alive despite severe attempts to put them out. Tantra is not magic; and the rites are not magic rites.

As Kālī has been regarded as the flowing active spirit of Time, the dark mystery that surrounds consciousness, so Tārā has been regarded as the female spirit of compassion deified in the form of Avalokiteśvara. Watchfulness over the sufferings of the world is the central theme contained in the name of Avalokiteśvara. His female *alter ego* Tārā has thus, besides the third eye on her forehead, eyes planted on the palms of both of her hands, which are held in the bestowing (*varada*) *mudrā* and the *abhaya mudrā* that guarantees protection. Tārā's motherly compassion is indicated by her shapely and full open breasts, which are never covered. Her motherly role of fecundity is emphasised by the rounded buttocks, heavy thighs and a rather rotund lower abdomen. In twenty-one different *mantras* she could be invoked, but the most adored *mantra* is *OM TĀRE TUTĀRE TURE SWĀHĀ*. (The pronunciation of *mantras* has to be specially acquired from a person-to-person, adept-initiate device.)

This, however, is the Vajrayāna Tārā. The tantriks of Bengal invoke Tārā in a far more repelling and dangerous form. This fact had triggered the terrors that the locality had been harbouring. This Bengal Tārā has four hands. Her profuse matted hair is held by a serpent in one plaith (*ekajatā*), and she wears a tiger skin. A dagger, and a skull cup form her two adornments. At her feet Śiva lies inert, symbolising the state of matter bereft of energy. (In the *Lāmaic Vajrayāna* the male is the active element, and the female the passive, as the various union figures illustrate; not so in the Hindu concept, where the male, as matter, lies passive, and the female, as energy, remains violently active. These differing views have given rise to the organisation of different *āsanas* formulated by adepts in either systems.) It is this latter form which has been causing so much disturbance in the Hindu minds of the neighbourhood. Not the Avalokiteśvara Tārā, spirit of compassion, but the Vāma Aghorī spirit of Nātha Tārā, the Nāga Tārā, the Tārā of the crematory grounds had forced herself on the people, who were intimidated to propitiate the deity in the best manner they could. It was an electric situation.

So, when it was obvious that the rites of Tārā would have to be observed, and blood, an unavoidable necessity for the rites, would have to be provided for, pundits, became busy. Blood-rites were unthinkable for a bārwari *pūjā* (community prayers).

There are compromises suggested indeed in the treaties. But these must have been the afterthoughts, as most compromises are. To modify Tārā was not something that could be accepted by the Lady in Saffron without some kind of protest. She was a total puritan in matters of rituals.

"Rituals," she said, "do not actually force themselves on you. One is at liberty to choose, and cancel, if not found suitable. But to have chosen, and then painstakingly go in search of a bypassing compromises is ridiculous. In fact, it is an insult on the very modes of the rituals. How could results be obtained by avoiding or going around the methods?"

The Pūjā

Night came. The imposing figure of the officiating priest in his red regalia appeared on the scene. Indeed his presence demanded respect, and much was expected of him.

In place of the usual water for the rites, the chalices were filled with neat alcohol brewed specially for the purpose and occasion. It was not the common drink. It was a special decoction collected from a person who knew. A heap of lotuses in half bloom attracted the notice of all. One thousand of these loutses, dipped in red (vermillion, sandal or blood) were to be offered with a special chant. Five assistants were supposed to be handing over things to the priest as he happened to stretch his palm. These assistants appeared to be fully aware of the rites, and their requirements. The rites proceeded with the precision of clock work amidst blowings of conches, cymbals, bells and drums. The twirlings smoke proceeding from the aromatic herbs and unguents burnt in metal urns spread a mystic haze over which hung a heavy perfume, almost intoxicating, yet exhilarating. The entire surrounding appeared to have come to life. Although the chants went on smoothly, a strange hush had solemnly descended on the narrow lanes.

All eyes were glued to the sublime image itself. The terrible Tārā wore a bewitching smile, incandescent in its subtlety. The modeller was meekly seated on the floor, but away from the ritualistic platform, which remained out of bounds for all, except for the few assistants selected and specially anointed for the occasion.

The image itself stood there dominating all other details. I still could see it in all its grandeur, bedecked with carefully arranged garlands of fresh hibiscuses, lotuses and the blue Aparājitā (*Clitoria ternatia*). The Latin name is vividly descriptive of the shape of the bloom. There are several flowers suggesting the same motif: *Adhatoda vasica*, *Artemasia vulgaris*, *Cressa asiaticum*, *Cressa cretica*, *Dichoroa fabrigaga*, *Nerium*, *Ochrocarpus*, *Thevetia peruviana*, *Toddalia asiatica* and *cactii*. All of these are specially favoured in the Tārā rites. (It is not difficult to read within the nomenclatures of these blooms their association with such names and places as Artemis, Asia, Crete, Peru, Dionysus and Thebes.) But none of these could supersede the simple hibiscus in importance. The involved physical similarities in the flowers with the symbol of Tārā are traceable to the cult and rites of Artemis (or is it the other way round?).

I was speaking of the image and the decor. The marine blue of the skin shone through the heaps of garlands and necklaces. The brilliant third eye of the forehead attracted the gaze of the concerned. In place of the gold ensembles serpents entwined the matted locks, the wrists and the elbows; even the tiger pelt used as a loin-cloth was held by a serpent belt. A tuft of hair was held in a serpent-knot atop the head where shone a resplendent crescent (an emblem of the Moon cult). A red rolling tongue stuck out of the full-lipped blood stained mouth. Despite the fierceness of it all, there was something on the aspect of the mother; specially in her eye off the looks which radiated a benign grace of superb peace and confidence. Was there a trace of heaviness at the abdomen of the eternal mother? But the fullness of her rotund things and the heaviness of her posterior spoke of her fertility. And that third eye: O, what an influence; fantastically captivating it was.

At her feet lay the limp body of a white male form, clad in tiger skin too. This was supposed to be the image of Matter bereft entirely of Energy, the lifeless intertia, and worshipped as Śiva (quiet), *kāla* (time) or/and *śava* (corpse).

The image stuck to my mind as one conveying perfect poise; and to my boyish frame of mind I did not find in it the least semblance of either fierceness, or ugliness, or obscenity. She was the Great Mother, the Restless Equaliser, Assimilator, Bestower of Fortitude. I loved her.

Tārā: The Eternally Embraced

With maturity I came to know more of Tārā. She has undergone a complete transformation under Tibetan influences of the *Mahāyāna*. Here, in Hindu rites, she is the Power released from Matter. But in yet another version, Tibetans accept Tārā as the binding force in creation. She is represented as eternally engaged with her *alter ego* (positive with the negative) in the divine embrace of consummation. The fiercely engaged seated union has been carved and painted in a thousand forms by a thousand artists. There are popular *tankas* (Tibetan scroll paintings) depicting the motif. How often on the streets of New Delhi have I seen foreign tourists paying through their nose for a copy of these 'queer' embracing pictures! These figures are avidly sought after by practising aspirants in tantra. It depicts all too vividly the message of Life, where the forces of creation and destruction are inseparably knitted in a cosmic togetherness. Speaking as pure abstract specimens of art and sculpture, this message of joy, fierceness, grace and passionate abandon, put together in one, is nowhere to be matched. It is abstract art *a merveille.*

She was known to India long before the Chinese scholars visited the lands (sixth century AD). Actually, there happens to be a form of Tārā known as Sitā Tārā. The sound reminds one of *Sitāra* (Astarte, Esther). Anyone acquainted with the Tārā rites would appreciate why my Lady in Saffron had insisted on the performances of the rites in a proper manner, or not at all. *In mystic rites the insisting exactness of the propriety of the way is of utmost importance.* Success depends largely on a meticulous observance of the given injunctions. Any slipshod transgression could lead to disasters. No, Tārā rites could not be observed in a residential locality.

Today Tārā is associated with Tibet and Mongolia, Indo-China and the Himalayan heights. In fact, the lady had a long established tradition of commanding devotion from the ancient world, eastern or western. Rome had conquered the east by forces of arms; but the east had finally *conquered* Rome by making it accept its gods and goddesses who, by and large, still command supremacy amongst the descendants of Rome. Actually no history of culture has yet been exposed to man where the spirits of the fierce and the benign, spirits of Emerson's Great Eater, and Ramakrishna's Great Mother, have not been energetically worshipped as aspects of the one and the same Power.

The image spread its charms over me. To my young eye it posed no ferocity at all. 'Ferocious', or 'pleasant' describes personal mood, or attitude. Tārā revealed to me her positive charms. All her negative aspects vanished. I had become her neighbour.

Several actions in the rites, however, which I observed very closely, intrigued me. I was seated closely secured by the side of my Lady in Saffron, away from the platform, almost unnoticed by the converging crown. I did notice, however, how all the people by themselves kept a respectful distance from her.

Mystic Details

(*a*) *The Water Jar:* I noticed that a big mass of wet clay had been brought from somewhere with much ceremony and fanfare. It was laid down ceremonially in front of the image, and patted into a round shape with a receptacle in the middle. In this were thrown several kinds of grains. On this was placed a large earthen jar filled with water from the Ganges. This water jar was painted with vermillion. The designs represented same *yantras*. Fresh foliaged twigs, mostly from trees known for mystic ceremonies, five different types in all, were now stuck into the mouth of the jar, the leaves fanning over the brim. In the middle of these leaves, and covering the mouth of the jar was placed a bowl filled with rice. On this bowl a green coconut with its stem attached was placed with the stem side showing.

Finally the *kalaśā* (the jar) and the coconut were covered by a piece of red cloth, over which garlands were placed. The *kalaśā* had to be 'guarded' now. Four bamboo shoots stuck in four lumps of clay were placed around it with mango leaves flagging each of the shoots. Nine rounds of red thread were to go around the four posts; and this 'guarded' the magic circle of the *kalaśā* which then represented the *soul* of the deity.

This made me inquisitive. Particularly the awe with which the clay was being handled, after having been brought with so much eclat, intrigued me beyond measure. What was that clay? From where had it been collected? Why people breathed a sigh of relief when it had been brought, and the ceremony of laying the water jar had been over?

I asked my mentor, the Lady in Saffron, just by looking at her. She replied through her silent looks. I knew I had to wait. Later. What she finally did explain gave creeps to my guts. A kind of emptiness overwhelmed me. The facts dwarfed my wildest imagination. It was not really so shocking; none the less it did shock.

(*b*) *The Clay:* It was clay collected from a dug-out, a special dugout where years back five types of carcases (human, canine, feline, foxen and ape) of animals naturally dead, or 'sacrificed' ritually, had been buried in. It must have been a sanctified and secreted spot where none could disturb the cadavers. In course of time the bodies would be turned into clay; and the clay collected from this reservior would be used for making the sacramental platform, as well as a rest for the *kalaśā*, i.e.. the water jar. (In *tantra, sādhanā* of a more serious and personal nature, a platform is constructed on the very bodies. Such an *āsana* is called *Pancamuṇḍī*, 'the *āsana* on the five heads').

Thus the water jar was of supreme interest and importance to the chief priest. The image attracted the attention of public emotion, and assisted the devotees to concentrate tangibly to an object of emotive dedication and delight. But the abstract relation of personal consciousness of the priest with the cosmic was established through the *kalaśā* where the five material elementary substances (water, earth, fire, air and ether) were invoked.

Beside the water jar there were two more things which attracted the attention of the *sādhaka*.

(*c*) *Yantra:* One of these was a *yantra* engraved on bronze, copper or silver with a particular design generally geometrical. In this case it was a silver *yantra.* I have seen it carved on gold plates. But the most captivating and intriguing *yantra* ever seen by me was a crystal one which a Mongoloid yogi had shown me at the foothills of the Himalayas. It was a massive (5″ × 5″ × 3″) piece. The edges were unhewn. To this day as I close my eyes I see it staring at me. To this day I do not know how and by whom was that *yantra* carved within the mass, whilst the crystal piece remained a compact whole without any sign of a joint anywhere. The *yantra* was embedded within the crystal. The yogi claimed that the *yantra* was naturally mined with the marks so carved; that no human hand did it. He also informed me that the *yantra* had been coming down from yogi to yogi for over a period of 1400 years of history known to him; and that he would not part with it for any treasure in the world. He mentioned some names amongst the previous owners, and many of them I recognised: Dattātreya, Ajaikapādā, Śankarācārya and Abhinavagupta. On my drawing his attention to a possible incongruity in chronology, he looked at me, smiled, and said, "All is fake and fraud; I, the crystal, the dates and tantra itself."

(*d*) *Maṇḍalā:* But to return to our narration. Besides the image, the *kalaśā*, the *yantra* another medium highly prized is the *maṇḍalā*, a geometrical square form within which various designs are drawn in coloured powders of five different colours, derived from botanical sources.

In esoteric gradations the higher a stage the aspirant reaches, he leaves behind the Image, the *kalaśā*, the *maṇḍalā* and the *mudrā* in that order, until he remains only with the self.

Now, to continue with the worship itself.

A Tense Situation

The great crowd thinned gradually as the night grew deeper, and the rites became more and more matured and involved. A sudden change of atmosphere became obvious. The air appeared to have been charged with, for the lack of any other expression, a presence; and unaccustomed vibrations put nerves in a tensioned state of 'expectation' as if something was going to 'happen'. The place, the time, the assembly, the very air we breathed seemed to be 'charged'. Do we call this 'solemnity'? Do we call this the dawning of power? Was it the effect of a presence? The high priest was merged. He was translated into another being. There was no stopping him. He muttered chants that could not be heard any more. His entire torso undulated like the hood of a cobra about to strike. The flames and the lamps suddenly grew in intensity. A strange calm fell.

Collection of the Flames

In the meanwhile we were expected to go out for the collection of fire from the crematory grounds at Maṇikarṇikā. For hundreds of centuries Maṇikarṇikā had functioned as the crematory ground for the Hindu world. The name itself bears testimony to its Lamaic connections. *Om Maṇi Padme Hum* is a celebrated Lamaic mantra. The significance of the word *maṇi* has already been described.

The legend associated with this name is very significant for those who want to get into the secrets of these lores and these rites.

(1) Lord Śiva had offered his appreciation of the austerity of the penance of Lord Viṣṇu. So carried away was He by the greatness of Viṣṇu sacrifice that he himself began to shake his head, and then from his ears the cosmic 'jewels' fell down in a tank which Viṣṇu had dug out with his discus for his daily ablutions. Since then the place is known as Maṇikarṇikā.

(2) The same legend appears at another place in the opposite form, in which Śiva was the penitent and the yogi; and Viṣṇu was the appreciator. In this case the *maṇi* belonged to Viṣṇu.

There are other versions. Those who know how to read through these mystic legends would know that on these banks from times immemorial yogic, specially Tantrà Yoga practices had been a tradition. And here at Varanasi, and in the legends, the Tibetan, the Scythio-Parthian, the obscure Nātha and Bhairava cults found a safe haven; and Maṇikarṇikā had been held in haloed esteem because of the special tantric 'power' ascribed to the sub-normal environment of the place. (Wearing a pair of ear-rings made of the horn of a rhino is an absolute necessity for a yogi of the famed Nātha community. In the legend of the Bhairava saint, Dattātreya (of whom we have already spoken) similar assimilation of several forms and rites has been suggested.

Anyway, a procession for "collection of the flames" winded its way towards the dreaded Maṇikarṇikā. The funeral flames of Maṇikarṇikā burn perpetually and have been burning ever since. The chief of the place is an undertaker who is a part and parcel of the rites. His is and has been a hereditary responsibility to supply the flames to all those who come here to borrow flames for the final dedication of all flesh to the bowl of *TIME*. From flame to flame, from dust to dust, the flesh terminates; but the hungry soul wanders until freed from the past hang-ups, and until it becomes one with the Cosmic Soul.

Tārā is a deity of the funeral grounds. She was being invoked within a residential locality. So, if Tārā has been dislodged from her usual habitat, as compensation for her temporary loss of abode-comforts, her favoured funeral flames had to travel up to her new site of invocation.

From the middle of a bamboo pole was hung a huge and well-decorated brass urn. This urn was properly consecrated and covered with garlands and incense. With the sound of cymbals, drums, bells and conches the procession proceeded towards the funeral grounds. Loud chants rent the midnight sky. Inhabitants of the locality must have taken a turn or two in their beds. 'There they go for the flames!' they must have cried and shuddered. The funeral flames were being brought right within the locality. What next?

The actual process was not a long drawn one. It appeared that the chief of the grounds had already been keyed up; and after an exchange of some hushed words (some cash must have changed hands), he threw into the urn a flaming torch, and flames leapt out of the urn with a ferocious glare. The devotees let loose a hurrah that should have rent the skies.

Now the procession had to turn back for its return journey. The joy of success at the picking of the flame-blossoms, electrified the dancing devotees. Conches and bells rang with renewed energy.

The New Path, the New Call

I had accompanied the din and uproar for about a hundred yards of the labyrinthian Varanasi. But then I was inexplicably overcome by a funny dazed feeling. I was not quite unaccustomed to this kind of sudden pulls. My hypersensitive mind, was receptive of the slightest massages peeping through the sonic field. I catch them almost imperceptibly, effortlessly, and then act involuntarily under the effect, till I reach the source of the disturbance. There *was* a call, and I *had to* answer. When one becomes a part of nature, one has to accept and fall in line with the logic of inevitability.

In the darkest of the dark nights, and on the ghats of the Gangetic Varanasi I got lost to my associates of the flames; I got lost to the rites that were being performed in my own neighbourhood; I got lost to surroundings and their bearings. Who was I? What was my errand? What was I supposed to do? I was a 'minus mind' existence, moving under a spell. My mind was in a state of void.

Victim in a Seance

As one dazed, under the influence of drugs, yet full of alertness in another sense, in another dimension, I continued tramping in another words. But I knew I had changed direction. I climbed down several flights of steps; then I climbed up what seemed to me an unending flight of stairs. Several stray bulls brushed my sides. Phantom clusters of men under the spell *ganja* and *charas* (*Cannabis indica*) were busy with their affairs in the lamps of dark among the ancient stone ruins by the river. Dogs barked for pieces of bones dragged from the cremation grounds. I continued climbing. And then a familiar smell made me further alert, impersonally alert. Aromatic unguents and frankincense were burning somewhere. The smell was too familiar. I could hear chants. Automatically a *mantra* began to tick within my consciousness. The Lady in Saffron always muttered it whilst guarding me on my *āsana*, as I sat on her.

A fire flickered somewhere. Towards this my feet now drew me. I stumbled against a stone thereshold, and badly split my toe. I felt the warm blood over my skin, and under the foot. But I did not stop, or as much as even touched my burning wound. Blood continued to flow.

I continued walking. I saw something extremely scaring. Not that I never had confronted such a seance. I was quite accustomed discussing such seances; but the realities of the situation made me lose heart. I continued the *mantra* as if it were my other self.

I recalled the place. It was the dreaded Nepali temple. This Vajrayāna Lamaite shrine is almost a hide-out near the Maṇikarṇikā funeral grounds. Few notice it. Yet it had been always there standing as the citadel of Bhairava Tantra practices; and people whisper that human sacrifices were made there not too infrequently. The altar there was set on *panchamuṇḍi*, i.e., over the five corpses. The most complicated *āsanas* were practised there. The place haunts in the subconscious.

Today, amongst the many sights for the tourists, 'Nepāli Khaprā' (the Kharpara temple of Nepal i.e., the Vajrayāna skull-temple), as the place is described, is a chief attraction for a type of curious and probably sick mind, not because of its fame as a seat of mystic seances, but because of the simple *mithuna* (copulating) figurines relieved on wood panels and red sandstones on the surrounding caves and walls. Similar popularity is attached to other seats of the same Bhairava rites, such as the Khaṇḍāria temple of Khājuraho, the Sun temple of Konārk, the Parashurāma, Rājārāṇī and Lingarāja temples of Bhubaneshwar. In fact, there are innumerable temples with such figurines scattered all over India.

Let the curious search for their type of food. The cockroaches and the vultures, the bats and the owls too have a right to search for the food of their respective choice. All are welcome to the skull-bowl. Time drinks off all the same; good is bad, bad is good. Vajrayāna carries the adept beyond the world of duality by accepting the duality.

I had been to this temple before in accompaniment with the Lady in Saffron, who had performed on sundry occasions certain *āsanas* and rites with me as her *alter ego* and apprentice. I particularly recall two such seances in which I had taken an intimate role: one was on the occasion of a lunar eclipse, and the other one, more important, was on a solar eclipse. I was not new to it; neither was the place strange to me. On important days in the Hindu esoteric calendar, like on *Śivarātri* or *Kārtikī* new moon night, I had gone there to participate in seances.

But I was new to the old yogi whom I had not seen before. He was *digvāsah* (having the space as his garment); besides his beads and the heap of matted locks, he wore nothing. He was seated on a human form, also naked, and appeared to be in a complete trance. This one was a woman.

At the Session of the Space Clad

Wide eyed I discovered gradually the figure lying naked under his seat. This was the favourite 'aunt' (previously spoken of) whose haunt had been the neighbouring funeral grounds. She had been widowed when a virgin, and because of her own prowess, as well as of her transcendental moods and preoccupations, she had been much in demand in similar seances. She has been known to be lying down in that state for over a fortnight, even from a new moon to a new moon. How many times she has fed me with her own hands. I still recall the fund of love this venerable lady bore for me.

Why was I called to this particular session? This would remain a secret to me. But I knew that I had missed a great opportunity offered to me kindly and gracefully. I kept quiet for a while. My mind was at a standstill. But in my subconscious i.e. the stratum of consciousness which responds despite the disturbances of the outer surface, suddenly got merged in the very essence of the *mantra* already known to me. The *mantra* itself became real to me, and sparks of lights of varied colours shot through the surrounding space, and settled between the brows, where the pressure of the bead had always remained as a red light warning spot. The spot perceptibly appeared to tingle and emit flames until I fell into a trance. Time stood still.

Had I really any *time* at my disposal? The rites at home were going on in full swing. The procession of flames must have reached its destination long back. The fire sacrifice, and the lotus sacrifice must have been finished. But who cared? Who to care indeed?

I was scared; I was anxious to get back; but all that on the surface. In my real depths I was at the centre of a tranquil quietitude. No kind of movement was possible at all. I belonged to there; I was of them; I had no will of my own. I was in the thick of the rites, consummating with relish every breath of the time. As many hairs there were on the body, stood alert on ends; thrill succeeding thrills sparked through the roots. I felt to cry, 'Leave me alone!', but actually I stay put. I was gradually being sucked in towards the burning flame, which was roaring in the pit.

Auntie's open body lay before me like a corpse. I recalled the relevant scriptural lines. Was I not already quite familiar to this part of a seance where a woman offered the sacred seat?

As I watched, she had appeared as a distant neighbour of another planet to me. Her staring eyes with their burning looks fixed on me expressed both some sublime rapture and undisturbed stillness of peace. The animation in the looks compelled me to adore her. I would love to be sitting there myself . . . . Gradually she turned into a ball of blazing light. I saw my body too becoming another ball of light, and the two balls were gradually coming together.

The Awakening and the Come-back

I do not know from where drizzles showered over me, and I shivered. Two beads fell in one mighty bounce before me, and a Hibiscus laden with ash. I collected them avidly, and hurried out of the temple. But before I turned my back on the temple, I bowed flat on the ground and closed my eyes. My mind wanted to go flat for poor auntie.

As soon as I had closed my eyes I was more than amazed to see my Lady in Saffron all in flames. From within the flames she smiled and called out, "Come, come at once . . . I wait . . .."

Now I began to run. But where?

Where must I go? Down the steps, up the steps, along the western banks, direct south through sands and stones until I reached the familiar ruins of the temple near the Chatuhṣaṣṭhi Yoginī temple on the far end of the river? To the sacred Boa tree? To the altar at our neighbourhood where Mother Tārā was being invoked? I was running, and saying within me, "I come, I come. I do not tarry."

I returned to the Tārā ceremony near our house, nay, just at the threshold of our home.

5

Flame Gatherings

Back to the Pūjā Rites

A solemn scene was in progress. My uncle, father and mother, and all my brothers were busy arranging the fringes of the ceremonies. . . . . A small crowd had gathered; curious, yet spellbound.

Many had been busy in self-inspired meditations according the Hindu way of offering personal worship. Quite contrary to superfluous knowledge regarding the much maligned Hindu milieu, many still hold on to this faith with a firm certainty about its final peaceful outcome. This reflects the tantric spirit proper. The otherworldliness involved in such tantric engagements with the self ascends astral heights on the two wings of mental discipline and ethical contents. Objective and idolatrous as this looks, its inner aim and achievements are directed to pure subjectivity.

The familiar surroundings of the otherwise busy lane at Varanasi had assumed an eerie heaviness. Things felt solemn and tense. Nothing looked relaxed. Intensely merged in personal efforts the throng had become unified, crystallised. Yet the total effect remained contained within a single purpose. It looked as if within a single embryo several lives were engaged in seeking individual growth and timely deliverance. The more this image tickled within, the more I felt amused.

The place was quiet and solemn,. reserved and spiritualised to a degree that could be felt as sublime; the vulgar and dross had melted away; the curious were no more; the engaging drama of excitement had given way to divine solemnity; and that hullabaloo was gone. Night had taken over. Soul reached a perceptual depth just in being there.

From time to time the chants from those who assisted the head-priest came clear and loud, but the head-priest was only repeating them without even as much as moving his lips. He appeared to be quite in another space altogether.

Tall and straight on his seat, in the lotus *āsana*, his eyes were fixed between his brows. He had been throwing butter-soaked *bel*-leaves (*bel: vilva: Aegli mermelos* or ash apple) in a flaming fire leaping from a huge pit made of sheet-copper. Other assistants were busy throwing other objects with rhythmic timings: franchincense, sesame seeds, sandal shavings and bits of unskinned flesh with the fur hanging on. Spoonfuls of the sanctified butter-fat helped the flames leap up and consume the offerings, marking the end of each chanted *mantra*.

A heavy aroma hung around the place. I could not detect the deterrent obnoxious smell one would expect reeking out of burnt flesh and hair. This indeed was very strange.

My excitement from the traumatic experience at the burning ghat and the Kharpara temple had not yet died down. The wounded toe had been singing. Blood continued oozing. But I could not mind less; the letting out of the blood felt better than nursing a throbbing blue-spot. All I was eager for was to get near at my Lady in Saffron, my ultimate shelter.

I could think, and reconstruct the fast racing lurid events. What could have happened if I had not been struck out of my dazed condition and taken out of what I had been cast into.

True it is that tantric sacramentals do not sanction causing harm to Brahmins. Not to speak of the human sacrifice, where neither a Brahmin, nor a woman could be used; even in the very complex *śava sādhanā* (cadaver-rites for attaining cosmic powers) the dead body of Brahmins could not be used. But fear does not bid any logic; and I had been off my guard.

The very first effect of sudden fear is loss of rational faculties, which confuses all senses, and even wipes away all memory. Fear is the most handy, and the most effective dope which could derange the mind of a victim. The weak of mind, and a sensitive one, provides the most conducive medium for mesmerism, as for the spirit's means of communication. A pronounced negative mind is as useless in these proceedings as a positive one; the best mind for a medium is either apathetic, or a *tabula rasa;* but never an opaque one. Sensitiveness is a must in these seances.

By then I had overcome the grasp of the unbodied fear; but as I rested close to the reassuring shelter, my Lady in Saffron, I became myself.

The Body Melts Away

But where was she? Did she belong to this world? Was she approachable? She appeared to have thrown around her an impregnable fortification. Although she had been surrounded by devotees all around her, none dared get too near. I looked at her closely and recalled the special rites of tantra known as *Bhūtāpasāraṇa,* along with *nyāsas* and *dhyānas* which are supposed to throw around the adept effective guards against 'anti-spirits', or spiritual obstructions. The most renowned examples of these are recorded in the *Mahāyāna* documents with reference to the ascension penances of Gautama Buddha; the Buddha sitting tranquil, quiet, still, safe and beaming with an inner light, against all forces of evil, all types of physical and mental temptations.

Here was the example of that supreme truth that this body melts into insignificance when the spirit takes over; that the spirit calls for no cover; that a person in spirit becomes an imperson as soon as the fleshly is transcended into the cosmic, indeed beyond approach. Time and again I had seen her in that very condition. Yet how novel and brilliant did she look, as she was seated within the circle of fire made out of eight fire bowls set around her, and fed by awe-struck hands, busy keeping the flames up.

There were other flame bowls too; three of them. Her hands were stretched out, the palms resting on her bare thighs, now covered with a film of glistening sweat. On these palms were set two raging bowls; and on her head rested a third one. My father was busy throwing some powdered ingredients into these three; and had been chanting *mantras* all the time. I wondered if her hands would get scorched, even roasted; or if her skull would split.

Trembling deep within, cautiously, I approached her, and quietly sat near her. No one objected; no one could, knowing fully well my relations with her. She was essentially mine; I hers.

But the fiery circle! And I still get intense as I recall. Between two of the bowls there was space enough for me to slip in, and get nearer her body. I wanted to close on her, and touch her as she was there. The heat was forbidding; but what could have forbidden me when she had been seating so close? At the moment the temptation to be near her seemed to be more overpowering than the flames. Just as I attempted to stretch one of my hands to have a feel of the ground within the fire circle, something electrifying lashed me back. The terrible shock benumbed my nerves.

Gradually I became aware of other figures. They had crawled around the spot. All of them had been chanting a *mantra;* but I did not bother to leave my grounds despite the reactions. Suddenly I took courage, and got nearer to her. Now I was just by her side. In a moment I was on her lap (in the now—familiar and accustomed *āsana*). The bowls on her palms kept blazing; but I was quite surprised to find that neither the flames, nor the heat from it made me scared. I did not feel them any more.

Fire Walking

As I am on this topic of fire and heat, I propose to digress here on this point. The digression relates to an incident when I actually was inspired to walk through fire. Because the incident also is connected with rites of a sort it seems relevant for a record here.

Today with the media and the press enjoying a field day, the miracle of fire walking enjoys much curious publicity in the west. The major habitats of this phenomenal exercise includes the islands of South Pacific, Fiji, Ceylon and the Tamil south of India. The fire-walking rites are also found popular amongst some people inhabiting the eastern sea board of Africa. The more curious could go to the relevant reference books, and learn more about the fire-walkers.

Amongst the tantrik Śiva worshippers of India there is a strong sect originated in Andhra Pradesh. This sect, known as the Jangamas, followers of Saint Vāsava's Vira Śaivism, has a very strong hold on the masses spread all over the country. Varanasi is, naturally, an important centre of the sect. The Jangamas had during the Maratha supremacy over north India acquired power and property, and had established a series of charities for the benefit of poor students and aspirants. The Vira Śaivas, also known as the Jangamas, have established monasteries, Sanskrit students in academies, yogic centres, as well as centres for training ritualistic practices. This area in the city where the Jangamas have their colony established, is known as Jangam-wadi, where tantrik monks found shelter. These monks quite often held rites strange and fantastic, so that entry to them, even as a witness, called for special sanctions.

The incident herein described should have taken place around the year 1923. In those days I was considered to be a specially gifted student of the Sanskrit academy, and a novice in the tantra cult. In order to indulge a young boy seeking spiritual pursuits, the elders included me within the invited guests from the academy.

It was a summer day. A summer dry in north India is not exactly an experience to write poems on. The barometer must have been reading 112°. I was elated to have been included in the group visiting the special rites. At about three p.m. with the sun still very high, I started for the place with three more senior students from the academy.

Soon we found ourselves amongst a swarm flocking around the Jangama monastery. There had assembled many strangers, not all of them speaking the same language. Soon I was lost in the crowd. And did this not suit me? I was on my own. I always preferred this; specially on such quests.

I was drawn by the human current. Courtyard after courtyard was crossed before I reached a wider yard (40×40 feet), where within a freshly dug out pit (10×10 feet) angrily sizzled a huge quantity of burning charcoal obviously prepared carefully over a number of days. A fire-rite was in progress. The heat was unbearable to me, although I had been standing several feet away from the edge of the pit. How the participants bore the scorching heat on their bare skin surprised me.

Soon arrived an orchestral group. The crowd formed a gap to allow the musicians pass through. This was followed by a team of shaven headed monks in wondrous regalia. Each member of the party held in his hand some venerable object appertaining to the ceremony about to be performed.

I saw a green coconut resting on a richly embroidered red velvet piece, which covered a silver platter beneath it. Another plate carried a golden *mudra;* on a silk cushion; and still another one carried an elaborate *maṇḍalā* pattern. Two monks guarded over the coconut from either side with bare swords in their hands. Soon the procession came to a halt. After about fifteen minutes of chants and prayers the head-priest reverentially held the coconut in his hand resting the fruit on his outstretched palm. And then snatching a sword from the hand of one of the guards he brought it down with such a mighty force that the green nut split in two. (Any one might give a try. It was no common feat of strength and accuracy, balance and boldness to split a green coconut by one single blow of a sword, when the fruit would be resting on the man's own palm.)

From the split coconut water began to flow; and it was sprinkled over the fire. All this while the team had been bordering on the edge of the howling pit.

Immediately after the preliminary sprinkling the head-priest with the same sabre in hand entered the pit, and started walking through it as if the floor were covered with the softest of carpets. His entourage followed his steps. The entire team crossed the burning pit, one by one, bare-footed, with their saffron robes flying about.

As the monks had reached the other end of the pit, and stepped out of it one by one, a big shout went up, and a deafening recital of chants created strange vibrations, within which I was lost.

Then the multitude was invited to walk over the embers, still burning in hot heat. Many hesitated. But some did not. More jumped in. and crossed over. Later still when others followed, I too took the risk, and crossed. Then with steps deliberate, mind fixed, and the chants on my lips, I went round and round the fire, until one of the monks bid me step out.

To come back to the main stream of the narration about the fire-penance of the Lady in Saffron. I was not feeling comfortable. My attention was again and again diverted to the pain in my injured toe. It continued to cause me pain. The toe was bathed in blood which still oozed, though some blood had clotted. Suddenly the cry "Hail mother!" rent the night sky. She clasped me tight against her breast (now I know how true are the Tibetan *tankas.*)

A Blood Sacrifice

The shout of joy was in praise of a successful completion of the arduous flame rite. The bowls of fire were to be removed from her hands. But before these could be removed a strange stillness fell on the assembly. The Lady took great care in tearing off a piece of the cotton from her loin-cloth. She tore the piece into several more pieces, and made balls of them, after each piece had been besmirched with the blood oozing from my toe.

These blood soaked balls were then thrown by her own hand into the blaze over her head. My back had been touching the liberal mass of her breasts. But my comfort was suddenly disturbed by a deep thorn driven sharply at the base of my neck; parallel to the spine, just where my hair line stopped. It was a thorn picked from the Bel twigs around her. So sudden was this attack that I could not even make a squeal; but of pain, again, I had none. She queitly collected a fwe drops of my blood. Gradually I lost consciousness. I felt her arms closing around me. . . .I felt at home. . . .

Dawn!

The familiar touch of the bed with the soft cotton cover; the aroma pervading the room. I knew so well; the ceilings, the walls, and above all that benign face with the diffused smile began to materialise.

Her hands were across my neck; her cheek to my cheek. "Come. Time to get going. The sun is about to rise; and we must go for a splash in the river even before the great god finds us late. Come. Let me help you."

That bath was refreshing.

Before we came out of the stream, she held me before her and threw a handful of some stuff out in the stream; and only then did I notice the beads of *rudrākṣa* and the ash-laden hibiscus.

She gave a gentle pressure on my shoulder; and then as we were climbing up the steps she remarked, "You are not ready yet. . . They were only hastening the process . . . Never hasten. . . Everything in its time. Seasons have to be respected. (Here she held me closer to her, almost embracing me very deep. Her protective affection soothed my nerves)...You have to go far, very far. Remember the lessons in the Yoga Vāśiṣṭha? It takes no time to miss the way, and suffer a fall. Enemies are all around. The counter-force always shadows the force, until the summit is gained . . . Care, care and ever care. . . . Carefully prepare. Correct preparation is helf the battle won. . . . Find the correctaguide. Then you shall have gained three quarters of the battle. The balance depends on your own efforts, determined efforts. . . .

The Seed Word: OM

"Never get curious. Never get tempted. Peace, peace and tranquillity. You recall the value of pause. Do you? Pauses between words make sense more expressive. She, the Sense, resides in the pause between a word and a word. You know *OM* is a *mantra* so constructed that in its repetition one must pause between one *OM* and another. This is no guess. It has been so designed. Say *O*, the lips part; say *M*, and they close; and before you go to *O* again you have to take time for opening the lips and positioning them again. May be a very short time, almost imperceptible; yet there is that pause; and She, the 'Sense' (*vāk*) resides in that *ardhamātrā*, the quiet half-pause. One would notice that almost all *bīja* (seed) *mantras* end either with an *M*, or an *NG*, or an aspirant sound, such as *UH* or *AH*. In each case sound continuity would be impossible. A new effort is called upon to make a new start. This provides the aspirant with the golden means of silence, pause and stillness. The sign for this is ˘ or ঃ. These are, therefore, regarded as important esoteric sounds (as well as signs)˘ wherever pronounced, adds peace to pronunciation, like the last *M* with the sign-end (म्)ঃ ; butঃ denotes a breath 'pause'.

Peace and pause are the two steps by which progress is gained gradually. Silences are the greatest of all achievements in the *mantras*. Hurry not; haste not; suffer not; fall not back.

"Why did you have to respond to the desultory, disengaging, delinquent call? Remember, guests arrive of themselves when the broth is ready. These are not class guests. Hungry, greedy, of no consequence. But good food, meant for special use, has to be kept carefully away from these interlopers. Forces of good are moving side by side along with the forces of the anti-gods; for they too are hungry. Don't you know that all good rites (godrites) provide for the anti-gods also?"

Slowly I began to recite the chant:

Nihanmi sarvam yad-amedhya-vad bhaved
-dhatāśca sarve-a-sura dānavāh mayā
rakṣānsi yakṣā-ś-ca piśāca sanghāh
hatāh mayā yātudhānā-ś-ca sarve.
apasarpantu te dhūtāh ye bhutāh bhūmi samsthitāh
ye bhūtāh vighna kartāra-ś-te gacchantu śivājnayā.

(Those who stand contrary to the forces I invoke are hereby destroyed by me. Thus are the demons and the anti-gods destroyed, as I destroy the *rākṣasas, yakṣas, piśācas and yātudhānas*. . . . Those physical elements who could cause disturbances, be warned by the orders of Śiva).

"Yes. The first one is vedic; and the second one is tantric. So you see, in any rites the need for caution cannot be overemphasised. One must protect one's interests against contrary forces. There is need for protecting the prepared food indeed before it is served and consumed. Else the anti-forces would gobble up the good. You had been drawn by contrary forces, who would have used you for their kind of power. They would have sucked all your preparations out. You had an escape. Thank the Mother."

"And what do they do with such power," I asked.

"Never good," she said. "Thieving is not good. Thieved power cannot be used for good. Electricity supplies us the power which we have to buy. Many thieve this power, and make do. They do not have to pay for this. This is evil use. This is unclean. They pose threat to peace and honesty."

'Power' and Miracle Men

"Even the great yogis who are adepts in leaving their bodies, and travelling without a body by the air, take great precaution about the preservation of their bodies which tempt the spirits of the lower order. . . ."

"What is that?" I interrupted.

"Of that later on," she said; and continued, "Yogis who tamper with this business of power-getting seek power to impress and influence people for their own ends. These are the cheap everyday miracle men of whom everybody, looking for easy gains, speaks. They hail such a freak, and collect around the miracle man. But these so-called gains are not only short-lived, they are also often sources of disappointments in conventional life, and also a retardation in spiritual life. Let me repeat, there is no short-cut to spirit; and miracles for personal gains are to be shunned. Remember that the anti-god is a master miracle maker of the lower spirits. They mostly deal with the palliatives, the external cures and things like that.

"Fundamental happiness of man depends upon keeping up a spiritual balance; and this counteracts the evil powers, which are also active. Is it not a miracle that in spite of all these misdeeds, and sins of men we still like to love, to speak truth, to seek happiness, and we want to mould our society for a better living? Where do you find a greater miracle than a simple flower, a butterfly on wings? In time you will realise the great miracle of love for another person; the miracle of an infants hold on you; the miracle of nature's provision for food in the breast of a mother. Nature is the greatest miracle spinner. This wonder of miracle is set at naught by the anti-force. That in itself is another miracle. Without the spiritual influence of the silent and unknown yogic power this world would have burst at the seams long long ago. The forces are always at loggerheads. Still the world and life hold on. What a miracle! Power, specially Mother-Power cannot be used by thieves and gluttons of the spirit.

"Those who had called you for participation in their rites were out to rob you of the power which you have so far stored within you, which is not little. To preserve is your supreme duty from now. Had I not been about, and specially had I not been engaged in a rite at the time, I might not have reached you. The drizzle, the beads, the flowers were your warnings. You did well by getting away my son. . . ."

"You did well too," I remarked with a smile. Then I frowned, and asked. "But I had seen auntie there. Was she under the same evil spell?"

Evil is a Blind Alley

"Evil? What is evil? What is good? We are all a dull compost of good and bad. A strange amalgam. Unless we have experienced good, what are we? The vanity of all vanities is to float on the inflated idea of self-adulation and self-righteousness. Make that mistake, and you seal up the progress towards growth. In yoga the aim is to merge ego into self. The self and the ego are lying mixed up like gold is in the ore. Yoga is to gain skill in cleaning the self of ego.

"By keeping our heads bent down for achieving good,—and *good* here means impersonal good, we remain on the path of good. This is correct preparation. Correct preparation, as I had said, is a battle half won. The safest thing about your auntie is that she has her head bent down for impersonal good.

"But it is not difficult to be misled. Remember how you had been carried away. That power in the Kharpara temple was a very strong power. But she would soon recover, and realise the loss she has suffered. By herself she is a very great yogini. But even the greatest suffer a fall. Rāvaṇa was a great yogi; so was Kansa, Aśvatthāmā, Jarāsandha, Rasputin of Russia. They fell by the load of their imperfections, and passion for miracles.

Never hold back progress. Wheels should not be run backwards, watches should not be winded any other way but the right one. Follow the way. There is no short-cut, no compromise.

"Did you notice the position of your auntie in the group *āsana*?," she asked.

"The yogi was using her as his *āsana* of course," I said. "But that is also your position as my *āsana*. Isn't it? What is then strange about it?"

"This is true. But in the process I am the giver. In her case she was the victim, and was being sucked from. In wishful dedication there is the virtue of positive gain. One could gain by giving away. In forced extraction there is evil. This would leave her very weak. I would not like you to be in her position."

Much later I had gone to the Maṇikarṇikā and find for my self how auntie did, and was not very glad to have seen what I did. She had been at a continuous *āsana* within that small temple for over three days without a moment's break, so reported the undertakers who lived there.

"And where is that yogi? Would he get away with this?" I asked the Lady in Saffron.

"Sooner or later they meet their match, as Jarāsandha or Aśvatthāmā found in Kṛṣna. Evil is a blind alley. One has to turn back; but I would like you to keep away from such yet."

"Why?" I asked.

"You are essentially mine. . .You are good. . .You will do good. . . Many wait...You will have to work hard, and get what only a few could get. Love. Love from all and sundry. It is time to turn back. Come home. Come home. I shall prepare you a special drink for building you up. It is time we joined the morning prayers, and receive the final baptismal blessing of *śānti* (peace)."

Before I close this chapter of the experiences, I must record here a strange fact. This locality, where sixty years back the ritual was witnessed by the author, had been a flourishing place of business. The Tārā ritual as I have mentioned had to run through three consecutive years, and it did. But for mysterious reasons, miraculously, the place now stands deserted. The business is ruined entirely. The people still recall those fatal three years when Tārā, the spirit of the dead and of the funerary rites, had been invoked within the area of householders. The Tārā rites were discontinued thereafter. I recalled my father's warning to the Lady in Saffron. "You should have known better. . . ."

* * *

The Cobra Man and the Flute

Let us also recall the warning of the Lady in Saffron about "Meeting the match." I had the occasion of being a witness to this kind of 'matching' several times in my life. One such I propose to record here.

After long years of mysterious absence a young man whom we knew very closely, returned in the mantle of a yogi, with the usual ensemble of beads, and red marks on his forehead. Unlike the other yogis, he actually had returned to his widowed old mother, who was very happy to have her *wayward* son back. She did not mind in the least that the erstwhile vagabond had become a very sobre-minded yogi.

What amazed the people about him was that he maintained an absolutely tight lip about himself, and was hardly seen engaged in any form of spiritual rites except that secretive silence. He never spoke to any body. Because of a secret understanding between the mother and the son, both of them plied their respective business of life smoothly in spite of the wall of silence. For his living the young yogi kept himself engaged in manufacturing with his own hands and nimble fingers a special kind of indigenous leaf (*kendu*)—wrapped cigarettes, which soon became quite popular. He was seen preparing them all day and up to late in the evening under a tree, seated quietly on a rather high platform. He used to keep them in neat piles of ten; and customers just put the exact price down, and collected the number of heaps they wanted. There was no exchange of words; for all knew that the man never spoke.

Only once was this rhythm broken.

A young mother frantically approached him once; and sought his help in a crisis. A cobra had entered her bedroom. Her baby was in the cot in the room; and the cobra had comfortably coiled itself right on the same cot.

Would he help? The agonised mother kept staring at the dry taut placid face. The stern face never smiled.

At this he was seen for the first time taking part in a world-drama after his mysterious return.

He quietly looked at the weeping and distressed woman; laid down his basket of tobacco, and left the place with her, without minding his wares, which were left unattended.

What he did was a miracle of the most astonishing variety, and he at once became the talk of the town. He had gone to the room; stood beside the cot; watched at the live cobra silently for a few minutes, and then lifted it up most tenderly by the neck of the brute, without any more care than it were a wet piece of rope. Soon he returned with his new found friend, and keeping him on his lap cosily coiled, started wrapping his cigarettes, with the same care as if he had returned from a cup of coffee, and nothing more.

People would have liked to know what became of the cobra; but none dared. And most felt that he would make no reply. This incident, understandably, had enhanced his esteem and reputation.

Soon the lane was swept back to its usual placidity, until in the quiet of a hot June month it stirred again with a new commotion.

Of the yogis of India the Nāthas as a sect are known for occult powers of some sort. They are known to have the power of leaving their bodies at will; roam aerially at will; and return to their bodies when willed. They could, reputedly, revive the dead through passing into their bodies; and offer people strange medicines for stranger diseases. How far these reputations were based on facts I have no direct knowledge, though from personal contacts with this sect I have found reasons to regard them with some authority and a great deal of occult power.

The Nāthas generally are a roving type, although their quarters have been scattered all over the land conveniently placed at rather necessary and practical distances.

On this particular day one of the Nāthas, by profession a snake-charmer, approached our hero, blowing merrily at his gourd-flute, which forms an important ensemble of a snake-charmer. The cigarette man watched him warily. To the surprise of all he spoke to him with a loud voice, "Move along; move along. Don't disturb."

The Dumb has Spoken

The Nātha man with an air of quiet defiance laid down his hanging bundles, made himself seated at a distance, and continued to play on his flute. Soon the cigarette man was seen pulling out from under his seat a brass flute which he began to play (or should I say counter-play).

I do not have the ability to describe what happened next; but the Nātha man with the flute thrown away from him, as if wrenched by a brutal force, groaned with a terrible pain, holding his belly with both the hands. He actually reeled in agony on the dust of the street.

The fight continued, a silent fight of forces, a combat of strange attrition, a meeting of arms in the field of some occult magnitude. A small crowd had gathered, but it kept an awesome distance. The place at once looked like an arena where two pythons were engaged at wars. Soon the cigarette man fell flat on his back with no power to move. His limbs appeared to have been glued to the stone surface. His bleeding mouth frothed and fumed; and he shivered. He looked most pitiable.

Meanwhile the Nātha man was blowing his flute jauntily. With a cry he leapt up a few feet, and fell down with a thud with the blowing end of the flute driven deep down his throat.

His mouth started bleeding profusely. Try as he would, the flute would not be pulled out of his mouth. He choked, and was about to die; his face had turned blue. He appeared to have exerted a tremendous power to pinch out a drop of dust from the street, which he shot at the cigarette man, and then on his flute.

Ah, the release came at once. But the cigarette man was jumping and dancing as if stung by a million bees. He had to throw off his clothes. The Nātha man at once reached for the discarded clothes and tried to put them away.

But soon as he had touched the clothes out came a live cobra and spreading his vicious fangs stung him with a brutish vengeance. The Nātha yogi fell flat, apparently dead or dying. The crowd, which was to have been amused at the events was strangely affected by the gruesomeness of the drama, and watched with their tongues tied to the roots of their palates.

The cigarette man now held out his hand to help him, and the dying man held on to this help, and sat down. In about another five or eight minutes he was gone with his mysterious bundle, but his flute remained silent.

Our friend, the cigarette man, resumed his work, rolling on the eternal cigarettes. In the excitement we never noticed what had become of the cobra.

I resist from narrating here a few more of my experiences with similar display of the occult power of yogis. But this was what the great Lady in Safforn had meant by 'meeting the match.' The Nātha yogi had met his match.

The New Brāhmaṇa

In the meanwhile I had been fully initiated and admitted *a la mode* to the state of sacramental Brahmanhood. I got bound by the Vedic code of the seven vows.

I. Tell the Truth (*satyam vada*).
   Do the duty, and keep to principles (*dharmam cara*).
   Do not get away from the exercise of what you learn (*svādhyāyāt mā pramada*).

II. Accept the Mother as divine (*mātr devo bhava*).
   Accept the Father as divine (*pitr devo bhava*).

Accept a stranger-guest as divine (*atithi devo bhava*).

Accept the guru as divine (*ācārya devo bhava*).

Symbolising these two sets of vows, I bore from that day across my left shoulder a bunch of cotton threads.

Naturally I felt a stage advanced; and now I could claim entrance into the many forbidden areas of mystic performances so long denied to me.

One of these was the practice of the direct rites of the worship of the Mother. This was an area specially reserved for a tantra adept. And I was not adjudged yet as one. Although I had been encouraged by my associations with my Lady in Saffron, formally, no special tantric initiation had been administered to me.

This is a very sensitive situation. I had not yet found a special guru; and without the guidance from one, it was dangerous to dabble in tantra and tantra rites. Not that yogis have not been recorded to have reached their apex through unassisted efforts, yet, basically, such a course must be avoided. It means danger, as it did for Livingstone to penetrate into the unmapped African forests, or for Magillan to dare the unchartered ocean wilds.

A Daring Secret

In the world of tantra where deep thinking and concentration involves a complex mechanism, such as the yet unknown nervous system, any action, or mis-action that involves an injury is likely to remain permanent. I have seen people lose their brain-function, speech, suffer from breath trouble, even burst cerebral arteries and die. Tantra admits no adventure.

But one of the symptoms of a blessed yogi is, that his actions are tinged with the characteristics of daring fearlessness. There is an urge in him; and he must push from on to on. If the guru is there, all right; but if he is not there, then even without him; let his coming wait; let him be in coming. Meanwhile he travels from on to on, daring and ever daring.

Such a suicidal impulse is indeed wrong and ill-advised.

But I was young, and too enthused to pause for cautions. Perhaps the influence of the Lady in Saffron, her unseen hand of protection had emboldened my young heart. I ventured on the path which few would dare alone, and at that stage, I was totally unprepared for such daredevilry.

In retrospect, as I go back to those days, and to that inexplicable dogged determination, to that resolve to do what I had set myself to do, I find no reason at all for justifying why I had to act as I did. I was quite alone in a wordly sense. My secrets were my own. Yet I felt all the time I was not alone.

Outside the immediate municipal boundaries of Varanasi (of the days I am speaking of) there lies a haloed ground around a large stone-bordered tank. Because the place, then a wilderness, used to be secluded, a number of historically famous yogis, had made it their abode over centuries.

Even to this day the place bears such memorable and noble monuments as the marble mausoleum of the great Swamī Bhāskarānanda, of Mātā Lokeśvati, of Goswāmī Tulsidās. Nearby on a boat we saw the much discussed and famed Harihar Bābā, a silent naked saint living within a ramshackle hut built on a frail craft. In the many books written by foreigners he has been referred to as Mauni Bābā (silent saint).

There, hidden within a grove was located the famous temple of Mother Durgā, where regular blood sacrifices are offered to this day.

Why I decided to offer a long penance at this place is still a mystery to me; but once the call came, I decided for it.

For nine days in the month of Aśvin (September-October) this temple comes to life, and throngs of devotees make a beeline to it. The unending stream of men and women keep the place warm, busy and interesting. The huge crowd actually did in no way disturb inner seclusion, if one wanted to reach it.

I decided to offer prayers for a cycle of nine days at this very tantric spot. The most ancient temple spot in the most ancient city of Varanasi lies just south to this temple almost sharing its borders. It is a Gaṇeśa temple. I found the secluded platform of this abandoned temple to be the fitting spot for my exclusive *āsana*.

Today's craze for money and the precious foreign exchange has inspired the city fathers to remould that haloed surrounding into a supposed tourist attraction. Some businessmen had to spend his sudden wealth in constructing in marble the tallest landmark on the Ganges, and call it Mānas Mandir (temple of '*Mānas*', a Hindi Rāmāyaṇa witten by Tulsidās and very popular in India as a scriptural wonder of the sixteenth century). The entire Mānas is carved in black lead on white marble walls, complete with artistically moulded coloured depictions in Venetian-glass stains. Against the modernised 'tourist' motivated layout, and the vulgar opulence of an ill-conceived structure, the sanctity and quiet grandeure of the ancient temple stands totally violated now. But the age old Gaṇeśa, the most ancient thing in Varanasi, appears to be quite content and indifferent to this modern look.

My problem was to keep myself away from the detection of my family. The *Navarātri* days, as these nine days were called, used to be a busy period for our household, too busy really, for anyone to bother about a missing boy.

But my mother would miss me. So I had to take her into confidence. She, of course, was not too surprised. Perhaps she did not see through it. She just expressed her approval for a proposed penance her son was about to undergo. I got her tied down to keep this as a secret. She, in her own way, always encouraged me in any spiritual pursuits.

The Hard Way to Yoga

The prayers involved strict discipline. Besides being careful about my daily intake of food, and restricting my sleep, I had to get organised to be seated cross-legged in the lotus *āsana* for the entire period. This involved hazards of sorts: ants, flies, sudden gusts of winds; even reptiles could make their appearances. The place itself was infested with probing and interfering monkeys. I had to get myself prepared to withstand all these external challenges with equanimity and grace. There could not be any deviation from the *āsana* once I had avowed to assume my seat on it. In his Yoga Sūtra Maharṣi Patañjalī has strictly enjoined on the aspirant how and where to set the *āsana*. So has the Gita. But I was fascinated by the haloed place. Yogis must have been sitting there. It was a *sīddhāsana*, i.e., an *āsana* already sanctified. I decided to bow to Patañjali, and side-track him respectfully, and rely on my faith and determination.

I had to recite my prayers from a book which I had to position in a way which would not need any special efforts for turning over the pages through the ceremony, or penance. On my left palm would burn a lamp filled with *ghee*, (melted butter), and which I would not set down, nor let go out until I finished my prayers.

It was a severe test for attention and concentration. But I myself had chosen to bring that upon me.

Everything went on smoothly. The first day was a very trying day. The wind was high. The place was full of flies. On my damp skin flies would land in myriads; and on the floor ants, ants. . .

But when I was returning home I was deeply satisfied with myself.

The second day was much more calm and easy. The beginner's tremors were no more; but the wind and the lamp maintained their confrontation.

'I was totally left to myself on the third day. A strong wind blew; but the lamp kept calm; the flies and the ants were there; and the pestering inescapable monkeys. But somehow I felt that I had become their friend and even their brushings with my skin did not matter much. I was fully absorbed in my prayers......*'sarvā vādhā vinir-muktah'* (freed from all obstructions, as the prayer itself assured).

But from time to time I became aware of a *presence*. At time a soft breeze, as from a fan, blew over my skin; and at times I could even hear some other voice keeping time with my recitations.

I knew enough by then to expect such disturbances from friendly or unfriendly phenomena. Such digressive preoccupations, whether friendly or unfriendly, under a penance, have to be recognised as digressions; points of disturbance. All externals must cease to be. A state of trance demands 'I' to be with 'I'; self to be with self; awareness to be with awareness. It is not the inaction of the dead; it is so much of activity that it looks still, like the massive clouds sailing along a seemingly quiet sky. The higher they move the quieter they look. In fact these features in the space are nerve centres of excessive action.

A Sign: A Friend

The prayer was finished, and I felt exuberant.

Then I noticed a *presence*. Indeed someone had been keeping me company.

I must describe this delightful man.

Indian figures, are not known for Pathan-like builds, nor for those of the Highlanders of Scotland. Indian eyes are accustomed to watching insignificant figures of a short size, and of a light weight. This small man was almost covered with a puck-like spirit of an elfin cherubin, because around him light looked more edifying and identifying than the shadows. He had a shaven but well-shaped head with a tuft of jaunty hair knotted at the top. He was wearing simple cotton of a golden dye and his upper body was covered with a piece of the same material, tied across his armpits and gathered on his chest. He was looking very practical in that outfit. His forehead was covered with bright sandal paste; and around his neck he was wearing a fresh garland of fragrant champak (*Mechelia champaca*, a family of Magnolia), a very rare flower for that season. He also wore around his neck necklaces of the holy *rudrākṣa* and a mixture of corals and red crystals. He was seated on a piece of grass mat covered by a deer skin and a piece of silk; he had with him a water jar with a handle for carrying along, and a bamboo stick as tall as his own size.

This had to be a *brahmacārī* mendicant, a roving yogi of the Vaiṣṇava sect, and no other. I was surprised about his presence there.

He had been smiling at me; and greeted me. "How good is your reading," he said. "Perfectly timed. . . . And how devotedly you were reciting. Obviously you do understand what you read."

Confused by such compliments from a seemingly knowledgable person I could only say, "Do I? This is Durgā Saptaśatī. Not so easy a piece to understand."

The conversation went on stallingly; as if one was having the feel of the other. But I could also feel the natural good grace. He was friendly and intending to assist me. . . . But who was he?

I would not ask him. I had learnt the art of waiting.

But he did not leave me all alone.

After I had collected myself, and my things, and started my treck back home, I found that he too was following me.

"Are you going my way?" I casually asked.

"Your way?" His puckish eyes flickered in amused mockery. "Have you found it already?" He was smiling.

Abashed I rejoined, "No. I am sorry. I was only asking. . . ."

"Let us be friends. All right? Nothing more. For how long would the prayer last?"

"All the nine days. Mother willing."

"That is very encouraging. . . . I never get to hear such recitations with so much feeling, specially from a new *brahmacārī*."

"How do you know I am a new *brahmacārī*?"

"Oh, there are signs. There are; your newly grown crop of hair for instance."

"Hair as a sign for a *brahmacārī*! That's a novel theory indeed." I laughed. "You are a happy chum. We are friends."

"Are we? Now hold this." What he handed me was a lump of sugar-candy, the homogeneous cottage type, an aromatic solid crystal. It is known as *misri*.

It was not yet time for me to break my fast. I had to report myself to my mother; finish my daily prayers to the family deity. So I was concentrating on how to store the candy crystal.

In a flick of the moment the gay *brahmacārī* was not there.

I did not find it strange; but I found it funny. The lanes of Varanasi are such as one could easily have hidden anywhere, or give a quick slip.

But I was not a little surprised when in the evening I met my Lady in Saffron on one of the bastion pillars (a *burz* in local tongue) along the banks of the Ganges.

"So you had no difficulty today in your reading exercise," was the sudden enquiry. But the accompanying funny smile in her eyes was most intriguing.

"So," I exclaimed, "you had been at the back of it all. . ."

"What do you mean I was at the back of it all, little *brahmacārī*?," she remarked provokingly. "I am here. I sell coconut shells. At times I sing. But you are a budding yogi, engaged in penance."

I got peeved in no time. "But you are mocking at my efforts." I protested. Her carefree banter had brought tears to my eyes. I really had never meant to offend her.

"I thought you would be pleased. Do you feel otherwise?"

"You ask me, and I stop."

"On the contrary I am pleased," she embraced me with that; and all was forgotten.

Why Yoga?

The next day unconsciously I kept looking out for him. When he did not come, I started my recitation. But again in the middle of the exercise, the effects of the same presence, the same aroma, the same breeze attracted my notice; but I remained unmoved, and continued with my reading, not moving a hair, not batting a lid.

On our way back I asked him if it was at all possible to have an experience of that supreme delight of perfect freedom which is the sole objective of all the yogis.

"Are you sure," he asked, "that it is the sole objective of all the yogis? Do not be too sure. It is necessary for you to know that objectives amongst the yogis differ much.

"Some are like light. The wick in the lamp burns out itself, but gives light around. Its entire life and living is motivated by causing light and peace all around. Look at the grocer. His objective too is to distribute all around what he has stored. But in doing so he still nurses another deeper motive; a profit, which is not bad in so far as he maintains his family in the process. But some want to rob, and rob too much; and hoard at the cost of the misery of others. See the cow. We give her straw, grass and most of the thing which we reject as the earth's leftover, or our own leftover. Yet what she bestows is nectar, strength, vitality, the very milk of life. Look at the bee. With commendable patience, research, discipline and perseverence bees amass huge stores of honey. They never do so with the objective of distribution, as does the lamp, or the cow. Because the bee robs, so he is robbed in return. Because the bee only stores for its own use, and has no mind for others, the objectives are not associated with happiness.

"Bees are labourers; not workers. They are sold to their fate. They slave without enjoying their work.

"Causing gain for selfish ends alone, looking after one's own interests alone is the surest means to stifle the real source of happiness.

"Look at the miser. He too has the objective of amassing wealth, or what he considers to be wealth. But he is morbidly afraid of having to spend it. The objectives must be very clear indeed. The more an objective pushes selfishness at the back in preference to the good of many, the more the action of man becomes a source of happiness. This is the nature of the *sattva guṇa*, the spiritual mind. This is the true nature of integral yoga.

"Perhaps now it would not be too difficult for you to imagine and accept that the objectives for men in pursuing their own motives cannot be the same. Yogis are also men. There are many yogis; but all of them are men, men who are bothered by the same enemies who bother all men. You must be knowing the enemies of men. Desire, passion, greed and unbridled temper. These confuse good for bad, and bad for good. Vanity and ego and jealousy, all are very forceful adversaries; but one day you shall realise that desire, lust for power, lust for things and acquisitions, lust for intimacy with men in general and with the opposite sex in particular are some of the most formidable enemies of joy in life.

Yoga is a Sacrifice

"Yogis too offer their life work for acquiring certain powers. Some like the lamp look out for the power of burning themselves for being good to others. They shed joy all around and guide people along the correct way. Some again want to acquire power to influence and impress the people around, and wield greater power over the mundane interests of common men, whom they victimise through their ill-gotten power. Some again have the power, but hesitate to come out and get involved to be of use to the public. Some are never even seen; and yet these last to influence, by their very being, the good conduct of forces worthy of their attention. They assist good men, who under the influence of good and holy spirit, do a lot of good. The preservation of the essence of good qualities of all creation in spite of the overwhelming threat from evil forces, is the chief duty of those spiritual beings who work to this end, but who are rarely seen to be working. Make no mistake, whether you could see them or not, whether you ask of them or not, whether you are able to rationalise their involvement or not, they are there; they are there as the billions and trillions of planets beyond your immediate ken are there; yet these influence the solar system; don't they?

"The billions of cosmic rays, sound waves, subtle vibrations in ether and even further subtler facts (which remain beyond the perception of the pragmatist, but which are visualised by those with keener perceptions), influence creation. Busy in the cosmic system, a power charges the subtle bodies of atoms. A busy fast field of action, with actions and reactions shooting at each other, finally emerges as the concrete creation we see. It appears as if even this has a mind of its own. All this is unnoticed, unnoticeable; and therefore the common man, as well as the confirmed hedonist would hardly care for this. They lack the necessary poise and patience.

"Yet this proposes the precise field for the spiritualists. They are the ones who are deeply involved in probing into this. Through their determined efforts they strive to establish a rapport, a concord amongst the contraries that blow around this abstract field. They worship 'balance' *samatā*, equilibrium, poise.

The Cosmic Concord

"Whilst metaphysicians and *tārkikas* (philosophers) argue this, and write many books, spiritualists alone 'experience' this and prove their point by 'doing' what they alone could 'do'. They thoroughly dislike talking, or writing about this experience . . . . *'Pray don't ask me to explain that experience of mine, my friend; the more I explain, the more the feel of it renews itself ever and ever'* . . . didn't Vidyāpati sing so?

"The wonder knot that keeps this universal milieu held together as a unit is this one truth, an universal truth. The seeker ultimately comes to discover and know. The one who thinks of knowing too much, has nothing to seek about. Experience illudes him. Truth keeps away from the grasp of the talker.

"The ultimate nature of matter (*vastu*, *padārtha*) baffles the ultimate physicists. Is matter gaseous, solid, liquid, mallible, collapsible or elastic? This is not known. It is not known what fills the pockets that are created between one atom and another in a field of atoms? Radiation? What radiates? How? This is the most baffling challenge in higher physics. Yet, our ancients, like the Buddha, Nāgārjuna, the other *jīnas* before them spoke of *śūnyatā*, or space as being self-animated, self-charged, self-illumined. *Śakti*'s field is the ultimate source from which all forms, action-reactions, primacy-ultimate, intelligence, destiny, and the like proceed. This truth experienced is called the *bodhi*. This is beyond logic. Truth is experience-sensed.

"The ultimate point is attainable by a climb-up; once there, all the world milieu spreads before the eyes as a toy museum, a play-house, a giant baby's whimsical sport-effects.

"The 'I' in you is the only predominant truth—predominant and independent. It is indifferent to everything else outside that single focal point: 'I'. 'I' alone prevails. Loneliness is its companion; and silence is its language.

"Do not look surprised. Have no doubts.

"I live in what I am describing. This is essentially and intimately *my* experience. It cannot be yours, or of anybody else. It cannot be translated, transmitted, even shared. It has to be one's own attainment, achievement, conquest, fulfilment. This ultimate phase of consciousness acts like an igniting spark within a single element. Some recognise it as electron; we recognise this as *Śakti* within Śiva, electron within atom. That *paramātman*—not God, but the Godhead, *chaitanya*, or supra-consciousness is the very essential heart-throb of the world milieu. It is the centre of all. In personal life it is Love; in cosmic concept it is Power. There is a cosmic concord that holds together the maniness into one-ness. I speak not in vain. No, I speak not in vain . . . .

"We who see this, and feel this, remain silent and away, as the night sky does. We are unable to talk like the man who knows of things too logically, too much in detail, analytically and fragmentarily. But their knowledge is of a different vintage.

'Night' and 'Day'

"To them knowledge is daylight. They hardly realise that mere knowledge is a still-born child; a blind lane. Claimed as daylight, such knowledge without experience is indeed a blind and thick night. The bookman lives in darkness. Logicians could claim this to be day-light but in fact and usage it is night, opaque. Seeing through visions, is beyond the pages of books. Experience is reality, and reality is experience.

"Knowledge is an instrument that assists progress but is neither the progress, nor a realisation of the goal. Realisation is the consummation of an ideal feeling; and love is its final reaction.

"Remember that verse in the Gita? The one on the mystic *night* and *day?* When this yogic vision goes to sleep (as does Viṣṇu in his *ananta-śayanam*), 'night' becomes 'day'. It is yogi's paradise; his exhilarated trance. The non-yogin shouts, I have seen; I have known; I have discovered' etc. But he has consummated no experience. He is in the dark.

Citizen of the Cosmic

"And yet, as I was saying, there is a cosmic bond; a relation. Let me draw for you a picture to impress on you how deep, unfailing and inevitable is this cosmic bond. When a star in the space misses its orbit, and hurtles down and down until it disintegrates and vanishes in the wilderness of space, its agony is recorded by the remotest blade of grass on this earth. A dew drop listens to the music of the seas, as well as to the currents of cosmic rivers of moisture that proceeds from the solar hot heat. The shriek of a distressed child watching over the dead body of his mother pierces a nebula, and the firmament shivers in agony, and a star is born. Yes, there is an underlying link but unfailing between the events that disturb souls here, and the cosmic soul.

"We are all citizens of the cosmic. The tragedy is that we have not only lost our address, but we do not entertain the remotest worry about having lost it. We are vagrants on the sea of life; and still we bother very little about finding our true bearings. It is time we awake and see for ourselves what we have done to our divine heritage."

As the frail, short, cherub-like stranger had been pouring himself out, I felt his mortal limitations almost transformed and transfigured. He appeared as an adept in the art of captivating his listeners. Oh! the vivid urgency of his fervent narration, and elevating them to his own plane of thinking. This personal style of his narration made all abstractions gradually unravel their mysteries. Understanding is a sympathetic response."

I kept listening—rapt, mesmerised, thrilled.

Sources of Power

"The mighty forces of science are too often recognised for their obvious uses in wordly life. Although this power is harnessed to man's immediate uses, when we consider the immensity of this perennial source of power, the amount that is drawn from it for our use in mundane life fades into insignificance, compared to the amount that could have been utilised.

"Do you realise that all this and beyond is filled with power? And all this power is just being allowed to go waste? We are busy making toys out of this power. Gadgets and military equipments! Bah! Its real potential lies in assisting mental and spiritual developments that finally would redeem man from the two heinous enemies, ego and possessiveness.

"What man has achieved is to secure out of an ocean of power a mere spoonful; and we, in our supreme ignorance and enormous ego, claim that we have made science achieve great heights. What blindness; what futility. What we achieve, in the final analysis, proves to be but the assemblage of a number of fragmentary facts. The substances of achievement in terms of the ultimate good of man remains, alas, unachieved, even unattended.

"Fragments do make up a whole. That is a mathematical fact. But in the field of mind, life, energy this is not true. Once detached from the source, fragments remain fragments, even dead, useless, inert mass. By themselves they might multiply, but never could they make back the whole.

"The energy we have been tapping for our use is so superfluous, so physical, that the real source of energy remains quite untapped. Why does such a situation arise? Why do we miss our link with the Source? It is because we get confused. It is a case of confusion created through greed, and desire for possessions and more possessions. That is why a little while ago I had called them enemies to spiritual efforts. We must discipline ourselves. We must establish a rapport with the Source.

"There is a mightier force exercising its influence over the universal phenomenon, inclusive of the phenomenon of the mind, which indeed extends much farther than our field of experience. There is power acting and reacting unseen even beyond the worldly mental plane. This is the mystic spiritual plane, which yogis, try to tap and cultivate. Cultivate this; and get into touch with this Power.

"Bear it in mind, that all science and logical knowledge refers to only a portion of the total brain-power. The major part of our intellectual thinking capacity is lying as a dead weight locked up in the chambers of the unknown; yogis are, as it were, trying to unravel this mystery by finding a key to this locked up chamber, so that it could be unlocked, and the vast untapped resources of total energy could be brought to the service of life, life beyond life, thus reorienting and revolutionising the very concept of function and purpose of life. Stretching beyond this obvious body-locked life, it extends life.

By the Ocean of Consciousness

"There is life beyond this life. Perhaps this could be better stated. This life is unending. It is a wave raised in an ocean. This wave has many more waves behind it, and many more waves ahead of it. Ultimately all is an ocean. An ocean of total existence. Ocean of consciousness.

"It exists within a given body. It is as much a fact as we could see with our naked eye. But to hold on to this as permanent and ultimate is as great a mistake as to ignore the other fact that all waves are but the swells from a vast ocean of consciousness, unending, undying. That ocean is basically more real. This is no mere idealism. Here idealism becomes the Real. One might, if one would, ignore the fact, but not without severely limiting the infinite scope of his understanding of the ocean of consciousness. An individual's personal existence is but a pin prick on the surface of the Pacific Ocean. To rely on this too much is compromising with false pretensions.

"To view life in its entirety, to view life against this vast canvas, to view this intermediate interlude of play-acting between the cosmic displays of creation and dissolution is the subject of metaphysics and yoga. Yoga is a practical application of theories already arrived at by logical thinking. Yoga is never a blind man's buff.

"In this effort the guru is the guide, and the only guide. Without his assistance yogic practices could be like the ludicrous effort of emptying the ocean with the help of a shell.

"For trillions of years many more trillions of grass-shoots have burst out from the dusts of the earth and shared the drink of the sun.

Not of the sun alone; of the moon and the stars; of air and the dews; of the rains and the thrills of life. I feel the forces, as the tiniest grass blade or the unseen insect does. While I feel, as I do now, I realise that I am not merely a human, a limited worm in the cosmic layout; I am much more. I transcend my being, my dimensions, my time, my history, my potentials. I am nothing compared to what I could be, and what I am destined to be. Within me, deep within the recess of my *antah-karaṇa* (the source of my inner power) I feel the call of this sublime region of totality.

"What am I? Only a pawn in this game of mazes, on the chequered board of seeing, tasting, hearing, smelling, mating, earning, competing, greeding, lusting? Am I a victim of these mechanical responses? Am I a prisoner of my wishes, or a pressured animal driven whimsically by wind-blown circumstances? All my organs are but the extensions of my body machine; and they function as my being submits to the call of those responses which actually are blown from the world outside. The antenna that receives these responses and submits to them is my mind, an imperceptible entity; an entity that has no limb (*ananga*).

"Imperceptible as it is, it perceives everything. The mind alone feels. It feels without any assistance except from consciousness. Like meets like. Breath merges in breath, water in water, fire in fire, smell in smell. Like light merging into light, consciousness merges into consciousness and becomes one. Each thing we find in the world, in man, in nature, is wrapped in consciousness, or if it makes you understand it better, is merged in the unseen ocean of consciousness. As moisture is inherent in water, or heat in fire, so is consciousness inherent in objects and lives, seen or unseen, small or big. According to their make-up, of course, some are more conscious than others. The crucible, where personal consciousness merges with cosmic consciousness, is the mind. When I absorb the other world through my consciousness, I only let merge a stream of consciousness into a sea of consciousness. This process we call feeling; our feelings are the catalytic agents for the outer world to be absorbed in us, and become a part of our personality.

"How grateful we must be to god that in his infinite kindness he has filled the canvas of life, the stage of the world with trillions of minute things, small objects, which we, even with our limited perception, could feel as belonging to us, or at least meant for us. The cooing of a bulbul, the swift flash of colours reflecting from the wings of a butterfly, perfumes coming in the dark from unknown plants and bushes. This belongingness is the glue that keeps us sticking to them, as through them to the world. The world is as I feel; and I feel as my mind minds to feel.

"Are you feeling tired? Am I boring you?" He suddenly stopped, and looked at me. What reasons had he, I wondered, to ask me what were my feelings, or how were my responses functioning? Was he really in doubt, he the master mind, the super teacher?

I smiled, and said, "Please continue. Do not stop."

"The Real is just an extension of this feeling," he continued. "Feel the Real, the One, the *bhumā* (*all*-ness) through the smallest of the smaller expressions: birds flying, the grass sprouting, insects breathing blooms changing, into colour, the wink of the dawn, the blush of the eve, the morning of lovers, the cry of the new born. Even the agonies of the failures, the miseries of the famished and the frustrated are our own friends, guides, gurus inasmuch as they show us the path, and link us up with in the Great Real. They teach us how to extend our consciousness from the finite to the infinite, from here to the beyond of the Beyond, from now to ever. Our feeling for the Real becomes a fact through our feelings for the minutest expressions of life. Where, then, is any room for discrimination?

Transcendentalism

"When I used to sit alone in the wilderness near the sea shore I made friends with the sands. Yes, with the sands. Every grain was living to me; and I felt an unseen bond existing between the grains and my consciousness. By the vastness of the ocean, the silent sombre sands stretched and stretched to eternity. I visualised and felt that the world in her embryo looked like the wilderness of water washing the wilderness of sands. A grand sculpture was in the making. The conscious self sprang into life from such nativity. In that wilderness nothing grew but the cactii; the crabs and the snails, the stuck-up jelly fish and the scattered shells; the myriads of insects and the ever busy gulls each one fighting for a place, a foothold in the ever-growing tree of life. What a vision! The theatre of this drama kept me amazed and more amazed as the sublime story unfolded itself morning and evening. The beach itself lay like a sow watching over her numerous piglets at her teats; while the vastness lay silent, lazy, inert, the grains of the sand fed on the radiating sun. Energy charges all life and consciousness, and composes into forms the unending mystery of the world flux.

"I felt each grain drinking and absorbing and growing into dales and valleys, hills and mountains, trees, rivers vegetations, and the whole basketful of gifts known as 'life'. I felt each grain drinking, absorbing, helping grow, populating, shaping, colouring the world we admire. The entire beach was pulsating with solar energy. The feeling was ecstatic, thrilling.

"And something more. Each grain drinking of the sun became a reservoir of energy, and the long beach was agitated to a pitch until I could hear the cry, 'Life! More life!' I visualised the mythical Nara in the vastness of water, and Nārāyaṇa in the brilliant sun rays which had turned the surface of the sea into a sheet of molten mercury. Was not this drama of the world originally composed by these two master artists of a myth: Nara (water) and Nārāyaṇa (the sun)?

"So you see, the small is not so small. Even the fragments are not to be neglected. We must see the immediate in the light of the eternal, and the tiny in the light of the massive. We must regard the small man, the poor man in the light of god who has for his abode your life, my life and the lives of all. By serving them we serve ourselves; by being kind to them we do justice to ourselves. To these small things we owe the higher things; the higher truth; the higher feeling,—god. And by fully feeling this we become not only an extension of god, but we ourselves extend and surpass the mere feeling of the various church-stamped gods. That is real transcendentalism, if you understand. Knowing god is not enough. Becoming is the Goal."

Suddenly the young yogi became quiet.

The sun was setting on the other side of the city. It was the time of natural calm. The blessing of silence cheered us.

But I had to ask. "How to find the guru?"

He smiled; pressed my hand and looked affectionately. "Gurus are looking out for disciples too. Do you not believe it? Look there. One is looking already for you, you lucky boy . . . ."

A little away, on the baffle pillar, at our regular place, the Lady in Saffron had already been seated. Under the spell of the quiet light her silhoutte attracted me at once; and before I could take my eyes away from her, my friend was gone.

So my strange discourse (was it a discourse?) with the strange Vaiṣṇava (I never found his name, but used to address him as Nārada;

the puckish Hindu mythical Vaiṣṇava saint) continued day by day.*

There had never been an appointment. I could neither time, no locate his exits and entrances. He appeared and disappeared, but wa always careful to select either a crowd, or one of my most engagin moments to make himself materialise. The picture never altered th same funny tuft of hair at the centre of a shaven head, the same sanda paste spread over a high forehead, the same champak garland an the beads, the same cotton clad light syraphim body of evanescer light—and the same enigmatic smile overflowing his eyes, lips, an the benign friendly face. Oh, I could see him!

The *ċsana* under his armpit, the *sitār* in hand and the bras water jug shining by his side, he jogged along with elusive steps.

"Where do you live?" I managed to ask him one day.

"That presupposes if I live at all. That is a vital question, isn't it? was the immediate and disarming rejoinder.

"Don't you then live?" I sounded deliberately mocking.

Beamed that unnerving smile. "Do *you*? Do men live day by da or do they die day by day?"

Another one of those sphinx-like riddles. He would never come t the point.

"You always wriggle out of my enquiries."

"Out of flimsy enquiries. Life is so short. And there is so much t learn and unlearn."

No; I never came to learn about his whereabouts.

A Case of Materialising

None the less he was very real. His concern in me was very rea His love for me, like a burning hope within, made me look out f him.

Today, as I recollect, I find that contrary to the Lady in Saffro Nārada was very voluble. But I can also see that he had been givi

*Years have gone by since the strange interlude. I cannot capture the unado ed simple way of his speech, half Hindi, half Sanskrit. His diction, his images, h syntax punctuated with fascinating gestures, illuminating expressions flowed and on. It was charged with the conviction of experience together with the ma spell of a master's love for a disciple. In retrospect all that fades into a confu twilight area stretching over years of barren trampled neglect. The rendering fr a still vivid memory of the precious words into a foreign tongue has not simplif matters. Of course, under the circumstances, I would falter in correct verbat reporting; but I am pretty sure that I have remained true to the faith of what had so patiently planted into my soul.

essons to a novice. Naturally he had to talk at length.

He showed my way in many of the basic querries.

He always spoke of fundamental things; but it was his earnestness, irectness and that special way of talking which made everything asy.

We had been discussing this topic of 'materialising into a presence.' of course, without knowing anything about the subject, yet depending entirely on my very limited empirical knowledge, pooh poohed he whole idea.

But he reminded me . . . .

"Once you had drowned in the flood. You were hardly a child of our. Do you recall?"

I was struck dumb at this reference. Very few knew about it. But he incident had been preserved as a treasured memory in the family; as long as my mother lived, every year on that day she went religiously to the Ganges and offered a mother's prayer to some known god *who had appeared and saved* the life of her child. But how could on earth this little man come to know of that mystery-incident?

It was like this.

A turbulent monsoon had put all the rivers in north India in a spate. It was a record spate. The stone banks of Varanasi had almost been overflowing, and half the city was under water. Near to where we lived, the stone steps ride over a steep bank, a portion of which jutted out into the grey mass of the furious flow. This current coming unobstructed for the last eight miles met its first obstruction on the west bank, against the walls of the Darbhanga Palace. So struck and baffled, the current receded with doubled fury, only to back again after drawing a fast circle. The resulting whirlpool offered terrors to boatmen and swimmers alike. But the jutting stone *burz* itself provided a rather safe perch for daring devotees, who would snatch a few minutes of seclusion for offering prayers to the rising sun.

My mother was one of the very few who sought this seclusion. That morning the lady was offering her prayers. Two feet behind her the angry current raged periodically, rhythm after rhythm, roll after roll, with a natural regularity. Every time the onrush dashed, the water swelled up, dashed against the stone jetty, over-shot it and jumped down, forming a terrific cascade, into the whirlpool below. The thunderous roar of the dashing currents and the falling cascade kept bathers ominously silent.

I was left alone on the bank, while my mother had been at the prayers in that most interesting of places, where the mighty waters jumped the jetty and came down on the other side with a roar.

I wanted to reach her. Before anyone could notice, my toddling feet were already in the water; and carefully I felt the stone steps under my feet. The feel of the sharp current sent through me a feeling of strange exhilaration. I thrilled; and took another step;—and another;—and another.

Oblivious of what was happening behind her, my mother was engrossed in her prayers, with eyes devoutly closed. The bathers did not expect any accident. Things were so well knit and familiar that accident seemed to be far away from all minds.

Then, oops, the little feet missed, and the little body toppled into the abyss below. Almost keeping up a timing, the huge mass of water rushing from the south, jumped the *burz* and down came the cascade. The tiny feet were lost under the angry deluge.

Came a sharp cry. My mother still deep in her meditation, was suddenly awakened by the stab of the cry. She looked back, but her child was not there. Before she could utter 'help!' my wet body was hanging head down, from a firm grip, and I was being steadied into the eager embrace of a frantic mother.

The helping hand belonged to a strange man clad in red silk. He stood taller than anyone around, and wore an awesome grimness. But a soft gleam radiating from the body could not be mistaken. How that stranger had materialised in that impossible place, how he had not been noticed before, and how a second after, (when the first consternation of a confused mother was got over, and when she was looking round for expressing her sincerest thanks)—the man was gone!! The *presence* had vanished! The only exit ran up a flight of about thirty narrow steps; and the time was too short even for a monkey to jump up the place unnoticed. But the man was not noticed; neither any trace of the man was left behind.

The incident was at once being talked all over the place. My mother trembling out of the shock of such an advent returned home penitently, only to go back to the place next day for offering a very special prayer conducted by a very special priest.

And since then the anniversary of the event was always remembered by my mother, who religiously appeared on the banks on that fixed day, and offered her special prayers.

Nārada, my Vaiṣṇava mentor, had been referring to that event, which almost all had forgotten, and very few at all knew.

"And you say that you do not believe in *materialising*. The fault with your type of empiricism is this my dear, that knowing fully well the limitations of so called experiences you still want to steady your beliefs and disbeliefs on the basis of these very limitations. This is good for nothing...You must awake. You belong to the other time. You have to get down to work. You are simply wasting your time by chasing your own tail and shadow."

What to Do with Power

I remember once I had asked him what it was that a yogi really sought. It was he who explained to me the two ways and objectives of yoga. One was the objective of acquisition of power; the other was acquisition of peace.

I always believed that yogic power was of greater value. With this power under control, one would do so much good to the world. Oh, how he reacted to this suggestion of belonging to the tribe of do-gooders. He did not hesitate to call most of them pitiable frauds, vain intruders in the comity of the saintly. The temptation of showing off power reduces the spiritual state of the person who indulges in it.

The pity of it all is that a power-weilder, even engaged in trying to do good to others, is finally a loser. Playing the role of a do-gooder a man enters deliberately into the dark realms of self-deception, and of self-pity. Service as a *dharma* has to be both detached and devoid of selfishness, even of ego. Real service belongs to the men of piety and modesty.

Other than that a conscious act of doing good is commonly vitiated by a secret craving for self-proclamation and self-adulation. It is extremely difficult to get rid of this weakness. Only the most discip-lined could succeed in offering service to the damned and the desti-tutes of life. Most of the so called do-gooders commit an act of hypocrisy against their own souls. Real service to the miserables on earth proceeds from a total submission of the last shreds of ego to the source of all good, i.e., God. Modesty, I believe is the mother of true service; the father being tolerance.

Everybody seeks power; more so mystic power. This, of course, is more than understandable. But everybody is not so sure about what to do with this power. Unless the objective is very clear, acquisition of power might act as a knife in the hands of a child; or bombs in the hands of selfish nations. If an indiscriminate tyrant enquires the secrets of atom, he might hold the peace of the world at ransom.

Big powers act as big gangs of blackmailers when they talk with military power to back their indiscipline. World is saved by power; and world is also destroyed by power.

Acquisition of liberal power comes from yogic discipline. And from yogic discipline, again, one has to learn the uses of power. This discipline has only one—aim total elimination of ego. Use of power, however, depends on another kind of yogic discipline: understanding and appreciation of social concord, social peace. The former call for self-discipline with self-education; the latter calls for impersonal appreciation of the good of all, where self, it at all, comes last.

As I narrate and explain this, an incident comes to my mind. This happened in one of the islands in the West Indies. This question of seeking power made me question, analyse and rehabilitate a young man who was keen on acquiring power.

Let me relate the episode. Illustrations from life are the most telling of teachers. It happened in 1969, in Trinidad. I was confronted by a young man who had approached me for seeking 'power'. According to him, he had 'tested' me and found that I had power enough to transmit. This young man claimed to have visited Tibet, and knew something about the Tibetan occult. But after being with me for over 15 months or more, (he meant that he had been regularly attending my lectures) he became restless, and badly wanted to come nearer me, and 'draw' some power. So I asked him very frankly what would he do with such power if he had it. The young man did himself much credit by frankly stating before me that all he had been looking forward to was to acquire vigorous power for tremendous sexual ability. In his idea the females in creation suffer from an everlasting rut, and to wield a real hold over them a man needs nothing else but titanic vigour with sexual ability.

Of course I did lend him power, but of another sort. I taught him the power of understanding love, mind, body, and womanhood. Today his home boasts of two pretty children; and his Spanish wife is an adorable lady proud of what she is and what she has.

His has not been the only case. I have met with a hundred cases of this type. I shall narrate for record only two more.

This other young man had come with a male companion. Both of them appeared to be under some traumatic tension. Their skin looked dry, famished and burning; their behaviour restless; even their fingertips twitched, cheeks trembled; and from time to time their tongues shot out with the hope of wetting a cracking pair of lips.

According to their own confessions they had been attending some of my lecture sessions which were always open and public. Obviously they had known me for long, but had been quite unknown to me. This happened in 1972.

They had been under some duress, some distress.

It was a spiritual distress; according to them a dangerous occult distress.

I begged them to be more relevant.

They thought that some powerful source situated in another country (in their case Venezuela) had been in spiritual communication with one of them; and through that one, with other two. Now as they were falling to act his bidding, he had been sapping their strength away . . . and things of that sort. They had tried to penetrate into the seances of the visting Indian yogis, and found them to be too superfluous. In my case, so they claimed, they had failed to make any penetration at all. This is how they reported themselves. (I am only repeating their views and observations.) This had given them the daring urge to come to me for assistance. . . etc. (World of tantra is filled with such lumber, and the air in the lower stratum is filled with poisonous impurities.)

I felt rather amused at their naive analysis of the situation, and tried to tell them that I had no idea whatsoever about the 'seances' they had been speaking of; and so far as this business of penetration etc. was concerned, I had always kept an open mind, and the idea of penetrating into my spiritual realm should not have occurred at all. I further explained to them that they should climb down to the level of the common human beings, and desist from considering themselves superhuman, with superhuman links. I narrated to them the great occult legend of Kṛṣṇa-Aśvatthāmā and of the curse wielded by the evil powers of the latter. Challenged by the fury of an evil spell cast by Aśvatthāmā, Kṛṣṇa advised all to stand clear of their mental obsessions, submit themselves entirely to the law of non-violence, and bear no kind of emotional reaction to what Aśvatthāmā wanted to do. The curse would certainly fail against the non-violent. The best way to remain at peace is to turn the mind into a zero. Stay at the common normal level, and the uncommon would not make a hit. Be modest. Peace is the fruit of a tree named modesty.

The third was a very sad and tragic case.

She was a Dutch girl born in Borneo. Through the transfer of Dutch powers to local hands her family was flung to Amsterdam. The family soon got disintegrated, and she, a girl of barely seventeen, found herself swept away to distant Surinam, a state previously belonging to the Dutch, and known as Dutch Guyana.

I had the misfortune of meeting her there.

She came to me for assistance after she had heard me over the T.V. As usual I welcomed her, and listened to her dreary tale.

Then I questioned her about her sex life. The poor thing had not had even 22 years of life to her credit, and she could easily count at least twenty persons with whom she had actively experimented on a dream known as compatibility, with the distant hope of building a home. The home was still her focus of attention; just to have a father figure to attend to, and a place for her nestling in absolute peace.

I felt much moved towards her plea for rescue. She hated the life she was forced to live, and which she had not sought of her own choice; and unless she would find a way out she would either turn mad, or would be forced to eliminate herself. (She was a beauty. Her health and charm was ruined. She sang as well as she painted. But she lived in a 'home' filled with dancing phantoms.)

I succeeded in pointing out to her that she is more than three quarters demented already, and that suicide would not be so easy for her because she loved life intensely. The only way was to stick to the man she had been currently hanging on to. It was of no consequence if the man was not white; he was more; he was an artist; and he, as an artist, loved her, understood her mind, and above all he loved the home he shared, and their child. Did he know all her past? Yes, he did. (He later spoke to me.) And was that not an entire south-window open for all the sea winds to blow in and sweep away the least speck of rubbish from her mind?

The urgency of my talk made her gasp; and she wondered how I knew so much information about her. Paramaribo was a completely new place for me; and it was quite impossible for me to be telling her so much details about her life in depth.

She ascribed my knowledge to my spiritual power, and I warned her, as usual, that the greatest spirit is the spirit of love; and one who has acquired this love power develops an insight into most of the troubled minds of the world, provided the troubles are genuine.

She, as well as her husband (now they are married) still write to me.

I owe the knowledge of this source of power, namely, the power of love, to this Vaiṣṇava saint. He taught me about two types of power. One power acts through miracles, and provides for easy cures of ailments etc. This power could buy friends, make enemies, set people mad, spell disaster, astound and mesmerise. Such power brings power, money, social adulation, special distinction; and heaps on its victims a crushing weight of vanity. They end in misery, and they find their own salvation (that is winning peace and happiness for their own soul) in a miserable jeopardy. (Lucifer, Rāvaṇa, Hiraṇyakaśipu, Attila, Hitler etc. etc.)

The other power is the power of love and peace. It tolerates, understands, befriends and shares. It goes out to the aggrieved, the isolated, the abandoned, the distressed; it considers a child as an adult, and an adult as a child. By its own power it turns tears into smiles, and raging passions into charming blooms. It is a power that mothers all, and provides all with a magnificent touch that reaches the very soul. With this power cementing a concord between two, all distinctions,—such as sex, age, social status vanish. The only reality that remains supreme is sympathy, fellow feeling, love without motive. It acts as a great power. I owed so much to my little comic Nārada.

6

The Female Factor

Fleeing Spirit

My Vaiṣṇava friend, I called him Nārada, had done me a great favour . . . .

On the eastern bank of the large tank attached to the Durgā temple (where we had met each other for the first time) stood a walled garden described before. It was a garden attached to a magnificent marble mausoleum. Some forgotten Indian prince had offered this as a homage to his guru, Swāmi Bhāskarānanda. The saint's ashes are buried here; but in a serene cottage within the garden a full-size statue of the saint is found seated in the yogic posture.

In his life-time, when the surroundings were covered with a wood, the saint had built his *rattan* hut exactly at the same spot. Here he had passed more than a hundred years; years of teaching and praying, but most times merged in deep *samādhi* (trance). He was considered, along with another great adept in yoga, the renowned Tailanga Swāmi, a divine personality. He subsisted on nothing except what fell to his lot naturally. (*Ājagara-vrata*, living on food effortlessly arrived.)

Irrespective of the changes in seasons Swāmī Bhāskarānanda never put on any kind of garments. He never went out in search of food or shelter. Soon his yogic fame brought about him some inquisitive followers, whom he formally taught from primary alphabets to the most astute subjects like metaphysics and yoga. His teachings are still available in print, and are quoted as authority.

Like Tailanga Swāmī (we shall speak of him in a different context), he too followed the haloed path of tantra yoga, or at least a form of it, and was an adept in the celebrated *Śrīyantra* (a mystical diagram which lays out the entire lesson and import of tantra *sādhanā*). The statue of the naked skeletal Swāmi seated in his favourite *āsana* has been placed exactly where in that very posture he had given up his ghost in a deliberate ascension of life, about a hundred and forty years ago.

Peace dripped from the wooded trees surrounding this secluded spot. Even during the early twenties of the century, as and when I used to visit this place, I invariably became aware of the strange vibrations, usually associated with places sanctified by penances of great spiritual personalities.

What with the charms of the place, and what with the blossoming trees that hedged the walls, what with the well laid-out gardens, and the fountain gurgling, the few anchorites moving around the place with a solemn grandeur of their own, this place had been a favourite haunt in my early boyhood days.

Whence I Came; Why?

All that is gone now. The purposeful enthusiastic powers of an organised municipality have turned it into a tourist attraction; they have modernised much of its pristine sylvan charm. Gone are the walls; and with the walls, the garden, the blossoming trees, the fountain, and of course, the anchorites.

I have a strong belief that like the people inhabiting a quiet place, and later shoved into the jaws of 'development', the spirit of a place is also disturbed. The quiet spirit that had charmed Job Charnok on the Bhāgirathī, has been dislodged by a drastic urban growth. The haloed romantic poetry and spiritual vibrations of Sutanati, Govindpur, and particularly of the hemlet of Kālighāt across the dark woods of Bhavanipur and Chowrangi Natha's habitat, is today a far cry from the nerve racking milieu of 'developed' Calcutta. As men flee places of turmoil to seek quieter spots, the unseen spirits, the actual guardians of man's spiritual contentment, also seek other places. Any one visiting such places as Tārakeśwar, Dakṣiṇeśwar, Tārāpīṭh, Brindāvan, Badrināth etc. would confirm that despite 'development' in facilities the places have lost their soul. The peace and contentment of the surrounding, the light-winged vibrations in the air felt fifty years back (when 'tourists'—buses, motels etc. were not there) are completely missed today.

The only exception is the age old Maṇikarṇīkā of Varanasi. We have bartered the solemnity of pure spiritual delight for the cheap pleasures of travel lust and sight-seeing. This is true of Amarnāth in Kashmir, Paśupatināth in Nepal, Rāmeśwaram or Jagannāth Puri. This, I have painfully discovered, is the case of St. Peter in Rome, The Stone henge in England, Nizamuddin Auliā's tomb of Delhi, Ajmer Sharif, Our Lady Guedaloupe's shrine in Mexico (what a sacrilege there!) or the renowned Alcazar in Toledo's shrine. In a short period of 35 years, the change experienced is deplorable. This spirit of the saintly, the vibration of virtue run away from noise, promotional gaudiness and lack of piety and reverence.

Here I used to await my friend Nārada. In fact, it is through his encouragement that I had grown familiar to this place. Most times at noon, when I visited the place, I took my seat in the southern part of the mausoleum, and fell into a state of trance. For the joy of it, soon I became a frequent visitor.

And here the friendly Nārada, a master, gave me so many of his instructions.

Once I had referred to the strange coolness and the embracing familiarity of the place. I remarked that the place seemed to me as familiar as if I belonged to it. But when was it? How? I did not know; neither could I remember, when could I have' first' come to the place. This sense of belonging to it was unaccountable; otherwise why and how did the familiarity of the place so enrapture me? "I wonder why this place should appear so familiar to me!"

"We all visit our dearest places again and again," observed Nārada in his usually mystic voice. There is nothing surprising; nothing to fear."

More surprised than ever I looked at him. I must have frowned in disbelief. What could he mean?

Only that little provocation was enough. He started his explanation. (Oh, how much do I owe to these explanations from my chance-bestowed friend!).

"No life is a first-time life. The scholar's insistent enquiry and dogged search for the 'first-time,' for the 'beginnings of things,' really appears to be so stupid. I wonder why people do not seem to stop and consider that searching for a point of time in history is a child's funny adventure for finding the lost pant button after he has grown out of his garments. A real search should be made for *why* I came; not for *when* I came. For in a much deeper and truer sense all the 'things' around us are 'first-time' things.

"Oh, how stupid it is to view time as a flat slate of continuity from a dead point to a dead point. It fact, time is so alive, so vibrant, so dynamic, and perpetual. Perpetuity is time. In fact, time is life itself. In fact, time alone is alive. We borrow our little cup-fuls of life from the immense time stream. Father-time, *kāla*; Mother-time, *kalī*—that mystic Lady of the Dark, who delights in her 'life-play': life coming, coming, coming and, going, going, going, from out of sight, to out of sight; from out *of* nowhere, to out *to* nowhere. Life as a living force delighting over life as inert, dead. That's the image."

My puzzled looks made him stop for a while.

"This is contradiction. Life alive. Life dead. I do not follow you."

"I know. But contradictions speak of hard boiled truth. When they do, they are known as paradoxes, which contain the seed germs of crystal truths. Easy to remember. Dear to part.

"Time is a playful girl, busy playing on the sea shore of space, filling and emptying her colourful buckets. There buckets contain the sea in fractions; while the sea itself remains unmoved, unchanged. When the bucket is full, it comes alive. When it is emptied, life becomes dead. But this is only referring to the bucket. In relation to the sea, does the filling or the emptying affect it at all?"

With that hammering direct question he stopped.

"No. Of course, it does not," I replied. "But what are you now speaking of? What exactly you mean to say?" I became more demanding. More critical.

But Nārada was the very essence of patience. The smile never left the face. "What am I speaking of?"

"Look," I protested. "The time was all right. Now you introduce space. Why space?," I enquired.

"Yes, I have introduced strange concepts. But please bear with me for a while. Through these new concepts I propose to lead you to the knowledge of 'whence' you came, and 'when' you came, and to 'what' you came. The word *when* is time-motivated; correspondingly, the word *where* is place-motivated. Do you follow?"

"Yes; I do now; but what is space, as different from time? Are they two? How?"

I did not realise that I was betraying signs of irritation. Nārada smiled again. And continued . . . .

"Remember for all times to come that there are no *two*, or more than *two*. There is only *one*. The *one* is the all-in-all truth, the *satyam*, the *brahman*, the *bodhi*. . . . The god, that we clumsily refer to, is only the last convenient resort our unending talks cling to as a sublime hypothesis.

nirvacanīyam: Anucchiṣṭam

" . . . There is no god except when realised as *reality*, *satyam*. When that realisation comes, it just comes; it dawns upon consciouness; it descends. Then, when it dawns, there is nothing else to be done but to be in it . . . yes, to be *in, it!* To be *it!* Not as a body in water. No. But as water in water, breath in air, heat in fire. What you realise is exclusively yours. Your experience. Beyond sharing, beyond describing. All description of it is limited. Because word sense is limited, description has to be limited. But experience is unlimited . . ."

I felt intrigued. I was being swept away by a sudden current t ideas beyond my depth. I whirled and whirled, fighting to come up floating; but his hand was already on my head. He looked deep int me and asked, "Do you not sit on the body of the Bhairavī? On he naked skin? In an *āsana*? . . . ."

"She is my auntie?"

"So? . . . Just an auntie? . . . . Just a related person like that? An nothing more? O, how foolish you could be . . . . The auntie vanishe in the *āsana*, as the body does. What remains is abstract. *Prakṛt alter ego*, and the vibrations. Govinda Pandit is your uncle. But h is also a doctor of smallpox. He is also an astute *Haṭha*-yogi. Isn't it But not always so. To a tiger he is just food, nothing else. No longe Govinda Pandit, the *Haṭha*-yogi. Nevertheless, could you deny he i a *Haṭha*-yogi? A master?"

"No I cannot," I asserted.

"But what is he? Your uncle? A *Hatha*-yogi? A mass of assimilate food? Really what then is he?. . . . Your auntie is your auntie. But sh is also a Bhairavī. As you sit in *āsana* on her body, what is she? You auntie? A Bhairavī? Or an experience? Could you describe that experience?"

I was so confounded by the question that for a few seconds I fel totally lost.

How real was the experience! How vivid! How saturating! Yet t describe faithfully the nature and substance of that taste of absolut thrill seems to be beyond words.

. . . But I was being watched. And gradually a voice whispered *anirvacanīyam! anucchiṣṭam!*" (Beyond spoken words. Undefiled b the tongue.)

Nārada had been whispering into my ears.

"Yes," I repeated, "that was joy. Beyond words. I feel. Just feel."

"This is *ānandam. Ānandam* is total. Always total. It could not b fractioned even for sharing. It could not be brought out even fo description . . . . Am I right?"

That impish smile. It was ticklish.

"Total *Brahman*." I admitted.

"Let me examine the point again," my friend continued. "Shall we? Look at my hands. How many fingers?"

"Of course ten."

"How many hands?"

"Two."

"How many bodies?"

"One, only one body."

"Now, look around. How many bodies?"

"Why? You; I; . . . many; many bodies."

"And now. How many 'I's?"

" 'I's? . . . . Oh, I see. Why, only one 'I' in all."

"Then, what about me? Do I also not see, think, act?"

"Indeed you do...as a different body. Not as a different 'I'."

"We all float," he explained, "in the same air. The air is one, and the bodies are many; the water, for the fish, is one, but bodies are many. And so on . . . . There must be one 'I', one consciousness, one Brahman, although all these appear to be many. Maniness is a convenience in everyday empirical thinking . . . ."

". . .The doctors," he continued, "are many. But when we talk of cholera, or malaria, or cancer. . .to them, these are only one. We are patients. As patients, we are many. In hospitals we share many numbers. But to the doctors, we are mostly abstractions. We are problems for them to solve. They treat us as individual cases of some disease; i.e., the patient is not at ease. Each of the many is a fraction of one. One is the only truth, the Real. There is not else but the One."

"This One," he said, "the 'I', then must be in every thing, even if, like the one air, we do not see it. This One must be in life, as well as in what has no life..."

"Now, that is yet again another form of confusion," he explained. "Confusion of the mind, understanding . . . . In the Gitā there is a line . . . ."

I held him there, and recited . . . . *Ajñānenāvṛtam jñānam tena muhyanti jantavah* (knowledge lies hidden in the darkness of un-knowledge, and creates confusion amongst the living).

". . . .And the Lord goes further," he remarked. "A beautiful simile."

Encouraged, I went on holding my finger up at him, "Let me try."

Yathol-venā vṛtam garbham tathā tenedamāvṛtam.
Āvṛtam jñānam-etena nitya yuktena vairiṇā.

(That one anti-thought, an enemy, eternally clinging covers the entire world of knowledge, as does the uterine membranes cover life within the foetus.)

Śiva, the Asleep

He looked happy.

"Therefore," he continued, "you see, that supreme knowledge too is one. Anything beyond this One is nothing but an extension of our ignorance. You call it an extension of our ego. There is no ego without a sense of attachment or possession. To acknowledge 'I' in a total sense is to get rid of attachment that creates confusion; but saying 'my' is to merge the self in a whirlpool of confusion of attachment and more attachment. That is anti-freedom. 'I' is an extension of the Subject; 'my' is an extension of the Object, which fetters the Subject. The fetter is ego. 'I' cannot possess anything without damaging its pure innocence. Yet, . . . and this is important, this 'I' could indeed be extended to the Infinite, only when not tied to ignorance, ego, the sense of possession.

"Such was the man Swāmi Bhāskarānanda, a creature of no other substance but Light. We call these men the enlightened ones. When 'I' is inflated with ego, you get men like Rāvaṇa, Śiśupāla, Napoleon, Hitler. Realised Truth needs a heart as pure as a lotus in bloom for the light to rest on. Are you following?"

"I think I do," I said. "Now I could figure out time as living. But the space is not as living as time is. Space 'is'; but time is more than just 'is'; it is eternally continuing, eternally passing; eternally in motion, change. Space 'is'. There's no change. Limp. Even the change that there is, is dormant. Undetectable. . . ."

"No!," he warned. "Do not go further. You say dormant; not dead. Remember the *ONE* of which we had been speaking? Even Space and Time are One. Life as an active vast ocean touches the shores of Time and Space; and rests on the static Space.

"For even an ocean at bottom rests on something; and all is a compact whole. Time is Space in activity. Space is Time asleep. So you see Śiva, asleep, inert, lying flat, and seemingly 'dead' under *Śakti*, Kālī. Śiva is a word formed from the root √*ŚE* which means 'to sleep'. Now you could imagine why we say, Time and Space are one like the moon and its light. We talk of them as *two* for the sake of convenience. Description, as we have been saying, is the least part of realisation. Realisation is silent. A yogi is a silent person. Śiva is silent. Kāli or *Śakti* moves with power in *mantra, japa, vāk,* utterance."

I winced under the heavy impact of this analysis. But I did not give up, or get lost. It was not new to me any way. Abstruse arguments came to me as swimming to ducklings. At our home talks between logicians and metaphysicians were an everyday feature. I was somehow familiar with abstruse talks and technical vocabulary. Yet this long talk was difficult to keep pace with, and absorb.

But Nārada was an adept in teaching. He would not tarry for long on the abstruse area. Like an expert weaver he picked up the broken strand at the right moment, and started as if nothing had interrupted our talks.

". . . .So you see," he continued, "Time could not be described as a principle having a beginning. Time has no beginning, as indeed space has none. Śiva is *anādi*. Kālī is *cit* (consciousness), the cosmic energy of conscious life. Beginning of things cannot be known. All beginnings are shrouded in mystery.

"Let me see if this could be explained more easily. A circle is a racing path traced by running points kept equidistant from a given point." As he had been talking he described a diagram on the white marble with the sandal paste which was always there in his water jug. "The points," he continued, "in the circle are held fast and close to one another. Naturally of these points none is a 'first'.

Sound Gems

"All of us, and all of such as we are, had had somewhere else a beginning. We have no direct knowledge of it in our present condition. We always come back where we had been before. Some feel it, some do not, depending on the subtlety of the feeler's sensitivity. Why? It is quite possible that you had been not be unknown. The Durgā temple is so close; and annually they come there for pilgrimage. And the place is so attractive. Swāmī Bhāskarānanda was your father's guru. Your father is within you. Do you, then, disbelieve to have been here before?"

"Of course," I responded. "I have been engaged in picking flowers from this wild garden. Why? I remember now, yes . . . . It was a strange experience . . . ."

"What was it?," enquired Nārada.

"I remember once I was busy picking flowers dropped from the branches on the grass . . . .*Bāsak* and *Camelī* (*Mimu sops Elengi* and

F. Arborescens). All of a sudden a serpent from nowhere appeared, and slid first underneath the basket, and then calmly climbed and coiled on the flowers gathered in the basket. I had nothing else to do but to watch. It was so beautiful, so gorgeous in its brilliant attire, spangled white and grey and black. It was a cobra. I began to a sing a prayer for Śiva. After a long while it left me . . . . But I felt so happy . . . . I do remember. Yes, I was here."

"Yes. You prayed to Śiva. But there are smaller caskets of sound. Little gem sounds. Like a small tiny seed that keeps enclosed within its shell even a great banyan, or any tree for that matter. These seed sounds contain within them great prayers; prayers of unbelievable energy and force."

Before he could say anything further, I was uttering, *Om namo nārāyaṇāya: om namah śivāya: om namo bhagvate vāsudevāya: om kling kālikāyai namah: om hrīng durgāyai namah.*"

He smiled at me and enquired why I repeated so many of them. And continued, "How many boats you need to cross the Ganges?"

Not to be taken back I retorted, "Depends. The time, the current, the nature of the winds . . . ," and I laughed.

"Why not only one dependable boat for all weathers and currents?"

"What about oceans?," I persisted.

"Is it so very impossible to secure a dependable boat to get across the oceans? Of course, a very dependable pilot will be necessary. But one boat would do I believe."

"Then why so many *mantras?* So many gods?" This time my question had an urgency. I wanted to bring this subject to him. I found now the opportunity.

Mantras

"This is a very honest question, but not that much intelligent. Unless one is blind, or to much bogged into a single-track thinking, one should be able to appreciate the charm of variety in objects. Have you ever entered a drug store? Have you noticed how many kinds of medicines are there, and how many kinds of bottles? Some on open racks for you to handle. Some are kept out of common reach. Some are too dangerous, or too complicated. But do you need all of them? Have you entered a drug-store ever to need all the bottles? Although you need one at a time, doctors have to keep at hand a number of drugs. The doctor selects, and gives you that one which you need. Good doctors do not prescribe a number of medicines for a single patient. But they keep many medicines; and at times, they even have to show off a number of medicines to build up the feeble confidence of weak-minded patients.

"Your spiritual guru prescribes for you a dependable *mantra*. He knows many of them. But you need only one. He will select. Even in your lifetime he could change this, and give you another *mantra*. That depends on your power of spiritual need and assimilation.

"Take for instance the gradual selection of your food. You start with the mother's breast. You go to cow's milk. Then to the solids. Then back to softer, even liquid food. This depends on the needs of the body, and the powers of assimilation.

"The principal motive behind these changes is to assist absorption and assimilation. The power to absorb may vary between body and body, mind and mind, depending on other factors. Do you agree? . . . well, you do. Variety and changes should not disturb you at all. Our ancients have passed through many experiences. The history of spiritual experience of the ancients of the East is too long and various. Like undeveloped children we reach for as many *mantras* as we happen to come across with. This shows how we suffer from lack of confidence.

"One alone is enough, if the guru has selected that for you. It is obviously a mistake to claim that one single *mantra*, like one single medicine, is good for all on all occasions. We do not feel for many. We feel for one, just one, but out of the many. This is the correct position. We honour and respect all of them; but we cherish and hold on to only one. This one is *mantra*. Your *mantra*. The guru-*mantra*. The one medicine that the doctor has chosen for you, for your help. *Mantra* etymologically means 'the sound that helps one to *get across* by constant mind-ing'. You mind it. Repeat it. Own it. Realise its powers. It would give you power."

Pennyworth of Powers

"Could you give me the powers?," I jumped at the prospect.

"What powers?" asked Nārada derisively. "What powers are you talking of? Miracles? Powers to kill or save a life? To demonstrate magic? To bring people under control? . . . Remember Ramakrishna? Here is a story from him. Listen . . . .

"One of the two brothers of a family of ferry-boatman grew tired of the life in a village. Sheer monotony. He wanted powers, so that he could play the miracle man, the spiritual man. He left home, and found himself a guru. In time he did succeed in acquiring powers. With the powers now earned, he returned home, and arrived at the old ferry; there he found his brother, the ferry-man, playing the same old ferry boat. The return of the brother in the spiritual garments of a saint made the ferry-man very proud. He made haste to carry him across the river to their village.

"Gradually the ferry-man asked his brother what special powers the brother had acquired.

" 'Plenty,' replied the saint. 'For example, I could cross this river walking over it.'

" 'But why?,' asked the ferry-man quite disappointed. 'We have this craft. And it does quite well. It takes only a copper to cross the river. Had you to spend all these long years just to acquire a penny-worth of powers? This game of acquiring power might be a jolly sport, but it must be very expensive.'

"So you see, a real spiritual quest is actually blunted by greed for powers. Besides, power by itself is a temptation. Have I not already explained this? It provokes ego. Provoked ego acts against spiritual peace. Joy, not power, is the key. Spread joy."

Then Nārada began to elaborate on the subject of love, the powers of unattached love for the fellow beings; love for the world. "The secret of power," he said, "lay in considering and accepting all as one. One must see one's ownself in every other manifested object. The same subject everywhere. That is the real power worthy to be acquired."

I got confused. I must have told him that my quest was for no powers, really. I am bent upon only one object. I wanted to be filled with the love-power like my Lady in Saffron. I wanted to be loved by her.

An Ancient Temple of Tārā

> "*Objects blown into ocean become saturated with salt; so all inert objects become animated with consciousness as they get in touch with conscious power.* (VI-I-30)
>
> "*A Guru is he, who by a look, a touch, an utterance could electrify the divine consciousness of his disciple through his grace.*" (VI-I-61)

The solemn music of the ringing verses of Yoga-Vāśiṣhṭa filled the ancient temple. Our sessions continued. The same solemnity; the same *āsana;* the same sound and smell; the same aura. The Lady in Saffron had been leading me methodically towards the difficult achievement of gaining a state of total impersonality, e.g., the art of detachment in attachment; love without reactive emotional stress; sleeping when awake, and awaking while sleeping. The fortnightly sessions at night were now held at different places. We had been selecting more and yet more secluded hide-outs.

The one hide-out we had finally come upon was an almost unnoticed and certainly neglected temple in a series of temples built by a lady, Rāṇī Bhavānī (eighteenth-century female devotee from West Bengal) on the banks of the Ganges.

This was the dreaded Tārā temple. The access to this temple had to be gained through completely ruined and dark subways. Every time I gained entrance there I had to hold her hands for guidance. The passage to the temple felt eerie with screeching bats and furtive rodents.

But once within the haven of the small temple yard, paved with red sandstone, the feeling changed.

Participating in Seances

At times we came across strange unknown faces in the temple. Some engaged in meditation, some engaged in rites. If fire had to be lighted, the Lady in Saffron would do it. But on days when she found a seance already in progress, she would just sit near the flaming altar and join the stream of the rites without any ado.

Fire, blood and sex formed parts of the rites. Today when I have become more than aware of the powers of sex, as well as of the misuses of sex, I recall those seances with as much veneration and awe as I would bear at the direct presence of the Divine, or before a cobra alert with his hood swaying.

Of course, I knew which of the participants would be my 'seat'. I also knew how before assuming the seat I had to worship the *āsana* with certain special types of flowers, and rice grains, and also with blood, if available. In those days I could paint my forehead with hot sacrificial blood without any compunction. I knew how to draw the *maṇḍalas* for such special purposes. The use of various coloured powders in the *maṇḍala* had its own meaning and significance.

Before starting the rites I had to sip a special liquid. The quality was insignificant; but the effect was electric. As I sipped the liquid I did not care to notice if the pot was a jade, a bronze, a skull. Significance was more important than the material object.

The word *significance* is often used in whatever context possible. Specially, novices show concerned eagerness to learn (not the rites, or the things used but) about the 'significance' of the objects used, of the diagrams, of this, of that. *Significance* points out to a certain definite meaning, and no other. This means a very special treatment of a *mantra*, a word or a rite; even of ritual objects. Whenever the word *significance* is used, the aspirant is expected to absorb the meaning of the word, and rest the mind on that meaning alone in the abstract, and wrench the mind away from its mundane everyday meaning.

Yoni and Maithuna (*Coitus*)

Yoni as a word means the female organ, from which life springs out. In fact it signifies the *matrix*, starting point of a 'life'. This word in usage at once projects ideas, expressed as well as unexpressed, associated with the female organ, and coitus; and by extension of this image, the lurid use of this organ for the satisfaction of lust, which of course, is never satisfied. In reality, however and in the context of spiritualism, specially in tantra, this word almost invariably means the matrix, or the supposed fountainhead of life in general. As such it is indeed imaged as the matrix of the cosmic power of creation.

Imaging the cosmic in any sense has given man the gift of creating handy and helpful images: the lamp, for the sun; fire flames, for registering the gratitude of the Aryans of the cold nordic regions to the forests; water jar with leaves dipped within, for the bountifulness of rivers and rains etc., etc.

Images, delicate, sensitive, and eloquent images, form picturesque homages paid by the imaginative, the reflective to elements and forces of nature.

Since these phenomena are too big to be contained within the temples (symbols in themselves) built by man, the seer poets invent and accept a fittingly appropriate form to contain the big within a small indexive representation, or symbol. In tackling with the mighty forces of the cosmic, it becomes necessary to be toying with ideas, and capture the immense into the secured box of an index.

In imaging the matrix of all lives, or the cosmic law which gives us the primal form of the nebulae, man has stuck to certain pictures of which the most popular in usage are the furrow of the field, the pit for the fire sacrifice and the *yoni* itself (not always of the human female; but of any female for that matter). I am emphasising this because I want to impress upon the mind of all tantra enthusiasts that to the real adept in tantra, a *yoni* never projects the erotic image of coitus and lust. True it is that it takes a very long and hard-core training to arrive at this objectivity regarding *yoni*, and develop this reverential attitude to the triangle between the thighs of an *uttara-sādhikā* (*alter ego*), who is a female. It is then considered as a *pīṭha* (a seat for seancic meditation). (My personal initiation from the bodily approach of the Lady in Saffron has stood me in lasting grace; and I found, no difficulty at all whenever occasion arose, to approach this zonal reverence in the proper and exclusive spirit of tantra.)

To be in direct contact with the famale triangle. (I am deliberately not mentioning the female 'body'; for there is nothing physically responsive in the act of seance in tantra. Unless the triangle is approached as an *āsana*, a *pīṭha*, it should not be approached at all without singular peril to the efforts for spiritual realisation. The triangle in that case would be nothing other than one of the many paraphernalia associated with, and necessitated by the ritual of tantric *sādhanā*.) One has to undergo years of penance and practice; hard cruel excruciating processes of self-chastisement, self-denial.

Of the six passions living within the body, the first passion is the most demanding, elusive, tenacious and obdurate. Whilst it takes prenatal roots, it survives the decay with years of the body, as of the mind. Its embers flicker within the ruins of even a palsied body.

Naturally yogis, in order to be free from emotional handicaps, aim their efforts at gripping this powerful incentive, and engage its fire for loftier uses; for this power (the *serpent*, the *lhādini*, the sex) is the power of creative urge. It lies at the root of all progress, even spiritual progress, which supplies really the basic motor to all progress. Spiritual progress that does not involve universal progress is progress in name alone. It is an empty progress.

Mastering this power has been the aim of many yogis, many techniques, many clans in so many different ways; *Rāja-yoga*, *Karma-yoga*, *Hatha-yoga* etc., etc. But on all hands it has been accepted that the perilous (often self-deceptive) tantra way leads to the easiest and the most rewarding results, because the basic tenet of the tantra way has been joy, happiness and living in the fullness of life.

Because I was lucky, I was initiated to the female body directly through the blissful gift of an angel. The Lady in Saffron had caught hold of me when the implications of sex and of sexual pleasures had been a closed chapter to my boyish years.

Yet there came a time when I did realise a strange awakening in me. I realised that my body was undergoing a change. When at first I noticed (and she noticed) the stiffening of the organ, which hitherto never responded to the close, closest contact with the bushy triangle, the Lady in Saffron smiled; and made a funny remark. She at once explained to me that the change had to be overcome through complete concentration on certain details, like the touch of the skin of the loving old lady. "Touch and smell are two very important lead-guides to perfect *samādhi*", she said. "The senses are there to absorb the world in its gorgeous glory, but no more; the use of the senses has to be sternly restricted to the purpose of absorbing the supreme sublimity of the magic of creation. *Indriyāṇi indriārtheṣu*, as says the Gitā."

And then the contact became deeper, longer and more warm, though more trying. Long was the process; longer the seances until the body became redundant to all feeling, and an unbodied steadiness descended on consciousness transporting it to the realms of perfect peace.

Where was the body then? Where the stiffness? Where the triangle? Where male, where female? Only *ānandam*; only bliss.

And thereafter, this body has been coming into contact with many such triangles. Even when the *prakṛti* belonged to different age groups, it realised the same bliss. In tantra-*cakra* the most edifying and the most relevant *alter ego* is a virgin in her teens, when 'power' radiates at its highest intensity.

At time an immature sensuous *alter ego*, demanding secretly other things, and expecting other responses has miscalled her partner as limp, lame, disabled; but never in life, during the process of the spiritual tantra seances, when engaged in the rites, did this body falter, quiver, extinguish.

If it has not, then, the credit goes entirely to my heaven-sent mentor, my own dear Lady in Saffron, who had, through her self-sacrifice, guided me through the 'razor edge path' of the labyrinth known as *latā sādhana*. It is through her long long seances with me as her *alter ego* that she had made me familiar with the unfamiliar, accustomed to the uncustomary, intimate with the forbidden, and thereby made me grow with the area of social restrictions and moral taboo. Naturally, when later *alter egos* appeared in life, that area reminded me of the original blessed experiences. I wonder what would have been my fate, as it has been in many other cases of the sort, if that one *yoni pīṭha* had not blessed me with the embrace, the touch, the smell, the taste, the sight, as well as the sounds of the *mantra* which has been humming and humming through the long corridors of my life.

Yogis alone contemplate on the *yoni* as being the matrix, the source from where the cosmic laws and the cosmic power help evolve all that is created, inclusive of the mind's interrelation with the supra-mind, as well as the suppressed mind.

Maṇḍala is a diagrammatic representation of not only this source of life i.e., the *yoni*, or the matrix, but in certain cases such a diagram holds within its very carefully laid-out lines the entire lessons for the practice of *tantra* rites. It is a symbolic representation of *tantra* power. Indeed a *maṇḍala* could be described as a meditational lesson entirely illustrated.

Thus, merging in the joys of the *yoni* always signifies complete trance, or *samādhi*. Those who know Sanskrit very well would know how to account for and explain all those hymns, *mantras*, illustrations and sculptures which project not only the copulating duets, orgies of a number of men and women, but also those word pictures, word images, similes and metaphors, even entire legends (like *rāsa*, or *vastraharaṇa*) and lores pointing to sexual images. To the dilettante, the charlatan, the opportunist, the irreverent and the ignorant, tantra does appear, no doubt, as a profligate's horrid, diseased world, a paradise for degenerates and morbid perverts; but even if there were no tantra around us, such minds would continue to have their fill, and satisfy their lust and rut from the thousand other means which urbanised civilisation stocks for easy sale.

Never is the *yoni* 'as conceived by tantra' conceived as an apparatus for coitus. It is indeed unfortunate, and a whim in nature, that this organ is used for both ingress and egress of life; ingress of life in the seed form; and egress of life in the form of the living body. In tantra, the mystic congress carries the supreme and solemn importance of life's greatest, total and ultimate sacrifice. It is the dedication, nay, the complete annihilation of the maddening desire of sex exhilaration to man's negation of selfishness and ego. It is an acid test *par excellence*. Suspension of the erotic in physical existence grants the seal of entry into the sacred hall of everlasting ecstasy.

The tantra-yogins make nothing of the ingressing congress. Why?

Because in the ingressing process the incidental fact of casting the seed is totally eliminated; because in this congress there cannot be, and there is not any lust or excitement. As such, a penetration, in the physical and erotic sense, is impossible.

(I have heard from Lamaic adepts from Tibet that cases of withdrawing of any accidentally ejaculated fluid, if not common, is not entirely unknown.)

As I say this I could hear the caustic chuckle of the sceptic remarking with a guffaw that this kind of statement is mere rubbish, a midsummer effervescence, that such a state exists only in imagination; that this is incredible. I would not die to convince them. That is the duty of an advocate. But in modest humility I would ask them if conjuring great lines of art wonders, scientific invention, poetical sublimity is possible for the common and the sundry only because they are, or happen to be literate. Would they propose that every individual who has experienced sex is automatically fit for a *tantra*-congress? Does not the creation and execution of a thing of art appear equally incredible to the dud of intellect and blind of imagination? Where is there a 'norm' in sensitiveness? By being what they are, and achieving what they have achieved visionaries like Kalidāsa, Michaelangelo. Leonardo, Tagore, Goethe, Einstein have stamped our mundane world with the signet of beauty and eternity. Just by exclaiming, 'I am incapable of believing it,' the egoist is pervertly trying to impose a personal standard to measure what is beyond the capacity of an individual, specially of one without the least training for the subject. We are discussing here the hard core of an infinitely complex phenomenon, of a very mystic and specialised esoteric subject. To pass judgement in a cavalier fashion on the seriousness and solemnity of an involvement in which the best and the most disciplined minds of all times have participated, is definitely vulgar, even obscene.

Since in all tantra involvement the primary requisite prescribed and insisted upon is the elimination of not only lust, but of any personal gratification, mundane, physical or spiritual, the question of utilising *tantra* seances as places and opportunities for consummating the erotic hunger of the perverse does not arise.

Those who feel differently, cannot enter the *circle*, much less assume the all important role of the Queen, the *nāyikā*. (Let us remember that in the Kṛṣṇa lore, or history (whatever it is), Rādhā was the *nāyikā*.) So secret and important is the function of this all important esoteric role that in the entire Mahā Bhāgavata Purāṇa, which records finally all the acts of Śrī Kṛṣṇa, the name of Rādhā never occurs even once as a 'person'. She remains the mystery *nāyikā* without any personal identity. The impersonality is the hallmark of a tantric participation.

The tantra adept attaches so much importance to the details of the rites for these seances that in everything collected for the purpose, the central theme must remain the *yoni* (not coitus, though). The names of the flowers used, their shapes, colours and smells, the utensils and their shapes and sizes, the aromatics, the food and the drink, the time and the place selected, the *āsanas*, the companions, the hours of the seances, the zodiacal convergence in pin-pointing the time of the seance, all these have their technical import for the adept.

Dangers and the Two Ways

This is why tantra teachings are restricted to a personal guidance. These are never to be exposed haphazardly. This is for the benefit of the aspirant, as well as for the novice. A faulty seance is a dangerous thing. In case the seance cannot do good, it will do bad. Effect it shall have to have. 'Even a small portion of this *dharma* does not go *in vain. . . .*' Indeed it has its effect.

Those who are acquainted with the gipsy-hymns, ancient dryadic songs, ballads and legends of mystery coming down to us from times immemorial, know how the 'heroes' are warned about the legendary 'two ways': the short one is full of dangers, but the other, though easier, is a long one. Tantra takes the short one, and accepts the challenges of dangers wilfully. Tantra dares the dangers. A tāntrik is a *vira* (hero). That is why in tantra each success registered finds a hundred fallen 'heroes'. Charlatans are warned away from attempting this. It is dancing on the hood of a cobra; riding a hungry tiger. Hobnobbing will not do. Dilettantes, conceits and cynics beware!

The Dead is not Dead

Convinced of the truth on which tantra seances were based and blessed by the Lady in Saffron. I delighted in personal undertaking of a sort. Hence my adventures in the Tārā temple of Raṇi Bhavānī.

Here, in this temple I had witnessed around the year 1924 a terrible incident which has left since an indelible impression on my mind.

It was the dark fortnight's end; *Kārtik* the new moon night. The whole city was engaged in the lamp festival. Mother Kālī was being worshipped here, there and everywhere. I had made up my mind to spend the night in the Tārā shrine. I knew that for this night the Lady in Saffron shall be keeping her *āsana* on the ashes and bones of Maṇikarṇikā crematorium. So I had to be alone. I had taken courage, and groped within the dark passage to the temple. That passage was an abode of cold fear and damp creeps.

Let me narrate!

On that day I was alone. Seclusion had become a favoured companion to me. The Lady in Saffron was not near. But how far could she be from me?

A lamp was burning within the temple. A single lamp. And a woman was busy lighting a fire, assisting a big, dark and strong man obviously engaged in a tantra rite. His features and attire, specially the matted locks held by beads of the *rudrākṣa*, his red cloth announced his efforts. None had noticed me; but I heard him asking her in a rough voice to watch out. "I heard a noise. Someone is approaching. It is time they came . . . ."

The talk was incoherent. But who 'they'?

The *prakṛti* was young, and good-looking. But she too was wearing a red dyed silk cloth which kept rustling in the dark. She too had the *rudrākṣa* and the coral beads on. She came out and looked into the dark passage. In her hand was a vermillion painted trident, the infallible sign of the female counterpart in a tantra rite.

Soon enough I realised that I should be getting away from all that; but as she had been keeping a guard over the only passage, and as I could suspect the expected approach of others, I held my breath, and hung around the thicker part of the darkness amassed along the walls of the inner temple.

All thought of sitting at a long prayer had vanished. I was not really afraid; but I knew I was not normal. I was under a tension. The silent build-up of expectations of the unknown course of events had charged my nerves; and the abnormality of the situation kept my inner self on fire.

I heard people breathing heavily. Soon two persons carrying a load materialised from the mass of intense darkness of the passage. I knew them to be the undertakers, the 'Dom'-servants (Dom: a caste of funerary undertakers, guardians of dead bodies) of the crematory grounds at the Hariścandra Ghats.

The heavy load they had been carrying turned out to be a dead body. It was the first time I knew what it was to have a dead body as an *āsana*. I felt like a tiger on the smell of his quarry.

I noticed the lady asking them something. They were answering in affirmative.

"All ready? . . . . Sure? . . . . Any one noticed? . . . . Be careful . . . How do you know? . . . . All right. Uncover, and carry it in, and wait within the temple . . . You will also have to carry it back . . ."

The white mantled body was then carried within the temple. I remained still for about an hour. Then, when I knew everything was in place, I expected everyone to be engaged. By and by the ground would be clear for me to slip out, I hoped.

The great tantrik was totally nude. He was sitting on the chest of the cadavar with its face up. A fire was being nursed by two men, by which the lady was seated in meditation.

A Seantic Hush

Confronting the tantrik each of them was seated on either side of the sacrificial fire. They were sipping out of the same brass-lined coconut vessel. At about two o'clock in the morning (a brass gong from somewhere announced every hour and quarters) I became aware of some agitation, and the flames leapt up. The tantrik groaned. The woman, at this stage, put away the piece of cloth she was wearing, and lay flat on her back. The man, then spat on the face of the cadaver. Did it stir? I saw with my own eyes the seat, that is the body of the cadaver, rocking . . . rocking. Gently, but unmistakably. Then I heard a squeamish noise. But with the spitting, calmness prevailed again.

What I noticed then was quite unbelievable. Because I myself have been a witness, I could now say with certainty that it was no magic, no mirage, no kind of illusion. In fact and truth the scene which was being unfolded was actually happening within the dimensions familiar to us.

The lady lay flat on the ground, just beneath the raised platform on which the cadaver lay, and on which the yogi was seated. The corpse appeared to stir again, this time giving a heavy jolt to the man seated over it. He spat again into the mouth of the corpse; this time all over his face, or was it inside the mouth? Then, for a while, all lay still.

Then I saw what I still see. The yogi from his *āsana* on the corpse scattered rice and flowers over the female form. He took some of the water from his jug and sprinkled it over the dead body. A chant began to vibrate in the still warm air. No bat moved; no rat or mongoose frisked past. No lizard called. Even the spiders in their webs lay stilled.

Flame from Water

One of the men handed to the yogi a flaming brand from the fire-pit. He took this brand, and held the flame between the thighs, on the yoni of the female and fixed it there. Somehow it stood there in flames. The yoni, then covered with some of the rice and the flowers, suddenly leapt up into a bright flame. I could hear a hissing sound. The tantric went on pouring water from his jug into the fire. Instead of dying out the fire leapt up and up.

On a much later occasion on another night by the banks of the Ganges in Garh-Mukteshwar, where I had been camping alone for a month for penance, I had the good luck of witnessing a much similar rite.

I was occupying a solitary hut. By that hut there was another semi-permanent cottage of a boatman, who had become my friend and support for the time being. That evening he had gone out to visit his family in the village. I was alone.

Yet not alone. After midnight I became aware of some strange vibrations. I had read that a shark, or a sea hunting fish becomes aware of its possible prey through minute vibrations received through masses of water. What appears to be an apparent quiet stillness in nature discharges unfailing messages to the sensitive. The quiet is not so quiet.

I came out of my hut.

Imagine my surprise when I noticed a tall naked apparition standing waist high in the flowing river, and offering water collected in both hands. Ganges water was being offered to Ganges. Stream to stream.

So far all was correct, and understandable. But every time he threw the water a stream of flames leapt up from the spot where the water fell and illuminated the surroundings.

I was about to approach him. But something held me back. After a while as I tried to proceed, I saw the form gradually enter the river, and totally vanish under the water. The apparition was gone. Was it? Then how do I recall, and re-live in the experience? Nothing in experience goes out for ever.

I did not know him. But my boatman friend assured me that the saint had been known in those part over years and years. He came and went. But no one had been able to locate his dwelling, if he had any. He was accepted as a great saint. He has been of assistance to many distressed souls. But none has been able to see him face to face.

Pancamuṇḍī

Thus I was to witness for the first time a tantric act of offering water into a pit, and make the flames leap up. In this case the pit was provided by the triangular source of all biological life; verily the spring of life. The female *vidyā* or *nāyikā*, (as the *alter ego*, is known technically) lying flat on her back, with arms and legs closely gathered was receiving the homage while appearing to have been a mummified corpse.

I was sweating profusely. But the *mantra* was with me, the one I used to repeat at the *āsana* with the Lady in Saffron. In fact I was then thinking only of her, and with a deep concentration. My personal being appeared to be all too insignificant to absorb the eerie phenomenon.

Suddenly I witnessed a change in the posture of the tantric. He was no longer seated on the corpse. He was found seated on the body of the *vidyā* lying on the floor.

The corpse began to move to one side. No. The two men were pulling it away. They carried the body to a deep pit already dug out in preparation of this ritual, and laid it to rest there. Then they covered not only the yawning pit, but arranged, or should I say, re-arranged the sandstone flags over it very carefully.

At once I became aware that there had been buried within the pit four more cadavers of four different animals. The place now stood sanctified as a tantrik *pancamuṇḍī* (five-cadaver) *āsana*. Many tantrik aspirants of the future would receive assistance from this sanctified haloed seat, I thought.

After what seemed to me hours, the pair rose and sat in a close embracing sex-bond posture, the female seated on the lap of the male, face to face, embracing very tightly in the time honoured *Puṣpaka āsana*. We are acquainted with this posture from the Tibetan scrolls. A heavy breath hung around the morbid moisture-laden air in the sanctum sanctorum. The aroma of incense burning in the fire (no incense, to my notice, was actually thrown into the fire) solemnised the sense perceptions. My nerves were on ends. I could be knocked down with the touch of a feather.

Suddenly I felt alone. I longed for company.

Then it happened!

The Curse

All of a sudden the lady shook herself free of the strong clasps of the tantrik, and sprang up, and reached for her garments.

Some catastrophe had befallen, which broke the solemn spell. Something had gone sacrilegiously wrong. Some dark sin had torn the rites apart. With a hissing curse the lady darted apart. She was breathing heavily. Her round eyes spitted fire in the dark.

The tantrik gave a howl, and reached for the iron trident that stood near enough. At that point I looked for the two men who had been there. But they were nowhere to be seen. Now for the first time, I missed them. They must have gone away as soon as the burial had been finished. The night was at an end. Somewhere a gong was beating the four o'clock beat.

The tantrik rushed at the receding lady. He could have tried more successfully to hold the hell hounds. By now thoroughly aroused and agitated, the furious lady began to curse terribly. "Fowl evil-minded corruptor!! Demon of lust! Vile fornicator! Curse on you! Curse on you! Let Tārā's wrath fall on you . . . . " She continued as she tried to run away.

But try as she might, she could not get away. The heavy trident bit into the fleshy left loin; but fell with a clang on the stone floor immediately, it being too heavy to hold. Unconscious of the wound, and of the running blood, she ran past me. I sprang into the still deep mass of darkness hanging in the corner. Was I reaching to a situation? Should I try to save a stricken woman? Was I capable of the task? Who cared? I just sprang up. Then all was blank. I had fallen into a swoon. The last thing I remembered was the figure of the tantrik following her, and then, all was blank.

It was very late in the day. I was being lovingly nursed by the Lady in Saffron. I was already bathed. My clothes had been changed. I was lying in the yard of the Tārā temple. Obviously the Lady in Saffron had been at some rites herself for bringing me to my senses. Then we two walked out into the open. She did not say a word. I was too weak to talk. Silent, tired and all spent out, I followed my mentor.

Years after I have watched that woman strolling on the streets of Varanasi as a poor insane lost being. The sore on her buttock never healed. The mercury in the vermillion must have spread all over her skin. The sores on the skin, specially the condition of the tender flesh on her back and the breasts, made her completely forbidding to touch. Always bothered and pestered by hungry swarms of flies she remained an object of pity and scornful derision for the indifferent streams of onlookers that passed her, until one morning her lifeless body was found by the river side.

Twilight Maturity

The Lady in Saffron had by now taken me out of my growing boyhood. Carefully and efficiently she brought me to the threshold of my manhood. At this critical stage all growing minds must experience, with changes in the growth of the body, a strange lonelinees. It is a kind of loneliness which is created by an awe of disacceptance by an intolerant self-absorbed social circle. Inevitably all men have to pass through these years of exile into a 'no man's land', when the girl friends of yester year would look condescendingly upon a stripling youth as 'ungrown', and the male relations would leave the 'lad' aside as 'undergrown'. It is the twilight period of maturity.

The Lady in Saffron covered my entire world. So I was personally indifferent to the changes, as well as the reactions. I was still a 'boy', yet no longer a boy. I would have liked to live on my dream-foods, and set out on my wish-journeys. But the Lady in Saffron was a stern realist, who used to bring me down again to the level of the life that ran around us.

I was physically much too developed and stronger than boys of my age. Thus I was about to be introduced to the closed subject of sex relationship, sex draw, sex hunger etc. I watched how others around me were engrossed in what they called sex interest, sex play, sex relations. The subject of sex floated around me as mosses in a lotus pond, unasked, self-gathered, living, but clinging too close to my ethos with an abhorring sense of clamminess.

But sex never could possibly gain the frivolity of 'play' so far as I was concerned. The deeper education and involvement I had gained through the exercises that the Lady in Saffron had exposed me to, made it impossible for me to look upon the thing casually or emotionally. Sex was no 'play, for me. It was to me a sanctity named LS.

Every time my growing friends talked about it with secretive interest and adventurous excitement, my mind rushed to the haloed triangle of peace and tranquillity which I had been accustomed to approach with utmost reverence. Females and the female sex triangle meant for me my Lady in Saffron and the thoroughly enjoyable seances in her company.

I knew how to venerate that spring of life. It was an *āsana* for me. The deeply intimate forms of *āsanas*, such as *Ekadhārī*, *Puṣpaka*, *Jānuyugma*, the practice of which depended on sustained training, had now been quite familiar to me; and together with the Lady in Saffron I used to keep in meditation, locked for hours in her quiet embrace. A hitherto absent lustre had spread over my skin. A sheen had spread over my locks, which were worn long in those days. I used to take regular exercises in swimming, boating and wrestling. My body was healthy and disciplined, and my mind was alert to the lessons of my Lady in Saffron.

She had taught me a line in Sanskrit:

Nipita kāla-kūtasya Harasye-vāhi khelanam

(. . . it is like Hara, i.e. Śiva, immunised by the drink of cosmic poison, to be playing with a mere serpent!)

Today, as I am nearing the mile-post of an octogenarian, I realise how significant is that imagery. First train; then practise; then meditate and achieve. Only then one could survive in life, and share the fruits.

She had also explained to me the subject of sex in another way, in another context.

* * *

Near to our home an annual prayer to mother Kāli brought a number of children together. Usually members of close families overnighted there for about three days. This arrangement kept the family bunched together.

It happened during one of these annual events.

A Sex Lesson

Of course amongst us there were individuals of different built of different ages, different tastes, pursuits and urges. One of the girls, bigger than the rest, got into a close relationship with a boy. Most times they kept together. Obviously they were having fun in some intriguing way. It way the height of a June noon. Children were supposedly kept away from the dangerous glare and the hot winds. We, closetted in a room darkened by special curtains, were supposed to be taking a siesta in preparation for the long night ahead, when there would be a stage play in celebration of the gala Kālī-*pūjā*.

But the supposed 'rest' at the siesta was no rest at all. Indeed it gradually had grown into a warm active affair, which disturbed the required rest.

A boy squealed and a girl whispered; a girl squealed and a boy whispered. Something was going on between the two mentioned before, and we too were hungering to share the fun. But no. Both of them kept mum about it, and significantly exchanged sly smiles. There hung a curtain of mischief-making.

I got my niece, a confidant, aside, and directly asked her about the goings on. She swallowed several times before she could indeed confide that they had discovered a new game. Very funny, and very interesting. She assured me, if I promised dead secrecy on oath, I could be included in the game; she offered.

But when I got introduced to the game (!), I found no fun in it. The entire exercise was nasty and very boring. The cowardly aura of secrecy, and the constant fear of being found out then held for explanations, sapped away all fun from the game. Indeed what could have been the special gamefulness in just being close to and handling each others genitals? But the girls found it very funny, and the boys felt heroic, promoted to maturer ranks.

I consulted the Lady in Saffron. I clearly recall her analytical talk on the subject. She explained at length the different functions of the different limbs of the body, inclusive of the sense organs. It turned out to be a captivating solemn session.

Body is a Kingdom

Soon I understood this *body* as an instrument; and the instrument always was applied to and engaged in serving a *king* who lived within and away from the body, and yet controlled it. This king was the *mind.* It is never seen, yet it rules. It controls and orders all our actions through the *body*. It was a grand disposer of joy and sorrow, rewards and punishments.

Like all kings this king too has around him a cabinet of ministers. Some of these are seriously disposed, and act with a certain amount of responsibility. Some others are at times prone to be light-hearted and gay. Some like Śakunī and Karṇa (characters in the epic Mahābhārata) would push the 'king' towards evil consequences under the garb of fruitful advice; some like Kṛṣṇa and Vidura would always advise infallibly for good results.

The body is the kingdom; the mind the king. This king receives we thorld outside the body through the instrumentality of the senses. These senses are eyes, ears, nose, tongue and skin, with separate and exclusive functions such as sight, hearing, smelling, tasting and touching. There are other order carriers, or executive agents to the king, mind. These are the means of speech (with lips, palate, and teeth, as aids), hands, tongue, feet and the two excretory organs.

For living a given life, these functionaries are essential. Failure of any one, or more of them, makes the body-kingdom proportionately mal-functioning. It upsets the body balance. "You will note", she said, "sex or sex organs do not function as 'necessary' for just living our own lives. I have a sex organ; but it has now gone out of function. I am old. You have sex too; but it has yet to function. You are yet young and immature. You are like the seed of a green mango. It cannot sprout. It is not matured. Both of us have sex. In one it has ceased functioning; in another it is not yet matured. Yet both of us are living beings. This shows one thing. Sex is not essential for personal existence although as a power it wields on the creative urge of life a most telling and overwhelming influence. Sex as a power is quite a different field, and we shall have to deal with that later on. Here we were discussing the 'game', and the crude organs." And she continued.

Our individual lives, according to her explanation on that evening, could thus ignore sex; at least could survive ignoring it. But the other senses and active organs are essential.

Sex is essential for the continuity of life. The more exposed a life is to external dangers, the more does it multiply, and maintain thereby a natural balance. The idea is to survive despite the destructive forces. Thus insects, fish, birds etc., lay much more eggs in proportion to the number that survives. This is because of the exposed nature of their life patterns, and because of the odds they have to face. Before these lives could mature, many die out. Animals, in comparison, produce a less number. Man normally has one life born at a time, because in the case of man the chances of survival normally are very protected.

Yet again, and strictly speaking, the individual human life can survive without sex, i.e., the sexual act itself, or the 'game' in question. Hybrids have no sex, mules for example; the insect world is filled with sexless creatures, worker bees for example. In the human world too imbeciles and eunuchs, as well as saints, monks and nuns live a kind of sex negated life; so far as reproduction is concerned, they are restricted to spiritual creations. Thus many of them have left great works of art and philosophy. They failed, indeed, to propagate crude life; but in a more subtle and abiding sense they helped to propagate the cultural identity of man.

Therefore, sex organs, however powerful, must be regarded in human life as an additional aid for propagation of life alone; but the actual fact of 'living' could do without their use.

"We shall explain this further," she assured.

She classified the organs into two sets: the deterrant or the negative set; and the inspiring or the positive set. One has been called satanic, the other divine. Both work at the indication of the mind; and both leave, by their interaction, a certain permanent change on the mind such as happiness, or sadness. Happiness, inspires to create more happiness, and distributes happiness. Sadness spreads depression, and kills urge. It is the nature of wise men to cultivate those powers which make men happy, and spread happiness amongst men and life in general.

Smooth and effective functioning of physical organs is essential for the joy of living. Only the diseased think of unhappiness. Keeping a balance in using the organs for their function ensures good living. In other words, life must be kept natural. Nature wants us to remain natural; that is to say we must keep our balance with nature.

Keeping this balance depends on the balance of our desires. Our desires sweep us away from balance. Desires of the eye, of the ear, of the nose, of taste, touch and the eye takes one to see things that excite the nerves, and create more desire and imbalance. Taste creates greed for eating more, and makes the body fall sick; touch, likewise creates eagerness for embraces with other bodies, and separation from them causes grief. Grief, dissatisfaction, sickness, imbalances of all kinds result in depression, and depressions confuse good thinking; and with thinking disturbed, the beautiful human life withers in a wilderness of morbidity and destruction.

She then began to analyse further, and took up the subject she had promised to explain.

She pointed out that the urinary organs are chiefly meant for releasing the poisonous fluids from the body, as drains function in a house. The solid wastes of the body are discharged by the anal passage.

"You urinate", she explained, "through a tube. This tubic shape indicates the high degree of functional planning in nature. We know that tube-forms are the best for functioning as drains. I, a female, too have a tube to pass urine through. But there is a difference. Whereas the male tube shows, and is obvious, the female tube is not so obvious. It shows only its tiny head. Because it is tiny, delicate, tender and essential, it is kept secured between a pair of padded flesh, which protects this essential tube-head from infections. By and by I shall show that to you."

I insisted to know why then, there was a difference. The elongated exposed male tube, protected by a skin sheath, and the secret tube hid in an orifice.

I received the answer. "Never rush at knowledge. When you are sitting with a willing teacher, she would explain. You question only after the teacher has finished."

Now she explained that mere living is not, and cannot be, the ultimate objective in the life machine. Life machine is a part of the world machine. It must have a purpose.

"Purposeless creation is an anathema to life. Nothing in nature is purposeless. Even if we do not see the purpose, we must have the humility to acknowledge that we do not know everything. The secret of knowledge has not been finally gained. God is manifest knowledge. The subject and object of the finality of knowledge is what we call God. God is manifest; and God is also a mystery. Purpose is inherent in knowledge. Knowledge without purpose is waste. This world, this creation is not a waste. It is too beautifully, too perfectly, too organisedly and accurately created to be described as a waste, or the result of a whimsical sequence of events. One of the names by which the title of God has been expressed is *ṛta*, which means the cosmic order. The Vedas did recognise this plan, discipline or order in creation.

"We, men, are destined to find out this purpose. To find out, and having found out to apply ourselves in fulfilling that purpose. The first stage in this quest is called *tapasyā*, discipline leading to realisation; and the second is called *yajñā*, or sacrifice. *Tapasyā* teaches one to prepare for sacrifices. Without sacrifice the purpose of the world shall never be fulfilled.

"As life must discover the mystery of the ultimate use of life, so life also must discover the most skilful way of utilising the body as a machine for achieving the purpose. At the application stage this body, not entirely without the mind, is necessary.

The Tussel of the Three Śaktis

The desire to achieve this releases a secret force. This is the spiritual force or the *sattva-śakti*. But as every force meets its equal and opposite force, this force too is dragged back by a sluggish inertia of negativeness, and forms the *tamas-śakti*.

"These two are always at loggerheads. And the more they pull at each other, the ensuing friction automatically releases a third power, or *śakti*; this is the *rajas-śakti*.

"The *sattva* is striving to function as the most helpful servant of the king (mind); but the *tamas* would have none of it, and must keep *sattva* away from the King's counsels. It is a force of detraction. Mind suffers this tension.

"Mind is thus a powerful agent to make the organs function. Mind must keep steady in order to keep the organs steady. Mind must know its tract, and follow it. When mind is detracted, *tamas* takes a hold, and destruction ensues.

"One of the chief and easy incentives to this detraction is released by which is also a important incentive to creative urge. In fact this urge relates to the power that maintains the perpetuity of life.

"It is very obvious that life-current has to be maintained. 'The strand of life must never be severed', says the Vedas. For this the creative urge has to be guided along the right lines, or the *sāttvik* lines. But this creative power, *sṛṣṭi-śakti*,or the sex power, easily falls under spell of temptation and misuse.

Sex: The Lhādinī

"Sex, like the mind, is not an organ by itself, yet like the mind it exerts all over our personality a telling influence. It is the *sṛṣṭi-śakti* (creative force), or *lhādinī śakti* (joy force). There is a joy in creation. 'Creation has sprung out of joy', says the Vedas.

"Sex as a power agitates the body machine. This power gives meaning to all we see, hear, breathe, touch, eat, drink and enjoy. Sex thrills us, inspires us, and by inspiring creates. It creates life, art, poetry, dance, literature. And so creating, creates joy, ecstasy, and enlivens life with a motivation.

"When kept under control this power fills life with beauty, sweetness and appreciation. This power bubbles with glee for finding a fitting expression, and extends the area of joy. This power offers our body as a profound sacrifice to the joy of the Lord, and our soul is lifted up as a flame offering to the Ulṭimate. By willingly burning it, as is incense burnt, or a candle set alight, we pay our homage to the Supreme Lord of life, or to life itself, if you prefer it that way.

"But when let loose, uncontrolled, and allowed to run wild, this very power would bring disgrace and destruction not only to the self, but also to the world around. It has the natural proneness to multiply. If it does not multiply joy in joy, it would multiply sorrow and grief, in sorrow and grief. It tempts and bemuses thinking, so that what man seeks and embraces as sources of joy and pleasure, finally could turn out to be the sources of utter despondence, frustration and morbidity, which is a dangerous mental disease.

"Like all sources of power, e.g., gas, oil or coal within the bowls of the earth, the earthquakes, the storms, the tides, the currents, steam, electricity etc., this power too could not be repressed and forgotten. No power could be eliminated. The sky, the water, the solar heat, the air cannot be eliminated. These could be misused or used; kept pure or get contaminated and polluted. When kept in order, and put to the use of life, they become the greatest friends of life, otherwise, worst foes.

"Sex is the mother of life. We call it the *Mother*, *Śakti;* (*icchāmayī*) the wishful one, the *will*. This we worship as the *Mother*. Misused and squandered, even love becomes lust; power becomes tyranny; joy becomes orgy and debauchery. Multiplication of life, an unavoidable duty of life to life, becomes a threat, a menace, and causes hunger, want, famine, war by causing over population. Over population is the curse of the *Kali-yuga* (Dark-age). And the source of it all is the misuse of *sex-power*, the *mother-power*. This is why we worship this power, and seek divine blessings for keeping it under control and discipline, so that we could handle this power with propriety and understanding, control and peacefulness; else we could become exposed to greed, passion, squander-lust and drunkenness. As a result we hunt for more and even more, and get lost in a nerve shattering wild goose chase.

"Nature is a benign and infallible force. Throughout the natural world all animals multiply; but the animals or insects never go against their seasonal call, neither do they look for lust. Animals, insects, birds and fish act exactly as nature wanted them to act and behave. That is why there is a balance in the nature-world. Many animals have become extinct through the forces of hunger and greed of man. Man alone disturbs the balance of nature. The *Mother-power* is disturbed and agitated by the misdeeds of man's hunger, and lust. That provides the meaning all the more to our concern for praying to the *Mother-power*.

"This is our *cit*, *lhādini*. It is the power that inspires consciousness, discrimination, joy, creativeness. Creation is joy expressed. A creation in art is an expression of divine joy. Destruction is joy repressed, and hate expressed. One is a divine joy, the other is a demoniac glee. One is progressive, and pro-god; the other is regressive, and anti-god.

The Nāḍī

"The mechanism of joy is very subtle. Some part of it is known, and most part is unknown. So far as the known part of the mechanism is concerned we know that throughout the animal body there spreads, like telegraphic and wireless systems of receiving and transmitting messages, a system of nerves. We call them *nāḍīs*. We control the known parts of this system by a discipline and exercise known as yoga; and when we get success in the yoga system, and gain the know-how of the sources of joy and consciousness, then from this known part we gain entry into the secrets of the unknown parts of this system.

"Again, for this we need the blessings of the *Mother-power*. Why? Because, as has already been explained, the *Mother-power* is the source of all our *consciousness;* this power is the *cit-śakti*. And this power is most active in the vital phenomenon of the birth of life.

"Contrary to common belief, this organisation of the body and nerves is responsible for producing the higher grades of life. One could thus plan to have healthy, conscious and vibrant children who could prove to be more conscious and more powerful than others. The best of the species is a product of conscious effort. It is the contribution of regulated, and disciplined use of the power of reproduction. And for this we pray.

"Prayer becomes an exercise of the submission of the worldly-self to a subtle cosmic-self; it sees without eyes, hears without ears, feels without skin etc., and distinguishes and analyses. In so doing it builds up personality, strengthens determination and fortifies self-reliance.

The Power System: The Nerves

"The common man cannot always pray effectively, yet he needs this power the most. How to help him?

"For supplying water to the common man we arrange to collect it before distribution, through the civic arrangements of the water works. Underneath the organisation of the civic authorities we supply power to all homes. This also looks after the other amenities of life. In the absence of power, life would suffer.

"Much in the same way certain human beings undertake the task of building up a 'power' source. Once the power is acquired, it goes to serve the needs of the common man. Men, or women who collect this power to serve are called the yogis. They preserve within themselves, as in a power reservoir, the power of helping mankind, so that man could act in the way they are expected to act. Hence the yoga system, and the yogis.

"This accumulation of 'power', and its distribution depends on yogic discipline, which, in other words, means the direct control of the nervous system, i.e., of the *nāḍīs*.

"The *nāḍī*-system is generally divided into three main parts:

(a) *nāḍīs* which carry outer messages in; (b) *nāḍīs* which distribute the inner messages, reactions to the different limbs for their respective actions; and (c) a third set which acts by remaining 'asleep' that is, by 'not acting'. It does not, and might not act; but it drives others to act. Of the three *nāḍīs* (bunches of nerves) the one asleep is *suṣumnā*, which, when wakened, awakes all i.e., *awake* in the spiritual sense. The other two are *iḍā* and *pingalā*. These two absorb sensations, receive and sort them out; and having done that, function as demanded and directed. But once the *suṣumnā* (the 'sleeping one') is aroused, the Unknown reveals itself. A new world with new dimensions becomes known under the full bloom of the lotus consciousness and Light.

"What kind of a world could be this that men, though very few, are driven to? Great minds, wealthy beings, powerful persons have been known to sacrifice comfort, safety even thrones in order to achieve this power and enter this new realm. What does it hold for men?

"It holds for men the best of all that men have been seeking all the time, down the history of human quest and achievement: joy, tranquillity, peace, freedom from want, mastery over the trickeries of the mind.

"It is a world of the fourth dimension, where limits do not thwart, restrictions do not hamper, fear does not retard, hopes are not frustrated. It is the world where the realities of all hopes find their fulfilment; where doubts melt into truth, like fog melting in the sun.

"By the grace of the designer of the human system it is a surprising fact that the scurce of *sı ṣı mnā* is set closest to the nerves which act as reproductive organs. The urge to create, to make life in life, to build up the seeds for life and cast the same in the field meant for this purpose, depends on certain nerve points, or glands; and these points are based closest to the organs which are used for excretory functions.

"Let us at this point take a quick bird's-eye view of what has been said. It is necessary at this stage to note all over again what factors act as 'aides' to create life.

"We must realise that it is life alone that could create life. It is a natural duty of life to propagate life. If life did not create life, it would perish. But total destruction is contrary to nature. Nature intends perpetuation of life. For the creative process body is the mill, the factory, the instrument. The body is wonderfully fitted and equipped to carry out this function.

"We all know that all factories and mills have to depend on a supply of some power for driving them. There must be a source of power which supplies the required energy. Beside this energy there is something else on which the correct functioning of the machines depend. This is the personal factor; the mind factor. A master-mind constructs a master plan, and sets it on motion, depending on an assured supply of energy, or power. Man master-minds a machine, joins it to power, and then produces.

"In the body machine too the requisite power for this function is supplied by, what we have already known as the *lhādini-śakti* (sex-power). It is the basis of all our creative urge.

"All power comes from some kind of fuel. Fuel reserves hidden power. The body's fuel is food. Food could be derived from the vegetable world, or from the animal world directly. The perpetuation of the vegetable world too depends on seeds. Seed alone, unaided, could not spring into life, although it stores the prospect of life. Seed, for springing into life, requires other aids, like helpful soil, correct weather, and timely seasonal aid from nature.

The Seed: The Gāyatrī

"We have rounded now a full circle. From the fuels in nature, to the soil, the seasons, the seed; everything finally depends on the solar energy, the sun. This is why we the Hindus regard the *Gāyatrī mantra* (which is an invocation to the power in the sun) as our greatest heritage in spiritual concentration. This sun power comes from the space as seasons and rains, and from the earth as soil, soil-heat, minerals and water. All is finally the sun power. All is *Śakti*, the Mother's warmth.

"Thus, earth, water, heat, air and the atmospheric or cosmic conditions are vitally essential for the correct type of fruitful germination. It is easy to detect and observe that none of these could be created by man power; and certainly not the power within the seed. No seed could be artificially created by man power. This is a gift from the unseen and the unknown alone.

"Seed given, man could sow it how, when or where he likes. But that is all. Like earth, water, heat, air and atmosphere life too is beyond the limited power of man. Man cannot create the elements; and man cannot create life. Neither can man guarantee the life-span.

"Nature creates this seed. We need seeds as gift from nature for the perpetuation of life and vegetation, and all that perpetuates from life to life. Seed is therefore the subtlest container of the essence of the solar energy. It must naturally be alive with a tremendous store of energy. The power stored in a seed is fantastic. You must have noted that great and well-built stone walls crack to pieces by the force of a seed of fig; the plant envelopes a building, and crumbles it like a biscuit within its root grips. The entire city and stone constructions of the famed Angkor Wat is being crushed by the grips and claws of the roots of giant trees. The seeds of these trees are sometimes smaller than spider eggs.

"But this seed has to be cast. It has to be cast from a body to the soil. Body is the tree bearing the seed of life. There the seed matures, and becomes fit to be cast. Once the seed is matured, the body, or the tree, finally realises that the time for casting the seed has come. Urged by natural power, the parent body takes joy in casting, and feels relieved. It were as if a duty fulfilled. It is life's fruition.

"But for casting and fruition a proper selection of appropriate soil has to be made. Seed cast in unprepared and unfit soil would not bear the best results, or even worse,—there would be no result at all.

Adoration of the Triangle

"Body too has its season. In season the soil gets ready. This soil is provided by that body which we call the female body. When this female body is ready to germinate, it notifies by letting out a flow of blood that like a river flows between the outer world, where the blood is noticed as a welcome indication, and the inner world within the body, which is called the embryo.

"It is natural for those interested in life and in the planter of life to be thankful to this soil, this flow, this extra heat that energises the body to receive the gift of the seed. It is quite understandable and expected that thinking people, whose thoughts always look into the spirit of a phenomenon, should adore this great gift from nature. Who would be grateful for a barren land, a wasteland, a land without the gifts of a flowing river, or sun and rains?

"In the human body this field, this source from which life springs out a new life, is the female genital organ which is situated very close to the urinary tube, and the sex glands that are placed at the root of the main three bands of nerves that run through and around the spinal column. We have already described all that before. Have we not?

"We try to take control of this entire area of Power through practising the tantra yoga, which accepts a spiritual view of life here, and beyond through the able use of the life in this body. Thus the tantra yoga is regarded as attached to the material view of life, without, of course, ignoring its spiritual possibilities. This is why we adore this area, this triangle; and by practising yoga in close contact with this area we try to understand, control and absorb this power, the sex power, the *bīja* power, the *lhādinī śakti*.

"But the soil by itself, however fertile and receptive, fails to produce without the help of the proper and healthy seed. If the seed itself is lacking in full vigour of healthy maturity, germination is bound to suffer. This is why we had occasion to mention that like the elements, man by himself or herself alone cannot create life. In creating life the mere sex act, or togetherness, or even casting is no guarantee for success.

The Seed

"This seed matures within the body of a male. All lives spring from the seed. This seed has to be cast into the female soil, where there is a proper cradle to receive the seed, and keep it in heat for gradual development through the vital powers that the body preserves for this purpose. This is the period of germination when life is allowed to grow and take root.

"We have described the body as a machine; but we have also mentioned that this machine, unlike its material prototypes, has a mind. This mind is subject to the fluctuations of emotions. Because the functioning of the casting of the seed into the prepared soil is regarded as a happy event, joy is a contributory factor in the creation of life. The female body may be in season, and the male body may have the seed, but the urge of working together may be lacking. They might be reluctant to function; afraid to function. They might be acting under secret reservations, inhibitions, even obsessions. Joy cannot be enforced on a being. It must effuse and gush from within. A Joyous union of the powers alone could result in creating a joyous life. A healthy seed alone could express this uninhibited joy in its final product.

"This duty of creating a joyous climate is essentially human. Human life alone can reach the subtlest apex of all emotions. The driving factor in human life displays the emotions with profit and taste by keeping the instinctive drive under careful control. Animals other than human beings, and the insects are mainly dependent on instincts. Not so man. In man instincts are kept beautified by an emotional aura. *Lhādinī* in man thus creates things of beauty; and the resultant crafts express joy, and invite others to share in that joy. This, men cultivate as a special power.

"Those who undertake the joyous duty of cultivating emotional fields are called the cultured in contradistinction from other types of animals. When a horse displays his skill, a monkey, a lion or an elephant performs in a circus, and gives joy, a pet gives companionship and responds to emotions, they spread joy. To that extent they too are cultured, civilised. Having control over instinct and emotion is to be civilised.

"The seeding and cultivation of life in the human beings, therefore, should not be left to the instinctive urge alone. The emotions involved in a union between the male and the female human beings, in order to be fully relished, must be trained to cause joy all around, without making any one concerned in any way unhappy.

A Happy Union

"A happy union of the two human beings engaged in the joyous function of creating a life presupposes a cultured training that keeps runway emotions under control; and the fire of passion within desired limits. For attaining a direct control over the sex-power, and put it to the heaven-designed natural bonds we sit at the feet of the *Mother-power*.

"There is a crime known as rape. It is a grievous sin. A crime is adjudged in a social court; a sin is adjudged within the perpetrator's inner sanctuary where dwells peace. Rape as a crime forces against one's will an act of joy and duty. It also causes, through uncontrolled indiscretion, ugliness, humiliation and sorrow. Nature guides and moulds, but never compels. To compel to act under force or duress is to rape. The rapist forgets this truth.

"The seed to be cast into the warm flow, on which the female egg floats, has to maintain, for proper incubation, a given temperature, which is determined by the body reflexes. The direct casting of this seed from body to body is the safest way to help it germinate healthily. This seed is susceptible to damage unless it is cast directly. It is so subtle that it records even the emotional state of the two at the time of casting. This emotional state at the time of casting should, therefore, be free from complexes, such as anxiety, fear, shame, retardation, greed, lust and mindlessness. Seed cast by a divided mind could yield neurotically damaged life. Seed nursed within a hesitant or unwilling embryo could equally damage a peaceful normal growth. *Lhādinī* in either case has *not* been pleased. Unless this willing joy is secured, it is likely that the growth of the seed will be affected, and the life it assumes might have to bear the load of blighted emotions. This is extremely dangerous, and is filled with ugly risks. The union of bodies shall have to be between two completely healthy beings, with complete understanding and willingness, so that the union produces a feeling of fulfilment of a divine purpose served, of a joyous act brought to its natural end.

"Because this seed has to be kept warm and healthy, it has to be directly cast deep into a warm channel where the egg waits. The male body has been provided with a syringe like organ. Besides draining out the fluids of the body through urine, this organ also acts as a syringe for injecting or casting the seed into a channel where the warmth is kept up through a fluid, that the mature and prepared female partner discharges, and that carries the seed to its final destination for correct germination. This protective state is known as the embryo. A new life starts drumming within an embryo with the casting of the seed into the floating egg.

"This is again the reason why the shape of the male organ is like a long syring, and why the female organ is a close lipped crevice within which the warmth of the life fluid is kept closely guarded at a given temperature. Everything must be prophylectic, inclusive of the mind, which should be the purest of the pure.

Drive for Joy

"This simple act of casting the seed would be too mechanical and boring unless there was the added drive for joy. This union of understanding and love is joy. Joy is the drive, the foundation of life. If this joy is lacking, if this situation is forced, covered by a curtain of secrecy, a sense of guilt, if this situation is clouded with overcast emotions and gloomy currents of anti-thoughts, of course the act of natural joy shall be loaded with senses of guilt and corruption, and kill all joy. That which kills joy is a sin. Joy should be known as joy by being universally acceptable as joy, and by producing further joy.

"You see how early in civilisation the human beings of a certain part of the world discovered the connection between life propagation, joy and the need of control over this joy. Because this propagation was so closely connected with the propagation of health and joy, those people of the ancient times also discovered the forces of self-control, and education in this power of sex. They knelt before this power, prayed, and brought their highest and most precious gifts to be offered to this power, and called it *Mother*. They worshipped this power. To consider this to be anything other than a natural expression of devotion and honour is to express a sad want of spiritual humility and cultural control.

"Our *āsanas*, our seating close together, our methods of meditation are all very closely connected with the sublime task of developing a correct attitude towards the mystery of life. *Lhādinī* as a power should not be confused with the powers of lust and debauch. Familiarity to the secrets of creation, and to the correlated areas of body and mind that aid the creative urge, proportionally reduces the feelings of romantic urgency, uncontrollable passion and sinful surmises. By reducing excitement, and monitoring the urge, the knowledge of *lhādinī* and the function of creativity, together, becomes a normal achievement of joy and fulfilment. The difference between the sources of real joy and ecstasy and the sources of lust and greed is the difference between heaven and hell, god and anti-god.

Worshipping a Nāyikā, a Yoni

"In tantra, and tantra *āsanas* our organs, our body-being, come close to each other's intimate and fully aroused conscious being. Thus we discipline our mind and body to regard these seats of joy and power in their abstractions. Remember that in tantra a *nāyikā*, a *Bhairavī*, a *vidyā* an *alter ego* is also worshipped as a *mother*.

Lustful behaviour is quite unimaginable in this context. The day is near when the very idea of a female would arouse in you the sentiments of having seen the Mother in the human form.

"When you become a man, and accept the life of a 'householder' (*gṛhastha*) you will observe things around the society you will live in, and find out how often does a wife suffer rape from a husband. The result is a broken heart, a damaged love, and a ramshackle make-believe home. All this need not happen if men could once believe that like all other education an intimate and practical knowledge, a tantra-bound knowledge of sexual behaviour is absolutely unavoidable. Few, if ever any, realise that such knowledge is neglected at the risk of missing the best promise to human life, viz., the joy of creativity. Let the detractors bark around the *yajñasthala* (the sacrificial altar); they too suffer and live in hell. The only salvation lies through an acceptance of the *Mother* as a benign *Śakti*.

Ignorance of Tantra

"The tragedy of modern existence is that men enter this most important, vital area of life without ever developing the correct attitude to life, home, woman, sex, *yoni*, lingam etc. By keeping most of this in the dark, man has deprived himself of the peace and nobility that is inherent in the duties of a householder.

"Tantra enjoins on the participant a severe course of discipline. Most of this discipline is addressed to life, here and now. But because of a sudden outburst of a negative philosophy, and its popularity through the unfortunate and unreal preachings of religious *maharajas* and *swamis*, society's interest in religion has undergone a morbid change. The interest in life as it is 'here' has shifted to the life that is promised 'elsewhere'. Too much of metaphysics has put out the light of truth, as too much of wood chokes out the flame of the fire-place.

"There is no 'elsewhere' in tantra, which conceives life as an infant in its mother's lap. The image is significant and purposeful. The Hindus image Gaṇeśa-Jananī, the Mother, in whose lap the *gaṇa* or the 'people' i.e., life, survives. How close to this concept is the image of the Pieta, the Madonna of the Christian church. It is the matrix where all genesis begins; the *yoni* of the nebulae. That exactly is the image of the Mother whose grace blesses life here and now.

"The breast of the Mother is the perennial source of sustenance, and the *yoni* of the Mother is the perennial 'source' for evolution of universal lives here. She is the matrix; the alpha of the process of genesis.

In this image survives the concept of the *kumārī mātā*, the virgin mother.

"This sublime idea is better stated in the language of tantra; and the attitude of tantra to the world flux is aimed at supporting this sublimity. The physical part of the Mother which sustains and maintains life is the *stana*, the breast. The Sanskrit root for the word *stana* (breast) means 'to grow from more to more'; to develop. And the other part, or limb of the same Mother, the expression of the same *śakti*, which prennially projects streams and streams of new lives, new thoughts, new products of art and intellect, new worlds, new universes—is called *yoni*, the triangle that tantra worships. That faith in tantra rests on this attitude, this belief.

A Practical View

"Tantra does not waste its efforts on the other-worldliness of life; it actually educates, and then trains man to be prepared best for the life as it ought to be faced and lived. Looked from this point of view you would not find it difficult to appreciate my interest in you. I am determined to bring the best out of you, as I expect that there are forces within you, which, when developed and brought out, would do a lot of good to the society you will come in contact with.

"A trained attitude towards life, a deeper appreciation of life, and an education about life would turn a man into a proper householder.

"He would be able, then, to live it so well that death would pose no problem for him. He would leave life, when the time comes, in great peace. You see that a correct appreciation of tantra has to bestow automatically the benefits of the next life. Take good care of this life, the benefits of the next life would automatically follow as night follows day, and day follows night.

"Death being the gate to enter into the next life, peace at the threshold of entry is essentially imperative. Tantra gives that.

"The importance of the knowledge of the mysteries of tantra could be understood in depth through an episode in the life of Ādi Śankara, the great Śankarācārya. Let me narrate it once again even if you have heard it. Legends are great teachers of esoteric truth.

The Change of Śankara

"In the course of his zealous efforts to bring all thinking giants of the land under one banner he finally approached the intellectual wonder of the time, Srī Manḍaṇa Miśra (who was later on known as

Swamī Sureśvarācārya, and who had a considerable following of his own). He was a householder, and he believed in the *dharma* of the *gṛhastha.* He was married to an equally great lady of beauty, learning and love. Ubhaya Bhārati, the wife of Maṇḍana, stood firmly between the two opposite objectives: Śankara's objective of giving Miśra the vows of a *sannyāsin*, and her firm desire of keeping her husband to the path she knew as the correct one for a married man.

"Śankara had to face this lady in debate; and at once she broached the subjects of the secrets of tantra, and the powers of *yoni*, as well as its immense significance. She talked of the contributions of love and sex in moulding life and society, and asked Śankara if he was speaking from theoretical erudition alone, or from a *realisation* of life as it has to be practically lived. She challenged the young debatee, if he had any experience of a woman's love as a power. She asked if his mother had blundered in bringing him to the world, or if she herself is wrong to have adored motherhood.

"Śankara was confounded by the directness of the learned lady's approach, and begged for sometime to get himself further educated along the line. When he returned to the scene after spending a long year in the society of a woman in luxery, he had visualised the nobility and grandeur of life as an aspect of Grace of the *Śakti* that inspires and conducts it. Although Miśra came under the immediate spell of young Śankara's call, Śankara himself gradually became an adept in tantra, and his hymn on the Mother (*saundarya-laharī*) stands unto this day as one of the most treasured esoteric pieces ever written on tantra practice. Nowhere else has the sublime *Śrī-yantra* been described with so much fervent feeling and depth, yet so beautifully. It is a grand piece of literature.

"If ever you find time, go, visit the great shrine of *Śrī-yantra* of Śankara's adoration in Courtallam in south India, in Śiva-Kancī, and in Śṛngeri. Meditation in one of these *pīṭhas* could spark vibrations of consciousness, which could benefit you, which could surprise you. (I did visit Courtallam, more than once. That experience has been recorded later.)

"Tantra encourages life. Tantra expects man to live in the fullness of life. But tantra also expects our life to be disciplined. Discipline gives direction. For enjoying a well directed life, man must stand with humility before the Grace of Śakti, the Mother. In that single truth lies embedded all the truth and mystery of tantra. Mother is the core of tantra, inclusive of the roles that these mystic *āsanas* play.

To bring in eros in such a context, in such forms of exercise and practice, is to condemn poison in spite of its ability to cure. Never see the Mother in parts. She is *yoni,* the ultimate, where we all vanish at the end of the life span, and the genesis where we all begin our physical existence. The Mother and the *yoni* together is the alpha and the omega of this education."

7

Voices from the Void

Joy of Sex

My introduction to sex life through the chance instrumentality of that relative of mine and her boy-friend offered to me a heaven-sent opportunity to welcome a new knowledge directly, from the Lady in Saffron. I could not have expected a better start with this complex field of knowledge. Her own exposed body explained much to me. Her correct emphasis focused a new light around a hitherto mystified area held out of bounds. The supreme importance of life's involvement with sexual powers gradually unfolded itself. Since that time whenever I had to face in life any situation conducive to physical sex participation it was impossible for me to regard these organs in any light other than sources of a profoundly laid out mysterious base of power. I still stand convinced that disciplined sex contributes to matured life the same urge and energy as a mother's milk does to the life of a growing infant, both being sources of the Mother-power.

I became convinced; and with the years the conviction grew, that the power of libido, *lhādinī*, guides the sex urges through creative channels. It creates joy; and joy sustains it. This power opens up a vista of joyous atmosphere; opens up a spirit of loving understanding, and self-submission; and brings the mind to bear willingly the treasured onus of humility in love. True love glorifies itself through wilful submission. To this mysterious power the human soul brings the highest homage; and the body offers the supreme sacrifice; and life itself through this sacrifice reaps the harvest of life. We know this to be a great *yajña*, where death and life play together for the achievement of continuity. In this *yajña* pain becomes pleasure, and pleasure offers itself to pain. If life is defied by death, death, in a sense, is also defied by this power of sex.

As time passed, my understanding of the *worship* of this power, indeed of the triangle, (and through the triangle of the world of the female charm) became clearer. An attitude of deep respect towards the female was gradually tended by my loving mentor; as a result I could not regard these areas of the body with scorn, condemnation, or even secrecy. On the contrary I viewed this power with the highest regard and awe that life reserves for the source of life. Because I had accepted, and I have been known to accept this regard for libido, or the power of the *lhādini*, with a religious veneration, I have also known to regard woman as an expression of joy, as well as of a source of mysterious power.

Not the Sinner

All of us are, when not fully aware of our responsibilities, prone to act irresponsibly. This accounts for our excesses in this area. But we commit excesses in other areas too, e.g., in the choice and quantity of our food, drink, sleep, need, possession etc. The harm does not lie in what we do, but how and how much we do it. The knowledge of the limit alone is not enough; the power to draw a line, and to be able to call a halt before the limit has been reached, has to be acquired. And this is acquired through understanding, analysis, care, practice and above all through the development and cultivation of the correct attitude towards these.

This is why, I have never been able to condemn a woman for her 'fall', or a man for his 'sin'. I have never felt myself competent enough to play the high and mighty role of the self-righteous. Such a false attitude has not been able to influence my thinking, or cloud my 'love' for humanity. The very idea of a 'fall', or that of a 'sin' is supposed to dislodge the esteem of a man for a man.

Dislodge from what? Dislodge from where to where? Is there any place outside of the Grace of that Power of Life? That Power of Love? If the entire universe is charged and saturated with the power of the Mother, how could I conceive of a 'fall' from her? Does that not sound absurd?

This was a supreme test for me. After I gained this understanding, things gradually started to explain themselves to me. My personal life rhythm underwent a complete change, I came to be convinced that I worship and adore the *triangle* because I belong to it, much as a child belongs to its *mother*.

What I Owe to the Mother

I could not view this mechanism of life's supreme source of joy, of creative urge, in a spirit of flimsy delight, sporting curiosity, temporary diversion from boredom, or hunger for mere erotic excitement. I felt all these attitudes depressingly negative, and in the final analysis, extremely damaging to the balanced development of a man's personality.

(In life, as I happened to have to swim through an ocean of humanity all over the world, I recall, and recall with great satisfaction, that I have been able to save a number of drowning and drowned souls by a simple exposure and analysis of the facts of the situation with a calm vigour and a searching touch of love and sympathy. Sympathy of man is essential to befriending a situation from where a brother could save a brother. Are we not the sons of the same Mother? But have I not saved myself from many a trying situation, thanks to the conviction about this Power.)

To me this functionalism of the life process was a positive endowment kept apart by the life force. It is a life which fulfills its ultimate objective by stimulating, cultivating and achieving the true purpose and meaning of joy in life. This force is the 'mother' of all joy.

The *Mother*, the *lhādinī*, is the power that thrills and inspires. It overflows life with joy and joy alone. A saint is he who spreads love and joy. The balance is itself too famished to be able to propagate a communion, to produce ecstasy, to overcome grief and suffering with the powers of love. Hence life is embedded in the Mother; and the Mother is involved in life. To be living is to owe to the Mother's grace.

This is divine. This is Nature's; this is natural. This is straight, and therefore this is called *ṛta*. This is also why we worship the Sun, Fire, Air, Water and the great Atmosphere filled with ether which is a cosmic blessing. We call these (together or singly) *pratyakṣam Brahma:* yes, these are the *pratyakṣam*, directly realisable, *Brahman*, the all pervading power. We realise the supreme, the ultimate through these primal, never ending manifestations. We worship god through these. We worship their universality, indiscrimination, essentiality, powerfulness, grace and eternity. All lovers are idolators, and all idolators are lovers. The tangible is an idea in form. Concepts vivify themselves by getting congealed to forms.

Degradation

This is also why we regard this body, which owes its existence, feelings and thought to these manifestations of the divine as, verily, the temple of God. All functions of this body have to be divinely willed and organised. No act of the body, when naturally motivated and naturally functioned, could be regarded as heinous or sinful, without bringing a degradation to the divine purpose.

(Talking about degradation and the judgement on degradation, I recall how so many have found it fit to avoid tantra and the tantra practices as degraded. Let me digress a little to speak of this.)

In a number of books on tantra mostly sectarian, or superfluous, or both, certain practices in tantra have been looked down upon. These have been criticised as morbid, obscene, debauched and outrageous. The European adventurers and conquistadors, supported by their priestly community have tried to justify their thoughtless vandalism through history by condemning the tantric practices as barbarous. Let me quote just one instance. While in Mexico, I have tried to penetrate into the secrets of the ancient practices. I was delighted to find that these were still practised in the established Catholic churches. (I was amused at a remark, celebrated as having been made by the current Pope John Paul, that if he were to call the practices observed in the Mexican churches as Christian, then he is not a Christian. I, of course, cannot avow for this apocrypha.)

Let me explain. People who have condemned human sacrifices, do not find anything to abhor in accepting *for the church* such abominations as human limbs, (hands, heads and feet of the human beings), when made in gold and silver. I could illustrate the point much more vividly and convincingly. But this is not the proper place to do it. I have gone into the intricate details of some of the rituals (I recall one in Cholula and another one near Kaaba) and found the old cosily asleep within the folds of the new. I have seen some of the ancient rites 'performed' on the stage, and at once visualised the grandeur and sublimity with which the so called 'victims' entered, and struggled to enter those rites of sacrifice, because they considered it to be a blessing to offer life for what they cherished as a divine faith. Those who know about self-immolation of the Jains, of Harakiri in Japan, of Thermopylae, Chitor, Bundi, of the Samsaptakas, and of Balaclava would agree that certain conditions do remove the horrors of death from minds resolved to make sacrifice.

I may be misunderstood. I am not supporting the act of animal or human sacrifice. The question is moot and controversial. We are accustomed to argue for and justify the existence of war, gestapo, gas chambers, holocausts induced by nuclear leakages, and by oil and other industrial pollutions; we are used to justify gas wars, germ wars, wars of attrition, wars of napham blasts and atom bombs; we are accustomed to justify eradication of whole villages, whole tribes, uprooting the lives and sustenance of millions for the 'benefits' of industry. In the name of politics, good government, civilising the uncivilised, we have grown accustomed to view these as inevitable tolls payable to a modern and civilised life.

But we feel morbid and scandalised about certain forms of rituals and practices. In all honesty, these rites were performed (and are still performed) and accepted as parts of reaching the sublime. In a culture where indiscriminate fornication is a pastime, indeed often a point of bravado and status; where the simple institution of prostitution has found many tones of sophisticated nuances, tantra rites have been called to question, and the earnest practitioners have been termed as rascals and orgists. As I say this, I keep also thinking of its misuses; of pretenders and frauds. Indeed I have observed closely in my life many of these so-called cranks whose actions indeed could prove to be horrifying. Yet I had the luck of appreciating sublime grandeur, the solemn tranquillity and the satisfying results of these rites.

The fact is that sensitiveness is a personal characteristic. Whatever is personal could become a race, community or state characteristic, depending on the mechanics of eloquence, preachings and publicity, in short brainwashing. Printed words, and projected photography have been playing a great part in convincing and transforming public opinion.

Danger of Public Opinion

It is easy for personal sensitiveness to grow into a national or community sensitiveness. But sensitiveness differs from person to person, from time to time in history; and human judgements based on sensitiveness and prejudice have been found, times without number, to have been stupidly erroneous. We have on record that persons found guilty of heresy and witchery at one time, and punished with fire and sword by a society, have later on been redeemed as saints. Criminals of one time have been hailed as patriots, even national heroes of other times. We have also seen this stream flowing the other way too. Nothing is more unreliable and fluctuating than judgements based on sensitiveness.

To depend on human judgements entirely often misleads one to grievous errors. Certain eternal values must be regarded as time-tested. The human heritage of values has to be acquired through the virtue of worthiness. A sense of degradation or outrage could well be provoked by ill-conceived personal knowledge, even personal opinions. To pause and think is to mature in time.

I have personal knowledge of incidents which I could have looked down upon as atrocious, degrading, depraved, even noxious. Anyone who has stood before the ruins of St. Paul's Cathedral and the Pool area of London after the bombing, or on the streets of Cassel in West Germany after the winter blitzkrieg would know of atrocity and degradation. As I passed through the Cambodian devastations, through the raped earth of Thailand, I could imagine the much more wild devastations in Vietnam, and be filled with a crippling sense of morbidity, cynicism and utter frustration.

What is then really degrading? The most degrading thing on earth is the callous disregard of the wastage of human material for purpose of commercial benefit. To have at least an aim for attaining the profound, the sublime, the eternal source of soul's tranquil joy, should justify the means, and redeem certain practices from being called names. The benefit of the doubt is never to be denied even to the avowed criminal. The law sanctions it; and the civilised practise it; or should do so.

Fortunately for me I did not avoid the challenges; and I did not hesitate to come closer to these experiences, thanks to the introduction to the closed mystic area by an astute *yogini*. I did not find anything to horrify or deter me, or keep me away from further researches. On the contrary, the forbidden emotions of scorn, shame, lust or fear never bothered me when I happened to get close to the subject. In consequence I pursued my quest with sublime unconcern about the sex, age or the consequent rites, whenever an opportunity of seantic session offered itself. As a result I learnt what I learnt, and became aware of the secret source of the tantric power.

Two such so called 'degrading and horrifying' incidents come to my mind. Let me relate.

Two Incidents of 'Degradation'

The first one took place about the year 1934.

It was at Ghorā Ghāt in Varanasi. It was a popular ghat (a paved stone embankment with flights of steps running into the river). Its popularity was derived from the fact that White tourists always came to this halt as a convenient place for stepping down from their carriages or cars, (I always wonder why the tourists cannot walk through the lanes of Rome or Varanasi) and climbing on to the waiting barges. By setting their cameras and binoculars from the decks of the boats they would form their 'firm' and 'first-hand' knowledge about Hindu India!

Lepers, beggars, drug addicts crowded behind a busy market under the shades of huge banyan trees, with the municipal lavatories fuming out their stink all around. Thanks to ever-abiding streams of the 'pitiful' foreigners the sizeable medley of lepers, derelicts, addicts flourished, hanging around the shades. Commerce in alms was good and easy.

Since at night no tourists were to be seen around, the dismal rejects of humanity settled to light their humble fires, and cook their scanty meals, before they could pair off under torn rags to wrench from life the little juice of joy that life had yet left for them.

Here burnt an open oven of a roadside tea stall. Two bare benches, and several cups, or fractions of them, adorned the establishment. Drug takers in need of sweets, milk or other like delicacies crowded within the narrow lane, which the sophisticated carefully avoided.

I was attending at this hovel to a very learned man, of my father's age, who generally kept his audience spellbound by his erudition and experienced anecdotes. He has been one of the wisest persons I have come in contact with. The dialogues reminding one of Socrates-Plato-Phoedo group used to race at a very high speed. Varanasi is still full of such wise cranks. Suddenly I witnessed a sight.

A dark man with matted locks, and of course specifically nude, covered only with the celebrated ash, was speeding from the riverside towards the dark lane leading to the famed Viśvanātha and Bhairavi temples for which Varanasi is regarded as a Hindu Mecca.

He was proceeding with a swing. But he had been cupping his hands between his thighs, and spooning the liquid flowing from his bladder directly into his mouth. Yes, I saw him merrily drinking his own urine. I rushed out to fully investigate and ascertain the phenomenon.

I returned not before another two hours.

During this time I had a very engaging conversation with him, and I realised that he was indeed a very high ranking tantrik yogi of the rare order of the Bhairavas; and his powers included lighting fire by looking at the wood, and drinking water from a glass without going near it. He has been to me one of the most adored and honoured saints so far. But I was not able to keep trace of him. They come and go at their own free will in the manner of wild winds.

My second experience was more involved, and much more terrifying. I knew that experiences shock and scare because of our own ignorance. Experiences to which one is familiarly accustomed cease to cause either terror, or surprise. Familiarity smooths and settles nervous excitements or shocks. I have seen men fainting at the sight of a surgical operation, a skeleton or even of simple blood flowing from a body. We used to dab our foreheads with blood from sacrificed animals, and experienced thereby imagined glorification. Some find the tantra temples too horrible, eerie or gloomy. I have known very devout Hindus shirking away from cathedrals, finding them too dark and old. These are personal reactions, and need not be generalised.

But that second incident really shocked me.

My younger sister, in mysterious circumstances, began to throw blood by mouth. No medication proved of help, until gradually she imaciated, and died in a few weeks. In accordance with Hindu custom she was to be cremated before the next sunrise. Sun is not to rise on a Hindu dead body, if one could help it. We arranged for her instant cremation at night.

In Varanasi a dead body is given its final wash by the banks of the Ganges. After wash and before laying the body on the pyre the body is properly groomed and dressed.

My sister's body too was taken to the Ganges, and bathed. Driven by a sentiment that in life she loved to swim the river with me, I had gone out in the flowing current holding her body in my hand. The body was brought back; with the intention of changing her clothes and giving her the final wrap. Naturally, to gain some privacy, I took the corpse to a darker and more secluded section of the burning ghats.

The river, placid and dark near the stone steps, had entered a small bay formation, and stood still within a vestibular pool protected on the riverside by a wall of wire-netting. This kept the rubbish from flowing back into the river.

Imagine my surprise when half through the ritual of changing the clothes of my beloved sister, I became aware of some moving spectres stirring the stagnant water, and wading within the slush with floating ease. I could hear the smooth muffled splashing sound that the water was making as it came into clash with these phantom bodies. Soon I could figure out a pair of black dogs scurrying for the half roasted pieces of bones. It was enough to give me a cold sweat.

But that was not all.

Before I could write off the dogs and attend to my business in hand. I noticed a figure;—the figure of a man! Of course he was naked, and his poor charred frame was skeletal-thin. He was one with the black-pool, the dark dancing shadows. But the hungry eyes, and the hungrier looks glittered like cut diamond points. Those burning eyes were set on me. He too appeared to be busy in searching for food out of the rejected and washed away mass of refuse of charred leftovers. He was actually holding a piece of bone in his hand, and wrenching portions with his teeth.

Well, it *was* shocking, even to me, accustomed by then to many similar so called abominable, nay, terrible seances. I picked up the body silently, and with the help of my other brothers, and my nephew laid it down on the pyre. Soon the flames would cover and lap what had been my sister in this world, and what had really been nothing more than an organised shape of natural properties, ultimately consigned to nature.

That dark night, the mysterious spell of the great flowing river, the several other unnamed pyres burning around the ash-laden stone platforms, the close touch of the stilled skin of my dearest sister, the swim and the wash of the corpse in the flowing currents of the familiar stream, the awe of death, the sudden barrenness of life's physical continuity,—all these together—had brought out of my inner being a different personality. I felt weighed down by the strange course of events. I felt the cold embrace of innui overpowering me. All I wanted was to rest a while; to come to grips with myself to sleep and ride out of the cajolings of life and death.

My elder brother looked at me and remarked that I could do very well wish a snatch of sleep. He suggested that I climb the steps to the tower of rest, standing by the funeral ghats. It had been built by a wealthy man as a gift for this purpose, that is, for offering rest to the tired carriers of a hearse.

I listened to his timely advice.

I climbed the steps. In my mind I was visualising the long tresses of my sister being consumed in seconds by the hungry flames.

I must have fallen asleep with a disturbed mind.

I do not know how long I was merged in the slumber when I experienced strange pull. I sat up and opened my eyes and saw a terrible spectre, dark, charred, emaciated and wizened, sitting very close to me, and watching me with a lifeless grin. I ran cold within me. My conscious self receded within me. But . . . I knew how to hold my breath, and wait for the unknown.

Before long I came to myself and confronted the apparition squarely.

This time he laughed a little, a mere chuckle as if we have come out of an episode of great fun. We were communicating.

"So, you felt the scorn for what I had been at," he started the offensive. "You, of all persons. You the darling of the Lady in Saffron; you who have been the favourite of the Bhairava of Baṭuknāth, and of the great *sādhu* Jitendra and the holy Mauni Bābā! I feel to laugh. You scorned to see me picking my food from a refuse heap? A little bundle of conceit, you are.

"Where was I wrong pray?" he asked and continued, "Have I not left life at my back? Am I not, so to say, already lost to the society of humanity? I cannot and do not choose to beg for my upkeep from a world which I have willingly left behind.

"The dogs live; the crows live; so live the fish, the vultures, and hundreds of other live. I mix with them, and share their food. In them is the Mother: in me is the Mother,—Mother, who as *hunger* resides in all, and sends all to hunt for food. The reject goes for the reject food; the dead goes to the dead.

"All right; think of this another way. That body you washed, is gone. In Maṇikarṇikā all bodies are finally cast away. Where do they go? I mean the material bodies? are they spirited away into the oblivion? Or do they continue to belong to the material world? Who or what absorbs them? Is She not the Mother? The power of the Mother? Cāmuṇḍā Kālī? If all this could be her food, why might I not partake of her *prasāda* (food blessed by her participation)? If she stops the process, how would the world order be maintained? What is the good of my being a Bhairava, an Aghori if I fail to attune myself happily with this world order? Am I not nature and the natural order personified? Am I not '*bhūtādhyakṣa*', an onlooker and assimilator of the '*bhūtas*' (functioned and functioning matter)? Personal feelings are redundant for the likes of me. Are they not? What do you say?

"This is the logic of the wheel. No great philosophy in it; just the wheel. Where is the doubt? It turns and turns; comes and goes. All is grist. Where lies the confusion? Where the scorn? Man suffers from his own conceit, and feels superior to other animals. In the eye of the Mother all are one and the same. From the birth of a star to the birth of a sand-fly, so far as the mother is concerned, all provides the same joy, the same pain. Life is life, and food is food. Why this false distinction?"

And then suddenly he gave me a big push. I fell flat on the polished cemented floor. With his two thumbs pushed between my brows, in a trice he jumped over my chest, and seated himself, as if on a corps. He began to chant a *mantra*, which later I found to be the *bīja* (seeḍ) *mantra* of Nīla Sarasvatī. I did not even try to disturb him. I did neither shriek, nor shake. All on a sudden he began to spit all around. even on my body and face. I lay still. Almost with a reflex lack of thinking I submitted, and tried to say something like, 'I am joy; I am the Mother; I am the terror and the tranquillity'. Gradually I passed out.

On my coming back to myself I found the figure vanished; the heavy weight from my chest was gone. I felt extermely light. My senses appeared to have gained in altertness. I came, as if from a dark suffocating cavern into the light and joy of liberation.

This was a time when the Lady in Saffron was no longer available in het mortal existence. So the experience just remained, along with others, interred in the silent tomb of my memory.

I can recall other instances of apparently scornful, degrading, perverse and obnoxious behaviour of these Bhairavas. But those I have mentioned should be enough.

In the world of the great spirit there is nothing stranger than man with his awful gluttony for material possession and lust for power. Yet we suffer these gluttons of vulgar show of wealth and power; we salute them as celebrities. Then what is obscene? What ugly? The ugliest in life is to live in untruthful pretence.

We may fail to realise the divine will, and like a spoilt child indulge in undue advantages of the parental favour. We go into excesses, and overspend the store of power, thereby depleting the stock; we degrade the dignity of man, and bring on our heads all consequent sufferings of a squandering fool.

Herein lies the need for the divine intervention, and for the realisation of the divine purpose. Who or what is degraded in the divine scheme of things? Who and what is holy and mighty? Who to judge? Who to exercise the final disposal of reward and punishment? The sense of self-righteousness acts as the heaviest stone that permanently buries the divine in man in the dark silences of a doomed cemetery. One must liberate oneself from ego and false pretences. It calls for exercising self-control. Control for longer, steadier, surer and more beneficial enjoyment. Thus we learn the mysteries of life and sex. Hence we 'worship' what is sex, i.e., the power in sex.

A Cradle of Mistrust

I had reached the thresholds of manhood. In the tropics the sun rises with a jump, and sets with a plunge. Soon I had to reach down to the facts. The Lady must have realised the necessity of guiding me along this hidden path with more alacrity and purpose, more care and intimacy.

Twice a month, and during the course of one year on certain special days, we were engaged together in the extremely complicated rituals which called for the highest secrecy, and a perfect poise in the mind. Our sessions gathered day by day more and more importance. I felt the itch for further knowledge, so that the very thrill of it supplied the drive for seeking it. During this period I used to be on a stringently austere discipline of food, sleep and behaviour.

This familiarity to what is known as sex areas had completely erased from my mental slate the vulgarity of the curious. I had no droll craving for physical possession. In these sessions I hardly ever experienced a retarding or negative feeling. I never faced the degrading excitement of eroticism.

Sex Challenges

Life is a strange pilgrimage. Along this pilgrimage, on different occasions, I have been compelled to seek shelter at many unknown places. I had to meet strange situations in which the powerful threat of uncontrollable sex stood against further progress like a live cobra ready with its hood, spread to strike at the least mistake and carelessness. Psychologically, at times, it often used to create a void, when the outer personality met with an eroding inner commotion. To say that life has never tested my nerves, that I have never faced the acute challenges from this power, shall tantamount a vain boast, and an empty claim.

The challenges came; but not the surprises. The familiarity with the entire topography of the body, as well as with the mental phases involved, stood guard against any hunger or burn. In the physical world total closeness at times could result in a total absence. The great and peculiarly sublime experience of transcendental joy (*samādhi*),—the thrill of finding the soul swimming in a pool of joy, made me look upon these things as temptations, much in the same way as toys tempt children. I am convinced that to a matured mind such flimsy and flitting pleasures offer no call at all.

Yet, one must bear in mind that the power of *avidyā* (evil genius)

1. Author's father.

2. Swami Bhaskarananda's shrine, Varanasi.

3. Swami Bhaskarananda's statue.

4. The shrine of Kamaksya, Varanasi.

5. The Manikarnika cremation *ghat* (note the white temple where auntie sat).

6. Bhairava temple, Varanasi.

7. The Chinnamasta shrine (tribal) at Rajarappa, Ranchi.

8. The Baijnath yard (where the 'circle' was organised).

9. Durga at Varanasi.

10. The Bhairava at Muktesvata, Bhuvaneshwar.

11. The *mudra* on the face of Parasurama shrine, Bhuvaneshwar.

12. Chinnamasta: according to Tantra-dhyana.
Clockwise: the yoni-vivrta (eviden
source of life-spring)

A black stone natural formation;

14. A sacrificial pit;

Lajja Gauri (the white goddess with head hidden).

16. The neglected temple at the Bhaskar Puskar tank, Varanasi.

17. The trunk of the peepal, where the saint had stuck the bead.

18. The Amarnatha shrine. Cave with the snow *lingam* in full resplendent glory. Author back row, middle, in spectacles.

could be as strong as the power of *vidyā* (native genius). In a much truer sense the good around us, and within us, is so profusely and intimately operative, that we often do not realise its existence. We do that only when that good is severely challenged. Goodness of health, air, water, breath, companionship is hardly realised unless threatened by fever, fret, disease and discomfort. There is in life, as in legends, always the possibility of facing a challenge which could spell doom and destruction in no time. All yogis are aware of it, and mentally prepare themselves to meet it. The Buddha had to face it; he won finally. Times without number, the great Viśvāmitra was challenged; but each time he fought hard, and finally attained to sainthood. The power and the challenges of sex never die; never. The sun sets only physically; in reality it never sets, never dies. The power of the sun shines and works for ever; so is the power of sex, which is nothing but a transformed expression of the solar energy working through our nerves, passions, desires and ambitions.

These challenges came in due course in my life too; but instead of lust, came love; then came sympathy and understanding; and lastly, poise. This was the gift of those hard practising lessons on self-control. Sex is so pervading a power that it has been imagined as a flute's charm. The flute charms the serpent; so the *lhādinī*'s call charms the sex urge. If the flautist plays well, the serpent dances at his beck and call; if he flunks, falters or hesitates, comes the sting, sharp, true and fatal. The call of *lhādinī* (sex) has been imagined as a human response to the call of the flute; Rādhā (the *lhādinī*) responding to the call of the flute of Kṛṣṇa. It has been symbolised as the happy correspondence between kindred souls seeking the joyous experience between two or even more persons. It is a practical expression of the natural vibrations electrifying the magnetic stream flowing between two opposite poles.

Only the select are initiated into, and allowed to grow with the form of *sādhanā* (training) for joy. I was lucky to have been introduced to this at a tender age. I lived and grew with it. This form of *sādhanā* offers me no strangeness at all. But as I recall those days, I still regard myself as an extremely lucky individual.

Warnings on the Road

Lest the indiscreet and the fraudulent make mistakes, and suffer through many cycles of agonies, several warnings have been solemnly sounded. Here are a few quoted.

1. *Nipīta kāla kūtasya harasye-vāhi khelanam* . . . (this has been already explained before) Unless immunised by a drink of the 'poison' (of lust and greed) none should go about toying with this form of *sādhanā*.
2. Learn to hold the seed. Never think of ejecting it. No; never. Not when one is at the *āsana*. If it appears to be a union, it is definitely not a union of the body. Souls get united beyond the body's grasp. Results explode within a supra-conscious field of transcendental experience. It is an experience of the sublime void, where power alone holds the reserved court.
3. Sit on the *āsana*, as if seated on a dead body. Even if there appears to be a stir, an agitation, a call to the warm flesh, parry it; master it; keep a firm hold on it, as you would do to hold a wild cobra, until it is put away in a basket. Dominate invitation from the 'dead'. You are the only one really 'alive' in a world which is dominated by death. It is a union between the forces, of life and death. If, in the process, death does not transform into life, remember, life, your life, would gradually wither as dead.
4. For attaining to such a degree of impersonality master all temptations, all fears, all external responses to sound, smell, touch, sight or taste. Remain steady in the absolute feeling of "*I am allness*" (*Bhairvoham Śivoham*).

In order to attain this absolute state of impersonality (nothingness), which is the only door to enter the state of super-personality, the grown-up aspirant has to seek a perfect guide, a guru. Then he is initiated into the fiery zone of *vāma-mārga*, (the left-way), the Mahāyāna canon of *sādhanā*. He hardens himself by making *āsanas* on the living and the dead, eating food of all kinds horrifying or inviting, waking for indefinite periods, sleeping for indefinite periods. (I had been attendant to one such yogi in Calcutta in the year 1936 who had been sleeping for over three months, and who continued to remain asleep for another six months; I used to wash and feed the body as if I were tending a plant. Finally, I became his good friend.)

In this state of trance, physical responses are reduced to a mere zero under a yogi's perfect self-control. Unless the yogin gains neutrality, that is, perfect impersonality, the cosmic forces could neither be invoked, nor absorbed. Without the blessings of those forces no one is able to project happiness and joy.

One should recall the privations that the Buddha had to undergo:

the temptations that Jesus had to face; the warnings of the Tibetan Lamas, while accepting this way.

Bodhi

We must never forget the acute trials of saints like the Buddha or Jesus before Buddhahood could be attained. They could survive those trials because of their complete control over impersonality. Like Ramakrishna of our times none of them had been attached to any sense of personal ownership, or personal gain. They belonged in life to the very elements. That is the state of the Bodhi, of being a Paramahaṃsa. No emotion disturbs a Buddha; his conscious self exists irrespective of his personal body and its senses; he reduces his feelings to a zero; he is an individual without any social symbol. The world is his home, the universe his boundary. Firmness and steadiness are the two pillars on which his will rests. He is beyond scorn, envy, jealousy, opinion, ambition, pride, anger, fear or passion. Indiscrimination is his religious faith, and equilibrium is his confirmed state. "Where the mind finds its joy, and self-control its prize; where the self, looking at the self, feels pleased with the self, there lies the bliss of the yogi." (*yatropa-ramate cittam niruddham yoga sevayā/yatra cai-vā-tmanātmānam paśyann atmani tuṣyati*— Gita.)

These words in the Gita describe the supreme state of *nirvaṇa*, the tranquil state where the tantra way guides the seeker through a very difficult, trying but a much quicker path. Tantra 'plays' with sex indeed; gets absorbed in sex, but does not allow the sex to indulge, covete, lust or get passionate. Tantra worships it; venerates and adores it. Sex in tantra is a bath in icy fire. It excites without losing calmness, loves without passion. It reflects the illuminated state of Grace as sunlight reflects the dewy innocence of the colours on a lotus just bloomed.

The Two Friends

Where would I have gained an insight into these secrets without the assistance of my early mentors, specially the Lady is Saffron and my friend Nārada. My Lady was motherly, loving, eager and confiding. She had been taking me almost by her hand from mystery to mystery, and through practical exercises which none but she alone could have bestowed. The path was arduous; hazardous; at times challengingly ugly, even revolting; but her hand would be there, and her calm tranquil tolerance. We were close; we got closer; at the seances even closest.

But often we were sent off to a thrilling trip filled with a sublime quietitude. It was wortth all that strain.

My friend Nārada was on the other hand funny, jocular, impish and frisky like a cherub-puck. Always eager to teach, under the garb of learning; give, under the garb of begging; love, under the garb of being loved, he would appear to me, at an hour of keen spiritual distress, as if we had met by an accident. He kept his brotherly hand always directly on my doubt-spots. While his sudden and unpredictable appearances were like drops of unsought mercy falling from the sky, his exits were like fog-phantoms suddenly melting away on a marsh. He taught me the simple virtues of love and patience; the arduous practices of penances and meditations; the stimulating joy of fellow feeling and service. Robinson Crusoe had his Friday; he was my everyday. So convenient; so much my chum.

The Fort by the Bank

I noticed for materialising his favoured locale was the quiet river bank. To the south of stream, on the western bank, there stood the old magnificent pre-British fort of the ancient King of Varanasi. With this fort was associated one of the most tragic chapters in the rise and fall of the princes of India mauled and bullied into submission by the servants of the East India Company.

One of those victims was this King of Varanasi, Chet Singh. Although a very small principality, because of the cultural importance of the city of Varanasi, a city which stood foremost in the Vedic tradition, where the Buddha had for the first time preached, and where he had lived long, this principality was held in high honour. In fact the prince was regarded as the symbolic unit of Hindu India. He was bullied and attacked because of his pledged traditional loyalty to the Nawab of Lucknow, a viceroy of the Moghul Emperor. Through all the political upheavals in Muslim India the King of Varanasi was always left alone, because of his special symbolic position. Here near the bank Warren Hastings was defeated, and made to run away, up the river, to the hut of a boatman, who saved him out of animal pity. But Hastings was not to leave Chet Singh alone. He attacked again with reorganised forces when he was supposed to negotiate.

Unaccustomed to the trickeries of war and peace, the king, tired of the killings, came to learn that Hastings wanted him personally as a prisoner. This meant a great humiliation to the symbolic role that Chet Singh, the King of Varanasi, was supposed to play. Instead of humiliating the whole Hindu community, he escaped to some unknown destination, never to be heard of again.

Under the window of the large fort there was a small sand bank, generally covered with grass. The slope was modest and inviting. Near by, further to the south the river had its main bend before entering the city limits. The place was quiet, and a still hush made one listen to the river's message. A strange vibration reported intense longings in me whenever I stood below the window on the green spot. Later I came to know that just above the wall stood the haloed grounds once distinguished by great tantra adepts. A series of surprisingly well preserved temples still commemorate their efforts and achievements. This should explain why that green spot stored for me feelings extremely sensitive. (I visited the spot last in 1983. Meditation here still brings almost immediate results.)

The Silent Man of the Boat

On the bend itself where the sand-dunes kept the flow sluggish, one could notice a solitary boat, floating midstream. It was a phantom of a boat, and it never moved. It was permanently anchored there. During the monsoons, when all this would be merged under an angry torrent of grey waters, the boat would be guided to the safety of the narrow channel passing through the villages.

On this boat lived one of the most renowned yogis of Varanasi. He was regarded in my early days as the guardian angel of the city. He had never been heard to speak; but he communicated whenever he wanted to, by just looking at the people. He has been known, and recorded by foreign interviewers, to have held long conversations without speaking a syllable. He was the famous Mauni Bābā, or the silent saint.

I liked to sit by this green bank and prepare my lessons. At times I meditated here. Perhaps the influence of the Ganges, or the several *Śakti* temples in the ancient fort, or of the saint's boat at the distance induced concentration easily. Mind seeks its own rest by chosing a harmonious surrounding.

Here the friendly Vaiṣṇava saint, my Nārada, met me on that day when I was almost tormented for knowing the secret of the hidden power in *mantra*.

I was aware that a *mantra*, a *bīja* (seed), as a mystic sound contained entire meaning and import of abstract concepts. Besides, by the special nature of their composition they were reservoirs of power.

But how? Why? My agony to get into the secret made me impatient. And lo! Nārada materialised to my great consolation.

A Laughing Stock

I had spoken of the pair of children who had been engaged in sex play, and who had invited me to participate. I had tried to, but in the process I found it so very boring and futile, compared to the secret sessions I enjoyed at the seances with my Lady in Saffron. Naturally I tried to convey to them in my own way, my most intimate and sacredly held ideas regarding the position of sex in human life.

They laughed, and called me a prude ((*bakwās*). But whenever alone, the grown-up fiirt tried to fascinate me. She, I believed, was fond of my ways. Whatever the reasons, she appeared to be determined to win me over to her games. At least so I believed. Temptation at that age grows in that hide-and-seek way. So she stuck on; and like a desperate angler wanted to fish me out of the doldrums of theological tantrism with the aid of her fascinations and charms. So she continued pampering me in every way; and at times even followed me. In defiance of what I believed in and what I practised, she always bemocked my claims on the power of *mantra*. Together with some boys, she often ridiculed me about my avowed faith in the *mantras*. She even challenged my faith in the efficacy of a *mantra*. Her idea was to bring me to submission through the weapons of public humiliation, blackmail and taunt.

I was being secretly tortured. It was not the torture of the mauled ego. It was not the torture of being a sporting victim to female wanton. It was the simple and innocent tortuer that a misunderstood friend feels in not being able to convey to another a point of ecstatic pleasure; or in not being able to share in a common source of happiness. Such an experience is I believe, unavoidable in the journey through life, specially when one has to pass through that 'no-man's land' in human growth commonly referred to as adolescence.

I felt I could influence her with my reserved charm, the real charm, the charm of the power of *mantra*. But I myself should be able to master the secret before I could presume to influence her to my way. Particularly her. She was so intelligent and so fluent a person.

Flesh Knows no Innocence

Naturally, I had to find out the sources and the mechanics of the secrets of *mantra*, the power of the syllables, the special arrangements of the syllables, their effects, their sound, and the corresponding responses of those sounds with corresponding nerves which influence and mould personality.

Imagine my cold surprise when I found suddenly Nārada sitting close to me and smiling. I was taken aback. Before I could open my lips he pointed his almost fragile index finger to something down, and said "Look!"

A serpent!

I saw it slithering into a crack between the stones.

"That was a she cobra, boy. These females are fascinatingly demanding and disturbing!"

I could feel the mocking ring in his voice. (Was I not thinking of a 'she'?)

But the incident itself left me cold.

It was a cobra. It had been lying coiled next to my feet all the time, and I had not known it.

I smiled in return, and looked at the receding serpent, and smiled again.

"They know the mind. However, they are harmless to harmless minds."

"Why then do they bite babies, infants, cattle?" I parried.

"They too have temper. Their moods get vexed at times and then they act thoughtlessly. Don't they?

"Do you think babies are innocent of thought? No! Even babies think in their own ways. Flesh knows no innocence. The very elements of which living beings are formed are plagued with the crying demands of fascination, procreation and multiplication. In order to guarantee this natural demand functioning naturally, powers of enticements, inducements, temptations have to be checked, and totally eliminated in favour of love.

"There is no innocence in flesh. It has to be earned by conscious and sustained efforts. There is no innocence even in nature, which looks so unspoilt at times. No. Even babies radiate their moods. They do. Only we fail to record them correctly. We are too hardened for that tender and delicate response. Watch the difference between the understanding mothers and nurses, and the un-understanding ones. Watch the likes and dislikes of babies to strangers, even to their own folks. The selective mechanism is at operation, may be too subtle for our observation. But it is there. Sensitive animals like serpents, squirrels, badgers sense subtlety of responses through inlaid mechanisms.

Bats do not meet with accidents in rooms crowded with spinning fans; rats run faster than men when threatened with plague; bees know best where their hunting grounds are; birds are more accurate recorders of seasonal changes. There are examples throughout the panorama of life. We too act under the forces of impulse, emotion. But because we are far away from nature, we break into tempers, and occasion more misdeeds than deeds of which we could be proud.

"A father kills a son; a husband beats a wife; a man gets drunk and brings disaster to the whole family. So the serpents. They get afraid by being chased and harassed. They too understand; but those who understand make mistakes too.

"But the fact stands that serpents as a whole are mysterious. They are wise. They understand motives, motives of *mantras*. *Mantras* are not and cannot be powerless. *Mantras* are expressions of power. As bubbles grow out of water, when water in under the pressure of power, so the sound expressions bubble out of the powerful minds of the saints when they are in *samādhi*; of course I am not speaking of false sounds which priests mechanically utter for a living."

Mantra

I looked at him with wonder. How did he know about my perturbation, and need for assistance? . . . But this was Nārada. The unpredictable Nārada, the flitting cherub who appeared to know me to a T! Did he conjure the serpent and find room for introducing the topic? I would not be surprised.

From him I had learnt that the power of *mantra* is recognised all the world over. It affects animals. Whereas the constant humming of the swarm of bees conveys the position of the source of the honey, or the hissing of the serpent paralyses the frog or the deer, or the sound from the tigress brings the tiger near her, in the case of the human beings, *mantras* evolute from a mind in the *samādhi* state. Only then the *mantras* become charged with that power of will which makes them *living*. *Sound* or *utterance* is the physical expression of the powerful inner will of consciousness. In a state of *samādhi* the will-power itself takes form in sound forms.

"Mind you," he warned at this stage; "I say will; not impulse, nor desire." And then he directed my attention to a very important lesson in learning, viz., distinguishing the proper import of words.

Will

On that day I understood how misleading desire was. Desire is to will what dream is to sleep, or bubbles to water. Kicks of desire are but momentary reactions of unguarded greed; they reflect our unbridled impulses, or whims. Some desires abide, while some die out even before they have taken any tangible shape. Desires die with the death of ego.

Desire, in order to abide, must absorb within its outer shell the power of will. Will is a powerful dynamo; attached to will human efforts become dynamic. This is not the case with wish, fancy or desire. Will metamorphoses desire.

Will is a driving force, and drives to consistent and persistent acts. Will shapes character; desire tears it to pieces. The former integrates; the latter disintegrates. One mothers; the other devours. Will enforces mind to determine, distinguish, apply efforts and labour for achievements. Muscles achieve, but muscles are commanded by will. Will is *Śakti, power,* the Mother. What we call reflex is also in a subtle way conforming to will, although this cannot be recorded or registered.

Will inspires and invokes cosmic consciousness (*cit*), and compels the intangible shape to shape into a form that becomes real to the determined mind.

To the mind, that has given a tangible form and shape to an idea, contemplated with the will of making the intangible tangible, a formed idea assumes the form of an image. In a way it is the spiritual image of his enlightened self. From the highest source of tantric authority we learn this truth cryptically, as always. "To worship it, become it", it commands. Without this 'becoming' there is no worship. There is no worship *without*. Worship *without* is a rite; it becomes a mere ritualistic form. The only worship, like love must be a continuous, penetrating and merging flow of energy from within. from within to within. "*Becoming it*' is the first demand for a successful prayer. *It is the soul in shape*. This is at the root of our worship of deities. This is the very basis of image worship. It may be Kālī, Mary, Buddha or Jesus. Unless a prayer makes the devotee 'become' it, the prayer has failed. It is like reciting a cook book in order to appease hunger.

The devotee worships the image; adores it; bathes in the joy that springs from a noble spirit of true submission. To realise a state of elevation through submission, he explained answers for the last three stages of a constant mind: singleness of application (*dhyāna*), living conception (*dhāraṇā*), and the final rapture of oneness (*samādhi*).

The Sound in Ether: Nāda

Then he proceeded to elucidate the subject of *mantra*, and the mystery sound, *dhvani*, in the cosmic *nāda*.

Any articulation is a random sound and no more. Why? Because it is the result of a mechanical process. Sound is the result of a clash, of a friction between two or more objects. There is no articulation in the void. The One is lonely (*Sah ekākī*—Upaniṣad). The stage of perfect oneness must necessarily be quiet, tranquil and peaceful.

Air, water and fire articulate and evolve sound, only when their quiet motions clash against something else e.g., air and space, wind and leaves, water and rocks, fire and wind. It could also be air and air; wind and wind; water and water; rock and rock etc. One must always remember that air, or wind is always the common factor in the phenomenon of sound. (cf. Sanskrit √*svan;* or Latin *sona*, *sonic*, i.e.; sound in air, *svanati* in Sanskrit means 'he/she/it sounds'.)

The air in the *prāṇa* covers a whole range of nerve sensations, *Prāṇa* is the vital breath, and operates mainly through the nerves. Will as a force, otherwise known as volition, stimulates action through nerves. In other words nerves respond to *prāṇa*, and obey the will. *Prāṇa*-responses are activised through undetected subtle vibrations. Any vibration must create activised waves in air or ether. Sound is a recognised source of vibrations. *Mantras* are based on sounds; *mantras* are based *in* sound vibrations.

By some subtle esoteric method, the ancient consummate masters and adepts of the highest grade succeeded finally in establishing a relation between sound vibrations and nerve vibrations.

The vibrations created by the different sound effects of Sanskrit alphabets have been referred to different nerve points. Anyone who has even a superficial knowledge of philology and formation of sound arrangements of alphabets (of the different alphabetical orders of the different languages of the world), would at once discover the perfectly arranged order of Sanskrit alphabets. The sounds of Sanskrit alphabets coordinate with the physical mechanism of articulation, or pronunciation.

This perfection of Sanskrit alphabets is not a guess work. *Mantra* adepts put this order to the uses of the demands of the nerves and the nerve centres. In other words, *mantras*, conceptually formed, are so arranged, and put to uses as to assist in bringing through the subtlest and the most secured way, the desired effects on the will and peace of an individual.

A *mantra* is the sound-image of a yogi's inner will. His soul's appeal vibrates through the nerves, and the message activises the brain by making appeals to the proper quarters. A *mantra* like an atom is a store-house of *power*; it is saturated with the *will* of the person who utters it under proper guidance. A *mantra* is what a yogi auditions in his meditative personality.

A *mantra* thus becomes a living source of power. Yes, living. Believe it or not. What radiates life is 'Living'; and *mantras* radiate the life force. A realised *mantra* vibrates, as the particles of blood in the arteries do; as the heart or the breath does. As does the heat of the skin, the light in the eye.

As the meaning of a word is inherent in the sound of the word, so does the power of a *mantra*-sound lie inherent in its vibration. The secret of *mantra* is the secret of ether; and that subtle form of ether resides also within our body, and expresses as radiation of thought, will, feeling and understanding. As the breath within the blood cannot be easily discerned, so the radiating principle of the nerves could not be easily observed. But the vibrations are there, and sound messages could inspire the communication between sound and vibrations; between vibrations and the awakening of the extra sensory responses.

This brings us to the question of ether, or space, or *ākāśa*. There is an indefinable power in space which animates it. And through this animation wave-lengths get evolved, and become carriers of the minutest sound that is produced by air movements in space. The planets move in the space. Millions of bodies move about. Even where the space is windless and soundless, there is still some power which radiates sound. We call it 'form in no-form! (*rūpa-arūpa* or *guṇa-nirguṇa*). The stillness of the night cannot be altogether so still. The sounds around us are either too subtle, or too high for our physical ear drums to pick up. The centre of sound is soundless. At its navel, or vortex, even the fire is supposed to be cool. At the centre of restlessness lies asleep the *Śeṣa*, the Ultimate,—*Nārāyaṇa* at peace. We sing of this truth in a hymn:

Peace is asleep on the coils of Restlessness
The abode of the universe is a single space.
To penetrate this is beyond all yoga;

This is Viṣṇu, Nārāyaṇa, the delighter
of the power of growth.
[*śantākāram bhujaga, śayanam*
padmanābham suṛeśam
viśvādhāram gagana sādṛśam
meghavarnam śubhāngam
lakṣmīkāntam kamalanayanam
yogibhi-r-dhyāna gamyam
vande Viṣṇum bhavabhaya haraṇam
sarva lokaika nātham.]

What would one not pay in order to identify this cosmic sound, the sound that clings to the whirling planets, the zooming stars, and forms a cosmic link between the seen and the unseen. The physical ear is not enough to receive this; we must develop our spiritual senses. Then alone we come to know the unknown. To be with the cosmic, one must realise to belong to the cosmos. (I am Brahman: *aham brahmāsmi.*)

Aum

This cosmic sound, the ideal *nāda Brahman* (the sound waves that bind all into one) has been formed into the great *mantra* AUM, (OM) the exact pronunciation of which comes to the tongue after a long practice under expert guidance. It is a combination of three sounds in one.

It combines, *inter alia*,

1. The obvious; the inferential; the world beyond inference.
2. Start; continuity and growth; return to the flux.
3. Tranquillity; energy; inertia.
4. Cosmos; order; chaos.

There are many more variants of the explanations of this *mantra*.

In articulating the sound *A-U-M* (wrongly and inaccurately pronounced as *OM*, a result of human hurry and impatience) the mechanism of articulation covers three stages of sound projection. These three stages signify the three esoteric stages of beginning, continuity and closure.

Let us explain this. It only illustrates what care was applied in the formation of these esoteric sound-seeds known as *mantras. Mantras* are never to be treated as random inanities.

AUM as a sound is composed of (a) an opening vowel uttered with open lips; and (b) a continuing vowel with squeezed lips, and then, (c) closing the lips finally with a lip-closing consonant that cannot be pronounced without the assistance which the previous vowel gives. 'A' as in 'saw'; 'U' as in 'put'; and just the letter M without pronouncing it as 'EM', (in 'pronouncing' which we take the help of the vowel 'E'.) The single M sound cannot be pronounced; and it brings the upper lip firmly down on the lower. It denotes the opening of Life with the sound 'A', and closing it with a firm clap, as death does. Death closes as 'M', which closes, in Devanāgari (Sanskrit) alphabets, the consonant community. The spirit of Life and Death; creation and disintegration; supraconscious, conscious, and dormant states of consciousness,—all are reflected in this sound. Yogis hold on to it. The vibrations of the three-sounds-in-one (AUM) have been time-honoured, and proved, more by their results than by dry casuistry and sophistry.

This *mantra AUM* (or *OM*) has been accepted in Japan and China, in the far away South-Eastern countries of Asia, in Indo-China, Ceylon, India, and the ancient Orient; it originated in and was accepted by countries and civilisations where 57 per cent of mankind lived. These people speak of highly developed languages based on Sanskrit, Greek, Arabic and Chinese. Any language unrelated to these languages is still called tribal, undeveloped. This group of languages, and these people, from times immemorial, have been using this *mantra* for awakening their spiritual consciousness.

AUM, the *mantra*, has been the *'seed'* sound for the Buddhists, Taoists, Mahāyāna and Hīnayāna tantriks, and of course for the Vedists. Even in the Semitic religions we find the use of a similar sound, '-hom', as the suffix of some other sound.

The sound has taken many forms, the more popular ones are *om*, *aum*, *hung*, *hum*, *hoom*, *ung* and '. . . *hom*'. Let us warn at the beginning, even at the risk of being taken for a non-believer, that variations do not much matter. The utterance with proper reflection and meditation shall reach perfection with gradual progress. The exact sound function need not matter much at the beginning; but it is necessary to be warned here that it does not matter 'much'; just 'much'. Indeed in reality it does matter, and has to matter. For, one must remember the lessons already learnt about the *prāṇa*-effect, or the vibrational effect of *mantra* and its repeated utterance. These vibrations cannot be ignored at all. Correct pronunciation results in correct vibrations.

But it would be equally a great mistake to ignore the 'sense' value of a *mantra* for the sake of the sound value alone. The sense value of a *mantra* appeals to the inner personality that gets merged in the joy of union; while the sound-value concerns the mechanism of the nerve-based personality alone. The first is the repository of bliss; the second is only instrumental. If the two could be synchronised, good enough. But if one has to demand the 'first' care, the sense-value must get the priority. Yet, the sound effects cannot be ignored. Bad instruments always create obstructions to quick and accurate results.

Meanings have been added to the three stages of the sound; even pictures of this sound have been variously drawn.

The exact pronunciation does not matter in the sense that exact pronunciation has been lost in the maze of hoary times; and what remain are adaptations of the sound in various parts of the world amongst various peoples. Whatever the guru, or the expert, personally directs by way of pronunciation, together with, and in the light of the meaningful concept, is to be practised as the seed *mantra.*

The picture-form, idol-form, symbol-form or merely an alphabetical form differs from system to system of alphabets, languages and racial characteristics. In all these outwardly differing forms the picture of a half circle with a dot (a crescent with a star) remains symbolically consistent. It signifies that in the ultimate objective of realisation outward forms do not much matter. Religion implies the recognition of the ultimate spirit of god.

Śabda Brahman or, *nāda* or cosmic sound concept is best illustrated by a circle. But the God-idea itself is the idea of the immense, and cannot be bound or restricted. Although ○ could image an idea, yet no image could completely bind up immensity as an idea. Hence this circular representation could not be correct. It restricts immensity, which is falsifying the image-idea. In order to suggest the image of unbounded immensity within a bounded circle's restrictions a part of the circle is left incomplete. Hence the crescent form. Thus never the circle (⊙) but ever the half circle, (i.e., ◡̇) is accepted as the truer representation of the *nāda Brahman.*

Yet God cannot be incomplete. The word 'God' is supposed to carry the most complete concept in any field of human thought. The God-idea is the ultimate realisation of any idea. It is the hypothesis, the development and the thesis. 'God' is the index, the infinity. It is the seed, the fruition, the continuity. Like the concept of 'God' a point too has existence, but no magnitude. And this is illustrated by the point within the half circle (◡̇), or the same half circle repeated thrice (◡̇) as the Śiva tantra followers do. The Māhāyāna tantriks of Tibet signify this by the single eye, ((·)). The stylised deformations of this basic idea might differ from country to country; but the basic idea holds.

Yogis Agree to Differ

Thus both in sound and shape *om* or *aum* as a seed *mantra* has been helping the yogis of all times. Yogis have no differences amongst themselves; their exercising paths do differ. Very naturally so. Yogis always maintain their regard for yogis. They do not argue; they do not differ as missionaries might. This is the difference between the realised and the scholarly; a wise sage and an advocating preacher. The first one is actively joyous, the second one is an energetic enthusiast.

One of the basic and significant signs of a true yogi is a spirit of acceptance and tolerance. Such tolerance comes from a grip on firmness. Compassion and forgiveness become the acclaimed virtues of a yogi. He forgives because he feels strong. In spite of this, the pursuit to the path of the Great Unknown has been tragically littered with ruins soaked in blood, fire and tears.

I recall how Nārada's voice used to falter whenever he touched on this point: viz., the atrocities indulged by spiritual freebooters, greedy arsonists and cynical marauders in the name of religion.

Only two vices could be held responsible for this crime. One is the lust of possession, and the other is the lust for power. Power to acquire, and to hold on to its acquisition.

Those who fight for this power are the demons; and those who feel the vanity and emptiness of it all, are the divine people who care for the beauty and love for life and the world.

Love as Power

"There is yet another kind of power", Nārada continued.

"This is the power to give and sacrifice," the loving Vaiṣṇava said. "Give love; give sympathy; give care; give friendliness and companionship. Give it near and far; give it to known and unknown, rich and poor, friend and foe, the deserving as well as the undeserving. A man of love does not sit on judgement on the poor showings of others. A man of love floods out the misdeeds of the evil doer, or the wrong thinkings of the misdirected, by an overwhelming surge of love. He soothes all inner burns by the balm of forgiveness. A man of love has so much love that there would not be left any place in his heart for doubt or hesitation.

"As has been said, love is a power; and like a powerful avalanche, a powerful bulldozer, it sweeps away and removes every angularity, all sense of difference. It needs courage to carry such power to its destined end; but the yogi is well equipped to carry such power with a tranquil grace. Remember the Buddha? The Christ? Those were the true yogis.

"Such power transforms a common man into a loving, compassionate, liberal person. This is godly power. A man of love is a man of god. The one who could bear this power without ego is a yogi. Lord Śiva is Śiva because he consumed all the poison that threatened life. Jesus is Lord Jesus because by his own blood he washed the guilt of the world. Śiva, or Jesus does not belong exclusively to you or me, this sect, or that commune. A yogi is a universal man. He belongs to all. If sin is everywhere, virtue is everywhere too. If there is darkness, there is light too. Darkness is nothing but light's hunger for more light.

"The yogi by a spiritual process could acquire power. But unless his mind is responsive to the suffering hearts around, unless he is inspired by the spirit of altruism, unless he himself cries for removing the tears of the suffering, he cannot go out of himself, and feel free.

"Liberation is not acquired merely for idling or vegetating. Liberation's power is elemental. Liberation is a birth right to be acquired more spiritually than politically. One must feel free as the elements: the air, the sky, the light and heat from the sun, the ràins and the sound. One must feel natural. The elements as well as the yogi relate their power to the source, the cosmos. Thus they are able to derive their power from the Cosmic Source. A man of God receives to distribute; takes to give; exists to bestow; works to serve. A man of God follows principles to maintain the balance of form and order.

"The yogi seeks this *ṛta*; this order; this ability to harmonise with nature. A yogi's chief achievement is to acquire skill in living, to act to keep himself engaged in others. But he has to keep clear of the deceitful trap of *asmita* (ego, I-ness), and acquire the submissive dedication of a servant of man. The 'do-good' people do good to 'others'. Who the 'others'? All is 'I'. Yet others are there; the anti-force. 'Others' here mean a contrary and fundamental anti-force. The forces of imbalance and disorderliness. The yogi helps fight this anti-force, and assists in the fight against disorderliness, selfishness, cynicism,—and brings about, or at least dedicates his life to the attempt of bringing about an order of peace and equality in the normal external functions of life, and a balance in its internal responses. This is action with personal detachment; war without malice; possession without being possessed; power for service; and fullness of efforts for further achievements. One has to be a dedicated yogi to wield this power. Such alone are called the Supermen."

A Powered Seat

The sessions were held regularly at the Bhāskarānanda mausoleum. To be there daily had become a routine. The Lady in Saffron used to refer to my absences obliquely, but gracefully, indicating her hearty approval. "Gather ye rose buds whilst ye may," she used to mean in her own language. She used to sing a beautiful song. 'Burn and burn until pure gold is obtained' (*Khūb koré tui purḍiyé śonā khānṭi koré né*).

There were no appointments. We had become involved in an unchartered *modus operandi*, and we could perfectly participate in each other's movements. Often at our doors he would drop in, and my father would look at him with significant smiles, which he would reciprocate. At times they would fall into a hearty but whispering conversation. The light of joy that beamed over the faces of the two indicated a kind of rapport for enjoyment of life in its fullness.

One of these days Nārada suddenly asked me if I was interested in seeing and hearing for myself what a good yogi might achieve.

Of course I was by then too involved to turn down such a proposal.

He introduced me to a particularly 'powered' place, where some sort of vibration was immediately perceptible. What a place!

Close to the mausoleum of Bhāskarānanda there used to be in those days a stretch of straggling woodland with a tank secreted within its forbidding thickets. Besides the tank in the wilderness nestled several abandoned unkempt ancient temples and crumbling structures. The surroundings appeared to have been unmarked, and avoided. Why, I had no idea. Porcupines, rabbits, the ever busy squirrels and the patient lizards, wild hogs and serpents along with hosts of mongoose and chamelion played and frisked amongst the cacti; *ākanda* and *bāsaka* shrubbing here and there amidst the thick growth of tall trees: mangoes, jackfruits, toddy palms, silk cotton, bakuls, mahuās, jāmuns, peepals and of course the king of such wilderness, the royal banyan with its hundreds of root staves supporting a gorgeously green and cool canopy. Innumerable migratory birds as well as local ones kept up a lively vernal orchestra. The eerie mystery and coolness of the spidery surroundings, would always keep off the casual stroller.

Today the solemn panorama, raped and exposed, has given way to a large cinema hall, and the associated vulgarities and noise. Commercial hooliganism has completely eroded the quiet solemnity of the days that are no more.

The tank exists to this day as an anachronism amidst the modernised tourist attractions. A little away, to the western side of the tank, hidden within a mango grove, there used to stand a quiet and modest stucco structure with a flat roof. It was a cubic structure hardly eight by eight, with a possible height of mere six feet. It looked like a box. The only door was locked from outside, and over this lock spiders had woven heavy webs. Besides the door, at a height of about five feet, a small window with bars carried light and air within.

The Statue

On a June afternoon, for no accountable reason at all (except perhaps the will of Nārada who had been keen on my confronting some yogic power) I had selected this mango grove, instead of the mausoleum, for my meditations. Why was I attracted to this wilderness is beyond me to explain, except that Nārada had introduced me here. He knew.

After entering the woods I stood on the stone banks of the tank. Inviting clear water stood below several flights of sandstone steps. I took off whatever little I was putting on, and took a thorough refreshing bath.

The bath completed, I entered the deeper woods. A brain-fever bird and a woodpecker kept up a lively dialogue. But the harsh sounds deepened the seclusion and thickened the mysterious feel of the place. It was so quiet, secluded and peaceful there.

I looked around hard for the source of that creeping sensuous pull, when I spotted through the grove a humble building hidden within the bushes. No sign of human life was around; not even a pedestrian's trace to the structure's only cobwebbed door. The ever-present monks were conspicuous by their absence. Under a huge jackfruit tree, its barks and trunk bursting with fruits as large as a year-old baby, there stood a brick platform covered with moss, and punctuated with uninviting holes.

I came to it, touched it, and decided at once to sit on it for my meditation. There was some electric contact there. What a seat! I took off my only cotton garment and folded the same to be used as an *āsana*. Very soon I realised that I had been indeed sitting on a highly charged sanctified seat.

I had dropped into the ocean of tranquil peace, and remained there, I do not know how long; but the sun was about to set when finally I came to.

Something was naggingly holding on to me, tugging at my entrails, as it were, and I felt to be held by a strong spell. Drops of cold icicle globules seemed to shoot through my spine again and again. This world meant so little to me then; and as a pilgrim walking over the space of another world I strolled, half-dazed, towards the forsaken cubic building in the distance. What was pulling me to it? I noticed the dumb dusty look; I noticed the cobwebs. But the familiar aroma of burning camphor, sandal and frankincense drew me nearer and nearer, until I reached the grated window. With the help of a few stone slabs I gained a footing and peeped into the room.

Imagine my surprise when my attention fell on a normally seated human form, clad in punctillious white, not allowing me to know if the form was that of a male or of a female. The face itself could be seen merged in quiet and serene beauty. Long locks were tied in a knot up on the head; and the cheek appeared to be smooth. A yogi (or a *yogini*?) in *samādhi*.

As I was standing there staring at the form, I wondered if it was alive, or dead, or merely a statue. For it to be a statue the hair was too alive, the skin too vibrant, the eyelashes, dark and young, too real. *Nivāta niṣkampatayā vibhāti yogādhirūḍhā iva mārutena:* description of Śiva in yoga by the poet Kālidāsa. (Looked like a yogi in trance, as steady as a flame of lamp in windless serenity.) Of course the whiteness and smooth folds of the garment revealed a freshness that could not have been even a morning old.

The Cry

I was still wondering if it were dead or alive; if it were indeed a marble statue. A lamp was burning. A few flowers lay scattered on the slightly raised stone platform on which the yogi kept seated on a deer skin. I tried with all my heart to ask the question, "Are you alive, yogi? Are you of us, of this world?" I must have asked the question. For immediately, as the question cried within me, a tearingly shrill note, echoing within the walls of the small room, hooted firmly, startingly and definitely, . . . but only once. The sharp cry, like a bird locked unawares within a closed room, and frantically trying to find a way of escape, knocked itself against the blind walls, and sensitively spiralled in echoes and counter-echoes, until the rustling autumn leaves in the wood outside absorbed the last faint vibrations within the thousand moans of its fallen leaves. And then the silence grew darker. Did it mean that the form was alive? When I was tempted to form another question, and test if the shrill affirmative note was indeed in response to my question, suddenly I felt a firm grip pulling at my shoulders. I was dislodged from my stone look-out.

I came dislodged. I was standing secure on ground.

That grip had shaken me to my depths. But as I looked at the tall imposing figure still holding my shoulder in his grip, I was shaken all the more. The figure looked familiar, but with the confusion raging through my mind I failed to spot him, as I should have done. The white cotton cloth around his waist, and the other end of the same cloth thrown around his shoulders, brought before my mind the tall lonely figure I used to see at the Catuhṣaṣṭhi temple. (The Sixty-four yogini temple referred to before. He was the one who had pressed the bead on my forehead.)

It took time for me to recognise and absorb him. I had never heard him speak. All I had heard from him was the incessantly poignant cry, 'Mother! Mother!'

No, he had not broken his vow. He had not spoken a word. But his gaze burned. Immediately turning around, he began to walk very fast. I began to run after him. Why, I did not realise. But I kept following, as if I had no alternative. He suddenly cut through a wood of sacred ash-apple trees. Belhattā was the name given to the wilderness; and no one dared enter and cross this section at night; never without at least a companion. He took a steady north-easterly direction until he had cleared the old waterworks complex. Then suddenly it dawned on me that the day was a Tuesday, and on this day the woods of the Bhairava temple attract a number of aspirants.

I was not mentally prepared to get to the Batuk Bhairava shrine at that hour. It was a difficult shrine. I felt that like another night's excursion to the Nepali shrine, I was being 'led' to a place where I should not go; not at least without the knowledge of the Lady in Saffron.

To an Āsana

But I had no choice. I felt tied hand and foot. The cry, 'Mother! Mother!' preceded me, and I kept my steps behind. We reached the shrine. But he did not stop there. Another five hundred yards to the west stood the almost abandoned shrine of Kāmākṣyā. The Mother's most mystic rites were performed here. It was a shrine of occult rites. Only on one day in the year, my mother used to bring the children here; but it had always to be the day time, when she sought blessings from the yogi of the shrine, who was widely respected, and . . . feared.

The sun had set for about an hour and a half. There was no moon. The place was blanketted under a dark hush. The tall figure had now slacked his pace; and was eagerly searching for some indications. Then I noticed a light.

At the back of the shrine, standing in the middle of a very wide yard, which covered almost an acre and a half of land, under an arched corridor a fire was alight. This roofed corridor built in stone, ran all along the four sides of the yard. But for the only door that gave access to this shrine, along the entire square ran this roofed corridor.

Before I could approach the fire I saw the Lady in Saffron waiting for me in the yard. But the tall figure continued his progress, until he assumed a seat. Some other persons unknown to me were seated around the fire.

Apparently a special rite was in progress.

The Lady held my hand, and the first question I heard, amazed me.

"Where have you left your *dhoti* (loin-cloth) dear yogi?"

Indeed I stood stark naked!

For the first time I realised that I had left my loin-cloth at the foot of the jackfruit tree, on the platform. I had used it as an *āsana*, but never remembered to pick it up. What a sight I might have made as I had crossed naked through the city's roads. She at once tore a wide piece of cloth from her saffron sari, and asked me to breach that between my thighs.

Then she put her hands on my head, and began to chant a *mantra*. I held my head down. Gradually I was led to a congregation. I could detect three familiar faces. One was the Vaiṣṇava saint Nārada; one was the Bhairava guardian saint of the Baṭuk-Bhairava shrine; and the third one was my silent friend, the tall saint, later known as Sadhu Jitendra of Varanasi.

There sat some other persons also. All of them were seated forming a circle. The Bhairava himself was throwing butter soaked offerings into the fire. The hissing sound, and the spreading fragrance, made me suspect fleshly substances being offered. A jug of drink was placed conveniently for all to help themselves. I noticed that the Lady in Saffron, and Nārada drank only from their personal water jugs which they always carried. I was given a drink from the Lady's jug. After the drink my mind experienced a kind of erosion, and gradually a new mind, more sensitive, more alert, more receptive emerged; and it covered my sense-world entirely. Various lights in dancing colours kept consciousness at a new level of delight. I felt the Lady in Saffron drawing me closer and closer to her body, as always in seances. Actually she appeared to be making room for a stranger, who was a Bhairavi, young, vibrant and well featured.

I heard the Lady in Saffron inform her, as she pushed me towards her, "Take this one as your own. Provide the *āsana* for him. . .Do not hesitate. . .He will bear it. . .He is anointed. He is used to the *bandha* (union). . .Only you must remain careful. Remember; I repeat; he is anointed. . .Do not cause him disruption. . ."

I was listening. I could follow her motives. But I remained dumbfounded. I realised that I had gone to the wilderness driven by the will of my friend Nārada, who wanted me to experience the direct power from a yogi. Now I realised that it was also the will of the Lady in Saffron.

I recalled how I was made to take a naked bath. How I was purified by the long meditation. I was built up through the miraculous meeting with the great yogic form. I was with a purpose guided to the spot by Saint Jitendra. And lastly, before going into the meditation I was being offered a new *āsana*, a new *sādhikā*, an unknown female *alter ego*. Obviously I was under a test, my first real test.

Yogeśvari

Nārada had promised, I remembered, to bring me to a direct experience with the power of yoga; and then he had vanished. The string of events that took place after the promise was significantly strange to me. The figure in *samādhi* under the banyan shade in the woods still held me in awe. He (?) was known as Mother (?) Yogeśvarī, as I had come to learn later. I was also to learn that I could call her, and ask direct questions, after a session of meditation, and receive answers in that shrill sound. When the same sound came twice in quick succession, as if it came along in the course of inhalation and exhalation, it meant a 'No'. This I have tested many times, and many times I found that the shrill sound was infallible.

How the white robed form came there, who she had been, what were the references, I never came to know; but I did hear from my parents that the apparition had been nothing but a memorial statue. Yet I am sure I found it to be alive whenever I approached 'her' for answers. Now when I go there I do not even feel to have any questions, neither do I ask any, and of course there would be no answers.

Neither can I approach her for answers. The openness of my mind has since been closed. Now when I go there, I too find her nothing more than a statue. The magic of bringing stones to life has long since slipped away from my weak mind. Only the strong and the fearless, the stout of heart and selfless could achieve and retain the secret mystery of the powers unknown. Now when I go, the banyan with its straggling umbrella-branches, the abounding jackfruit tree, the dry stone steps, the pulsating water in the tank remain mute, and send me no messages. Even memories pass into skeletons.

The agony of the growing youth fills the soul with many questions. Youth over, the ego of man gets too hardened to get immersed in and saturated with the spirit of true prayer.

That I owed the experience to Nārada, I had no doubt. That the place was also the favourite haunt of Saint Jitendra, I had no doubt. That both Nārada and Saint Jitendra had been working in league with my Lady in Saffron, I had no doubt.

As the unfolding events would tell.

8

A Pack of Four

I, an Āsana

Flanked by Nārada on one side, and the Lady in Saffron on the other I lay down on the bare floor, flat on my back. I was, as usual, nude, and knew what was going to happen. Who cared? On one side Nārada, on the other side the Lady in Saffron. The unknown *Śakti* sat on me in *Sukhapadmāsana.* The only other one who sat on a similar human *āsana* was the Bhairava himself. Of course he had his *uttara sādhikā* (*alter ego*) to assist him.

The hours of the night had passed in quiet solemnity. Tārā, Tārā Tārā! At the sudden cry of the Bhairava we all became alert. He was chanting, and we had all joined. The last lines of the famous hymn from the Mahānirvāṇa Tantra rang out through the quiet solemn void.

> HRING! Oh Destroyer of time! ŚRING! Oh the Terrific One! KRING!
> Thou who are beneficent! Night of Darkness . . . of opaque desire,
> Thou art yet the liberator from all bonds of desire.

Then it was followed by the lines from the celebrated Kālī hymn. The dark gloom trembled and shivered. Thrill after thrill followed in measured succession.

> Mother, this chant sung with care,
> this homage paid with the proper rites
> makes the souls of mortals purified,
> when together with the worship, they offer their souls
> to the pair of your lotus feet:
> this prayer sung through the midnight
> whilst the worship goes on,
> makes even the words of the demented flow with
> a sweet sense of poetry. . .

And soon after rose the solemn chants, repeatedly, like gong bells striking in rhythm, and resonating within.

OM HUM KṢAM YAM RAM LAM VAM KROM
OM HUM KṢAM YAM RAM LAM VAM KROM
OM HUM KṢAM YAM RAM LAM VAM KROM

followed by, *mahākālī bhairava sarva-vighṇān-nāśaya nāśaya hrim phat svāha...*

Then the hiss. . . the flame leaping up. . . and the familiar smell of the burning of the fur and skin of some animal. . .(*salomāsthi svairam palalamapi mārjāramasite. . .*) soon I got immersed. No smell, no light, no sound from the chants disturbed, or should I say, reached me; neither the weight of the one who was embracing me with her bare thighs. Her heels locked and pressed against the *kuṇḍalanī* point, a little below the *svādhiṣṭhāna granthi* (nerve point of the second lotus).

My consciousness stood at a standstill *like a lamp in a windless sky:* yet I did experience the feeling of being carried at a very high speed through masses and masses of light bodies, like shooting stars, through the 'starry meads' as mystery poems describe, until a blinding beam of light began to whirl around me shedding beams after beams of brilliantly waving colours, and I appeared to crave for some quiet, some peace, some tranquil pause, just to inhale, and cope with the thrilling breath taking experience.

Then suddenly dawned a period of tranquillity, with the speed still vibrating.

Have you ever noticed a frisking squirrel speeding up the trunk of a tree, and then waiting, and watching you for a split second? Have you noticed at that split moment the bristles standing still on its back, and yet thrilling with a strange expectancy? Naturalists call it rader charged action of the fur of the rodent. That pause from speed, that stilled thrill between speed and speed. Do you visualise? Some sublime satisfaction, some fulfilled glee of having what you always longed to have, bathing you with a cool delight. It is an experience that leaves the nerves not tired, but rejuvenated; not dismayed, but strengthened. It is a tonic that makes the mind dare. Dreaded courage takes further strides, and new hopes leap. The innermost being of consciousness, the soul's very identity, then feels secured; one feels utterly non-attached; a kind of disregard for anything that lacks the soul power.

It strengthens the being. Under its drive the feeling of allness of the soul becomes supreme. . .

How long shall I continue to describe it? It is futile. It is useless. It was a feeling of 'joy forever'.

In December, 1977 on my return to India, I visited that haloed shrine again. I had the earnest desire to meet the Bhairava. The day I had reached was the second anniversary of his ascension. But his *alter ego*, the same Bhairavi *uttara śādhikā* still lingered there, crumpled like a dark prune. I was not a little amazed to find that she had been anticipating the meeting. From her ready recognition, and eagerness I knew something was in progress. She was sitting outside her dark hovel, where she now spent her days, and 'nights'.

Some other Bhairavas had taken over. She was kept at a venerable distance.

"No, I am alone now," she replied to my enquiry. "The new Bhairava still needs some more years to mature; but this is how She wills: and we submit. I am training a new Bhairavi. . . Why not come next new moon night? . . . I hope you have not changed."

I was not the same adept, I confessed; and excused myself for the time being. She, however, smiled, and assured. "Even a little of this, stands in good stead at hours of crisis." . . . She had quoted the Gitā, my favourite 'bible.' "You will come back," she continued. "I will be there, though not in this flesh. Still I will be. Come again. There is never a going away from the path. Come back."

This was not the only time when I got lost to a feeling of supreme power, a bliss of profundity in joy, a recharging of the confidence of manhood in the personality of individual existence. A paradise lost reserves a paradise regained.

I had similar experiences on four more occasions.

Let me relate.

The Humble Saint

Once I too had asked of a saint the idiotic question, "How does it feel when one is in *samādhi*?" We have already referred to the touching lines of Vidyāpati, the Vaiṣṇava poet:

"Do not ask. It is indescribable. Each word spoken thirsts for another word. The more it is described, the more remains to be discribed." Tagore says it succinctly, "You and I together. None to intervene. Nothing to bar", or "Within the magic lake of mind I experience a honeyed stillness; but I fail to gather even a drop; for that celestial sweetness eludes human grasp."

No the contents of *samādhi* are beyond describing.

This saint I was speaking of had visited my humble abode in the holy city of Prayāg situated at the confluence of the two rivers, the Ganga and the Yamuna. Every twelve years here assemble all the different saints of the Hindu order, irrespective of modal differences.

On the appointed day in the heart of winter, a couple of million people. with at least five hundred thousand recluses, monks, anchorites, saints and *sādhus* (male and female) assemble for a ritual dip at the confluence, at a certain given time. From all over the great land of the Indian subcontinent, from the South-East Asian countries, and even from beyond. These godly people regularly assemble here on an appointed date. I have always felt intrigued how they keep scientifically so alert and accurate about the date without any media known and organised by the 'civilised'. It takes so much of organised publicity to collect about a hundred thousand people during the Olympics; without any fanfare of publicity, any competitive, incentive, how do the masses assemble periodically. What moves them to dare the harassment? What cudoes do they expect? How is it all organised? Who organises? That event has remained a wonder to me.

That year, winter was exceptionally exacting; and conditions became more trying because of an early winter monsoon with hail and sleet. It was a trying Kumbha, as the *sādhu*-fair is called. (I recall that to have been the only January when I saw icecles in Allahabad.)

I had returned from an early bath at the confluence of holy rivers; and was very busy in wasting my time with some friends talking of literature and similar uselessly useful subjects, to the delicious accompaniment of cups of tea and hot snacks. It was an extremely material moment of fullness.

When came a knock; and with the knock entered a frail form, about five feet three inches, light stepped, donning a simple beard, not too long, and wearing just a light cotton piece, which having covered his loins could hardly cover his frail body. Locks, turned copperish through over exposure to the sun, hung loose on a pair of indistinguished shoulders. The eyes were half closed.

Carried away by the youthful gaiety of nonchalance and fun, and excited by the hypnosis of uttering the wittiest and smartest remarks on Wilde, Shaw, Lawrence, Freud, Rolland, Eliot, Sartre, Gide, Jung, names, names and names, I ignored the slight person altogether. Taking him for a begging, mendicant I rudely directed him to try his knocks at the other door. He might succeed to draw the attention of my more devout mother.

And he knocked at the other door.

Imagine my utter shock when a few minutes later I found my mother entering the room with smiles spread all over her face, and introducing the stranger as my cousin Chakravarty, who had been lost in the Himalayas these twenty years or more. He had come to pay homage to her, who had given him suck when orphaned as a baby.

The last we heard of him was when he had been working at the Royal College of Nepal as the Head of the Department of English; but then one morning he was found missing. And only now my mother had rested her eyes on the prodigal.

I had heard of my cousin C, and of his spiritual greatness. Now I got an opportunity to see him at close quarters. At my mother's earnest requests, he obliged her by the longest stretch of stay at one place; for four days. He would not disappoint her. He said that he had come to attend the bath no doubt; but his chief mission was to have a 'final' meeting with 'one who had given him suck'. He should have been over fifty years in age; but he looked young; hardly thirty. He had not even greyed.

And gradually I came to be convinced of his sincere devotion to the life he led.

So, I could not resist to learn from him. I wanted to know from him what do saints actually realise in *samādhī*.

Feeling Free with the Supreme

"How does *samādhi* taste?" The question nagged. "This was the time," I thought.

Those four days were to me four years of reconstruction. The time I had passed at the university, engrossed in collecting learning of a different kind had been, spiritually, years of a wide waste with nothing of growth, or even of maintenance of what I had acquired.

Finding saint C within the precincts of my homely surroundings I indulged in some kind of mental refreshments, spiritual replenishments. It was a kind of indulgence that he condiscendingly sanctioned. He tolerated me with infinite patience.

Of the many questions the one I asked most emphatically was a direct one. "Why did he have to leave all his past duty-bound commitments behind, and take to this lonely path? What were its gains? What exactly did it offer? Why this yoga? To what end?"

I had already warned him not to trade with me the cheap common pretentions about filling the heart and soul with love, and come back for serving humanity with love etc. By now I had seen how such empty presumptions could lead to fraud and pretence.

If that were so true, filling the heart with love etc, why like Kṛṣṇa, other supermen had been able to fulfil their respective obligations to spirit, in spite of being fully involved in life? In fact most of the Vedic and Puranic *ṛṣis*, if not all of them, had served their times with dedication, in spite of the fact that they were householders? They did not seek total seclusion by embracing a run-away life, in order to equip themselves with the necessary power.

"Are you questioning me for your knowledge," he asked, "or, are you criticising my way of life as I live now? Are you angry with me brother?"

His eyes were half closed; his frail figure was held straight as he sat in the *Padmāsana* posture (as he always did); his voice was poised, smooth, calm and sonorous. The very picture would convince any cynic of the earnestness of his mission, and the depth of his 'knowledge' of things. He indeed was all spiritual. A man *realised.* He, to my mind, represented the quintessence of a yogic bliss. How contented and self-contained was his demeanour.

And where was I? Cut off from my regular line of power, away from the practices, covered by doubts, impounded by a willing slavery to 'reason' (as the Western thoughts had taught me to be), I had turned domesticated, practical. I was racing after 'success,' as I was bedevilled to understand and accept 'success'. I was teaching in those days, and knew no end of my conceit for knowledge!

Close-eyed, he was waiting for my answer.

"I am doing nothing of the kind," I said. "All I am asking, and I have got to ask is, why must one run away from life, and seek something intangible and immaterial, if the subsequent gain is zero, or less than zero? What do you get out of this stake? What? You have to tell me please."

The eyes closed, the body held straight and aloof, the voice sedate and cool, 'C' replied, "I have to, as you ask. And I will."

Then there was silence.

I recalled my old days. I used to be tolerant with such pauses and silences. I held my breath, and waited.

"I seek joy; eternal joy; joy for life; joy for the living."

"Do not talk rubbish." My irritation at having to listen to these cliches made me intolerant. "I have got sick of hackneyed phrases. If there is so much joy collected for the living, as you say and insist, you and the like of you—then, why am I not in joy? Why? Why is so much suffering all around? Since the Buddha and Jesus we have been accustomed to live on this poor pottage! Now enough of it!"

(How impatient and impudent I had turned out to be because of the grooming I had received in a soul-less university!)

"Your joy and my joy could be very differently sought and differently viewed. What do you mean by joy? Have you ever tasted joy?"

As soon as the question was asked, the closed eyes opened.

But that look! It was the glitter from a diamond in a dance hall filled with redundant people. A personal focus of attention in an impersonal crowd.

"Of course I had my moments of joy", I said. "So what?"

"Moments. . . ." he chuckled. "Like what? When? How?... Let me see."

"Art gives me great satisfaction", I said. "Art, literature. Good and noble literature. Art, literature, music. . . ."

"Pause. Pause. Hold your breath, and pinpoint exactly what you seek, and what you get as what you term as joy. Precisely if you may."

"I cannot. My sublimest moments of the most satisfying experience of joy come invariably from excellent pieces of sublime literature. . ."

"Like what? Give me an example, please."

I began after a moment's hesitation. "All right. If you insist. Shakespeare for example. . . ."

He did not allow me to finish. I smelt, somehow, that he had almost cornered his quarry after calculated stalking.

"Quote lines, for example. Quote." It was a stern command. And meekly I followed suit, and recited:

Our revels are now ended. These our actors,
As I foretold you, were all spirits, and
Are melted into air, into thin air;
And like the baseless fabric of this vision,
The cloud capped towers, the gorgeous palaces,
The solemn temples, the great globe itself,
Yea, all which it inherit, shall dissolve
And, like this insubstantial pageant faded
Leave not a rack behind. We are such stuff

As dreams are made on, and our little life
Is rounded with a sleep.

I remember that I had put my all into reciting those lines; and the effect created the desired solemnity.

Saint 'C' had kept his eyes half closed. His limp arms lay on his laps, fingers gathered into a prayer posture.

"How long did it last? How long does it last pray? This excellent feeling of feeling free with the supreme of all sensations?"

Feeling free with the supreme of all sensations! What a way to express ecstatic experience. I was impressed; nay overwhelmed. The magic of a profound presence, a close friendliness, was at work. And I quietly submitted, "Not very long I believe; not long at all. That's the tragedy. 'The Call eludes the sight and the touch. Has it got congealed in this vernal voice of the Infinite?' That's how Tagore cries. We all cry."

"No! Not all. My source of joy is a magic fountain. It is like the tap you use in your home. You open it, and leave it open as long as you want to have the water you need; and you close it, when you do not need any more. At your own free will at your beck and call it operates. If you wanted to use the shower for hours, days, months, years . . . well, it is up to you, the blessing of water pours, pours, pours. And soon as you want to stop, well, turn it off. It is essentially yours. It is within you. This fountain of joy. It is under your control. You command it; you maintain it. . . Yes this fountain of joy is all yours. Soul is the refuge of soul. Soul is the light of soul. Yoga bestows it; *sādhanā* prepares it; *samādhi* enjoys it; and the *sādhu* roams free from all 'whats' and 'whys', obligations and commitments. He is committed to only one thing; this joy, which he spreads; he brings peace to those who seek it. And there are so many who seek. I seek for instance. And you, if I have known you correctly. There is no tragedy but what we ourselves compose. We the poets; we the actors; we the audience."

"What is it that man gets in *samādhi*?", I asked. "Please make it clearer. We are getting lost in poetry."

"What is it," he counter-questioned in the known Indian way of teaching, "that man wants to get most?"

"Joy; happiness I suppose," I replied. "Or contentment may be, in a different language".

"That will do. Now, answer me. Do you feel clean amongst the unclean?" he asked. When I replied in the negative, he continued, "Then, how could one experience joy, call it contentment, when there is suffering all around? Yet man must seek and find joy. Else his life would be barrenly lived. Moreover, one cannot give what one has not got. In order to give joy, one must have joy. Then what is the solution?" he asked. "Enigma? Eh?", he chuckled.

"Not so," I said. "Buddha, for instance, might have to say that the solution lies in freedom from birth, or some other like rubbish, with which I have the least desire to meddle with."

He ignored my slight, and continued.

"To *feel* clean it is not enough *to be* clean; it becomes the duty of those who want to feel clean to make their surroundings clean. They have to work hard for it; but then, there seems to be no other way open. In a world left unclean there is no chance of feeling clean.

"So about joy. Man must work for the removal of suffering. Everything, every method, every devise appears to be sanctified, ethical, if it could remove universal suffering, sufferings of the living in body, sufferings of the mind, and sufferings from lack of expression, or communication. This equally involves economical suffering, spiritual suffering and political suffering. Whatever is done for removing these kinds of suffering is holy, god's work. This I believe.

"This is also what Rāma believed, Kṛṣṇa believed. This is why we call them supermen, gods, removers of suffering. Love alone should be enough to make the evil understand, and turn to the good way. But when love and understanding fails, as failed in the case of the Kauravas, then the violent way is the correct way. Only one way is left. The violent way. Because a duty cannot be given up. Then even a violent way becomes a way. Under the pressure of love and softness duty cannot be given up. Like *śama* (peace) and *dama* (control), *daṇḍa* (punishment) is also one of the assigned means of correction. Extreme in extreme cases. Not to adopt the same would be wrong. . . I understand that much. And I agree with you. But what makes a Kṛṣṇa a Kṛṣṇa? What makes a man a superman? What makes him a being apart?"

I had to reflect awhile before I could reply. "It appears to be his capacity of understanding, forbearance, wisdom, added to his ability to bring himself directly in opposition to the vile and the vicious, and fight it with strength and power, if, of course, his power of love fails."

I was not entirely pleased with my lifeless reply!

"You are not getting clear to yourself", he said. "A superman distinguishes himself from the common run of men by the great challenging virtue of involvement; involvement without the least selfish motive. The genuinely powerful must feel involved in the least of social transgressions. None should feel free of other lives. Lives are interrelated by an unseen and inscrutable bond of fellowship. One disturbed life sparks off a host of chained disturbances. Such imbalances must be rectified with a strong hand. Maintaining equilibrium becomes a demanding responsibility of the superman. Kṛṣṇa, and his active involvement with the society he lived in, for example. He was indeed a superman.

"But wishing is not acting. Acting without power is a weak action; and weak action generates a general weakness in *corpus socialis*. Therefore effective action calls for power; and this power to be abidingly effective must flow from spiritual ability alone. Again, look at Kṛṣṇa's life, which is a record of total love. Total dedication can come only out of total love. Without the backing of personal power how could one wield power? If some one has been himself lacking in love, what will he give? So the root of good intentions springs from the power of love, or the ability to love; in yogic language we call it *kauśala*. It lies in self-control (*dama*): that self-control which makes one fight for others without personal ends. It calls for tremendous resourcefulness in acquiring spiritual power, which could be charged from the yogic sources alone. This power is also known as 'Grace'. It is the Mother of all powers. The light of this power removes the darkest intentions of evil minds. This is the eternal power of ecstasy (*ānandam*)."

"What is exactly the nature of this *ānandam*?", I asked.

This time my voice reflected my earnestness. I felt that 'C' felt pleased, and perhaps more relaxed. He radiated perceptively an aura of peace and joy. We were nearing a desired point of agreeableness.

"What about the joy you received from your association with the saints you have met?" He paused menacingly, and continued in a much deeper voice, with his eyes almost closed, "What about the old Lady of Varanasi, your aunt? Did she not lead you to joy?"

"I have lost the touch. Now it appears to have been a thing of the past. In those days I would have risked anything for retaining that link with the source." As I confessed, my voice charged with emotion faltered. Was I not feeling like a lost lamb? He suddenly looked at me; raised his palm, and continued. "Now, supposing I bring the lost power back to you, which of these two kinds of joy you would like to have?. . . Not that I am proposing to bring it back. But let us talk. You had asked about the nature of this joy. Let us answer that. Which of these two kinds of joy is dearer to you, and why?"

I did not hesitate; I did not falter. The spirit of the Lady in Saffron all on a sudden enveloped me. All on a sudden I felt all hers. It filled me with courage. I wanted to be mercilessly true to myself. I said that I sought the joy of the inner spirit, and not the one derived from art and literature.

And at once came the question, "Why?"

Famous lines raced through my memory. Great sages have recorded this eternal answer in their words, words of all time. I just went on repeating, "What is that knowledge by knowing which all that is worth being known becomes known? . . . Know Him, and arrive at immortality . . .

"To get that by getting which nothing else is again to be got; the firm feeling of that which when felt does not permit even the most acute suffering to affect feelings.

"When one arrives at this, the emotional self is stilled and pierced; all doubts come to an end; and actions are rendered free of reaction."

But he stopped me, and said, "This joy is within yourself. It is like a flowing pipeline, supplying joy and sweetness from an eternal and unlimited reservoir. You open it and drink when you like, as I explained a while back. It is essentially your source of strength. From this strength you go from on to on."

That has been up to this day the best description of this source of power, nay, the best transcended description of the joy that springs from this power.

Was I not on that mystic night at the Kāmākṣyā shrine transcended to a region of light? But where has fled the light? Where? Where have gone the snows of yester years?

But I came to know of this mystery of love and power, bliss and eternity, yet again in the year 1954. This was about 12 years after the Prayāg meeting with Saint 'C'.

The Lost Leader

I had camped for some time at a height of 11,000 feet, away from the Tibet-Simla hills of the Himalayas. A group of young men from the universities were engaged in laying a part of the Himalayan roads. I was supposed to supervise their camp life, and discipline. The upshot was that I found myself in a thoroughly enjoyable role of a conscience keeper for those whose conscience was still found in a state of flux.

It so happened that I used to get away from the bustle during the evening; and one evening I lost my way in a deep forest. That part of the forest was notorious for pythons and bears. And I had descended to a considerable depth in a gorge, never realising how fast the evening with its darkness, could envelop a gorge. Along my climb up, there came a point when I knew I would not be able to make it, and must find myself a night's shelter. I went round and round in the mountain-puzzle until, tired and perhaps scared, I realised I had fallen into a loop, coming back to the same point. I was perspiring heavily. I was out of breath. I felt I was on the point of fainting. I carried neither a torch, nor even a match box. All I depended on was a chance grabbed rude stick. Eventually I came upon a rather flat piece of stone. Readily I rested on it and tried to gain my breath, take my bearings, and perhaps to think about the next course of step. I was thinking; but at the same time I felt I was about to pass out.

The unrelieved solid mass of sombre opaque darkness overpowered my senses. The forest's heavy breath steadily rose and fell, like the sleeping body of a mammoth python. Myriads of fireflies pinpointed the thick mantle of the dark. A strange vibration continued reporting me a message.

Somehow my mind was registering it. I ought to have felt lost. I ought to have felt scared. I ought to have been going through spells of nervousness of sorts. But no. Nothing like that happened. It felt as if I just woke up in my own room in the pit of a dark night, and found nature breathing more heavily and scaringly than it should. The familiar had become unfamiliar.

I realised that for me there was only one step to take, one thing to do. I sat in an *āsana*, and made myself as relaxed as possible in the circumstances, and plunged in taking a dip within myself. I got merged in meditation.

Soon the hills cleared, and I was floating into space, instead of being engulfed by the heavy weight of the dark surroundings, I was floating through a sea of light of many colours. The body that contained myself was left far behind; and I was clothed by a superbly delightful aroma. At times a few stars like fireflies just brushed my breath, and flew at a much faster speed. I found myself singing my favourite verses from Tagore:

I watch at thy beauty with all my mind's eye. . .
My eyes need no longer wander abegging.
I hear within me strange strings stirring;
A flute call keeps drawing me nearer
to what I always sought. . .

Then there came a moment when I ceased to exist at all; when to feel was to get lost in a sea of sheer delight. I must have passed out.

I continued perspiring heavily. I heard strange voices. The air felt warm, and the breath heavier with a thick smoke.

I saw a face peering over me. "You are safe; you are all right," the voice assured in clear English.

Gradually, out of the unknown dark, materialised two faces I knew. These were two of the boys of the camp. They had come out in search of their lost leader.

I Want a Guru

By those faces, I noticed, was standing a strange young man clothed in his superbly pure nudity. He must have been nearing his thirties, and looked aglow with a piping health. Spiritual glow dripped from every strand of his hazel hair. He stood over me like a Hermes by Praxiteles in his classic frankness and simplicity. As soon as I saw him, I was filled with some newfound energy; and I got up, and sat on the rude floor. The two students were busy wiping my sweat, and a blanket, most certainly borrowed, was thrown over me to stop a mild shiver. A lamp burnt meekly; and a fire crackled.

It was a cave, L-shaped, the front not being three feet wide and about four feet deep. After a sharp bend at right angles the cave ran in a broken ovalish shape about eight feet deep. I had been sitting in this part, on the bare rock bestrewn with ashes.

I paid homage to the sage only after he had greeted me in a very sincere and respectable manner befitting yogis. He must have received formal education in academics, as his choice vocabulary in Sanskrit and English, specially his distinct pronunciation of each chosen word showed.

I could not resist a smile. "So", I said, "you are the one causing this darkness, and confusion, the loss of tracks and the other things. You must be a troubleshooter of sorts. Thank you . . . But why? . . . Why do you call me? Why, at any rate this harassing recourse? . . . I feel puzzled."

I was speaking in Sanskrit, and at times we both broke into English. The two boys stood confused. They did not understand a syllable of what had been transpiring between us.

"I needed you badly sir . . . very badly indeed. Pardon me for arranging this forced meeting without warning you. I had heard of your coming. The hill people talked of you. I would have much liked to come to you. But you see how I stand. I am helpless in a way. I feel ashamed to have to put on borrowed cover to suit the ignorant. I feel so easy and natural as I am. And when I walk in my natural state, I see that I embarrass others. So I do not move from this cave. I needed you, sir; I needed you. So I called. You have to pardon me. You have come. That is the big thing. Thank you. Thank you indeed. Please accept this." He held out his hand holding a bunch of rhododendrons, in full bloom.

Accepting the charming gift I asked modestly, "Why . . . of all beings you must need me dear friend?"

"I need a guru. I badly need a guru. I called you for this. Please do not deny me the privilege. I need you. . ."

That insistent appeal could have shaken any being. The two boys stood dumbfounded, as they now half realised what had been passing between us.

Then he revealed his tale to me.

He had been found inspired even as a child. Born in a family of Brahmin Vaiṣṇavas he was picked by Christian missionaries, and educated by them. Soon the poor parents discovered a spiritual calling in the child, and became more and more concerned about it.

The mother was a devout Vaiṣṇava; the father was a traditional Vedic Brahmin. The conservative family had no other child. After his school-leaving test when he had been taking studies at the university, he came to his mother and asked for a 'release' from life in the everyday world. He needed permission from the mother to become a pilgrim along the path of eternity.

At first the father had objected, but after a time, when the mother could not bear the pangs of her son's separation from his soul's quest, she finally freed him with a heavy heart.

When he had left home, some twelve years back, the mother had blessed him, and told him that he should never forget God, and chant the name of Rāma, and she herself would protect him through the power of that name. "In Rama's name" she said, "I myself, and all the world come alive and alert. So Rāma Rāma Rāma. Go to Rāma."

I was listening with rapt attention to the new legend of the Great Immigration. Then he reported something that took me by surprise.

The Scribbled Words

He said that in the state of trance he often scribbled. But he could not decipher later what he did scribe. He asked me if I could assist him in reading what he had scribbled.

I went through the neatly kept first volume. The writing was clear enough. But the script offered a great surprise. These were written now in Bengali, now in a script very near to Bengali, but not Bengali, may be Oriya; and some other parts were written, most likely in some forgotten oriental language, the alphabets looking like cuneiform. While the scripts were varying, the language, where I could decipher, was speaking consistently in esoteric tantric Sanskrit, and loaded with *mantras*, *maṇḍalas*, signs, together with directions on certain rites. The language, I observed, at times broke away from pure Sanskrit to Prākṛt, and even to the straight current provincial dialects. The subjects hovered around the central theme, tantra and the tantric practices.

It was an entirely amazing discovery. Quite taken aback I looked at him. My wild eyes must have betrayed my perplexed bewilderment. But unconcerned he, a child so to say, continued to speak of his handiwork composition and the diagrams.

"Have I gone all mad? What are these? Why? Who gets these scribbled by me? Poor me?"

"On the contrary," I said, "they make excellent sense."

But I would neither explain, nor read out. I knew, I assured him, that the source from which he received these messages would one day reveal more clearly what he alone was not only destined to know, but was also the most equipped to know.

Finding a Guru

He kept the book aside, as if it were a bunch of papers of no consequence to him. His most insistent demand was that I become his guru. When he was about to fall at my feet, I held him by my hand, and embraced him. The pine fire was crackling. With the flame before us I drew him close to me, and gradually 'on' to me; as I was seated in the Vīra-āsana. He was seated on my left thigh, his back touching my shoulder and chest. I began to whisper in his ears. (The two boys had been stilled by now, and sat crouched in the farthest corner of the dark.) "Thou shall have no guru, O thou blessed one. One who had the mother as a guru, needs no other guru. And the *mantra* thou seekest lives vibrating within thee in its fullest glory."

"And what is it then?" he screamed driven besides himself.

"Of course Rāma", I said. "Did not thine own mother cover thee, with that *mantra* as thou had undertaken the *niṣkramaṇa* rite? (the journey out for liberation) . . . Now, take my advice. Regard the Mother herself as thy true guru, thou lucky one, the blessed one. Thou shall have all that thou seekest. A few years more. Wait and try".

Suddenly he jumped out of my embrace, snatched a burning wood from the fire, and danced out into the dark outside. The figure vanished; the flaming torch gradually faded into a dot of light, which finally was swallowed up by the thick jaws of the dark forest locked within the sharper jaws of the gorge.

Camping in a Blizzard

The third incident also refers to one of my journeys to the Himalayas. This time it was Kashmir; and the area refers to the northern range stretching from the Pir Panjoli, to the famous Amarnāth hills. One has to reach it by climbing a height of 17,000 feet at the Vavyan peak. The route lies through the Liddar valley, and crosses two steep climbs, the first, the Pissu Pass, and the second, the Machhar Pass. Then one reaches the source of the Liddar at the lake of Seshnag; from Seshnag a steep climb finally descends to the valley of Panchatarani where five streams form a beautiful confluence. The route is difficult, but not as difficult as the rest of the mountain pass. Up and down it goes for over eight miles until the valley of the Amar Gangā is reached. On the banks of the Amar Gangā rises a bare rugged steep hill which contains the famous cave of the shrine of Amarnāth, a self-evolved snow *lingam*, a miraculous ice formation* by itself.

I had reached the valley of the Liddar in the early part of the month of June, a time most unwelcome for a trip to Amarnāth. But I felt a strong call; and I had to make a start. It looked I had no

*Ice formations are no miracles. Yet this one was miraculous. This miracle of the formation has been pointed out and discussed in a book on Kashmir, *Kalhaner Dese* (in Bengali) by the author.

option. The weather conditions were not only forbidding, but the glacial state of the high mountains after the Chandanwari gorge and the Pissu Pass had created a special threat of sudden avalanches. Particularly because a team of English men had been rescued a week back from a glacial catastrophe, any further attempt to reach the cave was legally forbidden until August.

But I had to go. I obtained a special permission from the local authorities, and signed a bond for undertaking the pilgrimage 'at my own risk'. That was a menacing phrase. But once the call comes, nothing matters I believe.

I had to carry a complete commisariat on horseback, inclusive of a small tent. On another horse I had to cover the journey in four days.

On the evening of the second day I was overwhelmed by the weird howl of a nasty blizzard; and I had to take shelter in a dilapidated ramshackle which had once been a hut. The drover pony, carrying our succour and shelter was nowhere to be seen. The animal with his man appeared to have melted away. Being a son of the soil he must have sensed the catastrophe, and had already taken shelter.

The night was terrible. Rain and blizzard continued until 2 o'clock in the morning. On the point of utter collapse and exhaustion I discovered a being in the dark; but I could not figure it in spite of my best attempts. My mind must have gone out of conscious functioning for a while. A warm fire, and the smell from some burning drug, most possibly marijuana, brought my senses back.

A naked and emaciated old man, with a heap of matted locks, was seated in a corner. Had I met with this apparition in a museum, I would certainly have taken him for an epidermised skeleton. I had no energy left in me to probe further. I could still hear the breath and the sniffings of my horse. But the warmth, and perhaps the effect of the smoke flung me into the arms of a drugged slumber.

The Distance That Never Narrows

When I got up, dawn was just trying to get through a very heavy blanket of fog. My horse was munching, and occasionally stamping his hoofs. I was up. But the phantom-man was gone without a trace.

The drover had arrived, and directed me to pick up the journey while the sun did not get hot. A high sun would soften the fallen snow, and endanger the climb, more so along the steep descent to Panchatarani. The fearsome peak of Vavyan was looking me into the face; but I girt up, and made a start after two quick cups of black coffee conjured by the illusive drover.

I had not ridden much further from the bivouac when I became conscious of the same dark figure walking naked, bare feet on the white snow, and slowly climbing the menacing peak. Faint strains of a merry chant floated past me. It was a Śiva chant, punctuated by sudden breaks into the cry, 'Hail Amarnāth'.

While I wondered at the patience and the endurance of the little man, I also tried to reach him on my horseback. I gave the heel to the horse; but much as I would like my mount to overtake the figure at the front, and much as the beast would trot faster to a canter, no, I could not in any way shorten the distance. The figure, serene and unperturbed, would obstinately keep its distance.

It was no spectre. It was a reality. A fact. The drover was goading me again and again to keep to the tracks left on the snow by the fellow's bare feet. 'There is no danger there', he would encourage me, and I would drive on and on and on; but I failed to come an inch nearer the 'figure'.

Having reached the peak the figure raised both his hands and gave out a fierce cry, 'Hail Amarnāth,' and then vanished over the other side of the watershed. When my horse reached that spot on the peak, I looked for the footprints on the snow. They were not there; and nowhere again, all along the descending broad vista of the mountain's snow clad slopes, where the garrulous Panchatarani flowed at a distance of three miles. Even a sparrow, a flitting mouse, could be spotted against so white a background. But all I saw was snow and snow alone. The descent looked broad and smooth. An entire wide backdrop glistened in the sun. In fact it had been the wide surface of a river, now frozen. There was no place to afford cover even to a cat. But the figure had apparently melted into thin air.

The drover in despair shouted out his dismay, "Yah Allah. . .La illaha il-Allah". While he had his reason to break out thus, I too was shaken. But we held our peace between us. Noises made under extreme degrees of tension not only break through the silence, they often, break through the unchartered confidence-barriers, and go a long way in rehabilitating the shaken nerves. Who but a cynic, then, could laugh at the effects of chants and *mantra*?

Came the Panchatarani; and we should have pressed on through the gorge. But soon a nasty roaring blizzard began to cough and puff awesome portents, and the terrific cataclasm broke loose with a mighty roar lashing and pounding the walls of the mountain sides. The blizzard rushed through the long narrow funnel of the gorge sweeping everything before it. Rains, hails and biting winds made a shambels of the prospects of a peaceful enjoyable journey. There was no question of further progress. The scaling of the last pass was postponed to the next morning. In an abandoned stable we lit a fire and settled for a sticky shivering bivouac.

The blessings that climatic changes bestow on nerves cannot be fully appreciated unless life is lived in the open. The best of prayers have been discovered and sung by Zarathustra, or the Buddha under an open sky. Imagine the Vedic sages, the Essines, the saints of yore like Socrates, Jesus living closed within a sky-scrapping mansion in Manahattan and kneeling within closed doors, and receiving the Ten Commandments, the Lord's Prayer, the solemn *Puruṣa-sūkta* or the *Gāyatrī* over a voice from the radio.

The Cave

Early morning. The climate had changed. It was heavenly. A soft sun soaked our skin with a rippling delight. The horse between my thighs felt my delight, and responded to my happy tune. (My tunes, I have come to believe since, are better appreciated by horses). I passed the gorge all alone. The drover was left behind to look after the camp, and to prepare some meals for both of us. I had taken, however, with me a package of offerings (nothing at all could be expected in the icy wilderness) and a prayer book.

The horse was now descending to the frozen Amar Gangā valley.

Soon the cave shrine came to view.

High atop the mountain the mystic cave-mouth was bathed with a brilliant sun. The actual shrine was yet to be seen.

The horse kept trotting over the frozen course of the river, now and then munching at a mouthful of broken snow. The brilliance of the sun, a most feared cause for night blindness amongst the nomads of these parts, often hit the eye, although covered with goggles. The crisp air and the chaste sorroundings radiated the twin blessings of serenity and composure. My soul was flooded with delight.

Thousands of years ago the ancients had selected sublime beauty spots for their many pilgrimaging settlements. Their love for natural beauty and their skill in popularising and publicising those remote spots through sundry legends and lores defies the best efforts of modern holiday-spot seekers. It appears quite remarkable to me that the ancients of Greece, India, Japan, and I dare say of China too, always posted their holy places in sublime surroundings of seductive beauty.

Spirit seeks beauty along with Truth. Holiness is a complex feeling that sets in motion man's instinctive desire to rise above the petty, drab and embarrassing coercions of life. It releases the cramped spirit of liberal youthfulness in man, and it opens avenues to man's awareness of beauty, truth and love. A pilgrimage undertaken proposes a journey to the sublime. God is just another name for the sublime. Its abode is rightfully divined as heaven.

The cave gradually came nearer, and as I got near the foot of the hills, it got lost behind the hanging crags. The winding tracks, however, could be seen. I left the horse there, and began to climb slowly the rocky uneasy track.

A new vigour appeared to have activised me in spite of the strains of the previous days. I climbed like a mountain stag, and reached the mouth of the cave like a young boy drawn by some mysterious expectation.

It was a strange feeling to be alone for hundreds of miles, overlooking a snow-packed terrain and faced with hoary challenging peaks of perennial snow. Snow has its own silence; the silence of death.

Through the blinding sun I could detect some sparkling movements followed by flutters. The least sound would be heard a hundredfold in that quiet, serene rock locked panorama. Soon I observed that the flutter and the dazzle came from a pair of white snow pigeons. These were the proverbial companions of the Lord of the hills. I had been told so much about the mysterious pigeons of good luck. What luck could await me in a forlorn empty cave?

I entered the cave with the bundle of offerings in my hand. The surface was all packed with hard ice, slippery and dangerous. I had a fall at the very entrance. But soon as I gained my balance, and got up, I heard a consoling voice greeting me, "Take care. No hurry. You have reached."

We Meet Again

On nothing at all, but on a slab of ice that emaciated spectre was seated. I at once recognised the mystery man of the dark night who had guided my way through the unmarked snow. Now the distance had vanished. The same light and sparing body, the same matted locks heaped on the head, the same form, the same size. Yes, it was the same man wearing nothing around but the light. Yet it seemed incredible that he would, on his bare feet, cover this long distance, and yet outdistance me, although I was on a horse.

Amazed and thrilled at what I had at last physically found, something that I had ever sought, I bowed to the sage.

He remonstrated, and said that in a shrine social exchanges, greet-s ings must never be indulged in. "The only Lord is one, and there i he in all his glory. Bow to the Lord", he said.

There stood against the wall of the oval cave a three feet high *lingam* of snow, so perfect in balance and proportions that it would be incredible to accept that it was a self-made structure. With the waning and waxing of the moon the figure alternately vanishes, and reassumes its full shape. This is a traditional myth. But something struck me as very strange. Although the *lingam* was situated within the remotest part of the cave, it reflected a very bright luminosity. It was lustrous enough for photography (without a flash).

I bowed to the *lingam*, but kept standing.

"Sit here, near me," he softly commanded, and produced a small seat, drawn out from beneath him. I hesitated, and protested that his old bare skin needed it more than mine. It was his seat. (It was a broken sheet of galvanised corrugated iron, a leftover from some misty repair around the shrine.)

"My seat is here", he said pointing to the bare icy floor.

"When did you arrive?", I asked with some hesitation, covering my surprise as best as I could.

"I have been here ever since the last *Śivarātri*" (which was a couple of months back).

"*Śivarātri!*" I was shocked. "This place would be totally impassable then!"

"This place is impassable even now", he smiled. "Don't you know? But you still came. It must have been a hard trip for you, my son, and daring too, considering that all tracks have been covered by a carpet of snow."

"But you have nothing here to survive on. Not even fire. How do you keep yourself warm? How do you. . .".

He smiled again, and did not allow me to finish. "How do those pigeons survive? What fire warms them? How do the plants now asleep under the snow covering survive? Nature has enough warmth. Nature is life."

"The pigeons could fly to warmer places", I said.

"But they do not. They are here. And the plants; how do they survive? They never quit their places", he said.

"They don't survive without hiding", I parried. "Look, the panorama is bare of plants."

"Bare of plants? How do you know? What you see is fragmentary seeing. They are all around, and here; only they are asleep. . .Much is asleep in me too, much; and you do not see that. In this body so much is asleep."

I watched him in wide wonder, not understanding a syllable of this wild claim.

Reincarnation

"You look surprised. You can't believe. The warmth, thermal power of the sun, which tones up the pigeons, tones me up too. In body, that is. The same warmth is dormant in the 'sleeping' seeds and roots. That need not be surprising. Or is it?

"Let me explain. You see this body; and it is constituted of millions of cells. Each of these cells could be charged in advance, for safe storage, much as you get certain contraptions charged with stored energy. You take care of the body. But do you take care of the cells? I mean the energy potential of the cells? You look at these cells just biologically; not spiritually. How do you call it now? Thermal potentiality. (He smiled a little.) You certainly do know of it.

"But your knowledge proceeds along fragmentary paths. You feel confused again. Watch the monkey, the frog. They cover distances at great speed, in real leaps and bounds as you feel proud to describe your progress. But watch the serpent, the elephant. They move fast too; but you will miss in their way of progress your 'leaps and bounds'. They do not ever miss the contact of continuity; contact with the real as you say.

"If you kept your knowledge also attached to the inner potentiality of the system, torn away from the biological view alone, then you would have discovered and recognised the spiritual potentiality of the cells; the secret mystery of the energy potential of the cells; and then and then alone, you would have attempted to discover the secrets of getting the cells charged, as I, and many like me, get them charged; and you wonder. There is indeed nothing to wonder at all.

"So, as you see now, this question of dormancy in nature is in a way a question of charging for storage of energy also. These plants and the other lives which appear to be sleeping, are in fact engaged in the very serious and vital business of storing energy for the future, or for continuity, if you prefer.

"This body as you see, shall, at the end of the fever, also end; and leave no trace behind. You will say that nothing remains. Yet this apparent fact is difficult to live with. Something remains; the vital thing; the *prāṇa*. Extend the above theory, and one could easily see into the fact that the continuity of *prāṇa* remains unobstructed even when a body is surrendered to the elements. Through these elements, again *prāṇa śakti*, the spirit as we commonly call it, works, and blooms again, after the weeks of *prāṇa*'s winter, if you prefer to use the same imagery, are over. The spirit has no death.

"The spirit remains alive. The roots. The beginning of the things. . . . There survives life. The germ life; *bīja*; *prāṇa*. Life is more true, more real, more surviving than you imagine. Your reliance on the physical senses is a blinding faith. Yet the senses are agitated and activised by the nerves; and the reach of the nerve power, the reach of the extra sensory mind, is quite unknown, and unrealised by you. Is that not so? You forget that your senses are so organised and empowered as to receive and convey things within limits. But the unlimited could be sensed and perceived with the aid of unlimited power alone.

"You may, or may not perceive it; but it is there. The spiritually myopic cannot form a correct view of the world. Does it surprise you?"

Sweet Inaccuracies

Things began to become clearer in a new light. The language was halting; a bit mystical. There were uneasy gaps in the sequence and flow of logic; but what he said appeared to be perfectly logical in the final analysis. All he said was inductive. Not so much theoretical as perceptual.

But I persisted in asking in my mundane way. "What about hunger?" I asked. "Hunger for food; for a little fire to warm the skin. Without some outer heat the body as an object would be frozen."

"But I am not, as you see. I have survived. These are facts. The only way you would accept these for firm facts is when you put a watch on me. But you know even when you want to watch on someone you feel to keep a watch on, persons just before your eyes vanish in no time. From within the lonely dark a company materialises. The dark womb nurses light. How weak are our faculties! How weak are we! Don't you see?"

He started smiling knowingly. Obviously he had been enjoying himself. (The experienced knows that this is the precise indication for a proselyte, who comes to realise that the master is not only happy with him, but is about to bless him with knowledge.)

"Do we see all?", he began more sedately. "We do not. Could we see all? Yes we can. But we do not. Why not? Because we are away from the cosmic. But in fact we are in it, of it; if we realise that way.

"Obviously, therefore, there should not be anything that the body would not bear. The body is a mysterious reservoir of a mysterious power; only the source of that power has to be tapped. But in life what is happening? Neither do we realise that power source nor do we tap it energetically. The question does not arise.

"So, do not please disbelieve. Personal belief or disblief only betrays our own limitations. Our reasoning, logic, calculations are for a limited day-to-day use only. Are they not? It is so difficult for us to step beyond this. Reason, as we happen to know it, holds our understanding at a ransom.

"But the power asleep within us is great, immense; the *Brahman* as we know, as we identify. . . Yes I go without food for days. What of that? At times I have to. Because. . . .

Impatiently I stopped him to ask, "When did you have your last meal?"

"Meal? I do not know what you call a meal. Meal of the one is not the meal of the other. There are only a few given sources for storing strength and vitality that the body needs for survival. These are called foods, when these are absorbed into the body through the mouth. This food is our need. But mouth is not the only passage for putting vital strength into the body. That which supplies energy, strength, vitality to the body is called food, when taken into the body through the mouth. But our skin, our hair, our nerve system, even our thoughts absorb energy, vitality, direct from the source of all energy all vitality. . . ."

The Mother with Many Breasts

"And what is that?", I asked, a little bewildered; compromised.

"*Prakṛti*; Nature; the Mother as we love to call it. It is helpful for life, and to the living, to be less technical. It is helpful for life to accept a bit of inaccuracy, and sweeten bare facts. Facts are more dry than truths. Truths sustain. Facts form a heavy load; almost dead as lead. Truth is alive.

"You have studied literature. Haven't you? You know how great sages, wise men have deliberately written legends, fairy tales, epics in languages deliberately inaccurate on points of facts. As if facts did not exist for them. As if they had a scorn for facts.

"Why must we call this obviously unresponsive, and vaguely, perceived power 'nature'? Why? 'Mother' would be so much easier. Mother Nature becomes so homely. I know that this is 'inaccurate'. Hydrogen and Oxygen are facts. H_2O is a fact. More accurate. Accuracy must be a lifeless god worshipped by science. But Mother Ganges, Father Tiber, Mother Mary, Father Himalayas become much more significant and meaningful to the hungering soul which lives caged within this body's tangle.

"Even some laws of the mind and memory tell you that bonds of association, or relational contexts assist memory. Hidden in these beautiful and sweet inaccuracies a zest for living down the fire and brimstone of the facts of life assists us to survive. The facts keep on growing, until under their weight we lie crushed. The very meaning of existence lies dead under the load of learned facts.

"*Prakṛti*, our Mother, is also *prasūti*, who gives *birth* to life. It is the mystery-love source we image as the eternal triangle, the *śakti pīṭha*. The *trikoṇa maṇḍala*, the *hring-kling-aing* of the sound forms, continue to be always there with us, for us to tap from, for our sustenance. It is her pap we cling to, and suck from, in a hundred forms,—fruits, grains, water etc. She is the mother with a thousand paps planted all over her body. Only we do not visualise. We keep blind. We chose to keep blind. The ancients imaged and carved a goddess to answer this description of the theory. But we have remained unresponsive and ignorant; and we remain thirsty, although there is water just beneath where we stand. . . . That reminds me of an incident in Australia. . . .

"What more", I thought. "Who is this man? What is he? How comes Australia now?" I kept listening and. . . listening. . . .

"It happened in the great deserts", he continued. "A party had got stuck in the dry lands, between the Eastern Fitzerald river and the lake Macdonell. It was a dry basin and the trapped were on the point of breaking down under exhaustion particularly for want of water. Ultimately they had almost resigned to a desert death. They had lost their way, and with that any hope for survival.

"At this point they were observed by an Australian nomad boy, who had been searching and foraging for whatever food he could collect. The party, and its condition made him act fast. He took out from one of the desert bushes a long stalk of hard grass and making a pipe of it drove it through the sands. When the stalk had been pushed through a depth of about three feet, he sucked the grass pipe.

"Water filled his mouth, and he asked the others to have their fill.

"We all walk through the deserts of life. The life-giving drink flows just around and beneath us. We cannot become the natural nomad, and read and interpret the ways of nature. I have remained without food for days; yes; but I never felt hungry.

"And when you mention that, feeling,—yes, what is it? What is feeling? What is yoga? Is it not the mastery over feeling? (*yoga-ṣ-citta vṛtti nirodhah*—Patanjali) Sleep is a rest to the body. When does the body need a rest? When it is tired. The yogi has no right, as I pointed, to *feel*; so how could he feel tired?

"Kṛṣṇa ran his horses; and in time rested them, so that they could perform better. We too have to rest our bodies. But instead of going to sleep, we go into a trance. Patanjali says that a yogi could go into sleep for months because he does not need sleep in body.

"Why? Your nerves go to sleep when you get to the proper *āsana*. You know that from experience. Don't you? But you still would call for the *alter ego,* your opposite. Don't you? Why? *Be yourself.*"

I looked at him. Watched him. On a sudden rush of agitated delight I offered him the entire pack I had brought so carefully with me to be offered to the deity. No doubt he protested, but I had no use for any other snow symbol of a *lingam.* I had seen and touched what I always wanted to see and touch. When I asked him what could I send for him from civilisation when I reached that wilderness (I knew of a party arranging to start for the shrine in two weeks' time), he smiled and said, "Some air, some light, some earth and ether, and some fire."

I understood his riddle, smiled, and answered, "Yes, I shall send you some dry woods for your fire. But what about some food?"

He picked up the pack offerings. "Here is enough for the next three months."

A Misadventure

The fourth incident also, like the two previous ones, happened in the Himalayas, that mysterious landmass which has been nestling from times immemorial the great mystiques of the East, and to which even to this date souls in spiritual quest trace their pilgrimage.

The year was 1952. The place was near the meeting ground of Tibet, Kashmir and the range across the Chini valley. A journey of seven days on foot from the nearest bus outpost, Narkanda. The entire range was known for the Mahāyāna tantra system, and the cult of the Mother prevailed. Every turn of the road was protected by a mound with a white flag; and the single eye painted on all four sides stared at all.

I was on a mission, and I had young men to assist me. Although we were strictly asked by the administrative authorities to keep away from the villages, and particularly from the girls, two of the youths had erred as youths are privileged to do. The long stay in wilderness, with nothing to watch but forbidding pine forests around for ten miles, and the snows beyond, naturally the nerves of those urbanised excitable youths broke down. Drinking deep from the picturesque bounties of sublime nature is not everybody's cup.

They had to go in search of water, and fetch it over distances. They did this daily. But one day they did not return. I was so much withdrawn within myself that I did not notice their absence until at least 30 hours had passed, and one of the camp assistants, by now anxious, brought the matter to my notice.

A little more probe, a little more wait, and some gossips from two mountain pedlars made me suspect if they had been taken into captivity by the local tribes for interfering with their life rhythm, and (this sounded dangerous) for trying to tempt their girls.

In those remote mountain areas nothing more serious could have happened. The entire area lived under the spiritual influence of a female figure regarded as the *Mother* by all and sundry. She had been the living divinity for them. And it was the fame of this legendary being that had kept me so long glued to the terrible spot.

Taking some rough bearings I started alone for the village lying at a distance of half a day's walk down a gorge, one of the coldest gorges I have come across with. Except for the middle of the day sun hardly reached the gorge.

A stick in hand, I climbed down the pine-laden mountain sides, rendered extremely slippery by the fresh and drying pine-needles. By four o'clock in the evening I came across a gorgeous thundering cataract bestrewn with huge rocks torn down from the mountain sides by a perennially raging torrent. I had to cross these rocks with very careful steps. Before me gaped what could be termed as the only ford; but a slip from any of those smooth rock boulders might have sent me at least twenty feet down where the water was falling in a rage of cold white fury. Half a mile ahead there was a bend, and after the bend a heavenly valley overshadowed by a snow peak over fifteen thousand feet high.

The setting sun on the western side of the gorge, against a back-drop of a pine clad mountain, was sending its slanting upward rays of burnt gold. The entire snow peak seemed to be bathed in burning copper and gold. Only the splendid Himalayas could reveal such stunning beauty. And then the valley itself. For miles and miles, as far as eyes could see, from the branches of the high pines to the depths of the gorge, vines and vines of cascading briar roses had spread a riotous glee with bees humming, breeze murmuring, pines sighing and the perfume from the roses maddening the nerves, and cajoling the senses. What pieces of heaven the Himalayas keep tucked away from defiled human visions!

As against such a heavenly experience my mind was loaded with a gloom of finding out my two companions kept in the custody of tribals for crimes that they could have avoided. It has always been the criminal pride of the so-called civilised to assume those children of nature as backward and unworthy of organised care. They preferred all kinds of liberties against them taking advantage of their charity and hospitality.

I felt extremely depressed.

I reached the village. It was deserted but for a single crippled old man who was left behind. The entire village had moved out. I learnt from him that the two culprits were kept captive at the Mother's command. The people had gone out to attend an annual fair another three miles away. Across the gorge the drum beats could be heard floating from the valley. But the Mother's cave was another mile's walk from the fair grounds, which stood about three to four hundred feet below the cave itself.

The path, however, was not difficult to find. Before I had reached the cave, a man in red clothes, with overgrown hair and flowing beards was awaiting me, and to my surprise welcomed me by name, and informed me that the Mother expected me without delay.

The mouth of the cave did not at all indicate its largeness which was realised after about three minutes of crouching through a narrow entrance. There came a narrower passage; but one could walk straight through it, until a very wide hall came to view. Of course the view was hazily defined by several torches and a roaring fire pit. The floor was generally damp from drips from ceiling; and at one corner flowed a regular stream. The soft crooning murmur of the dark flow together with the crackling and hissing flame completed the eeriness.

Mātājī

Mātāji as the Mother was called, was seated singly across the blazing fire. In a minute my tall companion vanished into the gripping mass of darkness. I found the great lady seated on a cushioned *āsana*, which was covered with a tiger skin. She herself was covered with masses of beads. Around her loins a piece of red rag was carelessly thrown. I knew at once that she was wearing nothing, as the Bhairavis of the Paraśurāma or Dattātreya-Nātha order never do.

"I had been waiting on you", she declared. It was an extremely fascinating voice; melodious, firm and unnerving. "You did not notice; today is the fourteenth night of the coming new moon; and tomorrow's sun would dip into the dark ocean of a night without any moon. What a day to meet a young adept who had the fullest training from experts in the *āsanas* of the *vīra* (hero). But you are agitated over minor things, little bits of life with no substance. You have come for the boys. You will see them in a while. Be at ease. Have a drink. Sit over there; there's a deer skin. Everything has been kept ready for you. I wanted to have you here. O if I am not happy. Come closer."

She was of bewitching beauty; a proportionately sculptured figure in the best beaming health. It is always difficult to measure a Bhairavi by her age. But as a woman she was at her peak (*mahādevim mahāghorām muktakeśīm digambarām*).

The Two Come Close

An *āsana* opposite to her, but across the pit of fire, was pointed out; and I took my seat, still wondering at that stirring presence. At once ran through my spine the vibrations which are associated with the annointed circle (*piṭha cakra*). I accepted the drink without ado. My tiredness was over. The atmosphere, the welcoming voice, the aroma of the place, and above all the vibrations and the ethos of the consecrated *pīṭha* sent me floating along the all too familiar rhythm. It is surprising how things learnt in the spiritual way remain fresh like gold even if long tucked away from life. I rememberd the courageous consolation from the Gītā: nothing obstructs; nothing is destroyed. (*nehāvi-*

krama nāśosti pratyavāyo na vidyate). I assumed my own posture and remembered Varanasi Catuhṣaṣṭhī yoginī, and the Lady in Saffron. There was no getting away. Like a plummet heading down for the base of the depths, my conscious self merged into an experience of peace, serenity and tranquillity. That was 'It'.

I was asked to open my right palm. As I tried to reach her hand avoiding the flames, she stretched her right hand *right* and *through the flames*, across to me, as if the fire never existed; my hand was held in her grip. The flames leapt up all around my outstretched arm. I watched; the flames hissed and danced; but not a hair singed, neither did the least feel of the flames disturb. I recalled the fire walk at the Jangama monastery in Varanasi.

She painted my palm with some vermillion pasted in butter, and ordered me to have a look. As I did so, I saw just on my palm as on a TV projection, my two young misguided friends crouching against a corner in a room, where the walls were painted red. Before I could turn my eyes off, the miserable bodies changed before my eyes; and when I looked again, I saw the crouching bodies of the two wretches melting into an agonised festering and running sore, as if they were being consumed by rotting wormy leprosy, which was eating into their bones. Maggots were wriggling on the open flesh; and thousands of flies were pestering the wretched creatures. I shrieked in agony and closed my eyes in horror. I burst into tears out of sheer pity. "Help them Mother!" I cried. "Help them!"

The vision was over. I found the Mother's smiling face had been gazing at me fixedly.

"They must know what they are", she said. "They must know what they are to become. They must realise that life is a bliss for those who make it a bliss. Yet it is a hell for those who want it bedevilled.

"My son, there is no shortcut to joy, Joy like heaven, has to be earned; and once earned, has to be preserved with care. Do not worry. Come close to me. Let the two come close to One, aye, even less than One, to a zero. Before you return to your camp, they will find their way back. But you always wanted to experience this. Didn't you? Thus you will have the experience. The time is ripe. . . Come."

She sprinkled water on my head, and scattered a handful of rice all around.

And she blessed me with her consecrated company, and graced my poor body by a night long participation in a feast of ethereal delight of the highest spiritual experience.

I had been there for the next fifty hours and more. When I returned I knew that the spot between my brows, where Saint Jitendra had pressed the bead, had been singing. I knew from her that I shall always be having the use of a living *mudrā* if and when I wanted. Moreover, if I wanted my way to *realisation* to be the way of the power-charged *vāma tantra* I would never be wanting in finding a *sāttvik alter ego*, befitting the subject at hand.

Indeed, I did not find this wanting. She was true to her words.

If I am found to be reticent about recording details of this session, it has been so because I am still under her command not to give away the details. This is how the mystique of the secret *sādhanā* is maintained from person to person.*

The Burning Socket

In Cambodia, near the great Angkor shrines in a dilapidated small wild temple, where no one ever goes, and which never attracts the notice of the curious tourists I had come across a skeletal form with sunken eyes, dangling breasts. She was loaded with beads and serpents for garlands, and was staring at me with glaringly burning pupils looking from within dark hungry sockets. At that time I was very sick. Too sick to even correspond. All I could do to appease her, (and I longed to be near her and embrace her) was to snatch a handful of the wild *ākanda* (*calotropis giagantia*) which had burst out of the ruins around.

Again, that evening in one of the shrines, where I was carried for being nursed and cured, and where a prayer was being conducted, for a while, my eyes fell on the spectre; but, this time she was smiling at me. To my great amazement, I really do not know why, I was reminded of the great Mātāji of the Himalayas. I wondered how she could reach me there. But the fact of seeing the same person at several places does not surprise me any more. Take me, if you please dear reader, for a mad man who dose not know his own mind. But then who does?

Back to Our Narration

Yes; the fact of tasting bliss had become a reality there in the Kāmākṣyā temple-yard at Varanasi. Nārada was there, the saint

*This incident has been narrated in *Kinnar-Pahari* (in Bengali) by the same auther.

Jitendra was there, the auntie of Maṇikarṇikā was there, and of course my Lady in Saffron was there. I became initiated. I was introduced to the inner coterie, accepted within the circle.

But another person was there too. She was to become a haunting interest for me in my later years. She was the one selected by the Saint Jitendrà. Her development and demise forms another chapter of my experience.

9

Illusion and Reality

Lost to the World

Remember the *āsana* at the foot of the jackfruit tree? The haloed figure of Yogeśvari near the Bhāskara Puṣkara tank? For over a long while the wooded resort had remained my favourite hide-out for meditation. Bathing nude in the quiet tank was so exhilarating; moreover its utter seclusion was inviting. On days of boyish tensions I used to 'consult' the statue, and received invariably the answers with the hootings; one for 'yes'; and two for 'no'.

The love for seclusion (even by remaining away from the Lady in Saffron) was gradually growing. I was finding it increasingly uneasy to stay home. The Lady in Saffron, too, in her own way, was becoming more and more withdrawn to herself. She was growing sick of something; and had been at pains for having to conform any longer to mundane life.

I was feeling lonely. The long hours under the jackfruit tree did not give me the peace I sought.

One evening, lost in a mood of vacant restlessness, as I was strolling on the bank of the Ganges, the usual crowd streaming by, I felt the touch of Nārada on my shoulders. He was standing before me, and was smiling very knowingly. Without any introduction he came right to the subject, and asked me if I felt to accompany him to a far away place; if I would leave all this, and take to the way of the recluse; if I really was looking for peace.

I was over-elated. I almost jumped and grabbed at what I had been longing for. The proposal gave me a sort of release. I did not ask where, or how, or when. I was ready; he was ready; and we started out at once from that point. No looking back at all.

Suddenly he turned back, and stopped and stared deep into me. Before I could realise what he was doing to me, he had the thumb firmly planted at the point where the bead had been pressed by Saint Jitendra.

It was a sensitive spot; a special spot, as if something permanent had got planted there. As a result even the least disturbance in my psyche would get recorded, and set a series of reactions. The pressure from Nārada's thumb at once threw my mind into a psychedelic spin, and my consciousness began to experience waves of indescribable thrills. I appeared to have lost all control of myself, and found myself tossed on the crests of joy in a sea of ecstatic delight. I am not able at this distance of time to say how long the experience had lasted. But I could still recall that intensity, that delight.

A Room and I

I regained my consciousness in a warm room lighted by a single lamp, where several persons were seated in *Bhdrāsana*, deeply merged in meditation.

Before I could surface from the shock of that sudden transference from the ghats of Varanasi to a strange hide-out, there came the familiar touch; I heard the familiar voice; and felt reassured by the ethereal smile of the Man of Love. "You have reached", he said, as he beamed, and continued, "From here there is no falling back. Hereafter only progress; *Caraiveti*, the forward march alone. What a lucky aspirant. Let the light shower on you."

A strong cold wind had been blowing outside. The place was new, and the air felt much lighter. I could smell the familiar pine, and wondered if it were any part of the Himalayas . . . But it was not so. I was brought to the foothills of the Vindhya range, little away from the holy Chitrakoot, where Lord Rāma of the Rāmāyaṇa had built his cottage, and meditated. Quiet flowed the dreamy Mandākinī.

The Gentle Rāmadāsī

The Rāmadāsi sects are adepts in *Haṭha-yoga*. They keep the body clean, inside and outside, and decorate it punctiliously as one who would love to do the bed of the beloved. For here within the body resided Rāma. For them gaining success in meditation meant attaining the bliss through the privilege and ability of serving the Lord as His most intimate *alter ego*. One must live in the identity of being directly as the Lord's consort, *alter ego*. Service in its tenderest aspect is enjoined on the adepts. I have seen amongst these saints some who for all there lives lived, thought, behaved as a famale; they keep themselves ready to be received by the Lord in His 'inner chambers'.*

*cf. Poetry of Donne, St. John on the Cross, Hafiz, Tagore, Gibran, Blake, Kabir and the Sufis.

In later years of life I had to get close to the controversial theories of Freud, as well as the associated refutations by both McDougal and Jung. I understood the basic perverted states of some human minds, which would like to behave as males or females, even if it went contrary to their physical equipment.

I was closely associated as a boy of eleven with the only child of a wealthy father who kept her daughter covered with the charming make-belief that she were a boy. (cf. Queen Christina of Sweden). She urinated standing; and by some peculiar physical adjustments left marks against walls of the urinal, using male urinals all the time. She scoffed off her menstrual disturbances as mere periodical ailments; in order to hide her rounded smooth limbs, she wore loose garments; and sought company of girls all the time, in support of her male chauvinism, yet carefully avoiding the males all along. Had she not died rather early, I do not know what could have happened to her.

Freud might have come to her aid. But to come to the aid of the Ramadāsis sounds as fantastic a proposal as to suggest cures for the 'madness' of Jesus Christ or of the zeal of Muhammad. I could have written off the Rāmadāsi monks as perverts, had I not known them personally and closely. They, invariably cultivate a charm of behaviour which draws that admiration which a gentleman pays to genuine gentleness.

I have discussed with them the most involved texts in metaphysics. I have found them to be persons of very high spiritual and moral order.

Spiritual emotionalism is an area of intense involvement. In fact it leads man to perhaps the most traumatic, agonising, yet thrillingly joyous experiences in life.

Sex-intensified emotionalism is supposed to create seriously damaging upsets in life. Most murders and suicides, litigations and ruined homes are attributed to this area of emotional disturbances. In any case the sexually aroused find their experiences finally debilitating and tiring. In contradistinction the spiritually aroused have experiences of a totally different complexion. Pangs of spiritual emotionalism have made men deny the 'pleasures' of life; deny wife and children; make princes abandon their kingdoms, fathers abandon their sons, sons abandon the ties of homes, fathers and mothers.

Side by side with such cases as Anna Karenina, Lady Chatterley, Oscar Wilde or Profumo there are cases like the Buddha, Chaitanya, Meerā, Pingalā, St. Simon, St. Augustine and Chardin. Think of the young naked anchorite I came across with in the Khadrālā cave. Much of the human treasures of mystic creations in art and literature would have remained in the dark but for the fire and flame that illuminate the captive souls of these misunderstood 'madmen'. Hunger, sleep, envy, jealousy, fear of death, temptation for life all count as nothing to souls sparked with this kind of spiritual emotionalism.

Rādhā of Navadwip

I had met one of these Rādhā-cult saints in the sleeping town of Navadwip (West Bengal). This town is hallowed by the sweet memories of one of the greatest love-saints of India, Śrī Kṛṣṇa Caitanya Mahāprabhu, otherwise known as Caitanya.

The Vaiṣṇava sects of India owe generally a great debt of spiritual solace to his way of love; and particularly to those who believe in securing self-illumination through the rather arduous path of loving without attachment, dedicating without expectation and service without distinction. Caitanya and his cult believed intensely in the soul power of love, and in the state of supreme subjectivity attained through self-denial. This sect sings their way into the lives of people otherwise lost in the drunkenness of possessive life. They warmly believe that the ecstatic state of 'love in the Lord' becomes feasible by accepting this way of trance through music.

The denial of self-passion in the interest of fullness of life lies at the basis of the Rādhā followers, as well as of the Rāmadāsī Vaiṣṇavas.

A very subtle sense of total liberation inspires those who follow this path. They feel that the un-liberated cannot bring total peacefulness to the disturbed lives of the mundane. In serving these lives, sick with a hundred delusions, they receive their ultimate joy.

There in Navadwip I met this one (man-woman) I was referring to. 'She' was really a he. 'Her' age was above eighty; and 'she' could move about the yards of the shrine of Caitanya with difficulty, and was really housed in one of the smallest rooms at the end of the yard, and beyond the common sight of those who visited the holy shrine daily.

The Amazing 'SHE'

I approached 'her'; and looking at me 'she' at once dropped down her veil; and welcomed me in the sweetest language from behind the thin veil. Before I could mention anything 'she' asked me how my father was, and how was the Lady in Saffron whom 'she' openly called

Bhuvan? "You know me?" I asked quite perplexed at the power she apparently held.

"It is much easier to know other people's affairs than to know one's own self. Don't you agree?" With that question she smiled one of those seductive smiles which one could only expect from a trained and professional flirt known for studied communications without words. I was bewitched.

'She' offered me a seat within 'her' hovel which could hardly accommodate one.

Here 'she' kept seated all day and night, day after day, and night after night. None knew when 'she' would come out, when 'she' would get in. 'She' was a chimera-presence in the temple yard. None alive knew when 'she' had come there, or from where. The oldest of them knew 'her' to be an old lady. 'She' was always known to have kept herself in the best of 'her' decors, perfect in 'her' toiletries, make-up, and 'her' immaculately decorative dresses.

The walls of the insignificant hovel seemed to recede as she closed the doors. She offered me only a gesture of the hands, and said, "Here is a seat for you; here the water for washing your feet."

And I saw a seat, and a jug of water with a washing bowl materialise from nowhere. 'She herself' carefully held my feet, and before I could have protested, held them firm and bathed them, as a mother would a child's body, and wiped the same with a towel. As she was at it, she smiled charmingly, and broke into one of the sweetest melodies from the great poet Jayadeva.

Let me smoothen and brighten
The pair of feet,
Before I dye them red (with love).
Place them now on my head, love,
Thy touch, an antidote of lust;
Thy feet a fitting crown for my head.*

Then looking at me she said, "You seem to resent. Why? Why this ego? Why this sense of ownership when you do not own the body. It is the residence of my beloved. Is it not? Why must you think that you are you? This might be so as you see. To me you are as good or as bad as I am. The better part of me that is. It is far easier to feel

*Gita Govindam, XIX, 6-7

the infinity in others than within the ego-ridden self. The infinite is the only real; and these bubbles that detract with their finality really keep attention diverted. A guest is a welcome blessing from God. Isn't he? The guest is the Self come in person. Now command, what could I do for you?"

For a minute I held my peace; I did not know what to say. She asked again. "Don't you want something? Some entertainment for instance? Some nourishment? Something soulfilling? What is it? I shall see what I could do for you. Just be sure, and call for it. Go ahead now. Do not hesitate."

My sense of perception had been awakened like needles on the back of a porcupine alerted by the smell of carrot roots. I looked at 'her'. And what I noticed took my breath away.

There was seated before me no other a person than the Lady in Saffron herself! The heavy soft body, the cascading hair, the ample breasts covered with the beads, the inviting arms, the familiar posture, even the base of the great *lingam* where she used her *āsana* and where I kept seated on her. I almost swooned, but I heard my own voice uttering the chant "Mother Tārā! Mother Tārā!"

"Come, tarry not. Come. You shall have it. Peace, and love."

The session was brief but deep. Too deep to be described. In fact I have no language to reveal that experience. But need I reveal? No; because I was ordained to keep that a secret; but also because of another firm conviction. Wrenched from their proper context, the associated consonance and the attuned symphony to sing of these types of experiences, would be wrong. The narration would be vitiated with the dual poison of incredibility and pollution.

'She' had been an *alter ego* in all its nervous and spiritual senses. What 'she' materially or physically was, I had no means to feel, or determine. To me 'she' had been my Lady in Saffron; and the female in 'her' was fully radiated in its positivity, in its power, in its ignition and transmission. The promised peace and tranquillity became mine. When we had emerged from that small room, it was already dark; and the temple bells were ringing for the vespers. A slow clapping chant was being recited. 'She' joined the chorus, and began a dance.

The Great Dance

I wish with all my heart that I could describe that dance. I have read the description of the dance of Isadora Duncan as she danced in Athens, Vienna, Berlin; I have read of the skill of Ana Pavlova, of

Uday Shankar and their dancing ability. I have read the description, in the Bhāgavatam, of the *rāsa*-dance of the boy Kṛṣṇa. But the dance that afternoon I had viewed, defeats all telling. It was intangible to the senses, and yet it kept the senses gripped with an ever-elevating airiness because of which nothing appeared to be belonging to the world we reside in.

If there is some other dimension where reality gives way to the insubstantial supraconscious awareness, then alone that dance would relate to anything comprehensible, tangible or real. My joy flooded my inner being. That ethereal delight could have related to my supraconscious being alone. I was filled; but filled with a perfection of delight of an altogether different texture quite unreal to the realities which we know to be materially existing.

Up to this day I speak of her as a 'she'. Yet the fact was that she had been a he, a man, a male. And years and years of dedication to the Lord, as His *alter ego,* had transformed him into a 'she' not physically, not materially, but spiritually and ethereally which is more important and to the point, so that in another dimension, he existed as 'she', and enjoyed the companionship of the Lord of 'her' Love. One is what one feels to be. She stood as an example of that epigram.

It is this abstractness that makes the highly sensitive coitus form of the *Mahāmudrāsana* to be known also as *Śavāsana*, the 'dead' posture. It is certainly not what the uninitiated charlatans think as the male-female pairing. It is true that hundreds flee away from it, and keep away. It is more true that more hundreds try this and get destroyed irretrievably; and many more hundreds scoff at it, and call it fraudulent and hypocritical game of the scoundrel and the perverse.

I have not been able to make the Freudian postulates fit in with this direct experience. Those theories, however logical, remain logical, but unreal to me. These experiences, for example, thoroughly out of focus with logic, are still treasured by me as the most delectable and consummate ones I could recall.

I appreciate how difficult it is to believe this factually; but I also know how absurd it would be not to believe in such phenomena which are everyday occurrences in the twilight world of mysticism.

It is from this source in Navadwip that I received the priceless boon of the companionship of the only *alter ego* who had remained my companion for over a very long period. It was through my lack of patience, my over-zealousness that I had lost her association. And before I was ready to approach her again, she had left her material existence. But of that in time.

Before I come back to the episode of Nārada, I shall narrate here another experience, also in West Bengal. This happened much later. Since the area is the same, this is the best place to refer to this. The world of tantra is a world of mystic revelations which constitute the only realities for a son of the Mother.

Quest for a Bangle

During my stay in Trinidad a doleful mother approached me to do something for her very beautiful daughter who had been gradually losing her mental balance. She must have been about twenty years of age when she was brought as a subject to me. I knew of no magic; and I knew very little of a faith cure if there is any such cure. I had my own method of prayers. All I try is to make my spiritual consciousness penetrate the material awareness, or lack of it in a subject. Of the twenty odd years this poor girl had spent in this world, nearly six years were spent in a mental hospital. Because of the utter dejection of her mother I had promised her some help as best as I could. But for that, I told her, I had to go to India, and then on my return I could have given her some hope, if I could find an answer.

For finding that answer I had to pay a visit to a shrine several hundred miles from Delhi and nearly a hundred miles south-west of the city of Calcutta. The distance did not matter; but the communications were sadly left to the most primitive methods inclusive of spanning two rather wide rivers on country barges pushed by bamboo poles. The apology of the only track road was at the time under repairs, which had been held back for political reasons, *after* the track had been dug up. Normal walk on that track was impossible; wheeled transport was a dream.

When I was on this quest (for a 'cure') I was accompanied by a determined lady I had known for years. There was no way of dissuading her from undertaking the hazardous journey. We reached the shrine on foot for the last six miles when the sun was about to set. On the way we had nothing to eat; along the paddied expanse we hardly met with any people or habitation; and a slashing Bengal lowland rain kept us on our bare toes dancing over six miles of a narrow sticky walk. Utterly harassed and famished we looked for some shelter for the night, and some sort of succour. After a research of thirty minutes we came to the conclusion that we have to pass the night almost under the sky in the mosquito-laden heavy atmosphere. Food was out of the question. Not a soul was in sight, except some urchins returning from some school somewhere to some other village somewhere.

A large ponderous tank covered with festering fallen leaves and breeding mosquitoes stretched under a sad afternoon sky; and on its bank stood the lonely singular shrine. That miserable structure was my rendezvous. The closed doors were barred; but we had a glimpse of the deity, Mother Kālī of course.

I went to the pond, and took a hurried wash. My companion wanted to follow my example; but the sqeamish feminine slavery to forms stood in her way. She had to satisfy herself with just damping and brushing her sad sodden feet, and generally the portions of her much harassed body.

Her real worries related to the approaching night.. (There was no shelter worth the name.) A paddy-thrashing hut, with mud walls on three sides was all that stood at a distance from the shrine. It was unoccupied but for the bales of bare paddy-stalks, which littered almost all the floor in irregular heaps.

By now completely resigned to a dinnerless night (of course after a day of no lunch and no breakfast) I started to organise a fire under a small concrete covered pavillion situated in front of the shrine, and prepare for a night of penance. The vibrations were too loud and penetrating to be ignored. I suggested to the lady to take meanwhile a rest within the shed.

We had no changes of our clothings. If I had to offer my penances in the morning I would have to wash my clothes during the night, and leave them to dry so that I could use them in the morning; or agree to offer my prayers in wet clothes, and allow the clothes to dry on my skin. In a malarial situation the risk would have been great, specially to urbanised softies.

Of course she was free to decide the course she would adopt for herself. One thing was certain that there would be no offerings or prayers in slept-over clothings.

She Comes, Comes, and Ever Comes

The drama started after the lady had retired to the shed. In about another hour the sun would set, and the shrine, as well as the nondescript straggling village, surrounded by miles and miles of paddy fields, would be swallowed up by the growing dark surfs of gloom, made darker by the myriads of fireflies. I was about to get myself lost into the rather convenient feelings of non-existence, when I heard sounds of mild jingles caused by light steps accustomed to music. The vibrations elsctrified me. As I opened my eyes, now turned to the east, I saw a charming girl of about fifteen, carrying akimbo a healthy baby boy. Clad in a red sari, and decorated with vermillion and gold, she stood before me wearing a strange smile in half appreciation of my predicament. Her two hands were kept engaged in supporting the baby. I looked a. her feet. Not a trace of mud there. As she was facing the west, the red glow of the setting sun made her loose hair glow like hot copper, and her eyes sparkled with smiles and with a frank spirit of eager communication. She could not have been real, or was she the Real?

She looked like one of the commonest of village girls,—inquisitive, eager, and ready to be of some assistance. Very naturally, and without waiting for any preliminaries she asked in a typical rural dialect, peculiarly local, "When did you arrive? What have you for food?"

I was hearing; but my eyes were fixed on the glowing circle of the vermillion that separated her arched, long, black brows. '*Black like a line of beetles*', I remembered.

At once came to my mind other sensitive motifs: the one eye of the Tibetan Mahāyāna; the Egyptian beetle-sun motif; the Omega in Delphos; the *ankuś* of Egypt, the serpent of the Māyās the *vajra* of the Thais, the trident of the Cambodians, the loop of Shintoism. . .so many. . .so many. . . How fascinating could the mind become. Now seeing, now visualising, now imagining, now interpreting. . . .

But I knew that I should keep steady and alert.

I bowed to her, and paid my reverence. My forehead was on the floor.

"O! How strange", she giggled. "Why do you bow to me? Look there. There is the *devī*, within the room, closed. Why to me?"

Yes, within the room, closed. I knew it so well. . . Clapped within the seed-heart of the lotus of the thousand petals.

"I do not know where she stands", I said, ". . . or where she does not. She is where the unbudded virgin is: she is where the Mother in bloom is. Any virgin anywhere is worthy of honour. She is *Śakti*."

"I am no virgin", she said, smiling in full glory of revelation. The setting sun had spread its crimson glow all over the western sky of the palm fringed, wide spaced paddy land of Bengal. "Look this is my son. I am his mother "

"So you are. And yet you are the virgin. I know of several virgin-mothers. Are we not, all of us, the sky, the fields, the crop, the pond, the earth and the air, all, all her children? She is the eternal virgin. Do you have doubts? The Virgin is a Mother; and the Mother a Virgin. . .That's the Truth about the Evermore. Germ to Womb to Life to Fulfilment, to Mother and Germ and Womb. The eternal Womb; the eternal Virgin, as you might chose. The interim is a playful Mother's wandering lullaby, as she nurses. . ."

I avoided further talks, and asked her who she was.

As there were no habitations near about, and as the hour of the day was not suitable for a girl to be moving, how dared she to be at large, and with a baby to boot?

"I don't know what you are talking about. I belong to the village. I belong to here. This is my son Ganeś and I have just come down from my husband's place in the hills. But all this is by the way. The fact is that for the whole day you had nothing to eat. You must be hungry. Would you accept some popped rice from me? You will not refuse that humble fare I believe. Would you?"

I watched the engaging smile which actually made my curiosity tingle with a bundle of further enquiries.

Before I could figure out what to say, and how to say it, I watched the girl recede into the back bush, and vanish. Within ten minutes she appeared with a basket filled with puffed rice and some brown jaggery lumps. Then she threw an invitation to a poor man's fare for dinner, and explained that behind the bush in a hut people would be waiting for us. The hut could not be missed. It was located just behind the bush; and for all purposes the best time would be eight in the evening.

She did not wait for my answer.

In a god forsaken remote village eight o'clock was midnight; and through the dark our steps were hesitant. When we reached the place, we found a young man waiting for us welcoming profusely and apologising at the same time that he could not have gone out earlier to welcome us in this doped village.

What did dope it I enquired, rather casually. But I was serious; because indeed by now I had absorbed a lot of the special vibrations radiating throughout the locality.

We call it in our common parlance 'a weight', or something living in the air.

He perhaps understood the point of my enquiry and replied to the effect that the place was under the *protection* of a 'living' deity, made of common clay; and periodically was exchanged for a new one; only the inner core, a piece of bel-wood (ash apple—*egli mermelas*) continued to be inside the image of the deity.

The Girl Who Illudes

"Centuries back when this part of lower Bengal was covered in woods and shrubs, and had grown into a natural habitat for the Bengal tigers, when the lands hereabout had been lying beyond human civilization, a yogi had strayed into this place, and found this natural tank. By the tank stood a bel tree. Under this tree he had made his *āsana*. Later, this very *āsana* was consecrated as *pancamuṇḍī* (five-skulled-seat). He must have been here for quite a few years when he became aware of a young girl of about eighteen years of age, often assisting him, and bringing little offerings of food and drink for him. At first the yogi did not notice this. The Buddha also did not notice Sujātā. But soon he had reasons to make enquiries how in the wilderness a young girl could be seen. He decided to follow her, and find out for himself. He had made a full round of the tank, and as he came back to his *āsana*, he found that the girl had vanished. He tried this several times. Every time he did so, he failed; but every time consistently, and invariably the singular apparition vanished as it approached his *āsana*. He never found the opportunity to exchange words with her. He never tried to. He had other ideas. He kept his seat, and continued, apparently undisturbed, his penances. But the people around thought otherwise.

"Gradually he was losing his balance of mind. So people thought. He was found to shriek loud through the night, and the fierce words rang through the forest. Night jars screeched; jackals sent out dismayed yells. 'How far would you run away. How long? O thou illusive fascinator?' He would scream and howl. 'Some day I will catch up with you, O thou self-willed deceiver, the Charming Reality!'

"But who were the *people*", I asked, "if this was a dense forest infested with tigers?"

"Who were they? Let me explain. Of course the tigers continued. But with them some human tigers too began to prowl all about here. They were more dangerous. These were the thugs, the marauders, evil worshippers of mother Kālī, who always sought for a secluded spot, away from civil control. That helped their way of life.

"They too must have seen this girl at times. At least so does it appear. They too must have followed her. Their inquisitiveness made them search for the truth, and their failure must have finally told on their nerves. Would, they too lose their head as the sage apparently had? They held on to the saint, and asked him about what he knew of the girl. He must have answered them most incoherently. And they were drunk. Not knowing what they were doing, they began to beat him, and was about to kill him and offer him to the Mother Kālī. Strangely enough the saint submitted to their will. But he had a last request to make.

"According to the legend he had awaited this hour. Now that the hour had indeed arrived, they would have done him a favour by releasing him in the way they wanted to. No objection; no hesitation. But after his body had been so offered, he directed, the lifeless body should be entombed under his seat. When they would dig the ground, he said, they would come upon other things, which they should not stir. Then they should cut down the bel tree under which he sat, and make an image of it by modelling it with clay. He knew that they wanted to see and know the girl. But that part of the privilege must be left to them. He, however, assured them that the girl would never leave the consecrated haunt. Only if they were able, they could see her, and talk to her by their own efforts, and—luck. She herself knew where she belonged to. After that the saint gave up his life.

"When the grave was dug up for his internment they, to their horror, discovered within the hollowed sarcophagus skeletons of several animals, inclusive of human bones. They at once appreciated that they had disturbed a saint with powers to have reduced them to reptiles, or maggots.

"But he did not do so only because he wanted to be interned below his *āsana* along with those lives who had assisted him to capture within earthly dimensions, the haunting Reality that illudes the human grasp. Because of the saint's blessings that illusive 'She' would never leave this place unless desecrated by any heinous crime."

"Like what", I interrupted. "This mortal world is only full of crimes."

"Do you seriously think so?" he asked unconvincingly.

"There are crimes not articled in the books of law, and yet those crimes could send the souls to unending tortures even in this life and this body. Greed and envy; spite and passion; lust and unkindness. . . O there are so many."

"Well, I am no expert. But you see no one really lives here. And we do not allow people to reside permanently hereabout. We try to keep this place clean."

"Clean of men?" I chuckled.

"Clean of men", he repeated.

"Does the girl still appear?" I asked rather in a low key.

"Some claim to have seen her. I live not very far from here. I often pass here and around. I have never seen anything like that."

"That does not prove anything," I remarked. "Does it? We do not see what we do not want to see. How many times, for example have you stood before a rose, and admired its beauty? The beauty of the soul of a forgiving wife; how many times have you seen? Again, seeing suddenly the unexpected, we brush those strange experiences aside, and call them names instead, imagination, hallucination, spectres of sleeping ideas, or shadows of mental projections etc. Have you been seeking her? Actually hungering to see her?"

"Well? In a way." As he casually remarked, he lighted a cigarrette, and offered me one. I declined, and he continued. "And why not? After all. . .Its something to be talked of. . ." He could hardly suppress his rather wise incredulous smiles.

"Like the illusive yeti or the monster of Lochness? A tourist curiosity?" I laughed and allowed thereby an opportunity for him to give vent to his repressed merriment.

"Well, I have not seen anything so far. This much I could own. But I must also own that from time to time people have been reporting seeing her. She, in many respects, belongs to hereabout. Hence people come here. You should see the multitude gathered here during the *Kārtikī Amāvasyā* (the new moon night of October).

"She has been seen quite alone; but at times with a rather bulky boy held akimbo. . . . Well, let them see. . . . Let them talk. . . I do not have to believe. Do you?"

"I do not know how to reply. Belief like gold is so much mixed up with muck and dross. I have heard from pork-knockers in Guyana that in their search for diamonds many have thrown away in their eagerness real diamonds down the river taking them to be mere crystals, jades and pebbles. I myself have passed over many saints; have slept over many valuable unreturning hours. Who cares? He who does, is an expert. Belief too like knowledge is mixed up with cynicism and ego. We take pride in 'scientific' methods, 'scientific' knowledge; as if knowledge could be anything but scientific. But those who do believe, have to pay a bitter price before securing the longed for blessing."

The food served was bare boiled rice with no side dishes, except some boiled breed of water hyacinth touched with salt. We had to manage within the limits of the fare. But I could not resist asking him, "Where is the little girl who had invited us? Judging from her concern for us, we expected a sumptuous dinner; particularly when she was so richly dressed. Where is the charming girl anyway. . .?"

I could have continued with my half jocular tone. But as I looked at him, in spite of the dim lantern light, I was taken aback by his wide looks. His lower jaw had dropped causing his mouth to open a bit. "What girl are you talking about?. . . In this house no one lives really. Only pilgrims during the big festivals use it. I came here by chance today. I am a teacher in a school about eight miles away. I had to arrange for some paddy collection from my maternal uncle's lands. Only my old mother is with me. As you see, we had just some rice left with us. And mummy is so sorry to have to treat you with such a fare. No young girl is with us. Are you sure? . . . What girl? Young and charming? Was she carrying a chubby baby?"

Of course I did not allow the conversation to proceed. The phenomenon was obvious to me, but only as a phenomenon. But I was determined to probe further into it.

When we returned to the thrashing hovel, I made it clear to my companion that I am going to take off my garments, and wash, and spread them out. Hopefully they would get dry by morning. I would have to offer my prayers. I also suggested to her that if she cared, she could do the same, and use the mounds of hay for cover. In the dark nothing would matter anyway. In any case I shall keep out for the night. So she would be free to adjust as she would like.

Without waiting for an answer I walked away into the dark. I spread my washed linen along the cemented floor of the temple. And assumed *āsana*, before the small fire I had lit. I do not know when or how I got merged in my meditation.

Then something happened.

By about midnight I was astir by a new arrival. But I kept on meditating. Attention fixed between my brows, with eyes closed, the *mantra* came alive even more alive. But I distinctly heard the same *mantra* being uttered by some other male voice.

Kṣīrabhavānī

I had a similar experience while meditating in the remote holy shrine of Kṣirabhavānī, off the Ullar lake in Kashmir. As I had been praying with eyes closed, I heard a myriad voice singing along with me. At the end of the session I was amazed to. find myself alone at the spot.

At a certain point I wanted to touch water. I had kept no water for me, there being no vessel. Because of long practice, through reflex I happened to stretch my hand for the water. Imagine my surprise when I actually did touch it. Shocked I opened my eyes. Before me, in a bowl-like declevity in the cemented floor, there was water . . . . By my side sat a bearded yogin in *samādhī*.

The Light Breaks

The resonant choral sound did not bother me. But my poise was shaken when I observed that the lady had left the haystack and was comfortably seated by me, muttering some *mantras* to boot. I went back into my meditation. No leaf moved.

It could have been about two o'clock in the morning when I became aware of another female form, now seated very close to me. In the still and heavy air hung a delicately ethereal fragrance. It was intoxicating. My throat was dry; my skin hot, my head and body were damp with sweat. But, as usual I did not move. Suddenly I was offered a drink.

"Take a sip." There was no mistake in the tone. The voice was my companion's. But the language was Bengali, which struck me at once, because the lady in question did not know Bengali. But I would not be dissuaded. I knew better. I continued with my *āsana-śuddhi*; *bhūta-śuddhi*; *digbandha*. Then I began to recite the famous invocation:

Pancasal-lipibhi-r-vibhakta mukhado—
panmadhya vakṣasthalām
Vāsvanmauli nivaddha candra-śakalām
āpīna tunga stanīm
Mudrāmakṣaguṇam sudhāḍhya kalasam
vidyām ca hastāmbujai-r
Vibhrāṇam viśada prabhām tri-nayanām
*vag devatām aśraye**

*The deity I seek shelter in has fifty faces divided into the fifty alphabets. Her full-grown upright firm breasts cover the area between her armpits and her heart. On her crest is tied a bright crescent; and in her hands she holds a jar filled with the drink of immortality, a book, a *mudrā* and a dice with a lasso. Ah, she radiates her halo all around.

I continued with the *Matrikā Nyāsa* resolutely, without accommodating any diversion, until stood vivid before my eyes what I always longed to see, my Mother, the one I knew, the Lady in Saffron!

Then light broke, as also the first light of the welcome dawn. I was swept away by a torrent of what seemed to me electrocuted waves and waves of light and light, thrilling me all over, awakening every hair strand.

The joy of the state was sensitively wholesome, intangibly abstract.

Swept away by a torrent of what seemed to me to be light, *the joy of feeling free* was intense, yet quiet and cool. I felt no disturbance at all. A solemn quiet music was penetrating my being, and I felt as if I was floating through a garden filled with fragrant blossoms.

The wilderness had come to life. Early birds began calling, and I felt the gentle blowing breeze.

Tārā! Tārā! I cried fervently.

I was alone! The fire had subsided long ago. I made straight for the pond. I did not see my companion anywhere. I entered the hovel, and found her deep asleep cushioned between the straw-heaps. She stirred as soon as I had entered, and begged me to step out. I remembered that she had to dress herself, and quickly withdrew, wishing her a happy morning.

I was confused. It was high time I got out of the shroud of logic, I thought. If the arranged could get deranged through events that baffle cause, one should be intelligent enough to accept the truth, that the time to get upset has gone over the head. The excitement was too much for any pretence to equanimity. If the lady had been sleeping tucked safe in the hay stack, who was the one sitting by me? Was I getting all muddled, befogged?

I rushed to the *āsana* for any signs. The fire-place was cold. I covered my forehead with the ashes. But where had disappeared the hole with the water? The smooth surface of the floor bemocked my credulity. I rushed to the shrine, and with one hard push flung open the door, and kept staring at the deity. That was the only time when consciously, driven by the remorse of being deluded again and again, I felt to grab the deity, and shake her up for her cruel dumb pranks, which only whetted my longings. I yearned for her embrace. I became hysteric.

I assumed the *āsana* again. I wanted to get free of all conflicting thoughts, and get near Mā. I began my prayers, that would keep me engaged for another three hours at least. Subsequently, after her ablutions were over, my companion too joined me, and reverently occupied a seat, though keeping a distance.

But then the dreamy surroundings had come to life; and a priest showed up. He performed his normal prayers, while we waited. Then we received what we had come for, an iron bangle, which had the supposed power to put the girl's mind at peace. On our enquiry we found that our host, the young man with his mother had already left the village.

But I was determined to see that incandescent girl-apparition (!) again, if at all possible. I had to experience her sweet charm again. I was driven into frenzy by a strange urge. That extreme longing made me burst into tears. My companion was dumbfounded. Unabashed, unchecked I expressed to her my agony, the agony of the soul longing to come to grips with the subject of ecstasy.

Yet Again She

I was talking all the time; but my talks, I knew would not make any sense to her. She grew concerned at my state. Having set out in search of a cure for some demented girl in Trinidad had I got myself demented in the process? The priest had warned (did not he?) that this state of mind always portended something bad. I did not realise how true he had been. But to go into that would be too personal; and I choose to leave it there.

Hungry, exhausted and driven beyond her feeble state of endurance, my delicate companion wanted to get out of it all. She, I believe, was scared, specially at my change. The idea of a long journey back with a demented companion made her feel extremely nervous. She wanted to get away, but how?

At this time a bullock-cart appeared, and she fell to negotiate with the driver promising him a fantastic price. . . When we were about to leave the village an old lady stepped by the track with a basket in hand. She had brought puffed rice, and two lumps of molasses. She reported that a little girl had asked her to bring it for the strangers in the temple. In as much as we were returning, we could as well take the humble fare with us. "The road is long, very long", she remarked.

"Where is the girl", I asked. The immediacy of my ardent enquiry threw her into utter confusion. "Who is she? You know her? Go and bring her to me; if necessary, by the cuff of her neck. I will reward you." I insisted.

Her dismayed stare looked baffled. "I thought *you* had sent her", she replied with a husky voice but continued to peep into the cart. "Kālī! Kālī! She even had paid me some coppers, saying that the puffed rice be delivered on the cart. . . I myself had so much looked forward to seeing her again. A pretty girl Kālī Kālī!" And she bowed to the echoes of a long forgotten local legend, while I fell to cry openly like a child.

The cart man moved. The bullocks lurched philosophically. My companion accepted the dole on her sari-end which she had spread out. The cart gave a stronger jolt, and ambled past the bush, down the track, by now sun-drenched.

Then came to view the little hut from where the old lady had crystallised. I could see her tracing her steps back.

But I also saw the beautiful girl standing at the threshold of the hut bathed in sunlight, and smiling with a gay abandon. At my sudden shriek to my companion, "Look there she is. . . There! At the threshold of that hut. . .", my companion said, "It is the effect of continued hunger and thirst. You are raving", and she held me down for I was about to jump out, and get to that illusive presence.

The cart soon went past the track. No, my companion had seen no girl. Neither had she ever left the thrashing floor during the night!

And the only evidence of this *incredible* episode remained held within the sarī-end of my companion. We munched and munched, until I fell asleep on the jolting cart, somewhat soothed by the spring of the soft heap of straws covered with lairs and lairs of palm mats.

I noticed while getting down from the cart that she held a handful of that rice in her sari-end. "These are charmed grains", she said. I looked at her in silent approval.

But whilst crossing on the boat she slipped on its side, and fell into the wide river. With great difficulty we salvaged her; but the puffed rice, the remnants of the offering, the collected ash, everything, except the bleeding mercury (*sindūr*). was gone. We were drenched thoroughly. Only my diary was saved as the single evidence of what had been to me a stirring night, lived all alone, and yet not all so alone.

My eyes had never lost sight of the smooth running stream. In a while not a single grain of the puffed rice could be seen floating.

They had gone for ever.

A Mountain Shrine

I have been to the mountain shrine of Kāmākṣyā (different from the one at Varanasi, already mentioned), known to be the most powerful' shrine of all, in the north-eastern region of India. The shrine was built on the *śakti* emblem of *yoni*, the triangle. There is no deity there, neither any given form. The actual shrine lies deep under the earth. This subterranean shrine is nothing but a spring jutting out of a slit against the Himalayan range.

The legend has it that Lord Śiva had lost his wife sacrificed in a ritual observed by her father. In fact she had sacrificed herself by jumping into the fire pit of the *yajña* (sacrifice). This she did to mark her protest against her father's anti-Śiva stance. The bereaved husband began to roam on the earth almost demented with the dead body flung across his shoulders. Because there seemed to be no other way of bringing him back to his senses, Viṣṇu, a fellow god, gradually cut the body into pieces. The limbs, so dissected, fell piece by piece. Every place the pieces fell to, grew into a 'Mother Shrine' and was held extremely sacred to the tantra believers. The shrines were consecrated, so they hold, by the fall of the limbs of Śiva's consort. Of the most revered of these holy places Kāmākṣyā is one if not the topmost of them all. Here fell her delta, triangle: and here from a rock side spring jets out a water flow. The devout dip their hands in the small square receptacle of the spring and feel a rather warm slit in the rock, which draws their devotion.

All over the world, specially amongst the mountain tribes, reverence for springs and caves, gorges and subterranean flows has been a common feature. This area in the north-west border of India has been strongly under the influence of the Dravido-Mongoloid tribes who have contributed much to the *Mahāyāna* Tantra of Tibet, Indo-China and China. The female principle is held in very high regard. But Kāmākṣyā, like Delphos, is different, distinct and unique. Here all tantriks assemble on the break of the monsoons.

After the hot May-June months, before ploughshares penetrate the soil, the people around celebrate over three days, when the Mother is supposed to be having her periodical menses. This heralds her eternal virginity and fertility. In obvious symbolic parallelism the period is hailed; special rites are offered, and farmers never touch any digging tool, much less violate the soil. Sex is a taboo for these days.

Blood is given and taken as mark of successful prayers. Cloth pieces soaked in the Mother's blood-blossoms are distributed as blessings from the Mother-Spirit. The shrine is kept closed for these days; and special prayers are organised to last uninterrupted for four days and three nights. Great tantra adepts assemble and offer their prayers.

Kāmākṣyā is thus a great link in the chain of the tantriks and the *Mahāyāna* followers, because Kāmākṣyā symbolises the great triangle of the Great Mother. The *mahā-yoni* or the *mahā mudrā* is found here, and nowhere else.

There I had gone to have the 'virgin worship' performed according to the mountain rites. But that did not satisfy me. On my next trip to this distant place I was all by myself, but for a foreign tourist who had been visiting me then. His presence did not bother me, as he kept himself fully engaged in tribal songs, temple songs and with those Indian hippies who pass for god-men, morons or straight cranks.

So I was left to myself.

The temple is invariably closed at about midnight after the last *ārati* (vespers). It was at the time of the vespers that something happened to me. A song having come to my mind I began to sing. The small gathering got shocked because such songs within the *sanctum sanctorum* are hardly ever tolerated. But the chants came from authentic Sanskrit tantra texts; and none dared move, not even the knowing priest.

The music and the emotive words sent me into a trance; and I quite forgot myself. I was there, yet not there. The forms and norms of life did not matter any more with me.

As I came to, I found the temple hall and nave merged in utter darkness; and the silence was so solid that I could almost touch it. The prayer finished, I stepped out. The yard was flooded with a bright moon. I went out of the temple in search of my tourist friend. He was busy talking to some hippies.

But my inner hunger remained unfulfilled.

The very wide yard looked lovely. Staying there after the forbidden hour was considered dangerous. Yet in rare cases some infatuated zealots persist to sit out a night or two in the mysterious yard. I decided to meditate through the night all alone.

Next morning, I was on the edge of nerves. . . Under a deep tension, almost feverish, I could feel the pulls of a very strong magnetic call. I worked slowly along the line of that magnetism, until I was climbing the great Bhuvaneśvari hill. From the peak a sublime view of the magnificent Brahmaputra widened eastwards. To be there was to touch sublimity. At a distance of about two miles down the stream floated, like an emerald, the island shrine of Umānanda. I recognised at once that to have been the focal point. Did the island call me? Why?

Om Jvālā Jvālā Svāhā

I could hardly keep myself restrained any more.

That night as my companion had bolted the door of his room I was out in the temple yard again. It was drizzling. The sky was overcast; and occasionally was rent by thunder. Flashes of those lightnings left the dark, darker. Quite unexpectedly, and quite against the run of my normal health I began to develop the symptoms of a shivering ague. I wished I were heavily clothed. I wished a fire could be near about. But the dark was as thick as my mind; and I could not see my own hand; As I shivered, I searched and searched for the gate to the shrine.

I knew that at the mouth of the shrine there was a little shelter. I proceeded towards it; and missed the door. However absurd it might sound today, but the inescapable fact was that I missed it several times, until I found a fire, and perched close to it. My eyes closed as soon as I assumed a seat near the fire. At once I dropped into a deep meditation, like one drugged, or under some spell. Like a line loaded with lead I gained my depths in seconds. I had no idea of the hour of the night. When I came to, I saw a couple, both obviously *kāpālikas*, standing before me. No one else was about. The very stars had gone to sleep under a thick blanket of Assam clouds. A strange quietness hung from the trees. Only the inescapable sombre hills were busy standing guard over this eerieness.

Of the two, the full bloomed heavy limbed female held me in her grip, and guided me to the river, where a boat was waiting. The only ferry had stopped long ago. There was no one about; and ferrying to the island of Umānanda Bhairava at that hour was forbidden because of the dangerous nature of the cross-currents and whirlpools which hug the rocky banks of the island.

Yet the boat moved on. I have no recollection of the boatman. Was there a boatman? or was it the male figure who managed it all? Anyway, the stretch of the dangerous river was negotiated successfully. As we passed, we were suddenly challenged by a screeching flock of crows who roost on the trees and rocks of the island. The lady talked to them angrily in Assamese; and the birds vanished. The obvious absurdity of the bizarre situation brushed my mind; but only for a moment; for at the next moment the lady, a strikingly beautiful matured Bhairavi, well clad, properly garlanded, with hairs down, sent her twining arm around me and whispered, "Depend. Rely. Come to me. I am with you; and shall be with you. Be with me. Be yourself."

I have known myself to respond to such calls all my life even at the cost of personal dangers. I felt well protected and responded in a silent affirmative which she understood. In the quiet night, under a mystic sky the wide river flowed on its mystic journey. The water, the boat, the dipping oars, the rippling waves added to our solemn bond. Silence was the only language between us.

The next thing I knew was that I was climbing the rock of Umānanda Bhairava. I passed some ramshackle settlements. Soon I was seated at the very shrine, which never keeps open at that hour; but the fact was that we had descended into the deep pit of the shrine, where stood the famous *lingam*.

At the sight of the *lingam* and of a fire, I kneeled and began to recite along with other voices: *om yāng linga śarīram śoṣaya śoṣaya svāhā*.

Om yang linga śarīram śoṣaya śoṣaya svāhā
Om ram sankoca śarīram daha daha svāhā
Om parama Śiva
Susumnā pathena mūlaśringatam ullāsollāsa
jvala jvala prajvala prajvala Hansah So-Ham svāhā

Again, and again, and—again the terrible chant came out of me. I knew a crisis was at hand.

A Drink

The chants flowed on and on. The music came rhythmically at a racing pace. But all through I could recognise the voice that had kept me spiritually aware all my life; it was the familiar voice of the Lady in Saffron. From somewhere she had been chanting.

It must have been nearly two o'clock in the morning when I was suddenly touched, and a motherly voice whispered, "Drink".

But through my long practice my eyes remained closed; and I desisted from making a response. I heard; and did not hear.

But someone was trying to force me; someone was drawing me to her body, and insisted, "Drink! Drink from me. Have no fear. Drink!"

My face was pushed to something soft and tender, and I was drinking. But there was no cup; no physical hard brim ever touched my lips. But, none the less, I was drinking. Yes I was.

Then realities began to dawn on me. I realised that I had fixed my parched lips to a human body, and I was sucking at a nipple like a helpless baby. I had indeed been drinking from a living mother's breast; and I sucked and sucked to my heart's content. Once at it, there was to be no stopping. (But, how could there be so copious a supply? I wondered as I sucked.)

The warm soft touch of firm flesh, the light sweet taste of the drink, sent along my spine a kind of assurance from 'days that are no more'.

At this stage I became aware of a sudden itch between my (awakening) brows. The well known Jitendra-centre was signalling me. At once I felt assured of all protection and aid. I felt safe and strong.

I continued sucking feverishly holding the fleshy source dearly with both my hands.

All nights come to an end. On gaining my consciousness I found myself alone, breaking out of my sound sleep by the river side; I was under a tree. A cool breeze was fanning my fevered brow. But I was alone as alone could be. I had to finish my early morning bath; and I washed all alone.

Presently I could spot the holy pair, bathing. The male quickly came to me, and asked in a rasping voice, where had I been all the time; where had I spirited myself away. He wondered how could I effect my escape. Finally he confided, "What were the *mantras* you had been muttering? Those were great *mantras*. O Mā! I could not get beyond the circle!"

I did not ask him why he wanted to pierce the *mantra*-circle. The morning was too beautiful for such trifles.

"Familiar chants all of them," I said; "and so many had been reciting. Didn't you hear?" I asked him in all innocence and sincerity.

Before he could say anything, the lady smiled and remarked, "You missed a good chance; a good *āsana*; I thought you would do well with some assistance I meant good my son."

"But I had my assistance; I had my *āsana* . . . Did you not notice?"

"Who *was* she? How did she materialise in a situation like that? She was powerful; indeed powerful. O what a lucky young man. May the Mother bless you."

"You are no less powerful, Mother", I said in all politeness.

She looked at me with a strangely soft stare, and said, "Females, as a rule, reserve much more power than males, who would always do good to themselves to get into close touch with the female adept. Even Śivā needs the Śivā, as you know. Sneer not, reject not a female as a female. All is *Prakrti*; all is Mother."

"I know that mother", I said. "I alone know how indebted I am to this female power. I am nothing without that blessing. This one you saw has been all mine, always mine. I belong to her."

I was eager to get to the ferry.

They watched me with obvious amazement. My reactions, as I pronounced those words, could not be hidden. I was always proud of the Lady in Saffron.

However, I wanted to draw a prompt curtain over the entire episode; and begged for leave, after I had bowed to them.

The regular ferryman had arrived with some pilgrims and was ready to ferry back a fresh load. I jumped on the boat without delay.

As I was crossing the great Brahmaputra on the ferry, I broke into a song which my beloved Lady in Saffron had tought me. Why did she extend her protective powers to rescue me from the *Cīnācāra* of the pair of the Mongolian tantriks, must for all times remain a mystery; I had no capacity or will to interfere with what the Bhairavi would have proposed. None the less I felt sad. Very sad indeed. She had to come so near, so very near; and yet she did not make herself known to me as she had been accustomed to do years away.

The Mystic Pressure

But only then another emotive spring began to murmur deep within. That pressure from the bead of Saint Jitendra. Little did I, or could I divine at that time how that singular pressure would react in my life. Of course during the sessions of deep *prāṇāyāma* the spot still tingles with the familiar vibrations. But on many occasions when I was misled, confused or about to fall into a pit of dark insecurity, that tingling message suddenly sparks a deep vibrant warning, and I get saved.

This phenomenon of the tickle between the brows alerts me even now. Apart from the 'good thing' it does to me by radaring warnings of mishaps, or sending extra energies for receiving special charge of power, it acts involuntarily on certain occasions. But this has often proved sad, even tragic for others. I am not speaking of those special and personal occasions when I have intensely looked forward to some special powers in order to tide over some event, like a ritualistic session or even an important engagement. I could do well on such occasions with some extra vigour and concentration. Instead, I thought of those occasions when some unthinking person, having lost all balance, all logic, suddenly and unreasonably would go beyond the range of his temper or control, and attack me viciously for imaginary harms to cause me deep hurt within. I feel more concerned with the disturbed man. I cry within for *him*.

On these sad occasions I always pray that nothing unseemly might happen to the hapless person who hurts my inner truth, unsettles my inner 'man', which is inviolable, but which feels fowled by the wrong reactions. Automatically I become anxious for the safety for such foolish creatures; and pray again and again and with all sincerity that nothing unhappy might happen to them. I also cry at such times, even openly, 'Please stop these unwarranted insults. . . I do not want anything to happen to *you*. Please cool down"; but invariably my anxiety has been laughed at, and the price has always proved to be very dear to those who turn a deaf ear to my earnest warnings. To this day I feel much embarrassed for this brow-reaction; and I always stand in fear of it.

Often I reflect upon such phenomena. What purposes are served by the *yogins* in relating other creatures of much weaker powers to their own sublime abilities? How does the message operate? I have gone through many explanations, both Eastren and Westren, but more Western, regarding the logic behind these operations; but to me these explanations sounded then, and appear to sound even now, as loquacious indulgences in sophistry.

Logic and Dreams

The world of logic is in itself a jungle of words and word arrangements, which, while keeping the mind delighted on games of brainy-gymnastics, actually drives the heart and the emotional being, further away from living the life purposively. In spite of its vagaries, a life barren of the rewards of emotion, proves to be a life full of brambles without blossoms. Sorrow, suffering, joy, happiness are conditions of feeling; and make life worth-living, or not. If man could live on foods provided by logic and reason alone, this life could be correctly lived; but such graces from the unknown, from the mysterious world of the divine, as love for the fellow lives, beauty of the living nature, joy at music, the grandeur of dawn rising on an open sea, a bird coming to the window and singing, and many more such beautiful sweet tit-bits turn our tears to songs, our pains to sympathy. Would we not miss this sumptuous feast because in all probability we would fail to relate these events, with plausible reasonings, to the emotive satisfaction or dissatisfaction that we might end up with.

Often the modern psychologists attempt at explanations. Often by reverse process they appear to come to the aid of minds disturbed. But life is much larger than patches of disturbances, much nobler than political economy, much more efficient than electronic computers. There are droughts and floods in nature; but that does not disturb the eternal calm grandeur of the beauty in natural forms. The volcanic eruptions, the cataclysmic floods, the gruesome earthquakes too come with their own types of grim grandeur, and ultimately pass off, leaving behind a trail of suffering. Yet beauty holds. Nature with her mysterious attractions remains perennially intact. The sun would rise; the dawn would reveal and smile; birds would sing, and the crown of the Alpine snow would turn into gold at every sunrise and sunset. Nature remains beautiful despite her dark frowns and bloody claws. Nature and nature's beauty, life and life's beauty remain almost undisturbed, even if nature howls, or life wails.

There is hunger and poverty in society, oppression and lawlessness. World was never without them, and world will never be without them. But at the core of all these misfortunes lies man's heartlessness, a general lack of fellow feeling, a tragic want of the least awareness of an all covering Grace from the Absolute. Even a hungry man dreams. He could dream of bread; but that dream brings him a dream-joy. None the less the feeling of joy is his; and he tries to achieve it. Dreams might open doors to frustration, but a life without dreams is a life without achievement. Greatness is a tower that basically stands on realising dream messages. Dream is hope in other dimensions; dream is emotion recollected in a world of reflected realities. The basic fact holds true. And this fact is that life is lived with interest in the emotive personality. An emotive communication breeds sympathy, love and sacrifice. Bereft of these reactions, life becomes a complex biological mechanism operating under given physical laws. But we all appreciate the fact that life is not merely a mechanism. Logicality and rationalism are mental instruments for explaining given situations. The instrument of reason could explain, infer, even predict, and in many ways establish and condition order; but the Personality of Man, which enjoys or suffers, always has to live *by* these and *for* these emotional reactions.

The Tantra Way

The yogis talk of a state of equanimity, of balanced views of life, of tranquillity and detachment, of an abstract life living in the fourth dimension. Theirs is a heaven filled with personal dimensions of the Real. But these sages exist, like the medical men, for removing the mental complexes which prevent life from enjoying that beauty, love and joy which belongs truly to the essence of life. The magic of life ultimately depends on emotional balance. The bloom of life does not burst in a flat desert of parched sands of reasoning. Emotion not only provides colour and sweetness to life, but also adds to it the fragrant message of living in perpetuity through the seeds it casts.

This is where the tantric approach to the question of a successful life has appeared to me as much more vigorous and vibrant than the ascetic denial of life within the compass of living. I have always looked upon asceticism as a kind of betrayal of the very essence which inspires life with feelings of the sublime.

Seated atop the Bhuvaneśvarī hills, confronting the emerald rock of Umānanda Bhairava floating on the magnificent and wide currents of the Brahmaputra, I have often reflected on the beauties that life provides. The ugly, the hungry, the sick, even the so-called demented have been inspired by the warm and affectionate draw of this Śakti, this *lhādinī*; and these have produced great works of art and science, of beauty and usefulness. The drive, the inspiration, the energy, the powers of inventiveness, creativeness, these are powers that redeem life from the ugly and drowsy morass of indolence and frustration. Our struggle for survival includes the survival of the soul. By appealing to the Mother, the Śakti, to the Power and Energy that be, for infusing a material property with special gifts of blossoming into life, joy and perpetuity, by charging the inlaid dynamo of conscious will with special gifts of direction and achievement, (e.g., power to see more than the eye does, to hear more than the ear does, to smell more than the nose does, to become much more sensitive of touch than the mere skin does, to be able to divine and anticipate and predict much more than this common state of the mind does by appealing to the source of all this) we do not aspire to collar the supernatural.

In fact there is no supernatural. All is the Mother, Nature. There is nought but her. When we see the invisible, hear the inaudible, communicate with the future and the past as ably as we do with what we call the present, the ever-elusive present, we feel, and ought to feel, that we are in communion with the Mother. This way of reflecting on the powers of life, this way of achieving the powers of life is the tantra way. It says, "It is heinous to kneel before a power *without*, and beg for benefits. It is more heinous to refuse to kneel to the power *within*, and ignore its benefits." This power *within* is the only search of tantra. It searches, and it achieves.

The river flowed on and on. So did my reflections. And the ever-elusive phenomenon of the 'Mother's hand', which from time to time has blessed my life by becoming entirely three dimensional, at certain happy moments transported me to the fourth and a fifth dimensions, even if that was for the fraction of a moment. *Dhyānāvasthiṭa tadgatena manasā paśyanti yam yogino/yasyāntam na viduh surā-sura gaṇāh. . .* (The *yogins* alone in their vision watch this through their concentrated attention. . . . This has no end . . . . Neither the gods, nor the anti-gods found its end.)

Who am I? Why I get so near, to be cast away so far? There is a joy-stream flowing before me. Yet grief is equally true. I was so near my Lady in Saffron. Now I am far away. I remember the touch. Even the Mongolian lady had noticed my seat on *her* lap. Why I alone could not know it? Overflowing with self-pity I was standing along the queue that had formed for the morning entrance to the shrine. The subterranean gully was too dark and narrow to allow indiscriminate entrance.

The Beggar Maid

A little girl stood out of the queue. Presently she came close to me. She was, apparently, begging for food. It was morning; yet she was hungry. Of course I would give her what she wanted; but she had to wait, until I finish the prayers. No. She was insistent. "I have not eaten for the night. Good food is frying at the vendor's. Look! There, down the hill. Don't you see? Smell? Are you dumb? I am hungry. The shrine would remain. It is not going to vanish. Come out and give me some food first to allay my hunger."

Some pilgrims in the queue laughed at me? Some women laughed at her. Others were amused at my embarrassment.

The urgency of her begging, the complete lack of any argument and reason was more than compensated by her sweet insistence. Why I would not get out of the queue she could not understand. A loss of my 'turn' in the queue meant nothing before her hunger, Hunger was her logic, her goddess. "I am hungry. . . very hungry. . . Satisfy me first. . . . Your gods may come later. . . . They will not run away." Did I see a Mona Lisa smile break through the pink lips? Those last words rang within me . . . . I could recognise some message in them.

Te tuṣṭā sarva tuṣṭaśca yatra kanyām prapūjyate
Vidhi yuktā kumārībhi-r-bhojayeccaiva bhairavīm. . .

These lines from Rudra Yāmala come to my mind. . . (The virgin being fed and satisfied all the gods are satisfied. Feed the virgin. Through the virgin feed the Bhairavi, the consort of the Bhairava).

"What is your name little girl?" I asked playfully as I resigned to leaving the queue.

"Mālinī," she replied, and coyly smiled again. "Come. Let us go", she now commanded. "Why delay?"

(Mālini, I recalled, is the technical name of the Śakti in virginity; when she is of seven years of age.)

I came out of the queue and was led by her to the inn where indeed pies were being deep fried. The aroma was, of course, appetising. She ordered two plates. Two shares of food. Whatever she liked. I was all the time muttering the virgin mantra. . .

Aing hrīng śrīng hung hesauh svāhā

And she had been at it, ordering, arranging, commanding this, that, other details pertaining to cleanliness, saucers, spoons, pickles, and such other trifles. The floor-boys were on their toes.

"What a cocotte!" the manager remarked.

I was doing my *mantra*. A little later, it must have been an hour, I came to myself, when a crowd of customers was looking for accommodation.

The crowd was pressing. The girl was gone. Her share of food was only half eaten, and the waiter had presented the bill. I paid, and stared at the vacant seat.

The waiter had been watching me.

He smiled, and remarked, "She went out, and never returned."

"Are you thinking of looking for her." He began to laugh at my predicament.

"How long could she have been gone?" I enquired.

"More than an hour may be", he answered casually.

"Do you know her?" I asked.

"Who? Me? Know her? So many, pilgrims come and go, how am I supposed to know each one of them?. . . . A pretty child she is; I thought she came with you. She belonged to you. Does she?"

I must have looked like a fool with my vacant wide-eyed stare.

Gradually I murmured, "Yes, to me. I wish she did."

And with that I left the restaurant.

Thinking of the incident I remembered that I had not indeed offered any food during the prayers on the night before. Not even the butter-soaked customary sticks (*samidhā*) in the fire.

From the onrushing melee of the holy crowd a single line of a song came floating. The same song I had heard on the banks of the Ganges time and again. I had to find out who was singing. I followed; and the voice receded, until I came to the temple door. The crowd had melted away. The doors were closed. The song then was coming from within as I sat on the steps and began to sing to myself, "Who are you, the wishful Lady singing and dancing to your own times, clapping in glee all the time? Thou the arch seducer of perennial Time!"

Back to Nārada

Nārada too had his way of tantra. The mysticism inherent in the tantra way kept him, as well as his activities, quite mystified. But to me; he himself appeared to be the last mystified yet, to tell the truth, he and his pranks were quite beyond me. This amused him. He felt ticklish; and laughed profusely whenever I was left bewildered.

My days at Chitrakūta near the Mandākinī in the caves of Hanumān-dhārā were long and fruitful. I used to see Nārada at times; but most of the times he used to be away. I made enquiries at times about his sudden disappearances; from casual enquiries little could be learnt. All I could gather was that the activities of Nārada were accepted unquestionably, and his ways were looked upon with the greatest veneration.

But these were the days when I was getting seasoned to the way taught meticulously by the Lady in Saffron, (minus of course the nocturnal penance sessions with the *Circle:* and the *Prakṛti* connection; although the Mother symbol continued to draw a deep reverence).

Those who are accustomed to the urbanised way would not appreciate this hard training in the secrets of life and beyond.

I have often been confronted with this question of all questions: how could sex assist in the attainment of enlightenment in the field of spiritualism. In very many cases I pleaded ignorance; but in most cases I remained reticent. Why?

One of the most important and inviolable tenets of the tantra *śāstras* (treatises) enjoin on the aspirant maintenance of a dead silence about these practices, if one is seriously inspired to attain perfection along this line. The mystique of this path, by remaining beyond the reach of the ordinary, saves itself from misuse, and saves the enquirer as well from dangerously harmful experimentations. There is therefore, a very important reason indeed in maintaining the way of tantra as a secret line of defence from many lurching enemies.

What Tantra does for Us

Unlike the other systems tantra belongs to the path of Love and *bhakti* which trains men to love the world, the people of the world: and accepts the responsibility of preparing the world to face the problems of life. Life, not death, is the most important proposition to the tantrik. He craves for *mukti* (liberation), through *bhukti* (enjoyment, functioning, consummation of life).

This same idea about life is embedded in the basic and the most original thesis of the Bhagavat-Gitā. It postulates the noble idea of detached application to the functions of life, wholeheartedly, but without any personal concern for the consequences of devoted sincere efforts. Looking for good results is in a way looking for grief, sorrow, dejection. Expectations throw man into the octopus-arms of functional insatiety; and the residual depression, known as frustration, follows with a certainty. Pain and suffering caused by the mind that seeks to reach the limits of sensuous joy, has been at the root of most of our spiritual bankruptcy. We desire to be at the zenith of sensation. We fail; and this causes pains, problems and provocations. Even the highest minds suffer from doldrum periods of depression.

If life has to be enjoyed in its fullness, then all the organs, the instruments of functioning, must be kept under control. If life is allowed to get out of control, because the cravings of the instruments are taking control, then, the personality who owns this life is forced to a back seat, only to helplessly watch it being drifted away.

We see in life that for the sportsmen, for the athletes, for the defence personnel, even in the day-to-day civil life, for the massive band of technicians, craftsmen, scholars etc., severe and exact training is unavoidable. They have to undergo a strictly demanding course of training, and a sustained course of discipline to achieve what they are supposed to achieve. If this be so for the conventional life, then there should not be any doubt entertained against the necessity of a very careful and strict training for the proper uses of those instruments, on the perfect functioning of which the pleasures of life have to depend.

Having analysed this path of *bhukti*, tantra has applied itself to taking control of this body, and shaping its instruments up to an extent, so that a full enjoyment of life does not stand and does not have to stand against spiritual freedom, even against salvation in the positive sense.

According to tantra such spiritual emancipation through the body (without ignoring the functions of body and life), is quite attainable, only if all the acts that men do are dedicated at the altar of the ordainer of life, that is of the Mother-spirit, the generating power from whom springs all this and heaven too. Gītā recommends this attitude very emphatically.

Cast to the flames of discipline the waywardness of the sense organs; and then to the (trained) sense organs dedicate their sensuous functions. (Gītā, VI.26).

According to the Gītā the three most difficult emotional states of mind (which influence and overwhelm the functional apparatuses) are sex, anger and greed, (XVI.21). The origin of sex is libido; of anger is envy or intolerance; and of greed is possessiveness. These three have been termed as the three doors to 'hell' (the watchdog at the door of hell, according to Homer, has three heads). Hell in realily is a mental complex.

The tantra way intends to save the aspirant from this. Once he could keep his mind off this track, *mukti*, or liberation comes within his reach. He would enjoy all things in life, without getting entangled; his would be a deep involvement with life, without engagement or attachment. To achieve this subjectivity of the mind, and enjoy the objectives, is the tantrik's ideal goal. Hence the disciplinary exercises.

Wrenched off from the actual context, and seen (and then interpreted) from the outsider's self-projected vision, these acts of disciplining the most turbulent of the three forces that guide us to madness is often looked down upon as profligate, degenerate and even fraudulent.

There are tantra schools and tantra centres all around the world; and all over the cities of the world, flourishing under one or the other name. Tantra centres flourish under the generosity of deluded patrons, or (more often) under the paymasters who need these centres for uses often politically motivated. In recent years tantra dens have evoked a public hue and cry as centres for orgy and foul play.

The crux of the matter is that for a hundred of such urbanised sophisticated institutions, there could be just one genuine school of such discipline as saints like Nārada selflessly maintained. All that these joints look for is a genuinely gifted aspirant, or initiates who could withstand the rigours of routine, the bites of temptation, the flames of desire and indulgences, and yet come out as true gold from the fire of the furnace. The disciplined enjoy a sharper degree of sensitiveness than what the sense organs of the indisciplined could enjoy.

What Tantra Expects Us to Do

This is not the place where I could discuss the actual shapes and tones of these rigours. For that an entire compendium on tantra discipline has to be written; and tantra is not a subject for self-teaching. Of the many subjects of the 'self-taught' series tantra cannot be one. It is to be learnt from the guru, from the direct master, who accepts the pupil out of his or her engulfing love trust.

Once accepted, the initiate, then, enjoys every bit of that company. Love and understanding together forms the basis of this relationship. And then, like eating, sleeping, singing etc., sex too becomes an expression of a highly trained, and absolutely disciplined power which nature has planted in man. With the aid of tantric discipline even the joy in sex is elevated to a plane of ecstatic release in perpetuity. Then sex becomes a 'sacrifice' cf. Chāndogya and Bṛhadāraṇyaka Upaniṣads.

Disciplined libido is the source of the power which has the greatest potential value to human growth. Once the switch of this power-source comes within the reach of man, at his will man could mould his joy. Then the bonds of life would strengthen him without fastening. He becomes the *vira*, the hero, the strong man. Tantra views life clearly; and accepts death and the other life only as inescapable consequences. It does not prepare man for death; but builds him up for life.

The Lady in Saffron, Saint Jiten, Nārada, and others who had taken interest in me, were preparing me not as a saintly man, but as a manly man, which, in fact and practice, constitutes the chief aim of tantra education.

And for this I was taken to Chitrakūt, Ujjain and Nāsik (in that order). To Varanasi of course, I was tied by my navel string. I had to come back again and again to that hallowed place, where lived the Lady in Saffron.

I was beholden to Nārada when he gave me this break. His was the path of Love, *bhakti*. Although the superfluous would make an awful distinction between a Rāmadāsi, a Bāul and a tantrik, for the adept this distinction vanishes, because all of them are inspired by their enthusiastic interest in life's verve and vivacity, and all of them hold it very dear to their soul that life should blossom in that faith in love as it is divinely meant to be. 'Prepare and ever prepare' is the slogan of the tantra adept. 'Fight without fever', says the Gitā.

Although Nārada would be taken as a Rāmadāsi *bhakti* adept (and not a tantrik) by the common critic, he was as much a part of tantra as the tantriks are a part of *bhakti*. The two are inseparable; and all disciplinary practices inherent in any form of inner training depend *above* all on tantra. Are not all the ways the tāntric way?

Is not religion itself ritualistic? Voodoo, shaman, obeah, *prāyaścitta*, *puraścaraṇa*, *grahaśānti*, zodiacal invocations,—why, even the Lord's Prayer, Communion, Mass, Easter, Eucharist all, all of them are but the manifestations of shades of tantra. The Druids, the Orpheans, the Delphics knew the truth; the Māyāns, Aztecs, Incas, Tibetans, Egyptians, Shintos all are facets of the same thought channel—tantra.

Yet there is a subtle difference. That difference affects the outer shell only; the inner quest, its spirit and technique, almost always finds out a golden mean. As I say this, I recall (in recent years) my visits to Indo-China and Mexico, Brajil and Peru where I spent a stretch of exciting time. From these direct experiences I feel emboldened to say that tantra rejects the negative path. While tāntriks advocate consummation of the senses, while they lead others to partake of the feast, they themselves would survive on the minimum and the least. They are not the negative abstainers. They are the replica of complete *ānandam*, cheerfulness. They have no material attachment to remain shackled to the immediate cheer. From life to life. That was their dictum. To make room for happiness; to lead to happiness; to spread happiness; to watch happiness; to be near happiness and radiate happiness all around. Live in a 'family', as children of the Mother.

A Mother's Blood

After three most enjoyable months with Nārada in that wonderful sanctuary at Chitrakūta, one fine morning I was surprised by my mother, who was accompanied by my mentor, the Lady in Saffron. And I was led out of the *āśrama*. But that was not to be the end. Such attempts were repeated; and twice I had slipped out on my errand. I had left home, and attempted to join the company of the happy eternals. But like the first time, I failed to escape the entirely overwhelming but affectionate influence of the Lady in Saffron. She stood between me and my supposed 'freedom' as a mighty river between two rocks.

Then there came a shocking revelation to me, which turned my life completely.

After my three escapades I gave up thinking actively about leaving Varanasi and my home. One of these days my mother asked me to accompany her to her favourite shrine of Śankatā, near Pancagangā past Maṇikarnikā (all in Varanasi). On Fridays she would invariably be at the shrine. Most of the days I accompanied her on a boat. Innocently I did so on that particular day too.

As usual she had entered the nave, and got busy with her prayers standing before the altar. During the prayers she suddenly brought out a sharp knife, and just made a slit between her breasts, before we could bat an eye. Blood spurted out. Coolly she collected the blood even before my horror-stricken eyes. The blood was collected on a *bel* leaf. She laid the leaf down at the feet of the deity, and offered the same ceremoniously. The guardian of the shrine was watching her familiar face with eyes of horror. Never before in the shrine anyone had offered blood, specially at the sacred altar. To add to the horrible consequences of the extreme act the blood was not only human, but indeed of a Brahmin lady of rank, and that of a Mother! Before the horrified priest could say a thing, she had put my hand on her blood bathed chest and demanded from me the binding blood-vow that I would never attempt to forsake home for the unknown beyond, even for spiritual quests.

I was left with no option. The sickening sight of blood flowing freely from my mother's delicate and fair skin had shaken me to my depths. Like one mesmerised I repeated after her, "No, I will never leave this world of the householder."

Then she made me take two more vows. One that I shall not avoid married life when the time comes. The last one calls for some elaboration.

I could sing tolerably well, and delighted in singing. These efforts together with my efforts at the esoteric seances and the days of ever-increasing number of fastings etc., had severely told on my health. The *āsanas* did not help. A long trip to the seaside did not help. I had started spitting blood, coughing incessantly, and at times the heamorrhage became quite alarming. But I had no other accompanying symptoms of tuberculosis; not even the usual temperature, or associated depression. I kept hale, hearty, and indomitably energetic, which made the cure even more difficult. It demanded rest from nerve-exertions, abstention from physical strain, even from songs. Despite assurances from the Lady in Saffron, and from a Muslim saint, a new friend of mine, my mother lived a trying life of anxiety and uncertainty. So she drew out this third vow, "Never shall thee relinquish the non-vegetarian food under any circumstances. I have your mentor's (Lady in Saffron i.e.) permission for it."

I looked at her, and found this to be true. "The Aryans were meat eaters," she said. "What one needs is one's food. The balance is just a fad, gimmick. And it is not rare amongst the vegetarians. Do not encourage indulgence; and, if at all possible, kill greed."

I gave my word of faith to my bleeding mother on these three vows. After that she dictated to me some of the disciplines I had to maintain. One of these was to dedicate an yearly prayer in the name of a distant deity in West Bengal. This was Tārkeśvar. At the end of a five-year penance I had to acompany my mother to that shrine. It pained me to watch my mother go into a pretty long exercise of circumambulation stretching herself at full length on her nose and forehead, measuring the entire course, just crawling.

Superstition and Faith

Superstition! Primitive naturalistic faith!! There are other names to be called aloud. But those who shout have been found grovelling in the filthiest currents of other types of faith, beliefs and practices, much more abominable and demeaning than superstition. A faith not understood is condemned as a superstitious reject. Pure rationalism is more horrifying to any church than the most revolting attacks of Satan, which in itself is a named superstition.

I have ceased to bring every phenomenon to an explanation. Yet I am very wary of blind beliefs and faiths. There is in the very spirit of the sublime an aura of noble grace and openness, an aura of love and understanding which captivates me. To me the fullest expression of unrelated and unselfish love appears to be the sublimest magic of all. It is charming; it is a telling; it is captivating. It demands from man the utmost sacrifice that he is capable of making. It elevates soul, uplifts character, and injects into the frail frame of man the quality of endurance. Suffering is turned into joy, tears into nectar, losses into gain at the touch of unattached, unmotivated love.

Mankind has been trying the methods of war for giving peace; medication for curing the mind's ailments; stars and planets for securing their safety and commanding their fate; spells and charms to organise the disorganised. The result? Always a failure, always.

Dubious are the remedies which time has been testing ever so long within the laboratories of mind and outside it. But the spiritual panacea of being able to love without self, serve without profit, suffer without malice, possess without attachment has not yet been given a full scope, because every time someone tries it, the contrary forces bully it down. Yet it does not die. Resurrection has been promised along with the apparent death of faith and love. This truth has been illustrated in history time and again.

This love is attainable by spiritual endeavour alone.

Until such a day when human efforts could rationalise and causate the mysterious workings, methods of operation, active and passive reactions of the emotion known as love, all nervous feels shall remain captive within the unfathomed cells of what we sneeringly term as superstition. We call names and we show sneer mostly when we fail ourselves in our reasoning faculties and in our patience. How difficult it is to own one's limitations. Our own pride in our understanding, our faith in our infallibility and ability of the powers of reason are so superstitiously *tainted* and defiantly magnified, that when our personal reasons fail, we feel that all reasons have failed; and the card palace of the variety of rationality crushes down, and is blown to the winds! We, unreasonably, and impatiently, give it a name, and call out the name, however ugly it might sound. Calling an exercise an act of superstition is one instance of such egotistic outbursts of delusion. It only records our utter failure in calling for more sustained patience to go deep into a matter. We seem to be very critical of being regimented in thoughts. So far so good, accepted; but we continue to live under given conditions; we are accustomed to facets of actions and reactions; and through these inevitable conditioning we ourselves live a life of regimentation—one type of regimentation or another. Yet we pretend to keep away from regimentation. To be free from being brain-washed, to keep away from fixations, and live the life of the purest free thinker demands in man the utmost rigours of intellectual discipline (which in other words means intellectual detachment). The impatient and the superfluous, as much as the egotist and the vain miserably lack in this discipline.

Why do I love the one, and not another? Why do I respond favourably to one and slightingly to another? When selfish interests so demand, why do I make such sacrifices as I cannot imagine myself capable of making? Why do I subject myself to sufferings I find unimaginable to be undergoing? Why do I face disgraces despite the homely warnings of many? Why do I unaccountably embrace against all odds the one I hold innocently close to me? These are facts beyond the capacity of reasoning, or of psychologists. What passes through the mysterious chambers of the mind of a man in an asylum remains as closed a secret as what passes through the minds of an inspired soul in spiritual love.

The sombre shadows that darken the minds of the spiritually demented (very often, we later admit that these are the enlightened ones) remain a closed book to our ways of reasonings; so remains the 'gone-ness' of the hearts in love, love of a person for a person, of a person for a cause, of a person for the dedication to the ultimate. The secrets of the joy in love and those of love in joy, the secrets of the acceptance of suffering with the joy of bliss, breed, in a way, so to say, the germs of mystery. Mystery breeds what we sneeringly call superstition, and what we try to brush away with the pride of the ignorant about his vaunted knowledge. There are certain types of knowledge attainable through personal experience alone. There seems to be no other way (*nānyah panthā*). Of all superstitions a faith in love that serves, love that suffers and love that sacrifices remains the sublimest.

Psychologists try and rationalise animal events; scientists probe and deduct facts for further analysis. Water has been analysed; rose has been analysed. Even the lack of world peace is being analysed every day. Subjective analysis, objective analysis, both are being put to test and action. But with all that we fail to *make* a rose; or *make* a drop of water or an insignificant drop of protoplasm. We have not brought, we cannot bring, we will not bring world peace. Peace and Love, thus remain the sublimest, the most illusive, yet the most fascinating of 'superstitions'. The mystery of all mystery is this. That mystery shall always be there to haunt our strained faculties of the mind. Mystery is the frank admission of reason that it cannot move further.

My experiences in tantra have taught me this lesson. And this lesson like the spirit in the sunshine, like the joy in flowers, is deeply embedded in the music of my blood. I live because it lives within me. And this has to be attained by the blessings of the spiritual forces that are there. The forcible influence of my Lady in Saffron, of my friend Nārada, who taught me so much, entirely uncalled for, of Swāmi Sadāśivānanda of Rāmakrishna Mission of Varanasi, of Saint Jitendra, and of the innumerable spiritual souls who through their blessings had brought me into a close contact with the supreme joy in *sādhanā*, almost flowed down my path like the unbidden flow of Mother Ganges; this happened only because of their power of love and understanding. They loved me. Their love has been a blessing. This *Power of Love* came to them through their devotion to the tantra way.

Saint Jitendra had given me his shelter. He had taken me into his deepest confidence. I learnt the supreme knowledge of *latā sādhana* through his Grace. But all that happened like scenes in a Greek drama where chance, fate, and design each acted against a background of grinding demand, utmost rigour and absolute impersonality. Of that period yet later.

10

The Alter Ego

Mr Das: A Phenomenon

At about this time a singular event became the subject of a hot discussion in the locality.

The sudden disappearance of one Mr Das and his supposed death under very mysterious circumstances had been often talked about. Even the police had taken it for granted that Mr Das had died through accidental drowning. The ease had almost faded out from memory, until precisely, after a year the case flared up like wildfire.

Mr Das was a postmaster. His wife Sarala Das bore him a son, Kanai. Mr Das always appeared to levitate under a strange influence which was never accepted as merely spiritual.

Many thought him to be off his mind. But as a postmaster he did his duties to the entire satisfaction of the government as well as the public. Mrs Das was regarded as the very picture of a virtuous wife; indeed she was an extremely modest and pleasant person.

Mr Das often claimed about his direct connections with the world of the dead; and he was known to predict many things. He was known to sound timely warnings to people against possible catastrophies. Several times he had asked people to stop from undertaking a mission, or travel, or occupying a house. And later events showed that accidents had brought disasters to the transgressors. People generally listened to his warnings.

One thing however he could not do. Nobody could consult him for a solution, as he would not answer questions. He could only give warnings when he got 'the signs'.

He was a great devotee of the Mother. His daily routine of life included deep meditations and regular prayers at a temple.

(This was a Śakti temple at the back of Pātāleśvar, which is a celebrated yogic spot, mentioned in the books of antiquity recording traditions as old as 2700 years and more. The popular temple is still there, and could be seen, although neglected. What cannot be seen is the subterranean cell where tantric *sādhanā* used to be actually performed on grounds haloed by previous adepts. I am not sure myself why I attach so much importance and significance to the actual spots, *piṭhas*—where past yogis have realised power. After his son Kanai was born, he gradually began to lose interest in life, until on medical grounds he had to go on a long leave. In fact his wife in a way made him go on this leave.

But his involvement in meditation increased, and went on increasing, until he started spending long hours on the banks of the Ganges, often he sat through nights. He had completely lost his rapport with the outer world.

A time came when he stopped talking; and because of his moods he had to be kept within locked doors. He would hardly keep any cover on him. He would often break into strange and enigmatic languages. He shunned food and drink, and began to offer worship to his own wife, addressing her by tantra names. Whenever he could find an opportunity he would run down to the river, and sit at his favourite spot. Once there, he would stay put for hours and days in a state of transcendence.

In the city of Varanasi such a spiritual phenomenon was not a rarity. People talked, but hardly took any notice, or kept up the track.

One morning when Sarala, that is Mrs Das, had opened the door to look for her husband, the room was found vacant; the inner window, however, stood wide open. There was no possibility in normal circumstances to find any escape through the window, which had a clear drop of nearly 20 feet or more. But the man was not there, or anywhere to be found. Only the piece of the discarded loincloth was found on the river bank, where the river flowed down a drop of sheer fifteen feet. It was the season of monsoons. The river was high, and in floods. The current was deadly, and eddies made any swimming almost impossible. Since his cloth was there, he must have been there; and if he was not there to be found, where could he have gone in his naked state? The only inference that Mrs Das like others, would have arrived at was that he had thrown himself in the flood, and met with his eventual death. In that fast flowing current the body must have been carried away far and beyond.

Since Mr Das had been talking for some time of 'friends *calling him*', Mrs Das was sure that he had drowned himself.

This confirmation she received from her husband, who had *appeared* to her twice, and asked her to join him through the mercy of Mother Ganges. Her parents began to keep her under a vigilant watch.

For some time Mrs Das had been insisting on performing a regular funeral ritual for the peace of the departed soul. This she did with remarkable earnestness. But the priests were not ready to oblige before a year would pass. When the year came to an end, preparations for the funeral prayers were on.

I personally had been at her home, not a great distance from ours, the evening before the *śrāddha* (funeral prayers). The graceful lady, with her long black hairs spread all over her back was engaged in cleaning rice which was to be used the next day for the ceremony.

A Spirit Descends

All on a sudden she began to talk to me *in a man's voice*. The subject of the talk was the next day's prayer. The male voice informed me that contrary to what the people were thinking, the ceremony would never take place; for any attempt to displace him would be regarded as contrary to his peace. He was all right where and how he had been; and he would not tolerate any disturbance or dislocation. 'No prayers', *he* said.

I was shocked at this talk in a rude language from the sweet lady whom we had grown to accept as the very essence of good and virtuous womanhood.

Her mother came out. At once she found something amiss. As she tried to take the plate of rice from Sarala's hand, in a sudden expression of fury she threw the entire thing in the yard two storeys down.

Her case was being discussed by every one. In spite of the caution of the poor family a crowd began to make a bee line for curious interviews. (Stricken people are always eager to survive on spiritual morsels of whatever kinds, irrespective of logic or propriety.)

And within a week's time news began to circulate that her husband's spirit had descended on her, and that she had been doing incredible things, behaving unbelievably, and predicting events. Mothers with ailing children, wives with husband and in-law problems, even some spiritualists with their questions began to 'consult' her.

So far I was able to keep myself away from the seene.

That particular evening we had been sitting around a kerosine lamp, doing our 'home-work'. My elder brother Indu was also seated there. A neighbour, Kunja, a habitual opium addict, after closing his shop joined us. He wanted to talk to my brother. Both of them came to the conclusion that the entire thing had been a hoax. All the woman was calling for according to Kunja, was a bout of stiff whippings, and 'an effective male in her widowed bed'.

Simple deductions of complex problems always left me doubting. Moreover my personal knowledge of Sarala made me hold her in a very high esteem; and any type of dramatisation, hoaxes, double dealings, according to my view, was beyond her simple way of life.

"Let us pay her a visit," I suggested. "Why not you yourself question her and be satisfied?"

My voice exposed my annoyance at Kunja's banter.

Now, this opium eater, Kunja, like any other opium addict, viewed things as a wise crack would. His sarcasms were unbearable. He was notorious for his daring sarcasms, and was often roughly treated.

I quote an example.

A Magician

One of our friends, Shankar, a youngman, was reputedly a tantrik, and kept himself engaged in subjects bordering on exorcism. In this he copiously made use of wine and women. Although we kept ourselves away from his company, none the less we held him in some regard, and often people consulted him about directives when they needed any.

He was giving a 'show' at our home to entertain the children. One of the shows involved the art of mesmerism. He did mesmerise one of the girls from the audience, and made her read a letter in English language, which she did not know. She was made to eat some unedible things, and even hold her hand on the flame of a candle without any visible reaction from her. A needle was driven through her skin without any apparent sign of agony.

Shankar was next engaged in a new trick. He gave each of us a slip of paper and a blank envelope, and wanted us to write *in red* (we had been given a red pencil) anything in any language. Then the slips were to be placed within the envelopes which were to be sealed, and surrendered to him. We followed his instructions, and the sealed envelopes were back in his hand.

Then he started reading the contents without opening the envelopes, until he reached one which made him explode in anger. This was Kunja's envelope. The written words ran thus, "You are a damned hoax and a miserable fraud." To add insult to injury he had written this with a lead pencil. His call at Kunja by name in a terrible voice shook the audience. "If I could read the writing in red," he said, "I could read them in any ink. I could read your mind too, Kunja. How about telling the audience what you really are Kunja?"

One could have knocked Kunja down with a feather. My father came to his rescue. He just addressed himself to Shankar, and said, "Enough is enough. Kunja goes home, and uses an extra dose of opium. And Shankar, your shows are now closing."

Sarala Possessed

The incident was fresh in my memory. I could not take the bantering of Kunja against Sarala. Along with my brother we three made for Sarala's home, a walk of seven minutes.

It was past eleven o'clock in the night. The neighbourhood stood still. We had to climb up two flights of stairs to reach the second floor. The entrance to the apartment was closed. We knocked. Between the knock and the opening of the door by Sarala's mother a couple of minutes must have elapsed. During that pause the unpredictable Kunja made an unfortunate and the same indecent remark. "What these widowed young women need is a strong man in their bed as I told you", he said.

In the circumstances it was a very rude and shocking r mark to make. My brother felt embarrassed. But before he could say anything, Sarala's mother had opened the door and welcomed us. Looking at me she said, "Sarala was enquiring about you a few minutes back, and had asked me to keep the door open."

We were rather surprised at her remark.

We found Sarala seated on a simple bed laid out on the floor. Her bed was filled with lovely garlands and fragrant flowers. Visitors had brought brilliant nosegays for the satisfaction of the deity under whose supposed influence Sarala had been acting as she did. Everyone knew that it was the spirit of the blood-thirsty Pātāleśvar Kāli.

I have been lucky with these people 'under a spiritual spell'. Ignoring the other two she looked at me, smiled and demanded, "Why are you hesitating? Come, give me what you have brought. Oh, what a darling you are my boy!"

Sarala had been a vegetarian. But Sarala's husband was very fond of fried fish. Before I had come out of our home, I had gone to the kitchen, and secured a piece of fish fry, which I had kept hidden. I was not sure if Sarala would be found in her normal state, or if she would be in her possessed state. But I also knew if her husband's spirit was in her, he would like it. As a widow she would shun it.

Hearing her, to the amazement of all present, I produced the piece of fish, and handed it over to Sarala. When she began to eat it, everyone in the room released a gasp of horror. Sarala eating fish! (Under no circumstances a widow of the upper Hindu class would touch non-vegetarian food, or food prepared outside her own hearth. These are very strict taboos, and she, as a widow, had been abiding by the customs.)

While at it, Sarala suddenly addressed herself to Kunja.

"How Sir opium eater, how about your gay jests? Do you believe, or you do not? I dare you climb the steps to the roof, and bring from upstairs a branch of the oleander which, you know, grows in a tub on the roof. Dare you go, and bring it? Come, let us see, how truthfully you doubt . . . And the man I need . . . Why not you Mr Virility? Don't you take yourself to be the he man of many beds? Go upstairs I say, go upstairs. I shall meet you there with all my sex hunger dear! And we shall have a good time, O my strong man."

Of course Kunja dared not make the faintest stir. He was completely bemused and benumbed. His fingertips were steadily digging into my left arm to which he held on with all the he-power of his life.

Then came the turn of my brother Indu. She boldly asked him if he was convinced about the fact that the world of life stretched beyond the body.

I had brought secretly a handful of jasmines, her favourite flower, collected from our temple; but I did not find time yet to offer them to her. I had seen how she had raged at my companions, I ventured to make a personal move, when she smiled, and called me to her by a secret name. The dead Kanai used to call me by that name which none else used.

"Come Pandit, come. Bring me those flowers. You must not keep company of fools . . . " She stretched her hands, and I offered the flowers. She looked at them, and said. "Jasmines? For me? Why? Who loves these flowers? And who am I you think? You should have brought some *ladikennys* instead, which I like."

Kanai indeed was fond of *ladikenny*, a special type of sweetmeat the Bengalis in Calcutta make. But it is not eaten by some of the most orthodox, because fried sweetmeats are taboo to the most austere. In any case Sarala had never partaken of it. She, after her widowhood, had been living on a simple diet, once a day.

I ventured to reply, "You would not eat a *ladikenny*, would you?"

"Why not?" asked she "Do not mistake me for anyone else. You do not belong to those fools. Get away from them as far as you can. Keep far, far away."

At this point she expressed her desire to visit the washroom, and asked me to assist her. She had grown physically too weak under the strain of the nervous upset. I helped her to the room. I felt that others, inclusive of her mother did not view that move with much favour; but I had no fear. I held her hand, and helped her.

On our return, as soon as she came in touch with the bed, she broke into loud screams. Immediately she started shouting unutterable hard-core abuses and blasphemies, too hot for the tongue of so decent and tender a woman as Sarala. This time the attack poured on my brother. A copy of the holy book Gītā under her pillow had enraged her. My brother had secretly kept it there with intentions to help her. But she reacted horribly. The book had to be thrown out forthwith.

"You Are the Cure!"

For months Sarala remained a helpless victim. Now and then she would come back to herself. But most of the time she was under the the powers of 'possession.'

People would come and pay a visit, as if she were a deity. Many would consult her; and she would reply when she chose to. At other times when she returned to senses, she would bathe and dress and eat normally as if she were her good old self again. I would go near her, and she would take up my hand, and talk of her 'illness'.

Once I ventured to ask her what would be a good remedy for her. "You are the remedy," she replied to my amazement. "But you would not believe me", she said as she smiled, and added with emotion, "O how adorable you are!" I was too confused to say anything. But I still remember the fire in her eyes.

She was very insistent on performing the funeral rites of her husband, and she said if Kanai, her son, performed the *Śrāddha*, her ailments would cease. From this I could gather that she, as Sarala, did realise that she was ill. But she had absolutely no idea about the nature of her illness. She wondered why the *Śrāddha* was not being performed.

I noticed also that her hair, normally wavy and dark, in the usual course fell in cascades on her bare back; but under the spell, the same locks became a mass of tangled wires, matted into a coarse confusion; and no amount of care from her mother could disentangle them. On several occasions the mass of her dark hair was found dripping when she had not even gone near a bath, or water.

When it was noticed that for several months she had not had her regular menses, Sarala's mother became alarmed. She began to think about calling *ojhās* (samman priests reputed to tackle with spirits). But she also insisted that 'I' do something instead. She said that 'Mr Das' himself had made it clear that the cure had been in *my* hand. Didn't he?

I felt strange. What could 'I' do? During the spells Sarala had not only eaten food in huge quantities, inclusive of the tabooed *ladikenny*, but she had eaten even meat and fish, which she had never eaten before. The quantities of her intake were always spectacularly large. At times she ate and ate seemingly without stop.

Crime and Punishment

I consulted my Lady in Saffron. She of course had known of the case. She knew the family.

"Mr Das had been a pious soul", she explained. "He was eager to practise tantra. He dabbled in the esoteric practices, but he had no guru, neither much training. Naturally he had fallen a victim to the powers who seek such media for carrying out their mischiefs . . . It is unfortunate", she murmured. "Most unfortunate."

"What is so unfortunate?" I asked. "Mr Das had been a nice and happy man. He wanted to go in peace. He was well intentioned. If he had made mistakes, well, the Great Mother need not have punished him and his family this way. She should have protected her."

"For the Great Mother there is neither rewards nor punishment", she explained; and continued, "She loves you, me, the dog and the fly equally. She loves the tiger that hunts the deer, as well as the deer. She loved Rāvaṇa as well as Rāma. When Yaśodā punished the baby Kṛiṣṇa, she did not love the divine baby the less. Her ways are impenetrably mysterious. And how do we know for sure that in doing what she was doing she was not doing good to someone? Her mysteries are not confounding at all. We ourselves turn them to look like mystery. We measure things and distances by our own standards. Our standards are not her standards. When we measure the speed of the light from a distant star we do not use the same standard as measuring the speed of a train. Or, do we? She is the Mother spirit of all that is seen and unseen. Her standards, her ways, her logic must necessarily remain outside our easy computation.

"Want to reach her standards? Well, seek her; meet her *within* you. Then you will find that she is more real than all this you call real. More logical than your logic. Most of what we call mystery is a mirror-reflection of confusion of our own make. It is an admission of the limits of our reasoning. We make the mistake of applying the logic of the three dimensions to events of other dimensions. Mystery begins where logic ends. Logic ended, we cry like a little child who has lost control of the coloured ball which has gone out of his reach. It is there; he feels it; but it is not there; he cannot reach it. This wail of logic is what we call mystery.

"The Light from the Self alone could reveal her ways. Why must we be so logically motivated in unlooping her 'ways'? Kneel to her, ask for her love and favours. She alone knows the ultimate secrets of good and bad.

"But even the most pious, like the monkey-guard of the foolish king, could kill the object of his faith and love through a wrong emphasis of duty. You know the tale. A pet and trained monkey with an open sword stood guard over the sleeping king. But when he wanted to kill the troublesome fly disturbing the sleeping king, the monkey with a loyal fury brought down the sword on the fly with a force, and killed the king in the process.

"Even the most pious could take wrong directions. There are forces eager to lead him along the wrong way. There are many human monkeys living in this lane who would love to lead you along the wrong way.

So, in spiritual area too, one must be very careful about selecting the guru, the guide. Mr Das had been a self-opinionated *sādhaka*, and loved to keep things to himself, and never consulted other path-finders. Hence, his suffering; and now having failed the world of the fairer spirit, he is being tormented in the most gruelling world. I am anxious for Sarala, and her son Kanai."

"Then, why not help them?" I had lost control of my natural voice.

She looked at me, and simply remarked that something had to be done indeed. Suddenly she beamed a smile.

An Obeah Session

When she had reached Sarala's home she found that already a *sanyāsī-ojhā* (an obeah-man) had been preparing for casting the spell off Sarala. We watched the proceedings.

The massive *ojhā*, was middle-aged. He would be certainly the best remedy if weight could be a remedy. By the keenness of his eyes and the height of the gathered hair on his head, as well as by the heap of beads he had been wearing, he should have been the most effective *ojhā* in the dictionary. His chants were being muttered in a perfectly unintelligible cacaphony. All had been impressed by sheer absurdity.

Then he declared that the spirit had been a very powerful one; and any mistake would be most dangerous to his own safety and life. In this he finally proved to be correct. He called for the best food and the finest clothings; and when these were brought, he started his rites.

He asked several people to get hold of Sarala, and keep her under control. This was done, and the rites srarted. Both the patient and the doctor were seated within a *circle.* The patient's attitude was impeccable, and almost docile. The doctor had been muttering his abracadabra. The room meanwhile was filled with smoke from the burning inguents.

Things had been running on smoothly, except for a certain degree of tenseness caused by an enforced state of semi-nudeness of Sarala. For a reputed family known to social forms the embarrassment was understandable. But none dared to obstruct. Unaccountability of supernatural events calls for supernatural strength of toleration and forgiveness. *Man is pious mostly through pain and fear*. Few are gifted with natural piety which radiates piety all around. Such alone are known as godmen, *avatāra*, the divine in flesh.

Besides the family circle of about five members, we two had been the only outsiders. Since the Lady in Saffron enjoyed a high reputation, my presence was silently suffered.

Meanwhile Sarala began perspiring heavily, and started pulling out her scanty covers. The only cotton she had been wearing soon came off; but as she had been lying supine on her back, the same discarded piece of cloth now appeared to become her carpet.

Now the body was bare as bare could be; and the *ojhā* began to bathe her by pouring water from a jar. A very large copper pot filled with water stood by.

All on a sudden Sarala jumped up, and taking hold of the huge container by the two side-rings, shoved it up on her head, rushed out to the verandah, and threw the vessel, water and all, down in the yard. All this she achieved in one swift electric action; and we all stood amazed, considering the great strength she had to apply in achieving the titanic feat.

Between her raising of the water vessel and throwing it down she had dealt the *ojhā* with a cruel hard kick, sending the bulky man flying through the air like a carton box; and he fell on the stone floor with outstretched hands, on his poor nose, bleeding profusely in the process. Sarala, by now looking like a fierce maenad in her stark nudity, started pouring torrents of filthy raw abuses at her victim with obscene lascivious gestures which threw us into a confused state, as the Sarala we all had known was renowned for her modesty and voice, not All this, while she had been shouting in a strange *male* sweet nature, unlike the voice of Das.

The ceremony was in a shambles. She began to pull at the hair of the man, now stretched piteously on the floor, and held his neck in a vicious grip, until the poor victim began to froth in his mouth. We were not spared from her curses and her threats for bringing in a rogue for overcoming the might of a power that none of us dared challenge.

At this stage the Lady in Saffron quietly, unceremoniously glided into the picture.

Coolly, sedately the quiet Lady in Saffron entered the spell-bound arena, and tenderly held Sarala by her hand, and addressed Sarala as if she were addressing the deceased Das.

"Tell me Das Bhai (brother)", she said to the hearing of all, "why are you so upset? What must we do to relieve you of this horrible situation? We are very eager to be of assistance; but we do not know how. You do not have to suffer, and make others suffer too. You never liked it. You have always been good to folks around you. You must have been annoyed beyond your endurance to have to bring such a calamity on the lady you loved so much. Now confide please; confide in me. Tell me of your sufferings, and of the remedy."

The words acted as magic.

"Let that rogue leave at once", demanded 'Das'.

And of course the miserable *ojhā* had to leave.

Soon Sarala gained her peace, and slumped as if exhausted by a terrible bout of excess.

At the Lady's sign all left.

I too was going away when she stopped me, and asked me to be by her side as an aide. She asked me to recite the *Gāyatrī mantra.*

Then gradually she drew her own circle of lamps, nine in all, and carefully lay Sarala flat on her back on the floor. Her body now touched the bare ground. Her head rested on the thighs of LS who was seated in a lotus posture (*Sukha-Padmāsana*). Although away from her, Sarala's feet were kept carefully within the firey circle.

The fires in the pit lit by the *ojhā*, were still burning. I was chanting, and throwing inguents into the flames, although I knew that ultimately something else was to be thrown. LS herself was in a tranced state; but Sarala was keeping still, as if asleep. The drink LS had given her to drink might have been taking effect. Gradually and carefully LS rested Sarala's head too on the floor.

The poor patient's bare body appeared to be bathed in an ethereal lustre.

The lamp-circle was keeping its vigil in a merry dance.

Now LS studiedly took off her own last piece of cloth, folded it with care, and turning it into an *āsana* rested it on the still body of prostrated Sarala. As I had anticipated, she then sat *on* Sarala's body, (balancing herself between her thighs and the naval, just on the *svādhiṣṭhāna* and *viśuddha cakras*). Her gaze was kept fixed on Sarala's eyes, which were still closed.

How Sarala bore the weight of that bulky body will always remain a mystery to me.

I had by now lighted sixty-four lamps around the circle. As she stretched her palms I placed two burning earthen bowls on them, and placed a third one at the head of Sarala.

The Lady in Saffron had handed me a bag. I opened it now, and found that it contained some offerings for burning: *śatamūlī*, *apāmārga*, *sarpagandhā*, *droṇa* blossoms and *jatāmānsī*. These herbs I recognised; besides there were some feathers, furs and skins of serpents. There were other things which I could not recognise. Mixed in ghee and inguents I began to burn them in the fire as she devotedly chanted. (From her chants I could follow when to throw what.) The concoction took time to burn. The room was filled with smoke and a pungent smell.

Sarala appeared to be coming to life and to her senses. LS then turned her over, this time face down, and changed the position of her *āsana*. She sat on Sarala's back, i.e., on the *svādhiṣṭhāna cakra*. She was seemingly now pressing her down with her weight, until Sarala groaned. Blood began to trickle out, and the bare cemented floor bore a line of blood gradually meandering. Her menses had been induced. Finally, her senses revived. She was herself again.

After a long while Sarala spoke, and demanded in a male voice, "I want my old cloth back. . .There, there,. . .in the cupboard. . .No *śrāddha* (funeral service) without cremation. . .cremate me first. . ."

"Go and find the cloth for yourself", commanded LS. The terrible loud voice sounded quite unlike hers.

Sarala got up effortlessly, and approached a closet within the room, and brought out the piece of cloth which was left by the Ganges. She brought it back within the circle.

LS held the bare body of Sarala in an embrace, and made her sit on her lap, as a Madonna would carry the dead body of Jesus. The body was relaxing. Gradually the tangled mass of hair began to look smooth.

Fire was burning in the vessels. The abandoned piece of cloth lay folded within the circle. As it was thrown into the flames, which leapt up furiously, Sarala lost consciousness. LS started tying Sarala's own cloth on her.

I wanted to ask Sarala a question. But I never did. The occasion was much too solemn for any childish interference.

When I was watching at the fire and the consuming cloth, I regretted that I had not asked it.

But the male voice in Sarala faintly called me by name and assured that I need not ask for anything. Asking for anything was to kick at the back of time. "Never hasten time, (the Lady in Saffron had taught me, that. But to forget is human). Never kick at fire. Never blow up the air. If violated, these shall fail to respond to the living world in their friendliness. You shall remain what you are, the beloved of your protective angel. Ask for nothing more."

Glow-worms in Graveyards

Again and again I asked LS about the secret of this incident. Again and again she repeated just one thing.

"Tantra has two wings. One looks at the future. To think of the past is to go against the current of time and life; it retards progress, and keeps time waiting. Time suffers through a conflict of opposite forces. Time is always running from the past to the future. And the past dies with the birth of the present, which dies the moment it is born. There is really no present. The present is an illusion. A convenient pause to look at the past and the future from a supposed point. The point is not there. Present is an inference.

"Tantra is a great lesson of impersonality. It is the store-house of power that has to be used for the good of the future. Das did not work on that. He was engaged in the past. Our enemies belong to the past. The more we think of them, the more they grow upon us. Past broodings foster on the blood of the present. The past should be let alone in the past.

"Belong to the future. Think for the future; work for the future. There lies progress, bliss. In the future lies life. The past is dead. Future is hope; past is frustration. To delight in the past is to dance in the light of the funeral pyre. It is no use chasing glow-worms in a graveyard. Life lives in the future; dies in the present. Life lives outside of the graveyard of the past. Belong to the future, because the past could only keep you tied to the past. This would be fruitless, futile, foolish.

"This was the mistake in Das' *sādhanā*. Das got no peace; he got no direction. He became misdirected. So the currents from his past, which were too strong for him, sucked him within oblivion. From oblivion there is no comeback.

"If Sarala finds her way to the future, Das will vanish into the past. The past and the future should never be lumped together. They cannot be. Any attempt to effect this is misguided. Any attempt towards this end is bound to end up with such confusion as you have just witnessed.

"Currents flow one way, and keep the water pure. This is why in doing the *japa* on the rosary one has to go from a point to a point; one never goes reverse. Once the process is reversed, suffering must follow. Time is a free movement. Never obstruct time's freedom; for you cannot; and in the attempt you shall perish. You could even be confounded.

"The tantra I have been trying to put into your mind shall make you a *man*: a man reborn, a *dvija* (born for the second time, an enlightened Brāhmaṇa). These get involved in the positive alone; to the future, to progress. Belong to me. Belong to the future. Sarala is a free woman now."

Of all the different sources of knowledge LS was most critical of curiosity and gossip.

Sarala died at the full ripe age of 81 with her grandchildren about her. Forty-five years later.

In later years I have tried to recapitulate the events again and again. The materialists in their relentless logical delusion put forward their empirical standards for measuring facts that escape their dimensional logic. Naturally the basic mysteries remain unsolved. They would explain such phenomena by what they call variously as psychocentric reactions. They might tell me that what I have related is either my imaginary projections, hallucinatory reconstructions, or straight, a fig. A deluded desiring to delude.

But I know for certain that this is not so. This happened; and I witnessed it. The experience had been as much a part of the reality as the typewriter I am using, the shirt I am wearing, that picture hanging on the wall, the cat begging, or the kitchen sending out a smell. To deny it would tantamount an ostrich-like folly. But again, to explain, is to court frustration.

Our standardised measuring tapes are created to serve us within this world of three dimensions. But there is a fourth and a fifth, and so on and on, a seventh dimension too. Yes, it is so. There are things between heaven and earth Horatio. It is wiser to accept them, and attempt to establish a healthy communication, a personalised rapport. For these forces are principally helpful and kind, condoning, forgiving and generous.

"There are many rituals in the life of a householder", LS had once told me. "Your father would tell you of these rites, which are performed, when building houses, digging canals and ponds, cutting tree, building boats, marrying, casting seeds, nursing the baby etc. These forces in supernature are invoked, addressed to, and prompted to exert their blessings on these human efforts, which automatically clash with theirs, and disturb their peace."

Later in life, I found how true she was.

From the earliest dawn of spiritual history man has tried by every means to communicate with the neighbouring world of supernature. The gods and deities we conceive and adhere to are born of our conscious efforts in coming close to the world unknown. We believe these forces to influence, regulate and conduct our life patterns in various ways, although basically these forces are *unseen*. Is not life a temporary stretch of doubtful knowledge between the seen and the unseen?

The 'scientific' mind of the present world has questioned this area, and found some kind of rationale to bear upon the subject, thus 'giving to the airy nothing a local habitation and a name.' For those interested, the following scholars in the field could prove to be of value: A. Ostrander, A. Ivanov, O. Bagnall, W. Carrington, A. David-Neel, F. Edwards, E. Garret, A. Nyvov, M. P. Reeves, J. B. Rhine etc., etc . . . Their works which are available in print open up unfathomed areas of knowledge. It is interesting to hear what they have to say on common disbeliefs, which are always born of some kind of prudish confidence on acquired knowledge. It is time, according to them, that we make a double check on our so called accepted concepts about the supernatural.

Let us bear in mind, always bear in mind, that tantra as a proved 'science' calls for practical experience, and direct personal application and exercise. Mere theories do not count in Tantra.

We are ourselves prisoners of our own chain of logic, which when extended, becomes an extension of our ego.

But I had seen the Lady in Saffron during that rite in a complete different light. It *was* 'obeah'; witchery; wizardry; Sàmman; call what you like. Supplicating to the supernatural forces for setting right what the supernatural had damaged, is as old a practice as *Śunahśepa* in *Ṛgveda*, or Ephigenia in Homer. Why? The history of Rome and Carthage are filled whith human sacrifices, let alone those cultures which the expansionist greed of Europe had destroyed without much thinking. But what about Circe, Medusa, Clytemnestra, Cassandra? Even the sublime life of Jesus had to be set against the legend of a son-sacrifice watched by a virgin mother. Echoes of Ebrahiem, Eid, the Eucharist still run through the most adored members of the Jews, the Muslims and the Christians.

Sacrifices, blood sacrifices, have their beginning with human sacrifice; and as rites these have been preserved in a symbolic form through one or another practice that survives within the new forms of the old rites (cf. the PYX rites).

The Inhabitants of the Shades

My own younger sister was involved in one of these 'fits'. But it had happened when the Lady in Saffron was no longer with us in body.

But I was very much there; and I had taken control.

She had very long hairs, and although short (5′3″) she was chubby, loveable and a favourite to all, specially after she became a mother.

Her husband was a simple and good man, always helpful to people. He lived with his younger brother at his ancestral home. It was because of his affectionate temperament, and because of the extremely friendly disposition of my sister that all of them lived together.

The incident happened when she had conceived for her third child. She was cleaning her room on the third floor of the house, looking upon an open abandoned place where under a neem tree stood a grave belonging to some Muslim saint. Close to it several graves remained scattered, as is usual with these unnamed graveyards.

Taken in by the glories of a post-monsoon sunset she mindlessly hung by the balustrade runnig along the roof, and perhaps continued combing her long hair, meditatively crooning a melody. The branches of ancient tree shaded her efforts; and the graveyard below looked grim and silent. Evening, the border line of day and night, of man and nature, was chosen for combing hair on the border line of a home and a graveyard; and that too by a woman with a child born, and yet not born.

Sandhyā kāla (evening time), *sandhyâ bhāṣā* (mystified language), *sandhi-pūjā* (prayers offered when two times meet) are considered significant in tantra rites. This is a significant moment when the course of time's smooth flow has to be kept appeased through prayers. It is entering in space from one global atmosphere into another. Yogi's remain very carefully disposed at such times. These forces of *sandhyā* are the inhabitants of the 'shades'.

The portents were too grave and serious. Almost tempting fate. But the poor mother had been completely oblivious of the situation.

Suddenly by some catastrophic force she was carried away over the balustrade, and her unconscious body was flung over. It was later found stretched over the saint's grave.

I came to know of this nearly four days after the incident. During this period she would come to her senses now and then, only to get lost again in her wild incoherent talks that spoke of strange things. Again and again she would refer to her youth, her long hair, her love for her husband, and of the child yet to be born. Again and again she would threaten the family for taking no care of the proximity of the graves, and throw all kinds of insults at the neighbouring spirits. She, poor thing, could have been a little more careful in combing her hair in the evening and keeping away from the quiet resting place of the saint.

The amazed inmates searched for many remedies. Doctors had been on constant attendance. She was heavily drugged into induced sleep. But her talks would still flow out, though faintly. This meant that her brain was at work at a terriffc speed; it was excited and heated. Any time a blood vessel would burst. Fingers were kept crossed.

Away from home I was engaged at a penance; but news would float, and I became aware of the position. I came to see her. She reacted, and asked me quietly to get away. She spoke to me as if I were a stranger. I did not even touch her. I retired to the graveyard. Seated amidst the graves I started a penance, and came away from my seat only after my sister came to her senses. This had taken me more than eight days.

I did what I did because of the fact that LS herself used to take me for my lessons to a similar graveyard. This was situated adjacent to the home of Sarala. I still visit that place when I visit India, and my home town. I was never interested in the *spirits* of the life beyond. I knew from my father that *these* were there to bless and assist all of us; they seek nothing except to be left at peace; and a simple modest acceptance of the fact that they needed this peace.

Often for designs of our own we try to secure their 'assistance' in order to get things 'done' in life, which they have forsaken. We do not, and our acts do not permit them to be left alone with their peace. Often we want their power to act in ways they do not relish, and thereby upset their moods. They have moods of sort. Their supernature and superpoise are brought down to the level of our nature, and the associated chaos of that nature. At such misuse they react violently and make their presence known by creating panic and terror, even by what one would call destruction. It is good for us to remember that in creating what they are often forced to create, that is, panic and terror, they too subject themselves to much agony. They get much upset in the process without intending to get upset.

The panic, in this case, was brought to a balance, but I had to visit the secret seat near the Catuhṣaṣṭhī Yoginī shrine where the persence of LS was always eloquently alive.

I had to report to her, and thank her for saving my sister's life.

Talks from the World Beyond

But I was not so interested in pursuing supernature. I knew it was best to leave it alone, and if at all, pray for the lost soul. Nothing like prayers. I had Vedic authorities for recognising such spirits, and for appeasing them. The hymns of Rudrādhyāya would make this clear. Atharva Veda is particularly conscious of these powers. I got my views confirmed by a *yoginī* in Cambodia when I was visiting Angkor Wat.

My attention was concentrated on only one objective. I must reach the source of that power which gives joy, spreads joy, charges the the being with joy, and inspires life with the sublime spirit of Love for Life and the Living

I also know that to acquire this power in its full glory assistance

from an *alter ego* is essential. I had a good start in this inasmuch as
fate had given me the boons of a saintly father, and a friendly Lady
in Saffron. But then I also knew I needed a *prakṛiti*, an *alter ego*, a
virgin who alone could confer and grant the drive of initiative, the
consecration of the final being, the total sacrifice of self in a con-
flagration of the egoistic greed.

"The blessed need not worry. Why must I?" So I thought; but does
not such a trend of thought by itself betray the presence of some
worry?

But unknown to me this restlessness was being recorded somewhere.
So, inevitably, a discussion did crop up one of these days.

Besides the Śiva temple, the one where we had studied the Yogo-
vāśiṣṭha near the Chatuhṣaṣṭhi Yoginī shrine, I had also fallen in love
with two more places: one, where the rite of the cadavar was watched
by me through the grace of LS. This was the Tārā shrine behind the
Gopal temple of Rānī Bhavānī.

The last one was more conducive to my temperament. The great
Ganges flowed past the fort walls. The place itself was abondoned for
all practical purposes. The shrine of Sarasvatī was very rarely visited
by any outsider. Only a paid caretaker offered worship in his humble
way. He knew me as a frequenter, who would often slip into the
lonesome quiet, and meditate.

Once he had boasted to me about the pristine glory of the temples
protected by the royal beneficence of the House of Kaśi Nareśa, when
the place had not been as derelict. But those days were no more. The
reputation of the Mother's diabolic power worked against its
popularity. No wonder; it was indeed the shrine of the dreaded
Mahāsarasvatī

"If you know what that signifies, boy, you would run", the old
caretaker warned.

No old man. I would never never run. Even in her terrible aspect
the Mother would not scare me away. Why? Because she would still
be a Mother; my Mother. I sought her in the forms of Mahāsarasvatī, Vajrayoginī and the White Tārā. Are they not, all of them, the
same? Tārā of Tibet, the White Goddess of the Nordics, Manjuśrī of
the Buddhists, Kwan Yen of Shinto? Why must I fear?

I would find peace. None would disturb me there.

Yet at the same time I was restless. Why this restlessness? I came
out of the temple; crossed the wonderful garden on the expansive
terrace: and stood under the carved roof of the coupola looking over

the sedate quiet river flowing along the crescent embankment on which stood the ancient city. At a distance, on the opposite bank, where the river had taken a sudden bend westward, before it started on a northward journey, the fortress of Ramnagar stood out in the growing dusk. Little fires were lit on the small country boats where, at the end of the day, tired boatmen were busy baking their humble fare.

The mighty river dominated the life around, and gave to a transitory dream-play a touch of eternity.

An old man, sitting alone on the bank was singing a song.

But I had no peace. I was bursting with questions.

Why is it that the Mother is so fond of fire, blood, sex, wine—objects that excite to mislead, and mislead to excite?

I had to get myself steadied through penance, sacrifice, austerity. *Peace is a flower that blooms on the lake of restlessness.*

I was restless over thinking of blood, virginity, sex, wine, drugs. I was restless if I had found the real truth at the bottom of the mystery. I had raised the topic with my mentor time after time. I insisted that I must see the light behind these rites. But time and again my vision would be disturbed as if by a blur, which like a film of fog over my glasses would prevent me from seeing what I craved for seeing. As soon as I was confronted with the compactly close *āsana* between the two opposites, not doubts, but questions, jumped out of me, and disbalanced my absolute submission. My peace got disturbed.

I had undertaken an eleven-day penance. I would partake of a single meal prepared by me under trees. And what was the meal? Some vegetables thrown with the rice boiled in the same pot.

But on that last day even that food was put off. The evening meditations over, I was engaged in the fire rites. Soon I became aware of the usual vibrations. Before long I discovered the presence of LS even at that remote hide-out. She was standing just by me. She greeted me wtth a smile, and sat by me. I did not make any reply when she asked me why I was so disturbed.

And she started another session of explanation. That night I learnt in depth of the mysteries of the body-machine; of the mysteries of mutation, transference, transmission and evolution of the substances of the human organism, and their effect on human life, consciousness and personality.

Why Prāṇāyāma?

I visualised life and body as expressions which owe their existence to the power that, as cosmic energy passing through millennia, gets evolved into what it is. As such that energy never leaves life, and abides within and urges for expression. To let it be released is to be in touch with the Ultimate Source of that energy.

As psychic energy it activates two systems of nerves; but a third system lies dormant, as if it were at sleep. This is the *suṣumnā*. All tantra rites are focused at awakening the sleeping *suṣumnā*.

Suṣumnā has for its root the *kuṇḍalini*, an area of dormant activity set at the end of the spinal cord; its other end is held as it were, within a clasp formed by the other two sets of nerveflows, the *īḍā* and the *pingalā*, at the base of the nose, and between the eyebrows. Hence the adept at meditation concentrates on that spot.

These two streams of energy, also described (for the sake of convenience) as the 'solar' and 'lunar' energies, get mixed with the third stream of energy, described as that of 'fire'. The confluence of these three terminates in a flare of effulgence that illuminates understanding, opens up the door of the dormant power, awakens the 'sleeping serpent', and finally, the cosmic energy is released.

Thie *is* possible. This is not just a theory. This has been again and again shown, investigated, found correct, proved, yet doubted. That is the way of the sceptic. 'The sceptics smother their soul', says the Gītā.

The breathing exercise known as *prāṇāyāma* assists in this undertaking. The inhaling breath is drawn up (no matter through which nostril), and this is the vital oxygen laden breath known as *prāṇa* (note how oxygen, and with that, an open and free air, is vital); the exhalation throws up the impurities of the body-factory which, through this 'inhalation and exhalation-exercise', operates the pumps and the blowers of the body-machine. The exhalation has to be done through the nostril opposite to the inhaling one. Go on pumping in this way. Go on and on and on . . . as long as one could. For hours, days, nights, weeks, months, years. But a third and very important stage has to be remembered simultaneously.

Between the inhalation (*pūraka*) and exhalation (*recaka*) there is a vital second stage (*pūraka* is the first stage; and *recaka* is the third). This is the *kumbhaka*, where the breath is held within before exhalation. Suspension of the breath gradually leads to the suspension of the sense perceptions. Once the doors of the outer senses have been closed, the doors of the inner senses open up. These senses show way to the liberation from all physical aches and mental anguish. This keeps the human being tied to the chains of sex, passion and greed. All sufferings bubble out of the turbulence caused by these three burning drives in the flesh.

Looking at the world we divide it into two contrasting psychic states: the conscious and the unconscious. But when we reflect on the spiritual origin of 'life' as a phenomenon related to cosmic energy, we could agree with the Gītā that what we call the conscious state is really the unconscious; and what we call the unconscious is *the* actual conscious state. We accept the obvious, and deal with it. We neglect, or even worse, (for even neglecting calls for the drive from some conscious energy),—we remain ignorant of the latent source of energy from which we drive all our drives.

This is the cosmic energy. For want of a better term acceptable to rational man we call it cosmic, whatever it might mean. It is foolish for us to remain attached to this dominance of the conscious state. We turn and twist, and want a recess from this torture of having to remain stuck to a perpetually conscious state. This is how sleep comes to us as a welcome recess. But how many of us *do* sleep totally? We might sleep long; lie flat horizontally; but how many of us could sleep deep, that is, sleep vertically? The rousing of the *kuṇḍalanī* power is a vertical process, a wilful sleep-state, where sleep is total, as total as the Mārakaṇḍeya Caṇḍī describes: '*sleep that binds creation in crystallised adherence*.'

What we reject, ignore, do not care to know of, is the source of this conscious power, which remains to us unconscious, almost dead. It is this unconscious state which has to be communicated with. *There lies our total liberation.*

Why we must do this *prāṇāyāma* (the breathing exercise)? We have only one aim. Many aims are no aims. Aim must be one. One or none. This aim should be, and is arousing the *kuṇḍalinī*. Hit it; hit the 'serpent'. But when it leaps up, (eventually it will) one must contain it. Containing it calls for tremendous power, breath power. The aim of the *pūraka* and *recaka* cycle is to contact the *kuṇḍalinī*, and when it rises, when it is touched, we need all our energy to keep it in check from spreading its tremendous impact upsetting everything.

This power of holding the breath is produced by the well nursed *kumbhaka*.

Let us repeat here the stages over again.

(1) Fill in the breath by *pūraka*; (2) hold the breath by *kumbhaka*; and then (3) gradually release the breath by *recaka*, and then to fill

again . . . and so on.

Pūraka would send the breath all along the region of the lungs and the heart up to the diaphragm; *kumbhaka* would agitate the region lower to this, up to the naval; and finally, would take care of the entire sub-naval regions inclusive of the *recaka* anal base. From this *mūlādhāra* point to the *maṇipura*, the upward journey of the *kuṇḍalinī* power, once established through this *prāṇāyāma*, makes it much easier a proposition to continue the progress until the *ājñā* and finally the *sahasrāra*, which is the supreme goal.

The stirring *kuṇḍalinī* agitates the *ājñā* set between the brows. Here unite the two opposite sets of nerves as in one (cf. union of the opposite forces, male and female as we call them). It assists in settling in a final calm at the *sahasrāra* point; for no *opposites* now remain to agitate a stir. Here there is no more agitation; here is peace; here the opposite forces unite, Śiva-Śakti, Bhairava-Bhairavi, *lingam-yoni*.

The Secrets of Mithuna

My impatience made me feel that we were avoiding the point; that we were off the point. We had been going along at a tangent.

But I was anticipated.

"Do not get impatient", she said. "Soon we shall arrive where we have to arrive." (That smile again! Oh LS how much gracious you have been to me!)

"The process of this awakening and uniting takes a toll on the senses of the adept. The very act of arousing this power is also the act of closing the powers of the senses. These senses act mechanically, as these should; and the urge, the drive behind these, which makes these covete, greed for, slave for, stops altogether. The machine acts as a machine. Then all living bodies are seen as prompted by the mechanical powers alone; and no body, no form appears as particular, special—to the adept. This has been stated in the Gitā in another way:

> Like the drop of water held on the leaves of lotuses the actions of life leave no smudge on the consciousness of that yogi who acts because he *has to* act; he sees and sees not; hears and hears not; feels and feels not; smells and smells not; eats and eats not; walks and walks not; sleeps and sleeps not; breathes and breathes not; speaks and speaks not; spends and spends not; accepts and accepts not; opens and opens not; closes and closes not. Whatever

is done, is done mechanically, as the instrument of the Master Power.

"So staying in the Ultimate position of the instrument, even sex, acts as a machine for reaching the salvation stage. Sex being the most compulsive power in the human system, agitates the most, disturbs the most, and misguides the most. It rushes the entire process of living to a hazardous disaster; and finally deprives man of his senses. This is driving the senses to a negativising anti-force.

"When through the rousing of the *kuṇḍalinī* the same senses are defused, remember, the infusion of the sublimer senses is automatically inspired. The dulling of pain is not sublimating it.

"Sex as a source of power, as a special generator to distribute power all over our creative urge should not be deadened, dulled, negativised. On the contrary we must find other resources to activate it for sublimating its creative faculties. In order to train the tiger one must remain close to the tiger. Master the serpent by serving it. order to master sex organs, one must remain very close to the sex organs. If an opposite body sets me on fire, I shall cling to that fire, to that body, and discover the secret of the source of the power, and utilise it. To run away from that situation is a psychic negation of the self. Negations breed complexes. What could be a bbtter method than to regard it as the Mother's Seat? What could put an exciting instinct move at ease other than cultivating constant familiarity under circumstances and atmosphere conducive to spiritually sublime thoughts? In uniting through the consecrated *āsanas* sex liberates us from carnality. Instead of seeking erotic excitement, the adept is trained to focus his attention to securing pure joy, and to that *ānandam* which is not loaded with sensuousness. '*kāmo gandho nāhi tāye*', says the Bengal *sādhaka* (There is no shred of erotic sensualism in it). This way is called *sahaja*, the simple way in Bengal. *Smara pari rahitam* (without the presence of eros) says the tantra hymn *Karpurādi*.

"The body gets attuned with the ideals of this *sahaja* method: and the mind becomes fully trained to reach the depths of the source of the sex power without the associated responses, which are mechanical, biological, instinctive. The instinctive reflexes have to be overcome through the control of the *ājñā cakra* (Medula).

The Partner in the Circle

"The opposite partner is the seat of Śakti. She is Śakti 'Herself'.

The adept seeing any female anywhere automatically brings his devotion at her feet, for the Mother is there. This ideal attitude liberates him from depraved thinking.

"This is not easy. It has not been easy with you; it has not been easy with me to prepare you. It will not be easy with you to meet others, select from them, and discard or accept. For one genuine, there could be a hundred fakes, novices. Even those who wish well, mean well, ultimately succumb to a fall. (How very true was she. Now I know when it is too late.) The inner *dhātu* (essence) secretes automatically with the least reflexive disturbance. Before the mind gets into a checking state, the moisture of the limb concerned releases its control.

"So trained must the thought be, so attuned to the ideals, that the opposite forces would not appear as opposites at all. Two halves make one; and that one becomes identified with the indivisible Mother. In such a state the reacting physical reflexes cease to operate. This has been achieved in your body. Do not fail me.

"Any female would do. Any. But those who have their time engaged much more in physically arduous activity, those who, because of their labour incentive preoccupations find very little time to indulge in erotic sensuousness and sophisticated self-adoration (quite common amongst the bored city dwellers) are the most suitable. These are the essential archtypes. These have been held in high esteem. Objectivity about regarding the body as an instrument, a carpet, an *āsana*, an article of adored offering of devotion, is the essence of this exercise. You have noted in the Mahābhārata that most of the *higher types* have associated with these archtypes to beget offsprings of yogic order: fisherwomen, tribal women, nature gods and goddesses. All these are but the archtypes of the cosmic *anima.*

"Wives are generally discarded as partners in *āsanas* because of their mental association with the balance sheet of the day-to-day life of the household; as well as because of their mental awareness about those physically performed, and carnally consummated situations as sex partners.

"It is too much to expect wives to remain objective to sex when they had the experience of coitus for reproduction, and for the thrills of eros. To accept their erstwhile sex partners as subjectivised spirit-partners is to make an already complex situation infinitely more complex. Wives are best avoided and kept away from getting involved, although in exceptionally liberated cases of very strong minds a husband-wife team has been found to function. But the best to choose is from the completely uninhibited. There have been great *sādhakas* who have trained their wives to a degree of impersonality that makes fitting *āsanas*. This is difficult; but not impossible. This is to be avoided, but not prohibited.

"Old wood is not suitable for a house post; neither, for that matter, is young or green wood. Seasoned wood alone is the best. In planning a building all materials have to be properly seasoned, baked, steeled or toned. This is equally true of the state of the *sādhaka* as well as that of the *sādhika*. She has to be fetched before she gets enmeshed with too much experiences, too much maturity in association with life's down-to-earth demands. The fight of life and temptations from life make her body and mind unfit for tempering. Rivers are at their utmost purity only at the spring.

"The young alone could seek the ideal. Revolutionaries are made of the younger stuff. The young dare; the young dream; the young spread their wings for achievement of the impossible. Hanumān, Aruṇa, Icarus dared the impossible when they were young: but by doing so they did no good to themselves. The youth could afford to be daringly indiscreet; but all acts of indiscretion have to be compensated. Hence the young of mind and body should be secured, tempered, trained, tried, seasoned, and *then* accepted as the *alter ego*. Hence tantra insists on *prakṛtis* of the sixteen, seventeen, eighteen range. They are naturally dynamic. Their responses are both keen and urgent. They alone could discharge the radiative, dynamic power which could inspire the *kuṇḍalinī*, and bring life to the *suṣumnā*.

"The upward flow of power reaches the *sahasrāra*, and fuses personal consciousness with the cosmic thrill. Bodies relax: senses lose their functions! Mind gets pin-pointed. A total suspension of reminiscence disengages cognition from past memories. Mind is then entirely occupied by the one and only one feeling of *ānandam* that cannot be described, but can be enjoyed.

"Seated within the mystic circle, and filled with the joys of food and drink as the very essence of Nature and of the Mother, feeling secured in the perfect and undisturbed contemplation of the geometrical symbols that tantra prescribes, the yogi unites with the *alter ego* in the appointed *āsana*, and feels himself part of the cosmic process until his 'conscious-feels', and the 'conscious-feels' of the cosmos become inseparably one. The two, like widely separated octaves in music, still merge their tunes, in spite of the differences in frequency. In such a case as in the case of music—the effect is enhanced, and gains through the apparent difference. The union of these contraries, of the seemingly opposites, bestows the qualities of depth, volume, reach, harmony and resonance. *Sublimity is an outcome of the union of contraries.*

"The dual existence of the opposite sexes is accepted, and yet restricted. Whilst this is accepted as an instrumental fact, it also shows that duality could be eliminated through consonance of frequency. Wood through burning in gradual order becomes fire, flame, heat, finally cinders and ash. At a certain stage the fire, the flame and the heat become inseparable. They are 'plural' only to the outer view; but they exist for themselves in a mystic singleness. Good musicians keep tabla pairs (Indian drums) tuned octave by octave in several sets.

The Cakras

"The most celebrated of these circles has been symbolised in the *Śrī-cakra.* There are some other *cakras* which are also used (*siddha* and *kāla cakras*). The hours must be carefully selected for the night, and the participants, preferably, should be *several.* Such *āsanas* are meant for infrequent exercise, generally once a month, on the fifth, eighth or the fifteenth of the dark fortnight. A *śakti* may be in any natural state, and her being in blosssoms, or seasons need not affect the actual rite, as such natural courses are expected in the functioning of the physical cycle of the *Śakti.* The blood, potent with ovular energy, and containing estrogenic substances, in fact, assists radiation which one expects within the *Śakti.*

Adoration of Yoni or of the PYX

"On some bygone hoary day in far away Assam at the holy shrine of Mother Kāmākṣyā the yogis must have discovered the special hidden power of a *śakti* in blossoms. Hence the shrine is famed as the *virgin shrine*, where the blood of the female in blossom has been adored down to our present days (as already stated before).

"Seated in her *āsana* with the *puruṣa*, the human form of *Śakti* is a goddess now, the Mother herself; her body has to be ritually washed and cleaned; decorated and massaged with perfume; bedecked with clothes and jewelleries. With vermilion on the forehead, with a clear dot between the eye brows, red paint on her toes and feet, sandal paste decorations on her face, she shines as the very replica of the power that streams from body to body.

"And now for 'the spring head' itself. Yes, the *pubes* itself is carefully idolised and decorated with ritualistic veneration: vermilion, sandal, rice, grass, and flowers, even the chants and the *ārati*, and of course the final ritual obeisance as to a Mother. And why not? Is not that the Supreme *pīṭha*? The pit of the world-flame? The nave of the mystic world flux? Once upon a time man used to regard this region with utmost veneration and awe. It had been a primordial draw for all who cared to regard the life-force as something to wonder about, something beyond human comprehension, something which only descended as a motherly blessing for the continuance and preservation of the life-force. In human and animal form it carried the same importance as the furrow carried for the cultivators of the field.

"The same primordial draw under an atavistic pressure and subconscious stirrings continue still, and fling the human kind towards it as if pulled by a centripetal force; but not with that primal veneration and awe, regard and submission. Instead men are drawn towards it as children are drawn towards the closed door in the house, to the forbidden fruits hanging in the garden. And like children they feel as conquistadors, victors, he-men if they could violently rifle the door, and rape and plunder what has been secretly and mysteriously kept away from them under one or the other pretext. Instead of veneration, violation has taken over, and the sacredness of sex has been, through man's possessive and dominating postures, turned into an object for lust, lascivity and temptation. Sex has even become an object of sale and barter. So far away are we driven from the original position that the mentioning of sex in connection with the practice of tantra evokes automatic suspicions and attitudenous condemnation. Tantra affords the urban cynics a wide field for sarcastic humour.

"Elevated to a pitch of venerated exclusiveness the *subject* herself becomes sublimely aware of her pubic regions, and of their importance in life, and she feels deep within a spectral glow that lifts her up above the scale of the common mortal. (I have invariably noticed this spiritual change descending on the *subjects* whenever I have participated in this rite, or have been a witness to the rites performed by others.)

"The *subject* appears to consign herself totally into the belief that she is none other than *Śakti* herself, the Mother in Life.

"Not the pubic parts alone, but all the other different parts of the body, the several joints of the frame, the vital glands that determine the secret *ojas*-supply to the body and mind, the *cakra* points, are all singly and separately consecrated and adored. This is known as *nyāsa*. The environs, the surroundings, the five primary material forms, the firmamental directions, even the trees and the animals are brought into the picture; and their blessings are sought through the *śuddhis*.

Power in Mantras: Japā-Ajapā

"*Mantras* are repeatedly chanted, but these have to be picked up with care, specially the *bīja mantras* (seed formulas), and held with care and veneration between the two sets of nerves, with the same tenderness as a flower bud is held between two tender leaves. The image is significant, almost symbolic. A flower bud is held within the palms of the protective leaves; a prayer is held between two suppli-cant palms; and a *bindu* (life-seed) is held between two labias where a bud waits eagerly to enjoy its full blossoming. In its aesthetic subli-mity this commonly derided and befowled phenomenon responds gleefully to the Power that bursts into the Creative Mystery without the least urge for consummating a carnal sensuousness. *Śakti-unmeṣ* and *bindu-nipāta* are no exercises for the voluptuary.

"A great care should therefore be observed in the performance of this chanting. The vibrations of the recited chants matter as much as the complete understanding of their inner meanings. Indeed there are *mantras* without any 'meaning'; but there is none without an effective vibration. For this purpose a mechanical training of the tongue has to be cultivated simultaneously with the spiritual comprehension of the *mantras*.

"But the exercise itself calls for a rigorous practice and infinite patience on the part of the aspirant."

"Utter all the Vedic alphabets", LS had once directed, "as arrang-ed, and in sequence, one after another, strictly in the order set (A to Z). Then recite the *mantra*. Now recite the alphabets again, but by the reverse order, (Z to A). In this way the *mantra* would be placed bet-ween the two sets of the alphabetical recitations, one from A to Z, and the other from Z to A. These three steps, taken together, means the recitation of the *mantra* only *once*. It takes a lot of exercise of the tongue, and a further lot of patience and keen attention to complete this course, known as the *puṭita* course, i.e., the course in which the seed has been preserved between the two sets of the *mātrikās*, or the '*she*' alphabets. The *mātrikās*, as an accompanying musical perfor-mance, helps the aspirant to maintain the basic balance of vibrations, much as the base drone helps to maintain the musician's octave in spite of his free movements over the entire range of all the keys. The vibrations of the *mātrikās*, like a drone, assure the aspirant to maintain his orchestral symphony with the cosmic sound world. The scale is never lost; neither is the aspirant misled. In other words the frequency of the vibrations remains in this way floating always at the same level.

"While this process goes on, the *mantra* itself abides safely within the pair of the *mātrikā* series. Whilst moving from A to Z, the movement is known as the right, or *dākṣiṇa* way, and is called *japā*; the movement from Z to A is the left way, or *vāma* way, and is called *ajapā*.

"These *japā* and *ajapā* movements, the *dakṣiṇa* (right) and the *vāma* (left) movements are best remembered by a final illustration. Now listen: (i) *japā*, A to Z: (ii) *mantra*: (iii) *ajapā*, Z to A: . . . This completes one circuit. If one has to recite the *mantra* twelve times, then this formula has to be repeated twelve times; if a hundred and eight times, then the formula, complete with *japā* and *ajapā* has to be recited a hundred and eight times. (I have known of yogis who have done this for practically for years and years, thus completing chains of recitation a hundred thousand times. Many do it daily for a thousand times). A complete cyclic turning is effected by the simultaneous action of *pūraka-kumbhaka* and *recaka* of *prāṇāyāma*. Ceaseless and effortless must be these external rites, so that the internal concentration is not allowed to be disturbed at all.

"This is the way of reaching the stage of esoteric tantra meditation. What must be taken care of are the three vital controls of breath, mind and that control which faces the final acid test of perfect indifference, the literal indifference of the yogin, namely, the control over sex excitement leading to the control over the least disturbance of the seminal (or for that matter uterine) fluids. The least sign of the presence of these chemicals completely destroys the very objective of this rite. Tantra *āgamas* have enjoined the directive *smara-parirahitam* (i.e. devoid of lust) for this rite.

"We have spoken of the *ojah* (power vivre) in the body. This *ojah* is generated by the same process which generates within the testes the seeds along with the fluids in which the seeds float. That power which generates the seeds, by exerting the desired body and mind control, instead of generating the physical seed, generates within the body-machine, and what is more, within the conscious personality of the being, a 'field' of potency which could be best described as magnetic and spiritual. This is the source of the esoteric 'seed' power of *bīja*, and *bindu*. It charges the aspirant's consciousness. It is the same with the uterine fluids. Man's spiritual, mental and physical development depends on the preservation of this fluid (*bindu*); and its misuse creates loss of vitality, leading to an imbalance in his development."

(How and why such powers are generated shall be explained in a while. But instead of making a report in my own language I prefer to report direct as the Lady in Saffron had explained. Although after so many years I will not be able to reproduce here verbatim and faithfully what she had explained in Bengali, yet so impressive and penetrating was her explanation that I still could recollect the sequence, the images and the free flow of the lesson.)

Joy of Only-ness

"Now, something happens when the male and the female genitals come to form a union. Remember that those who think of these genitals, or of the union itself, in the light of what they are habitually accustomed to, (vide, experience, training or imagination) have not, and cannot have the least idea of what I am talking about. Neither those, who enter into this area without the strictest and the most disciplined prior-training of the mind and body, could ever conceive of this. You yourself would not have been able to conceive this mystery in its right and proper spirit had I not taken personal care of you while you had been a child, innocent, free from motivation or inhibition, and free from any past experience which needed to be cleansed.

"I am not deliberately, for the sake of avoiding any digression, and at the same time ensuring pointed concentration, speaking here of the cumulative effect on your present birth the blessings of your past series of lives, which, taken together is certainly, though incidentally, a very forceful factor in moulding and shaping your destined place in life. An eighth child, as a Brahmin child, born in the lap of an entirely Vedic *ashram*-like household, in the city of Varanasi, living on the Ganges itself, surrounded by some of the most revered yogis, and by some of the best classical teachers of our time, you might consider yourself a singularly lucky, well placed aspirant to absorb what you have absorbed so far, and what you are going to absorb further. Look at my relationship with you. Why? The other brothers and sisters of your family, living equally close to me never came into that contact with me into which you jumped as if drawn by the hands of destiny.

No, not environments alone, not nurture alone, there is yet a third unseen factor that determines our moves in life; an unseen hand that writes our history as it has been planned. But I must not digress. That is quite a different kind of knowledge which cynics, once again corrrupted by the logic of induction, fail to appreciate, and spend precious time in arguing about will, prowess and destiny, endlessly and uselessly.

"I am keeping all that aside, and concentrating on this subject. This is indeed vital for you; and you must absorb what I say. Just listen to me, and stick to what I say. Never never abandon this track of concentration, and with all your determination master the discipline that teaches you the supreme philosophy of indifference. 'Like the withdrawing limbs of the tortoise' as the Gitā illustrates.

"Since loyal, devoted, unflinching persistence and tenacity alone is regarded as an absolute precondition to success in this path, few dare, and fewer succeed. Most take a cavalier chance and fail. These same unfortunates and sad failures carry with them the most depraved conclusions about tantra. Many indeed attempt to participate in it as vultures approach dead bodies or dogs and hogs approach human filth. It is also a type of hunger. It inflames and burns them. Whatever they see, they see from the outside, and in the light of their experience with the females or the males as the case might be; and whatever they feel they would feel in the light of their imagined or real experience with body-play. Training in tantra is a discipline in objectivity.

"In reality these scoundrels are to be kept far away, as dogs and pariahs have to be kept far away from where a *yajñā* feast is being cooked. The smell could bring them about, as it brings swarms of vermins and flies; but in fact the feast is really being prepared for the welcome, the elect, the invited and the deserved. Tantra is for the elect. It is not an orgy in which all could participate, as all are not accustomed to the rigours of such mental and physical discipline. Recall what you yourself had to pass through.

"The enjoyment in tantra is *a joy of only-ness*. It demands a training of the senses to deny, reject, discriminate in order to voluptuate, consummate in absolute singleness, and at the level of absolute subjectivity. Success in this means to feel the 'bodily' without the body; the sensitive without the senses. This other type of joy has to be consummated with the other types of senses, other types of organs. It bestows other types of quiet ecstasy, and the presence of duality vanishes totally. You know from experience that this is possible and attainable.

"Now you are no more a child of yester years. You have grown. You have passed through organisations of schools and colleges, and acquired knowledge of another kind, of another society. Your present education has graded you up at the cost of innocence, faith and acceptance Humbleness as a virtue has totally disappeared. Hence I have to change my way of teaching as I had been accustomed to do.

"An electrochemical field is created as soon as a male and a female unite. A chained series of reactions at high voltage emit voluptuous sparks which, as if in a sweep, affect and obliterate all senses of discretion and restraint. The very force of the excitement unleashes hidden desires and fierce hungers, which float along the shores of sheer carnality; and then man is hardly able to swim back to his normalcy. Of the physical reactions which are detectable, under the pressure of carnal desire the two most obvious changes are noticeable in an increase in bodily temperature, and a shortness of breath. Man's entire personality undergoes a tremendous change under this carnal dominance.

"If you notice, these very symptoms could also describe the condition of a *sādhaka* in his supreme state of union with the Self. Yet there is a difference. Whilst the libertine returns only too quickly from his coveted climax, and falls into an immediate state of torpor, sloth, fatigue and depression, under the influence of tantric experience of pure sublimity, no such reactions prevail. In the case of spiritual union man, or the *sādhaka* does not *return* until he chooses to; and whilst he is there he not only enjoys the still quiet thrills of being in the *seventh heaven* of liberated love, but what is remarkable, he feels stronger, more energetic, more vibrant, more light. In other words whilst the former fills the flesh with death, the latter fills the spirit with life. It is a big difference, if you understand.

"As the electrochemical field *Śakti-kṣetra* sets into active operation, a whole field of higher consciousness gets infused with powers ready for radial discharges.

Special Generator: M-A-N

"There is a deep difference in the structural pattern of the male genitals and the female genitals. Whilst the male genitals are electrical on the exterior and magnetic within, the female genitals are patterned contrarily. If they were not so, during a union there would not be a total functioning as two into one. The female genitals are magnetic on the exterior, and electrical within. The two together create a field of cosmic force. It forms, as it were a microcosmic replica of the macrocosmic field of cosmic energy.

"Sudden uses of terms like these, which now are being used, could confuse. But as I warned before, it would be explained in a little while. Remember that the term cosmic has not been used to confuse the alert mind. If the term 'cosmic' or 'cosmos' could not be conceived by any, then, to that extent, a novice is not to be chosen for this degree of tantra exercise. That path is not yet his. Simple as that. But the contact with the cosmic is the very basis of the final aim of tantra. Tantra power is the cosmic power passed through a special generator that is a M-A-N and his conscious self.

"A body comes into deep contact with another body through the various *āsanas* you have experienced already. *Yonī-āsana*, *Sukh-Padmāsana*, *Latā-āsana*, *Januyugma-āsana*, *Ekadhārī-āsana Puṣpaka-āsana*, and of course *Śavāsana*. Some of these you know, and some you do not. All *āsanas* are not for all. According to the *prakṛti* and according to the *puruṣa* these *āsaṇas* change. But *Śavāsana* and *Sukha-Padmāsana* are the two in which the pair could keep merged for hours and hours.

The Nāḍīs

"The psychic currents that infuse the cosmic conscious nature of the individual, and which flow through the invisible, passages, or conduits, known as *nāḍīs* which report the variations of the cosmic to the consciousness of MAN. The guru alone could give precise instructions during the union, as it progresses, as to the actual conduct of the disciples. When he is sure, only then the guru leaves the pair alone. The guru remains responsible throughout, and thereby undertakes a role very dangerous to his own spiritual self, even to his physical being.

"The explanation offered pertains to the invisible psychic power operative within the body machine. Like any other power this power too is invisible. Its presence is experienced through the results it produces. The presence of the electric power, which is invisible, is noted when a bulb lights, a fan moves, a wheel spins. This is true of solar power, hydraulic power, fire power, steam power etc. Power is abstract; only the generating motor is visible through the objects it moves.

"So is the cosmic power within the *nāḍīs*. It is invisible, as the *nāḍīs* themselves are, but we have learnt to accept their presence through the effects they produce, and we experience the effect through that dynamo of the human body known as the brain system, and through its allied actions known as sensitive feelings, and emotional counter-effects.

But the invisibility of the source of power, of the power itself of the *nāḍīs* should not disturb us. Take the case of the so called medical miracle of the Chinese operation of acupuncture. Our ancient books actually had recommended cures for the body as well as for the mind through such methods as *sūcikābharaṇa* (needle-therapy), *vaśīkaraṇā* (bringing one under mental control), *sammohana* (mesmerism), hypnotism and other psychic treatments of the sick of mind and body. We used to neglect them, for want of 'scientific' acceptance. This, of course means, finally, acceptance by the Western opinion. And I am pretty sure, gradually the West too shall become aware of the phenomenal methods and cures that the Eastern wisdom has accepted. The lessons of inductive logic will also form parts of scientific knowledge. The forces of the mind, of the developed mind, of supraconsciousness, i.e., the yogic forces would also be accepted and honoured. You will live long to witness this change. So much for 'science' and 'scientific' acceptance.

"Now to come back to our lesson.

"Human energy is polarised into two opposite and different processes: one anabolism (*dhṛti-śakti*), and two, katabolism (*śūti-ṣakti*). Anabolism, or *dhṛti* helps to conserve; ketabolism, or *śūti* assists to disperse the energy along some fixed channels. That the human body is thus under the influence of a bisexual operation has been imaged into the male-female form of Śiva-Śakti as is seen in the image of *ardhanārīśvāra*. These images, *yantras* and *mudrās* are full of meaning. Gitā examples, '*Prakṛti delivers under my management. Pṛakrti is the yoni, I cast the "seed". This dual character of the cosmic in creative activity supplies the principle of perpetual evolution that carries the universe on and on.*'

The adept in this *āsana* remains merged in the *feel* of the cosmic, and the flow of energy circulates up and down, *iḍāpingalā-suṣumnā* from *kuṇḍalinī*-point at the *mūlādhāra*, to the *sahasrāra* point in the centre of the brow, spreading over the entire cerebellum, and shooting through all the *cakras*; and the *sādhakas* remain merged in what is known as *kaivalya* (only-ness), *ānandam* (joy), or *brahmānandam* (cosmic ecstasy). This is not a personal consummation, a selfish enjoyment, but this is like building up a reservoir of water with the ultimate objective of supplying the entire people with a precious drink. That aim of *being of use* to all is the ultimate utility of yoga. Do never forget that. Never be selfish."

That was indeed a long session.

Why had I chosen that remote abandoned temple of Mahāsarasvatī for my personal seances, and why on that evening, when I had been hovering between the unmapped area of faith and fear, doubts and revelations, I had decided to spend the night under the coupola I cannot explain today. Like many events in the past that evening with its tremors of restless questions too would have been lost into the forest of fugitive memories.

But for the gracious touch of LS, all have not been lost.

Her unannounced and sudden appearance had changed the course of events. The humble caretaker knew the saintly lady. Before leaving the temple door unlocked for our use he had made arrangements for a fire-ritual, and had spread two pieces of woollen carpets. These humble folks at heart are indeed very generous.

That long night had ended very quickly; and when we came out, and stood on the high walls watching the dark, cool, silent river, the eastern bank was touched by a ruddy gold bloom. Devotees were bathing. Bells were ringing all along the bank in the thousand temples that border the riverside.

LS left me alone standing, watching, wondering. Those days still tempt me by casting their long shadows along the lonesome memory lane. The light of other days around me has grown too dim now.

LS had explained once the mystery of sex in tantra *sādhanā*. That was years and years back. On this occasion the subject was again dealt with from another aspect.

But this was not the end.

It is a subject that goes on and on coming again and again confusing the mind until actually practised. It is amazing to realise how much of our conscious-self is charged with this power, which we regard just as an instinct. It is in reality much more than an instinct. Because we are accustomed to using it mostly in misuse and abuse, our subconscious always wanders about finding justifications for what we are engaged at.

In fact sex is a tremendous force of the highest magnitude; and in the human body we suffer to play with us without much thinking, or even knowing, what to do with it. Because of our misuse we are in doubts; because of the doubts we feel guilty of abuse; and because of this sense of guilt we are perpetually looking for justifications. One of the ways for justifying our wrong acts is to point our fingers at others either as the real guilty ones (as if the guilt of one justifies the guilt of another), or as the one we have been able to 'catch' in the act, and play the 'saint'. Saint-playing is the commonest game of the pervert.

A Cup of Coffee

In the years 1929-31 I had been much confused in spirit. Agitation was at its highest; and the *rajas* in the being was most turbulent. I suffered from sudden heat in the body (not fever, which creates a sloth and a weak feeling), and from that common complaint concerning the agitation in the nerve centres, called, unthinkingly, headache. Things were not eased out by the political situation of the time. Being too much involved, I had to hide away from the common search for political agitators for some time. This had been the hardest period of my spiritual preparation. I was alone, unknown, in a far away, practically deserted area; far away from the nearest railway station; and cut off from my natural habitat, the Indo-Gangetic plains.

Here I had suddenly met with a stranger.

I was approached by some people to bring help to a man who was a stranger speaking an unknown language, and who was physically exhausted to the point of fainting.

This was a very old man. Tall, well built for his advanced age, and clearly a tantric yogi, who should not have any suffering from any external difficulties. Seeing me he beamed up. I came to discover that his mother tongue was Telugu. Besides his mother tongue the only other language he knew was Sanskrit, and perhaps a few words of English. He did not know Hindi, which the local people could understand, but could not speak, their language being a tribal form of Rajasthani.

Being from Telengana the old man was a coffee addict. But coffee he did not get for days and days ever since he had left his mountain cave by the Tungabhadra. He was on a pilgrimage on foot to Brindāvana, near Mathura in Uttar Pradesh, a distance of about 8 to 9 hundred miles by the artery road. But he had got confused at a certain point of his journey, and reached Ujjain and Mahākāleśwar temples. From there he again was given a wrong start. Instead of heading for the north he had been walking towards the west, and had reached the wilderness of the Vindhya hills where I had been 'serving' in the capacity of a domestic servant, and where my identity was completely unknown. It was his total ignorance of the local dialect which accounted for the marathon stretch of his troubles.

There was no coffee to be had; but I prepared a substitute with the help of a drug, and a drop of caffein. But he cared not for the chemicals. His craving was more related to his soul; he missed the aroma of his native brew.

What he had been looking for was a cup with the steaming liquid in it, with its inimitable aroma. And he explained that what the soul hankers for is not the substance or the shape, but the essence, that which 'crystallises the knowledge of the five sense organs' as says the Gītā (the *tanmātras*).

I wanted to get close to him, and something happened within the week which made me stick to him.

Nazri: A Source of Power

I used to go out for long evening walks, and for early morning walks though not so long. I had to collect milk from a tribal milkmaid who lived down the hills. On my way to the milkmaid, quite early I bathed in a lake at the foot of the hill; and then I set out for the milk. At times I used to visit a temple known for a *śakti pīṭha* (a specially consecrated shrine haloed by a realised saint).

After a few months I became aware of a *śakti* vibration, and spotted it correctly as coming from the milkmaid. According to the customs in Rajasthan, where girls of a certain class are in short supply, she had been betrothed soon after her birth; and the first ceremonies of the betrothal were over when she had been only five. She only knew that she had a husband; but she had no more knowledge of him; she did not even know him, or recognise him. But in her own shy and modest way she had been a natural follower of the *śakti* pattern of beliefs and sites. Kālī was a very popular deity of the tribals.

One side of the lake was bordered by a sheer rock about 20 feet high, overgrown with hanging bush that none dared disturb. It could be approached only by swimming across. As the banks around had no resting place, a swim across meant a swim *across and return* for a foothold on the same bank. This seemed hazardous to many. So none dared the swim. The little lake was very lovely.

I discovered that swim to be very rewarding, as I had discovered a tiny cave. I also discovered that the place was known to some others, who had been making use of it.

Suddenly this girl, Nazri, whilst dealing my share of milk, one day, just mentioned if I had ever visited the cave. I was struck dumb and amazed. What and what she knew! I wondered; and the wonderment did not leave me for the whole day. I was thinking of LS, and had earnestly been asking for her advice. (In extreme moments I still do it, and find happy results.)

One of my friends, (we used to study together the history of the growth of Parliament in England, and certain revolutionary literature) Ramchand, accompanied me that day in my evening walk. We often walked together. The entire area was known for cobras. The saving grace was that the place was also the natural habitat for peacocks, who lived on snakes, specially on the cobras. So his company gave me some kind of support, as he had the rare ability of smelling a cobra from a distance.

It was a full moon day. I had been fasting. Ramchand came for a long walk to the local *śakti* temple, a good three miles away from the lake, and across the poppy fields (opium, besides, cotton, was the chief agricultural product of that harsh land). This amazed me because Ramchand avoided going there.

One evening, about three months back, I had visited the temple with Ramchand. Earlier that day some animal was sacrificed by the tribals in the temple, which was known for animal sacrifices of sorts. As soon as Ramchand's eyes fell on some blood at the foot of the sacrificial yoke, he, a devout Jain, fainted away. When I found this very Ramchand ready to accompany me to that temple again, of his own accord, I was really intrigued.

The situation became more intriguing when I met Nazri there bedecked in a regal attire, resplendent in jewellery. She was not alone, several other tribal girls with some unknown men had gathered. Nazri welcomed me to a seance, for it was indeed a seance they had organised. It was a new moon night. Ramchand was smiling. An old man of the group spoke to me, 'Nazri knows you. You practise on your *āsana* in the cave. Nazri also uses the same *āsana*, only at other times, carefully avoiding a clash. None is invited here; the deserving just comes. Ramchand knew you. So you are welcome. Please have a seat and fill in the quota."

Long before I met the old man of Telengana I had already been in

Nazri's circle for sometime. But the doubts again had been eating through my sternest efforts; and I recalled the warning of the Gītā, 'Doubt is the canker of the soul'. Having found the coffee-loving old man there I felt to consult him.

But Nazri herself was an *assigned* soul. She used to assure me now and then; for after the first period of hesitant acquaintance she grew so attached to my company that often at the noon hours she would, unknown to others, climb a tree, and descend into my room through a window at the second floor, and spend a delightful time discussing various points in yogic exercises.

I studied her efforts, but I was not quite convinced. Day by day doubts were mounting up, and I had to get me thoughts across to somebody. For some reason LS was not within reach. She generally is near me always. But at times she went out of reach, when no contact would be possible. I had been passing through a period of mental plateau. Perhaps LS knew what I was seeking, and what I needed. Hence the old man had strayed into this god-forbidden waste land. I had reasons to suspect this connection.

Dahuti

One early dawn after my bath, and on my way to the milkmaid, instead of taking the direct route I had decided to pass by an ancient broken temple where the old man had taken his shelter. He said he had been recouping from the strain of the hard journey.

I found the temple vacant.

Thinking that he might be still washing in the lake I walked out. This was a very quiet corner of the lake. Usually no one came to this side. On a jutting piece of rock, overhanging the water of the lake the tall big figure was found bending over, almost doubling himself. In the morning haze of November he looked like a genie from the pages of Alladin of the Lamp.

On approaching him, very cautiously, I found him engaged in the most difficult *Haṭha-yoga* rite of *dhauti*. My eyes fell on a long piece of white fine linen, (or was it silk? No; it could not be silk, for silk does not absorb; it must have been linen). One end was hanging from his nostril, the other end was hanging, in all, probability from his anus; and he was gently pulling it out from the lower end. Another piece of linen was laying in a heap by his side. I knew that it had already performed its task passing through the other nostril. I watched him for some time, and then leaving him to his peace, I slunked away to my daily chores.

That evening we had started our usually friendly discussions. I learnt that the *Haṭha-yoga* exercises are not required by those who are lucky enough to have the blessings directly from a *siddha-yogini* (emancipated female), who is the most adorable teacher possible along the path of spiritual emancipation. I felt that he was referring to LS. I kept silent. He continued.

The Kuṇḍalinī — to end of chapter

For days and days he remained my great preceptor; in a way my final preceptor; my eye-opener. There was no doubt whatsoever that he was 'sent' by the will of LS. He was the complementary to LS, as far as I was concerned. LS was all practical experience. She lived in *kuṇḍalinī*. But this old man was all knowledge. I wanted to know more of *kuṇḍalinī* from LS. She always kept me off saying; 'Gather ye rose buds whilst ye may'. Time would come for *kuṇḍalinī, and you shall meet* the person who shall teach. "You see", she said, "I know so little. I only know *that I am*. I could only give myself. Take it. *It is all yours for the taking.*"

But this old man was all *jñāna*, knowledge. He told me only what LS in all pobability had asked him to tell me. How, otherwise. I could explain my meeting this *lover of coffee?*

"The Fire of *kuṇḍalinī* is a real fire. It may not be able to light a lamp or boil your pot with this fire. Such domestic fire does not enlighten your intelligence, or spark delight in you. In the absence of that fire fear overcomes you, and the dark inside makes you grope and tremble much more than the darkness outside. If that fire was not there, processes such as agitation, excitement, thrill and inspiration would not have acted at all. By calling them nerves the materialists only help push the real question aside. They don't have the mechanics of further knowledge. But the *kuṇḍalinī* is fire; and that fire is as real as love is real; sex is real; hate is real; jealousy is real; ignorance is real.

"As a strange force it lies dormant, asleep, and has to be awakened. Unless the awakening comes even sex cannot function. Limpness does not agree with sex. Sex is taut, strung high, under tension. And heat and fire alone could intensify the limp, and make it produce the higher octaves, as in well-strung drum rhythms.

"The mental world also has its octaves. The seven octaves of the nerve world are the seven *cakras*. Who could start singing in the first octave and end up with the seventh one? Let alone the human voice, even a drum, a piano, a viola could not be so set as to help the first octave climb to the seventh.

"The human nerve world alone, by the yogic process, could elevate consciousness from the meekest ebb of awareness (i.e., the first octave, the *mūlādhāra*) to the supreme seventh octave, the celestial octave, where consciousness, like a tranquil lake of light, reflects itself in all its glory (i.e., the seventh octave, the *śahasrāra*).

"To consider this *kuṇḍalinī* as the power of sex, as many explain, is not only outrageous and foolish, but baffling and negative. Many an ignoramus insist that the Christian rite of Mass is a phallic rite! Hendonists draw their power from vanity of indolence and ignorance.

"*Kuṇḍalinī* as a power has nothing to do with the occult, although the occultists mention this power again and again. Actually *kuṇḍalinī* as a power is active throughout a man's personality and essence. A man is what he is because of what *kuṇḍalinī* makes out of him. The mechanised man eats, digests, defecates, sleeps, mates and dies; all this helplessly and mechanically. The body-machine does not need the *kuṇḍalinī* power. It uses the *ājñā* power, the power of reflexes (Medula).

"But there is besides this mechanised man another man, the real man sleeping within the human dody. That other man sings, admires, receives and expresses in poetry and literature, art forms and inventions. He images the future world; images his own self in the shape of gods and goddesses; identifies his ideals and is agonised for not being able to achieve what his urge prompts him to achieve. We know that the source of this energy, which consummates subjective joy, is called the *lhādinī*, which is an aspect of *kuṇḍalinī*, the *aghatana-ghatana patīyasī* (the lady of skill who could achieve the impossible and the incrdible).

"The stream of *kuṇḍalinī* saturates with its energy the entire area of perception. It is this flow of energy that inspires men to achieve, promote and create. It ensures constant progress. Indolence is an anathema to *kuṇḍalinī*. *Kuṇḍalinī* creates, and delights in creating, opening up all the windows to heaven and earth so that a man with awakened *kuṇḍalinī* perceives all times past and future, enjoys all that the sense perceptions and the super-sense perceptions could add to a man's justification for life here.

"You see how easy it is to confuse this entirely voluptuous ability with the sexually venal erotica.

"*Kuṇḍalinī* holds the secret of other skills as well. One of these is the power of keeping and holding the living world 'under a spell'. Men may not be made aware of the true nature of things. If they ever become aware of world's true nature, they would get upset, confused; they would get berserk. *Kuṇḍalinī* holds them under her spell; she holds them all 'in thrall'. *Kuṇḍalinī* fully awakened, personal consciousness would receive the full impact of the terrible nature of this up-side-down chaotic world, and man would naturally like to run away from it. That accounts for the presence in men of an innate touch of escapism.

"But there is no running away. Hence the dope of *kuṇḍalinī*. It sleeps and sleeps, radiating its influence to keep the body and mind together. Only the 'elect' would dare *open up the locked door*, face the sleeping python, and wake it up, and offer a battle to overcome it.

"The Gītā says that what we call the waking state is but the sleeping one; and what we call the sleeping state is indeed the waking one; that the day to the spiritually awakened is the night to the mortals; and what appears as night (ununderstandable mysticism) to the mortals, is the waking state (state of full awareness) to the spiritual beings. The fully awakened yogi goes back to sleep again, (this time) taking leave of the ways of the world. He maintains an indifferent attitude to the ways of the world. Between creation and creation the *Primal Being* sleeps. He who understands the secret of sleeping *kuṇḍalinī* understands the actual powers of *kuṇḍalinī*. Man does what he does only because *kuṇḍalinī* is asleep. Awakening is difficult; therefore the process of awakening is called the process of yoga, or the mystic way. There is nothing occultish in this very clear and very real analysis of the primal force of *kuṇḍalinī*.

"In a world where all are asleep, who is to awaken whom? The only way one could claim to wake up is to depend on some mechanical or personal assistance. These often fail; and there is no guarantee that this world would invariably work.

He could not Create by Himself

"Hence there is the use of the *cakra sādhanā*, where a combined effort from a number of persons is necessary. Even in the so-called non-tantra ways a *samāja* or a *satsang* (a socialising congregation) is necessary. In *Haṭha-yoga* alone the yogi works by himself. But how difficult this yoga is. If the *cakra sādhanā* is pestered with the dangerous possibility of a sensuous fall, the *haṭha sādhanā* is also pestered with a silent sinister possibility of going berserk. (cf. uncle Govinda's case before.) Only the firm of purpose, the firm of will, the disciplined of the body and the mind could succeed in either.

But of the two, the *kuṇḍalinī cakra sādhanā*, the tantra way, is by far the easier, because it does not lead the human body and mind through the almost dementing process of negative rigours.

"The negative way, the way of so called abstinence, is called the *asura* way in the Gītā (demoniac way). 'Know them to be of demoniac habit who suffer all the elements of the body through abstinence, and make Me, the inner being, suffer as much'. In nothing, in no pursuit, no man by himself alone could achieve abiding success. Behind the seeming success of every individual effort a series of persons has been at work. It must be realised that in life no man is alone. Life depends on life; and the living world survives through an unseen, and therefore, bond of interdependence of spirit and will. The admission of the power of this spirit is contained in the empirical concept of prayers. Life has been created by united efforts. *He could not create by Himself. He could not love Himself. He sought the second*, says the Vedas.

"What happens if during his efforts the practising yogi goes wrong? Have you yourself not met such men? Have you not brought aid to many of them? Many fall, before one succeeds; and that one becomes the saint, the superman, and offers the guideline to many. We call them the Christ, the Buddha, Rāma and Kṛṣṇa. These are not born every day, in every age. Because of this hope, the smaller must seek the higher.

"The importance of guidance cannot be overemphasised. The importance of the loving guidance of a guru means to the practitioner the importance of breath to the body; of procreation to life. The guru is the one who organises the group; guides the group; leads the group; becomes the centre piece, the *cakravartinī*, the Primal *śakti*, the *pradhānā nāyikā* in the group. And in tantra the guru is a She; that She becomes a *whole* only when tied to a He. This is simple; this is difficult. This is popular; this is unique. This is easily understood; this is easily forgotten. You must not again forget. You forget too often. Do never doubt. There lies the pitfall. Beware of suspicions.

Conflicts in a Junkyard

"You have now noted that the supermen emerge out of the common run of men; and that gurus are helpful to individual seekers. But because a person is a superman he cannot be held as a god by everyone, although to some he must naturally appear with the importance of a god. He may be *his* god, and could serve the purpose of a god for *his* devotion and submission.

"Similarly, every woman cannot become an *alter ego*. Wives are wives by virtue of matrimony. In marriages we hardly take into consideration the spiritual qualities of the bride. As such, marriages often remain incomplete unions of souls. But in selecting the *alter ego* that which is of supreme importance for consideration is the complementariness, the exact similitude of the essence of the person chosen. To this extent a guru or an *alter ego* is, for the seeker, a predestined boon.

"We have already discussed the subject of personality in the light of both essence and mechanism. Most men accept life and death as a helpless mechanical process with a pinch of the sense of inevitability; and during their circulation in the world fever act no better than machines. Birth and death are biological facts, and as such refer to medical science and sociology. One cannot include the Vedic Brahmanas, or, poets like Vyāsa and Vālmikī, or the great sages like Buddha, Śankara, Rāmānuja as just mechanical dross.

"Individuals live and die within the scope of their individual interests and fascinations, successes and failures. The real man is beyond this everyday personality. The real man lives within his being, in his essence. Often the outer man and the inner man are found engaged in a conflicting war between their respective mechanical roles and their essential calling. Arjuna's confusion on the battlefield of Kurukṣetra is an illustration of this conflict. No other person in the vast battlefield, not the noble Karṇa, nor the just Yudhiṣṭhira, nor the heroic Bhīma suffered from this conflict. But the sensitive Arjuna was torn between the two personalities that lived within him: one the mechanical man, and the other the essential man; one was *triguṇātmaka*, and the other was *guṇātīta*. (*Guṇa*=essence; subtle classification of dull, active and spiritual aspiration in all beings; *triguṇātmaka*= compounded of the three *guṇas*; *guṇātīta*=sublimated beyond the conflicts of the *guṇas*.)

"Man knows what he wants, but does not know where to put his hand for it. What he puts his hand on is not what he wants. Some know exactly how and where to find it, although it is impossible for them to define what they find.

"Others think that they know what they want; but every time they try to describe what they want, they feel that they have failed to pinpoint what they wanted. This is because the man of the moment lives with the moment, thinking that the moment is the time to live in; but the man of spirit lives in the spirit of things which is not bound within the moment. Naturally the conflict is there, and would remain there until a solution is found. Sooner or later the man of spirit is able to point out to the man of the moment his folly in trying to collect his happiness and satisfaction from the things he collects around him. Before long he would discover that what he has been living in is a junkyard. Then does the spirit win over matter; and the select individual wins over the mass mind.

"Love too is a power. While it indeed is a power with the man of spirit, it is just sex exploitation (which is never satisfied), and erotic dissipation with the mechanical man. The expression of the reproductive instinct is not an expression of love. Love fulfills; while eroticism is hungering, languishing, and famishing. The mechanical man engaged in a sex act only functions; the man of essence radiates in love. The first effort just reproduces a specimen; while the second alone inspires a superman, i.e., a man of special skill and power.

The Power and the Witness

"But *lhādinī* or sex is so absorbing a power that nothing concerning life could ever escape it. Call it art, literature, reproduction, politics, religion, music. In fact all expressions evolve out of the sex urge. It is there. To deny it is a supreme folly, ignorance. The sin does not lie in using it, but in abusing it; misusing it. The way of abstinence is the way of repression. The way of sublimation is the way of tantra.

"These so-called religious preachers want to bring in a period of peace and love through changing the world. But are changes really possible? How far could man change man? How far is man's power limited? What is power? From where is it derived?

"If we study the link between an individual's power and the principal source of power, it would not take long for us to discover that the process of emanation of power does not depend on our personal energy. There is a constant source of energy. By some eternal process once a radial field of power gets established, it continues to respond all the time. Because of its eternal nature it goes on operating whether we are aware of it or not. Even the power of individual awareness is derived from it. This we call the cosmic power. Cosmic forces are eternally operative. Power springs from it. We cannot instigate it, influence it, stop it or start it. God is only 'the witness', says the Gītā. God is just the manager, *adhyakṣa*. And the cosmic power, *Prakṛti*, ejects (*sūyate*). *Atmān* is *akartā* says the Gītā. (Conscious power has nothing to do, but to watch on.) This *ātmān* neither acts, nor gets affected (*na karoti na lipyate*). This acting God (*puruṣa*) acts only according to the essences of *Prakṛti*. When we say '*we* do'. '*we* act', we indulge in a folly. We feel that we are the actors; in fact we are not. The cosmic power has been acting; and irrevocably it would continue to act through the different expressions in what we call nature, man included. In this sense what we call God is also helpless. This must be understood, before one speaks irresponsibly about predestination, fate or destiny. A Hindu's sense of predestination may not be confused with the Hellenic *nemesis* or Fate. A true Hindu knows that fate has to be countered by action.

"Yet Man is not that much helpless. There is an eternal battle going within man to outreach his powers with which he is armed. He, the Man, could by his individual efforts change the *tamas* into *rajas* and *rajas* into *tamas*. (In other words the categories of the essences could be gradually purified from the more dense and dull stuff towards the more spiritual, lighter, and purer stuff.) This is the basis of the *cakras*; the basis of the awakening of the *kuṇḍalinī*. A perpetual motion of constant activity raises the man from his commonality to his superiority. *Activity is Siddhi. Action makes the man.*

Sex as Power

"We appear to be too small to change the general pattern of nature, of which man is a part. His cravings and anguishes, his sufferings and conflicts are based in the nature of the cosmos. Redress lies through individual effort. The individual however has the ability to transform himself and guide his own destiny; for destiny for the individual involves many cycles of his being. The cosmic process of evolving and dissolving has neither any accountable beginning, nor any foreseeable future. As long as the law of cosmic churning is operative, the individual by his efforts could, if he so wished, and worked for it, bring in changes in his personality as well as his essence.

"The individual who is in control of his change is in control of his power, inclusive of his sex power. He has to be; because the sex power is the most telling power in his making, in his shaping, in his extending himself into the future. All other personal powers move at the behest of the sex power.

"Sex brings minds together; sex binds companionship; sex creates and amuses; sex delights; sex preserves, conserves and dissolves at a momentum that is hard to check unless taken care of. Sex exerts the greatest influence over the society around. Sex is the power that could lead men to utter destruction and dissipation; sex is the power that could lead to sublimation. Sex integrates; sex disintegrates. Sex keeps the body and the mind in a state of perpetual slavery; sex supplies the basic energy for man's ultimate liberation. 'Those who suffer a fall on the ground, get up with the support of the ground', says a popular wise crack in Bengal.

"When sex is agitated, the flow of energy is at its highest. Nerves do not discharge so much vibrations, cells do not burn at so high a rate in any other form of activity as in the sex activity. (This includes all types of creative activity in art, literature, music, histrionics etc.) Joy and pleasure reach ecstatic heights through their draw on the sex power. Sex reaches by its activity the maximum scale of the human octave in its rhythmic vibrations. The act of physical sex lends its excitement in a moment of shock which cannot be contained. And the same height and the same degree of joy could be attained, and retained for hours and hours if that sex power is tackled in the way it should be tackled. In the physical sex act a material dissipation runs down the body, and recouping the lost cells becomes a rather long process; but the spiritual act of sex elevates human aspirations, and confers on the power of consciousness the abilities of keener perception, and wider sensitivity. The question of dissipation or of langour does not arise in this case at all.

"The immense power released and conserved through the spiritual exercise of the waking of the sex power, which lies dormant in the *kuṇḍalinī* gradually brings out of man his spiritual personality, and helps, wherever possible, to release his latent faculties for universal benefit.

"As an immediate blessing of this release, a field of special vibration spreads around, which is often visible, and is called 'aura'. Its presence is 'felt' by others, in more or less degrees, depending on the purity of perception of the observer, and freedom from any inhibited 'pull-back' of the person concerned. Such 'aura' has been even photographed by those for whom photographic reporting appears to be an infallible proof. The entire body limits, under such conditions, of the person concerned gets tensed and vibrant, and the resulting extra radioactive waves create an area around him so charged as to cause this phenomenon of 'aura'. From times immemorial spiritualists of all times and climes have been referring to such phenomenal discharge of power through a change of atmosphere, or visibly through the presence of 'aura'.

Astral Presence

"When this power in a man reaches its highest stage, then the individual personality splits, and evolutes a new second personality of essential being. This new presence is then known as an astral personality, or an astral body. This is how you yourself have experienced several times the presence of an unexpected person amidst unknown people when that person was least expected.

"You have heard of the astral presence in history, in scriptural evidences, in other narratives; and many of these you yourself have rejected as nonsense. But, again, you yourself have also gathered many evidences to shout out from the house top that what people disbelieve is their business; and what you have experienced is yours. It is not that much an urgent necessity for you to go and convince people. You are no missionary. You have no mission. The fact is, if you are aware of it, if you are convinced, then, continue to develop this power; acquire this aura; possess this power of going out of your material body, and assume an astral body, and feel for others, when others in their essential selves grieve and wither away. Man suffers more in his essential self than in his material self. Suffering is abstract.

"It is hard to believe this at the first instance. But when one ponders over it, one does not find it difficult to see that man suffers more in his essence. His material body suffers from materially diagnosed ailments, and the material scientific methods prescribe medicines of material value. But when man suffers in the mind, when he suffers from hidden complexes, when man is unable to check his ways although he knows and recognises his shortcomings, it is the essence that suffers. Then the sufferer goes to the psychiatrists. But the psychiatrists themselves have developed a science in their own way; and the way depends on empirical logic, and material gadgets. Their way lies mostly through instrumental measurements and findings. In the process the essence remains untouched. The more they depend on mechanical diagnosis, the more they lose their touch with the essential being that really suffers. The cause and the source of the malady remains untouched. Naturally the common cures suggested are, in all cases, palliative. In contrast, tantra leads to the inner chambers of the essential man.

"A man of essence alone could diagnose an essential ailment, and find out a remedy. This relates the curer to the patient through the ties of energy, essential discharge of power, the sex power, the radial effects of the bright *kuṇḍalinī*.

"For one genuine *tantra-tapasvī* (expert in the art of retaining the thermal power conserved from the source power) there are a hundred faked ones. It is much better not to act on behalf of a suffering soul unless the actor himself is free from all sufferings. He suffers who nurses unfulfilled desires. He is in total joy who has nothing to seek for himself. At the end of the journey lies the abode of peace. The peaceful alone gives peace.

"Sex as a store-house of energy holds tremendous powers."

I am the Furrow

I remembered Nazri. During a seance at the Devi shrine away from the poppy fields, Nazri's entire body seemed to be on fire: and I failed to keep my concentration fixed to the subjective field. Ramchand, and two others who were there, had been disturbed in their concentration because of the excessive radiation that emanated from Nazri. I was the only one to have kept his cool as long as I did. But I too ultimately felt assailed by a superior pull.

Next day as I was about to get across the lake, and enter the cave, I became aware of another presence. That was Nazri, the charming Rajasthani *Prakṛti*. I found her seated there, laughing bewitchingly. She was a beautiful girl in her prime of youth. The word 'bewitching' fitted her the most at that time. Such external beauty casts spells, for which witches are known. Great sages when required to be 'bewitched' for serving the purposes of 'gods' were bewitched by beauties, organised by the scheming gods. She had anticipated me. She explained how such bewitching powers too, emanate from pure seances. What she had said I got verified from my (good for nothing) book learnings later on.

Woman has been accepted as fire in the great Upaniṣads. Her sex has been imaged as the pit where fuel is on fire, emitting the smoke signs of call, inviting flames of call projected from within the vulva, and help keep the burning of the world *yajñā* aflame all the time. The smouldering coals within eject sparks of energy, which catch up with the cooperator who seeks from the fire and the flame the energy that he needs for further activity. It is only when completely immersed in and infused with this energy that the bodies erupt in the fruits of the action, and produce another life filled with energy and vigour.

Away from all this Vedic sophistication Nazri used her own simple phraseology, the innocent charm of which I cannot recapture after so many dry years of my life. But what she had said, perfectly conforms with that the Tibetans have to say, what the He-Vajra Samhitā has to say. Tantra bases its rites on a pragmatic view of life. Only those who do not have the direct knowledge of the reaches of these practices visualise, with a sick vision, unlicensed indulgences and debauchery in these practices.

Nazri said at one significant meeting the following message, it still burns within my innermost consciousness like the perpetual fire burning in Maṇikarṇikā: "Nano (for that was how she called me: it means 'my little friend') I am not here for long. I am happy to give you what I have. For others I have a body, a sex, and my beautiful youth. But for you I am the vigour, the energy, the abstract. *I am not the sky, but the soil; not the soil, but the furrow; not the furrow, but the heat in the furrow that hungers for pacification through delivery of fresh blossoms.* I was in search of your touch; your receptivity. You and you alone came to me here in this impossible part of the country to receive this. You do not know why you came. You do not know from where I come. You do not know where and when shall I pass away. In this life, at this moment this alone is real that *I am with you* and that this body as a spring is giving unto you a drink, the strength and vigour of which shall extend beyond this life of yours."

I was stilled by those stunning words. I was amazed at her earnestness. It was not a public practice. It could not have been made public. It was not for everybody.

"If we have to keep cooked food covered from flies out of fear of the poisons they may cast," she said, "we see the need of covering this practice from the human flies filled with poison. By uniting with the *prakṛti* the *puruṣa* unites with the universe as a whole. By churning out the energy from the dead matter the adept transforms the world through the power acquired. *Sexual union is the embodiment of the creative mystery secreted within the cosmic play.* This could create; yes; but what could create could also destroy. It is very simple to understand, Nano. And it is wrong and foolish to avoid the creative function out of fear that in it lies hidden also the destructive function. Pray to the destructive function; appease it by supplicating; keep it calm and controlled, checked and under a leash; but for the sake of the world and for your own self do not avoid the forces of creative energy.

"This is hidden in the images of the goddesses Kāli, Tārā, and Camuṇḍā. The very sight of these is repulsive and fearsome: their blood hunger, their skull cups, their bone necklaces and girdles, their daggers and swords, their nude dances over dead bodies. Oh how repulsive; how deterrent; how brutal; yet how engaging, fascinating, mystic!"

1932! The words still ring in my ears.

Yes. But what are we otherwise, when we rape and plunder; when we force intercourse on pregnant wives; when we disrespect human dignity and creep like worms and bacilii from one orifice to another orifice, with satisfying glee, having nothing at all to do with the upper regions and the inner cells where the human essence languishes, crying for a touch of recognition. Who cares for the heart of a hired woman? Who cares for the consequences of those irreparable psychological damages that we cause by enforcing our lust and madness on the bodies of the *prakṛti*. Would we allow these worms to sit on judgement on the tantra practices, and accept them as the gospel truth? The horrors of life and mind are a hundred times more horrible and repulsive than those tantra images, which after all help us consolidate and assimilate the conflicting function of energy, which create and destroy at the same time; and by the process of destruction makes room for a youthful, fruitful, and beautiful creation.

Those who think that these rites imply sexual abandon, blood orgy, terror and licensed acts of fornication at will are victims of their own sick thoughts, own hallucinated images. They are under the pressure of their own nightmare . . . .

"Do you not see," Nazri had told me once, "that almost every known *Śakti* shrine bears on its walls figures carved in sex embraces? What about the sacred and valued *tankas* of Tibet with the copulating fierce forms? Our home has one hung on the walls of the sanctuary. My mother had taken me the other day to the Dilwara temple. How could such obscenities command the veneration of centuries, and recognition of art? Far from being obscenities, these project on depraved thoughts to the adepts. They read other messages in them, and would feel helpless without them. But this is how the common man views them, and describes them. And, what is even more amazing, accepts them. If they did not, why should the detractors have crowded on them century by century? Have you not noted amongst these embraces stray pairs of fierce disposition locked in vigorous outbursts of energy. They seek the many into one, and the one into many, as their many heads, many hands and many feet denote. You do not imagine them to have many sexes or many breasts. For, the 'female' remains one, and the lips that the male adheres to are just one pair. *Śakti* is one, but desires are many. *Śakti* allows itself to be drawn into the fierce, the ugly, the calm and the beautiful with a solemn equipoise."

An excited Nazri appeared to be a transcended Nazri.

Symbolism is at the basis of this approach. Those who live and think and practise in symbols feel nearest to the abstract and the absolute. Those who are muddled up with the so-called realities of life, like food, fear and fornication, often ridicule the life-force illustrated through the known symbols. The howls of jackals at the moon leave the cosmos undisturbed. Stars do not lose their lustre when children hurl fireworks at them. Symbols are, and would remain the subtlest and the truest reporters of the ideal and the cosmic.

Tantra has achieved in the spiritual world the realities of capturing cosmic energy from the most vibrant source available to man, namely man himself, and woman. Only the most prudish would ignore this burning truth. It is entirely based on yogic principles and practice. Yoga insists on discipline; and tantra attests that discipline by making man confront his inner enemies.

I remember particularly a night during this period. It was the night of the Govardhana, following the new moon of Divāli, the celebrated night of lamps. To the tantra practitioners there is no other night as significant as that one. As usual I was set for a twenty-four hour penance. For some reason this limited period, that year in Rajasthan, got extended to forty hours. During this long session I was in the cave all alone. At about ten in the night I swam back, and was returning home via the Kāli temple. I had to cross a rather thickly-set grove along the way. It remained abandoned for its ugly reputation of being a haunt of cobras. I saw a dancing light within the dense copse, and felt interested. I entered the copse. Babul (*mimosa arabica*), neem (*melia ozadirachte*) serpent plants and cacti crowded the spot.

I saw Nazri with a chased Rajput scimitar in her hands, dancing the terrible dance of death and destruction (*pralaya*). The old saintly Telenghana rover lay on the ground as a corpse. Two flames on either sides of his unconscious body sported dancing flames, and Nazri was dancing, bejewelled, dazzling and resplendent with a gorgeously decorated red and gold girdle of the finest *zari* (gold thread) around. Embroidered bits of mirrors, stuck on her skirts and girdle, sparkled in a thousand shooting light points. Her long and dark hair was set loose, but was held by a tiara; her bare breasts were covered with many beads and necklaces; her lips were red with *pān* (kind of green leaves chewed with catechu, white lime and betel nuts), but redder with an enthralling joy. The sinewy vigorous movements, the electrifying gyrations, the forceful stamping of her feet threw around her circles upon circles of thrilling vibrations.

Before I could gather my runaway senses, and gain my poise, she gave me a mighty pull. In a trice I was carried away high and far spinning through at what seemed to me a cyclonic speed, and soon got lost to all senses of dimension, measurement, norm and proportion. I was, as it were, and as it should really be, transported by a powered drive to regions beyond my personal reach.

There was no moon that night. The thickness of the dark around was almost impenetrable. Village men under the distant neem trees had been thumping the humble Indian drum; and a tabor was keeping accompaniment to some crude Divāli songs. From the fields the fragrance from miles and miles of poppy again and again wafted its opiated breath, and projected images of thrill and fulfilment. There was a nip in the early hour breeze, and at times I shivered.

A peacock sent up a shrill cruel male call. It had sighted a snake; and was pouncing down upon it. In the babul groves young ones of the turtle doves began to make noise. The cacti and the neem blossoms filled the dark with aromatic dreaminess.

Moments passed like years and years of joy. Excitement makes moments of joy short-lived; while peace and poise make the same moments live for ever.

Hardly had I been merged in such a voluptuous self-abandoning ecstasy when I felt a sudden pull again. She felled me down on the bare earth, and sat upon my chest.

I lost consciousness.

As I came to, I found myself lying in the yard of the Kālī shrine. The early dawn breeze soothed my hot temples. I opened my eyes to have my fill of the blossoming sky with its blush spread over. Ramchand had been trying to revive me with a song. Nazri, normal and beautiful as ever, was standing by with a glass of milk. Her head was red with sindoor. Her bold eyes looked bolder at me through the dark lines of collyrium. She was chewing *pān*, and her eyes smiled. "Drink this, and break your fast", she said with rare sweetness.

I looked at her; accepted the glass filled with life; and drank to the last drop.

Six months after I had left Nazri's hill-town, I heard of her sudden and mysterious death.

She was being carried as a bride on a horseback, her husband on another horse. Before she had reached the threshold of her husband's village she slumped on the back of her mount.

Nazri was found dead. She never touched her husband's home.

11

The Virgin and the Holy Family

A 'Virgin' Rite

But all this is far away and long ago. The impenetrable silence of the stream of time has carried the events beyond my reach forever. All that remains of those halcyon days are the charmed whispers along the memory lane, and the sound of the footfalls of other days through the corridors of lost glories. The days in the Vindhya hills and Rajasthan, the old Telenghana *Haṭha*-yogi, the young Ramchand, the everlasting Nazri all float past as sailing ritual-lamps down the eternal Ganges, winking feebly through a descending veil of my stand fog.

That which always remained with me as a rock like solid support throughout life was the power of LS. It was she who had introduced me to the sublime teachings of Yogavāśiṣṭha, to the eloquent verses of the Gītā, to the store-house of the epic Mahābhārata, and above all to the concept of oneness.

It was she who had taken me by my hands, and guided my steps through the hazardous, undergrowth of tantra, through the intricate processes of tantra practices, and finally to the seances of the tantra adepts.

But in my inner mind droned the quest, the only quest, the only enquiry,—viz., the hows and whys of the adoration of the Virgin. But LS had never failed me. She always advised "Wait! Prepare! Time has to come to the worshippers of Time."

Another Divāli festival came. As it fell on the auspicious day of the moon, Monday, this Divāli night was regarded to be of a very special esoteric value. The moon and the Moon-Lady have been casting their mystic influence the world over on all tantra, or esoteric rites.

On that night of nights I was taken to a mysteriously hidden temple of Kāli in the locality of the historical Pātāleśvara. This temple was associated with two very important facts. One, it was very close to a *sādhanā pīṭha* associated with the tantric practices of the sage Śankarācārya; two, the temple and the deity bore the reputation of having witnessed the celebrated Pāncamuṇḍī rites, where in the days of yore even human sacrifice was said to have been performed.

In my youthful days when I was associated with the underground activists of the patriotic camp, dedicated to drive the foreigners out of the motherland, I was shadily aware of the existence of this subterranean temple, and its consecrated *vedī* (altar). As children, we used to cross ourselves while passing along this temple. And passing by that place at night was beyond the courage of the ordinary man, much less of a child. Oh yes, the very dusts along the lane at that point felt eerie.

On our entry into the temple we found the signs of an elaborate preparation for an absorbing Kālī prayer, inclusive of the 5-Ms. Rituals had actually started already with an unknown priest occupying the main *āsana*. In course of time a goat was produced, and slaughtered; the severed head was offered, and pieces from the meat, all skin and the fur, were carefully set aside by the right number, and ritually offered into a raging fire-pit. As the night grew past twelve I found that at least twelve persons had assembled in a smoky hazy hall where only oil lamps fought with the enveloping darkness and sweating damps. Of these, inclusive of LS, three were females. Of the other two one was a young girl of about twelve.

Again and again I looked at her. Obviously she had been keeping fast for the day. Her face showed signs of preparedness and readiness. Her eyes wore the charm of dreamy awayness. Small as she was, she looked as much concerned. The radiating vibrations were unmistakably perceptible.

Bathed and decorated, she was soon made to sit on a platform covered by a red carpet surmounted by a tiger skin. On this she sat in the lotus posture.

The ceremony started.

In solemn choral rhythm the chants flowed on.

> *Om Lling Kaumāryai namah* (Bow to the Virgin—Om Lling!)
> I divine Thou O Virgin with the three eyes:
> I divine the saffron toned one, riding a peacock;
> I divine the four-armed one
> donning the weapons *Śakti* (power), snare,
> the goaded crook; as also the *Mudrā* of protection;
> the decorated brilliant one, drunk in her own glory.

The chant went on. I was getting lost in a stream of sheer delight, flowing into an ocean of brilliant tranquillity. The music rose again in paeans of resonating verses:

> Mother O Mother, certain it is for him to get over the bites of Eros, once one gets merged in your true self. The sacred delta (where meet the powers of emergence, sustenance and annihilation) rests in union with the heart of the dead; whilst you keep smiling at Śiva (the male negative matter and virtue), who holds you high as you get engrossed in the joy of union that ejects the ecstatic sweetness of creation. Divine, and divine until the diviner gets himself merged into the dead of night . . .

The chant was too terrible for me. I held on to my peace somehow with my limited and feeble powers. It made me shiver like barley beards under an autumnal breeze. All on a sudden the ever consoling hand was on my back, then on my head.

With an effort I opened my eyes.

I found the little girl stretched on the platform. Lamps burned all around her. One of the ladies set three burning bowls on her head and palms. The smell of burning meat and unguents with the *bel* leaves oppressed the atmosphere. The virgin glowed in the light of the flames. Then suddenly she lay still as a corpse.

"What next?", I thought.

Beatitude

Solemn rang the words; solemner rose the paeans resonating through the dark. The dim lamps flickered, and made the stilled shadows dance against the walls. To minds saturated with suggestive symbolism the imageries of Sanskrit language evoked thrills of sublimated joy until stilled by the quiet grandeur of ecstasy. Consummation of delight appeared to have been suspended on the resonant surface of choral harmony and music, which has its own mesmeric effect; to that was added the charms of verbal dignity and poetical fascination.

I ceased to remain 'I', and the incorporeal feeling wafted away in waves upon waves of liquid delight. "Sheer *ānandam* (joy) confers complete courage", I recalled. "Then why worry about disease, decay, death?"

Once this firmness of mind takes care of man's innate restlessness, all else would follow up smoothly, and the drama of life, instead of posing complex situations, would become a thing of joy, a graceful involvement without any personal attachment. The free alone could enjoy; and the happy alone could spread happiness.

That was beatitude indeed.

So I know that the rite enacted before me was not merely an end in itself, nor an act of self enjoyment. I was gradually becoming a part of the whole. The presence of LS had elevated the tone of the ceremony, vitalised its efforts, secured its results, and pin-pointed a secular initiation.

Meanwhile the others too had been busy in their own ways. The seriousness with which the solemn rites were being performed in absolute secrecy, later made me think of the abuse such rites were subjected to due to a commonplace curiosity for experimentations, as well as a greed for a commercial drive for easy money, easy power, easy influence. It really encouraged venality which remains intelligently camouflaged by a colourful fantasy of spirituality. Due to such prostitution of an age-old and time-tried ritual in the interest of selfish possession I have often come across painful and shameful reports about these rites described by the casual and the unauthorised in very derogatory terms. I could see why most of the 'performers' (in such tantra sessions) have been derided in the past, even punished by law. I dare say they deserved the treatment. But just because of that I am not going to condemn the system. We do not condemn any system by the standards of misuse that it might sustain in the hands of charlatans and frauds. We do not condemn the judiciary by the standards of the corrupt; neither medicine by the standards of the quacks; nor the system of law, order and government by the standards of bureaucratic standoffishness, or the haughty indifference of the well dressed tyrant.

I remember that the Dalai Lama, who had previously been quite kind and liberal (in his Indian exile residence) to the Western visitors and the Western Press, had to draw the curtain down on the exposures from the irreverent and indiscriminate journalists who had been busy in bringing heaps of misguiding rubbish on the haloed system of Tibetan tantrism. The tantra treatises warn again and again not to have these exposed to the uninitiated. There are very strict guards, both moral and physical, against the conveyance of informations regarding the inner rituals and practices to the outsider and the non-initiate.

Naturally I stood amazed at the rites I had been observing.

She is the Consecrated One

The Virgin, now a deity, was lying flat on her back. Lamps were burning all around a well marked *maṇḍala*. The high flames from the ritual fire-pit were casting strange shadows. The young *devī*, seemed now lit up by the outer glow, now by an illumination that gradually was consuming her personal ego, probably even the consciousness of a physical existence.

I was particularly watching her wondrous looks. Judging by the looks alone she did not seem any longer to belong to here. She had apparently lost all communication with us, who sat at the foot of the platform where she lay. She was merged in herself.

Later I learnt that she had not reached that impersonal state by her own inner faculties, although the faculties, and their receptivity were tuned by years and years of training. Actually that state of perfect impersonality, which was brought about, was made to descend on her by the very rites. The adept was the one who transformed the little girl-medium into the cosmic spirit of the Mother. She was transformed indeed into the Mother, the Great Virgin, who had been looked upon as the only source of Power by peoples of all lands and all times. Such psychic transformations are possible, and are enacted, but these could not be confused with a state of mesmerism, or a lack of will power. Although so transformed, she grew acutely conscious of her spiritual role and of her physical obligation. Indeed her awareness was all the more keen and alert.

For two hours the silence persisted. The flames kept rising. Smoke engulfed the room. The inner chantings kept mind busy. Clothed in a blanket of silence, gradually we merged into the void. Bodies embraced bodies, hands locked hands; feet locked feet, and the eyes closed (so that the third eye gets opened). Above all vibrated the consummate thrill of it all. Some unearthly cool flow of delight descended from the top of the being, and moved down, down, down the spine, and gradually soothed all feeling, nerve by nerve. Consciousness, they say (Gītā) is an upside down tree; the roots at the top feed the yet ungrown leaf of the manifold branches with a surfeit of beauty and serenity, ecstasy and the tranquillity. It was a sublime experience. It was transcendental living beyond our time.

I sat through the embrace. I was overwhelmed by the immensity of that experience. I felt every grain of that subterranean dungeon coming to life and speaking to me in a language which I always sought to hear. And I heard.

I was hearing it even when the first breeze announcing dawn fanned my relaxed nerves, and the cool hands of LS protectively patted my head. 'Peace on you; be brave.' She was singing.

Come to me Mother,
Rest on my heart.
Let me watch at your glory.
You watch me, and I watch you, eye to eye . . .
None should watch this love play between the two of us,
O Mother . . .

In lost moments I still sing that melody.

Pity the tormented soul which cannot get lost to the world around at certain supreme moments of living.

But that Virgin never left my thoughts.

No. She had not been an adept herself. She was too young. Pretty; fascinating; ethereal. Yet she was no ordinary being either. She had *something* in her. She, I knew, was bound for a future. Persons without a future are dragging on a dead life.

I asked LS who she was.

"She is the consecrated one", was her pithy reply. Thereafter the curtain was firmly dropped. I was not curious. I applied the discipline of indifference.

Gradually, however I came to learn further.

Wandered through Heaven and Earth

Near to our home lived the world celebrated saint Śrī Śyāmākānta Lāhirī, better known as Lāhirī Mohāśoy. He had a son, who was a good friend of my eldest brother; and his great grandson was my chum. I used to visit the home of Lāhirī Mohāśoy quite frequently. When I was able to know myself, Lāhirī Mohāśoy had left the world; but from my father and from LS, who had been an ardent admirer of Lāhirī Mohāśoy, I knew almost every bit of the great *Haṭha*-yogi's reputation. He too used to visit the Catuhṣaṣṭhī yogini *pīṭha* and the adjacent *Bhadrakālī* temple.

At Gaduresvar, where the Lāhirīs still live, we had great fun in and around the many dark lanes and corridors always dotted with Śiva temples. In the hot summer days these dens used to shelter us, from a scorching sun.

One day I was seated in one of these temples, all by myself. I must have got lost to my outer senses, when I felt that someone was calling me, I looked for the centre of attraction, and found a boy standing and laughing. Actually he was calling me.

This was a demented boy of the Mālākars. They were craftsmen engaged in making silver filigree decorations for clay modelled deities with foils, and chipped and splitted white reed corks. In the nature of all guild crafts the art of silver filigree work with foils and corks had descended on the Mālākars for over the centuries.

One of the boys of the Mālākars was a victim of visions. As he read in the same school where we used to go, his sudden appearance with a charming grin of simplicity interested me. I was aware of his fits of visions.

He promised me a journey to the higher regions of consciousness within a moment. But no one used to take him seriously. He was taken for a man 'without' a proper mind. Yet I thought, LS thought, and the great contemporary Gōpīnāth Dādā (elder brother) thought that the boy's claims were not quite flimsy. He was indeed a visionary of a very rare type. Saint Ramakrishna Paramahansa we learn, was subject to such visions.

I often wonder which of us has a proper mind. Men who run mad after money, sex, drinks, excitements, sudden fame etc., and who cause and have been causing much harm to society are often taken seriously, and honoured. They represent our political and social interest. They often base their doings on apparently sound logical stands. I wonder if these foolish or god-drunk people, speak of the 'other worlds', are actually mad. 'Oh, why am I just a half-mad do nothing; why you don't turn me into a full mad one?', asks fervently a Bengal Baul (the mad one). Bauls are a singing sect half-hippy half-gypsy, but fervently dedicated to self-search.

Spiritual 'madness' is an accepted feature of the seeker after truth. I was not to be dissuaded by Mālākar's so-called madness.

We approached each other, and he asked me if I was interested. Near by was a *Śaktī-pīṭha,* a Durgā shrine of the ancient times. An attached garden was crossed, and we climbed atop a hill of ruins.

It was usual with Mālākar to relate his experiences. He did not talk to all; but he did talk. He used to have long sessions with Gopināth Dādā, who had been a world renowned tantra adept (Mahāmahopādhyāya Pandit Gopināth Kavirāj). Because he had been a secret follower and admirer of my father we were quite close to each other. In my spiritual difficulties I used to consult him in the absence of LS.

That particular evening Mālākar was in a mood to talk. In his talk he described his 'space' journeys from different 'solar' systems! He actually described the 'places' he had gone to, and experiences he had enjoyed. To listen to him was to be convinced. Very few could concentrate on what he used to 'prattle'; yet very few could just ignore him as a fool. His teachers in the school did not. This was so because at times when the teachers would find themselves confused over certain problems, he would come forward with an easy solution, or, with the necessary information, or at times even with predictions. He could almost accurately predict earthquakes, sex of unborn children, death of persons and accidents. He would just shriek out his warnings. Naturally people concluded that Mālākar was afflicted by a strange kind of madness which cannot be ignored, neither treated as a medical problem.

With him, as he talked, I used to race over the many places we hear of in our ancient treatises, as well as in the lores of the peoples of other faiths.

The report of his interviews with the immortal sages like Sanat, Sanandana, Sanātana and Sanat-kumāra, (the first four human creations who refused to settle and propagate; and carved out for themselves an abode of immortality), with the Aśvins. (celestial medicine men), with Vaśiṣṭha (a sage) and particularly with Nārada (a sage) became more and more engrossing to me. I did not have my doubts in these matters in those days specially when he used to relate; and I used to feel quite happy in his 'mad' company; and what was more, with him by me, I felt so complete in myself.

It is this poise in Mālākar that had kept me attracted to him. He was mentioned often by Gopīnāth Dādā, as well as by Saint Jitendra. LS herself used to confirm my attraction for the new find by her smiles. At times she sounded sarcastic as she piqued, "How about your heavenly journeys on the fancy chariot driven by your new friend?" And as I blushed to the tips of my ear lobes, she at once consoled by remarking, as usual, 'Gather ye rose buds whilst ye may'. She had two Sanskrit verses in support of my quests, which she called 'Mādhukarī-Vṛtti' (the way of the bees). One of these verses said:

"Fake jades assume the role of diamonds when set in gold. By the virtue of good company alone even a dunce gets matured in better thoughts."

And the other one went thus, "Even a worm reaches the head of the elect, only by keeping company of flowers in a garland; even blocks of stones assume godliness when the saints accept them as worthy of their worship."

Then she would start singing: "Burn, burn, burn! Pure gold alone shall outlive the fire!"

I was never offended by her sarcasms, which like the shafts that train a wild elephant, never stopped to make me a better and more improved person.

This Mālākar had brought me to the hill of ancient ruins at the back of the shrine of Durgā. Sun was about to set. Things were becoming sombre. But Mālākar was in his usual trance, and was busy talking in Sanskrit, which he did not know. He demanded that I pay absolute homage to Lord Śiva, because, he said, we had been standing in the direct presence of the Lord in the mount Kailasa. He, the Lord, according to Mālākar's statements, was then engaged in a game of dice with Mother Pārvatī, deciding the final fate of Mālākar himself. He felt his presence in the snowy heights so realistically that I found him actually shivering. I touched his goose-fleshed skin, which felt cold like ice. I paid my homage, but more to Mālākar than to the supposed presence of the deity.

Soon he urged me with a voice of command, "Come; my fate is going to be decided tonight. I would need your cooperation . . . Come . . . Come . . ."

The Breath of Darkness

A little distance away at the end of a blind lane there was a derelict wild space of about half an acre surrounded on all sides by tall ancient cut-stone buildings. No entrance was possible from those sides; the western side alone had a ten feet opening, commanded by two firm wooden gates. But these were always kept padlocked.

We reached one of these padlocked gates. Mālākar stood for some time before the closed gate. And I *saw* the padlock getting loose by itself. He pushed the gate open, and goaded me, 'Come; there is no time. Śakti waits."

I used to visit the place as a primary school-going boy when I was doing the first readings of the Vedas at the recitation stage. I was visiting it again after about ten long years.

What I witnessed that day was past my comprehension. What a total devastation. The whole area stood as an abandoned derelict wilderness. Our Vedic school appeared to be a thing of the past, a howl along mystic corridors.

Why are the *sādhanās* always, or mostly, associated with places dark and sinister, wild and abandoned? The subject has always intrigued me as mystifying. The aura of mystery is further enhanced by atmospheric oddities, I know. But why such aura or induced mystification should be necessary to *sādhanā* has often worried me. I have spent some hours on considering this subject in depth.

Later in life through my own practices I have come to learn some revealing facts.

It is not that the *sādhakas* select eerie haunted places for their exercise and practices. It is just the other way. Because of their steady communion with the spiritual world, and because of the 'temptation' of keeping near to their gracious will force and sympathies, the spirit seekers make unfrequented habitations their temporary homes. In our ignorance we associate these places with the haunted.

In the dead of a dark still night an empty house, or a busy hall, a courtroom, the familiar corridors of government secretariats feel different. One is able to locate at such places, specially when abandoned, the feel of a hundred eyes prying, a thousand eyelids winking, a million breaths passing over the shoulder.

It is not that every one should feel it. Every one does not feel the same way our own presence at a meeting, in a hall, even in our homes. Visitors come and go; our nerves do not register all such goings on in the same way, all the time, every time. These are the natural fluctuations of our own nervous conditions. The alertness of our field of attention does not maintain a level. Communication with the outer world, much more with the inner world, and with the world beyond our immediate perceptual comprehension, is not easy; neither does it reflect the same importance on every one. Our sensations differ with our state of health, perceptual keenness, or the want of it.

But generally speaking, certain places, because of their abandoned nature, record the spiritual vibrations, which in populated surroundings fail to register the required in-depth responses.

This accounts for the presence of so called 'creeps' in certain places, while at other places, specially at places which are always frequented, the 'creeps' are not felt. This is no place to discuss if these 'haunted' places always are blessed with spiritual 'presence'. But for the time being, let us accept, even as a hypothesis, that there are conscious 'presences' hovering all around us, mostly governing our good and bad motives, and attempting to bring about a balance between our desires and fulfilments. The ethical balance of the world at large is by and large guarded by these forces. Indeed the phenomenon proves to be extremely helpful to us. When we decide not to disturb their equilibrium by invoking them too often, neither to corrupt their moods by putting their powers to strain with the evil intention of bringing harm to others, these mysterious forces, whatever these be, actually and 'normally' feel 'good' to render us good, only if we let them be, and leave them alone. Loaded enterprises often backfire.

The Yantra and the Embrace

At a corner of that abandoned place there stood a plum grove: the prickly sweet berry-plums for which Varanasi is very famous. Stooping precariously through the grove we came upon a rather prepared mud polished yard, where flourished a bush of jasmines. It was the peak of the June month, when greeneries in general are under fire from the north India sun. But the jasmine, to my pleasant surprise, was in full bloom. Very close to the bush stood a tall champak; and the fragrance was intoxicating. The frangipani in their imperial dignity and beauty stood in a row of three plants. Besides these most coveted blooms, the humble oleander and the homely pious hibiscus marked their attendance. At a glance I took in all this, and wondered who had been gardening in this abandoned place.

The ground was smooth and well done. An elaborate *Śri yantra* (an extremely difficult diagram demanding the highest skill) sanctified the place. It was, as it were, a licensing stamp on the tantric rites. I recalled how this *yantra* was adored by the ancients. How the great Śankarācārya worshipped this *yantra*. It is revered at Śringerī, Kurttalam, Kanchipuram, Tirichinopoly (all in the south of India) and at Kathmandu in Nepal. This *yantra* has conferred the highest esoteric experience to renowned yogis besides Śankara whose great psalm *Saundarya-Laharī* is a masterly adoration of all the features of the sublime *yantra*.

I was watching the surroundings, and soon became aware of the familiar primary vibrations. Mālākar asked me to be seated and help lit a fire. From under a block of stone, where a large hole came to view, he brought out some mats, a pitcher of water, and some utensils, and the necessary paraphernalia for conducting a full-fledged tantra rite.

Who would conduct the rites, and for what purpose, remained still a mystery to me; but Mālākar proceeded sedately, unconcerned about the surroundings, unconcerned about my hesitations. He, on the contrary, was firm, definite and sure of his steps.

A fire was soon singing merrily. I was seated at one end, and observed for the first time that the *yantra* appeared to be 'alive'. I observed certain movements in its different sections, mostly done in triangles. Those who know the secret of this *yantra* know how important it is for the invocation of this *yantra* to have the direct assistance from an *alter ego*. (A remarkable evidence of this *yantra* could be seen at Varanasi in the shrine of Kāli worshipped by the famed Tailanga Svāmi).

Time passed. The evening was getting deeper and deeper. The first two hours of the evening were already at an end.

Then gradually I felt a stranger coming up stealthily. As I was watching this quiet approach, involuntarily my eyes turned towards the gates, which remained, as ever, closed, but before I could collect my confused thoughts all on a sudden I became aware of another presence, this time too close to me.

Naturally I received a shock from these inexplicable visions. The surrounding walls were too high for any one to climb and jump unnoticed. No entry was possible through the closed gates, on which I kept my eyes glued: but I found no one making an entry again. Yet on hearing a slight rustling by my side I found the figure of LS sitting in a yogic posture. She had arrived!

I wanted to touch her, and confirm that hers was a physical presence. But I did not dare. I found that I was still only an onlooker. What was being performed remained an act of absolute esoteric rite between a male and a female, both lying on the bare ground, but within the *Śri yantra*.

Any one concerned with this *yantra* knows very well how the male principles are interlocked with the female ones within this adored *yantra*, and how from that single union evolute one after another, like folds and folds of lotus petals, many other triangles all in their own way interlocked. The images of man and the universe, of the universe and the cosmos, of macrocosm gradually presenting the finality of microcosm, all are contained within the design patterned on that single *yantra*.

The female who had been lying on the *yantra* on her back had been covered by the bare body of a male, face to face. Identification at that stage was out of question. The flames were bright; but the mind was not in any shape for looking for identity. Gradually a change in my awareness became perceptible. My conscious being, suddenly gaining a kind of buoyancy, started experiencing a sudden haze, gradually giving way to a semi-lustrous feeling of joy that floated around. A soothingly soft light engulfed all awareness effusing an inspiring *esprit vivre*. The thrilling experience of ascendance was perceptibly overwhelming. In a consuming personalised joy of such singleness who is to pin-point what? Who the recogniser? And who the recognised? Who am I? Where had vanished the sense of 'I'? Without that sense of 'I' how could I have identified that which was not I? Whither had fled the will force that would proceed to identify?

The Sacred Chant: The Sacred Union

I found myself chanting; nay, not chanting alone, but actually visualising the great *mantra*, through a choral fullness.

Ka E Ī La Hrim
Ha Sa Ka La Hrim
Sa Ka La Hrim Śrim . . . .

The chant went on and on and on. Each time the sonic effect came fuller, nearer, arterially warm.

Gradually I saw a great red glow enveloping the identity of all the surrounding distinctions. In that conflagrational redness the 'I' in me swam like a bud thrown on a Niagra of liquid light. Countless morning suns put together could not outshine that brilliance. Yet it was red with a smooth coolness generally associated with sandal paste and the moonshine, the white lily and the touch of a stream of yoghurt. I would never have spoken at length about this feeling; but it was so strange, this feeling of contrariness, of a contradiction, a paradoxical situation in consciousness, that the more I reflect on it today, the more it strikes me as something quite phenomenal.

(And I must confess to another failing. Although I have been trying to portray to the reader the picturesque and vibrant sensation, I find human language to be too ineffectual to describe the thrill with accuracy.)

As far as I knew there was only one more male besides me. He was Mālākar. Who then could be the male in embrace? As I was at it, there floated, as I mentioned, the image of the female presence, the youthful and beautiful presence which spread a captivating aroma. A soft incandescent light bathed the surroundings in orange red. But soon enough still another vision floated up. The former two had now been well postured in a befitting description of *Śavāsana*, the male atop, chin to chin, toe to toe.

The newcomer, yet another female, had been decorated in garlands and floral ornaments. A floral bow was in her hand, and floral arrows too. She also held in her hands the noose and the goad. She had been smiling all along. Taking several firm steps towards the pair, the ethereally emblazoned female form stood on the back of the reversed male. Before I could look at her, I saw two more female forms, equally bedecked, standing on both sides of this fantastic group. A dark blue light from the ground steaming upwards was meeting the red light above. I was dazed to look further, and was about to faint.

I was held up straight into the seated posture. The grips around me were strong and confident. As I settled to a quieter balanced state I wondered whose was the grip.

The touch was unmistakable.

I tore myself from that grip. Something was happening to me and I could no longer allow myself to get so drifted. By what I saw, I felt, I knew that under no circumstance I should lose control of myself. There should be an explanation to all this. To explain is to get steady. These phenomena, whatever they were, must become understandable. They must become essentially mine, a part of me. How long was I to be drifted like this?

The spell broke. I found Mālākar seated alone on the *Śri yantra* and a little apart from him was seated a girl I never knew. The group had vanished.

Mālākar laughed.

"You could not bear it", he said. "I was always telling you that these sensations are real; as real as you and I, and all these are. Or you could say all these were unreal, as you and all these are unreal. Both ways you would be correct. I bring them as I will; and I see them recede from me as I wish. Why these come to me so easy I do not know, but I do know that I am not here for ever. As you have been thoroughly prepared for these rites, and yet as you are still filled with questions, I have brought for you this *prakṛti*. Only do not ask me who she is. She is *prakṛti*, and no more. She would one day explain everything to you. Only I shall not be here too long. She will be for some time more, but that too would not be too long. You only have to come for her, here, or the other two places you know so well.

One the Saraswati temple in Raja Chet Singh's garden on the river bank; and the other the back of the Kāmākṣyā temple. She would be coming to you at the bidding of Saint Jitendra.

"Now let us move . . . ."

In a minute we were out of the garden. Once out, to my utter amazement I found that we were only two. Confused I asked him about the girl.

He laughed and said, "They say I am mad. You see how mad you are. Did I not tell you that she would come whenever you wish. You are not wishing her now. You are wishing something else. Your mind is now asking for explanations. You would have them in time but not her. Mind can have only one thing at a time. Either explanations; or a spiritual *prakṛti*."

The Tragedy

Yes, I had the explanations.

But from my own mentor. She too confirmed that Mālākar was very right. Mālākar, like my old friend Narada, a past master, was born for a short stay with us. None believed him. None took him seriously. He would pass away before his time. But what he had given to me shall remain yet for a while, until . . . .

That 'until' would be my undoing. I was introduced to this most difficult and ancient way of elevating consciousness with the aid of the *prakṛti*. But I failed to keep the boon of *prakṛti*-participation on the subjective level. I got involved in personalised objectivity; in the emotional sub-sphere. I lost my poise. That was a much later accident in my life.

It came rather late; but it came; and with that came my fall. I fell through the mystifying play of *prakṛti*, playing false to my call, to my quest. *Prakṛtis* came to my life in enchanting forms, and that which is strictly forbidden in this path stood in my way. I failed to keep myself detached in the final moment of the union.

Those pseudo *prakṛtis* come, as they do, in the lives of every unfortunate *sādhaka*. They come and cause the 'fall' by tempting through the consuming path of physical craving for a momentary thrill. I forgot that such thrills are always to be consummated only on a spiritual level.

My power took a downward course, and I lost the chance of sending myself up. Let me explain.

Tantra Sādhanā: Will

Tantra or tantric *sādhanā* is not an exercise by itself. It is not the acquisition of cheap powers over the mind, or the body like mesmerism, or occult on the one hand, or like glorified acrobatics, physically motivated skill on the other. Tantric power is acquired through great efforts and strict applications. It calls for assiduous training from an adept who from the position of a guru could command, conduct and regulate the efforts of a disciple who has totally submitted his will at the feet of the guru. "Hellish suffering for those who enter this *circle* with erotic desire in mind", says the Devi Yāmala.

This power, when acquired, makes man live in the light of his inner self. He becomes acquainted with his real nature. He confronts a new world. Nothing in that world answers the accredited laws of the world once known to him. He finds himself a composite phenomenon of several selves, one living within the other, and each having a level of consciousness characteristically different from the other.

It is true that the grades follow a direction from a lower to a higher level; that is to say, rising from a lower state of consciousness. While the lower state of consciousness could only visualise and appreciate the material aspects of things and their values, the highest state of consciousness gets itself free from the limitations of time and place.

It enters a state where all known sets of dimensions give way to a field of specialised appreciation. Then the *sādhaka* is able to comprehend the unseen, the uheard, the untouched, the undying, etc. From the lower stage, where we stand, this highest stage appears to be a traveller's wag, or a blind man's dream; but on actual test this state of consciousness empowers the ordinary man with an extraordinary gift of doing things which the ordinary man cannot do, functioning in a manner which could go quite contrary to all known natural laws.

Such exercise of power makes us look into the so-called laws of material science from a new angle. Scepticism about facts held *unscientific* becomes gradually relaxed, and we make new enquiries into the mysteries of the unknown.

Of course all this depends on the revelation of novel sources of power; it is another kind of power stronger than what we draw from physical laws. Not fire, steam, water, electricity, oil, gas, etc., but power from soul, power from 'Grace', power from the unseen fountain of all power.

But at the source of all power there is the property of *rajas*, which is potential heat, liable to be generated through a friction of the forces of the *opposites*. There is no heat (*rajas*) without friction. There is no friction without 'two'.

The tantriks had known this secret for over hoary centuries. They called the opposites *Puruṣa* and *Prakṛti*, the male force and the female force. Science calls them now negative and positive. They also found that the mind of man is primarily charged with the power of consciousness (*cit*) without which no knowledge would be of any value or effect. Nose alone will not do; the power to smell is required. Eyes alone will not do; the power to see is essential. Muscles and bones and joints alone will not do; but the will, the purpose, the effort to move them is called for.

As a source of power *will* is of the essence. Tantra cultivated this power of *will* and called it the *mother* power. Not the limbs, not the body machine, not the outer world with which this body-machine is related, but the will, and the motive behind the will is the primal power of movement that prompts the individual to come into or get into contact with the outer world. How far *out* is that '*out*' depends on the extension of the individual's personality.

Tantra thus sets the personality of the individual on an unlimited and eternal journey through mental space. It is difficult to believe it; more difficult to accept it; but once accepted and exercised upon, the results themselves continue proving the facts with emphatic eloquence. Tantra is practical. Theory works very little for tantra. Theoretical tantra is helpful to understand, but the power in tantra could be acquired through practice alone.

The source of this power as we know is *kulakuṇḍalinī*. A number of books attempting explanations of this power even from biological, anatomical and 'scientific' points of view have flooded the market. These books are loaded with technical jargons and psychoanalytical explanations.

The mere fact that they sound 'scientific', that they are couched in a jargon beyond our need, or beyond our comprehension, makes us believe in their authenticity and plausibility. A host of proper names mentioned like (Freud, Jung, Blavatsky, Laughlin, Weiss, Ellenburger, Adler, Lazarus etc.) pressurise whatever *theories* these Western wonder-books mean for the readers to swallow. Most of this Ideology is consumed in the name of the scientific. Because *kulakuṇḍalinī* is the source of the power of consciousness, *cit*, we shall attempt to deal with it from the point of view of consciousness alone.

The Futile Scramble for 'Yet More'

Years have floated past since Varanasi. I was no longer the simple boy who had accepted LS with a free mind. My mind had grown complex. Like the changes in the shapes of boulders knocked down by glaciers and torrents into the stream of the Ganges, my thought pebbles could hardly be related now to their original simplicity. The instructions of LS did not convince my sceptic stand any more. Sophistication, and what is worse, book-learning (what learning!) prevented me to appreciate the simple beauty of those poised words of wisdom. Images had changed; imageries had changed. Words had got heavier; thoughts had grown more involved. The sheer ravages of time had rendered my memory, once photographic, now almost opaque; and seeing through clearly had become a hazardous undertaking. But the sculptured engravings of profound experiences remained true, fast and loyal to form. The contents remained as cogent as when they had appealed to a youth's mind. *Quest for the Unknown* having been a challenging adventure in spirit I had never tired of sacrificing every other thing to the discourses of LS, whose words, now although disjointedly, often knock within my brain.

There was a time when I had been very much exercised by enquiries on sex, and sex exercises; the sacrifice of the sexual *longing* to the *dedication* of the sex offerings posed no problems at all. I had learnt from that time that if man has to create, he must know what is he going to create. Else, 'hold' is the word. Do not create the haphazard, the unwanted, the imperfect. Do not address the pure soul to the devil of dross.

True it is that the primary founction of life is to propagate life. But how many of us are mechanically and dutifully so fitted as simple animals are, for accepting sex as a natural function for procreation and nothing more? How many view sex as a mechanism for serving nature's purpose? Instead, prompted and goaded by ego, we run to sex with the urge of Eros. We gravitate around this source in lustful scrambling, and look for the leftover moments of immediate and forbidden joy, (forbidden by nature; forbidden by nurture; forbidden by utility and usage). No wonder that we find ourselves impoverished and hungry scramblers, screaming for more and still more. We never remember that the source of all the wealth of energy and eternal life could enrich us only if we cared to halt the scramble, and attended to the higher purposes of our real calling. We would, if only we could, live sexually as men second, but animals first; for animals neither rape, nor lust for unions in and out of seasons.

This I had learnt from LS; and that at an early age. I knew of the human body and its function quite in a different light. That could have been the reason perhaps why she had imparted to me all that she could; and today I am trying to expose the mystic knowledge to those who care. This knowledge has been taboo by the wise as their most secret knowledge. This knowledge has thrown around it so many guarding fences, so many restrictions. It is filled with so many restrictions. It is filled with so many pitfalls. Once fallen, the dark abyssmal pit would suck in a man's personality, mind, memory, senses and everything.

Yet I am revealing what is regarded as a heinous transgression to reveal. I know in this I have her support. I shall give all: yet not *all.* Something shall have to be kept back; and that something has to be essentially very personal.

Sex-dens with Borrowed Haloes

I have seen in India in some of the so called *āśramas* of some of the very popularised and advertised yogis, where youth grovel in the mire of utter degradation. In the quest of extra sensory transcendental experience hundreds have licked the dusts, gone berserk, and have been subject to humiliations which could have been spared to the blossoms of a generation which needed fruits and seeds for posterity; but which have become moth eaten even before the cells of perfumes got matured.

Life is a Dead Song

During one of my journeys through Europe in West Germany (Kassel) a mother put before me a magazine reporting photographic evidence of what had been taking place in one of the popularised *āśramas* in India. She pointed out to one of the photographs, and screamed. "You see; that could have been my own daughter. And I know of one whose son has died, God knows where, in some part of Nepal, trying the clammed hell of a *kuṇḍalinī.* Whatever that might mean. I hope I do not injure your feelings . . . ."

The large spacious hall in the photograph was filled with youths (males as well as females) in the nude; all of them were in a semi-somnambular, semi-psychic state of consciousness. A few had been totally unconscious; while some others were trying to revive them. Some were probably screaming wild, as was evident from their wild looks, shooting eyes and painful contortions. Obviously they had been under the grip of hallucination induced by dangerous drugs. Almost all of them were non-Indians, mostly whites. The figures reminded one of the Bacchaic scenes recorded in Greek and Indian sculptures; or of the crowd of the damned on Rodin's gate.

What did they go for? What did they lack in their own white lands? To what did they make such a supreme sacrifice? What have they achieved? Why had their own world failed them? How far their quests and longings spring from their roots, from their inner consciousness? What new meaning for life they wanted to discover?

I ask and ask. The questions screamed out of me. LS, oh LS why are you so dumb about this? Why don't you guide?

There must be an answer. If the answer is not provided despite all our much inflated scientific achievements, life itself would remain a hollow bombastic scream in a wasteland where no sun rises, and a fierce fiery wind howls and howls.

On the banks of the Ganges at Varanasi, on the dusts of Brindavan, on the tucked away beaches of Goa, in the ravines of Nepal, Sikkim and Bhutan, even in the underworld lanes of Bombay, Jaipur, Delhi and Calcutta youths of prosperous Europe, Australia, Canada, USA languish in decay of body and soul. Their newborn random harvests of love and chance, hang in baskets they symbolically bear on their backs. And they track, rove, play along the dusty streets in rubber beach slippers, making an arid and addled picture amidst a lively and contained populace.

I wonder what that unlucky basket contains? A future for man, or a carcass from the past? What are they looking for? What do they really find?

The sensitive suffers. These youths also suffer. And the answer to their suffering lies through their coming to an understanding with the meaning and purpose of life, and the steady and unbroken work with devotion. This is the way to achieve some meaningfulness that would provide them with a final home for their soul to taste peace. Life is a dead song without achievement; how to achieve the meaningfulness of life is the intimate subject matter of tantra. To analyse is to understand, and understanding is the beginning of solution. Understanding is the budding of Love.

Hence the caution before I speak. There is no miracle in this knowledge; there is no real mystery. It is so logical, so obvious, so cogent that it could be followed even as a theory easily. Danger comes at the stage of practice. Before entering the deep waters of the Pacific for a swim across, one must prepare in so many ways the mind, the body, the brain, the emotions. In eating, sleeping, walking, exercising, hearing, smelling, loving, understanding, seeing, dreaming, thinking, discipline first, discipline second, discipline third This is the preparation. Tantra practice is like playing with live poisonous cobras, as has been said and could be repeated a thousand times. It is an exposed live mire of a thousand volts. Caution in this field cannot be too much.

This period of discipline cannot be short-cut. It has to take its full course. If that sacrifice of time and energy becomes impossible, then the practice of tantra is not *to be undertaken.*

Through some accidental play of luck and fate I was accepted by LS. Because I had kept close to her, body to body, and skin to skin, I had received from her the lessons in direct form. If I have gone in my later life, from yogi to yogi, adept to adept, pilgrimage to pilgrimage, it was not because I was lost to my way, nor because I was in search of other sensational feats; it was because the joy of the tantric spirit is an irresistible joy. It is inherent in the spirit of that joy that adepts would call and invite and respond. Tantra forms sacred esoteric brotherhood. It builds a family. It establishes a 'club' like a drinking club, a bridge club, a Free Mason Lodge. The tantrik is neither alone, nor selfish.

Why Meditate: Ojas

It is from LS I first learnt (of course as answer to my queries) why we meditate. Of course it has been answered before and more easily, too. But speaking in depth we have to refer to some special type of rhythmic, subtle agitations that help us maintain the equilibrium of the thinking mind. It is this rhythm that keeps the body at peace and the mind tranquil. Many refer to it as Alpha rhythm.

What they mean by it I cannot fully explain. But we know it as *ojas*. The total units of *ojas* a full human life cycle could form and utilise has been measured as 3, when 100 units of *ojas* take human consciousness to the supreme state of *kaivalya*, or transcendental bliss, from where all power flows. Tantra-pursuits supply these fugitive units; and a single life cycle might not be enough to collect it.

Meditation is a process by which this rhythm of *ojas* is daily, hourly and momently kept at a perpetual state of regular beat; and some like the Zen, keep the eyes fixed on objectives; and some like the tantriks keep the vision fixed between the brows, and wait for the *opening* of the third eye. When it does, the inner being of the meditator is flooded with an effulgent aura of purest delight.

Such meditative balance completely controls all conditional reflexes. Pain or suffering apart, such tantric meditations ultimately help control gravitational effects, retinal movements, heart spasms and breathing, even sudden muscular failures, and assist healings. There is an evidence from a Western researcher that he has himself seen a Lama in Tibet covering 300 miles on the roof of the world in 30 hours. Many have seen people covering impossible distances as if on wings. I had seen that spectacle in going to Amarnath, which I have described before.

Many wonder how the *yogins* in the snowy Himalayas keep warm without fire or cover. LS did not wonder. She explained that the body in its subtlest form is composed of that shape of matter which we cannot see. There is a process of perpetual 'cooking' of these subtle forms of matter. She called them *renu* or *anu*, which come into being and disintegrate like so many floating bubbles. The only difference between the nature of bubbles and the *anus* is that *anus* have the tendency of keeping clung together; they never stay alone in singleness, neither do they remain still. Each time they burst, they transmit heat. The adept keeps concentrating on this process within his body. As this is maintained, it ultimately reaches the source of all heat and energy. And then he keeps his body out of all decay or suffering from external changes of heat and cold. Power in the field of Life comes from the mutation of these *anus*, through our breath intake. These *anus*, are as heated and powerful, (within their own limits) as the sun and the sun-spots. What the sun is to the universe, an *anu* is to the individual life form.

I have made further enquiries about what I state from some physicists; and they felt wonderstruck through what they heard. They informed me that the contention of LS totally agrees in principle with the theory of ionisation of air, and of the formation of electrons from intake of oxygen etc., which I myself have not understood too much. All I understood was the fact that somewhere modern science sees what my LS sees, and tantra proposes.

LS and Her Science

In recalling this phenomenon today, as described by LS, I become aware of two other associated ideas. The first of these concerns a reference to the Hindu ancient myths which describe a set of, what they call, innumerable 'spiritual' *ascetics*, who are supposed to be *too small to be seen, too numerous to be accounted for, and too much associated with the solar agitation* and with the solar 'sacrificial fire' (sun-spots), so that they are described as 'the children of the sun'. By nature they are described as volatile, provocative, agitated and bad tempered, although their inner nature is saturated with the grace of doing good. These are mythically called the *vālakhilyas* (always in the plural). Along with such characteristics as agitation, speed, discharge, of electric power, vitality and cosmic knowledge, they have the added quality of invisibility. One of the most remarkable qualities of the *vālakhilyas*, which makes them distinct is that even God stands in 'fear' of these, and 'grants' them the pride of the first place. Gods may change but not the *vālakhilyas*. Ideas may change, but not the Principle.

(I wonder how the description, and the purpose they serve, fit in with the description of the atomic structure.)

The second aspect that intrigues me about the description of *ojas* by LS concerns modern physics, and the knowledge it has revealed to the 'scientists' ever since Einstein, Bose and Eddington. The entire concept of space and time, the concept of Euclidian geometry has undergone so categorical a change that the universe could no longer be described but by certain abstract signs, conveying inlaid meanings. When I consider these aspects of what is science, and what is mathematics and physics and astronomy, I take a second look at what LS had said about the human body, the generating and dissolving rhythms of such cellular balances which involve even the intellectual personality of man. What a magnetic field is this body of man! What are its potentials! What its possibilities! One has only to grasp it. Having grasped, one has to engage oneself towards evoluting one's own self to the highest state of consciousness, which achieved, man could become a superman, like Kṛṣṇa, Chirst, Zarathustra.

This body of man has enough power stored within itself. All its organs have been dulled by misuse and unuse. This accounts for the changes in sensitivity from individual to individual, and from the tribals to the 'civilised'. I am now learning to accept the fact that the civilised have successfully rendered their own organs incapacitated through abuse, misuse and unuse. With a pinch of some chemical, some drug, the civilised add acuteness and sharpness to their senses, and induce hypnosis, transcendence, etc., powers acquired temporarily, again just to indulge, to dissipate, to smother the natural potentialities of their organ. Cats play with their own tails. Children derive creative pleasure by floating bubbles in the air. Men make a game of themselves.

How true was LS; now I realise. I have now discovered from readings of some experimental findings in the Boston City Hospital that drugs and meditation could be connected by the following physical changes in the organism of man.

Under the influence of psychedelic drugs there is an immediate and sharp increase in the Alpha rhythm which could be registered in man. It is a vibrational rhythm created by radioactive substances, as in Helium gas. Because of the fact that the body of man is under the constant active agitation created by the forces of transmission and mutation, the radioactive principles and the resultant Alpha rhythms influence man's higher and subtler personality.

The use of drugs brings about a decrease in breathing rate, which leads the body to consume limited oxygen. This partially explains how yogis survive on the altitudes of the Himalayas.

A decrease in breathing rate, as well as a decrease in blood pressure have also been observed by the experiment referred to above. An increase in the electric resistance of the skin is another observation recorded. But the most significant observation refers to the dramatic fall in the level of lactate in the blood.

The sad aspect of Western materialism is that it always puts to test the spiritual findings of the East in the crucible of science with a view to explode their credibility. It accepts truth as truth only after casting the findings of the eastern mystics in their set moulds which are unfortunately limited to the interaction of chemistry, chemical processes; and these are yet not fully discovered. We can discover only that which exists; but we cannot adduce any justification to the hows and whys of that existence. Could we? Not always. Mysticism assists there; and so far, we have been noticing, what mysticism explains in its own way is accepted by the Western method as probabilities; they are enslaved to their *scientific* researches. Most 'seers' in science are unaware of their blindness.

LS did not know modern science. Neither did the simple Mālākar. Yet the vision and the depth of experiences, the range and the scope of their information astound me even after the passage of all these years. I could not ignore them despite their lack of scientific training.

Mālākar Leaves for the Beyond

Until Mālākar died under very strange circumstances I used to keep his company. We used to sit at *āsana* on certain nights of the dark fortnight at the Sarasvatī temple of Chet Singh gardens. Every time the apparition of the same girl came: every time there was the full quota of three *prakṛtis*. This was entirely due to Mālākar's personal intervention. At times I saw LS there: and having seen her I felt quite free to do what I did.

Mālākar did not 'die'. He had formally *taken leave* of his mother. He sat in his usual praying room, on his *āsana* alone. His mother found his lifeless body stretched on his *āsana*. According to the usual concept of death this '*taking leave*' and abandoning body for further space journey sounds rather phony.

I learnt of his death from a follower of Saint Jitendra.

When I reached Mālākar's house I found there a number of his school-mates, besides the usual collection of the relations, most of whom had been lamenting the early death of a *spiritual soul*. (Now they recognised that in the mad world he alone lived with sanity.)

But not his mother. "He came to me to bless this home", she said. "We did not accept him. So why lament now? He had done his duty by me; and from me he would never be separated. I believe what he has promised to me."

I was so surprised at the way she had accepted the grief of a son's death. I realised the meaning of the great verse in the Gitā: *those who fall from this yoga are again born in homes of their own kind, a clean and well provided home . . . .*

There were others there. LS, and Saint Jiten and our homely Gopīnāth Dādā, who had made a name all over the world both for his erudition and for his yogic abilities. Gopī Dādā had been an ardent admirer of Mālākar. He used to narrate many anecdotes of his association with Mālākar, who, he said, always confided to him his experiences of the great celestial journeys.

Suddenly Saint Jiten left all of us alone, and in his own special way began to dance crying *ma-ma-ma!* He was quite known for these 'mad' dances, Quite unexpectedly he pulled my hand, and began to dance with me almost hooked within his left arm. An electric current passed through my being. I held his two hands, and went round and round, until I felt I could not take that any more. I was fast losing my sense. I felt faint. If LS had not held me high, and sang her favourite tune to keep my spirits high, I would decidedly have fainted.

From then on I kept nearer Saint Jitendra. He had been my childhood friend; and he still took me for a child, and he himself appeared to become a child when near me.

He had been a famed yogi now. It was said that he could perform miracles. I myself had been the cause of having him perform some minor 'miracles' for me. Whether he could perform miracles may not be to the point; but he himself was a miracle. The ease with which he used to anticipate questions, and provide answers for them, would make any one believe that he was indeed a great thought reader. The immediate pull of his magnetic draw (and I learnt from others, he used to draw his favoured ones) could make one believe in his mesmeric powers. The ease and felicity with which he sang his songs, talked to cats and birds, anticipated rats and lizards, corresponded with crows and kites would make one accept that he had been a past master in ventriloquism, and more. He looked and behaved every inch as an old seaman from a Nordic saga. (Oh! I loved that man!)

But he had been above all a marvellous exponent of curious gimmics, of miracles and games of cheap popularity.

As was the person whom even he adored.

Purwā Bābā

This was the famous Purwā Bābā. (*Purwā* in local Hindi of Varanasi means a clay terracota cup.) He was given that name from a strange fact. He was a dumb man for all practical purposes. The only sound I or anyone else had heard from him during my experience of about twenty years was a sudden hysteric outburst of *kwaon kwaon kwaon kwaon*, half-puppy and half-peacock sounded through the nose. It was a mixture of complaint and protest against the teasing hordes of urchins who often disturbed him too much.

There was reason.

Bābā used to keep seated on a neglected piece of broken stone projection near a public stand pipe at the junction of the Viśwanātha lane and the Bhūteśvara lane. It is a very important, and the most frequented spot in Varanasi. Millions would churn around the place on days of festivity. But since the corner, where he sat, was close to a municipal garbage dump, none went near and none would waste a look on it. He was thus taken for a part of the garbage, and totally neglected for a demented reject.

This would be the way of the Aghorīs. These are the *piśāca siddhas* (adepts in control of the forces of the dark world of the greedy and the blood thirsty). They do not communicate. People left offerings for him; and the urchins found him a mine of little gains. They came; they saw; they robbcd; and ultimately they teased the mindless(?) fellow. Unaccountable generosity of man is always taken for madness. Then he screamed helplessly; and the urchins fled helter skelter, laughing, as if in their victorious glee. I am sure this was a game he wilfully played with the children whom he liked to come near him and to entertain. For the urchins he had been a game.

A shallow rainwater drain passed in front. In the evening a fire would be lit on the stone-paved drain itself, as if it were a hearth; and a meal of rice and vegetables, all mixed together would be cooked in a large earthen pot by some of the shopkeepers around. A crowd of hungry men, and a pack of dogs would wait for the meal. The rice, the vegetables, the wood and the pot itself all came out of daily donations from the people around. They took Bābā for the greatest of the great. But when the meal time came he would, once in a while, condescend to take a handful, thrusting his bare hand into the boiling pot, and lick up what came by just like that, without ever bothering to wash his hands before or after. I have seen his messed up hands being greedily licked by the street dogs! Often he would share with them the licking. The rest of the food would be distributed equally between men and dogs. At the end everything, the pot, the wood and all signs of the cooking went to the garbage.

But not the small earthen drinking pot in which people offered him milk. He took sips occasionally, but the dogs lived a great life. The pots were carefully preserved by him near his head, as if these were his treasures. The least attempt to dislodge any of these would provoke him to immense rage.

I am still at a loss if this was his way to underline a commentary on the values of material possessions for which men keep a guard like dogs on bones.

And this speciality brought him the title of Purwā Bābā the 'cup saint'.

This reminds me of an African shoemaker (retired) in Trinidad who lived in a rented two-room tenament on the ground floor. He lived actually under the porch, because the two rooms were filled with empty beer bottles. As soon as a bottle was emptied, without much ado he would throw it over his shoulders and dinn! it would go into the heap. Each time he would remark "That's how the emptied make a heap, and much noise, ending in what? Rubbish!"

The Aghorī and the Dogs

During my travels in Kanya Kumari (Cape Comorin) in 1977 I met with an Aghori. He had a whole pack of dogs following him wherever he went. In the evening he would stand by the sea, where the charms of the magnificent sunset brought every day hundreds of tourists. People around the Aghori would light a fire about the time for sunset, make a hearth of stones, and boil rice with fish and vegetables together.

He had been under a vow of silence for more than forty years of his stay in Kanya Kumari and would watch over the proceedings. When the dogs and the men were fed, he would vanish away. None would follow him.

I wanted to. But I do not remember how he got lost to my sight. Seated on the dark and lonely beach I was reflecting on this case; even at my nightly *āsana*. Next day at noon I was passing through a wilderness; and there he was, standing before me, not even two feet away; and smiling. 'Namah Śivaya', I said. 'Namah Śivaya', he replied, though his eyes smiled again. I walked on; after three or four steps I looked back. He was gone.

This is the way of Aghorīs. They move about, and never halt.

In the hotel at night I became restless. The great sea at the land's end of India lashed against the rocks. The sound of the surf added to my restlessness. I came out, and stood under the sky where the casuarina trees, like sentinels, were standing against the lashing sea winds. A grove of delicate frangipani breathed the exotic fragrance of its Mexican ancestry. My mind carried away from the surroundings, was again and again going back to the old man with the dogs. I went back to the actual place where the embers from a smouldering fire still breathed with the puffs of wind. A few boatmen were sitting together and drinking. I gathered from them the fact that the ritual had been going on without a single day's break for the last twenty years, and more. No one else was around. I felt so lonely.

There was a straight record of 63 years for that yogi, and all the time the man had been as old as now.

This was nothing new to me. Credibility of such rather unnatural(?) events depends much on the credulity of the listener. But credulity is often the target of ridicule from those who have got themselves enslaved to what they call logic, or rationality. Every day in life things happen for which no reason offers any explanation. The nature of rationality, scientific thinking etc., undergo changes every now and then. Such changes have been taking place with such fundamental phenomenon as the shape of the earth, the locus of planetary movements, the shape and nature of time, the origin of species, to name just a few. Yet when we are confronted with perfectly verifiable events for which science or experience cannot offer an explanation, the sneer of the incredulous is ready to contest veracity.

Phut-Phut Bābā

I remember a winter night in Varanasi. It was drizzling. The winter monsoon was taking a toll of almost freezing human beings and cattle in northern India. My mind kept busy under the cotton-stuffed quilt about Phut-Phut Bābā.

He had been an ancient man occupying a seat near a fire on the banks of the Ganges at Dasaswamedh Ghat, and opposite to the marble statue of another yogi. Day and night he made the puffing sound with his mouth, 'phoot-phoot-phoot-phoot' at the rate of two in three seconds. Later I learnt from *prāṇāyāma* lessons that this was one of the classical forms of *recaka prāṇāyāma*.

Even in Varanasi, he was considered to be a spiritual person, of a very high order, obviously, because of his weird practice. He had nothing much to say to the people. He was as good as a dumb freak. Suddenly the entire town looked amazed at a special event.

The Ganges was in floods. In every eleven or twelve years the monsoon flood at Varanasi reaches unusual levels merging a good bit of the town. Phut Phut Bābā's seat was within the danger mark of the flood level. The people around were eager to afford Bābā a safe place to remove his seat and the fire pit. The old man would not hear of it, although it was the dreaded eleventh year.

A day came when the water touched his stone seat; one inch more and the fire would be out; and the seat would be merged. But nothing further happened. Bābā did not have to change his seat. The water stopped there; and the town stood amazed at this. (Easily explained as a case of coincidence!)

Somehow Bābā just knew when the water would stop rising: for in certain years much before the monsoons Bābā would casually change his seat to a higher place, but near to where he used to sit.

That winter night I decided to have a look at the naked Bābā, who had only a little fire to protect him. The sound 'phoot-phoot-phoot' was clearly audible through the still night. I came near the seat, and stood by, looking at him. He had been alone, but to all appearances he even did not notice me.

I saw what I had come to see; my credulity came to an end. But what of the sceptics? Would they stir out of their beds?

I went back to the safer and more comfortable security of my quilts.

Credibility of such events depends only on those records which people have to report from experience. But then these reports are brought to a thousand other points of scrutiny. To 'prove' something incredible is a reverse type of mental function born of perverted ego.

I am not too keen on bringing home to the incredulous the logic of credulity. I have been, and still am, dependent on my experiences. This is one of the reasons that I meticulously avoid all types of drugs and alcohol.

To continue with my experience at Kanya Kumari.

The next day at Kanya Kumari had been a wet day. From about four in the afternoon the rain was heavy. I went out of my hotel, and wanted to experience the fire-ritual of the Bhairava of the dogs. It would be funny to watch a cook busy cooking on the beach lighting a fire under that heavy rain.

Armed with an umbrella, and protected within a good English raincoat I found myself at the site. I had noticed the smoke from the distance; but I expected the fire to burn under some sort of temporary shelter. But no. The expectant team of dogs kept seated around. The few devotees were busy cooking, and the Bhairava was standing with solemn unconcern, just as an indifferent onlooker. However incredible it might sound my duty here is to record what I had witnessed.

Amidst all the shatterings of the foul weather; that area of the beach, where the drama was taking place, remained bone dry. None was using an umbrella; no other shelter, or any ghost of it, was even conceived of. The team merrily was busy doing what it did every day. Incredible? Granted. But I had witnessed it all the same.

The Aghoris

The Aghoris never cease to amaze me. Whether they are the Bhairavas, or the Bhairavis, or the Nāthas or the Pāśupatas (different spiritual sects differing in their subtle forms and rites, but one and the same in principle), they and their ways fascinate me much more than the other calmer types of spiritualists, who answer to the expectations of the sophisticated. I have found that the Aghorīs are much more stringent and demanding in their forms of self-control. They look fearsome; they keep an exterior garb of anger and bad temper; but these are their protective shields, as is their habit of smearing the body with ash, keeping naked, wearing the heavy locks, occasionally having live serpents with them (as are mascots adored) and finally, they always seek weird places like crematory grounds, cemeteries and garbage dumps as their favourite abodes. They appear to be the spiritual editions of the modern hippies.

We have spoken of the Nātha yogi who played with the flutes; we have spoken of Govinda Pandit and the pundit who performed the Tārā prayers; we have spoken of the Bhairava who was found drinking his own urine, and the one I met at the cremation of my sister. Yes, they are a queer lot. My great friend of the Bhairavanātha temple, the one who conducted the seance at the Kāmākṣyā shrine, along with auntie, and even LS, appear to me as belonging to one sacred and mighty tribe. I worship their memory.

So was the saint Jitendra. He was indeed a Bhairava, although many did not accept this. Most Bhairavas are what they are; the real truth is known to them alone. "The Śakti followers are adepts in secrecy; the Śaivas are known from the signs; and the Vaiṣṇavas are recognisable from their manners . . ." says the adage. Friend Nārada was a great Vaiṣṇava.

But of all the Bhairavas I have seen at close quarters none surpassed in causing me so much surprise as did Purwā Bābā. He was not only a Bhairava, but a *piśāca siddha*, which means that he had very direct rapport with the world of the 'dead'. The spirits, they concede, are all about us hanging around, and protecting us; but which could cause us terror, harm, even violent death, if uselessly disturbed by selfish invocations. *Piśācas* are those unbodied spiritual beings who survive on the dead and the dead bodies, human or otherwise. Such is the crude belief. But there are more things to be known about them. Remember the *siddha* at Maṇikarṇikā at the cremation of my sister? Terrible! Isn't it?

If we know about Purwā Bābā we would understand Saint Jitendra and his predicament much more. Let us wait until we know a little about Purwā Bābā.

I shall describe only one incident.

This came in the month of *Baisakh* (May-June). With a party of four friends I was passing through the familiar lane, when I became conscious of a most inviting fragrance of fresh jasmines. The smell alerted me. I looked back. Bright lights, and an unaccountable assemblage at the distance attracted me. My friends laughed at my interest, and remarked about my fits of saint hunt. None the less I had to go.

And I came to the spot, where I found the old saint seated, in the lotus posture and apparently without life. None could dare declare for sure if he was indeed dead. There have been instances before of signs of apparent death inclusive of the stoppage of heart beat in a person who was really in the extreme trance, or *kaivalya samādhi.* This is induced by *kumbhaka.* (Incidentally this is one of the many reasons why a good Hindu hesitates to accept the death of Jesus on cross; or in other words why he does not find it difficult to understand that Jesus must have been still alive when his body was taken down from the cross, and removed to a hidden place for special attention. One must pardon this incredulity of the Hindu, who does not suffer from any hangover about legends of Osirian or Mithraic origin, about accepting death in a few hours on an instrument of torture of so great a saint and master as Jesus, the soul of all saintliness.)

They were waiting on expert verdict. It came in about two days, during which the body remained in the lotus *āsana* without any appreciable change in it. Thereafter the body was pronounced to be without life, placed into a stone box, and immersed in the Ganges.

Saint Jiten was one of those saints who were called to pronounce on the Bābā's passing away. He had been a constant follower of that *piśāca siddha* Aghora *yogin.* Another of those who had pronounced the death was my Gopī Dādā.

I could quote other instances to show the degree of Saint Jitendra's high calibre. But these are not necessary for our narrative. We have seen him at the Yogeśhwari wood; we have seen him at the Kāmākṣya-Maṭh. And now we shall see him as the *alter ego* of this virgin whom I had met at that session in Pātāleśwar. This I reserve for the next chapter.

12

Moth for the Star

A Saint's Companion

From my childhood I was close to Saint Jitendra. But time, as also the sudden disappearance of the Saint from Varanasi kept me out of touch with him; and with that had gone that constant vibration which signalled my deep affinity towards him.

But in later years a small coterie of select brotherhood grew around the saint; and most of the members were known to me, although they were not aware of my special and intimate contacts with him. Proving the past is a dissipation of ego; it is the future that a man of efforts desires proving.

Through the association of this brotherhood I had come to know of certain developments in the life of the saint. A chance reference by one of them to the latest persuasions of the saint made me get deeper into the hide-out where he had made his *āśrama*. The followers, just a few, used to assemble there.

On the very first evening of my new attempt I found a famous vocalist singing to the delight of a sizeable audience, and to the delight of the saint. He was almost smothered with nosegays of jasmines. The exotic aroma of burning joss-sticks floated in the air. I was trying to make myself as much invisible as possible, and kept crouching in the corner, opposite to where the saint had been sitting, surrounded by close attendants.

Devotion and service are the two facets of the same coin of close friendliness. Service becomes a lifeless routine without the tender touch of devotion. Without service devotion becomes pampering and sentimental. Saints anywhere must be attended to, physically that is; they are too unmindful of their physical needs; and although suffering means nothing much to them, continued neglect of attention to the body could wear out the physical frame.

Besides these two attendants I also noticed a young girl of about 14 (I could not really judge her age. Though she looked well built, she appeared to be just a cuddling plaything); she was sitting not only close to him; but she had been almost sharing his *āsana*.

Sharing the *āsana* of a yogi is a very serious thing. I have spoken of the Nātha yogis before. These, the Vaiṣṇava Bāuls and Bairāgis, the Bhairavas hardly ever prosecute their ways without the closest association of an *alter ego*. Keeping company with the opposite sex is as much of importance to them as keeping fire near them, although it means to them, as to all *sādhakas*, keeping association with poisonous snakes.

Āsana

Sharing the *āsana* of a yogi is a very special privilege. The *āsana* of a yogi is a consecrated object; and in most cases it has been consecrated by the guru at the hour of initiation; and often it is inherited from the guru. In the esoteric world an *āsana*, a *kamaṇḍalu* (hanging water jar that a yogi is never without), and a stick are the constant companions of the man who has embraced the life of yoga.

Saint Jiten was an *avadhūta* and as an *avadhūta* he had to care very little for these strictures. Yet an *āsana*, is an *āsana*, and cannot be even touched by the laity who have not been duly canonised. It is too personal an object to be shared by any member of the commune.

I remember an incident.

The Daṇḍi Swamins of Varanasi

This happened when I was a boy. It happened in one of the Śankarārārya monasteries in Varanasi. The monastery is still there, situated close to the Kālī temple at Dasasvamedh. Swamis known as *daṇḍīs*, from their habit of carrying a daṇḍa, a flagged stick in their hand, mostly devoted to personal penances and propagation of Vedantic learning, and practice of yoga as enjoined by the great Śankarācārya, lived there. Once they take the vow, they change their name; never go back to their past; never refer to their caste, or relations; and remain steady to their pursuits until they die. Each one of them respond to the call Nārāyaṇa (God) by replying Nārāyaṇa.

For their living they depend on 'chance' food. They do not go about begging. At noon they would go out and call at only three places (and no more) their plaintive cry 'narāyaṇa, narāyaṇa, narāyaṇa' three times. If in this way no response comes within the limited nine cries in three houses the poor crier has to go without the only meal he could have for the day. They are not supposed to visit the same locality again and again.

They only accept cooked food for immediate meals. Irrespective of what is offered, salt, bitter, hot, sour, sweet—they usually mix up the whole lot in one amalgam, and *offer it to their body* in the process of offering *havi* to the sacrificial fire. They do so with a significant chant which I remember, as I, myself recite that every time I eat or drink.

Brahmā-rpaṇam, Brahma havir
Brahmāgnau Brahmaṇā hutam,
Brahmaiva tena gantavyam
Brahma karma samādhinā.

(What is for offer is Brahma; the offering is Brahma; the fire offered into is Brahma; the one who is offering is Brahma; the offerings reach Brahma for the fulfilment of Brahma's peace.)

A *daṇḍī* does not comment on his food; he does not thank or participate in any social formalities: but blesses the home where he has been, even if he has to go back empty handed. He does not accept money.

I am used to seeing them, and entertaining them ever since I know myself. Once my mother had the luck of offering food specially prepared for a very old *svāmin*. From our home we always had to leave requests at the monastery for a *daṇḍī* to grace our home at lunch. We of course mentioned the number we expected to entertain. Accordingly they could pay their visit at the appointed hour.

On this particular day the old *daṇḍī svāmin* came. My mother washed his feet duly, and wiped the same with a new saffron coloured cotton towel. This and a coloured piece of loin-cloth and a new straw *āsana* with new earthen water jar were the *svāmī*'s ensemble before he could sit down to partake of the meal.

After the *svāmi* had left we discovered, when we ate, that the entire food was terribly bitter to taste. This accident had happened because the salt used was grinded the previous night by our servant on the mortar slab on which, immediately before his use, without his knowledge, someone else had grinded the bitter leaves of neem (*melia azadirachta*) for preparing a medicine.

But the *svāmī* had not even made a grimace; and throughout the meal, and after, maintained his usual cheer.

These were the *daṇḍī svāmins*; and I was close to them, and their monastery.

A Tiger Fight

On a noon day having nothing else to do I had decided to visit the monastery, if not for anything particular, just to listen to the discourses in Sanskrit, where the old chief of the *maṭha* (monastery) used to teach the anchorites.

On that day I found the place strangely silent. None was about. I had no idea that on that new moon day, which was also a Monday the monks were busy in a day-long special penance.

I found the place quiet. No one was about. My eyes fell on the well spread out *āsana* arranged cosily in the south-eastern corner of the long veranda. It was a low, wooden platform, spread over by carpets. The most interesting feature of this secluded and solemn *āsana* was a large tiger skin with the two glass eyeballs staring out of a very large head which was not exactly wearing a welcome smile. This skin with a head was spread over the carpet.

I was hardly eight years at the time; and I have been accustomed to looking at this tiger head from a respectable distance. I had never had the opportunity to have crossed the rubicon of this sanctum sanctorum. Stealthily I advanced towards the tiger; and soon had the head under my armpit. I imagined to be throttling it with all my might. A tiger fight was in progress and I was proving to be much too stronger for the poor tiger without a body.

The great fight went on and on; and all the time I was on the sacred *āsana*. How long I had fought I have no recollection, until I was awakened by a strange din.

The entire monastery had assembled near the *āsana*; and the members were staring at the daring impunity of a mere lad of eight, who had committed the supreme sacrilege of having ridden on the *āsana*, and even falling into sleep there. The sanctified heirloom had been demanding for ages regular worship from the inmates of the *āśrama*, that *āsana* having been used by (so it was reputed) no less a person than the great Śankara himself.

In the eyes of the horrified congregation I should have fallen striken with a malady, paralysis or dementation but nothing happened; and they were surprised. I had grown into something in their eyes!

But I was coolly held in the arms of the old *svāmi*, and felt very confused; yet not too confused to utter the all important sound 'nārāyana, nārāyana'.

Well, every one present had to respond 'nārāyana, nārāyaṇa' and with that invocation the spell had broken.

I had indeed a long sleep. It was late afternoon. Time for me to go to the Ganges, swim and sit for the vespers. All that the *svāmī* asked me was if I had enjoyed a good fight with the tiger. The astounded inmates could not appreciate the abject leniency of the octogenarian. But I just replied in the affirmative and smiled, and whispered, "It was a great fight."

In return he too smiled and said. "That must have left you tired. You have overslept. This *āsana* gives peace to all. Run to the river. It is time for the vespers."

I still recall the looks of disbelief and horror shooting from the eyes of the inmates, and whenever I had visited that place again they invariably asked me if I felt anything special while on the *āsana*.

"I do not know. I had fallen asleep", was all I could say.

The Female Nexus

So I was saying that sharing the *āsana* of a yogi is a very serious thing. And none could share it without damaging the aura of the *āsana*. In this case the *āsana* was shared by a girl. I know that an *alter ego* has as much power as the ego itself. In the case of the Nāthas, and the Bāuls as in the cases of the Bhairavas, Bairagis and tantriks the close presence of a female, always an *alter ego*, is of as much importance as the presence of an *āsana*, a *kamaṇḍalu* and a *mālā*. But keeping a girl near, they warned, was as important, and dangerous at the same time, as keeping a flaming fire close by, or keeping cobras around the neck.

We the common minded, often under the lash of our own ego, pass judgements on these yogis who keep a close association with women. We forget that they keep a closer association also with live cobras; that they are almost never attacked by tigers, leopards and other ferocious animals although they keep within the dangerous bounds of these; we also seem to forget how they go about the neglected villages of India, and bring so many types of medical aids to the folks who depend so much on them. I feel that we, the common, should never apply our standards of ethics and behaviour on those who live apart from us, in their own worlds. Our norms and their norms differ. We might not show a due regard to them; but democracy demands at least to let them have the full run of their pattern of living as long as they do not interfere with others.

These yogis, having their own ways, usually work in close association with all the so called 'prohibitions' that are usually regarded as contraband to spiritual growth. There are the *ripus* (enemies to spiritual life) (temptations); through setting examples they make it evident that the so-called sources of temptations could act as close friends to the spiritual growth, only if they are tackled smoothly and in a perfectly friendly way. To react to anything anyhow is to cause shock to the spiritual dynamo. The secret is to get above the field of reaction. When no external temptations tempt and threaten mental poise, then and then alone a yogi could be called *paramahamsa* (the ideal man).

This is not a totally novel way of reaching the spiritual self. The first Christians knew it. There was a time when the members of the Catholic ministry, even Popes, used to lead a normal married life. For a very long time in the history of Christian spiritualism, association with the opposite sex had been regarded as one of the most serious and necessary penances for saints to attain beatification.

In the history of Christian beatification we hear of saints who have shared beds with nuns, for the exclusive purpose of practice in rigours.

In Islam the Sufis as well as the Imams, known for their piety and spirituality, have not run away from the closest association of the opposite sex. Almost all of them led to their credit, a normal married life. The Darvishes I have come in contact with often seek their *alter ego* at the actual hour of mystic rites. That is how in Islam instances of great spiritual power are found amongst women also.

I have moved amongst these.

During my earlier stay in New Delhi I often visited the world famed tomb of Nizamuddin Aulia whose spiritual powers were recognised by the entire contemporary Muslim world. Even princes and emperors stood in fear of his powers. The vain and arrogant amongst them paid him deferential homage, and tyrants often mended their ways under his restraining advice Powerful Sufi saints weilded great influence on the rulers. Early sings of cruelty in Emperor Akbar's early life were very much controlled by the spiritual intervention of Saint Salim Chisti of Fatehpur Sikri, near Agra. The mausoleum of Saint Moinuddin at Ajmer is held by the pious Muslims next to Mecca in holiness.

The Living and the Dead

I had been a constant visitor to the Nizamuddin shrine. I have had strange experiences in this shrine. And I still find the place soothing to my disturbed spirits.

One evening I had gone there alone to offer my prayers. Actually

I had gone to take certain notes on the nearby tombs where the remains of some of the great literary giants of Urdu, Persian and the rather newly budding Hindi language were buried. Whilst working in the ruins around, I felt to pay a visit to the shrine.

By the time I had reached the shrine, the sudden dark of the tropics overwhelmed the darkly arches of the corridors to the shrine.

Ancient stone steps climbed down the sides of the corridors to reach a tank where the pious generally wash themselves before entering the main courtyard. I finished my ablutions in solemn silence. No sound penetrated the high walls; and the shades thrown by the hanging branches of the neem trees standing on the other end of the tank did not help much in removing the gloom.

I was passing through the corridor, and was keeping my eyes set on the little shade of dim light across the passage opening on to the yard.

I heard someone breathing. Some living things had been lurching in pools of darkness gathered in the recesses of the longish corridor. The sound of breathing; a powerful vibration; a pull. I stopped, but did not look back.

"Stretch your palms", came an order (in Urdu) in a very husky voice.

Of course I did stretch my hands and palm, but where was the source of the voice? All I touched was the darkness; I could spot the source. Suddenly I felt a touch, cold, skinny, aged, although I felt the tenderness of the female heart. I turned around. I saw nothing but a pair of burning eyes staring at me. A toothless sound hissed the command, "Hold this, I have been waiting. Go behind the shrine, and climb the steps to reach the poet's mausoleum in the garden. Sit close to the *mehendi* (*lowsonia spinosa*) grove. Wait for me. Do not succumb. Do not hesitate. Run. Run. Time waits . . . ."

Before I could take a breath or bat my lids, the voice melted away in the surrounding stillness; the bright looks closed, bringing down the impenetrable blanket of deadly darkness.

I had no spleen to wait and ascertain if indeed there had been any physical form. If the token was in my hand, there had to be someone as tangible behind the token.

Fear is a reaction to many situations other than the sudden failure of contact of the known to the known. Any attempt of contact between the known and the unknown is accepted as some sort of spiritual aberration. We go for it, if we do, through different agencies; joy being one, and that joy coming through music, art and human relationships. Love and wonder are also spiritual, and we entertain quest for these spiritual contacts. But when the spiritual jumps down upon us unbidden, and from unexpected quarters, we feel shocked specially when we fail to connect the event with any known cause. The 'unknown' causes fear.

For me a spiritual blessing or a spiritual appearance was not entirely unexpected. I held my breath; pushed back my curiosity; and acted as bidden. I came to the grove directly, even without paying my usual homage to the holy tomb in the shrine.

An old fakir was seated, doing his rosary. On seeing me, obligingly, he moved a little, making room for me. Then I observed something; but only then. On the marble floor lay what apparently looked like a corpse covered with a white sheet. I knew that shrine too well; and took a seat near the body, but keeping close to the old fakir. I knew corpses are not brought in that part of the shrine, neither are they brought in that condition.

Gradually I became aware of someone sobbing piteously. It sounded like the muffled cry of a distressed soul in extreme agony. In that half-dark scented garden, under the jalousies of the marble canopy the entire scene breathed of a page from *Alf Laila.* For the first time I 'wanted' to know what was all this about.

The fakir consoled the sobbing person. "Do not worry", he said. "Look the man who could help us has finally arrived. Praise be to Allah. Take heart. He must have brought the cure for your daughter. Was not that the prophecy in your dream?"

Who the man? What prophecy? Who waited for what? What did I bring with me? Nothing. I had come on an errand of fact-finding history, and just lingered on aimlessly. I had been carrying on researches on some tombs; and why have I been involved in what looked like a romantic episode?

"My son", the old fakir was communicating, "You are welcome. Use what you have brought. It has been a very long vigil; and the life in that body is about to expire, if it has not expired already. Make haste. Use what you have . . . ."

What have I? I thought. What madness is it?

But the fakir continued. ". . . Make haste as I said. Remove the sheet, and do the needful. Let the long vigil end."

There was something in the husky voice of the old fakir. I acted at his bidding and removed the sheet. A young girl's body came to view.

The soft scent from the *mehendi* hedge, the shrine with only a flickering lamp burning, the mystifying patterns drawn by the delicate smoke from the burning joss-sticks, the muffled sobs, the fragile body of a dying young girl stretched on the marble floor,—all was indeed real, as real as jalousied light from the first hour of a faint moon covered with a heavy haze. All that together, conspired to cast a spell on a situation quite out of my grasp. The unreality of it all appeared to transform the objects before me into a half-fairy, half-mystic romantic oriental tale. To me, particularly, the least romantic transfiguration becomes an extremely engrossing event.

Under the strains and stresses of real life the fragile filigree of romanticism is often subjected to harsh treatment. Grim reality demands firm action, and threatens total obliteration for the hesitant and the lazy.

In appreciation of the serious nature of that sombre situation I tried to draw a stern face, expose a cold heart, and remain unmoved by a pathetic setting. Something stirring deep within made me feel, however, the tremors of a gripping series of events that was to follow.

With all that, I could not, despite my mood, possibly remain totally passive. What lay before me was a living, real, crude and challenging situation. By some unseen design I have been chosen as an agent to the revival of this apparently dead girl; and I was expected to play my part. But, good heavens, how? How on earth? A blank sense of utter helplessness and the total inadequacy of my feeble powers made me eagerly seek some assistance.

The case before me was one of an extreme stage of tuberculosis. The face was the palest I have ever seen. There was no sign of any life. The cheeks bore some colour; but the lips were red. The mother (I discovered that she was the mother keeping the week long vigil) was still sobbing. She came quite close to me and whispered in half choked words, "Hurry up my son", and continued, "This is the seventh night of my vigil. I trust that my prayers have been answered. You have come like destiny to save this girl. Now do not hesitate, or tarry. Time is running out; or has it run out already? . . ."

Boldly I took my face very near to the girl to see if there were any signs of life left. Finding none, I placed first my palm, then my cheek against her cheek, and found it to be still warm. With a passive objectivity, and with an electric movement, before anyone could bat an eyelid, I thrust my hand under her chemise and felt near her heart, while with the right hand I felt her pulse. The life waves in the artery flowed feebly and intermittently. No time to lose. Surê. But what was I supposed to do?

I myself felt to cry.

I felt the heaviness with which I always associate the advent of the forces of LS. I fervently wanted her to know what I must do? What must I do?

I waited. I wanted LS to come close, close, closer. I visualised her smiling and approaching me; but with her approach the trance was gone. I felt miserably confused.

"Are you looking for something my son?" The old fakir intervened. "Look I hold something in my hand. It is a tiny, tiny bead. It dropped from your hand . . . . I noticed it drop. Yes. Now hold this; here."

He handed it to me.

I did not know what bead it was. It was some vegetal product, too tiny to identify. I recalled the apparition that had thrust something in my hand while I was entering the shrine, and passing through the dark corridor.

As I was watching the bead, I dropped it again; and again the old man picked it up, and said, "Thrust it through her nose. She cannot swallow now. Thrust it through the nostril, and blow through your mouth. Blow."

In a trance I did as I was asked to do.

We all waited.

By about the middle of the night her breathing became normal, and her body became warm. I asked the mother to warm some milk, and try to give it to her, a few drops with brandy and honey.

I have no recollection how long I was in that state of *kumbhaka*, but I felt run down. I was heavily sweating and breathing more heavily. The fakir brought out a glass of drink, and held it to my lips. By the time I came to myself, I recognised the old woman of the dark, standing at a distance, and chewing with comfortable relish betel nuts with *pān* (betel leaves, taken with lime and tobacco).

I watched her hard, and challenged within to know why had she used me to do what she was herself capable of doing. I never liked to be used as a medium in those types of exercises. The incident, and the demands it made on me, really annoyed me. But from what she said, and by the manner in which it was said, I could gather that she was aware of LS. Naturally she was questioning my loyalties. But I would be honest to LS, and to no one else. She followed my point luckily at once, and kept her peace.

"Now you could leave", she threatened me; "your erand has been well done. If you so wish to pay me a visit later, I shall always know you, and welcome you. Now leave."

Threat or no threat my visits to the shrine of Nizamuddin Aulia continued, and I still frequent the place. The old lady was never seen by me again.

Islamic Shrines that Impressed

Remember the shrine in Ajmer, the most popular in the Islamic world, next in merit to the Holy Mecca and Madina? This is haloed by the supreme spiritual glory of the Sufi Saint Moinuddin Chisti. I have already made a mention of this shrine in passing. I could narrate a number of incidents that happened to me in this shrine. But apart from their irrelevance in this context, I refrain from loading this narrative any further.

Yet I shall refer to one of them.

I knew an old yogi who had travelled more than once the length and breadth of India in search of spiritual experiences. I had enquired from him which of the holy shrines in India according to his experience appeared to him to be the most powerful one.

The old man answered, "Ajmer Sharif".

I knew the legends of both Lalla Deed and Nuruddin Rishi. So I asked the old man to relate his experiences. But the legends were not to be ignored. Nuruddin had surprised his mother by making a rock burst in milk. She had been demanding her maternal due. She said that as a mother she had given him milk. And now when he was about to abandon her for the forests, what arrangements had he made for her provisions. At this challenge he commanded the rock to pour milk for his mother; and the stone yielded milk from a spring. The surprised mother gave him permission to pursue his own way of life. Lalla's legends are known to the Kashmiris who sing her songs to this day.

The Call Unresponded

I immediately agreed with the old man. Indeed the Ajmer shrine radiates powerful vibrations for those who are tuned to receive. On one occasion, when I was praying quite alone within the mausoleum of the saint at night, I was approached by a young man. He waited until my prayers were ended. As I came to, he asked me if I was interested to experience something. At this I smiled, and remarked casually, "What would I do", I said, "with experiences that come and pass away like summer clouds. I was looking for something more tangible; more sustaining; more personal."

I was taken around the yard. In a dark corner I noticed a series of steps going down. The entrance was otherwise barbed. Only once in a year that cage was opened. Some great spiritual soul had his *āsana* there. He had the very rare power of levitating, as Hamadani of Kashmir, and Lalla Deed had been reputed to have possessed. He was known to have been present at two places at the same time.

Incredible as it might sound, the acquisition of the power of levitation is not an idle imagination, or a wild dream. It is as credible and possible as a piece of iron floating on the sea, or speaking to people a thousand miles apart, or watching shows happening miles and miles away.

What had been regarded incredible appears today as familiar as toys in the hand of children. What has been regarded as perfectly credible thousands of years ago is looked down upon today as incredible. The early apostles found the 'dead' Christ appearing before them, and talking to them; Saul became Paul because of the appearance and ministration of a person quite away from him. Swami Vivekananda changed his mind to accept Kaṭhia Bābā as his guru when the physical presence of Ramakrishna Paramahansa directed him otherwise. There have been historical evidences from men not accustomed to telling lies, of the simultaneous presence of the same person at two different places hundred miles apart.

Credibility is a mirage chased by the sceptics riding on the hobby horses of learning and rationality. 'There are more things between heaven and earth' than what could be gripped by the iron hand of reason alone. Modesty is a virtue that teaches more than is imagined it could teach. And opinion must be withheld on a subject which has not been studiously gone through and absolutely mastered. It does not do science or the scientific outlook, any harm to study a subject before passing judgement on the strength of ignorance. Patanjali's *Yoga Sūtra*, and Vijñāna Bhikṣu's great commentary make no secret of the process of achieving levitation. I am quite sure, given Patanjali his chances, and fulfilling his reason-based steps, man could process himself to the state of levitation. LS had times without number demonstrated this talent without making it look like a great feat.

But to continue with my experience in the Ajmer shrine.

I knew of the saint, and was now eager to know him more. He was no more in flesh; but the graces of these saintly beings far outlive their physical body. As I looked by my side to talk again to the young man, I found I was alone, and in that dark, wide and empty courtyard there was no one else. It was past one o'clock in the night. On the other side of the yard, in front of the mausoleum a group of singers from Iran and Afghanistan were singing for the pleasure of Sheikh Moinuddin, the great lover of music. (Music has been a mysterious link between the seen and the unseen for many of the spiritualists. Mirā, Guru Nanak, Śrī Caitanya Mahāprabhu apart, almost every Sufi saint is fond of musical accompaniment, musical atmosphere for the promotion of their elan, or *ojas*.)

I was amazed at the sudden disappearance of the young man, and looked at the dark passage going down. Unaccountably I found the door ajar. I went in, but did not know what to do. I was unconsciosuly reciting some Vedic verses. Behind me step by step, the same verses were being sung in a female voice. I had to look again and again. I had to. But my eyes failed to penetrate the blanketting darkness. I came to a squared declivity, which in the dark I could feel was filled with water. I felt as if I knew about this water tank (let me call it a tank. It could hardly have been a two feet square hole). I sat by its side. I did the usual *āsana-śuddhi* (purification of the seat); *bhūta-śuddhi* (purification of the elements); *anganyāsa* (steadying of the limbs of the body); *kara nyāsa* (steadying of the joints of the fingers in preparation of the *mudras*) and started *prāṇāyāma* (breathing control).

Soon I got enveloped with an aura of conscious radiation. Waves after waves of vibrating thrills kept me, as it were, on crests of huge South Sea breakers; to be dancing on those rolling crests as on the hoods of a hydra-headed snake, was to experience the sublime. This to me was no joy of the voluptuary; but it was that kind of joy which, for lack of any better expression, humans describe as transcendental. One needs the super senses to examine the full impact of 'super-life', 'super stratum'.

Gradually from a distance the voice of the *muezzein* was heard calling the faithful to kneel in prayers. It was after four o'clock in the morning. Time for the first oblations, the first salutations had reached. I began to climb up.

On the steps at the mouth of the cage I saw a female figure standing, waiting on me. I did not know her; but she said she knew me. We talked for some time, and I found that she had been in search of an able *alter ego* for her ends . . . .

I am much ashamed to confess that I failed to answer her inner needs, as I was no tonger the same adept; and the very presence of a young and beautiful woman made my body crumble into a series of agonies. In spite of her many assurances I failed her. For the time I felt unfit for an *āsana*.

My failure on that dawn fully illustrates what could happen to a person attacked by his inner enemies (*ripu*-s) even while on the verge of success. Those who live in the spirit of things have to live in the world of the opposites without the least affectation. To be near the opposite sex, near the serpents, near the tigers and leopards, near starvation and near the flames are practised by yogis as matters of fact.

The Draw of the Opposite

Without opposites there is no ignition; without ignition there is no transmission; without transmission there is no possibility of fusion; without fusion there is no chance of heat, motion or, radiation. This is as much true of physical opposites as of spiritual opposites. We all seek for our complementaries. Until the complementaries are with us, and become intimately and intensely ours, fused and interfused, there is no chance of a total transcendence. This physical exterior drama not only symbolises the inner drama, but the physical provides the very vessel for drawing from the spring of the eternal drinks.

Again and again our built-in difficulties challenge this fusion. Because we are faced with many problems, inner as well outer, personal as well as social, spiritual as well as physical, sensitive as well as intellectual, organic as well as inorganic, the yogic way is littered with hazard; but if surmounted, it also offers the most effective success. Prejudice and fear surround and entangle us like coils upon coils of serpents, benumbing us with their hot breaths before we realise how each moment by moment we are losing a life and death battle.

In attempting to unite we might split. In attempting to create a fusion, we might just bring on chaos. In attempting to turn two into one, we might break the one into two. This is indeed a dangerous game. We must prepare long and steadily to battle it out, and attain the final victory of the spirit over the forms of the immediate. It is victory of life over death; light over darkness and the real over the unreal.

At the finality of all thinking there is the space; and this space is the field of energy. This space-filled energy, or energy filled space, gradually is transformed into the duality of the principles, the fundamental principles of the opposites. There are the two; necessarily the two are not at war. The relation between them is not one of conflict, which is the general nature of the material world of forms and qualities. It is in an evolute state. Before the evoluted forms crop up, the fundamental duo remains a single concept of space filled with energy. This is the one; the two in one; the one in two. This is the concept of Śiva and Śakti. This is the field of tantra. It is for this 'I' seek 'you', 'you' seek 'me'; the incomplete seeks the complementary. There is no feminine and masculine in it. There is no sex in it. It is a principle, not what is called temptation.

Grace and Mystics

This truth is not achieved through mere practice. Practice leads to experience; and from experience one advances towards the consummation of the 'total'. That too is just an experience: an absorbing all-in-all experience. But experience itself is assured by Grace. Without the blessing and intervention of Grace, practice as an exercise leads only to a certain level. The world title holder for a muscular and strong body may not have the courage of Lawrence of Arabia, or General Rommel. The physically insignificant Gandhi proved to be a tower of strength. Body could be cultured through discipline and exercise; but courage depends on 'Grace' or personality, which we call the inner make up, or character, or *guṇa*. A fruit is a fact; but to participate in its taste and to enjoy it depends on Grace. Techniques cannot guarantee the final peace. The world of experience like the world of opinion is exclusively a personal world.

This experience cannot be transmitted, translated. The mystics speak of it; and having had the experience do not like to justify or rationalise it. The mystics are strange creatures, wide away from our empirical forms, idioms and aspirations.

When we try to understand the mystics through responses in the stratum of our empirical needs, we baffle ourselves; and of course we baffle those around whom we have gathered. We ourselves have got to change our thought perspectives, thought dimensions and thought aspirations. We must learn to see things as they ought to be; not only as they are.

That might take a long time. To see things as they are is dependent on a long exercise. This depends on mental discipline. This kind of mental discipline is yoga. But then having seen things as they are, the way leads further on. After having seen into things as they are, one has to see things as they ought to be. The first set of the seers is the yogi; but the second set is the mystic.

No one expects miracles from the mystics; neither should one expect to find prophets amongst the mystics. A mystic is not a mystic until he has reached the dimension beyond this world and the world realities. He knows that Space is an embryo within which the world is what an amoeba is to the human body, or an atom is to the entire ocean. Tantra practices to lift human energy from the body level to the world level; from the world level to the matter level; from the matter level to the energy level; and from that to the level of space and energy. To talk of sex against such pursuits is both irrelevant and irreverent. It goes off the point.

Back to Saint Jiten

That is why I was not the least perturbed by the presence of those older ladies around Saint Jiten, nor did I find anything unfamiliar in seeing that young girl there. In those days the whole city of Varanasi was filled with the rumours of the fall of this particular saint; as well as the supposed fall of my Gopi Dādā. Both had become victims of gossips related to the presence near them of young and beautiful girls! Those who handed out the rumours really had nothing to do with the life and activities of these yogis. We who used to keep close to them found in them more than enough power of restraint, piety and subjectivity.

The selection of an *alter ego* is as complicated a process as the selection of a Dalai Lama in Tibet. Not the external circumstances determine the selection so much as some esoteric signs and portends. I have seen such selected *alter egos*, and had the opportunity to be near to them for days, months and years. I could vouchsafe unhesitatingly that in all cases (within my knowledge) a well selected *alter ego* after full training becomes a Bhairavī par excellence; and that dynamo of energy could charge many a tantrik into activities that conduct the world order.

The Young Bhairavī

My close association with this one gained in depth after the session in the Pātālesvar Kālī shrine, which has already been narrated. In the dark mystic state of that night I could not fully recognise her as she lay on the platform. But later I could identify.

Not only did I identify, I also came to know that the whole episode had been planned by the very kind Saint Jitendra who from my early boyhood had been taking so close an interest in me.

I learnt austerity, discipline, ascetic self control as inner powers, when judging from the outer ways it seemed that I was involved in life and its demands. Most time Tāntriks and *Haṭha-yogis* are found leading a normal mundane life. It is not unusual for them to be mistaken for common sensuous beings. This apparent contradiction is a garb wilfully worn by the adepts of the highest order to keep the inquisitive away from pestering them with disturbing enquiries. "Without earning a bad name", they say, "one does not get the nameless".

I learnt from her the very difficult art of keeping long fasts; keeping seated for very long hours; to concentrate amidst a lot of distraction to be quickly absorbed in the higher planes to keep simultaneous watch over several planes of human life and its activities.

She was young and tender. I could have learnt much. Although junior to my age, although less conversant with book learning than I was, as a field of potential power I knew she had been far above many. In fact without her assistance the saint would not have reached that elevation which he did. This was his own assessment.

How far her lessons would have assisted *me* has remained ever since a moot question. But the climate of India of those hectic days was very different, and I got, in spite of myself, sucked in by the huge eddies formed by the political torrents of the time. We had been at war with the British at that time. It was a war of attrition.

A Drift

It was during this period that I was driven from pillar to post, both spiritually and physically. The physical law that an object could stay only at one place at a time had been at work within my inner being. Politics and hatred on one side, spiritual emancipation and love on the other could not have lived together; and politics had swept me away. I came into contact with forces which had nothing whatsoever to do with the inner rhythms or the music of the soul. These people never knew about the different octaves in which the consciousness of man could work, and could be made to work. I proved to be an anachronism amongst them.

But the spiritual forces in me helped them a great deal, because these forces had moulded my character as one determined to follow any pursuit with zeal and fearlessness. These qualities the underground activists prized, and they in their own way had been busy at moulding me to their purpose.

I had drifted away from Varanasi; I had drifted away from my regular *āsana* and discipline; I had drifted far far away from that rigidity of purpose which holds the body-machine high above the usual fascinations of the world, specially of the opposite sex, whom I had always learnt to regard as the basic seat of *prakṛti* and the temple of *Śakti*.

Due to the drifting winds I had come into contact with certain characters who had been past masters in the ways of the world, and the way of all flesh. To them my undisturbed youth, my health, my chastity offered the greatest curiosity, as a strange animal would offer to the animal catchers.

Why is it that when the mind and body take the greatest punishments from the world in its secular challenges, when nerves are at an end, and muscles ache in the agony of carnal calls, when anxiety and uncertainty like the two jaws of an evil carnivore gnaw and mash the reserves up, when the entire psyche faces annihilation through drastic challenges,—then suddenly, the locks of restraint break down and the gates of all fortification are flung open, and man falls a prey to the temptations of an immediate and easier course of relief?

I am at pains to have to call them temptations. There is no temptation in the outside world. The nest of temptation is built within, gradually, hive by hive, pocket by pocket, gland by gland. Unless man has stored up elements of temptations within himself, no outer forces could tempt him. It is like drawing water from the ears. If there is no water inside, no water from outside could draw a drop out. In this respect all cases of so-called temptations are instances of the victim victimising himself. Self-hypnotism is the greatest enemy for the development of spirit. Temptations are the reflections of our own secret desires.

But there is always a turn back. In tantra this turn back is both immediate, and radical. In tantra and tantra alone the sins of the fathers are refused a visa to the area of spirit; for man is what he is because of his own efforts. He could eradicate, and completely eradicate the past, and come out in the open virginity of natural protection, for the Mother is always there to embrace.

The Two Who fell

I had come back. But I had been in hiding. What with the university career, what with the political involvements, what with my personal fascinations for literary activities, I had grown a little slack on the sides of the spiritual pursuits, although I had not given them up. I had been receiving assistance during this period at Allahabad from three males and two females who had been very close to me. The final test came when a young lady had offered her 'love' to me; and I had accepted her in love. But the way I had accepted her completely upset her; and the more she came near, the more she became convinced that there is a pattern of love beyond the walls of the body which is more sustaining, and immensely rewarding too.

But tragedy struck her too early. In her serious attempts to reach the peak as early as possible she had been denying herself the physical sustenances of nutrition and rest. Soon she died of tuberculosis. This again shows that the path of tantra accepts rigours of a different nature; but no rigours on the stamina of the body. The body is the temple of consciousness; it is the very shrine of *Śakti*, the Mother. And it has to be kept in top condition as a shrine has to be kept. Food, rest, habits and even things generally accepted as luxuries are not forbidden in tantra when utilised for the main purpose. But the indulgences of an Epicurian voluptuary, of a sensuous Hedonist are entirely ruled out in the persistent practice of tantra. Sense organs exercise the acuteness of senses, but refuse to get dependent on objects outside.

The other one kept on the path a very long time, but then wanted me more than the path itself. Ultimately she went mad, and finally ended her days in an asylum. For her the return journey back home had been completely overgrown with impenetrable undergrowths.

Mā Ānandamayi

It was about this time that I came to know of the eminence of two great ladies. One had attained the state of sainthood, and was widely known as Mā, the Mother, (Ānandamayi the Blissful One). I have seen her on several occasions, but my mind was wrapped up in the doubt which is characteristic of young age, specially when the mind is exposed to empirical knowledge, and to the poor traps set by the three dimensional science of the West.

Despite all the vicious forms of autocracy and fanaticism the mind of the East always flourished under the canopy of star laden skies, above the desert sands (as did the minds of the first Judaic immigrants from Egypt); atop the snow covered mountain peaks of the sublime Himalayas; along the torrential rivers of Iang Si Kiang and Hwang Ho. From Japan to Java and Ceylon, from Champa, Siam to the banks of the Jordan and the shores of the Galilee the teeming surges of humanity over the centuries have been experimenting with the dimensions of the reaches of consciousness in man. Whether it led them to the openness of the prayers of the Rigveda, or to the labyrithian rituals of the Yajuh or Atharvan, or the solemn hymns of the Zend Avesta, or the cool compassionate realism of the Buddha, or to the mystic delights of the Lamas of Tibet; or the early psalms of the Dead Sea Scrolls and the Essienes, or to the sincere devotions of the early Christians, or the deeper voices of the mystical chapter of Iranian Sufism in Islam,—the openness and the liberalism of the Asian in the realm of spiritual thinking has enabled the Asian mind to flourish along a free way. This has not been the case with the West, despite a growth of empirical logic and material science. This failure is partly due to the regimented and organised dogmas of the western churches, specially the churches before the encyclopoaedist. An organised religion shackles its own freedom, but accumulates power; and power corrupts all except the free and the lonely.

In our younger days we had been the victims of Bentham and Mill; Spinoza and Descartes; Voltaire and Hume. The freedom in the West that came after the First World War with Einstein and Jung, Marx and Engels, Eddington, Dewey, Russel, Rolland, Croce, Bergson, Hesse and Santayana made the Asian mind recall the freedom of Greek thinking, of the neo-Platonists, of the early Christians with such later disciples as Eckhart, Juan de Broix, Aldous Huxley and Theiland de Chardin.

Out of touch with my Lady in Saffron, away from the banks of the Ganges, enmeshed in the whirlpools of politics my mind and body suffered a battering from which a come back was not that easy.

One afternoon I went to pay a visit to this Mā. A cynical mind does not claim the best of receptivity; and I found that the crowd around Mā was the same mundane mass—crowd of mediocrity who assemble only to collect some immediate blessings or 'cure', solutions or sudden 'gifts' of material values, which their passive efforts or timed selfishness do not normally deserve.

For the first few minutes I just kept watching the curious congregation. Gradually I was getting worked up by the futility of it all, when suddenly I felt that someone was looking at me.

It was Mā herself. And what a look it was. No one ever has succeeded to describe that look. She had been looking at me through the corner of her twinkling eyes, and that noble face bathed in the red of the setting sun beamed with a motherly indulgence. Mā was a beautiful and very charming woman. Her elan or *ojas,* her power, her aura almost tingled every hair root on my body. I had never before seen such great beauty in so sublime a form. If beauty could indeed bewitch any one, the Mother did with hers. I remembered:

īṣat sahāsa-mamalam paripūrṇa chandra
—vimbānukāri kankottama kānti kāntam . . . .

(She was smiling with her eyes, and shedding the mild graces of a full moon shining on a cloudless sky, so that her complexion vied with the sheen of purest gold . . . .)

I stared at her; and knew that she had held me. She spoke to me from the distance, and at once declared my business by replying to my enquiries before I could even speak to her.

I went next morning; and next morning and next morning. Why, I do not know. I felt drawn.

I went morning, afternoon, evening.

Until one fine day on the peaks of the Vindhya-vāsini hills, where I was looking for a day's stay, and not at all expecting to see anyone there, I found her seated alone on the steps of a cottage door half reclining against a post. "Vālārka-candra-prabhām" (glowing like the rising sun and the moon). From the looks of her eyes I knew that she no longer belonged to this world. She had been merged in absolute trance. (Mā is hardly seen alone. The crowd is always around her.)

Soon an attendant old lady appeared from out of the cottage. She begged me to assist her, in taking Mā down where a car had been waiting. "They never thought", explained the old lady, "that she would go on a trance just now. She had been eating her scanty breakfast of oranges, and suddenly went limp. Look the trouble now. I wanted her to finish her breakfast."

She waited a little, and tried to push a spoonful of the carefully peeled orange into her mouth, in vain.

"Might I try?" I asked hesitantly.

The old lady took a full look at me, and without saying anything handed me the spoon and the bowl.

As I held out my hand near her lips she opened them, and with great seeming efforts swallowed what was put into her mouth. She had taken thus about four mouthfuls, when she opened her eyes, and smiled with her eyes. Only Mā could smile like that.

Some people had arrived by now to find what had happened. Before she left with them, she asked me to search for the house a little down.

I got my shelter for the night; but how did she divine what I had been looking for. And why did I look for a house when she could have given me much more? We indeed do not know what we want; what we get, prove by their worthlessness the basic hollowness of all wants. To be able to know what one wants is the beginning of fulfilment.

I knew we must meet again.

We did, once, twice, thrice. But I could not come nearer to her. She was always surrounded. On my return to India when I attended the last Kumbha Melā at Prayāg (where after every twelve years the spiritual population of India assembles for a ritual bath, and where the assembly of the mendicant saints continues for a month) I stepped into a tent reserved for her stay. As usual she was in a state of trance for the best part of the day she had been there. A crowd was singing devotional songs. Hundres came to see her from a distance. But I was wondering that having just returned from the West Indies for a visit to India why I had to come to the fair with an indifferent mind. Moreover why had I entered that tent, of the thousand other tents, and why did I see her whom my soul had been seeking?

She was known to Saint Jitendra; she was very well known to the yogi Gopinath. She was still regarded, as the highest specimen of a spiritual soul in India, a woman *paramahamsa*.

The Path of the Lonely

Then something strange happened.

This was after the Vindhya hill incident; and much before the return from West Indies.

I had forgotten Saint Jitendra. I had a subconscious recollection of the little saintly virgin at the Kāli temple. Without anything definite in my mind I had paid a casual visit to the temple. Some young men had been preparing for a journey to Tibet. The elaborate preparations indicated their imminent departure in a day or two, when on seeing me they invited me to accompany them. Why I declined I do not know.

As I had stepped out of that temple, where I could have expected some message regarding the virgin, who I felt sure, must have reached a very high stratum of spiritual power, a friend of the olden times came to me.

I was asked to be present at the *āśrama* of the saint Jitendra.

How he, or anybody had come to know of my presence there, or even at Varanasi I do not know. But the man said, "You are wanted by the saint at once. A catastrophe has struck . . . ."

The virgin I had been searching for . . . .

She had entered into a trance, and never came back to senses. After a vigil of five days and nights she had been declared as one liberated; only the body was there; and the body had to be consigned to the flames. I was chosen and called upon to take charge of the solemn funeral.

The saint, as I knew, used to live in the deeper parts of the lanes in Varanasi. His place had been the pilgrimage of many. That day he had need of me. I felt embarrassed.

On arriving I was told that the saint had been waiting on me somewhere else, away from the main city in the wilderness of Kāmākṣyā.

As I entered the threshold of the ancient temple yard I became aware of the familiar vibrations. No one was needed to show me the way from there.

At the back of the yard, and behind the temple, on the varanda lay a body, covered with a white sheet. The sheet itself was loaded with flowers and garlands. Gentle whiffs of smoke twirled around the body from the hundreds of joss-sticks. An elaborate circle in white and red surrounded the body. On the floor, near the body, solemnly sat the saint, his hand holding hers. It was difficult to believe from the vivacity of the skin of that tender hand, the flexibility of the joints that the body was lifeless. The saint's head was bending down. I wondered if he too was in trance.

Two more renowned yogis of Varanasi were sitting on either side. On the other side of the yard a party was engaged in chanting religious melodies. Death to the Hindus opens the door to liberation, and is a moment of 'celebration'. Such deaths had to be very effectively celebrated.

But who was she?

A strange stare on the face of those around turned a grim subject grimmer. I could feel that I was not only expected, I was almost held essential. As if the body belonged to me.

I approached cautiously. Was it she? I began to think. Was the body really hers?

Yes; so it proved to be. It was she indeed.

I laughed within myself as I realised the position. Did I not, on my own account, go to the Kālī shrine in search of some information regarding that virgin on the platform? And here was she, the selected *alter ego* of the saint, my childhood friend, my secret mentor and aide. I recalled how the saint's name was getting tainted by rumours about his close association with a virgin. Now she was gone.

Holding my hands the saint withdrew to a corner of the yard. There under a *bel* tree he gave me some instructions.

Apparently he had been much moved by the incident. "I had need of thee", he started. "She had been undergoing her meditative penances over months. Gradually the period of meditation, specially of *kumbhaka* increased in duration. A time came when she lost touch of everything; and sang melodies all the time. For the last nine days she did not come out of her trance even once. Finally, I had to intervene; and I went into her room. It was too late. She had aleady ascended her due station. She was born with power. She came only for this short duration. She always talked of you. Somehow your auntie had some prior inkling about things that had to happen. She had even warned me. But in these matters one has to follow one's own path. *Is it not the path of the lonely traveller*? She has gone to where she belonged to. For her there is no more coming, neither going. Now you have to play your role."

Suddenly he stopped.

I looked at him. "But there is something I must tell you. I had been waiting on you", he said finally.

What was it?

He explained.

He had located her even as she had been a baby. The saint was quite ware of her past, her previous courses of life. She had been a Tibetan *yoginī* whose progress had been interrupted by an unthinking lama. Because she had withdrawn herself from him before any serious harm could be caused, the affected lamas, who really wanted to flourish on her, by depriving her of her independent powers, have been still in search of her. Some of them had been around in body, but what is more dangerous, some of them are around even without body.

She had been in her life before the last life, born in Kāmbodja (now Compuchia). There, to this day, lives the famous colony of the Chām adepts with their effective brotherhood of tantra. For years she had been their only Bhairavī. She had been a Bhairavī for the last seven lives in a string. Of these she had known of the last two. Ultimately she had come to me for shelter, knowing that she could be safe here. The only thing she had enjoyed was the seances she had with LS. (In many of these seances I had accompanied her.) LS had not at that time revealed her identity to me. This too was as planned.

Then came the time when I had receded from the entire milieu. In common language I had 'failed'; I had 'fallen'. I knew that I had betrayed myself, my calling. For me not one life, but many many lives have to be passed through before I shall again experience what I had experienced with LS, in Kāmākṣyā, in the ruins of Angkor Wat, and of course in the company of this virgin.

It is the spirit of this virgin alone which sparked from body to body and hunted me in many forms; but no time could I any longer stay steady. The excess of *rajas* in me again and again drove me to the dull dark regions of *tamas*.

Yet I had my role to play.

The saint was very anxious to save her body from pollution. She had been anointed when she was a mere child of five. She had her Mongol strains; and she could visit many at most places; but always a virgin.

Those who knew about the spiritual milieu at Varanasī, knew about the mystic practices that even today certain yogis love to strive for. Quite expectedly they were aware of the strange life and practices of this girl. She had been carefully prepared for a set purpose; and the stories of that preparation had set a new current of legends. The nature of those careful preparations, the care with which that training was being given were familar only to those who kept a very secret knowledge of the Tārā *sādhanā* of the Lamite school. Spiritual yogīs from such haunts as Nepal, Sikkim, Bhutan, Ceylon, Arakan, Sikiang, Thailand and Cambodia often used to visit Saint Jitendra.

Ignorant of this rigid course of training the people of Varanasī, like people anywhere, whispered and talked about the imaginary orgies. A blissful combination of powers was set at naught be cynical irreverence of some mean urban gossips.

This is a very common threat to the peace of the adept. The necessity of selecting seclusion, and withdrawing from the public gaze and public communication is thus enforced on the tantra practitioners.

I must try to narrate the balance in the saint's own words.

"You have known me for long. I needed her; as I needed you. She assured me that she had been keeping near you. Your failing did not escape her notice. But these temporary setbacks do not, and need not, permanently retard a practitioner. The Lady in Saffron was of great inspiration to her. Now she is gone; this was her own will; and she must go.

"We must see that her journey is not hampered; her body is not molested . . . . Make a note of it."

I was shocked to hear that. "Her body molested? This body?" I was aghast.

The saint looked at me. "That should not cause you any surprise. Recall the rites in the Tārā shrine behind the Gopal Mandir? Remember the dead body, and the *āsana*?"

"How could I forget?"

"Well; that was the body of a male. This one is that of a female. This female is a virgin, and a consecrated one at that. Although she herself is powerful enough to protect her mortal remains from being used as *āsana*, yet for her to react is to keep contact with this world. That would cause her enough pains, the pains of a falling soul. That would delay her liberation. That could upset all her plans. Friends are meant to be of assistance in crisis. It is best to consecrate her body in a fire bath, and reduce the body to ashes. But until it is done, it has to be protected and kept under the strictest guards."

"Guards? What guards?", I asked dismayed. "Guide me please."

Guarding the Dead

Then I came to learn a new knowledge. This was the knowledge of the books of the dead. Many of these books have been destroyed by those who did not understand the significance. Many have condemned these as sources of sorcery and occultish perversions. Even the invaluable records of the Essienes, the Egyptians, the Mayans (and now probably of the Tibetans too) have been destroyed, and are being destroyed for one reason or another. When mankind should have mastered the knowledge of the unknown more and more, mankind is getting farther and farther away from the truth about the unknown because of his own destructive spirit, specially when such a spirit is fostered by his own immense ego-pack.

Like the humans, the spirits, I learnt, are also in wait for communicating with such emancipated soul. The presence of such a soul even for a while is of immense benefit to them. The higher spirits, like visiting professors, transmit some relief to the suffering spirits. In the Mahābhārata this sort of incident has been narrated more than once. The most famous of these are the ones related to King Somadeva, King Ambariṣ and King Yudhiṣṭhira. The suffering spirits howled for a longer stay of these holy spirits amongst them, as their presence had brought them immense relief.

Apart from these suffering spirits looking forward to the chance passages of the higher spirits, there are the evil ones. who are always on the prowl to pounce upon the progressing spirit, and bring evil portents to stop the progress. In the epic Rāmāyana we see the progress of the yogi Hanumant being retarded again and again by such evil forces as Surasā; and Simhikā Kṛṣna was confronted by Pūtanā, so was Rāma confronted by Taḍakā. The evil forces are there to hold back the forces of progress. This is true of the yogic progress also; this is true of the progress of soul also. Using the human cadavar for spiritual purposes is as old a practice as the *Vetalas.* Consult the Lākuliśa sect; consult Bhartṛhari and Paraśurāma himself.

A new knowledge was dawning on me. I remember the mystic lines of the Gītā, "*Even yogis stuck to the path of the Moon, the smoky dark, nightly path of the southern equinox* (*fail to reach their ultimate liberation and*) *are forced to suffer come back.*"

I became quite aware of the responsibility I was shouldering. I was to assist not only in carrying the dead body to Maṇikarṇikā; but I was *never to lose my physical grip* on the body. Then having reached the funeral grounds I would myself, with the assistance of the *yogini* Auntie, bathe the body and decorate the corpse as if the virgin was offering herself as a seat in the final *Śavāsana.* Her naked body was to have been covered with a loose white sheet, as the body would be laid on the pyre, a red heavy silk garment would be thrown over the whole pile of woods. Then, carefully the white sheet would have to be removed, thus keeping the body entirely covered, yet without any cloth or garment with knots or stitches on. The hair will have to be combed, and let loose from the height of the pyre. Until the hair burns out along with the red cover neither the body nor the pyre should get out of the gripping touch.

"Nothing shall happen to you. The *yogini* will be there to guide you. Nothing shall happen. Be emboldened and act as I bid", he assured.

Nothing did happen.

But . . . .

The *yoginī* herself had been acting very funny. Again and again she found excuses for me to run errands, so that I could leave my grip to go somewhere else. But I did not. Then she pronounced her most effective sentence, her most vicious technique. At the bathing and dressing she suddenly drew my attention to the nudity of a young woman's body, and her own embarrassment to have me near when she would be engaged in that ritual immersion.

But I knew better, because I had been warned.

Saint Jitendra had asked me to seek assistance from *yoginī* auntie; but he had also warned me. "She herself could look for a chance to have the body. Never lose the grip."

I recalled the part auntie had played on me when I was a small boy, and how LS had intervened. I also recalled how auntie had given herself up to methods and forms quite contrary to the way of the Bhairavas. So when Saint Jitendra had been warning, I remembered that the *tāmasa* way of tantra too could be effective; but it could also lead one to the ways which could spell disasters. The Atharva Veda is filled with such powers of miracle: *vaśīkaraṇa*, (erosion of will) *māraṇa* (bringing death), *uccātana* (destruction), *sammohana* (mesmerising) etc., which belong to the worldly sphere alone, and could at best be regarded as interference with the general ways of life.

I did not openly cross swords with her, and obeyed her directions in every way possible; only I did not let go the grip. I kept the body touched to mine.

But she again raised the point of washing her body. I could not but recite.

yasmin sarvāṇi bhūtāni
Ātmai-va-bhūd vijānatah
Tatra ko mohah kah śokah
Ekatvam anupaśyatah (*Iśa up.*, *VII*)

(The atman is the source, and all these (differences) are mere evolutes thereof; and in the atman all differences become one. Where, then, is any scope for confusion, or for affliction when all are seen as one?)

Finding no other means to get me away, she appeared to have been reconciled to the realities of the situation.

I had placed the body successfully on the pyre. Now was the time to remove her garments. I covered the whole pyre with the heavy piece of red velvet, richly embroidered with the famous Varanasi gold *zari* thread. Then carefully I untied her sari, and began to pull the same. The sari was coming out smoothly. Suddenly it stopped in between the movements; no attempt of mine would allow an inch to come out. I was compelled to pass my hand at the point of obstruction. My hands touched the body. I felt. Very warm. Was she alive?

Shocked, I put my hand near her heart. Obviously the heart was not only moving, the body itself was about to take a turn. So puzzled was I that I could hardly keep the balance of my mind. Things had been happening. It was dark. The shadows of the solid stone embankment walls, made darker by the high-power electric arc lamps, which guarded the Maṇikarṇikā cremation grounds, came creeping over my senses. I felt two persons standing on either sides. I felt breath over my shoulders. But I did not look. Gradually I was losing my senses.

"Let me help you", came auntie's grating voice. "Move, Let me do it."

Very simple and under the circumstances, quite a helpful and natural suggestion. But I had not entirely lost my senses yet. My eyes suddenly fell on two black dogs waiting on me, looking at me from almost under the funeral pyre, close to my feet.

I looked at auntie. I looked at the dogs. It was not unusual to see dogs around the crematory grounds. So trained and accustomed to these grounds are these dogs that they roam about fearlessly even around the burning fires.

But I smelt a rat. It is a kind of feeling that is not emotional. It is a feeling of the other senses which pulsate the inner spiritual personality of the being, which the psychoanalysts describe as supraconscious. I looked at the dogs again, and then at auntie, and held tight on to the body. All the time I was uttering hymnal chants from Atharva Veda which invokes the spirit of agni (fire) for driving away the evil forces that hover around the dead in a crematory ground.*

**Antar-dāve jukutā sve-a-tad*
Yātudhāna-k-ṣayaṇam ghṛtena
Ārād rakṣāmsi pratidaha-tvam agne
Na no gṛhāṇā-mupa tītapāsi
Rudro va grivā aśarait piśācāh
Pṛṣṭīr-vo-api ṣṛṇātu yātudhānāh
Vīrod vo visvats vīryā yamena samajīgamat

Let this lethal offering in the fire, O the sacrificing priests, destory the demoniac antiforces. Let them be caught in the natural flames, and consume themselves. Let those who attempt to disturb be totally distroyed. Let your throats be severed by the destroyer Rudra, those who seek to live on human flesh; let Rudra crush your ribs; let the poison herbs assist you in reaching fast the abode of death. (6:4:1-1-2)

Then I began to talk to LS; and almost cursed her for being so cold and callous to the whole situation. Where was she?

The *mantra* from the Atharva Veda coursed through my mind. I repeated it over and over when I felt that the dogs were vanishing away. One of them passed very close to me, and I dealt him a severe kick with my left foot. To my surprise he did not make a reflexive howl as any dog would make even as a protective gesture. But the great fact was that they had disappeared. Now, relieved, I stared at auntie. She too had been perspiring.

I gave a fresh pull at the sari; and it fell at the foot of the pyre in a heap.

Our scriptures lay it down for us to prepare a body carefully. Clothes might be put on; but obviously that was meant for helping the people around from embarrassment. Otherwise a body has the right to be consigned to the elements in the same undress in which it was ushered into the world. Nothing belonging to the world need encumber the body. Washing and cleaning is a must. After that it is to be decorated, and carefully massaged and rubbed with things as would assist a fast ignition and end. The body ready, prayers have to be chanted. These prayers take care of undoing the mental ties of the deceased.

What is the mind? What is the emotional body (*manomaya koṣa*)? Whatever it might be, it is the root cause for the development of individual personality. This personality grows with the assistance of the sense organs and the active limbs. It is therefore enjoined on those who prepare the body to insulate the organs (the "nine doors", ears (2), eyes (2), nostrils (2), mouth (1) excretory organs (2)=9) with gold pieces. (I believe that this custom of covering the 'doors' with gold has come down to the Indian funerary rites from Egypt via Iran where the well-to-do used to cover the body entirely with gold, gold filigrees etc. I have reasons to believe that the Aztecs and the Mayans did something alike.

I was given specially marked gold pieces for use on this occasion; the one to be placed on the *yoni* being specially marked with a special *Devi-yantra* embossed on a very thin plate. Although the body was not open to my view, I followed the instructions correctly. What amazed me was that as soon as one was pushed into the mouth, the lips which parted, appeared to close at once. This made me happy and satisfied. I felt the response, and it gave me the message that all had gone well.

By this time the guard of the crematory grounds had sent on to me the ceremonial fire gathered from another funeral pyre which was in flames. I was about to set the pyre to flames, when very feebly and unconvincingly auntie said, "But you should re-check if the girl is alive. I noticed some movements. Didn't you?"

I looked straight into her eyes, and said firmly, "How did you know that there were symptoms of life still existing? I had approached you for assistance; and that too I did at the behest of the saint. Instead of assisting me, you enforced on me all your pranks to deprive me of the body, and deprive me of the pleasure of fulfilling the obligation I owe to the beloved saint, who has been my friend over the years, all along my spiritual life. How could you attempt such a thing? You know that in this path there is not and cannot be any hurry. You hurry and hustle, and you fall. This is not the first time you are doing this, but you will never learn. You know that I am protected. I am safe. I am totally resigned to your kind of greed for acquisition of special powers. Auntie, love is power; the sublimest and the chastest power. No other power could match the power of love. None has loved you, and what you have been searching for is not really liberation, but this power. But you have ignored the power of love, I am sorry for you auntie. Really sorry."

She kept staring. I was about to put the flames to the pyre.

As is prescribed I had to put the flame to the face after going around the pyre seven times. It was difficult for me to go around with the grip on. I was not to let go the grip until the hairs were burnt and the outer cover was burnt out and dropped by itself. But I deviced a means. I went round the pyre with a long log in my hand; and with the log tip I kept my close touch. The other pall bearers were assisting me in various ways without having the least inkling about the battle that was going on between the two old sinners.

Then she said meekly, "Do not worry now. I promise to watch over the body. You do the rituals with your mind at ease. I pledge my faith."

"Thank you", I said and looked at her face, now streaming with tears. I listened to her, and trusted her. But I had also pledged to the saint. So I did what I was doing, without any outward change; but inwardly I had changed. I became relaxed, and I really could attend to my prayers.

As I watched the flames leap up, and cover up the mortal remains of a spiritual angel in flesh, I sang with my full heart the great hymns from the Atharva Veda, composed for such sublime occasions and recited by all of us. The noble hymn really elevated the sentiments that all feel during such times irrespective of religious affiliations or social motivations.

> O earth, cover up this body as a mother covers the body of her child, to protect from the inclemencies of weather...Go thou, the immortal *Puruṣa*, to the solar clime through the light that the eyes had, through the breath that the life had, through the other senses of the different organs to the regions of atmosphere, space and cosmos, and the atmospheric moisture would assimilate the body moisture; while the crude body would be assimilated by the world of vegetation...O *Puruṣa* who is being accorded the send off (*preta*), let no inner faculties of yours ever abandon you, neither may thine active functions of limbs abandon thee; in the after-life may thee not suffer from the want of faculties. Let not your shelter, which is as good as a tree, suffer thee; let not the great earth refuse thee a safe shelter; enter the world of the menes where Yama rules (the god of assimilation and balance).*

The hairs were on fire; I was now helping the flame to lick around; and the unguents, gums, butter, sesame seeds, heaps of sandalwood and camphor did the rest. The flames leapt up. Now the other companions shared their responsibility of making the flames rage in a roar.

Suddenly the fire leapt up in one brilliant flame; and I was mesmerised to watch that within those dancing, leaping, howling flames quietly sat LS with the body on her lap. As both of them lay in a quiet togetherness; one protecting, the other protected. I felt a strange peace descending on my soul. Vision? Hallucination? A strange eruption blowing up our state? Why must I doubt? It was LS; no less.

**imid vā u nāparam divi pāśyasi sūryam n.ātā putram yathā sicābhyenam bhuma ūrṇuhi* (18:2:V:10)...
ajo bhāgas-tapasa-stam tapasva/tam te śocistapatu tam te arcih yāste śivāstvanvo jātavedas-tābhir-vahainam sukṛtānu-lokam.
yāste śocayo ramhayo jātavedo yābhirāpṛṇāsi divamantarikṣam/ojam yantamanu tah samṛṇvatā-mathetarābhih śivatamābhih śṛtam kṛdhi (18:2.1:8-9)
ma te mano maso-r-māngānam mā rasasya te/ma te hāsta tanvah kim caneha/mā tvā bṛkṣah sam vādhiṣṭha mā devī pṛthivī mahī/lokam pitṛṣu vitvaidhasva yamarājasu. (18:2:III:4-5)

Atharva Veda

I entered the Ganges. The waters were so cool and embracing. On the other bank of the river the sun was rising. The first beams were already there on the quiet orange sky. Pigeons were flying around, dipping in the mid stream, and perching on a floating piece of bamboo that the thoughtful guardians of the banks had left floating. The love for animals and birds to these meek Hindus is so genuine that it acts without any show.

A Pyre in a Forest

As I am on this topic of the funeral pyre of the virgin of the saint's *āsana* I find this to be the best place to describe yet another fire which had consumed an old man, the old man of the shrine.

Readers might recollect an incident which had taken place in a Cāmuṇḍā shrine in the forest near Haldwani and Ramnagar.

It was a forest famed for tiger hunt. The trees were considered very valuable for furniture and building. These were red wood, samong, catechu, acacia, cedar etc. The forest was overgrown with tall elephant grass. Numerous brooks ran through the ravines, and lower down, the collected water had made a wide marsh land before forming a stream to flow down to merge into a river. In between was formed a large lake. On the banks of this lake, partly covered with lotuses, stood the shrine of Cāmuṇḍā, the, divine spirit of death and devastations. Only the very select tantra adepts chose this deity, generally hidden away from the masses, for their special worship, which goes to the extreme forms of blood, sex, alcohol and drugs. The very extreme nature of the form precludes the ordinary from dabbling with the rigours of the rites. Generally the Cāmuṇḍā devotees believe in the value of induced physical emaciation. They never keep a seemingly strong or well fed body, and their penances demand the hardest of trials.

I had chanced into this shrine through the directions of an old man, who had assured me of some benefits if I could venture to sit there in meditation.

I was never afraid of such adventures. On the contrary I embraced such lucky opportunities. On my reaching the spot one afternoon on the back of an elephant provided by Havildar Sher Singh, a friend of mine, (who in his own way tried to dissuade me), I stopped under a boa tree. This was the tree I was to find out according to the directions given.

To the surprise of the mahout (elephant-driver) I decided to get down by the big banyan. Hundreds of aerial roots shooting down from the branches had quietly entered the dark moist earth below. The wide expanse of the immense lake was crowded with millions of lotuses at different stages of bloom, unbloom and decay. Swarms of bees filled the quiet with a mesmerising buzz that held my attention almost under a spell. I had never seen with my naked eyes so vast an expanse in so sombre a place where no trace of human habitation could be noticed for miles. Yet the simple charm of the surroundings was fascinatingly breathtaking. I wanted to drink in full the wild virgin beauty and its romantic aura.

I beaconed to the man to stop there with his elephant, and wait for me. I wanted to be left alone.

He hesitated. He informed me that the place was no good for being alone, because it enjoyed a sinister reputation of sorts. Besides being a favourite haunt of the notorious *tarai* tigers, the temple near by was haunted. It was known for animal sacrifices; indeed sacrifices were so common that predators of the forest often shared the leftovers from those dubious rites.

Then, explicably and suddenly he stopped. He hesitated, and looked around as if for any chance eve droppers. "A skeleton has often been noticed hereabout", he whispered, "hungry for human blood." He finished.

He could have added more to his list of negatives. But my determination was not to be stalled by such descriptions. The charm of the place, its outlandish beauty and draw, the immensity of the prevailing calm, the vertical depth of a quiet loneliness, the many-coloured shifting shivering shades, the canopied greeneries, the tale telling footmarks made me follow the twists and turns of a bewitching woodland.

I decided to take my fate in my own hands, and sternly asked the old man to leave me alone. "No skeleton", I quipped, "would gobble me up", and with that smart remark I decided to push ahead.

As I moved on, alone, knowing fully well that he would wait on me until my return; and in a little while I could hear the thuds from his country axe cutting branches from trees for a meal for his elephant.

There was no trace of a path. The lake was the only guide. Yet I imagined to be following a given route. Often I had to go around stagnant pools, and brambly growths, marshes and clusters of acacias and the sensitive 'touch-me-nots'. Frogs jumped all about, and I could imagine that the other reptiles too would not be far away. Myriads of water birds of sorts like ducks, cormorants, darters etc., kept the otherwise bland surface busy. Far away the majestic swans held their sway. Now and then the famed red neck ash gray cranes moved with their corporal steps. The fascinating lavender and mauve of the water hyacinths kept away from the mind the curse the weed has brought to the rivers and waterways of Bengal. Huge lilies, reminding of the great Victoria Regina of South America, spread their brimmed leaves, and a gay sun sparkled over the dew drops collected on their green plates. The lake shimmered as a bowl of quicksilver. It was impossible to think that only five miles away a miserable creature known as man was busy sweating out life through his multifarious machinations, and schemes of self-destruction.

I had a vague recollection of the way to the temple. The route was marked, they said, by the presence of a huge banyan, leading to a wild bamboo patch, and confronted by some oversize jack-fruit trees and catechues. Sher Singh, who had described the route thus, had said, "You will not miss it."

After a dazed walk of more than an hour sense dawned on me that my friend Sher Singh's description fitted more his experience than my adventure to discovery. I had lost my way, and I decided to climb a tamarind and take my bearings.

Before I could gain a fairly good foothold on my perch, I was confronted by the combined opposition from a host of our erstwhile tailed ancestors. Their behaviour, extremely rude and threatening was unbecoming of that sense of kinship. Any violation to their group life, and they would charge. I could do no better than beat a quick retreat. But before I did so, I imagined that I had sighted a red flag fluttering in the wind. In all probability that should be, I thought, the locale of the temple.

Further progress became heavy; and every moment it was getting heavier. Obviously I had lost my way. The more I hoped to be proceeding, the more I got entangled in the lianas and the irritating stubborn bushes of wild opuntias, acacias, the earth hugging triple thorns and touch-me-nots. Any moment an accident could prove fatal. But I kept ahead. Some irresistible draw was acting on me. But the threat of animals kept lurking behind my other mind.

Then it happened. Just in front sparkled upright a gray band. That instant death rose about a foot from the ground, and confronted me with its wide hood spread in fury. I was about to take a step back (a sure way of bringing the total wrath of the brute on me); almost from nowhere a kite screeched loud and shrill; and I froze. In that split second it dawned on me that the best protection under the circumstances was to freeze totally. Thereafter started a primal war of survival between a screaming life, and cold silent death.

Breath by breath time ticked away. The menacing hood stood firm and erect. The shooting split-tongue moved in and out with electric precision. A pair of intensely bright black and cold beads, standing out from the head, kept a deadly vigil. The imperceptible oscillation of taut and steady muscles near the neck rose and fell rhythmically. I kept my eyes glued to the unwelcome intruder. A fraction of a second's inattention, the slightest sign of uneasiness would bring the nasty fang down on its imagined adversary. I watched and kept my cool. A steady perspiration bathed my forehead, and damped my armpits and neck. A cold shiver ran through my belly.

Then the unpredictable took over.

A sudden breeze, unusually strong for this hour of the day, shook the woodland. Bamboos whined; neems and ceders whizzed and murmured; fallen leaves rustled along the ground; muffled groans of distant branches aroused a forest from its slumber. In a split instant, from the branches atop, something dropped with a cry, and the hood turned, and fell with a lash, missing its victim, a bundle of brown quivering fur.

The drowsy forest grave out a tearing fierce howl, as if bent on pulling apart all oppositions. Swarms of monkeys mad with a violent rage began to run helter skelter. Before I could realise what was happening, the mother monkey had caught hold of the neck of the receding cobra, and began to rub its mouth against the nearest tamarind with a savage diligence, vigorously, methodically, viciously.

Monkey and Snake

I recalled a similar incident on the steps of the Durgākuṇḍ in Varanasi, where a colony of monkeys had settled, and gave it the attractive name of Monkey-temple.

That mid-morning I had come out of the Bhāskarānanda temple, and noticed a small crowd assembled to watch a battle in progress. A monkey was seated on one of the steps, with his head doubled down, as if searching for some lost nut. Soon I realised that the fellow was engaged in a hunting game, too dangerous for any animal to indulge in. The good humoured crowd kept up an excited conversation, and watched the proceedings with a keen interest. Some object tucked in a hole between the stone steps attracted the monkey's attention. He was taking his hand again and again near to the hole-mouth, and trying to tempt out a jutting hood. It belonged to a cobra. The reptile appeared to realise its predicament; but it played helplessly to the tune set by the monkey because of its instinctive reactions to such a provocation. Every time the furry brown hand would approach the crevice, the hood would come out with an indicisive attempt to strike at the elusive hairy adversary. The nearer the hand dared, the further the hood jutted out; the faster struck the motion, the quicker receded the arm. Flash by flash the game went on and on. It was developing indeed into an engrossing drama. The hand that tempted was the left one; but unseen by the defending cobra the right hand of our illustrious ancestor kept poised and balanced for some calculated strike.

And the chance came sooner than later. The left hand almost touched the crevice, and out sprang the angry hood. About ten inches of the striking body offered the break to the monkey at last. Before we could bat our eyes the right hand of the monkey held the hood in a vicious and killing grip; a great pull followed, and the body of the helpless cobra began to wriggle and coil around the hairy hand.

Oblivious of what was happening to his hand, the monkey now applied his attention to giving a vicious rub of the hood against the stone flags mathodically, calculatingly and watchfully. Each time he rubbed for half a minute or so, he would bring his hand to his nose. and have a good look at the mess he was accomplishing of the killing hood. Thus the rubbing went on and on; the inspection went closer and closer, until what had been a cobra's proud hood and fang was reduced to a stump, limp and bloody. The monkey, having squared her ire, threw the mess away in utter scorn far out into the stagnant water of the tank. All that remained of the cobra's power and venom were some expanding rings of silent water.

I knew that monkeys enjoy taking an upper hand against poisonous snakes in order to protect their offsprings, as do peacocks, hawks, owls and eagles. The law of the jungle that day acted in my favour, and I continued my journey to the temple. There was no question of going back.

A Funeral Scene

The watery expanse of the lotus-laden lake, had by now (unknown and unrealised by me) created another type of threat, which made my progress all the more hazardous. Swarms and swarms of bees of different species had built huge hives; and the least false step on my part would have brought upon me a major disaster.

At this hour I became aware of the smell of burning hair and flesh. Although that suggested a big fire, no smoke was to be seen. Yet the smell was too strong to be ignored. On climbing a small tree I not only discovered a fire, but also noticed the temple. I was now sure for the first time that the Cāmuṇḍa temple was situated by a crematory ground near the lake, when the lake and the surroundings were alive with people.

On reaching the actual spot I found that a cremation was in progress indeed; but an accident had thrown its three frail attendants into confusion. It was a group of hill people who lived hugging the notorious *tarai* (lowlands infested with forests) of the Himalayas. They eked out a miserable existence through cultivation and wood-gathering. They were the daily neighbours of elephants, tigers, deer and snakes, and lived at their mercy.

The cremation related to a relative mauled by a tiger. According to his last wishes he was being cremated by the holy grounds near the temple. Since the burning had gone by already more than half, most half friends had left. Unfortunately an unforeseen disaster had overwhelmed the group. Under the power of the flames the carcass had bent, and the impact had thrown the flaming and charred mass on to the ground. Those who know, would realise the hazards of putting up that burning mass on the flaming pyre again. Although the poor attendants were busy at it, their efforts, instead of solving the problem were adding to their hazards all the more. I thought I could perhaps assist them. As I offered my help, they looked at me with an eye of distrust. I could read into their trepidity and consternation.

They had their reasons to be wary of such help. In their mind they had been harassed by a fear complex. This concerned a legend attached to the place. The crematory grounds, as well as the temple, they said, were under the influence of an 'evil' spirit. That spectre had been sighted by many. "A few seconds back", they whispered, *She* was here; and with your approach *She* shied away. *She* is sure to come back . . . ."

"Why?" I enquired, as I tried to interpret their nervous looks.

"*She* wants the carcass . . . . *She* eats the flesh . . . . *She* is of the nether world."

Instead of explaining, the mystery was getting all the more thick. I was keen on knowing more. But I had also to be back to my elephant; and the guidance of these people would be of great assistance. So I decided to apply myself to the task of putting the slipped mass of carcass on the pyre again.

After what I did for them, they brought me to my elephant. I left the place resolved to come back to my quarry. Who was this mysterious *She*?

At about this time when I was obsessed with the haunting idea of discovering the mystery of the *forest-She*, I was surprised by a visit from my parents. I was particularly happy to have my father near me. Imagine my astonishment when in a day or two my father referred to no other a subject than the temple of Cāmuṇḍā.

"This temple has been a favourite haunt of *yoginis*," he said. "I am surprised that you have made no attempt so far to locate that very important spiritual spot."

"But the place is haunted, and has a very uncomfortable reputation," I remarked. "Uncomfortable, and alarming."

"So are all the great haunts of the *yoginīs*. But anyone interested in *bhairava-siddhi* of tantra must seek the blessings of such places. Pilgrimages are not made for nothing. The aura of a place casts influence on the later *sadhakas*." After that he said nothing. The subject was closed.

Before I could arrange for any transport for the old man, one morning he surprised me by disclosing that he had visited the temple, and that his labours had borne him the desired fruit. What the fruit precisely was he would never explain. But my mother began to pester me now. She wanted to pay a visit too. It was a holy place, she remarked. Knowing fully well that she would not be able to undertake that hazardous journey without transport, I approached Sher Singh, who arranged for a well fitted bullock-cart.

As we approached the temple grounds, there was a visible change in the ethos of my mother, and she whispered, "This must be a haunted place. Never venture to come here alone."

"But daddy did. And so do many devotees. Are you afraid?"

She kept quiet. At this time a number of crows began to call. Jackals, dogs, vultures and crows are close associates of the tantra milieu.

The Temple

The temple itself was stone-flagged like many other temples in India. Considering the sombre reputation of the surroundings the temple proper was kept in a state of fairly good preservation, but for the cracked yard, which had suffered from the growing trunk of an over-aged peepal tree. A veranda supported by flat stone pillars ran along the three sides. The fourth side was barred; and beyond the barred place stood the sanctum sanctorum, the *devi*'s nave standing behind a pair of wooden doors. Although the brass-knobbed ancient doors were coming off the hinges, and although the passing breeze made the old contraption groan in agony, the deity had been safely tucked hehind. And I could feel a tremor gradually growing within my spiritual consciousness. An aroma of incense hung in the air.

The weird and eerie feel of the place made my mother go dumb. Although she folded her hands ritually, and moved them again and again nervously to her forehead, she did not betray the least interest in going near the temple doors at all. Instead, she tried to take a rest on the round platform surrounding the peepel. Suddenly she gave out a mild scream, and I smiled as I looked at a great lizard ambling away from the base of the platform towards the safer cover of the bushes beyond. My mother tried to be wiser, and advised "we should try pray from this place without disturbing the grated seculsion."

I laughed at the predicament of the poor lady, and remarked, "But father had visited the place all alone; don't you remember?"

She quipped against my casual frivolity. "Ghosts are friends of ghosts", was all she said, and glummed.

"But we have come all the way to the deity. How could we pass over her, and not pay her our respect by opening the door, and placing some flowers? I have collected all these lotuses only for this purpose."

"Open the door? And offer flowers? Not while I live," she remonstrated. "You shall not try even as much as to cross the door", she commanded. "Let us leave the place alone." So saying she began to move away. I had to follow her a little distance. The cart was near, and she did not hesitate to get into its safety. But before I would follow her, I made an excuse, and ran to the lake for a wash, and for some fresh lotuses as well.

I gained entry into the temple yard from the back trap door, in order to avoid my mother.

I rushed to the trapped door, and dashed it open. No one was there except the black and red deity, watching at me intently through her wide open glass eyes. I took my seat, and offered the flowers, one by one, completing the number nine. Then I sat at meditation, and kept myself engaged in *japa*.

I rose to a sharp and demented cry from my mother. I turned back, and saw her hinds receding fast through the gates.

And then I discovered the cause of her panic. The form of a naked and charred skeleton, which had almost no belly, stood before me, in the yard. Two lumps of harsh and dry flesh oscillated from her chest, almost drawing out the skin with their weight. The lumps hung around her socketted belly. The only part alive in her aspect was the pair of eyes, bright, hungry, dry and fiercely red shot. Her canines projected from her toothless mouth. A store of matted locks screamed around her necks, but a knot was heaped none the less on the top of her head. It appeared the mass was held by a human bone. Beads of sorts dangled around her neck. As I watched her still, she also was looking at me very keenly. Suddenly she let loose a loud and hoarse peal of laughter. That my blood did not run cold was because I had concentrated on seeing in her my beloved LS. And she calmed. Then I watched her proceeding towards a small square pillar standing in the middle of the yard. It had a bowl-like receptacle cut into it for receiving particularly the severed heads of animals that were sacrificed there.

She was dipping her skeletal fingers into the bowl, and scraping its walls drew out something, and licked the same with famishing eagerness and earnestness.

As I watched, she attempted to withdraw.

"Wait", I cried aloud. "Wait Mother! Wait! Do you not know why I came here? Only to see and touch you. To touch your feet. I have brought something for your delight; something fresh and red like the blood which is so dear to you." I held out the red blossoms, the few lotusues that still remained. And with the blooms in hand, I approached her.

And there she kept standing, naked as the bare sky, sparing as a cherry tree in late autumn, and engrossing absorbing as a rainbow touching the horizon of a sea. Her hollowed belly, her long neck, her skeletal presence, her bright hungry famished ravenous eyes, her toothless blood tainted mouth held me spell bound. As I watched I was overwhelmed by her spiritual immensity.

I began to sing and pray what I had been singing and praying ever since I knew me as a child in my father's bed.

na mokṣasyā-kāṅkṣā na ca vibhava vāñcchā-pi ca na me
na vijñānā-pekṣā śaśimukhi sukhecchāpi na punah

at-s-tvām samyāce janani jananam yātu mama vai
mṛḍāṇt rudrāṇi śiva śiva bhavāntti japatah . . . .

(Let who care for liberation, wealth and knowledge. I do not entertain in the least any desire for personal happiness. All that is at an end. Now all that I seek from Thee O Mother, is an end to this cycle of birth and rebirth, and sing all the while Thy name: Mṛḍāni... Ruḍrānī . . . . Śive Śiva Bhavānī . . . .)

She stood half crouched, like a bird about to wing away from its perch. But her watching eyes had been fixed at me. Presently she dipped her fingers again in the bowl, and licked avidly. As I pushed forward, and placed the lotuses near her feet, she ran to the trap door, and vanished. I gave a chase; but before she gained the dark cover of the forest, she turned, and blessed me with a last look. I felt I read her message. I felt I was standing under a protective umbrella named LS.

I came back to the squat pillar, and dipped my finger in the blood bowl, and dared in all faith to put it to my taste as an object of benediction and grace, and remembered that many a pious Christian would similarly suck out of the waifer bread on Good Friday the blood of the noblest of sacrifices that the oriental legends have reverentially preserved. To my utter surprise I tasted nothing but aromatic honey. Hopefully I looked at the trap door again. Then with all reverence I touched my forehead with the finger.

Back in the cart we were solidly dumb: mother with her trembling heart, I with my heart singing in divine glory. Only when my mother reached home, she supplicated as only a mother could, "Keep away from that awful path. That path is not for a householder."

But I could not listen to a motherly command. Shankar could not; Gautama could not; Khudiram, Dinesh, Bhagat Singh, Badal could not. The bug of inspiration and dedication first destroys the links between the individual and his emotional world. The call of the inner spirit is an echo from the barrens of solitude. I had to go back to the temple; and I did.

That morning I woke up with a desire to visit the temple. It was a very strong desire. I could not have shared my thoughts with any one. I went straight to the mahout, and he readily agreed to give me a ride on his elephant.

As usual he ambled away with his elephant after I got down a little distance away; and to his enquiry whether he would have to wait for me, I replied that I wanted to be alone; and that I did not know when shall I return. So, I said, he could go. He was too puzzled to make any remark. Finally he left me to the mercies of the forest.

I reached the shrine fighting against forbidding grips of the spreading roots and tentacles of a sprawling ancient banyan. Within the shrine there was nobody to be seen. A burning lamp indicated that the place was inhabited.

I was more than surprised to discover a new phenomenon. I saw an old man in *samādhi*. The figure of the lolling and skeletal Cāmuṇḍa in a seated posture with the skull pot lifted to her lips was awesome. But my real attention was fixed on the yogi. Was he alive?

I waited. I saw no movements. He might have been in a trance. I was watching the image in the meanwhile. Gradually my body relaxed; and my conscious self spiralled along a defined track into space. I was receiving messages. I was being asked to *do* things. I reached for the water bowl (a *kamaṇḍalu*).

It is safer to swallow a lump of potassium cyanide, or kiss a live rattle snake on the lips than to interfere with a tantrik's *kmaṇḍalu.* But I was not acting out of choice. I helped myself to some water, which I held in the cup of my palms. I sprinkled the same on the head of the seated yogi. At the contact of the water the body fell down on the floor. I undid the legs at once and stretched them. I poured some water through his lips. Gradually the man revived.

The unkown man addressed me by my name which was not known to the people around. Some older people of Varanasi alone knew that pet name, and LS used to call me by that name, when she did not address me as "My child"

It became now clear that I was summoned by the yogi's spiritual force. He was gifting me his *asana* (a grass carpet), and his brass *kamaṇḍalu* just in exchange of a favour. His time had come. He was ready for his funeral pyre; he would have his body burnt there immediately.

I hesitated. I could be held for murder. I needed a medical report of death, although these spiritualists are burnt or buried on the certificates of other spiritualists, and in the presence of witnesses.

He asked me not to worry. He assured me of the necessary technical assistance. All he wanted was to have my assurance. I was to help him out of the shrine, carry him near the pond, and help him on to the pyre, and finally, set fire to the body.

In the circumstances I realised that I had no choice in the matter;

and I promised.

On reaching the funeral ground I was surprised to discover that some people had already arrived there bearing a dead body for cremation. It was the body of the mother of the village doctor. With that information everything became solved. The doctor offered me the technical protection, and I was able to consign that saint's body to the flames.

I still feel that old man in *samādhi* in my bones whenever I am very seriously disturbed. But that shrine of Cāmuṇḍā, (the Sanskritised form of a tribal power Cāh-Muṇḍā (Muṇḍā is a tribe) appeared to me as a mystically powerful spot. It has the reputation of having been the *sadhana pīṭha* of one of the ancestors of the now defunct hill royalty of the Rajas of Kashipur, a branch of the Nepal royalty. I had the good luck of being with the old Raja who was a tāntrik of a very high order.

That shrine, the pond, the crematory ground, its sombre influence affected me with a compulsion, which forced me to return to that mysterious haunt time and again before I left Kashipur permanently, but that noble and divine *She* never again came to my view. Luck must be a miserly sunrise. It does not shine too many times.

I recalled the last days with my LS. She would not warn me as my mother did. There is an essential difference between an emotive sense of self-preservation and a spiritual sense of self-elevation. LS was no more; yet LS really never had died in me. My mother spoke; and at that time who but LS spoke. "I am with you. Do not hold back in fear. The path of tantra is a path of no fear. It is the path of the, *vira* (hero)."

Last Search for LS

Today as I sit to recollect and consider the dismal failures of my life, side by side with blessings I have been lucky enough to receive, without having any particular claims on such blessings, I wonder if my subsequent indiscriminate entanglements with *prakṛti* were not due to some desperate suppression of inner hunger. I must have been craving for achieving something in life, but I was forgetting one of the most important warnings of tantra.

Never get attached. Was I not too attached to Varanasi, LS, Saint Jitendra, Nārada and the shrines? Attachment of any kind keeps freedom in a leash. Real freedom is enjoyed only by the liberated. And the liberated must never get attached. This is not a passive or negative philosophy. On the contrary, only the unattached could fulfil the role of an active positivist.

My emotional nature, craving for love and more love, had opened a trap for me. I had been searching for the company of LS. After I got myself steadied from the whirlpools of politics, when I returned to Varanasi, I found the little coconut shop empty. A barber was carrying on a miserable saloon there. He could not, neither any one in the neigh bourhood could, give me any information of one, who had been to them a crazy insignificant, wild, half-naked, half-witted hag.

I searched for her all the same. But she had vanished seemingly for all practical purposes.

I do not know why I did not ask my father about her. But later events made me suspect that he, the ancient and saintly person did never get out of touch with the 'old hag', who for others, had lost her brain.

I was in the university in those dys. The University of Allahabad was eighty miles away from Varanasi, I lived in a hostel. One night I had a terrible dream, in which again and again the huge Siva *lingam* and the yard came to view, and the serpents which could often be seen coiling around it kept staring at me. Visions had meaning for me.

The Protective Hand Unseen

Often when my mind goes vacant and opaque I visualise the momentous last seance with LS. Whenever my soul rides at a high pitch, she with her love and charity, sustains my inner spirit, and I feel safe like a fledgling under its mother's wings.

And yet in my heart of hearts a deep-rooted evidence often sparks a flash; and I question myself, 'Has she really gone to the Evermore?' If so, who has been coming to me at odd hours, and at odd situations? Who was my guide in that distant lonely night when in a lost moment I was confronted with the super powers of a Mexican *alter ego* on the banks of the Atawalk in Oaxaca. What was her name? Marina? And that seance in a dark night by a darker stream's dream current? That night could have been my last. But no; I am still very much alive, and some power had been protecting me, guiding me decidedly, unfailingly? Who again was with me in the Moon cave of Huana Picchu, the Moon neighbour of the sun-dominated Macchu Pichu? Or, over the immeasurable impossible apology of that flimsy bridge, spanning a gorge of several hundred feet with my old man's steps, shaky, unsure, quivering? Who was that girl, who appearing from nowhere gave me courage, and spoke in an intimate voice, "Once on this track, there is no turning back." Or, at the cave of the Royal dead? Did I not swoon away in my *asana*? I had fallen down from the rocky platform. I had hurt myself. Whose hand was it that revived me, and first aided the wound, and then vanished? In the wild expanse of Macchu Pichu where miles and miles could be viewed at a glance, whither had fled that illusive Florence Nightingale?

No, LS had not gone for ever. On the contrary She has been with me ever and anon, step by step, holding me up when I fell, extending help when I needed, cutting me down when I, in my ignorance, over-taxed my ability, and attempted to achieve what was not within my grasp. That everlasting, unfailing, eternal She has never left me since.

I did go astray. Again and again and again I had played the truant, the runaway. For monts and months I did not even know if I had a guardian angel giving me succour; I cared not for else except my sky high ego, and that tremendous warmth of life which guides youth along the precipitous path of self glory, the suicidal course of running into the arms of self-adulation and *passionate* streams of infatuated self decay.

Track Back

I still recall that afternoon in my hostel at Allahabad. Suddenly, half through my exercises with Legouis and Cazamian, I felt the kind presence in the room. The doors were closed and bolted. Yet the familiar smell of the body of my LS pervaded the hot air of May. I looked at the door, and felt that She was standing at her full height; but before I could take stock of the situation she had vanished.

Real or phantom, the experience had robbed me of my poise. The finals of the Masters examination were close at hand. It would be dangerous to be disturbed; to be forced away from my studies. But I could hardly pay any attention to anything else. I recalled with shame that I had not known her for these three or four years of sensuous self-adulation and careless bohemianism.

That night I could not sleep. The memory of hundred and one seances with LS raced through my howling memory. A strange and dry barrenness oppressed my soul; and I took the six o'clock train to

Varanasi drawn by a strange irresistible longing to meet someone undefined. When I reached home, I found my father waiting for me. From him I learnt that LS had been ailing for sometime; and it would be best for me to find her out at once, and meet her.

The information was confused, vague, and in a way futile, because father could not at all tell me where I could find the venerable old lady. I went to Gopī Dādā. He did not know. But he assured me that I shall find her out if she wanted me to meet her. I went to Saint Jitendra. He too did not know; but he knew that I would be helped, if she really meant to see me. "It is her worry; not yours", he assured.

I kept on searching, and came to the auntie at Maṇikarṇikā. She had not seen her for years, but she asked me to try the old shrine at Kāmākṣyā. I went to the old Bhairava; and he winked at my enquiry, and asked me to take a seat.

After a wait of an agonising half hour he came back, and asked me to try the ancient shrine at Agastyeśvara. "Within those lanes there is a heap of abandoned neglected rubble. Climb the hill; look well; you will discover a tower...There!"

The lanes were too narrow for the sun to penetrate except at the height of noon. Eventually I discovered the hill of debris, and the leaning tower of a crumbling temple. Soon as I had sighted it, a change came over me, and I was being drawn towards a definite destination. I cried softly, 'Auntie', and began a song.

At the far end of the decline of the hill a dell had been formed of cactii and shrubs: *artemesia, calotropis gigantia, clitoria*, oleanders, datura etc; a huge neem provided the shade and the necessary humidity.

There stood the ruinous temple deep down the rubble heap, and tucked away from human sight. I climbed down very cautiously. The vibrations, now 'loud' and clear, grew intense, insistent and frequent. "Auntie!", I whispered. That soft sound held. I was caught up in a whirlpool of power. I shot through the few paces, and found myself within the temple. There was she, leaning against the plinth of the *lingam*, seated on the *gauripaṭṭam*, the very repeat of the picture in which I had first discovered her at the Śiva shrine in the Catuhṣaṣṭhi lane. In one sweep of my look I swallowed the bitter truth. This was the end.

Her heavy breasts had shrunken. The lumpen weights pendulum-wise rested over her emaciated thighs. Age had been gnawing as at an old oak. I could see the ultimate ruin of a delightfully familiar dignified figure. Only the aroma, the strange captivating sandal-touched aroma, that recalled my childhood days, hung all over the place. (Of all the senses, the sense of smell, I find, is the most powerful recapitulator of the past). Her wide eyes, bright, now trance-laden and half closed, pierced through me. I found myself helplessly watching her. I sat close to her, and took her hands into mine; and did not know what to say.

I collected just enough energy to whisper into her ears, "You cannot go now. Do you hear? No...I have need of thee yet. I need thee more now than ever. I have sinned."

She held me within her arms. Strangely enough the embrace felt strong and fully responsive. There was no weakness at all. Energetic, deep and firm was the hold as if she were intent on giving me all she had to give. I wanted to cry out for help; but something had been gradually keeping me up against the irresistible break-down. Yet I was feeling a kind of warm courage gradually building within. Her body was giving way; but the fire of will seemed to be at its height. Suddenly I felt that the end was near. I felt disturbed.

The Last Āsana

A world without her was inconceivable to me. Although I had kept myself away so long from her, although within this time my way to tantra had suffered from diversions of several types, yet deep within I knew that she had always been with me. Hers had been the courage, and I felt courageous; hers had been the boldness and directness, and I was what I was; hers was the nagging inquisitiveness that made me nag and persevere in my persistent efforts. In moving around, I was being moved by another perceptible force. I was like a tired swimmer relaxing on the flowing stream just by keeping afloat: Although the stream had its will on me, yet I hoped that I shall finally recover my strength, and swim to overcome.

Now she wanted me to swim again. Although seated reclined, I became aware of her steady revival; and she was holding me in the same *āsana* as she had started years and years back when I had been a mere boy. She asked me to 'prepare' her.

I consecrated the entire base of the triangle; painted, as she used to do, the pubis with *sindoor* and *ghee*, (mercurious oxide mixed with melted butter . . . . Mercury, somehow is regarded as a very powerful medium in tantra, and is known to be creatively as effective as the 'seed bearing semen' of Siva); then I lighted a lamp, and burnt some joss-sticks. Thus prepared I covered the space between the thighs with the red oleanders. The space began to grow before my concentrated eyes, until it covered my being, my imagination, and became all in all, the all effulgent gate-sublime for all life and creation. The usual effect of a flaming aura covered my essential being. My hands could feel waves and waves of radiant flame; and the more the warmth clung, the more tightly I held on to her. After a while, at the very peak of the intensity when I was about to give out a cry, a change came over me. A quiet protective ease descended on my nerves. A stream of cooling delight submerged me, flooding my entire apperceptive being.

Body to body we were locked now, and the beads around her neck, hanging between us, came alive. I felt the sparks that radiated from that mass. She was moaning certain *mantras*, which I partly recognised as the famed *Aparājitā hymn*. Then she was busy consecrating me: *Om Hrang Hring Hrung Hraing Hraung Kṣaung Grah Turu Turu Svāhā*.

I do not know why I began to cry at his point, but was at once stopped by a strange event. Her breasts, limp as they were, came flowing with milk! I looked at this with amazed wonder. "Drink! Drink!", came the soothing command. "Drink, and grow strong. This is me. This is it. This is for ever."

And I drank. I sucked and sucked. I do not recall how long. How much. There are times when no measurements count; when our standards get obliterated. It was one of those unending stretches of time.

All power, all energy, all effect seek a material medium to express itself. Vitality is not matter, though it could be sent through matter. That milk was matter, medium, yet not mater. It was the essence.

It was powerful. She knew I would need power to fulfil her commands. She was preparing me.

A White Screen in a Picture House

The crude mass of this body has so telling an effect on our consciousness that we often allow our senses to get obstructed under its pressure. Against this wall of flesh and bones our subtle energies, like a torrent against unbending walls of rocks, dash, recoil, fume and froth, and dash again. Progress becomes retarded, only to rush out the next moment with doubled vigour. We forget that in this world of matter mass is just an expression of something that indeed craves for subtler expressions, using the body as a medium.

Consciousness, life, feelings, will-force are just the motives trying to communicate something locked within this dumb mass. What is that? How is that? Are the human beings alone subject to functionalism? What functions? How? Why? Who or what inspires? Where is that source of energy that supplies the will to see, to hear, to touch, to smell, to wonder, to striva, to compete, to adjudge, to classify, to write poetry, paint pictures, carve stones, build houses, pattern gardens, invent ships, guns and atom bombs?

We forget that this body is not all; if anything, it is but an obvious presence as is the white screen in a picture house. On it the world drama reflects, and in the process of the interesting stage play, involved in its emotional impact, we accept to wilfully forget within that dark hall that we are, and have been 'made' to cry and laugh by some projections on a screen. We have been forced to identify our past and future, and our very selves with the happenings on the screen. We, the three dimensional beings, thus staying in the dark hall, willingly sacrifice one of the dimensions, and conform to that two dimensional absurdity. Mesmerised by the charms of a show, we contribute to get ourselves identified and equated with what is indeed a chimera and a bluff.

And if this were possible, why then could we not exchange this strange-drama for stranger happenings in another location, and another perspective, with another drama demanding our flight to a fourth dimension? There is a dimension beyond the acepted three; and we are able to realise the magic of that dimensional expanse only if we were able to lift ourselves up our spiritual altitudes. There is a fourth dimension. What we accept as the be all and the end all of our lives is but a promotional achievement of a secondary force which makes us keep engrossed with what is but a mere projection. The reality of the things remain quite hidden beyond our grasp.

Most of us explain this foolish involvement as the gimmicks of *māyā*. It is not unreal; but it is complex; and its greatest impact on our consciousness is to keep us charmed and deluded for the time being at the cost of the eternal, The Real, The Truth.

In the world of active participation, where life and death play the trapeze at great risks, but to the amusement of the temporary spectators, we are completely covered with this mesmerising skill of *māyā*. As the foetus in a womb is kept afloat soothed to a sleep although covered with the life fluid that, on its birth, shall be discadred as dirt, *māyā* too keeps us afloat in this world with a view to give us the opportunity of a New Birth. No more birth in body; but a New Birth in Self. When we are born, and if we are ever born in the *real*, all this we are surrounded with shall be discarded as mere dirt. To accept this obvious as the *reality* is *avidya* (ignorance); and to be able to get at its true nature is to be blessed with *vidya* (true knowledge), which the Buddhists worship as the spirit of *Prajñā Pāramitā*, and the Jains worship as Sarasvatī.

I was in my own world of thinking, totally lost to the immediate circumstances. But she was tracking my thoughts like a faithful hound tracking the steps of her erring pup. I had been too much moved by the threat of the looming tragedy. I had accepted her for granted. I had lost the sense of dimensions, and forgot to measure that my LS cannot be eternal. Now that I had discovered her after all the years, and found her at the threshold of life and death, at the checking point of the departure lounge, I could hardly think properly.

The hand was held within hands; the bodies were closely locked; the beads were pushing through the flesh; but I could not keep back the terrible fact that she was going away for ever.

I broke down. As my head rested on her breast, I broke into unmanageable sobs. I felt fingers pass through my hair. I felt her palms drawing my head deeper into her breast. I was besides myself with remorse. A sense of sharp grief overwhelmed my better senses, and between sobs I spoke with difficulty, and said, "I have been neglecting you, auntie. I have been going astray. I deserve punishment; but this once give me a chance. Give me a last chance."

The Last Ṛide

She began to speak. She asked for some water. I held the familiar *kamaṇḍalu* to her mouth. She would not touch her lips to it. "Use the cup", she said. And I used the brass bowl. She took a long drink, and then said, "Even if I do punish you, even that would be a blessing to you dear. Remember the brush strokes we used to receive at the Kāla Bhairava temple? This is the way of the Bhairavas, an open and true way, provided you keep true to yourself. You have been, so far, true to yourself. You have deceived no one. Before one deceives another, one has to deceive one's own self. In the complex world of the mind the injuring has to get injured first; the violent is first violated.

"Have you indeed any reason to be so despondently self-abusive? The *ātman* is ever-Pure and ever-strong. So don't pour impurities on what you love most through an idle self-reproach. Melancholy is a poison that overpowers clear thinking. Death is Truth; the only truth. Death is Time in the open. Confront death in the face, and learn to respect. Do never give up, or give way; do never crouch and cringe before the Lord of all Life. Death is the charioteer for carrying life from a world of No-More to a world of Ever-More. Do never feel that in this mortal carnal life, acts of momentary accidents entirely rob the spirit of the inner man's true stature and solid gifts.

"Potentiality is a sleeping root, undying root which springs back to life under sympathetic watering and systematic care. In this world of ends there never is an end; because nothing ends entirely. Rise up: struggle; awake; for life is a process of perpetual striving.

"The boat may sway: but through expert piloting a destination is finally reached. Nothing in life is lost for ever, and no loss carries a writ of final end. All falls assume and store the possibility of a rise. Only wake; take heart; struggle and strive. Effort is pregnant.

"I know . . . who else would know? I know that you had a very hard time. You had to pass through a phase of howling temptations. You have fallen a prey to the nagging of flesh: but recall how many times in the past you have come out with a strong heart. You have been initiated in the art of *āsanas*; you have been on the road to the fearless *vīra-vrata*, the vow of the strong. And I am by you. I shall remain so.

"Yes, these years, long long five years have been the most demanding; but they have been the most formative too. In the journey of life, pitfalls not only test you, betray you, but also form you, train you. You are out of the morass. Why then must you feel yourself let down? There is no finality in this restless erratic life. Come closer to me. You have not forgotten. How can you forget? Before you do, you have to forget yourself. Could the guru be forgotten?

"In a much sublimer sense the seed cast by a guru grows in the spiritual embryo of the disciple; and its period of gestation is indetermined; but there is never a miscarriage. If not in this flesh, in another round of life, in another home, another form, this seed has to sprout and take roots, and bloom. Had that not been true, this world, and all its natural laws would come apart, and chaos, instead of order, would have prevailed.

"Do not cry. This is no moment to break down. Am I not going from a temporary *caravansarai* to a permanent abode? True it is, that I am going away for a while, from your physical presence, but only to reside in your permanent self. This body has its debts to pay off to the five elements, and it has to be paid. In death we become one. In life we remain separated. Life is a divider; death alone is the equaliser. Do not remain away from me. Have the last draw from me. Come closer. I have been calling you for this. Don't you understand?"

As she stopped for a little breath, I handed her the brass bowl; and she drank a little again.

The day was drawing closer; and the distant ringing of a bell announced that in the temple of Agastyeśvara the devout were busy. The placid pace of life felt least disturbed by what was taking place in a broken temple not too far away. And on a sudden the dark dungeon of the sanctum sanctorum, where the *lingam* had been keeping watch over the last act of a great and sublime drama, a sudden effulgence enlivened the remotest corner. Against that light even the boas cringed instinctively, and began to crawl along the floor.

LS opened her eyes, and looked at her departing friends, and called out, "Go, and crawl to your freedom, but do not forget me."

As she whispered these very strange words, I looked at her bright face, and was surprised to see a clear halo of light, like a ring, a coronet, gradually form and surround her matted head. I was shaken at the phenomenon. And then, and then alone, she commanded in a cool voice, "Embrace; embrace me totally, as of yore; meeting me face to face, I will not be able to throw my legs around your *cakra*, but you can. And you shall. Take off the clothes, and touch the water. Then come. This last time; this most intense time. This shall be with you for all the time . . . ."

Suddenly I stopped her. "I am not the same one auntie," I said. "I feel pure and simple no longer."

She did not allow me to finish.

She stretched her hand towards me, and said in a husky voice, which was difficult to recognise as hers. She appeared to pull at my *dhoti*, and cried, "Remove, remove, remove . . . . Time is passing. We have a long way to go . . . . Come close. Closer, and closer to me. You shall not regret . . . . Come, Come."

I did not regret; and I do not regret.

Time passed as time passes unknown to the two in an 'embrace', bathed in a soothing celestial light; and all records of memory merged deep into an unfathomable ocean of sheer delight, which defied time and space. That last meet together, that last seance, that last ride together in the celestial wilds of immensity and abstraction.

I was unnecessarily worried about the state of my mind, and more so about the state of my body. I felt loathsomely impure about my body. Not too long ago it had been submerged in the mire of uncontrolled passion. Now I felt reassured; resurrected. I felt cured.

I felt her palms blessing my head. "Do not despond," she said. "I shall not fail you."

As she attempted to speak to me, to my horror I noticed that she was slouching helplessly. Her body, limb-wise, that is, was gradually going out of action.

Carefully I laid her down flat on the ground. The snakes had now returned, and drew closer, and coiled close to her body. The circle of light kept hanging around her head still. I offered her again some water.

Lesson a la fin

Suddenly she began to speak with a new vigour.

"Finally you have come back. This is reassuring. I had been waiting. And I would wait. I needed you now. I could not have disposed with what was not mine. Come near me. Nearer and nearer. Thus we had begun. We had begun in one way, now it has to be reversed. You now, instead of me; you have to be active. Remain active. You are the reservoir of my activity. Only do good with it.

"What is good? Do not bother. Good is when you feel good. In creating joy, spreading joy. God's greatest achievement is the humble flower, the tiny butterfly; man's gratest achievement could be to wipe away a drop of tear, and replace it by a smile. That is always good. Do not go deeper into subjective discussions. Words lead nowhere.

"Deal with life, and death would take care of itself. The only thing that is sure, that does not need assurance is death. Life is in the soil; life is in water, air and earth.

"Those who keep closer to these are the children of god. Keep closer to them. Their *paurușa* (male substance) is real *paurușa* (the vital energies of virility and valour); *prakṛti,* likewise reserves the most effective energy at the volcanic level, able to erupt at any time if properly ignited and agitated. The *kșobha* (agitating concussion) has to be invoked. It is the nature of *purușa* to be electric outside, but magnetic inside. The nature of *prakṛti* is the opposite of this. It is magnetic outside, and electric inside. When together, the intensified field of power created by a sublime frictional effect, which images and symbolises the cosmic effect, effectually sparks off energy in the personality of a human being, then the consecrated is blessed with the tantric power. And this is found more easily in the unsophisticated, in the simple children of the soil, in the tribes, in the working people. The prisoners of forms, manners and etiquette find it hard to respond dedicatedly to this form of exercise. Their consciousness is mostly charged and occupied with images of their own sickly making. In order to construct the future of man, our own inner personalities have to be thoroughly reconstructed in the simple light of nature.

"What you call the high, the noble, the select, the privileged are but paper dolls playing roles on a stage. They come and go. But the soil remains, the earth remains, and the work here on earth remains. They never change. Keep close to the children of the soil. They shall survive. Theirs is the tantra. They enjoy contentment. Simple is their view of life. Not theirs whom you call elect, special, high.

"Why must you cry? Is it for this that I had built you up? I come, and I go. You are the one to bid me a grand farewell. Yet it is not a farewell. I shall always keep near you. Only remain true, sincere, loyal to our vows, our *āsanas*. I am yours for the keeping. Would you keep me? Could you promise me that?"

The beads seemed to have acquired some life, and began to move. I was horrified to notice that two live snakes were wriggling within the heap of beads, and trying to carve out a placc. I had known them before.

As her body was half-reclined on mine, I could not avoid the feel of the creatures, and the automatic shudders, which she must have felt, made her break into a smile, however faint.

She passed her hands over them, as if to reassure me of their harmlessness and friendliness.

"Not afraid I believe." She smiled, and then she looked at me. How could I describe that look? A mother's look.

I knew that she was looking at me like that for the last time. She was injecting me with all her charms and aura. My eyes filled with irresistible tears. I forgot to be afraid of those reptiles.

When love overwhelms, love alone remains predominant. Other feelings give way to the spirit of unattached love, like fog before the sun. Fear, spite, jealousy, avarice, anger, any other negative emotion must be flooded out by such a forceful transmission of love. Why do men not love enough before trying to 'correct'? But then, such love calls for patience and forgiveness. Above all it calls for an impersonal abstraction. It is attachment with detachment. It is absolutely important to acquire the supreme virtue of non-attachment in order to be able to forgive. The attached are by definition already tied, already enslaved. The attached are themselves not free. How could they be non-attached? If they are not entirely non-attached, their love too would be the love of the attached, and therefore, not free. The experience of drinking liberated love gives the experience of drinking peace. I was indeed reassured.

"These are my secret, gurus," she said, pointing to the serpents, "and they too have now come to bid me farewell. They know where I am going; and they too would not leave me alone, even in my life away. O my pets."

She passed her plam over them again.

"It is not for nothing", she continued, "that the image of snakes again and again comes into the area of transcendental perception as well as into the area of the process of transcendental meditation. *Kuṇḍalinī* is imaged as a serpent; the rousing of *kuṇḍalinī* is imaged as the uncoiling of a snake from a deep slumber. Siva, Tārā and many other Vāma Margī (leftist) images like Gaṇeśa are associated with snakes. We the Hindus are not unique in this. There are gods and goddesses of other lands associated with snakes. The python has been worshipped in some of their temples. Snakes have always intrigued magic and magicians. In the *Mahābhārata* a snake has uttered the most practical and wise truths about life. We have to learn many things from snakes before putting their bad temper or their poison in the forefront, and fear them. For one poisonous snake there must be ten non-poisonous ones.

"Yet we are always against them. Even in the *Mahābhārata* we have been against them, although we image Viṣṇu as the greatest protector and friend of the snakes. Viṣṇu is the lord of consciousness.

"Life and consciousness are essentially coiled up, and could be uncoiled only at the hazard of both. The solar energy and its source, the sun, are imaged as Lakṣmi and Viṣṇu; and consciousness is imaged as a snake the lord is resting on.

"These images talk to you, if you understand their language, and know how to communicate with them. The image is your own thing; you conceive; you perceive; you communicate. Else it is a picture, an idol, a piece of wood and nothing more. This spiritual communication, this spiritual consciousness, this spiritual awakening is all imaged by snakes. No; snakes are the friends of aspirants. Don't be afraid, because there is nothing to fear.

"But when a life is threatened and provoked, disturbed and teased the immediate protective reaction is anger, or a show of anger, and if necessary even aggression. Do not feel disturbed; you will not disturb; you have nothing to fear. Befriend them, they become friendly. Ask your mother. At your home in the *agni kone* (south-east corner) under the first floor, in the dark room, there lives a pair of snakes. These are cobras, white cobras. She leaves food for them every day, and assures them protection. And they protect her. And the day they are disturbed, they would leave the home; and you all have to leave that old home. This is true."

I was of a divided mind. Should I make her talk? Or, should I assist her in keeping her energy conserved? The words were flowing at an easy speed. No hurry, no rush. The thought sequence, the active marshalling of facts ranged from the memory mass, came in a crystal-clear stream, as if she were at the prime of her life. Where was the gloom, the tiredness, the malfunctioning from the looming death? I wondered, hesitated, quailed.

But not she. At once came the question, "Have you anything to ask? Any question? Any doubt? Do so now . . . or, never, never."

I knew that when the lamp of life finally is about to go out, it flickers, for the last time very brilliantly. I have seen that a man known to have been stone deaf for years suddenly received his lost ability only minutes before his death. The sudden spurt of energy in LS, instead of gladdening me, actually saddened my heart. She was going . . . going. I have also heard of the dead returning to communicate; but I also knew that souls such as LS are very hard to be communicated to by the sundry, only because their spirits are of an order far more subtle and far more liberated for the common man to get into contact with. The liberated are abstracted beyond any recapitulation.

Exiled from the Land of Consciousness

The voice had fallen silent. The afternoon sun was scorching all things in existence. In the distance a pair of woodpeckers droned their tap-dialogues. A hawker called out his wares, *kulfi malai . . . kulfi malai* (ice-cream).

"I had so much to ask", I said; "so much to learn. I do not know anything yet. I am still in the land of nowhere. How far am I from the poise and contentment of Yogavāsiṣṭha. How easily I have slipped; I have erred. My respect for the human body, my regard for the power-seat in the female, my equanimity against odds have been eroded time after time. I am still in exile from the land of consciousness. I needed you so much now; I am still a bundle of questions. I have no other friend. What could I ask now? How could I deprive you of your last moments of peace?.... O if I do not feel utterly helpless." I screamed.

"No you don't. You never shall do", she assured. "There is no now or then for peace. Peace is peace. Either always, or never. There is no fragmentary peace. Peace is total. You watch around. You shall see that from the west, where the sun goes to sleep at night, and life feels cold, the peace of the sleeping would descend on earth; it is the peace of hooded consciousness; of death.

"It is itself disturbed. Too disturbed to be of any good to mankind. If it is itself disturbed how could it bring peace to others?

"The world of the future would very much like an arranged peace. But arranged peace is no peace. We have to earn the peace of the essence; the radical peace. It is the peace of the lotus in the morning sun, reflecting on a lake's surface. Peace is a state of love. There could be no peace without love. Peace is total; peace is eternal; peace is unattached; peace is its own protection, its own power. None can protect peace. It sounds like an empty claim. Peace is self-protected.

"Peace is of the heart; not of the head. Man cannot win and secure peace through the application of head alone. Feel . . . feel . . . feel . . . Feel unattached. That is the only way.

"The peace I talk of is of the inner strength. My peace is with you, the world, the universe, . . . *ā-Brahma-stambha-paryantam* (wide, wide until you reach the space and the outer space, the nebulus and the navel of creation) as has been said. I am here. I am not here. I am because my body is; yet I am much bigger than this body, stretched far beyond the measurement of human time. I am going to come; as I had come to go. I have all the time in my hands; and I have no time. Until the sun rises . . . Ask . . . ask. Do not hesitate; do not keep back. What is it thou seekest? (*Ki Chās Tui*—This form of pronoun like TU in French, Russian colloquy, denotes in Bengali deep affection.)

Aura

Gradually the darkening shades within the room began to get alive, and I noticed a kind of glow covering her emaciated body. Round and big at her head, the aura got thinned at the foot, until I felt that she had been lying on the bed of a supersize banyan leaf.

I have learnt of auras since, and have studied the phenomenon of plasma. I have spent devoted hours on the study of experimentations carried out in this area, in Europe and America, particularly in Mexico. But on that evening I too was surrounded with this aura. In fact I was myself seated within the protection of this aura, the halo as the devoted would term it for describing a saint.

As the area of the aura began to expand, and as the faint light within the room became alive with this phenomenal glow, I noticed the pair of snakes getting restive. They gradually uncoiled from around the neck, and slithering from the body of LS tried to seek rest over my body,

When a boy, I used to borrow various kinds of snakes from the professional snake-charmers who swarmed the lanes of Varanasi. I knew the electric, sensuous, muscular pressure sent by the thin scaly wrigglings of the elongated body, and soon observed that there was a method in their movements. They wanted to coil the two bodies into one, and cause pressure around the hip joints.

Latā Sādhanā

My eyes widened. I looked at her. A faint smile streaked between the pale lips, they had became brighter, deeper, eloquent.

"You see; how my friends are resting. This is the ultimate test for peace. You are at peace. *Peace and love shall be your most friendly powers, if you could keep away from such enemies as vanity of human possessions, and envy for the possessions of others.* Power is and could be yours only when you are dedicated to use your efforts for bringing in peace. You could see for yourself. The snakes love you as much as they love me. This is the test."

How precise is Sanskrit as a language. In translating what LS had said I have to write long sentences in English, yet her Bengali (like Sanskrit) was so pithy, precise. This last sentence in italics, for example in Bengali would be: *Shanti pābi, jodi ahang bhāv nā thaké.*

"This is the ultimate secret of *lata sādhanā*, the female entwines the body of the male like a creeper, as do these snakes. The erotic in the human body creeps through the body and becomes love and understanding. That is Śankara's burning of *kāma* with the third eye. You know the legend. That is the end of *sādhanā*. Let the serpent lie tame as a friend clinging to the body.

"Didn't you seek the secrets of the *latā-sādhanā*? The male-female *āsanas* clinging over long hours are parts of this *sādhanā*. The (cadavar)

Śava āsana too is another type of *latā sādhanā*. Did you not want to know?

"Watch them, the two, the male and the famale. O they lie quiet on you as two earthworms, like two hands joined in prayer, yet how powerful they are. Death in life, life in death."

I was wondering how could she know what I had been seeking within my mind. But I was a fool. I should have given up wondering about her. Science could have explanations for all her feats, as she herself defied science. She was prescience, ultra-science.

Latā Sādhanā and Sex

"Of all the emotions man suffers from", she explained, "sex and sex-oriented emotions demand the most vital sacrifice. It is the most demanding and the most daring of emotions, it is also the most self-centred, next to hunger. It adores the self most, and hates to share its joy and consummation. It is wanted the most, it is regretted the most. It is creative; it is destructive. Is is joy, it is sorrow. Bow to sex, the *lhādinī*.

"Any emotional upheavel generates heat. Heat is an effect of combustion; unless some object is consumed or burnt, there can be no heat. In other words, whenever excess heat (as in temper) is generated in the body, it must be inferred that something vital in the body is being burnt. (No combustion, no heat, vice versa).

"The substance which is consumed by any emotional imbalance, and causes heat is a vital organism within the body. These are called *gūḍha koṣas*, or *āśayas* (cell-glands). These *koṣas* are always changing, giving place to new ones. The speed with which these changes spin around keeps the body warm, or in heat. Food, breath, water-moisture are the media through which these cells are maintained, and a constant balanced supply of the cells is kept up, despite the constant consumption. We age and decay because the mechanism that replaces the consumed cells becomes gradually defunct, and new cells cease to replace the consumed ones.

"The importance, therefore, of using these cells economically cannot be overemphasised. Sudden outbursts of emotions, as much as the slumbering quiet of tight-lipped suffering (which causes more damage, as slumbering fire does) cause exhaustive damage to the cells. At times the speed of the supply of the cells fails to cope with the demands made on the system. This causes the failure of the nerves, and diseases of various complicated nature, even a sudden paralytic closure of the uses of certain organs and limbs of the body follow. Even madness, which is nothing but a short-circuiting of the brain nerves, may be caused by these failures. Control of emotions (otherwise called passion, temper, *krodha*) is of supreme importance to love and peace.

"It is not difficult to understand how important it is for man to maintain the equilibrium of nerves, which is a step towards maintaining the inner peace. A man of peace alone is a powerful man. He alone is able to bring peace. A saint is one who radiates peace like a lamp in a stormy night.

"But as emotions continue to make such damaging demands on the nerve system, sex and sex-aligned emotions wreck the dynamism of creative energy. And because such a loss causes the most serious damages to vitality, to that dynamo if you prefer, the technique of using sex, and of preventing its misuse, has to be learnt. To love is to understand. Experts have to be consulted, and lessons have to be diligently practised through application of sustained discipline and understanding.

"He alone could use a car or a horse who could control it. Hence one needs a licence to drive a fast vehicle through crowded places. If for driving a fast vehicle one should need a licence, the spiritual man too needs a licence for controlling this source of dynamism planted within the human system, and known as sex power.

"As one is never sure of one's mastery over the control of such machines without coming into close contact with the machines, the control over the most vital of these powers, namely, the sex power too, cannot be deemed as complete and dependable unless one has *practised* it through the most challenging process of keeping the closest contact with it.

"By keeping the closest contact with it alone one could sublimate entirely this emotional adversary, and gain peace.

"The lairs of sex demand run into the deepest levels of personality; and even the highest of the spiritual beings are known to have been victims of the persistent gnawing of this obstinate emotion even as they think that they had mastered it. Regular and disciplined cultivation of a close relationship with sex alone would completely eradicate the dark after-effects of the retarding draw of the same power. There is no other way considered as effective and sure as the tantric way: that is keeping close to this aspect of the physical body through promoting a 'religious' attitude.

"Abstinence is not the best way of utilising the gifts of nature. '*Those are demons indeed who thoughtlessly suffer the mass of limbs through repression*'—(Gītā). Nature has not created anything redundant within the human machine. By maintaining the theory of abstinence in yoga we are out to make a fool of god, and of his greatest manifestation, viz., the wondrous balance and economy in nature. Real yoga teaches for 'control', that is, control for use, and good use. Control never implies negativising. *Bramhmacarya* means the period of schooling of this control.

"The best use of nature-given faculties is to put them to the most controlled and studied exercise. A controlled mind enjoys itself through application. This is not rejection, negation or abstinence.

"The misuse of the dynamic possibilities of the *lhādinī*, the power that enjoys itself through a voluptuous consummation of creative urge, causes the same damage to the body and mind as the batteries of a car, which would get damaged through the misuse of the copper plates placed inside them. By misuse, disuse, and overuse that dynamism, which is god's greatest gift to mankind and life, could be entirely and irreparably damaged. Because sex gives supreme joy, therefore man and man alone, as no other animal, misguidedly engages himself in extracting the first and the last drop of joy through the indiscriminate uses of this power. This is a suicidal mistake. Indeed it is suicide of body and mind.

What Man has made of Man

"Look what man has done to himself and to the world through such misguided and misplaced zeal. Look at the great treasure-house of nature and the natural resources. Man's greed and impatience have almost denuded and certainly raped every department of these treasures by indiscriminate exploitation. Even the animal and the social worlds have not been spared. What have we done to the balance of natural biology, ecology and geology which together kept man supplied with the most essential needs for his survival, e.g., pure air, pure food and pure water. What a mess we have made of them now.

"The vandalism does not stop there. Look what we have done to our own body-machine. We have been misusing them ever since the times of Solomon and Māndhātā. We function most pitiably through our own disregard of the senses. We overuse, and underuse. In both the cases we misuse, upset and disorganise. The owl, the vulture, the eagle could see more than we do; the dog could smell more accurately than we do; the snake, the bee, the fish have a keenêr hearing sense. The sensitiveness of flying birds and hunting bees is amazingly electromagnetic. The human body too has been equipped with this electromagnetic shield to afford sensitive communication; but through our own disuses and misuses that shield lies blunted, frustrated; and we look for miracle-men for their powers, when we ourselves could become store-houses of miracles, because we have been naturally filled with a potentiality of radioactive field of communication and knowledge. A yogic training alone could recover for us our lost senses, and inspire us with the faculty of natural and automatic, fore-knowledge.

The Serpent Motif

"These snakes too", she continued, "know what is going to happen. They are now restless; and like you, they too are clinging on to me. That is how they bid a farewell. They do not grieve like you. Why must you grieve? Don't you realise that I am out for a much better place? Man's better possibilities open up with departure from this life. The *cakra* has to be turned from on to on. In 'running' with the *cakra* alone we run along the path of the better prospects. Without 'running' the *cakra* there is no liberation, no peace."*

I was crying. She felt it. She could hardly lift her hands; but the vibrations were growing in intensity as well as in frequency. The strange light around her body was getting warmer and warmer. Somehow now I felt wrapped with that light.

She was almost in my arms. I was holding her as close to my body as possible under the circumstances. It was naturally uncovered as usual but for the beads of shells, bones, seeds, crystals and Tibetan corals. Her head rested on my shoulder; the mass of tangled hair brushed my skin: the warmth of her body, then at a feverish height, radiated through my skin.

The pair of serpents had changed their position, and had been wrapping our body tighter and tighter. The fever in her body made

*In reporting this last dialogue, as well as in the dialogues carried on before, I have used, for the sake of easier understanding many modern phrases and scientific terms. Of course LS had spoken her own language, and taken help from her own technical knowledge of Yoga and Saṁkhya treatises which abound with technical words. I recall her using words as *samvit*, *taḍit*, *caumbik*, *ananta*, *antarikṣa*, *saura*, *antah-prajnā*, *spanda*, *mahākāśā*, *srișṭi-kendra* etc., by which she meant supra-consciousness, electric, magnetic, space, atmosphere, solar, subconscious, vibrations, cosmic nave etc. I do not think it necessary to load the text any more with those Sanskrit words.

me sweat. But I was determined not to go off in a swoon. I knew that the end was not very far.

I am Arriving

". . . No; not very far now. I am coming closer. I am arriving. But this is not the end. This is only the beginning. It is a beginning for which the life-long preparation, and the many many preparatory efforts through cycles and cycles of lives look like links in one long chain.

"*He lives who knows when and how to leave. Death alone reveals true life, and life's truth.* What we call death is the beginning of the Everlasting. This is the most solemn moment for a voyage to the Great Beyond. Do not grieve at this moment. Do not load this moment with any thought other than joy and fellow feeling, good wishes and a wish of no return . . . . Wish me no return.

"No return I said. Yet there is always a kind of return which is of the spirit. The spiritual shall be everlastingly present as the good weal, the blessing, the grace.

"This mind which is a store-house of cravings and frustrations drives the operation of the body to sickness. To be liberated is to be liberated from this mind. A mind-laden soul is the suffering *jīva*; and the soul freed of the mind is the soul of eternal values, the cosmic Atman. It has no individuality. But when the individual seeks and prays, when the individual submits and kneels for assistance, the same soul responds, as it must, but in the shape and size of an individual.

"*There is no seeing but of a point; there is no time but of a moment; there is no communication but through a well recognised individuality.* This is why devotees could see and communicate with the unsubstantial and the liberated who reappear in shapes and forms easy to communicate with.

"There is no return I said. Yet whenever you shall need, and may your needs find an end sooner than you realise the needs, whenever you shall need this 'other I', the soul, which assists all, shall appear to you in a known form. That is not indicative of any restraints or impediment to liberation. That is really indicative *of* liberation. The liberated alone could appear unrestrained in luminous shape for assisting prayers. For receiving that emanence one must keep oneself in readiness at all time. Always feel calm, clean, holy and simple. The simple attracts more rapidly than the complex, or the ceremonial.

To Where it Belongs

"Soon all this shall be over. This mass would then be a burden unto you. Carry this to where it belongs. To Maṇikarṇikā, to the flames and the ashes, to the Ganges flowing to the open sea.

"Your auntie at the cremation ground has the information. She is getting ready. She is busy preparing the pyre. You carry the body through the Tripurā-Bhairavī lane. Rest the body at Mānasa Kāli. Then proceed to the end of the Maṇikarṇikā Lane, where the steps take a right-hand turn. At the municipal office of death registry you shall find everything ready. But all this just for two points. Get them clear.

"This body shall not be touched by any other human hands. You and you alone shall bear it. Look at the corner. There are two bamboo pieces and some ropes. Cover me with the rags you find, and bind the body on the bamboos. Then drag the bamboos. I shall assist you at every step".

She did.

"Let me die this once", she continued. "I shall then belong to Time. You shall consign me to the elements. No fear, no grief. Promise?"

I did not have to answer anything. I held the body and recalled that first day when she had taken me to the Siva shrine in the Catuhṣaṣṭhī lane, and made me sit *on* her, making her body an *āsana.*

The serpents had vanished; and I felt that the room had suddenly broken into a myriad voiced light that sang as it revealed, and revealed as it sang. Waves and waves of thrill impassioned my deepest cords with a feeling of buoyancy, amplitude and expanse, and I felt that I have become a neighbour of the sun in the farthest limit of space. I could see and feel the myriads of souls seeking solace from this one journeying soul, and the power that it shed in its passage, filled my being with tremendous urge and initiative.

Although the snakes had vanished I felt the intimate pull and draw of their coiling around my waist and below my navel. The vibrations in the two delves on either sides of the pelvic bones electrified my spinal column; and again and again I appeared to jump out of the situation. But I held on, clasping the body skin to skin. This agitation at the *svādhiṣṭhāna-cakra* made me look at a world spinning at a very fast speed.

A pale moonlight had been waiting outside. The ruins and the rubble heap looked like mountains in the moon, glorified and transformed beyond recognition.

A Deity Born

Without the realisation of total emptiness, there is no visualisation of Reality. There is an emptiness of the mind, and an emptiness of consciousness. Once it is realised, against the background of this emptiness, the desired subject begins to assume an objective shape. Then and then alone is a deity born, and visualised. Because this is beyond any description, the only method of communicating this feeling must take recourse to a language of symbols and signs, of abstract expressions to point out the abstract. These are the *mudra, yantra, mantra, āsana, maṇḍala* and of course the image. But the deity itself is of the mind and mind alone. And a void mind alone could contain this.

An emptiness had gradually overwhelmed me. It was a sizeless, seamless, shapeless void without air, smell, touch, sound or tint. All on a sudden I could see the beloved shape of the Lady in Saffron fading away into the void. She seemed to float along for a while in a tiny diminutive shape, until she twinkled as a star in a moonless tropical sky.

I could then realise that a brightly attired and bejewelled young lady, crimson in complexion was smiling at me. Her third eye was clearly visible in all its brilliance between the brows. I recognised the form to be that of *Devī Mātangī*, but did not know what to do. I was looking for that dot of light that had been the Lady in Saffron. My Lady in Saffron.

"Yes", the voice of LS appeared to be saying, "that is what all this is going to be. All is me; all was me. To leave you alone is not what I want, or what I can. I would never do it. Do not get depressed at what you had been passing through. All *prakṛtis* are but my natural forms. That you plodded through the rough and tumble of the many who had come across your path has only helped building you up, because you had never lost touch of me. Do never despond. The way of no return has never been found in spirit yet."

All on a sudden I heard her voice singing. And I listened, until I joined her:

parityaktāh devāh kaṭhina-tara-sevākulatayā
mayā pancā-śīte-r-adhika-m-apanīte tu vayasi

bhavād-bhīto māta-s-tava yadi kṛpā nāpi bhavitā
nirālambo lambodara janani kam yāmi śaraṇam . . . .
pṛthivyām putra-s-te janani bahavah santi saralāh
varam teṣām madhye durita sahitoyam tava sutah
madiyo-yam tyāgah samucita-m-idam no tava śive
kuputro jāyeta kvacidapi kumātā na bhavati . . . .

(I have now reached the eighties of my life, and have left all other forms of worship, as these demand the rigours of complex formalities. I feel scared now. Without your blessings. Mother, to whom shall I pray now? . . . . All other children of yours are much simpler than this tainted one. But should you abandon me on that count, Mother? It would not appear quite fitting for a mother, who is known to bear a special care for the bad one.)

Through all this praying and singing I was busy to follow her directions meticulously. I got down the bamboos. The rags were indeed red silken wrappers. I rubbed *śindur* all over her body. I arranged the beads. Finally I laid her on the bamboo litter and tied the ropes around. Then I offered to pull. The body seemed not only too light, but it appeared that I was pulling a wheeled barrow. The going was smooth: and the directions were clear.

Alone I mounted the rubble heap. As I dragged the load, a strange hearse it must have been, some of the dislodged bricks and debris rolled and made a noise, making the night birds fly about. I reached the comparative smoothness of the lanes. In a city like Varanasi, where every day the craziest of people are engaged in the craziest of acts, none noticed that I was dragging a dead body by myself. In any case at that hour of the night I might have crossed on the way only a few. For some strange reason the dogs, a number of them kept following, never barked throughout the lone journey.

Joy Its Own Reward

I had been brooding on my life. I learnt how important it was for man to be engaged in some form of spiritual exercise, we call *sādhanā*. Under the influence of a spiritual discipline alone man could evaluate the changing state of the world drama. I felt that no state of the body could be regarded as filthy, or dead, or dreary. No action could correctly be described as pure or impure, proper or improper. Beyond all these distinctions the body is and remains to be the *āsana*, the *pīṭha* of the supreme essence. It cannot be otherwise

Where then there could be any objection to be in God all the time? Why a special preparation for the invocation of the spirit? Why a special form, a special edifice, a special messenger? At all events man is in god: there is no escape from that. The difference arises only in feeling about this basic and unchallengable truth, which is a fact. No function of the body could really be described as filthy, evil, bad or sinful. Before such a description taints an action, it taints the dweller of the body, the promoter of all actions and thought. To keep the purity of the pure we ourselves have to remain pure. There can be no relaxation from our duty to remain pure and truthful. *Nothing taints me without tainting my inner being.* Nothing. The motive alone reduces all functions to bad or good, joy or sorrow.

That which increases through giving and sharing is joy; that which in itself is its reward is joy; that which sublimates not only an individual, but the entire surrounding, his society, his age, his time, is joy.

But that which leaves behind a trail of morbidity, a chain of dejected and frustrating reactions has to be termed as sorrow. Dejection is sin, because dejection is no virtue. Dejection negates. The negative is sin, and sin is negative. Positive alone is Śivam, Kalyāṇam (good). Positive alone is virtue. Sin is fear; fear is sin. Fear is not sought for; yet it thrives in the underworld of mind. Dejection too is not sought. Unsought it overwhelms us, and we find no way to keep it back.

When man has to fight morbid sadness, despondency, he brings a pattern out of himself to destory himself. Yet again he is capable of bringing another pattern out of himself to fight the menace. That personal pattern is determined by what and how far he could visualise the counter-power to morbidity, dejection and sloth. When the correct positive, affirmative method of countering evil, morbidity and sloth has been found, one realises it to be the blessing of the Mother. Sing to that power. Raise the voice in singing its praise. Sing, sing, sing. The soul in fear cannot sing. Sinners cannot sing to please their inner being. Demonstrative, exhibitionary skill of voice is no singing. Those who are the beloved of the gods sing and pray, paint and create. All these are signs and gifts from the Mother's blessings. Arouse the state of consciousness, feel the all-ness pass through the stages of gradual ascendance until it reaches the supreme state of tranquillity. That is bliss, the region of liberated delight. This liberation gained, all is liberated.

Perpetual Movement leads to Achievements

But the liberated has not arrived at the end of the journey; he has only reached the actual starting point. Does he stop there? Is there a *kumbhaka* (witholding of breath) in the Realised State?

No! *Perpetual movement leads to achievement.* Divine agitation is the essence of ecstasy. From the stages of liberation there is no stepping back. He has to move on and on, and descend to the level of the common man, to *jana-nārāyaṇa* (god as the man on the street). The mass waits for inspiration from the man of the hour, the divinely inspired man. Instead he becoming the god of the dumb mass, the dumb mass becomes his god. He becomes the servant of the mass. He, the liberated, cannot leave the mass because he has arrived. *No man is free until the last one is free.*

I passed through the lanes of Tripurā Bhairavī chanting the prayers, and thinking of the liberated and their ways. I stopped at the yard in front of the solemn Mānasa Kāli. The Bhairava of the shrine had been waiting. He lifted his water pot, and sprinkled the body. He placed a garland reverentially.

The Water is Cool

I came to the Maṇikarṇikā Ghāts. Auntie had kept everything in readiness, and it took me no time to consign to the flames what had been my dear Lady in Saffron.

The cool breeze of the hour before dawn fascinated my consciousness, and made me take a good look at myself, at my relationship with this strange lady. I tried hard to think what the world without her would feel like. The flames were lapping the body with intense hunger. I was petrified to see the two large snakes crawl through the ash-covered sands, and approach the pyre. Soon they could be seen wrapping around the flaming body. And I visualised the Lady in Saffron sitting on it, with two fire vessels resting on her two palms, and another on her head. (This was the second time I had a flame wrapped vision of hers at Maṇikarṇikā.)

Was I looking at a hallucination? A figure coming to life through the impulse of my living wishes? If I did, so what? The thrill of it was a pure thrill still. And—it had its own message. That message is a reward.

The auntie of Maṇikarṇikā was telling me, "Take a good look at her. She is yours for the asking. She can never abandon you."

No, it was not a self-projection: a hallucination. Indeed she never abandoned me.

Once in the depths of the Guyana forests when I with my family had been thrown in a position of no help at all, I had seen her smiling at me from the waters of the turbulent Kangaruma, that flowed into the Potaro. Again when another day I was writhing in pain and fever in the abandoned jungles of Cambodia, where I had slipped in illegally, hoping to offer prayers at the Śiva temple of Angkor. And when I thought I was dying, I saw her beaconing me to come up and follow a track, until I met a Buddhist monk who saved my life.

That was not all; I again had seen her, coming out of the dark beyond the hills by the side of a shrine in Japan, where I found tucked between folds of mountains and tall trees a red painted open tiny shrine. I longed for a second; and she was by me. Until the morning we had been together.

Another time, in Cairo, the plane was late; and we were stranded because we did not find an accommodation. With my two children, heavy with sleep I had to come out of the Nile Hilton for want of accommodation. I stood by the car, facing the river. The car man would take me to another hotel too dismal and forlorn for a feeling of safety and hygeine. As I came out of that hotel, tired and at nerve's end, and as I was occupying the seat by the driver, I saw her in the car waiting for me. I led the car to the next hotel which we occupied for our stay in Cairo.

But, even in the morning we got transferred to the same Nile Hilton as charges of BOAC!

I have seen her again and again directing me to take the course I took in moments of utter confusion.

The body burnt until the first lights of the sun with me. Her glory beamed through the woods on the opposite bank. The ghats got filled with bathers. Temple bells rang from the thousand shrines that crowded the banks of the Ganges at Varanasi.

Bare footed, bareback I walked by the bank, until I reached the ghat where she used to sit at evenings and sing.

I entered the river.

The water felt cool.

Glossary

Āsana: A convenient posture of keeping seated for long hours of unbroken meditation. Also means the series of physical 'exercise' to keep the body 'fit' and active for long periods of endurance and concentration.

Aśvatthāmān: A character in Mahabharata, attempted to sacrifice himself to gain divine redress.

Aghoras: An extreme sect of Bhairava.

Arhat: A Buddhist saint.

Avalokiteśvara: A form of the Buddha worshipped in Tibet.

Abhaya mudrā: Open right palm with fingers straight and up to denote "protection".

Ananta śayanam: Bed of eternity.

Asmi-tā: Asmi=I am; Asmi+tā=The subconscious egocentric consciousness that upholds the supreme ego of 'I'.

Avatāra: A divine descension in life-form. A strong belief held by Jaina Buddha and Hindu thoughts.

Bhairava: Tantrik saints known for their pious habits and modes.

Brahman: The cosmic consciousness, distinct from *Brāhmaṇa*, a realised man of peace, equipoise and learning, the top-knotch class of human beings.

Bhagīratha: A king in the epic supposed to have brought the flow of the Ganga down to the sea from the Himalayas.

Brahmachārin: See page 70.

Bīja: seed, i.e., a tiny sound that stores the potency of growing into a full-fledged fruit-bearing tree of spiritual realisation. Index-sound or word(s) bearing deep significance, and used for repetition in meditation.

Bandha: Literally is a 'knot'. Erotically it means male-female physical union in a close-knit seat; an *āsana* where irrespective of physical nudism a perfect poise sublimating the pulls of libido assists the conscious state to reach the supra-, even cosmic, consciousness. where time and space gain perfect stillness.

Bhadrāsana: Yogic seating posture where folded crosslegs are so arranged as to keep the heels pressed under the opposite thighs.

Cit-power: Consciousness.

Chhanda: Rhythm.

Cakra: (Circle) esoteric session consisting of several male and female members engaged in meditative rites.

Dattātreya: Datta, the son of Atri. One of the greatest tantra adepts.

Duryodhana: Anti-hero in the Mahabharata.

Daśaratha: Father of Rāma.

Durgā: A goddess with ten hands who in a spiritual confrontation killed the buffalo demon. (Dougga-plaque, see illustrations of the lion riding goddess from a different land and culture).

Durgā Saptaśati: A holy recital consisting of 700 couplets contained in the Mārkaṇḍeya Purāṇa (book of chronicles).

Gṛhastha: See page 70.

Gita: 'Song Divine' included as an episode in the epic Mahabharata and held in the highest honour by all Hindu spiritualists.

Gati: Motion.

Gunas: Inborn natural modes, with three different aspects: (a) *Sattva* (b) *Rajas* (c) *Tamas:* farthest from the essence (a) *Sattva* is true to the essence of the 'object'; (b) *Rajas* is the struggling agitated stage of life's efforts to reach (a) which (c) struggles to pull back to its dull inert area.

Gaṇeśa: Elephant-headed god. Petted 'son' of the goddess Durgā, or Pārvatī. Deity of success. (*Gaṇa*=mass, proletariat; *īśa*—lord). Gaṇeśa is a deity of the masses.

Haṭha-yogī: A yoga practitioner who controls the body in every possible way with a view to win over its disturbing elements.

Japa: Repetition of a given name or syllable or both leading to meditative concentration. 'Telling' the Bīja'.

Jīva: The living spirit in the body also known as *ātman*.

Kalā: Explained at page 38.

Kuṇḍalinī: Supposed esoteric source of consciousness, in a sleeping state, which when awakened, lights the seven strata of consciousness.

Kṛṣṇa: Hero of the epic Mahabharata later worshipped for his personal eminence as a beloved deity, along with his *alter ego* Rādhā.

Kurukshetra: The final battlling grounds in the epic Mahabharata.

Kālī: Mysterious spirit of Time, worshipped as a goddess.

Lotus: Esoterically means the last of a series of seven stages of consciousness known as *sahasrāra*; a stage of perfect peace and emancipation.

Lhādini: Power that enthuses activity.

Lingam: Emblem (generally of stone) representing Śiva.

Mahāmahopādhyāya: The highest honour conferred on a Sanskrit scholar by the British Crown, when it ruled India.

Mantra: Esoteric syllabic constructions of deep significance for telling on either beads or just mentally. It could also be a few words of spiritual value as indicated by a spiritual guru.

Maṇḍala: Esoteric diagramatic patterns done in colour which in themselves are subject to interpretation.

Mahābhārata: The longest epic in the Sanskrit language leading to a feud of two sets of cousins.

Mahāyāna: One of the two Buddhist schisms.

Mani Padme Hum: Seed mantra for the Mahāyāna sect.

Muskil-āsān: An Islamic mendicant.

Mahāsana: An āsana in which an *alter ego* is physically embraced.

Mudrā: Gestures of palms and fingers denoting a language of expression.

Mahānirvāna Tantra: Celebrated treatise on tantra theme and practices by Agamavagisa.

Nādī: Perceptive and apperceptive nerves.

Nāgārjuna: A very learned Buddhist saint whose fame had gained for him a status in Chinese paradise as a deity.

Nāyikā: *alter-ago* in tantra practice.

Nila-Sarasvatī: Same as Tara, Nila-Tara. Goddess of the Mahāyāna order, accepted in Tantric-Hinduism.

Nirguṇa: Anti-*guṇa*; Non-*guṇa*,

Prakrti/Purusa: The power and form aspects of all creation.

Prāṇāyāma: Guru-guided breathing exercises, leading to an ability to face esoteric difficulties in realising spiritual contentment.

Pushpavati: Woman in menses.

Paśupati: Name of Śiva: controller of Pasu (evil passions; animals).

Paramātman: Ātman is identified in a living object with consciousness. But the cosmic consciousness that pervades all is *Paramātman*. See Brahman, which indicates 'space'; *Paramātman* indicates 'consciousness.'

Pratyakṣa: Directly seen (realised).

Prayaśchitta: *Puraścharaṇa-Grahaśanti*—These are rites of 'atonement' with a view to ward off evils.

Pradhānā Nāyikā: Chief female in *cakra* (see *cakra*).

Ṛgveda: One of the four Vedas, (Sāma; Ṛg; Yajur; Atharvan).

Vedas are the earliest of all spiritual authorities for the people who now are known as the Hindus.

Rudrākṣa: (*Eleocaripas ganitrus*) Fruit-seed used as beads in strings, specially dear to tantra anchorites.

Rāmāyaṇa: An epic on the life and exploits of the hero Rāma.

Ṛtulā: Woman in season i.e. woman in menses.

Ṛṣi: Term denoting Vedic ascetics.

Sādhanā: Esoteric practice with a fully dedicated mind.

Sādhaka: Adept in *sādhanā*

Śakti: Siva—cosmic power source.

Śakyāmuni: Name of Gautama, the Buddha.

Sthiti: Opp. *gati*, static stillness.

Sthāna: Selected place of esoteric choice.

Śivam: Ecstatic state of aesthetic bliss.

Sannyāsī: See page 73.

Sitā: Consort of Rama (Ramayana).

Sunyatā: Nihilism.

Sukhapadmāsana: One of the seated postures. Crossfold legs with heels on opposite thighs.

Śivaratri: The night of the fourteenth moon in the dark fortnight in *Chaitra* (May-June) dedicated to Siva-rites.

Suṣumṇā: *Kuṇdalinī* is composed of a set of three streams of nerves of these two are known a *Idā* and *Pingalā* (afferent and efferent); the third *suṣumṇā* is a tough band that does not appear to have any responses, and so is called the sleeping one. This is skirted an either side by the two streams of *Idā* and *Pingalā*. Yogic practices aim at arousing *ṣuṣumṇā* from its 'sleep'.

Vāma Tantra: The two ways of tantra practice are known as *vāma* (left); *dakṣiṇa* (right). While the 'right' way is adopted by householders, the uninhibited *vāma* way is reserved for the abnigated adepts.

Vajrayāna: The extreme and difficult form of Mahāyāna calling for *alter-ego* participation.

Vānaprasthī See page 73.

Vidura: Character in Mahabharata; half brother of Dhṛtarāshṭra. He was a spiritually motivated man

Yoginī: Feminine of yogī, a spiritual person in quest of transcendental peace.

Yoga Vāśiṣṭha: A highty esoteric yogic treatise in Sanskrit (now available in translations) written in a dialogue form.

Yonī: Matrix; the source, the spring of life; the section of the female anatomy from which new life springs. *Yun*=the yoke that 'joins' the 'is not' with 'is'.

Yantra: Esoteric diagrams with systematic meaning explained by an adept.

Yajña: Sacrificial ritual in which fire is the central deity.

List of Anecdotes

Index